Burcu Adıgüzel Mercangöz
Editor

Handbook of Research on Emerging Theories, Models, and Applications of Financial Econometrics

Springer

Editor
Burcu Adıgüzel Mercangöz
Faculty of Transportation and Logistics
Istanbul University
Avcilar/Istanbul, Turkey

ISBN 978-3-030-54107-1 ISBN 978-3-030-54108-8 (eBook)
https://doi.org/10.1007/978-3-030-54108-8

This Springer imprint is published by the registered company Springer Nature Switzerland AG.
The registered company address is: Gewerbestrasse 11, 6330 Cham, Switzerland

Introduction

Financial econometrics is the application of statistical techniques to financial data. Financial sector data have many different characteristics from other sector data. For instance, their variances and standard deviations of returns are mostly relatively large. In these extreme returns, the distribution of daily asset returns is not normal, but generally heavy-tailed, and sometimes skewed. The autocorrelation of returns is largely insignificant. The distribution of returns is non-stationary (clustered volatility) and approximately symmetric with increasingly positive kurtosis as the time interval decreases and has a power law or Pareto-like tail. The mean and (especially) the variance of returns are nonlinear. Volatility shows positive autocorrelation and scaling and has a non-stationary log-normal distribution. Therefore, modeling and forecasting financial data is very important for financial professionals.

New technological inventions and rapid trade globalization have brought us into a new era of financial markets. Especially over the last two to three decades, several new and derived financial products have been created to meet customers' demands. Therefore, finance experts currently use more sophisticated statistical techniques.

The goal of the book is to provide many financial econometrics models, theories, and applications together. The most important benefit of this book to the body of literature is the fact that it is a resource that addresses all econometric techniques for financial data and sector in an integrated manner. Although there are separate studies on each model, there are not many studies in this way. In addition, this book aims at helping more researchers in understanding the application of econometric techniques for the financial sector. It provides a comprehensive discussion on financial econometrics and solves financial problems by many econometric techniques. In addition, since there are some basic package programs for implementing financial econometrics, some authors of the book provide financial econometrics theories and models by supporting applications with a package program.

The topics included in the book are financial market data and time series characteristics modeling and composition, equilibrium and regression models, limited dependent variable models (logit and probit), vector autoregressive (VAR) model and cointegration analysis, volatility models such as ARCH, GARCH,

TARCH, panel data analysis, big data analysis, and analysis of some financial theories such as capital structure studies.

The book consists of eighteen theoretical and empirical chapters. The first chapter explains and deals with time series characteristics. In the first chapter titled "*Exploratory Classification of Time-Series*," an exploratory analysis run is advised before running more specific statistical studies so as to enable the researcher to acknowledge quickly and easily to what extent his study's aims may be reached, based on the available data, and provide an overview of the likely results. Therefore, the more information may be extracted from the data concerning their structure, the better it is for further studies. Concerning multidimensional time series, a task not well solved by principal component analysis is their classification. The proposed new hierarchical factorial classification provides the identification of homogeneous groups of series as an alternative/complement to PCA. This allows us to clearly identify unidimensional groups of time series, whose consequent modeling may take advantage of the classification: indeed, it may be expected that time series belonging to the same group may be described/forecasted by a similar kind of model. Moreover, the issue of a representative time series for each group allows us to first model this one at the best and further apply the same kind of model to the members of the group, if necessary, with little variation of the parameters.

In the second chapter, titled "*Predicting the Tail Behavior of the Financial Times Stock Exchange/Johannesburg Stock Exchange Closing Banking Indices: Extreme Value Theory Approach,*" the focus is mainly on the application of financial econometrics to Johannesburg Stock Exchange (JSE). There are issues that are related to reliance prompted by volatility clustering in the South African financial markets. To overcome these issues, a novel approach is developed by applying the extreme value theory (EVT) distributions to predict extreme losses of the five South African Financial Times Stock Exchange/Johannesburg Stock Exchange (FTSE/JSE) indices. In addition, the chapter provides a basis for future researchers for conducting studies on emerging markets, more specifically in the South African context.

The third chapter, titled "*Financial Econometrics and Systematic Risk,*" analyzes systematic risk. Systemic risk is a concept that has gained much popularity over the past few years, especially after the 2007–2009 financial crisis. It refers to measuring and quantifying the probability of a systemic crisis where a possibly large number of financial institutions default simultaneously. In addition, this field of research also covers the contribution of institutions to systemic risk and their exposure to systemic risk. The literature of systemic risk is very extensive. One way to categorize this literature, although non-exhaustively, is to look at the use of methodology rooted in network theory and financial econometrics. The papers which make use of network theory analyze the existing interrelations data (such as inter-bank loans relations) to map the network of institutions or extract the network applying financial econometrics methods on frequently available data of those institutions (such as stock market returns). In addition, there are papers which use only financial econometrics methods, without deriving a network of institutions. All in all, financial econometrics methods are very popular in systemic risk research. There are many survey papers on systemic risk literature, but their focus is rather on the systemic risk indicators than the underlying financial econometrics methodology. This chapter contributes to fill this gap.

The fourth chapter, titled "*Monetary Policy Shocks, Financial Heterogeneity, and Corporate Dynamic Investment Activity*," contributes to the literature that reviews how different level of leverage and cash holding firms react to monetary policy shocks. From an academic point of view, the findings of the chapter assemble a bridge between the existing literature that accumulates monetary policy shocks through high-frequency event study approach to corporate investment dynamism and the background that focuses on macroeconomic aggregates as an interpreter of asset returns. The practical implication of the study is that investment managers may be aware about the importance of leverage and cash holdings in explaining differential investment activity to monetary policy shocks. Company decision makers should consider the impact of various policy instruments on corporate investment and take an active response in advance.

In the fifth chapter, titled "*Oil Price Scenarios: Its Economic and Fiscal Impacts on the Kuwait Economy,*" the author empirically explores the effect of oil price assumptions on selected macroeconomic variables in Kuwait. Since oil is the most important driver of economic growth and the main factor to sustainable development for Kuwait's economy, falling oil prices weaken the fiscal position and growth. Therefore, fiscal policy has a crucial function in passing on or mitigating oil shocks to the economy. The author uses the SCPD macro model, which is a structural macro-econometric model with policy simulation and long-term planning capability, to estimate the impact of scenarios on the forecast of oil prices from 2018 to 2030. In great detail the author discusses Kuwait's economic and structural exposure and vulnerability to oil price volatility. This chapter's contribution focuses on economic growth, fiscal policy, and oil shocks to the economy. The chapter revealed that high oil prices have a positive impact on GDP growth in Kuwait. However, oil price shocks might cause negative macro and fiscal dynamics, while higher deficits and financing needs will make market environments unstable and volatile over the medium-term period.

In the sixth chapter, titled "*Exchange Rate Sensitivity of Firm Value: Evidence from Non-financial Firms Listed on Borsa Istanbul,*" the author analyzes exchange rate sensitivity of firm value. Given the importance of exchange rate dynamics on financial stability in emerging markets, it is crucial to figure out how the firms' sensitivity to exchange rate fluctuations differs. In this regard, this chapter investigates the reaction of the firm-level and sector-level returns to the changes in the exchange rate. For this purpose, firstly the coefficient of sensitivity to the changes in the exchange rate is estimated at the firm level. In the following step, firm-level characteristics which might have an effect on the FX sensitivity of firms are examined by allowing for possible distributional asymmetries. Few studies exist in the literature which investigate the asymmetric nature of currency exposure of firm value as it is considered in this study. In this chapter, as a contribution to the existing literature, the inherent asymmetry in exchange rate exposure is directly modeled and the role of firm characteristics differing along the empirical distribution of exchange rate exposure is examined via adopting quantile regression methodology. In short, the main contribution of this study is to identify factors determining to what extent FX risk is priced in stock markets. Specifically, the robust positive association between the on-balance sheet net FX position and FX sensitivity of firm value implies the role of hedging practices. Moreover, this study reveals other firm-level dynamics governing the FX sensitivity of firm value. In this context, empirical results indicate that the degree of engaging in international operations, profitability, firm size, and growth opportunities are statistically significant factors. Thus, both the relevance and popularity of the examined issue for emerging markets as well as adopted unique econometric approach in this chapter add an interesting dimension to the book.

The seventh chapter, titled "*Limited Dependent Variables and an Application on BIST-100* (*Istanbul Stock Exchange*) (*Logit and Probit Models*)," explains logit and probit models. Binary independent variables do not cause any problems in classical regression models; however, if the dependent variable takes on values 0 and 1 (dummy variable), this may cause various problems in the regression model. If the dependent variable takes on a value between 0 and 1, the errors of the model will also take on a value between 0 and 1 and the errors will not show normal distribution. If the dependent variable takes on two values (0 and 1), instead of using linear regression models, it would be more appropriate to use models in which the relationship between the dependent variable and the independent variables is nonlinear. In this book, where emerging models, theories, and applications in financial econometrics are discussed, the model that should be used in situations where the relationship between dependent and independent variables is not linear is qualitative choice models. For these reasons, the inclusion of these models in the book is extremely important.

The eight chapter, titled "*Vector Autoregressive Model: Model and Analysis*," explains the vector autoregressive models (VAR). Single-equation models may not be sufficient to explain some events in finance studies. Because there can be a multifaceted and complex relationship between variables. In such cases, the VAR developed by Sims (1980) is used to explain these events. The VAR model is a regression model that can be considered as a kind of hybrid among univariate time series models. The VAR models are generally defined as alternatives to structural models of large-scale simultaneous equations. The VAR model is an econometric model that generalizes univariate autoregressive (AR) models. All variables in the model are treated symmetrically with an equation for each variable explaining the development of the variable, depending on the lags of the variable in the model and the delays of all other variables.

In the ninth chapter, titled "*Construction of the Monetary Conditions Index with TVP-VAR Model: Empirical Evidences for Turkish Economy*," the author conducts a study for a variant VAR model. Monetary conditions index (MCI) was constructed for Turkey covering the period of May 1986-—October 2018. MCI was calculated using time-varying impulse response functions obtained from the time-varying parameter vector autoregressive (TVP-VAR) model. TVP-VAR models allow the change of index weights over time and provide better reflection of the changes in monetary conditions during economic crisis, regime changes, and structural arrangements. Analysis of the time-varying structure of the index components demonstrates that the transmission from interest rate to economic activity is quantitatively higher compared to the exchange rate transmission channel. According to the empirical findings, MCI successfully captured the 1994 and 2001 crisis periods and the monetary tightening experienced in recent years. The index that constructed in this study could be used as an important indicator to reflect monetary conditions.

The tenth chapter, titled "*Monetary Policy Regimes, Fiscal Implications, and Policy Interactions Among Developing Economies*," macroeconomic-financial linkages and policy evaluations have given new stimulus to the study of business cycles, international spillover effects, and policy making. In addition, the evaluation of interdependencies, heterogeneities, and co-movements among different sectors and countries has become a modern requirement. Then, there has been a considerable amount of analysis of the performance of monetary policy rules, fiscal implications, and their interactions in driving the transmission of certain shock, especially during the recent global financial crisis and successive post-crisis consolidation. In addition, even economic-institutional issues, often not directly observed, and the transmission of certain shocks, often idiosyncratic, now need to be evaluated from a global perspective and in a unified framework for either developed or developing economies. The approach and the empirical implementation addressed in this chapter propose and develop econometric methodologies in order to give a valid contribution to such topics and thus improve the recent literature on macroeconomic-financial linkages when evaluating international shock transmission and investigating policy interactions in multi-country dynamic panel setups over time. Interdependence, homogeneity, and commonality are also identified in order to account for policy implications and suggestions for decision makers. Although recent studies have found the presence of relevant interdependencies across countries, the recent recession and successive post-crisis consolidation have shown a substantial degree of heterogeneity, with some common behaviors, in macroeconomic-financial linkages among countries and sectors. These linkages may have changed over time due to different transmission channels and institutional and economic implications. Thus, when formulating policies or forecasting, several issues need to be considered, such as relevant interactions between monetary and fiscal policy when accounting for international spillovers, how additional transmission channels allow shocks to spill over, and how economic and institutional implications matter in driving shock transmission. The chapter develops an extension of a time-varying structural panel Bayesian vector autoregressive model in order to deal with model misspecification and unobserved heterogeneity problems when jointly modeling and quantifying multi-country data using the information contained in a large set of time-varying endogenous macroeconomic-financial variables. A hierarchical prior specification strategy and Markov chain Monte Carlo implementations are defined in order to calculate posterior distributions of conditional generalized impulse response functions and conditional forecasts reacting to unexpected perturbations in the innovations of the factors in the system. The performance and functioning of the model are described by conducting an empirical application over the last two decades for a pool of emerging market countries, with particular attention to the most recent recession and post-crisis consolidation. Here, given the structural framework, one is able to match endogenous variables (describing the real economy and financial markets) to additional time-variant factors in order to capture unobserved heterogeneity and dynamic misspecification when investigating transmission channels and economic-institutional interdependencies affecting shock identification and spillover effects. In this context, Bayesian methods are used to reduce the dimensionality of the model, structure the time variations, and evaluate issues of endogeneity.

From a modeling perspective, a relevant degree of homogeneity in the spreading of the spillover effects matters among real variables and even more among financial sectors. Thus, unexpected country-specific shocks directly affect a country's own output growth in the financial dimension and then in the real economy because of consistent cross-country interdependencies. When dealing with not directly observed economic-institutional issues and additional transmission channels, the common component in the real and financial dimensions tends to matter more because of consistent interactions between monetary and fiscal policy, mainly during the aftermath of the Great Recession. In the aftermath of the Great Recession, the intensity of spillover effects sufficiently decreases behind more coordinated fiscal actions, mainly in the financial dimension because of stronger cross-country interdependencies. Thus, there would be significant benefits from fiscal consolidation without delay and that there is a need for caution against excessive faith in fiscal structures. From a policy perspective, the empirical results highlight that fiscal consolidation has played a central role in the disinflation process. Nevertheless, a number of other forces have also contributed, such as economic-institutional reforms, structural reforms, and access to global capital markets. With ongoing post-crisis consolidation, following the notably expansionary monetary policies of major advanced countries, many emerging market economies have experienced a significant process of international financial integration characterized by the rising importance of international financial flows and larger gross external assets and liabilities. However, further reforms in goods, service, and labor markets, which improve economic efficiency, are needed to boost potential growth.

The eleventh chapter, titled "*The Impacts of Transportation Sector and Unemployment on Economic Growth: Evidence from Asymmetric Causality,*" describes a study based on asymmetric causality analysis. Causality analysis is an important activity in economics and various branches of science. In this chapter, causality analysis is evaluated asymmetrically. Relations that cannot be detected by classical causality analysis can be observed in asymmetric causality analysis. Analyses were started with stationary tests. After the vector autoregressive (VAR) model was established, the stability and assumptions of the model were examined. Granger causality test was applied to the stable model. According to the results of this test, no significant causal relationships were found between the variables. In addition, the relationships between variables were examined by asymmetric causality analyses proposed by Hatemi (2012). In the application part of the study, the causal relationships between the economic variables of the USA were examined.

The twelfth chapter, titled "*ARCH Models and an Application on Exchange Rate Volatility*," explains volatility models and conducts an empirical study by using volatility models. For the correct pricing of financial assets and accurate estimations, there should be low volatility in the price movements of an asset. Volatility, an indicator of risk, is calculated by various models. Since changes in asset prices are not linear, volatility in asset prices is determined by the ARCH-GARCH models, not by the classical regression method. ARCH-GARCH models are needed to determine the volatility of any asset and to determine the factors causing this volatility. ARCH-GARCH models, which determine the volatility, which is extremely important for the financial literature, will be an important contribution to this book and the literature as it is an extremely important subject for financial econometrics.

In the thirteenth chapter, titled "*Using COGARCH Filtered Volatility in Modeling Within ARDL Framework*," the author explains and uses a different variant of volatility models. There are various studies in the literature to determine the impact of volatility of financial asset on another variable. Usually, in these studies, volatility was modeled using stochastic volatility models and discrete GARCH models. This chapter is differentiated from other studies by obtaining the volatility through the continuous GARCH (COGARCH) model. Moreover, the chapter gives an example of using the COGARCH filtered volatility in the ARDL bounds test approach. In addition, the reader is guided on how to apply the proposed approach by giving an example with R codes.

In the fourteenth chapter, titled "*Performance of MS-GARCH Models: Bayesian MCMC-Based Estimation,*" the author employs a number of robust econometric techniques to investigate the dynamics of exchange rate from the nonlinear perspective. Despite the abundance of studies on the behaviors of numerous economic and financial data from BRICS countries, nonlinearity has not been exploited to the fullest yet in the modeling and forecasting of such important variables. This chapter is an attempt to bridge this gap, specifically, as used in the investigation of the behaviors of the exchange rates in BRICS countries. Furthermore, the chapter provided a practical guide for assessing volatility using MS-GARCH with different estimation methods (ML and MCMC). The chapter compared various estimated MS-GARCH models using ML and MCMC to review their performance and features. This chapter can be a good reference when facing modeling exchange rate problems. Overall, this chapter particularly intends to enhance the understanding of the patterns and movements in the exchange rate of BRICS countries as well as asymmetric regimes in exchange rate in general.

In the fifteenth chapter, titled "*Volatility Spillovers Between Oil Prices and BIST (Borsa Istanbul) Dividend Indexes,*" the causality in variance (risk spillovers) between oil prices and BIST (Borsa Istanbul) dividend indexes returns is investigated. This chapter differs from the literature in the following aspects. First, the author uses the causality-in-variance test procedure developed by Hafner and Herwartz (2006) to investigate volatility spillovers between oil prices and BIST (Borsa Istanbul) dividend indexes due to the various advantages of this procedure. Second, there is no empirical study that tests the causality in variance between oil prices and BIST (Borsa Istanbul) dividend indexes returns. Third, the author takes into consideration two dividend indexes to better understand the sensitivity of the companies with high-dividend yields to oil price shocks. The causality-in-variance test results suggest a significant one-way volatility spillover effect from oil prices to BIST dividend indexes returns. This significant effect appears due to the higher sensitivity of the BIST dividend indexes returns to the variation in economic activity caused by oil price shocks.

The sixteenth chapter, titled "*Panel Data Analysis*," explains panel data analysis theoretically and gives an empirical study about the analysis. Econometric data—horizontal cross-sectional data (unstructured/undated), time series (dated regular frequency), and mixed (panel)—are defined as data. Cross-sectional data are data used to indicate the change of any variable relative to different units in a fixed time unit. Time series, on the other hand, are the series showing the change of the values taken by variables according to the frequency values (year, month, week, day, hour, etc.) in time. Unlike the two data types above, panel data, which comprise composite data, accommodate both the horizontal and vertical (time) dimensions of the data. Panel data are both spatial and time dimensional data. Therefore, researchers who want to examine the change of a group (each observation value in horizontal section) over time with econometric tests frequently need panel data analysis. By using panel data methods, more reliable and healthy results can be achieved. In this chapter of the book, in addition to other chapters, panel data analysis is included. In panel data analysis, testing of stationarity of variables, revealing the cointegration relationship between variables, and determining causality between variables and panel regression methods are included. The above analysis is included in an application example with its steps.

The seventeenth chapter's title is "*An Amalgamation of Big Data Analytics with Tweet Feeds for Stock Market Trend Anticipating Systems: A Review*." The global markets are becoming more complex in the current scenario due to the nature of economics and its dynamicity. Therefore, the trade market remains unpredictable and largely varies in respect of economics, social, and weather conditions. The key challenge in trading is to predict the market trends based on various key factors, for the best investment plans. As the data technologies are rising, the resources for building prediction models are considered a crucial responsibility; therefore, the inclusion of researches on big data analytics, machine learning, and data science can be an added advantage in achieving the effective stock predictions. These research criteria's would help the marketing groups in making automated trading based on training and patterns provided to the machines, and thus, the efficient stock predictions are performed by the machine learning algorithms to recommend the best trading plans.

In the eighteenth chapter, titled "*Capital Structure Adjustment Speed: Evidence from Borsa Istanbul Sub-Sectors*," the author explores the validity of capital structure theories and the existence of the target debt ratio, which have been discussed for a long time in financial literature. If the firms have a target debt ratio, the question of whether a target debt ratio is critical for the firm's capital structure can be answered by determining the adjustment speed of firms. This chapter is expected to contribute to the literature on the existence of the target debt ratio by determining the adjustment speed. Moreover, in the macro dimension, it is expected that the determination of the adjustment speed of sectors and the determination of borrowing tendencies in the crisis and non-crisis periods will contribute to policy makers.

It is hoped that this book will provide the resources necessary for researchers, teachers, engineers, managers, and practitioners to adopt and implement econometric techniques to financial data and the financial sector. It aims to provide a comprehensive discussion on financial econometrics and solves financial problems by many econometric techniques. The target audience of this book will comprise professionals and researchers working in the financial sector, while it also comprises research experts and practitioners in the field. But the book will also be beneficial to teachers, students, engineers, managers, and practitioners, who will find this text useful in furthering their research exposure to pertinent topics in prioritizing and directing their own research efforts in this field. This book is expected to bring different research backgrounds (due to its cross-platform characteristics) together in order to form effective research groups all over the world. Above all, availability of the book should be ensured to as many universities and research institutes as possible through whatever graceful means can be found.

Contents

Exploratory Classification of Time-Series 1
Sergio Camiz

Predicting the Tail Behavior of Financial Times Stock Exchange/Johannesburg Stock Exchange (FTSE/JSE) Closing Banking Indices: Extreme Value Theory Approach 31
Katleho Makatjane, Ntebo Moroke, and Elias Munapo

Financial Econometrics and Systemic Risk 65
M. Hakan Eratalay

Monetary Policy Shocks, Financial Heterogeneity, and Corporate Dynamic Investment Activity 93
Mahbuba Aktar, Qu Wenzhou, Hijbulla Al Mahmud, and Mohammad Zoynul Abedin

Oil Price Scenarios: Economic and Fiscal Impacts on the Kuwait Economy 109
Sedat Dizmen

Exchange Rate Sensitivity of Firm Value: Evidence from Nonfinancial Firms Listed on Borsa Istanbul 141
İbrahim Ethem Güney, Abdullah Kazdal, Doruk Küçüksaraç, and Muhammed Hasan Yılmaz

Limited Dependent Variables (Logit and Probit Models) and an Application on BIST-100: Logit and Probit Models 167
Lokman Kantar

Vector Autoregressive Model and Analysis 197
Murat Akkaya

Construction of the Monetary Conditions Index with TVP-VAR Model: Empirical Evidences for Turkish Economy 215
Coşkun Akdeniz

Monetary Policy Regimes, Fiscal Implications, and Policy Interactions Among Developing Economies 229
Antonio Pacifico

The Impacts of Transportation Sector and Unemployment on Economic Growth: Evidence from Asymmetric Causality 267
Sultan Kuzu Yıldırım

ARCH Models and an Application on Exchange Rate Volatility: ARCH and GARCH Models 287
Lokman Kantar

Using COGARCH-Filtered Volatility in Modelling Within ARDL Framework 301
Yakup Arı

Performance of MS-GARCH Models: Bayesian MCMC-Based Estimation 323
Lawrence Diteboho Xaba, Ntebogang Dinah Moroke, and Lebotsa Daniel Metsileng

Volatility Spillovers Between Oil Prices and BIST (Borsa Istanbul) Dividend Indexes 357
Barış Kocaarslan

Panel Data Analysis 375
Hasan Huseyin Yıldırım

An Amalgamation of Big Data Analytics with Tweet Feeds for Stock Market Trend Anticipating Systems: A Review 397
Deepika Nalabala, M. Nirupama Bhat, and P. Victer Paul

Capital Structure Adjustment Speed: Evidence from Borsa Istanbul Sub-Sectors 437
Turhan Korkmaz and Aslı Yıkılmaz Erkol

About the Editor

Burcu Adıgüzel Mercangöz was born in İstanbul in 1980. She got Associate Professor of Quantitative Methods degree in May 2018 from Inter-University Council in Turkey. She is a graduate in business administration from Istanbul University. Then, Dr. A. Mercangöz began her master's studies in quantitative methods in the Institute of Social Sciences at Istanbul University in 2003 and held a master's degree with a dissertation on the topic "The effective usage of logistics information systems in the logistics firms" in 2005. While doing her master's, Dr. A. Mercangöz commenced her academic career as a research and teaching assistant for the Faculty of Transportation and Logistics at Istanbul University in 2004. Following her master's, Dr. A. Mercangöz began her Ph.D. studies in quantitative methods at the same university in 2005. She holds a Ph.D. with a dissertation on the topic "Network models and an application in supply chain network optimization" since 2010. Dr. A. Mercangöz is now a faculty member of Istanbul University Faculty of Transportation and Logistics. Dr. A. Mercangöz speaks English. She is married and has two children.

Exploratory Classification of Time-Series

Sergio Camiz

Introduction

Forecasting in advance the evolution of a stock market is the dream of all investors. Thus, the problem is largely studied in financial literature with a tremendous amount of papers aiming at modelling in the best way the market, in order to predict its behaviour at some close or far horizon. Indeed, the close horizon currently adopted for automatic trading led to dramatic effects in 2010 (*CFTC* and *SEC* 2010). Presently forecasting is considered rather difficult, in particular due to the large number of stocks, which requires a tremendous amount of parameters to be estimated. Hence, the preprocessing of the observational data on which to estimate models, in particular concerning their dimensional reduction, becomes a task of relevance. In this framework, principal component analysis (*PCA*, Jolliffe 2002) is largely quoted as a method of reference (Guo et al. 2015; Yang et al. 2017). As well, *PCA* finds its space in techniques which combine it with more sophisticated methods, such as kernel *PCA* (Ince and Trafalis 2007; Nahil and Lyhyaoui 2018), independent component analysis (Chowdhury et al. 2018), support vector regression (Chowdhury et al. 2017), and neural networks (Zhang 2018). The same papers are rich in bibliography on the subject.

Indeed, as in many other fields of investigation, *PCA* is used in finance in an instrumental way, as a technique of data reduction, preprocessing, etc., without taking advantage of its exploratory abilities, which may enlighten the researcher in his quest of understanding, prior of trying to model what he is dealing with. In particular, dealing with multidimensional time-series, such as stock exchange prices,

S. Camiz (✉)
ISPC-Consiglio Nazionale delle Ricerche, Rome, Italy
e-mail: sergio@camiz.net

B. Adıgüzel Mercangöz (ed.), *Handbook of Research on Emerging Theories, Models, and Applications of Financial Econometrics*,
https://doi.org/10.1007/978-3-030-54108-8_1

and their study and modelling may take advantage of exploratory studies, able to put in evidence mutual relations between series and partition them according to their behaviour along time. Indeed, since long the idea of applying exploratory techniques as a first step of any quantitative study was recognized successful (Tukey 1977). In particular, exploratory studies "let data speak for themselves" (Benzécri et al. 1973–82) and allow the scientist to have a very deep insight of the data, through a truly "detective work" (Diggle et al. 1994), without the need to apply models and statistics. This approach is appropriate when real multidimensional data tables do not cope with the conditions required to apply correctly statistical methods. This is particularly relevant when dealing with time-series in which the independence between observations is not satisfied. On the opposite, the results of an exploratory technique may lead to better define models. While exploring, it is common to identify structures and relations in the data—to be checked later—without the need to extensively use statistical tests, which would increase the risk of type I error, that is, assuming as relevant, noteworthy, or significant what is not. Camiz et al. (2008) successfully adopted this strategy to study *Pinus pinea* L. leaves as tentative pollution bioindicators and could identify otherwise unexpected models. There are many reasons in favour of this strategy: (i) it may be applied to any kind of data, regardless their nature and distribution; (ii) it does not need to define any a priori data structure or distribution; (iii) no independence between observations is required; (iv) it is not based on *p*-values, whose use and misuse have been recently severely criticized (Reinhart 2015); (v) it contributes to the creation of the correct hypotheses to test (Camiz 2001; Camiz et al. 2008); and (vi) it helps in the identification of the models to build.

Dealing with a multidimensional time-series, that is, a set of synchronous ones, an exploratory study may aim at identifying their correlation structure (in the sense of the mutual linear relations between time-series), some patterns common to subsets, patterns of homogeneous observations, etc., all issues which may deserve being confirmed through more appropriate tools. As for modelling, it is likely that time-series clustered together by an appropriate classification method may be suitable to be described by models of the same kind. For such a task, *principal component analysis* (*PCA*, Jolliffe 2002), the best known exploratory tool, may not be fully appropriate. In fact, concerning the variables, *PCA* only provides their contribution to the extracted orthogonal factors and their correlations with them, which are usually taken into account to interpret the factors; moreover, the quality of their representation on the several dimensions indicates whether a reduced dimensional reconstruction may be considered satisfactory or not. Considering time-series as variables, their exploratory *PCA* is feasible (Bry 1995), issuing principal components which are time-series themselves, describing orthogonal patterns of variation along time. Sadly, considered a long time, they may be difficult to understand and interpret. Orthogonal and/or oblique rotations may help in identifying directions more correlated with groups of variables, but this means a second treatment, based on the choice of an approximate solution in a predefined number of dimensions, usually unknown; the same *factor analysis* requires applicability conditions (independence of observation, multi-normality of residuals), which are usually far from holding (for further reading, see, e.g. Harman 1976; Jolliffe 2002). In addition, *PCA* may not be used for forecasting, because of its exploratory nature and because the structure of correlation between time-series may vary along time and, dealing with a whole data set, *PCA* may not describe what does not belong to it.

The classification of time-series may be an interesting adjunct to *PCA*: the partition of them in homogeneous subsets is not provided by *PCA* results, unless by observing the common gathering of some of them around some factor. It is known that the primary motivation in holding a diversified portfolio of stocks is to reduce risks (Solnik 1995). Thus, such a partition could help an investor to organize its shareholding in a more balanced way, by selecting shares of different groups with different behaviour, which may contribute to reducing risks. Unlike the classification of units, which is largely discussed in literature (see, among many, Anderberg 1973; Gordon 1999; and in particular Lebart et al. 2006, for clustering in the frame of exploratory multidimensional analysis), little was developed for variables, for which the same criteria are adopted: thus, the correlation coefficient is taken as a similarity index, and single, average, or complete linkage criteria are usually employed. As specific methods, we may quote Lerman (1981), with its probabilistic hierarchical method called Likelihood Linkage Analysis. More close to *PCA* spirit may be quoted *VARCLUS* (SAS Institute 1999), a divisive algorithm which creates clusters by trying to get them as one-dimensional as possible; the *K*-means-like method proposed by Vigneau et al. (2006), which creates a principal component associated to each group; and more recently Chavent et al. (2011).

The alternative proposed here, *hierarchical factorial classification* (*HFC*, Denimal 2001, 2007), aims at classifying variables by building a hierarchy, that is, a complete set of encapsulated partitions represented by a dendrogram. The hierarchy on the variables is built according to a *PCA*-like method; hence, for each node of the hierarchy—that is, a group of variables—*HFC* issues a principal plane on which both the variables forming the node and the units, as seen only by them, may be represented—just as in *PCA*—and consequently interpreted. By cutting the dendrogram, a partition results, and *HFC* provides—for each formed group—a *representative variable*, which summarizes the common pattern of variation of the clustered variables and, as such, may be used in place of them, in particular while modelling. Indeed, the modelling of a single time-series for forecast may be easier than that of a multidimensional one, and applying such a model to a small set of series highly correlated with it might be more successful than building a very complex general model.

The method has been tested in several frameworks: in plant ecology (Camiz and Denimal 2006; Camiz et al. 2006; Camiz and Pillar 2007), climatology (Camiz et al. 2010a, 2014), and dendrochronology (Camiz et al. 2010b; Stafasani and Toromani 2015; Camiz et al. in press), proving its complementarity with *PCA* and its advantages with respect to a classical hierarchical classification of variable methods. Thus, *HFC* joins the two methods, ordination and classification, in a single tool.

In this paper, *HFC* is proposed, and its results are compared to *PCA* through a case study concerning the time-series of the daily stock prices of Brazilian financial enterprises.

The Data

The time-series of daily prices of 17 stocks of Brazilian financial enterprises have been daily recorded in the period 27/10/2009–13/4/2012, for a length of 610 auction days. Their names and acronyms are reported in Table 1, with their descriptive statistics.

As two series, *SULA11* and *CIEL3*, had a change in the nominal value during the study period (1/3 and 3 times, respectively), their prices have been adjusted to the nominal value of the last observation all along the observed period. Moreover, for the analyses, all series have been standardized.

The Analysis Methods

Principal Component Analysis

We base our study on the fundamentals of *principal component analysis* (Benzécri et al. 1973–82; Bry 1995; Jolliffe 2002; Lebart et al. 2006), the best known exploratory multidimensional method, whose essentials are sketched in the following. Given a quantitative data Table ***X***, crossing *n* units by rows and *p* variables by columns, *PCA* builds a set of *principal components*, new uncorrelated variables obtained through linear combination of the original ones, valued on the same units, whose relative importance is ordered according to the amount of information of the original data table which is synthesized by each one. The principal components are usually interpreted as *factors* corresponding to the main sources of variation of the data table. Graphical two-dimensional representations of the pattern of both units and variables on the planes spanned by pairs of factors revealed a most helpful tool for a progressive study of the original data table that may be carried out step by step, from the simplest most evident relations to the most hidden ones.

The basic principle of *PCA* is to consider the *inertia* of a data Table ***X*** and to decompose it into uncorrelated *factors*, whose decreasing inertia sums up to the table one. As *inertia* of a data table, we mean the weighted sum of squared centred values appearing in the table, which in exploratory data analysis is considered a measure of the *information* contained in the data. Thus, most exploratory methods aim at getting optimal results by maximizing the inertia. The principal components are linear combinations of the original variables obtained from the decomposition of either the correlation or the covariance matrices between them. In fact, one may refer to the singular value decomposition (*SVD*, Abdi 2007) to show that the elements of ***X*** may be written as $x_{ij} = \sum_{\alpha=1}^{p} \sqrt{\lambda_\alpha} u_{i\alpha} v_{j\alpha}$, product of the square root of the eigenvalues λ_α—measuring the inertia—hence the carried out information, of the αth factor, with the corresponding eigenvectors u_α of ***XX'*** and $\sqrt{\lambda_\alpha} v_\alpha$ of ***X'X***, respectively. In addition, $c_\alpha = Xu_\alpha$ provides the principal components and $\sqrt{\lambda_\alpha} u_\alpha$ the correlations between the original variables and the principal components. The Eckart and Young

Table 1 Names and acronyms of the 17 Brazilian stock time-series, with corresponding descriptive statistics: minimum, mean, maximum, variance, standard deviation, and coefficient of variation

Name	Acronym	Minimum	Mean	Maximum	Variance	Standard deviation	Coefficient of variation
Banco ABC Brasil	*ABCB4*	8.500	12.651	17.500	3.138	1.771	0.140
Banco do Brasil	*BBAS3*	11.000	16.623	22.100	6.231	2.496	0.150
Banco Bradesco	*BBDC3*	6.650	11.167	17.300	6.960	2.638	0.236
Banco Bradesco preference shares	*BBDC4*	7.800	11.622	15.620	1.990	1.411	0.121
Banco Industrial e Commercial	*BICB4*	21.400	25.799	31.350	3.235	1.799	0.070
Banco Pan	*BPNM4*	25.260	31.670	38.410	5.658	2.379	0.075
Banco do Estado do Rio Grande do Sul	*BRSR6*	22.480	28.336	34.980	7.184	2.680	0.095
Bolsa de Valores Mercadorias e Futuros	*BVMF3*	11.250	20.769	33.300	32.846	5.731	0.276
Cielo	*CIEL3*	33.150	45.547	65.100	34.224	5.850	0.128
Balcao Organizado de Ativos e Derivativos	*CTIP3*	8.300	11.638	13.990	1.121	1.059	0.091
Itausa Investimentos Itau	*ITSA4*	21.810	29.320	33.210	4.191	2.047	0.070
Itau Unibanco holding	*ITUB3*	25.550	36.017	43.530	11.728	3.425	0.095
Itau Unibanco holding preference shares	*ITUB4*	3.780	7.311	12.200	3.958	1.989	0.272
Porto Seguro	*PSSA3*	17.340	21.607	28.970	10.620	3.259	0.151
Redecard	*RDCD3*	18.480	26.392	36.400	15.460	3.932	0.149
Banco Santander Brasil	*SANB11*	12.840	19.346	25.950	10.238	3.200	0.165
Sul America	*SULA11*	12.700	16.972	20.910	4.408	2.100	0.124

Source: Author's creation

(1936) theorem proves that the best reduced dimensional approximation of X—that is, the one which minimizes the non-explained inertia—is obtained by limiting the sum to the first r largest eigenvalues. Thus, *PCA* is essential for a critical study of the data table, by considering first the most relevant information and further the least one, this way favouring the interpretation of the factors which mostly influence the composition of X. This may be obtained by studying the correlations between principal components and original variables as well as the ordination of the units along the principal components, which are usually represented through graphics. As a side result, it is widely used to reduce the dimension of a data table, aiming at minimizing the risk of losing essential information. Indeed, this practice may be heavily criticized, since no consistent control is available to fix this dimension, despite the many methods proposed in literature: for a critical review, see Camiz and Pillar (2018).

On the planes spanned by pairs of factors, the units may be projected in an optimal way, thus maximizing the represented inertia and approximating their reciprocal distances. To the principal components, *principal axes* are associated, defining planes on which the original variables may be projected as vectors. Here, the cosine of the angle between vectors and axes corresponds to the correlation between the variables and the principal components. Additional variables, observed on the same units, may be projected as *supplementary elements* according to their correlation with the principal components. This way, they may be used to help the interpretation of the principal components but as well to show the ability of both factors and original variables to estimate the supplementary variables, in the sense of the linear regression.

In the case of time-series, the principal components are orthogonal time-series themselves. In decreasing order, they are most correlated with the original ones. When these correlations are all positive, they may describe a kind of weighted average time-series, but otherwise they show both agreement and oppositions between them. Thus, their interpretation as time-series may be sometimes difficult.

Hierarchical Classification

The use of hierarchical classification in an exploratory analysis, albeit computationally cumbersome with large data tables, is advantageous since it provides a complete set of encapsulated partitions, which are optimized according to a chosen criterion. This way, which partition to choose is an issue of the analysis instead of being an a priori fixed parameter. In order to build a hierarchy, the algorithms are usually agglomerative: at the beginning, given p objects, (i) each one is considered to form a group alone (a singleton); then (ii) a numerical index of pairwise association between groups is chosen, which allows (iii) to create an association matrix containing the initial values for all pairs of objects; then, (iv) a rule is defined to update the association matrix each time two groups are merged, and (v) an objective function based on the association indices is chosen, whose optimisation is taken as a rule to identify which pair of groups must be merged at each step. In addition, (vi) a method must be chosen to decide how to obtain a partition from the built hierarchy. Then, (vii) iteratively, the following agglomerative steps are repeated—until only one group results—namely, (vii.i) the pair of existing groups optimizing the objective function is identified, (vii.ii) the pair is merged in a new group, and (vii.iii) the association matrix is updated, by withdrawing the values corresponding to the two merged groups and including instead the indices computed for a pairwise association of the new group with those still existing. This procedure provides a hierarchy, which is usually represented by a dendrogram summarizing the association between objects and corresponding to a complete set of encapsulated partitions. Eventually, (viii) according to the choice done at (vi), the user may decide which partitions to take into account. As based on four different choices, a data set may be classified in several ways, depending on (ii) the choice of the association index, (iv) the optimization function, and (v) the criterion for the redefinition of the intergroup association after agglomeration. For details, see Anderberg (1973), Hartigan (1975), and Gordon (1999); for the method to detect optimal cut-points of the dendrogram to get a partition, see the review of Milligan and Cooper (1985).

Hierarchical Factor Classification

A special attention deserves *PCA* of pairs of variables, which produces two factors only: unlike the orthogonal time-series issued as principal components of a larger number of variables, whose explanation—in particular those following the first one—may sometimes be obscure; in this case it is easy to prove that the first one synthesizes what the two variables have in common and the second which are their differences. This easiness of interpretation led Denimal (2007) to develop his *hierarchical factor classification* (*HFC*, see also Denimal 2001), a method which deserves being taken into account when studying time-series. The method combines in a single procedure the classification of variables with a factorial representation in the same exploratory spirit of *PCA*, as well as a simple—albeit not optimal—classification of the units. In addition, the *HFC* results may be very easily represented on *PCA* graphics, this way providing an integration of these methods which gets even easier its use.

In order to build a hierarchy on the set of variables, *HFC* associates to each built group a *representative* variable, which summarizes all those in the group and uses a sequence of *PCA*s of pairs of such representative variables of the groups previously built. It operates as follows:

1. At the beginning each variable (either standardized or not) is considered to form a group alone—a singleton—and clearly representative of this group. Then the iterative algorithm is based on the following steps (see Denimal 2007, for the technical details).

2. All pairs of existing groups are compared through their representative variables, which are submitted to a non-normalized *PCA*, i.e. the *PCA* of their 2×2 covariance matrix. Note that the two eigenvalues sum up to the two representative variables' inertia: it is easy to understand that the first one carries the amount they share and the second one the amount of their differences, respectively.
3. Among all these pairs, that whose *PCA* second eigenvalue is minimum is selected: this means that the pair whose differences are minima is sought.
4. The two groups of variables corresponding to the selected pair are merged, and the resulting group forms a new node of the hierarchy.
5. Given the new node, the first principal component of this node's *PCA* is chosen as its representative variable. Indeed, based on the interpretation of the factors issued by the *PCA* of a pair of variables, it summarizes what the variables of the node have in common, a kind of compromise between them.
6. The first eigenvalue equals the first principal component's inertia, which is a share of the total inertia of the variables in the node. Note that this inertia may be very large, since the *PCA* is based on the covariance, depending on both the number and the inertia of the variables gathered in the group.
7. The second principal component represents the amount of differences between the variables composing the node, which are expected to be as little as possible.
8. The second eigenvalue summarizes the inertia of these differences. It may be proved that in the iterative process, these second eigenvalues are non-decreasing; thus they may be used as indexes of the hierarchy. The choice of its minimum value at each step ensures that the formed groups are indeed the most homogeneous.
9. To each node of the hierarchy, two principal planes are associated: on the first the covariances/correlations between the variables belonging to the node and the two principal components are represented as angles cosines, while on the second one the scattering of the units—seen only by these variables—may be studied. Due to the meaning of the principal components, an easily associated partition (albeit not optimum) of the units in four groups may be done, according to the concordance-discordance of their values on the representative variables of the aggregated groups. This way, the relations between representative variables of different nodes may be used to understand similarities and differences among the corresponding groups of variables.
10. If the variables are p, the steps 2...9 are repeated $p - 1$ times, obtaining a complete hierarchical classification of the variables.
11. To obtain a suitable partition, one may cut the dendrogram at a given level of the index. Indeed, it is important to avoid to create groups containing independent variables. For this task, we supposed that the hierarchy index may not exceed 0.7, the opposite of what Jolliffe (2002) recommends for a factor to be considered relevant.

It must be noted that the first principal component issued at each step is a weighted average of the variables forming the node: if its correlations with these variables have all the same sign, it may be taken positive, and it has a weighted centroid position within them, thus justifying its use as a representative of them. Should they be opposite in sign, the representative variable refers to a *dipole* of variables, which identify the same representative variable with an opposite meaning. In this case, the dipole may be split into two subgroups, and a representative variable of either of the subgroups had rather be sought. In the case of time-series, the representative one is a weighted average of those forming the group, and as such its pattern along time may be seen as a proxy of the pattern of the others; on the other side, the series of the differences may describe their variation along time.

It results that the two principal components of the last built node of *HFC* are usually highly correlated with the first two principal components of *PCA* performed on the whole data set. Thus, their interpretation may be quite similar. Indeed, both methods are based on the same geometric space of *PCA*; hence the representative variables of all nodes may be represented as supplementary elements in the ordinary *PCA* principal planes, allowing an interoperability between the two methods. Note that the representative variables of the different nodes may not be orthogonal; thus their interpretation may be referred to the corresponding group of variables: nevertheless, it may be proved that the second eigenvalues and the first of the last node sum up to the total inertia. This will allow an evaluation of the inertia lost due to a chosen partition.

The application of both *PCA* and *HFC* to the case study has been done through specifically developed functions of *R* (R-Core Team 2013) in a Linux-based personal computer.

Results

Principal Component Analysis

In Table 2 the eigenvalues issued from *PCA* of the 17 time-series are reported together with the corresponding share of total inertia, its cumulate percentage, and the threshold value for significance of the said share, according to the Brokenstick test (Frontier 1976). This test assumes the distribution of the shares of total inertia as it was randomly broken into—in this case—17 pieces and considers random the eigenvalues whose value is lower than the corresponding test. According to it, here only three eigenvalues are accounted for an inertia share larger than the threshold, hence worth to be taken into account. On the other side, Jolliffe (2002) recommendation—to take into account eigenvalues larger than 0.7—would suggest here 4 relevant dimensions; the Josse and Husson (2012) test, taken from the *FactoMineR* package (Husson et al. 2017), suggests up to 12 non-random dimensions; the Rencher-Bartlett test (Rencher 2002), which estimates whether the non-considered dimensions are spherical—hence random—admits up to 16 dimensions. This gets quite difficult to take a decision about the non-random dimension of the data set (see Camiz and Pillar 2018), for an experimentation on the subject), should it be relevant

Table 2 Eigenvalues issued from principal component analysis of the 17 time-series of Brazilian stock prices

	Eigenvalues	Percentage of inertia	Cumulate inertia	Brokenstick test
Dim. 1	8.408	49.459	49.459	20.233
Dim. 2	3.831	22.537	71.996	14.350
Dim. 3	2.629	15.464	87.460	11.409
Dim. 4	0.920	5.410	92.870	9.448
Dim. 5	0.311	1.829	94.699	7.978
Dim. 6	0.253	1.486	96.185	6.801
Dim. 7	0.180	1.057	97.242	5.821
Dim. 8	0.141	0.827	98.069	4.981
Dim. 9	0.078	0.456	98.525	4.245
Dim. 10	0.063	0.369	98.894	3.592
Dim. 11	0.056	0.329	99.224	3.003
Dim. 12	0.044	0.258	99.482	2.469
Dim. 13	0.032	0.187	99.669	1.978
Dim. 14	0.019	0.113	99.782	1.526
Dim. 15	0.019	0.110	99.893	1.106
Dim. 16	0.013	0.078	99.971	0.714
Dim. 17	0.005	0.029	100.000	0.346

Besides, the percentage of corresponding inertia, the cumulate, and the Brokenstick test value. Note that three eigenvalues are accounted for a percentage of inertia larger than the test
Source: Author's creation

for further studies. As our aim is exploratory, we decided to consider in the following the first four dimensions, which summarize 92% of the total inertia: we do not think that the further dimensions would significantly modify the overall understanding of the data structure. Here the first factor summarizes nearly 50% of total inertia, the second and the third 22.5% and 15.5%, respectively, with the fourth accounted for only 5.5%, for a total of nearly 93%.

In Fig. 1, the 17 time-series are represented on the circles of correlations on the planes spanned by factors 1–2 on the left and 3–4 on the right. In these graphics the cosine of the angle between each time-series—represented as an arrow-vector—and each factor corresponds to their correlation, whereas the length of the arrow, considered in respect with the circle radius, corresponds to the share of the time-series jointly described by the two factors generating the plane. Thus, on the right, we see 10 stocks highly correlated with the first factor, whereas the other 7 are opposed 3 to 4 along the second factor, apparently showing a very low correlation with the first one. Hence, we may hypothesize that the first factor is a kind of compromise of the time-series in the said group, whereas the second may represent a compromise of the four stocks positively oriented with it, together—but with opposite meaning—with *BPNM4*. Indeed, the two other stocks—*RCDC3* and *CIEL3*—are poorly represented on this plane, but appear pretty well represented along the third factor. Eventually, the fourth factor shows some correlation only with *BBDC3* and *BBDC4* opposed to *ABCB4*, indeed difficult to interpret.

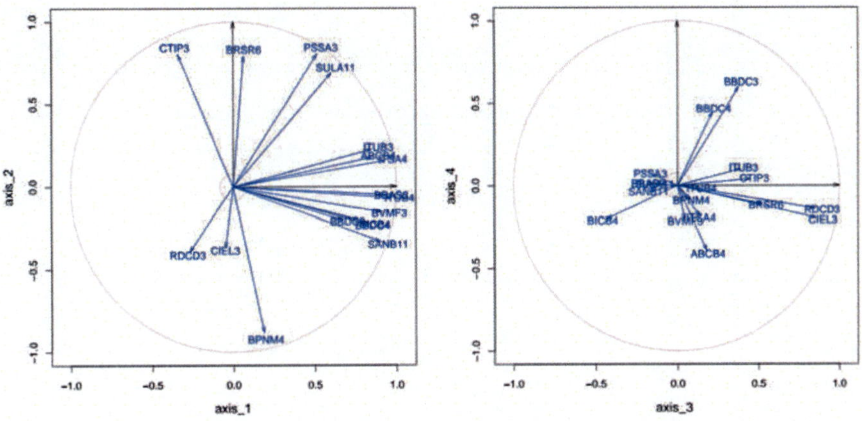

Fig. 1 The circles of correlations issued from principal component analysis of the 17 time-series of Brazilian stock prices on the plane spanned by factors 1 and 2 (left) and on the plane spanned by factors 3 and 4 (right). Source: Author's creation

These remarks may be better grounded on the results sketched in Table 3, where for each time-series, their correlations with the four factors are reported, together with their cumulate quality of representation on the progressively increasing dimension factor spaces. There we see that only nine stocks are correlated with the first factor for more than 0.8, with three others, *BBDC3*, *PSSA3*, and *SULA11*, with correlation higher than 0.5. To the second factor are highly correlated four stocks, positively *BRSR6*, *CTIP3*, *PSSA3*, and negatively *BPNM4*, whereas with the third factor, only *CIEL3* and *RDCD3* show high correlation. If we look at the cumulate quality of representation of the time-series, we may observe that with three dimensions only *BBDC3* and *BBDC4* are less well represented: in fact, their medium correlation with the fourth factor raises their cumulate quality, so that with four dimensions the quality of the analysis is very good, with all time-series represented for over 80%.

In Fig. 2 the daily observations are represented on the planes spanned by the same pairs of factors as before. On the plane spanned by factors 1 and 2 (above), the days follow a continuous pattern which starts with central values of the first factor and negative of the second during the first 175 days, then a shift towards more central values of the second factor until day 230, then extreme positive values along the first factor until around day 270, again more central values for the first factor with positive values of the second one between days 275 and 415, then extreme negative values for the first factor and central for the second one until around 540, and eventually central values for all in the last period. These remarks are supported by the larger contributions to the axis formation of the days of the commented groups: to the first one, larger contributions come positively from days 226 to 274 and negatively from 432 to 519, whereas to the second one contributes negatively the first days until 162 and then positively from 275 to 310 and from 343 to 389. Looking at the pattern on the plane spanned by factors 3 and 4 (below), we see

Table 3 Correlations of the 17 time-series of Brazilian stock prices with the four principal components issued by their principal component analysis and cumulate quality of representation on the generated spaces

	Correlation 1	Quality 1	Correlation 2	Cumulate quality	Correlation 3	Cumulate quality	Correlation 4	Cumulate quality
ABCB4	0.849	0.721	0.176	0.752	0.176	0.783	−0.392	0.937
BRSR6	0.063	0.004	0.790	0.628	0.520	0.899	−0.111	0.911
BICB4	0.829	0.688	−0.217	0.735	−0.435	0.924	−0.200	0.964
BVMF3	0.911	0.831	−0.154	0.854	0.044	0.856	−0.206	0.899
BBDC3	0.668	0.447	−0.200	0.487	0.374	0.627	0.597	0.983
BBDC4	0.815	0.664	−0.223	0.714	0.210	0.758	0.444	0.956
BBAS3	0.924	0.854	−0.049	0.856	−0.169	0.885	0.010	0.885
CTIP3	−0.342	0.117	0.802	0.760	0.452	0.964	0.042	0.966
CIEL3	−0.047	0.002	−0.366	0.136	0.856	0.869	−0.195	0.907
ITSA4	0.932	0.869	0.157	0.894	0.136	0.912	−0.185	0.946
ITUB3	0.849	0.720	0.226	0.771	0.387	0.921	0.103	0.932
ITUB4	0.971	0.943	−0.068	0.947	0.139	0.966	−0.017	0.967
BPNM4	0.188	0.035	−0.880	0.811	0.081	0.817	−0.085	0.824
PSSA3	0.514	0.264	0.803	0.909	−0.156	0.933	0.070	0.938
RDCD3	−0.268	0.072	−0.392	0.225	0.851	0.949	−0.138	0.968
SANB11	0.904	0.817	−0.330	0.927	−0.167	0.954	−0.035	0.956
SULA11	0.601	0.361	0.687	0.833	−0.132	0.850	0.007	0.850

Source: Author’s creation

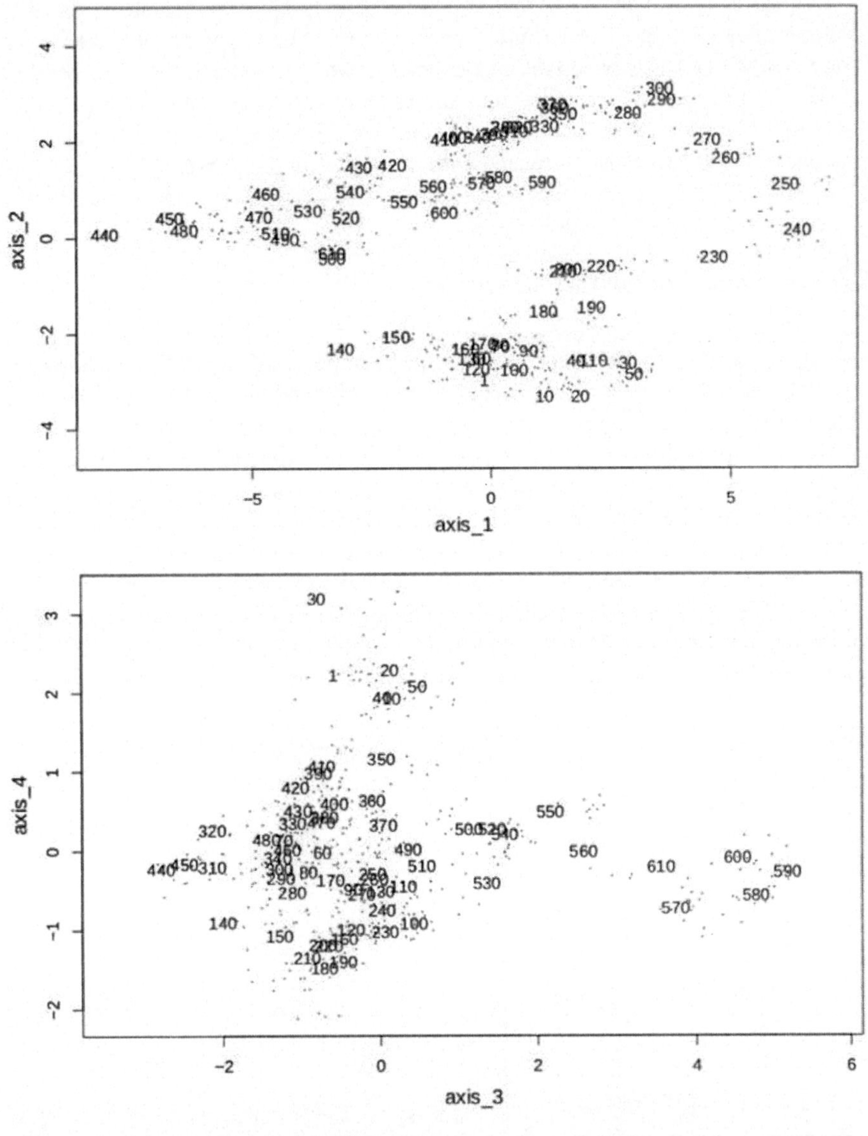

Fig. 2 The daily observations on principal planes issued from principal component analysis of the 17 prices time-series of Brazilian stock prices: on the plane spanned by factors 1 and 2 (above) and on the plane spanned by factors 3 and 4 (below). Source: Author's creation

two extreme periods: the last 70 days on the positive one of the third factor and the first 55 days isolated on the positive side of factor 4. These days contribute highly to the axis formation, together with the extremes on the opposite sites that are not clearly separated by all others; thus, on this plane a kind of homogeneous pattern of days results, from which the two said sets separate independently.

Summarizing, we may say that two time periods are opposite along the first factor, corresponding to lower and higher values of the larger set of stocks most correlated with it, whereas on the second factor, two opposed periods correspond to those with alternate values of the four stocks more correlated with it. On the other side, the third and fourth factors put in evidence the higher values in the extreme periods of the stocks most correlated with the corresponding axes.

Hierarchical Factor Classification

In Fig. 3 the dendrogram representing the hierarchy built by *HFC* is shown: it explains the relations between the studied time-series based on the *PCA*s between representative ones. As usual, the level of the node in which two branches are gathered corresponds to the hierarchy index, which measures their differences. Unlike the hierarchy built on units, in this case it is not enough to inspect the differences between the indexes of the subsequent nodes to obtain a consistent idea of possible partitions (here one may imagine two or three groups), since the resulting groups may gather uncorrelated variables, something nonsensical. Therefore, we had rather looked at Table 4, in which the basic elements of the construction of the hierarchy through *HFC* are reported: from left, the node label, the number of groups of the corresponding partition at that level, the labels of the gathering groups,

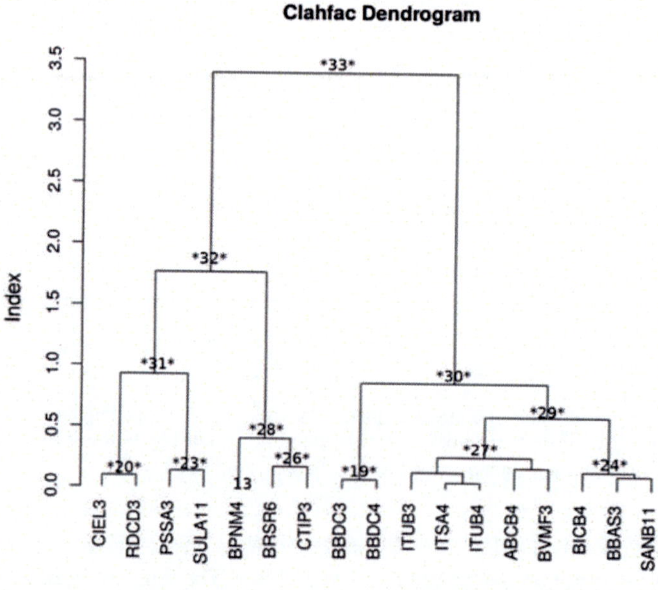

Fig. 3 The dendrogram produced by the hierarchical factor classification algorithm applied to the 17 time-series of Brazilian stocks prices. Within asterisks are the names of the nodes and the partition classes. Source: Author's creation

Table 4 Hierarchical factor classification construction of the hierarchy on the 17 Brazilian stock time-series

Node	Number of groups	N1	N2	Node size	Eigenvalue 1	Eigenvalue 2—index	% Local inertia 1	% Local inertia 2	% Global inertia 1	% Global inertia 2	Cumulate global inertia 2
18	16	10	12	2	1.951	0.049	97.566	2.434	11.478	0.286	0.286
19	15	5	6	2	1.930	0.070	96.487	3.513	11.351	0.413	0.700
20	14	9	15	2	1.906	0.094	95.298	4.702	11.212	0.553	1.253
21	13	7	16	2	1.893	0.107	94.629	5.371	11.133	0.632	1.885
22	12	11	18	3	2.820	0.131	95.559	4.441	16.590	0.771	2.656
23	11	14	17	2	1.865	0.135	93.232	6.768	10.968	0.796	3.452
24	10	3	21	3	2.751	0.141	95.112	4.888	16.184	0.832	4.284
25	9	1	4	2	1.830	0.170	91.504	8.496	10.765	0.999	5.283
26	8	2	8	2	1.829	0.171	91.438	8.562	10.757	1.007	6.290
27	7	22	25	5	4.394	0.256	94.487	5.513	25.847	1.508	7.798
28	6	13	26	3	2.423	0.405	85.671	14.329	14.255	2.384	10.183
29	5	27	24	8	6.553	0.592	91.715	8.285	38.548	3.482	13.665
30	4	19	29	10	7.619	0.864	89.815	10.185	44.817	5.082	18.747
31	3	20	23	4	2.843	0.928	75.393	24.607	16.722	5.458	24.205
32	2	31	28	7	3.499	1.767	66.444	33.556	20.583	10.395	34.600
33	1	32	30	17	7.715	3.403	69.395	30.605	45.384	20.016	54.616
Sum of the hierarchy indexes						9.283					54.616
First representative time-series					7.715				45.384		

From left: node label, number of groups formed at that level, labels of the gathering groups, number of time-series clustered at the node, first and second eigenvalues of the PCA associated to the node, corresponding percentages of local and global inertia of both eigenvalues, and cumulate global inertia of the second eigenvalues

Source: Author's creation

the number of time-series clustered at the node, the first and second eigenvalues of the *PCA* associated to the node, the corresponding percentages of local and global inertia of both eigenvalues, and the cumulate global inertia of the second eigenvalues. The most relevant column is the seventh, reporting the hierarchy index, i.e. the second eigenvalue of the *PCA* run on the two representative time-series of the gathering groups. This is a measure of the differences between the aggregating series, which essentially depends on their correlation. We chose to take into account the 4 last nodes, resulting in a partition in 5 groups, because the index corresponding to this partition—0.592—does not seem to represent a too low correlation between the series in the fifth node, whereas 0.864, the index of the following node, does, at least according to Jolliffe (2002) recommendation, this time the other way. Hence the five groups of the obtained partition are as follows: *19* (composed by *BBDC3* and *BBDC4*), *20* (*CIEL3* and *RCDC3*), *23* (*PSSA3* and *SULA11*), *28* (*BPNM4*, *BRSR6*, and *CTIP3*), and *29* composed by the eight others (*ITUB3*, *ITUB4*, *ITSA4*, *ABCB4*, *BVMF3*, *BICB4*, *BBAS3*, and *SANB11*).

In Fig. 4 the time-series belonging to each of the four upper nodes are represented on the circles of correlations issued by the *PCA*s associated to the corresponding node. The order is *33*, *32*, *31*, and *30*. The reading is analogous to the usual circles of correlations, the cosines of the angles between vectors, and axes representing the correlation between time-series and factors: in each graphic, the time-series belonging to the node are represented in blue, whereas the two principal components of the two merging groups are represented in red. We comment these graphics including the values of the correlations between representative time-series reported in Table 5. The first one corresponds to the upper node *33*: here, the two time-series *30A* and *32A* representative of the corresponding nodes are nearly orthogonal (correlation = 0.123) between them and close to either of the two factors *33A* and *33B*, respectively—hence highly correlated (0.995 and 0.975, respectively) with them—and poorly correlated with the others (0.222 and−0.106). On the opposite both time-series *30B* and *32B* are badly represented on this plane.

Thus, we may say that the representative time-series of *33*, whereas representative of the subgroup *30*, is not correlated with the *32A* since they are nearly orthogonal, and indeed the corresponding time-series form two well-distinguished groups around their representative one. In particular, those belonging to *32* form a dipole, with four positively and three negatively correlated to *32A*, but the bundle is not as tight as the other. This is clearly visible in the second graphic on the right, corresponding to the node *32*: in this, the two dipoles *31* and *28* join forming a dipole, but they seem poorly correlated between them (0.474), so that *32A* is not so highly representative of a homogeneity, albeit correlated with both of them (correlations 0.874 and 0.740, respectively). Furthermore, in the lower row of the figure, the node *31* forms clearly a dipole, opposing *20A* and *23A*, and *30* separates clearly the group *19* from *28*, close around their representative series. In all the shown nodes, the medium-low correlations between the representative time-series of the two joining groups justify the choice to consider a five-group partition.

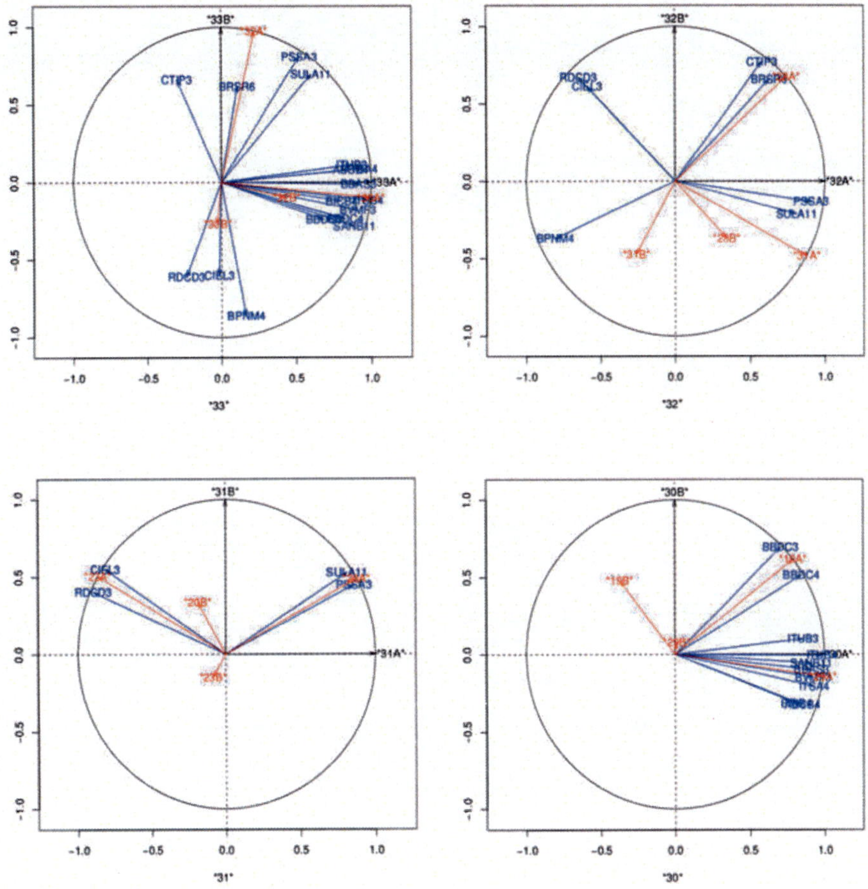

Fig. 4 Representation of the time-series of the 17 Brazilian stocks prices on the circles of correlations corresponding to the PCA of the four upper nodes of the hierarchy issued by HFC spanned by the corresponding principal components. In blue the time-series and in red the representative ones (indicated with A) and those representing the differences (indicated with B). Above, left: node *33*; right: node *32*; below, left: node *31*, right: node *30*. Source: Author's creation

In Table 6 the correlation matrix between representative and differences time-series of the five groups are reported: we must remark the correlation between *19A* and *29A*, 0.692, sufficiently high to raise the question whether to split or not the node *30* in two groups and that between *20A* and *23A*, −0.508 negative, which—even being medium—suggests to split the dipole into two different groups. As for the description of the correlations between the time-series corresponding to the differences, we may observe that they are usually relatively low, with some exceptions, such as those between *29B* and both *28A* and *28B* and that between *29A* and *20B*, whose interpretation may not be easy.

Table 5 Correlation between pairs of representative time-series of both nodes and classes and those of nodes, resulting from the HFC of the 17 time-series of Brazilian stock prices

	33A	*33B*	*32A*	*32B*	*31A*	*31B*	*30A*	*30B*
33A	1.000	0.000	0.222	−0.436	0.406	−0.459	0.995	−0.027
33B	0.000	1.000	0.975	0.099	0.804	−0.166	−0.100	−0.271
32A	0.222	0.975	1.000	0.000	0.874	−0.263	0.123	−0.270
32B	−0.436	0.099	0.000	1.000	−0.485	−0.474	−0.444	0.176
31A	0.406	0.804	0.874	−0.485	1.000	0.000	0.323	−0.322
31B	−0.459	−0.166	−0.263	−0.474	0.000	1.000	−0.440	−0.033
30A	0.995	−0.100	0.123	−0.444	0.323	−0.440	1.000	0.000
30B	−0.027	−0.271	−0.270	0.176	−0.322	−0.033	0.000	1.000
19A	0.769	−0.245	−0.068	−0.242	0.058	−0.367	0.789	0.614
19B	0.374	0.011	0.094	−0.444	0.298	0.215	0.371	−0.476
20A	−0.130	−0.621	−0.635	0.655	−0.873	−0.488	−0.067	0.297
20B	0.512	0.026	0.139	−0.139	0.189	−0.338	0.507	−0.111
23A	0.582	0.778	0.888	−0.180	0.864	−0.504	0.501	−0.261
23B	0.150	−0.225	−0.186	−0.155	−0.088	−0.151	0.172	−0.064
28A	−0.129	0.788	0.740	0.673	0.320	−0.514	−0.207	−0.081
28B	0.101	−0.368	−0.337	0.370	0.474	−0.425	0.137	0.165
29A	0.989	−0.060	0.161	−0.464	0.366	−0.431	0.990	−0.144
29B	0.036	0.243	0.245	0.742	−0.146	−0.687	0.011	0.077

Source: Author's creation

Table 6 Correlation coefficients of both representative (denoted with A) and differences (denoted with B) time-series of the 5 groups of 17 time-series Brazilian stock prices issued from HFC

	19A	*19B*	*20A*	*20B*	*23A*	*23B*	*28A*	*28B*	*29A*	*29B*
19A	1.000	0.000	0.129	0.332	0.235	0.096	−0.213	0.210	0.692	0.056
19B	0.000	1.000	−0.365	0.291	0.149	−0.157	−0.230	−0.325	0.436	−0.325
20A	0.129	−0.365	1.000	0.000	−0.508	0.150	−0.029	0.621	−0.109	0.463
20B	0.332	0.291	0.000	1.000	0.333	−0.056	0.009	−0.266	0.518	−0.076
23A	0.235	0.149	−0.508	0.333	1.000	0.000	0.536	−0.195	0.534	0.221
23B	0.096	−0.157	0.150	−0.056	0.000	1.000	−0.242	0.255	0.179	−0.204
28A	−0.213	−0.230	−0.029	0.009	0.536	−0.242	1.000	0.000	−0.193	0.680
28B	0.210	−0.325	0.621	−0.266	−0.195	0.255	0.000	1.000	0.112	0.522
29A	0.692	0.436	−0.109	0.518	0.534	0.179	−0.193	0.112	1.000	0.000
29B	0.056	−0.325	0.463	−0.076	0.221	−0.204	0.680	0.522	0.000	1.000

Source: Author’s creation

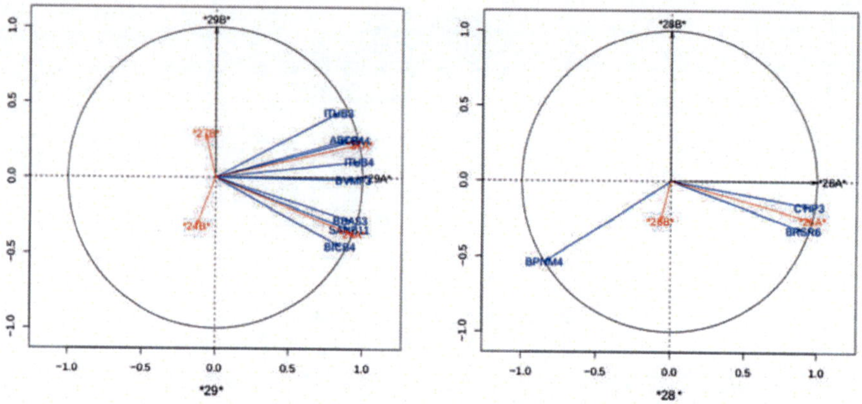

Fig. 1.5 Circles of correlations corresponding to the classes *29* (left) and *28* (right), of the 5-group partition issued by HFC on the 17 time-series of Brazilian stock prices. Source: Author's creation

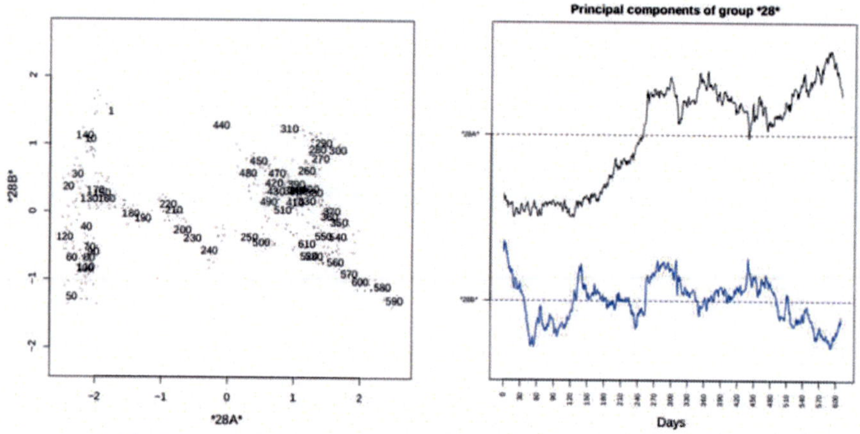

Fig. 6 Left: the pattern of the days on the factor space associated to the group *28*, hence as seen from the time/series of the group. Right: the pattern of the two principal components of group *28*. Source: Author's creation

We complement these results by showing the representative planes of both groups *28* (left) and *29* (right) in Fig. 5: the others are less interesting, since they only involve two time-series each. The node *28* is composed by two groups, whose correlation is 0.824, pretty high, thus, it makes sense to consider them as a group: *28* is a dipole gathering *BPNM4* (which represents itself) with the already formed group *26*. In Fig. 6 some other representation concerning the group *28* is proposed, namely, the pattern of the days on the space spanned by the group's factors and the pattern of the factors along the time-units: indeed, their interpretation may be the same but based on opposite representation. Such graphics, with the corresponding interpretation, may be proposed for all groups and nodes, but we limit to this one, as an example. On the left of Fig. 6, the pattern of the days on the factor space associated to the group is shown. Here the time-units are represented according to the three time-series belonging to it only, as summarized by the two group's principal components. Hence, this graphic may be interpreted just as those in Fig. 2, limited to the time-series gathered in the considered node or group. In this case, the pattern is very different from the global one, represented in Fig. 2 (above), with marked variations resulting along the second (vertical) factor at the two extremes of the studied period. As usual, their position is interpreted according to the orientation of the time-series on the corresponding circle of correlation (Fig. 5 right). On the right the pattern of both representative and differences time-series along time is represented. Here, whereas an overall positive trend may be observed in the first representative time-series *28A*, in the second more relevant negative variations result at the extremes of the observation period. In both periods it is certainly due to the opposite behaviour of *BPNM4* in respect to the other two stocks belonging to the group during those years.

Discussion

In Fig. 7 the representative and the differences time-series corresponding to both nodes and groups issued by *HFS* are projected as supplementary elements on the circles of correlations issued by *PCA* on the factorial planes 1–2 (left) and 3–4 (right). This allows to represent their correlations, this way showing their reciprocal relations. In the circle on the left, it is evident the position of the representative series *33A*, *30A*, and *29A* very close to the first factor, hence indicating very strong correlations (0.998, 0.994, and 0.991, respectively). Thus we may argue that the first

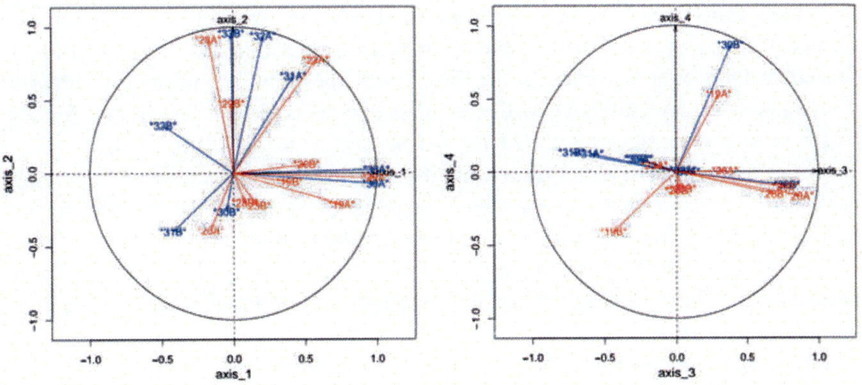

Fig. 7 Representation of the representative time-series of both nodes and classes issued by HFC on the circles of correlations corresponding to factor planes 1–2 (left) and 3–4 (right) of PCA. Source: Author's creation

PCA factor and the representative series of the nodes *33* and *30* (*33A* and *30A*, respectively) correspond very highly to the representative series *29A* of the group *29*, something not shared with other nodes and groups' representative variables: note that the other most correlated representative series with the first factor is *19A*, whose correlation is worth 0.755, a much lower value. As for the other representative series, the *23A* is more weakly correlated with this factor (0.577), and the following ones—*28A* and *20A*—are very little negatively correlated with it: −0.172 and −0.161, respectively. On the opposite, it is relevant to observe that to the second factor of *PCA* are highly correlated *33B*, *32A*, and *28A* (0.959, 0.940, and 0.914, respectively): thus, this factor is correlated to the series of differences *33B* of the last node, which is between *32A* and *28A*.

This confirms the need to split this node, since its two issued orthogonal series are correlated with the orthogonal representative series of the nodes which join there. On this plane, the representative series of the group *23* (*23A*) is well represented, meaning that it may be thought as nearly a linear combination of the two factors and opposed to *20A*, which is not really highly correlated with this plane. Thus, not even the node's representative series *31A* is very correlated with it. To get a better description of these series in terms of factors, one has to look at the circle of correlations on the plane spanned by factors 3 and 4 in Fig. 7 (right). There the representative series of group *20* (*20A*) is correlated to the third factor (correlation = 0.577)—as does *32B*—and *19A* correlated with the fourth factor, as does *30B*, indeed a difficult issue to interpret, since they belong to different nodes. Summarizing, on the represented factor planes, the five groups of time-series seem clearly distinguished. Nevertheless, only the first three factors of *PCA* seem to be sufficiently interpretable, as correlated with the representative series of some groups: the first with *29A*—the largest group—the second with *28A* and distinguishing *28* and *29*, and the third with *23A*. Indeed, the comparison of the principal components with exogenous time-series could contribute to their understanding.

All this information sets us in condition to examine in detail the correlation matrix between the 17-stock price time-series, reported in Table 7. There, the stock prices have been rearranged in order to distinguish clearly the correlations within the five formed groups, enclosed in the submatrices along the diagonal, from the other. Indeed, a high coherence results in them, with the only exceptions of *BPNM4*, which is negatively correlated with the other two series of the group, and *BICB4*, which is poorly correlated with *ITUB3* (0.458) and with some other.

In Fig. 8 the pattern along time of the time-series issued from both analyses are reported, once standardized to ease their comparison: on the left the first four factors issued from *PCA*, in the centre the first representative variables of the four nodes of *HFC*, and on the right those of the five groups issued by *HFC*. In the four-factor pattern (Fig. 8 left), one may recognize the high- and low-value periods, in good accordance to what was observed on the factorial graphics in Fig. 2, while commenting their position along the years on the factors and their contribution to them. Apart from the daily fluctuation, the first factor seems initially stable, then increasing to a maximum, then decreasing until a minimum, and then recovering. The second one, after a period of stability, increases; then it remains constant,

Table 7 The correlation matrix between the 17 time-series of the Brazilian stock prices

	CIEL3	RDCD3	PSSA3	SULA11	BPNM4	BRSR6	CTIP3	BBDC3	BBDC4	ITUB3	ITSA4	ITUB4	ABCB4	BVMF3	BICB4	BBAS3	SANB11
CIEL3	1.000	0.906	−0.444	−0.374	0.315	0.126	0.094	0.249	0.139	0.157	0.028	0.083	0.111	0.099	−0.276	−0.146	−0.028
RDCD3	0.906	1.000	−0.590	−0.507	0.380	0.113	0.156	0.132	−0.026	0.010	−0.176	−0.114	−0.108	−0.128	−0.472	−0.362	−0.250
PSSA3	−0.444	−0.590	1.000	0.865	−0.626	0.549	0.399	0.164	0.233	0.566	0.584	0.428	0.506	0.330	0.311	0.427	0.230
SULA11	−0.374	−0.507	0.865	1.000	−0.449	0.478	0.302	0.228	0.267	0.627	0.612	0.495	0.568	0.430	0.407	0.571	0.350
BPNM4	0.315	0.380	−0.626	−0.449	1.000	−0.592	−0.709	0.284	0.291	0.030	0.077	0.266	0.032	0.311	0.312	0.172	0.427
BRSR6	0.126	0.113	0.549	0.478	−0.592	1.000	0.829	0.015	−0.042	0.409	0.274	0.079	0.344	−0.016	−0.322	−0.068	−0.300
CTIP3	0.094	0.156	0.399	0.302	−0.709	0.829	1.000	−0.192	−0.354	0.069	−0.149	−0.333	−0.083	−0.414	−0.671	−0.417	−0.642
BBDC3	0.249	0.132	0.164	0.228	0.284	0.015	−0.192	1.000	0.930	0.714	0.521	0.691	0.374	0.549	0.322	0.564	0.585
BBDC4	0.139	−0.026	0.233	0.267	0.291	−0.042	−0.354	0.930	1.000	0.733	0.667	0.822	0.550	0.700	0.550	0.731	0.756
ITUB3	0.157	0.010	0.566	0.627	0.030	0.409	0.069	0.714	0.733	1.000	0.888	0.890	0.757	0.705	0.458	0.693	0.606
ITSA4	0.028	−0.176	0.584	0.612	0.077	0.274	−0.149	0.521	0.667	0.888	1.000	0.951	0.904	0.840	0.713	0.788	0.760
ITUB4	0.083	−0.114	0.428	0.495	0.266	0.079	−0.333	0.691	0.822	0.890	0.951	1.000	0.832	0.878	0.759	0.851	0.866
ABCB4	0.111	−0.108	0.506	0.568	0.032	0.344	−0.083	0.374	0.550	0.757	0.904	0.832	1.000	0.830	0.669	0.743	0.686
BVMF3	0.099	−0.128	0.330	0.430	0.311	−0.016	−0.414	0.549	0.700	0.705	0.840	0.878	0.830	1.000	0.795	0.823	0.884
BICB4	−0.276	−0.472	0.311	0.407	0.312	−0.322	−0.671	0.322	0.550	0.458	0.713	0.759	0.669	0.795	1.000	0.846	0.888
BBAS3	−0.146	−0.362	0.427	0.571	0.172	−0.068	−0.417	0.564	0.731	0.693	0.788	0.851	0.743	0.823	0.846	1.000	0.893
SANB11	−0.028	−0.250	0.230	0.350	0.427	−0.300	−0.642	0.585	0.756	0.606	0.760	0.866	0.686	0.884	0.888	0.893	1.000

The contours along the diagonal enclose the time-series of the same group

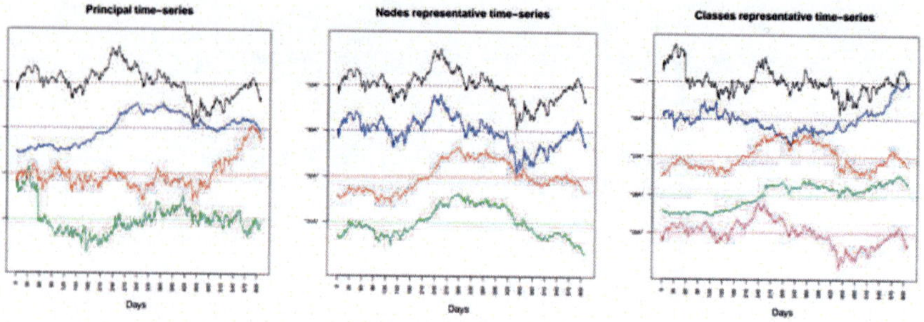

Fig. 8 Representation of the pattern along time of the time-series corresponding to the first four factors issued by PCA (left); to the representative series of the four upper nodes of HFC (centre); and to the representative series of the five groups issued by HFC (right). Source: Author's creation

slightly decreases, and keeps constant to the end. The third factor is relatively stable for most of the time, until a strong increase takes place towards the end. The fourth factor shows a sudden fall nearly at the beginning and then, after a relative stability, slightly increases and further slightly decreases.

Unlike the observed four factors of *PCA*, which appear very different from each other, being linearly independent time-series, the representative series of the nodes (Fig. 8 centre) are pairwise similar and similar to the first two factors, respectively: indeed, we already checked the very strong correlations between *33A*, *30A*, and the first factor of *PCA* and the analogous ones between *32A*, *31A*, and the second factor, so no further comment seems necessary. As for the representative time-series (Fig. 8 right), we find a similar pattern of series *29A* and—less—of *19A* with the first factor and the nodes *33A*, *30A*, a similarity of *28A* and, more, *23A* with the second factor and the nodes *32A*, *31A*. In addition, a similar pattern results between *20A* and the third factor. Indeed, considering the low correlations between the representative time-series of the five groups, one may wonder whether the factors are true ones, differently contributing to all time-series, or simply describe the differences between the groups themselves.

In Fig. 9, the pattern along time of all stocks time-series are represented gathered by group, together with their representative time-series. Note the highest agreement of the time-series of the groups *19*, *20*, and *23* in the above row of the figure between them and with their corresponding representative one: it could be expected, given the high correlation between the only two time-series composing these groups. Looking at the groups *28* and *29*, more important differences emerge, namely, in the group *28* between *CTIP3* and *BRSR6*, the latter showing a daily oscillation much more important than the previous and a relevant difference of both with *BPNM4*, which has an opposite pattern in respect to the others. Indeed, should one be really interested in detecting representative time-series, he/she had better split this group in two, consider a representative time-series of *CTIP3* and *BRSR6* only, and use *BPNM4* as a singleton. Note also in the group *29* the behaviour of *BICB4*: indeed, starting from day 470 it is slightly decreasing, whereas all others are growing. It is clear that a graphical representation of the pattern of all stocks

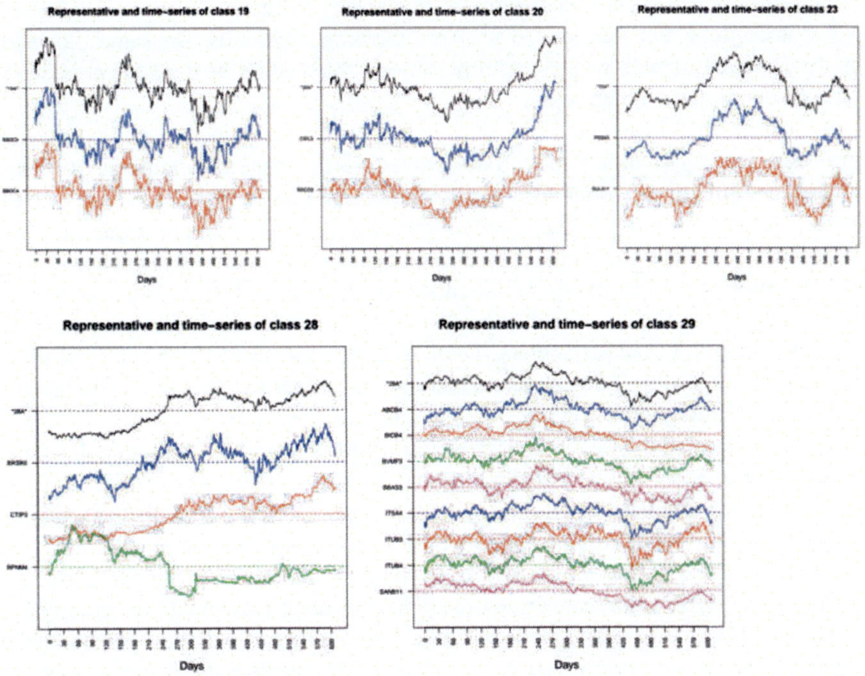

Fig. 9 The pattern along time of the time-series of each class together with that of their representative one (in black). Above, left to right: classes *19*, *20*, and *23*; below, left to right: classes *28* and *29*. Source: Author's creation

along time, grouped this way, may be of highest help to have a consistent idea of the stocks at hand. Indeed, only these two stocks get questionable the choice of five groups done according to the hierarchy building results. A careful observation of their pattern in Fig. 9 shows that their particular pattern may be limited to a part only of the observational period, hence to some specific issue concerning them in some days.

Unfortunately, due to loss of exogenous information concerning the considered stocks in the observed time period, a true interpretation of the shown results is impossible.

Conclusion

The studies on the behaviour of stock prices along time may be very useful to investors, which may be interested either to buy stocks strongly correlated with exogenous parameters, whose improvement along time may be predicted, or to spread the risk by buying stocks whose different behaviour may prevent a simultaneous collapse. Exploratory analyses are not suitable for prediction, a goal which only well-built models may deal with, but reveal very helpful to understand the time-series structure, which may lead to a better modelling afterwards. The same allows to study the relations with exogenous time-series, which could be used for prediction after an appropriate modelling.

It is clear that *PCA* and *HFC* address two different kinds of problems: *PCA* provides principal orthogonal time-series, which concur additively to the multidimensional time-series formation. Should one had in place exogenous time-series, strongly correlated with these extracted factors, he/she may argue that the exogenous influence the given ones in an analogous way: this is the sense of the interpretation of the factors. As for the modelling, it is likely that the time-series of a group may be fitted with the same kind of model fitting their representative one, with a minor variation of the parameters. Thus, *HFC* reveals useful for the classification purpose, while adding further understanding to the factorial structure revealed by *PCA* and providing a better aid for the modelling.

The application of these methods to the case study showed 3–4 orthogonal factors which explain most of the data inertia and subdivide the 2-year prices in time intervals of a particular behaviour; then five classes are found (six, if we separate *BPNM4*), with a quite different behaviour along time. As said, the interpretation of the found patterns and of their differences could be only done by comparing them with external information concerning the Brazilian stock market and its underlying economy: sadly, this revealed impossible, but nevertheless it was beyond this paper's aims, which were rather to introduce *HFC* and its main features. Indeed, such interpretation would clarify to what extent the found results could be useful for the interpretation of the data at hand within the Brazilian economy framework of that period.

Following this study, further developments concerning stock price time-series may be oriented in different directions: *(i)* a check for the stability of the correlation structure along time and consequently of the found factors and groups, *(ii)* the search for exogenous parameters explaining the series trends and thus suitable to be used for prediction, and *(iii)* the modelling of the time-series for forecast. Some attempts to deal with the first one have already be done, both on the stock market (Camiz and Diblasi 2013) and on other contexts (Camiz et al. 2010a, b; Camiz and Roig 2011; Camiz et al. in press), and are currently under improvement. The second direction would apply to two-way exploratory multidimensional analyses, aiming at identifying the relations between two data sets based on the same units: this would lead to check to what extent either set may be described through the other; see Tenenhaus (1998) for the illustration of several methods. Suitable programs are currently in progress to carry out these tasks. As for the last one, the modelling of the representative time-series of the considered classes could provide information on the modelling of the individual stock prices: in fact, it is expected that their major trends may correspond to those of the representative one, hence modelled the same way.

References

Abdi H (2007) Singular value decomposition (*SVD*) and generalized singular value decomposition (GSVD). In: Salkind N (ed) Encyclopedia of measurement and statistics. Sage, Thousand Oaks, CA, pp 940–945

Anderberg MR (1973) Cluster analysis for applications. Academic Press, New York

Benzécri JP et al (1973–82) L'analyse des données, vol 2. Dunod, Paris, France

Bry X (1995) Analyses factorielles simples. Economica, Paris, France

Camiz S (2001) Exploratory 2- and 3-way data analysis and applications. In: Lecture notes of TICMI, Tbilisi, GA: Tbilisi University Press, vol 2. http://www.emis.de/journals/TICMI/lnt/vol2/lecture.htm

Camiz S, Denimal J-J (2006) Classifications hiérarchiques factorielles de variables. Revue des Nouvelles Technologies de l'Information 6:383–388

Camiz S, Diblasi A (2013) Evolutionary principal component analysis. In: Trabajos Completos, XLI Coloquio Argentino de Estadística. Universidad de Cuyo en Mendoza, Mendoza, Argentina, pp 680–685

Camiz S, Pillar VD (2007) Comparison of single and complete linkage clustering with the hierarchical factor classification of variables. Community Ecol 8(1):25–30

Camiz S, Pillar VD (2018) Identifying the informational/signal dimension in principal component analysis. Mathematics 6(11):269

Camiz S, Roig FA (2011) Evolutionary analysis applied to tree-ring chronologies series. In: Actas E-ICES 6. Malargüe (Mendoza, Argentina). Comisión Nacional de Energía Atómica, Buenos Aires, Argentina, pp 30–37

Camiz S, Denimal J-J, Pillar VD (2006) Hierarchical factor classification of variables in ecology. Community Ecol 7(2):165–179

Camiz S, Altieri A, Manes F (2008) Pollution bioindicators: statistical analysis of a case study. Water Air Soil Pollut 194(1–4):111–139

Camiz S, Denimal J-J, Sosa W (2010a) Exploratory analysis of Pacific Ocean data to study "El Niño" phenomenon. Revista de la Facultad de Ciencias de la UNI 13(1):50–58

Camiz S, Maulucci R, Roig F (2010b) Exploratory analysis methods applied to dendrochronological series. In: Papu O (ed) Actas E-ICES 5, Malargüe (Mendoza, Argentina). Comisión Nacional de Energía Atómica, Mendoza, Argentina, pp 61–67

Camiz S, Denimal J-J, Purini R (2014) New results of multidimensional analysis of TAO/NOAA data on "El Niño" phenomenon. In: Hucailuk C, Núñez N, Molina E (eds) Actas de trabajos completos E-ICES 9. Comisión Nacional de Energía Atómica, Buenos Aires, Argentina, pp 24–45

Camiz S, Spada F, Denimal J-J, Piraino S (in press) Hierarchical factor classification of dendrochronological time-series. Annals of Sylvicultural Research

CFTC, SEC (2010) Findings regarding the market events of May 6, 2010: report of the staffs of the CFTC and SEC to the Joint Advisory Committee on Emerging Regulatory Issues. Technical report. U.S. Commodity Futures Trading Commission and U.S. Securities & Exchange Commission, Washington, DC

Chavent M, Kuentz V, Liquet B, Saracco L (2011) ClustOfVar: an R package for the clustering of variables. arXiv preprint arXiv:1112.0295

Chowdhury UN, Rayhan MA, Chakravarty SK, Hossain MT (2017) Integration of principal component analysis and support vector regression for financial time series forecasting. Int J Comput Sci Inf Secur 15(8):28–32

Chowdhury UN, Chakravarty SK, Hossain MT (2018) Short-term financial time series forecasting integrating principal component analysis and independent component analysis with support vector regression. J Comput Commun 6(3):51–67

Denimal J-J (2001) Hierarchical factorial analysis. In: Govaert G, Janssen J, Limnios N (eds) Actes du 10th international symposium on applied stochastic models and data analysis, 12–15 Juin 2001. Université de Technologie de Compiègne, Compiègne, France

Denimal J-J (2007) Classification factorielle hiérarchique optimisée d'un tableau de mesures. Journal de la société française de statistique 148(2):29–63
Diggle PJ, Liang K-Y, Zieger SL (1994) Analysis of longitudinal data. Clarendon Press, Oxford, UK
Eckart C, Young G (1936) The approximation of one matrix by another of lower rank. Psychometrika 1(3):211–218
Frontier S (1976) Étude de la décroissance des valeurs propres dans une analyse en composantes principales: Comparaison avec le modèle du bâton brisé. J Exp Mar Biol Ecol 25:67–75
Gordon AD (1999) Classification. Chapman & Hall, London, UK
Guo Z, Wang H, Yang J, Miller DJ (2015) A stock market forecasting model combining two-directional two-dimensional principal component analysis and radial basis function neural network. PLoS One 10(4):1–19. https://doi.org/10.1371/journal.pone.0122385
Harman HH (1976) Modern factor analysis. University of Chicago Press, Chicago, IL
Hartigan JA (1975) Clustering algorithms. Wiley, New York
Husson F, Lê S, Pagès J (2017) Exploratory multivariate analysis by example using R. Chapman & Hall/CRC, London
Ince H, Trafalis TB (2007) Kernel principal component analysis and support vector machines for stock price prediction. Inst Ind Eng Trans 39(6):629–637
Jolliffe I (2002) Principal component analysis. Springer, Berlin, Germany
Josse J, Husson F (2012) Selecting the number of components in PCA using cross-validation approximations. Comput Stat Data Anal 56:1869–1879
Lebart L, Piron M, Morineau A (2006) Statistique exploratoire multidimensionnelle: Visualisations et inférences en fouille de données. Dunod, Paris, France
Lerman I-C (1981) Classification et analyse ordinale des données. Dunod, Paris, France
Milligan GW, Cooper MC (1985) An examination of procedures for determining the number of clusters in a data set. Psychometrika 50:159–179
Nahil A, Lyhyaoui A (2018) Short-term stock price forecasting using kernel principal component analysis and support vector machines: the case of Casablanca stock exchange. Proc Comput Sci 127:161–169
R Core Team (2013) R: a language and environment for statistical computing. R foundation for statistical computing, Vienna, Austria. http://www.R-project.org/
Reinhart A (2015) Statistics done wrong: the woefully complete guide. No Starch Press, San Francisco, CA
Rencher AC (2002) Methods of multivariate analysis. Wiley, New York
SAS Institute (1999) SAS Online Doc, Version 8. SAS Institute Inc., Cary, NC
Solnik BH (1995) Why not diversify internationally rather than domestically? Financ Anal J 51 (1):89–94
Stafasani M, Toromani E (2015) Growth-climate response of Young Turkey Oak (*Quercus cerris* L.) Coppice Forest Stands along longitudinal gradient in Albania. Seefor 6(1):25–38
Tenenhaus M (1998) La régression PLS: théorie et pratique. Editions Technip, Paris, France
Tukey JW (1977) Exploratory data analysis. Addison-Wesley, Reading, MA
Vigneau E, Qannari EM, Sahmer K, Ladiray D (2006) Classification de variables autour de composantes latentes. Revue de Statistique Appliquée 54:27–45
Yang L, Rea W, Rea A (2017) Financial insights from the last few components of a stock market PCA. Int J Financ Stud 5(3):15. https://doi.org/10.3390/ijfs5030015
Zhang H (2018) The forecasting model of stock price based on PCA and BP neural network. J Financ Risk Manag 7(4):369–385

Sergio Camiz, 73 years old, was born in Roma, Italy. He is married with five children.

He got his Master in Mathematics (Abstract Algebra) at Roma University in 1969 and PhD in Science (Data Analysis) at Paris IX Dauphine University in 2002.

He has been Professor at Sapienza University of Roma since 1979 until 2017, where he taught courses in both mathematics and statistics at the faculties of architecture, medicine, and sciences. He is still in the faculty of Doctorate School of Landscape and Environment of Sapienza University of Roma.

He is currently Associate Researcher at Cultural Heritage Science Institute (Istituto di Scienze del Patrimonio Culturale) of Italian National Research Council (Consiglio Nazionale delle Ricerche).

He carries out researches in theoretical and applied data analysis, specifically focusing on applications in archaeology, natural sciences, ecology, sociology, and political sciences. He edited 6 books and published over 160 papers in scientific reviews and congresses' proceedings.

Since long, he keeps a strong international cooperation with scientists in France (since 1996), Argentina (since 2004), Brazil (since 2002), and Peru (since 2007), with regular yearly interchanges for both research and teaching.

As a freelance photographer in the past, he carried out nine personal exhibitions, five in group, and supported nine doctorate workshops.

Predicting the Tail Behavior of Financial Times Stock Exchange/Johannesburg Stock Exchange (FTSE/JSE) Closing Banking Indices: Extreme Value Theory Approach

Katleho Makatjane, Ntebo Moroke, and Elias Munapo

Introduction

The financial industry, including banking and insurance, is undergoing major changes. The insurance industry is increasingly exposed to fatal losses for which the requested cover is only just available. Since the early twentieth century, with the rise of financial markets, volatility predictions have become a vital issue. According to Šiml (2012), volatility is a bulbous risk factor, and it critically impacts the prediction of risk measures such as value-at-risk (VaR) and therefore volatility clustering, meaning that extreme returns come in clusters, which indicates that it is a highly vital facet of return distribution and must be controlled in risk management models. Additionally, Makatjane and Moroke (2018) document that modeling the volatility of markets gained much attention after the introduction of generalized autoregressive conditional heteroscedasticity (GARCH) models by Bollerslev (1986), in which Ardia et al. (2016) indicate that the GARCH model is currently a prevalent tool in risk management. Besides, the world has experienced so many financial disasters in the last century that it has compelled financial market participants to elaborate on refined methods for risk estimation and management. VaR applications became popular during the 1990s, after the inauguration of JP Morgan's VaR system and RiskMetrics. Currently, VaR is a widely-used risk measure to quantify the maximum amount of loss for a given portfolio, at a given time horizon and confidence level, with a pre-assumption of normal market conditions (Gaye and Demiralay 2016).

K. Makatjane · N. Moroke · E. Munapo (✉)
North-West University, Mmabatho, South Africa
e-mail: Ntebo.Moroke@nwu.ac.za; Elias.Munapo@nwu.ac.za

B. Adıgüzel Mercangöz (ed.), *Handbook of Research on Emerging Theories, Models, and Applications of Financial Econometrics*,
https://doi.org/10.1007/978-3-030-54108-8_2

Due to financial disasters that are caused by changes in economic environments, and expectations from investors, Bauwens et al. (2014) emphasize that GARCH-family (or GARCH-type) models yield biased estimates as the parameters of these models are time-invariant. Massacci (2016) explains that financial returns are however fat-tailed; hence, risk measures that are computed during tranquil periods are not informative in periods of turbulence. Obviously, this shifts the attention from the center to the tails of a conditional distribution of returns and to the concept of tail risk. This can be difficult to measure in practice, since the conditional distribution of financial returns during periods of distress may not be appropriately described under standard parametric assumptions.

The problem of using GARCH models to model volatility dynamics is the assumption of conditional normality, which is often rejected by empirical results, as demonstrated in Danielsson and de Vries (1997). This designates that extreme losses have a higher probability of occurring as compared to those following a normal distribution, because their moments are higher than that of the normal distribution. Furthermore, it is well-known that emerging market returns depart from normality significantly, and this departure is greatly influenced by the behavior of extreme losses. Sigauke (2014), on the other hand, warns that risk measures estimated by utilizing the sample quantiles that are from a normal distribution while the data is fat-tailed are unreliable.

Due to asymmetry and fat-tail in financial returns, GARCH models are unable to capture this time-varying process. That is why Klaassen (2002) improves these models and introduced regime-switching models, which are known as Markov-switching GARCH models (MS-GARCH-family type) in order to capture and model the periods of high volatility and low volatility simultaneously and further capture the asymmetry in both regimes. Because asymmetry regime-switching GARCH models are restricted to the assumption of normality as in single regime-switching GARCH-family models, these models are unable to model and predict extreme values; hence, a theory that considers these extreme events is the so-called extreme value theory (EVT). This theory aims to monitor and predict extreme losses in an efficient way. Beytell (2016), on the other hand, discovers that using EVT in conjunction with risk measures gives reliable market risks, whereas Wei et al. (2013) show that EVT relies on extreme observations to derive a distribution of random variable tails. In that manner, the risk is measured more efficiently than by modeling the entire distribution of a random variable. The link between EVT and risk management is that EVT methods fit extreme quantiles better than the conventional approaches for heavy-tailed data. As a result, the EVT distributions to predict the risk that is related to extreme values caused by the financial shocks and financial instability in South Africa (SA) are used.

The purpose of this study is to recall some fundamentals of EVT and to improve the academic literature by studying the tail behavior of stock returns and the associated risk for five major banks in SA (ABSA, Capitec, FNB, Nedbank, and Standard bank). The conventional extreme value approach by first filtering the data to capture some of asymmetry, dependencies, and extreme relationships in the stock returns is extended and thereafter applying ordinary extreme value techniques. See, for instance, Sigauke et al. (2012), Sigauke et al. (2014), or Beytell (2016) for more on this. In this way, not only better in-sample tail estimates are obtained, but more importantly, this will also provide better predictions of future extreme return levels. An additional advantage is that the independently and identically distributed (i.i.d) assumption behind the EVT-based tail-quantile estimator is less likely to be violated (Maghyereh and Al-Zoubi 2008). From now, the usefulness of EVT in modeling extreme events in the banking market is explored. The remainder of the study is organized as follows: the section hereunder describes the review of literature, while the subsequent section discusses the modeling framework. Next follows the results and discussion, while the final section gives concluding remarks with some ideas for future work.

Literature Review

Classical EVT has developed two commonly-used extreme value distributions (EVD). Coles et al. (2001) stress that the asymptotic distribution of maxima or minima by a Gumbel, Fréchet, or Weibull distribution may be approximated under certain conditions. The EVD is a unified form of these three distributions. Ideally, if one wants to model values that are extremely below or are extremely high above a certain threshold, the distribution Pareto generalized (GPD) is said to be a good candidate [see, for instance, Hosking and Wallis (1987), Davison and Smith (1990), and Zhao (2010)]. In order to evaluate the tail behavior of extreme observations, EVDs may be used to estimate high quantities of these extreme values (Danielsson and de Vries 1997). Studies in financial modeling have gained more practice in recent decades. The generalized extreme value (GEV) and the GPD distributions have turned out to be increasingly in the mainstream of financial risk distributions because they have recently been applied to banking and finance, actuarial, insurance and reinsurance, and stock markets, among others. The moments that these distributions produced have never been seen in any other study but in Tsay (2014). Nevertheless, these EVDs are firstly introduced by Fisher and Tippett (1928). Mondlane et al. (2013) compare three EVDs, namely, the Gumbel, Fréchet, and Weibull. These authors use a parametric expression that depends on real shape parameter ξ and discover that when $\xi > 0$, this informs a Fréchet family case, while $\xi = 0$ resembles a Gumbel family case, and $\xi < 0$ resembles Weibull.

The GEV distribution, however, falls under a family of continuous probability distributions that are established inside EVT. Beirlant et al. (2006) disclose that the GEV is the only edge distribution of correctly normalized maxima/minima of i.i.d random series. Jenkinson (1955) uses the following standardized random variable (rv) $s = \left(\frac{x-\mu}{\sigma}\right)$ to derive the GEV distribution. $\mu \in \mathbb{R}$, and it is also known as a location parameter, and σ is the scale parameter, and it must be greater than zero to avoid undefined solutions. Given a time series $(X_1, \ldots, X_n)$, which consists of a sequence of i.i.d rv, the maximum values are given by $M_{xn}(X_1, \ldots, X_n)$. However,

Davison and Smith (1990) suggest a justified alternative EVD which describes the distribution of excess over high or low threshold. This distribution is referred to as the GPD. The advantage of the GPD is that it utilizes more sample information, for estimating the tails, than GEV which cognizes only the BMM (Zhao 2010). Šiml (2012) declares that another density function of maxima or minima (adhere as excesses) is defined in GPD. This limiting distribution of maxima or minima can be estimated in two ways under peak-over-threshold (POT) approach (1) GPD method and (2) Hill's method. First, the GPD method utilizes normal fitting techniques like the MLE, etc., while the latter provides a formula for estimating a shape parameter.

*Similar to GEV distribution, GPD contains three subfamilies of distributions according to the val*ue of shape parameter ξ. Having a density function (df) with $\xi < 0$, Šiml (2012) shows that this is a short-tailed Pareto II type, i.e., uniform or beta density function. When $\xi = 0$, this presents a thin-tailed density function that is represented by a normal, gamma, or exponential density function, and finally, $\xi > 0$ gives a heavy-tailed density function with tails that decay like power functions, such as Pareto, Student's t, and Cauchy and Fréchet distributions. Therefore, in determining the quality behavior of the tail, the shaped parameter of the GPD is dominating.

With the aim to present some of the basic techniques and methods of risk management, Skřivánková and Juhás (2012) apply EVT methods where peak-over-threshold (POT) and its generalized version peak-over-random threshold (PORT) approaches are employed. These methods are suitable for special types of excess loss. Their results indicate that all the parameter estimation methods lead to the positive value of extreme value index (EVI), hence concluding that the considered distribution is heavy-tailed. In studying the EVT for finance, Rocco (2014) discusses two parametric methods for fitting extreme values. The procedures are (1) block minima method (BMM) and (2) POT method. Both methods can be used under the maximum likelihood estimation (MLE) to estimate the parameters of the distributions. Recently Dombry (2015) has proved consistency of the maximum likelihood estimation (MLE) methods which are used in this study to estimate the parameters of both the GEV and GPD distributions. The BMM is based on the assumption that observations come from a distribution satisfying the extreme value condition so that the maximum or minimum observations follow approximately a GEV distribution. But Dombry (2013) contradicts that the properties of the MLE rely implicitly on the assumption that BMM has exactly the GEV distribution, not its approximate. In many situations, this strong assumption is unsatisfactory but lies on the domain of EVD (Dombry 2015).

On the other hand, Sigauke et al. (2014) applied an autoregressive moving average GARCH (ARMA-GARCH) to the All-Share Index (ASI) of the Johannesburg Stock Exchange (JSE) and used the filtered residuals to fit a GPD distribution. Empirical results show that the Weibull class of distributions can be used to model daily return data. The ARMA-GARCH-GPD model produces more accurate estimates of extreme returns than the ARMA-GARCH model. One way of mining upper extremes from a given data is to take the exceedances over a predetermined high threshold. POT distributions, such as the GPD or the generalized Pareto-type

(GP-type) distribution (see Verster and De Waal 2011) and referred to as the generalized single Pareto distribution (GSPD) in Sigauke et al. (2012), are also used in the studies of Sigauke and Verster.

Nonetheless, the conditional tails are successfully estimated by the GPD after filtering the return series by a GARCH process. Previous researchers focused on both the left and right tail of the distribution without examining whether the extremes in either tails are similar. However, Maghyereh and Al-Zoubi (2008) extend these classical unconditional extreme value approaches by first filtering the data to capture some of the dependencies in stock returns and thereafter apply ordinary extreme value techniques. In that way, they obtain better in-sample tail estimates and provide a better prediction for future extreme return changes, with the main advantage that the i.i.d assumption behind EVT-based tail-quantile estimator is highly achievable. Chikobvu and Chifurira (2015) fitted the GEV and GPD models with a higher degree of accuracy to the JSE mining index. The author uses the BMM for GEV and POT for GPD with the MLE for parameter estimates. In assessing VaR, the arithmetical estimates indicate that both the GPD and GEV outperform the fitted normal distribution, as the movement is furthest in the lower tail. Additionally, inferior estimates from a GEV are produced relative to that of the historical VaR, and furthermore, GPD provides slightly more conservative estimates for adequate *capitalization*.

In fact, Hung et al. (2008) study the impact of fat-tailed innovation process on the performance of 1-day-ahead VaR estimates using three GARCH models, namely, GARCH-normal (N), GARCH-Student's t, and GARCH-heavy tail. The results suggest that for asset returns that exhibit leptokurtic features, the VaR estimates generated by the GARCH-HT models have good accuracy at both low and high confidence levels. These findings suggest that heavy-tailed distribution is more suitable for energy commodities, particularly for VaR calculation. In their study of evaluating effects of excess kurtosis on VaR estimates, Baixauli and Alvarez (2006) examine and evaluate the accuracy of VaR estimates that are generated from several models by considering different distribution forms that are commonly used in the related literature, such as normal, Student's t, logistic, and Edgeworth-Sargan distributions. Their performance is evaluated using different procedures such as chi-square goodness of _t test and found that the Edgeworth-Sargan distribution outperformed the other three distributions. Assaf (2009) introduces EVT methods by estimating the maximum daily loss and computes VaR in each market. The results of this study show that the VaR estimates based on the tail index are higher than those based on a normal distribution for all markets, and therefore, a proper risk assessment should not neglect the tail behavior in these markets, since these may lead to improper evaluation of market risk. The results would also be useful to investors, bankers, and fund managers, whose success depends on the ability to forecast stock price movements in these markets and therefore build their portfolios based on these forecasts.

Methodology

Following McNeil et al. (2015) and Bee and Trapin (2018), suppose that the asset return r_t at time t can be described by the following time series specification:

$$r_t = \mu_t + \varepsilon_t, \tag{1}$$

where μ_t is a time-varying mean and ε_t is the error term that can be expressed as

$$\varepsilon_t = \nu_t \sigma_t, \tag{2}$$

where σ_t is the time-varying dynamics and ν_t is an i.i.d process with $E(\mu_t) = 0$ and $\mathrm{Var}(\nu_t) = 1$. The distribution of ν_t, specifically its tails, is the focus in this study. Both BMM and POT are used to estimate the tail regions of the innovation distribution and the associated risk. The POT is based on the Pickands-Balkema-de Haan theorem which hypothesizes that the distribution of the observations in excesses of certain high threshold can be approximated by a GPD. But with the BMM, the observation period is divided into nonoverlapping equal periods, and this restricts attention to the maximum or minimum observation in each period. The created new observations, according to Ferreira and Haan (2015), fall under the domain of attraction conditions and below the EVD denoted by G_γ for some real γ parameter. Maghyereh and Al-Zoubi (2008) emphasize that ν_t should be i.i.d and it is critical to apprehend specifications for μ_t and σ_t such that ν_t is strictly a white noise process which does not contain any time dependence when applying BMM or POT.

Return Series Modeling

As a first step, pre-filter the return series with an ordinary time series model, taking into account the observed FTSE/JSE return dynamic, in order to obtain an i.i.d residual series. The econometrics literature suggests many different models for the time series dynamics. In this study, use a Markov-Switching exponential GARCH subject to two-regime (MS(k)-EGARCH(p,q) model for the volatility with skewed Student's t-distribution, by incorporating MS(k)-EGARCH(p,q) and hoping to capture the observed characteristics of the FTSE/JSE banking indices. Our choice of MS (2)-EGARCH(p,q) model is due to its ability to capture the stylized features of volatility. Specifically, MS(2)-EGARCH(p,q) increases the flexibility of the conditional variance specification by allowing (1) mean, regime process, variance, and distribution of the series. The latter are critical for the decryption of the empirical results, since the differences between these models and common one-regime GARCH model are directly associated with them. Ideally, a random walk with drift usually models the mean process of an econometric or financial time series. For example, in a short period of time, Taylor (2008) and Mills and Markellos (2008) present the quality of the stochastic process over the structural model as in (1), (2) an asymmetric response of volatility to positive and negative financial shocks, (3) the data to determine the power of returns for which the predictable structure in the volatility pattern is the strongest, and (4) long-run volatility dependence.

With MS(2)-EGARCH(p,q), the skewness that often occurs with the financial time series is taken into account; this helps to know on which side of the distribution the extreme quantiles and extreme frequencies of the tail distribution of the return series. Ardia et al. (2016) divulge that the past negative observations have a larger influence on the conditional volatility than the past positive observations of the same magnitude which allow different specified distributions. As in Bee and Trapin (2018), use a skewed Student's t-distribution with regime-dependent shape parameters for the error term $\varepsilon_t(S_t)$. By letting S_t to be an ergodic homogeneous Markov Chain (MC) on the finite set, Bauwens et al. (2014) then disclosed that $s = \{1, \ldots, n\}$ and the transition matrix P is defined by the following probabilities

$$P_r\{S_{\mathrm{t}} = i | S_{t-1} = j, S_{t-2} = N, \ldots\} = P_r\{S_t = i | S_{t-1} = j\} = p_{ij} \tag{3}$$

that has the following invariant probability measure $\pi = \{\pi_{ij}\}$. Assume that the chain is initiated at $t = 0$ implying that $\{S_t\}_{t \geq 1}$ are independent by definition from $\{u_t\}_{t \geq 1}$. For more reading see Cruz and Mapa (2013) and Rapoo and Xaba (2017). In order to accomplish the covariance-stationarity in each regime, the following condition must be met $\beta_k < 1$. To leverage the regime shifts, specify the MS(2)-EGARCH(p,q) as

$$Y_t = \mu_t(S_t) + \nu_t = \mu_t(S_t) + \exp{[\lambda_t]}\varepsilon_t(S_t). \tag{4}$$

Test for Independently and Identically Distributed Extremes

Independently and identically distributed tests are based on the dimension of correlation with spatial embedding. The discriminating statistic that is used here is the dimension of the spatial correlation. Even so, adopt the procedure of Wang et al. (2006), who used the nonparametric method known as Brock-Dechert-Scheinkman (BDS) for testing serially independent series and nonlinear plan in a time series. The test is based on the series integral correlation described as

$$\mathrm{BDS}_{\mathrm{m.M}}(r) = \sqrt{M}\frac{C_m(r) - C_1^r(r)}{\sigma_{m.M}(r)}, \tag{5}$$

where M is the embedded points of the space with m dimension, r is the radius of a sphere centered on X_i, C is the constant, and $\sigma_{m.\ M}(r)$ is the standard deviation of

$\sqrt{M}C_m(r) - C_1^r(r)$ which is the correctional integral. Reject the null hypothesis of i. i.d when the computed probability value is less than the suggested significance level.

Extreme Value Theory and Risk Measures

In this section, EVT methods for estimating and predicting tail behavior of FTSE/ JSE returns and the extreme risk related to the tails are discussed.

Extreme Value Theory

The purpose of this section is to summarize the set of results of the EVT necessary to develop the theoretical foundation for this study. For more readings on EVT, see Sigauke et al. (2014), Maposa et al. (2016), and Bee and Trapin (2018). The modeling of extremes may be done in two different ways: modeling as set of minimum values and some set of minimum values below some low threshold. In this way, there are two significant results where the asymptotic distribution of minima is modeled by BMM under the GEV distribution, while the second significant result concerns the distribution of excess over a given threshold and shows that the limiting distribution is the GPD.

The Generalized Extreme Value

The GEV distribution falls under a family of continuous probability distributions that were established inside EVT. This was to cartel the Gumbel, Fréchet, and Weibull families which are also known as type I, II, and III EVDs. Given a time series $M_{xn} = \max\{X_1, \ldots, X_n\}$, we therefore follow Zhao (2010) and Calabrese and Giudici (2015); define the GEV distribution as

$$G_{\text{ev}}(\xi, \sigma, \mu) = \begin{cases} \exp\left(-(1+\xi s)^{-\frac{1}{\xi}}\right), \xi \neq 0 \\ \exp(-\exp(-s)), \xi = 0 \end{cases} 1 + \xi\left(\frac{x-\mu}{\sigma}\right) > 0, \sigma > 0, \tag{6}$$

where σ is the scale parameter, μ is the location parameter, and ξ is a shape parameter which indicates the tail behavior of a distribution. When $\xi > 0$, the expression is valid for $s > -\frac{1}{\xi}$, and this corresponds to the Fréchet tail. But, when $\xi < 0$, the expression is valid for $s < -\frac{1}{\xi}$; this corresponds to the Weibull tail type. For the former, $s = 0$ at the lower end point, while the latter, $s = 1$.

The Generalized Pareto Distribution

In EVT, the GPD plays the role of a natural distribution model for excesses over a reasonably high threshold. In other words, GPD plays the same role as POT and also the same as the BMM on the GEV distribution (Maposa 2016). According to Arnold (2015), the shape of ξ in the GPD is equal to that of the corresponding GEV. MacDonald (2011) and Nortey et al. (2015) showed that for a sequence of observations say $X_1, \ldots, X_n$, the extremes $x - u$ of some suitably high threshold u can be well approximated by GPD(ξ, σ, μ). Chinhamu et al. (2015b) also discover that a two-parameter GPD with scale parameter σ and shape parameter ξ has the following representation:

$$G_{\xi,\beta}(x) = \begin{cases} 1 - \left(1 + \frac{\xi x}{\beta}\right)^{\frac{-1}{\xi}}, & \xi \neq 0 \\ 1 - e^{-\left(\frac{x}{\beta}\right)}, & \xi = 0 \end{cases}, \tag{7}$$

where $x > 0$ when $\xi \leq 0$, $0 \leq x \leq \beta/\xi$ for $\xi < 0$ and $\beta > 0$ (Tsay 2014; Chinhamu et al. 2015a)).

Risk Measures

Risk measures are historical predictors for investment risk and volatility, and they also form an important component of the modern portfolio theory (MPT) which is a standard financial approach to evaluating a stock or a stock fund's performance compared with its benchmark index. The proposed risk measures for the SA banking sector are discussed in this section.

Value-at-Risk (Var)

VaR is the most common risk measure in the finance industry, and it has been recommended in Basel II accord. Considering the loss L of a portfolio over a given time period Δ, VaR is a risk statistic that measures the risk of holding the portfolio for the time period Δ. Assume that L has a distribution function F_L, and then Brodin and Klüppelberg (2014) and Bernard et al. (2017) define VaR at level $\alpha_\epsilon(0, 1)$:

$$\mathrm{VaR}_\alpha^\Delta = \inf\{x\epsilon\mathbb{R} : Pr(L > x) \leq 1 - \alpha\} = \inf\{x\epsilon\mathbb{R} : F_L \geq \alpha\}. \tag{8}$$

Typical values of α are 95% and 99%, while Δ usually is a day or 20 days depending on the intuition of the research.

Expected Shortfall (ES)

For risk management, transfer pricing, and strategic capital allocation, stock markets need to break down firm-wide losses into contributions from individual groups or trading desks, to see how the stock price return denoted by R is being decomposed into the sum of each group's return r_i, that is, $R = \sum_i y_i r_i$, where y_i is the weight of the ith group in the total portfolio. Nevertheless, Acharya et al. (2017) compute ES by

$$\mathrm{ES}_\alpha = -\sum_i y_i E[r_i | R \le -\mathrm{VaR}_\alpha], \tag{9}$$

where R is the stock price return, r_i is the sum of each return's group, and y_i is the weight of group i in the total portfolio.

Conditional Tail Expectation (CTE)

The loss distribution above the quantile does not influence the risk measure. Therefore, choose conditional tail expectation (CTE) because the measure addresses some of the problems with the quantile risk measure. By adopting theorem 3 of Yang et al. (2015), then the study follows and computes CTE as

$$\mathrm{CTE}_\alpha(X) = E[-X | X \le \mathrm{VaR}_\alpha(X)] = \frac{1}{\alpha} \int_{-\infty}^{F^{-1}\alpha} x f(x) \mathrm{d}x \tag{10}$$

Glue VaR Risk

This is defined by a function with four parameters. Glue-value-at-risk measurement can also be harmonized in a large range of contexts if the parameters have been standardized. This allows Glue VaR to contain the risk of mild tagged losses that are between VaR and CTE. Hence, Glue VaR is computed by Eq. (11):

$$\mathrm{GlueVaR}_{\beta,\alpha}^{h_1,h_2}(X) = \omega_1.\mathrm{CTE}_\beta(X) + \omega_2.\mathrm{CTE}_\alpha(X) + \omega_3.\mathrm{VaR}_\alpha(X), \tag{11}$$

where ω_1, ω_2, and ω_3 are from the notation $\begin{cases} \omega_1 = h_1 - \dfrac{(h_2 - h_1).(1-\beta)}{\beta - \alpha} \\ \omega_2 = \dfrac{h_2 - h_1}{\beta - \alpha}.(1-\alpha) \\ \omega_3 = 1 - \omega_1 - \omega_2 = 1 - h_2 \end{cases}$.

The choice of this measure is based on the omega ratio as a tool for effectiveness measurement, and it also helps in dividing a set of investment outcomes into two groups: the area of profits and the area of losses. Furthermore, no other study has applied this measure for risk assessment for financial market risk.

Goodness of _t Tests and Backtesting

In order to validate GEV and GPD together with the proposed risk measures, use the parametric goodness-of-fit (GoF) tests and the conditional and unconditional backtesting procedures. For the GoF, the Shapiro-Wilk (S-W) and Anderson-Darling (A-D) tests are used. The A-D test is a modified Kolmogorov-Smirnov (S-K) test which gives the tails more weight than the K-S. The critical values of the A-D test are calculated using a specific region. This offers a more sensitive test and the advantage of calculating critical values for each distribution (Saculinggan and Balase 2013). Hence, the A-D test is estimated by Eq. (12):

$$A_n^2 = n\int_{-\infty}^{\infty} \widehat{F}_n(t) - F(t)^2 \frac{\mathrm{d}F(t)}{F(t)(1 - F(t))}, \tag{12}$$

where $\widehat{F}_n(t)$ is the Kaplan-Meier estimate based on the sample of residuals and $F(t)$ is the distribution under the null hypothesis. If all observations are complete, then $\widehat{F}_n(t)$ coincides with an empirical distribution function. And the S-W is estimated by Eq. (13):

$$W = \frac{\sum_{i=1}^{n} (a_i x_i)^2}{\sum_{i=1}^{n} (x_i - \overline{x})^2}. \tag{13}$$

x_i are the ordered sample values and with a_i being the constants generated from the means, variances, and covariances of the order statistics of a sample of size n from a normal distribution. The null hypothesis that the random sample comes the normal distribution is rejected, if the test statistic W is less than or equal to W_α the critical value for the significance level the probability of α type I error. The conditional and unconditional backtesting procedures that are used are the Kupiec likelihood ratio (LR) test for unconditional coverage, which was established by Kupiec (1995), and Christoffersen test for conditional coverage, which was developed by Christoffersen and Pelletier (2004) as an extension to the Kupiec test, and lastly the Basel II green zone which was modified by the Committee (2019). Kupiec (1995) proposes the LR statistics LRUC to accurately estimate the risk violation rate and computes the test as follows:

Table 1 The Basel II zones

	Confidence level			
Zone	90%	95%	99%	Multiplication factor
Green	0–32	0–17	0–4	3
Yellow	33–43	18–26	5–9	3.40, 3.50, 3.65, 3.75 or 3.85
Red	≥44	≥27	≥10	4

Source: Bank for International Settlements, the Basel II; Authors' creation

$$\mathrm{LR_{UC}} = 2\ln\left(\frac{(1-p)^{n-x}p^x}{\left(\left(1-\frac{S_n}{n}\right)\right)^{n-x}\left(\frac{S_n}{n}\right)^x}\right)\tilde{\chi}_1^2. \tag{14}$$

However, Christoffersen and Pelletier (2004) extend the Kupiec test to take account of the serial independence of violations (i.e., extreme clustering), and the test is computed by Eq. (15):

$$\mathrm{LR_{cC}} = -2\ln\left(\frac{(1-\pi)^{\eta_{11}+\eta_{12}\pi\eta_{21}+\eta_{22}}}{(1-\pi_1)^{\eta_{11}}\,\pi_1{}^{\eta_{21}}(1-\pi_2)^{\eta_{12}}\,\pi_2{}^{\eta_{22}}}\right). \tag{15}$$

Note that Eq. (14) is an asymptotic chi-square distribution with one degree of freedom which according to Agresti and Kateri (2011), Kallah-Dagadu (2013) estimates as follows:

$$\chi^2 = \sum\nolimits_{i=1}^{k}\frac{\left(n_{ij}-\mu_{ij}\right)^2}{\mu_{ij}}, \tag{16}$$

n_{ij} is the set of Ks observed counts, and μ_{ij} are the expected counts under the null hypothesis. With the Basel II green zone, the market risk is covered due to its activities, and their capital requirement size is calculated as Eq. (17):

$$\mathrm{Cap} = \mathrm{Fact} * \max\left(\mathrm{VaR}_t(0.01), \frac{1}{60}\sum\nolimits_{i=0}^{59}\mathrm{VaR}_{t-1}(0.01)\right), \tag{17}$$

where Fact is the multiplication factor reported in Table 1.

Data Analysis and Discussion

This section presents results from empirical analyses of the data. The results are summarized in tables and graphs; and the aim is to model the extreme losses of stock price returns and explore the effectiveness of risk measures for measuring the risk of investment.

Exploratory Data Analysis

Five-day business day FTSE/JSE closing banking indices from JSE are used. These cover the total period of 02 January 2008 to 20 April 2018. The plots of the logarithmic closing stock returns are shown in Fig. 1. Relative dynamics of the FTSE/JSE closing banking indices are observed for the specified period. It is also noted that the mean of returns is constant, while the variance oscillates around high volatility (instability) and low volatility (tranquility). This implies that FTSE/JSE closing banking indices have volatility clustering. It is very much evident from Fig. 1 that the volatility of FTSE/JSE closing banking indices had increased significantly during recent times, especially from 2009 to 2012. Nleya (2015) states that this occurrence is ascribed to the panic in the markets that is caused by global financial crises.

Xaba et al. (2015), on the other hand, find that few banks have most condensed stock returns, while others have prevalent stock returns. As uncovered in Fig. 1, both Capitec and FNB have most reduced stock returns, while the remaining three banks have vast stock returns. Before executing the main analysis of the study, a few basic issues, for instance, the normality of stock returns, are reported in this study as recommended by Cox (2017). Descriptive measures are utilized to additionally

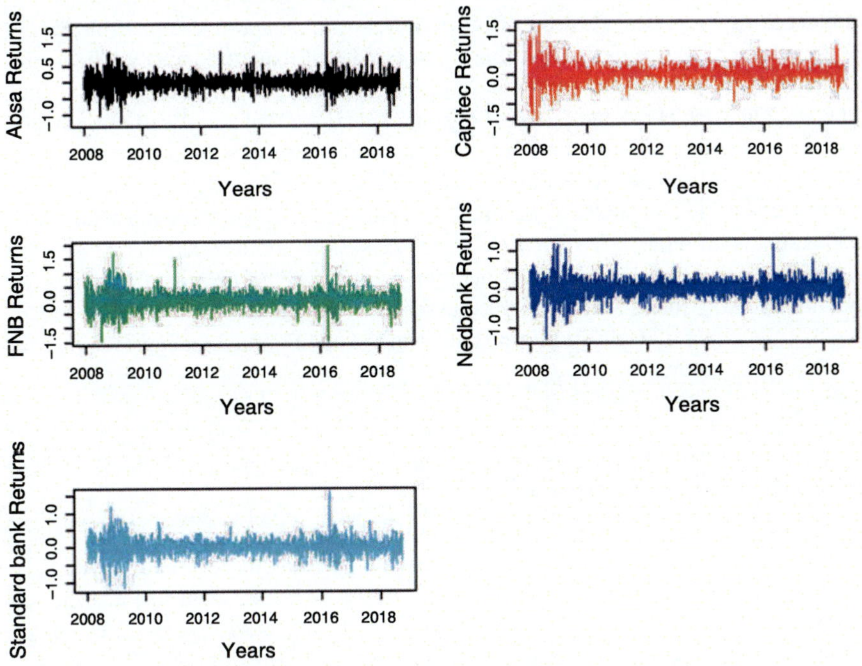

Fig. 1 Five-day returns of FTSE/JSE banking indices. Source: Author's creation

clarify properties of the returns for a predefined time, and the outcomes are accounted for in Table 2.

The unconditional standard deviations as reported in Table 2 are relatively comparable. The mean and standard deviation of the ABSA, Nedbank, and Standard Bank indices are similar to each other. The Capitec index, however, has the highest standard deviation. The magnitude of the average return is very small compared to the standard deviation. Mokoena (2016) and Beytell (2016) in their studies report the same results. The five return series considered all revealed kurtosis above 3, indicating that the return series are all leptokurtic. Another feature of the returns series is the presence of skewness. In fact, all the indices are negatively skewed confirming the results of the J-B, A-D, and S-W as all the three tests reject the null hypothesis of normality. This slight negative skewness indicates that the lower tail of the distribution is thicker than the upper tail and decline in returns is more common than their increases. According to Vee and Gonpot (2014), Khula and Moroke (2016), and Korkpoe and Junior (2018), stock markets are described by boom-bust cycles, and such cycles feed into the volatility of the markets.

Markov-Switching Exponential GARCH

This section presents the results obtained from the proposed MS(2)-EGARCH(p,q). Using a maximum likelihood method, estimate the EGARCH(1,1) of Nelson (1991) subject to two regimes. Skewed t-distribution errors to capture the possible fat-tail performance of the empirical distribution of FTSE/JSE banking indices. The conditional mean parameter denoted by mean (μ) is statistically significant for all the three models. The ARCH (α) and GARCH (β) parameters are also statistically significant, indicating the presence of conditional heteroscedasticity effects in the stock price returns in each regime. Additionally, stationarity is met by summing together the estimated ARCH and GARCH parameters in each regime, and these are found to be all less than one. That is, $\alpha + \beta < 1$ (Klaassen (2002). In addition, skewed Student's t (δ) parameters are positive and statistically significant, signifying that the returns are not normally distributed. The gamma parameter (γ) is statistically significant, meaning that the effect of negative return shocks on the conditional variance is higher for stock in price returns.

In-Sample Goodness-of-Fit

To confirm whether or that a skewed t-distribution is correctly specified, use the J-B, A-D, and S-W to test that the null hypothesis of the estimated empirical distribution of the returns is a standard normal distribution against the alternative of the estimated empirical distribution of the returns other than a normal distribution. The results of the study tabulated in Table 3 suggest that the empirical distribution fitted to the MS

Table 2 Descriptive statistics for returns series

	Mean	Median	Std. dev	Skewness	Kurtosis	J-B test	S-W test	A-D test
ABSA	0.0002	0.0001	0.2062	−0.0727	3.9313	1383.6(0.001)	0.93(0.001)	30.9(0.001)
Capitec	0.0012	0.0003	0.2191	−0.1002	4.9362	5639.9(0.001)	0.15(0.001)	72.64(0.001)
FNB	0.0005	0.0006	0.2583	−0.2414	4.3399	1995.4(0.001)	0.69(0.001)	85.9(0.001)
Nedbank	0.0003	0.0001	0.1969	−0.0111	3.7922	1514.0(0.001)	0.87(0.001)	41.3(0.001)
Standard	0.0003	0.0001	0.2015	−0.0539	4.0258	1718.7(0.001)	0.87(0.001)	43.9(0.001)

NB: values in () are probability values of the S-W and A-D, respectively
Source: Authors' creation

Table 3 In-sample goodness-of-fit tests

	Absa	Capitec	FNB	Nedbank	Standard
Tests	MS(2)-EGARCH(1,1)				
A-D	0.028(0.001)	0.66(0.002))	0.27(0.05))	0.21(0.004)	0.19(0.002)
S-W	0.96(0.008)	0.99(0.005)	0.99(0.003)	0.99(0.001)	0.99(0.009)
J-B	0.269(0.006)	0.87(0.008)	0.96(0.004)	0.93(0.009)	0.88(0.005)
LM	0.970(0.123)	0.500(0.487)	0.500(0.517)	0.510(0.508)	0.532(0.902)
Q test	2.266(0.007)	2.870(0.001)	1.128(0.001)	3.999(0.006)	0.630(0.006)
BDS	0.498(0.751)	2.472(0.156)	0.498(0.365)	0.499(0.129)	0.500(0.122)

NB: Values in () are P-values of A-D, S-W, J-B, LM, Ljung-Q, and BDS tests
Source: Authors' creation

Table 4 Maximum likelihood estimates for the GEV

Bank	Block size	Minimas	ξ	se(ξ)	σ	se(σ)	μ	se(μ)
ABSA	22	150	0.052	0.049	1.325	0.084	3.151	0.115
Capitec	23	143	0.398	0.231	2.289	0.328	6.810	0.857
FNB	15	219	0.219	0.048	1.809	0.074	6.131	0.411
Nedbank	30	110	0.072	0.162	1.319	0.325	2.999	0.100
Standard Bank	258	13	0.166	0.450	1.321	0.774	8.006	0.418

Source: Authors' creation

(2)-EGARCH(1,1) is a skewed t-distribution. Therefore, the empirical distribution of a skewed t-distribution is correctly specified. This is also conformed with the results in Table 2 where the skewness coefficient indicates a skewed distribution; also, the GoF test revealed non-normality in returns series.

Frequency Analysis of Extreme Quantiles

The FTSE/JSE closing banking indices stock prices are fitted on GEV for block minima and GPD for peak-over-threshold, and the method of the MLE is used estimate the parameters, and this allows simple approximations for both standard errors and confidence intervals (See Bee and Trapin 2018). Summarized in Table 4 are the MLE of the GEV distribution. Using different block sizes, a positive shape parameter is estimated indicating that the five banking indices follow a Fréchet family distribution for all the block size frames considered. The results, however, are in accordance with the finding of Coles et al. (2001) and Chan (2016).

A GPD distribution is estimated using the MLE method through POT. According to many authors such as Luceño (2006), Bee (2012), Arnold (2015), and Bee and Trapin (2018), among others, the GPD is a two-parameter distribution that has only a scale parameter and a shape parameter. Use a mean excess life plot to select a threshold for the GPD presented in Fig. 2. For each bank, different thresholds are selected. The pattern change for a very high threshold is apparent here, but the

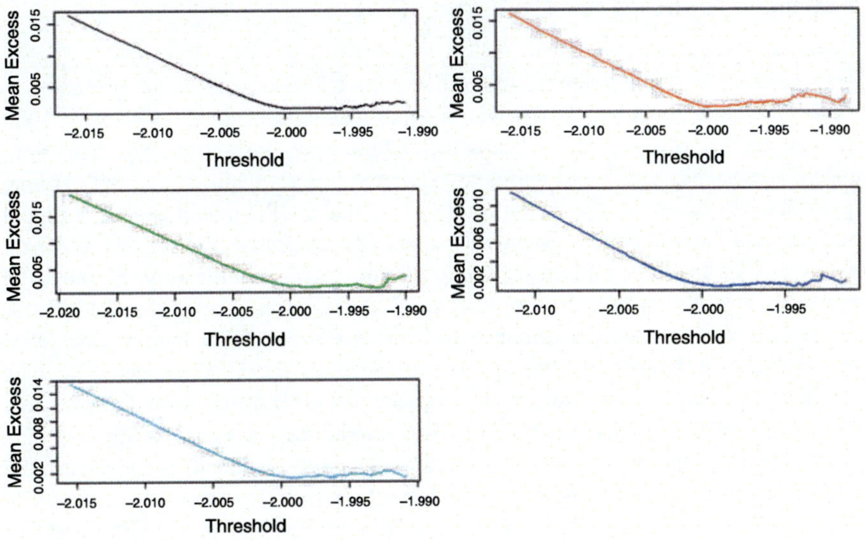

Fig. 2 Mean excess for threshold selection. Source: Author's creation

Table 5 Maximum likelihood estimates for the GPD

	Threshold		Extremes	Estimated parameters and standard errors			
Bank	p	u	n	ξ	se(ξ)	β	se(β)
ABSA	0.979	−1.997	677	0.185	0.005	−0.083	0.016
Capitec	0.538	−1999	688	0.085	0.003	0.443	0.034
FNB	0.563	−1.998	463	0.220	0.006	−0.069	0.018
Nedbank	0.567	−1.996	695	0.174	0.005	−0.058	0.018
Standard Bank	0.668	−1.998	313	0.167	0.005	−0.040	0.019

Source: Authors' creation

disturbances in relation to sampling errors are considered relatively small. Therefore, $u = -1:997$ for a return of ABSA, $u = -1:999$ for a return from Capitec, $u = -1:998$ for FNB, $u = -1:996$ for a return from Nedbank, and finally $u = -1:998$ for a return from Standard Bank.

We then proceed by estimating the GPD by the use of the MLE procedure, and Table 5 is the parameter estimates for a GPD model. The shape parameters for the five bank returns are all positive. This implies that a fitted model was a type II GPD, which is known as a Fréchet GDP, as the slope of the model falls faster near the selected threshold and produces infinitely long and thicker tails. The left tails of this type of loss distributions are fat, i.e., the probability of occurrence of extreme loss was higher than that of a normal distribution (Kourouma et al. (2010)). Furthermore, the estimated parameters are efficient because a threshold denoted by u is near zero, which makes the estimated model to be more robust and reliable. For instance, see Brabson and Palutikof (2000) for the efficiency of GPD parameters with a small selected threshold.

Extreme Quantiles for GEV and GPD

True values of extreme quantiles of a GEV and a GPD distribution are presented in Table 6. Unlike Jocković (2016) who change a sample from 15 to 45 with 1000 MCMC replications, this study keeps the sample size constant at 2575. This is to ensure consistency and avoid biases of estimated models while estimating extreme quantiles. The results of the current study prove that a GPD model and GEV model performs similarly at both 95% and 99% quantiles, respectively. The 95% and 99% extreme quantiles for a GPD distribution do not change significantly. Equally, the same findings are deduced from the GEV distribution. Using the RMSE for assessing the prediction performance for both GEV and GPD models, the GEV model shows a better performance as compared to the GPD model. The bias estimation is less for a GEV model as compared to a GPD distribution. For instance, by looking at the ABSA returns, the GEV model has at most 10.6% less bias estimation as proposed to GPD distribution. But with Nedbank, for instance, the GPD distribution produces RMSE of 24.6% which is higher than that of the GEV model by 7.1%. In general, all the RMSE for GEV are less than that of GPD, and this gives the GEV distribution better quantile estimates for all the banks.

Extreme Value Theory as a Risk Measure

Four common risk measures that are known as VaR, ES, CTE, and Glue VaR risk are used to compute the risk for FTSE/JSE closing banking indices. To show the results

Table 6 Extreme quantile estimates

Bank	Model	95%	99%	RMSE	Model	0.95	0.99	RMSE
ABSA	GEV	9.801	9.873	0.038	GPD	9.938	9.937	0.144
	Quantile mean	9.818	9.932		Quantile mean	9.818	9.932	
Capitec	GEV	23.335	26.493	0.160	GPD	21.138	21.144	0.185
	Quantile mean	21.124	21.144		Quantile mean	21.124	21.144	
FNB	GEV	23.961	28.898	0.173	GPD	20.555	21.135	0.248
	Quantile mean	21.124	21.144		Quantile mean	21.124	21.144	
Nedbank	GEV	23.609	28.098	0.175	GPD	20.520	21.132	0.246
	Quantile mean	21.124	21.144		Quantile mean	21.124	21.144	
Standard Bank	GEV	23.730	28.631	0.178	GPD	21.125	21.145	0.225
	Quantile mean	21.124	21.144		Quantile mean	21.124	21.144	

Source: Authors' creation

of the EVT as a financial risk measure, risk measures discussed in the previous chapter are estimated and the results presented in Table 7.

For the GEV distribution, taking the extreme losses from the ABSA bank at 99%, VaR is 1.206. This indicates that 99% of the time, the bank is expected not to lose more than 1.206%, while the expected loss using ES at 99% is 0.984%. Nevertheless, while using CTE, the extreme losses for Standard Bank are 11.061. The implication here is that the highest losses expected by this bank are 11.061% daily. Looking at Nedbank, not more than 0.878% losses are expected daily. Glue VaR risk indicated that only 3.077% losses for Capitec bank are expected daily. Similar interpretations can be made for GPD model. CTE for the GPD model indicates that the extreme loss of not more than 11.201% is expected for Capitec bank, while Glue VaR risk gives the smallest expected daily losses of 0.842% for ABSA bank, Capitec Bank, Nedbank, and Standard Bank, respectively. Park and Kim reveal that a 1-day change in the financial market's value would not decrease by more than by 0.842%. To take into account market liquidity constraints and Basel regulations, 5-day risk horizons in addition to the more typical 1-day horizon are being considered.

In general, Glue VaR risk produces fewer risk computations as compared to other three risk measures. Table 8 reports the average computation of the risk measures for the five banks. The results confirm that Glue VaR risk reveals few risks as compared to other risk measures for both the GEV and GPD models. For instance, while comparing VaR_{95} and Glue – VaR $Risk_{95}$, Glue VaR $Risk_{95}$ shows 2.36% less bias estimation than VaR_{95}. At 99%, Glue VaR $Risk_{99}$ reveals 0.418% less bias estimation than VaR_{99}. This is reported for the GEV distribution for all the banks. For the GPD distribution, Glue VaR $Risk_{95}$ as compared to ES_{95}, for example, presents 0.843% less bias estimation, while 99% Glue VaR $Risk_{99}$ shows 8.323% less bias estimation compared to CTE_{99}. This implies that the computation of economic capital using Glue VaR risk is more conservative than using other risk measures

Table 7 Computed risk measure

		Generalized extreme value model				Generalized Pareto distribution model			
Bank	*P*	VaR	ES	CTE	Glue VaR-	VaR	ES	CTE	Glue VaR
ABSA	0.95	1.738	1.413	3.211	1.572	1.140	1.370	8.479	0.842
	0.99	1.206	0.984	5.351	3.074	1.140	1.890	10.719	0.953
Capitec	0.95	4.775	4.419	7.727	1.572	2.195	3.070	8.456	0.842
	0.99	4.625	4.072	10.781	3.077	2.195	3.070	11.201	0.953
FNB	0.95	4.775	4.419	6.270	1.573	1.582	1.874	8.081	1.572
	0.99	4.191	3.976	9.405	3.073	1.582	2.592	9.699	3.074
Nedbank	0.95	1.607	1.293	3.585	1.572	1.156	1.363	7.895	0.842
	0.99	1.091	0.878	6.212	3.073	1.156	1.869	10.137	3.074
Standard Bank	0.95	6.771	6.512	8.319	1.572	1.227	1.482	8.292	0.842
	0.99	6.345	6.175	11.061	3.074	1.227	2.132	10.987	3.074

Source: Authors' creation

Table 8 Backtesting of VaR

Banks	Model	*P*-values for Kupiec test				*P*-values for Christoffersen test			
		Risk measure	Level	0.95	0.99	Risk measure	Level	0.95	0.99
ABSA	GEV	VaR	Losses	0.517	0.378	VaR	Losses	0.207	0.885
	GPD	VaR	Losses	0.919	0.877	VaR	Losses	0.865	0.987
Capitec	GEV	VaR	Losses	0.517	0.522	VaR	Losses	0.476	0.939
	GPD	VaR	Losses	0.796	0.950	VaR	Losses	0.871	0.994
FNB	GEV	VaR	Losses	0.529	0.902	VaR	Losses	0.801	0.739
	GPD	VaR	Losses	0.668	0.872	VaR	Losses	0.701	0.885
Nedbank	GEV	VaR	Losses	0.650	0.872	VaR	Losses	0.698	0.839
	GPD	VaR	Losses	0.694	0.682	VaR	Losses	0.980	0.794
Standard Bank	GEV	VaR	Losses	0.697	0.232	VaR	Losses	0.578	0.815
	GPD	VaR	Losses	0.712	0.872	VaR	Losses	0.898	0.988

Table 9 Average computation of risk measures

Model	CI	VaR	ES	CTE	Glue VaR risk
GEV	95%	3.933	3.611	5.822	1.572
	99%	3.492	3.217	8.562	3.074
GPD	95%	1.460	1.831	8.241	0.988
	99%	1.460	2.311	10.549	2.226

Source: Authors' creation

under the GEV distribution. Therefore, the conclusion made is that GEV and GPD estimates of Glue VaR risk under different confidence levels exhibit analogous characteristics as observed from VaR, ES, and CTE. Generally, it is noticed from Table 8 that GPD distribution has fewer bias estimates for all the risk measures as opposed to the GEV distribution. This makes the GPD distribution more superior than the GEV distribution, because for $GEV - VaR_{95} = 3.933$ and $GPD - VaR_{95} = 1.460$ which give the GPD model 2.473 less biasness than the GEV, with 1.78% for ES, while $GEV - CTE_{95}$ gives 2.419 less bias estimate than $GPD - CTE_{95}$ (Table 9).

Goodness-of-Fit and Backtesting Results

This section of the study presents the goodness of _t tests for both GEV and GPD and the backtesting results for the proposed risk measures.

Goodness of _t Tests

The A-D and S-W tests for GoF tests are used, and the results are shown in Table 10. Nonetheless, Stephens (1977) recommends these for the GoF for extreme value

Table 10 Goodness-of-fit tests for GEV and GPD

Tests		ABSA	Capitec	FNB	Nedbank	Standard
		Generalized extreme value model				
A-D	Statistic	0.415	0.551	0.541	0.415	0.157
	P-value	0.335	0.156	0.165	0.334	0.954
S-W	Statistic	0.062	0.074	0.106	0.068	0.024
	P-value	0.362	0.247	0.093	0.301	0.926
		Generalized Pareto distribution model				
A-D	Statistic	0.279	0.136	0.364	0.545	0.278
	Prob	0.648	0.978	0.44	0.162	0.652
S-W	Statistic	0.049	0.018	0.049	0.085	0.047
	P-value	0.52	0.983	0.526	0.176	0.561

Source: Authors' creation

distributions. Chikobvu and Chifurira (2015) and Maposa et al. (2016) also use these tests for testing GoF for both GEV and GPD distributions in their studies. The null hypothesis that the returns follow either GEV or GPD is not rejected (p-values are not significant). Hence, the FTSE/JSE closing stock price banking indices are fitted very well with the specified distributions. This implies that in extreme market conditions, it is thus possible to estimate the potential losses for stock and commodity indices.

Backtesting Risk Measures

To evaluate the accuracy of the risk measures, a backtesting procedure is used, and the estimates are given in Table 8 in the text and Tables 11, 12, and 13 in the Appendix. While backtesting the estimated risk measures, a predicted loss is compared to the actual loss observed on the next day. When the actual loss is greater than the estimated risk measure, exceedances have occurred. For VaR, a statistically expected number of exceedances over the VaR curve are expected. Tables 8, 11, 12, and 13 provide results of backtesting risk measures from GEV and GPD models, respectively. The null hypothesis is that the risk model is correctly specified and accurately predicts financial risk for the five banks. Nevertheless, both the Kupiec test and the Christoffersen tests suggest that the null hypothesis is not rejected and the conclusion is that the four risk measures for both GEV and GPD produce reliable, efficient, and unbiased risk estimates for both 95% and 99% confidence levels. For long time period such as 10 years as it is the case in this study, the models produce suitable risk estimates. According to Bee and Trapin (2018), these long time periods are indicated by high probability values for losses at all selected confidence levels of all the tests used.

During ES backtesting, both tests produce high probability values, indicating that the estimates of GEV and GPD at all levels are all very suitable. Furthermore, GPD values are valid for all tests at all quantile levels and for extreme losses. There is a strong evidence that GPD is a more adequate model for VaR and ES estimations, as compared to the GEV model in both 95th and 99th percentiles. Besides, a capital adequacy directive forced market risk analysis through banking supervision in 1996. In today's market risk analysis, the methods used continue. The calculated risk measurement values must be multiplied, according to Kourouma et al. (2010). That is, on a daily basis, each bank must meet a capital requirement that is conveyed as higher of its previous day's VaR number which is measured according to the specified parameters and an average of daily measures on each of the preceding 60 business days, multiplied by a multiplicative factor. The same interpretation can be made for CTE and Glue VaR Risk.

Basel II Green Zone

Table 14 summarizes the outcomes of the regulatory backtest on the risk measures. The values in the Table show the number of times in backtests, which are used in 1 year (250 trading days) by risk measures in all three zones. The test is ranked as follows (1) a green zone, if in a window of 250 trade day the number of exceptions reported is 0 to 4, (2) a yellow area, if there are 5–9 exceptions, and a red zone, if there are more than 9 exceptions. Neither of the risk measures avoids a regulatory penalty, with all of them slipping into the yellow zone, which imposes a penalty between 0.40 and 0.85 times the VaR for calculation of the market risk charge (Bee and Trapin 2018).

Interestingly, the hybrids with 250 days of data perform uniformly throughout all the risk measures. This gives an annual average penalty that ranges from 23% to 65%. Generally, all the risk measures show that both the GEV and GPD distributions are good estimator models for extreme losses for the five banks' stock returns. At 99% confidence level, the risk measures do not produce the most worrying results. For example, ABSA only produces zero exceptions out of 250 observations. Nieppola (2009) notes that there is only a very small likelihood, which is less than 0.01%, that an accurate model with a correct coverage of 99% would produce as much as 10 or more exceptions. Hence, the current study finds that the risk models has estimated extreme tail losses with adequate accuracy for all the banks.

Conclusion

As the volatility in the oil markets increases, implementing an effective risk management system becomes an urgent necessity. In risk management, the VaR methodology as a measure of market risk has gained fast acceptance and popularity in both institutions and regulators. Furthermore, EVT has been successfully applied in many fields where extreme values may appear. The current study aims to empirically investigate the tail behavior and the associated risk for the five FTSE/JSE banking indices in South Africa. To achieve this, use GEV for block minimas and GPD for peak-over-threshold and estimate the parameters of the two distributions via a maximum likelihood method. Then later estimated the extreme risk on the tails of the distributions.

All the parameters of the of the GEV distribution are found positive and significant for all the banks studied with a shape parameter greater than zero. This stipulates that the FTSE/JSE closing banking indices are fitted with a Fréchet family distribution. Moreover, a GPD, the parameter estimates are found significant with type II GPD, known as a Fréchet GDP, as the shape parameter is greater than zero. This gives more efficient parameters for the GPD as selected thresholds are small. Also Juárez and Schucany (2004) discover that the MLE for GPD has the highest efficiency when threshold is near zero. Similar results were found by Brabson and Palutikof (2000), whose study shows efficient GPD parameters with a small selected threshold.

For the sustained loss and risk, VaR, ES, CTE and Glue VaR risk are estimated for the five banking indices. At the probability of 95%, ABSA bank, for instance, had a VaR of 1.783. This indicates that the expected loss on returns is not more 1.783% in worst-case scenario within the 1 day. The same interpretation is done for the 99% with an expected loss not being more than 1.206% in 1 day. With the expected shortfall for the extreme loss of ABSA, the expected conditional loss is 1.413%, which is smaller than the VaR by 32.5% for GEV modeling. Computation of economic capital while using ES was found to be more conservative than using VaR. The GEV estimates of ES under different quantile levels unveil analogous characteristics as perceived from VaR. Similar interpretations are made for GPD. For GPD ABSA returns index, VaR is estimated at 1.140% for the 95th percentile for the left tail. According to Park the expectation here is that a 1-day change in the financial market's value would not decrease by more than 1.140%. To take into account market liquidity constraints and Basel regulations, 5-day risk horizons in addition to a more typical 1-day horizon are considered.

Kupiec and Christoffersen tests suggest that estimates of the four risk measures for GEV and GPD cannot be rejected. The distributions for long-time positions produce suitable risk estimates. Chinhamu2015b has discovered that these long positions are indicated by high probability values for losses at all selected levels. Similar findings are recorded by the current study. On average, both tests produce at most 81% of risk accuracy at 95% significance level for Kupiec test on ES estimates, while at 99% produced 67.9% on average. The Christoffersen test on average produces 73.9% at 95% on ES estimates and 64.6% at 99% level. It is worth noting that 99% estimates produce lesser risk estimates as compared to 95% estimates. This indicates that 99% estimates are more reliable than 95% as the expected losses in 1 day are less than expected losses at 95% level.

Basel Committee on Banking Supervision, herein known as Basel II zones backtest results, give more understanding of risk analysis. The test is classified as follows: (1) the green zone if the number of exceptions reported in a window of 250 trading days lies between 0 and 4, (2) the yellow zone if the number of exceptions lies between 5 and 9 and (3) the red zone if the number of exceptions is more than nine. Neither of the risk measures avoids a regulatory penalty as all of them slipped into the yellow zone, which summoned a penalty between 0.40 and 0.85 times the VaR for calculation of the market risk charge Bee and Trapin (2018). Hence this clearly shows that risk distributions in this study had estimate extreme tail losses with adequate accuracy in all the banks.

Financial risk is any of various types of risk associated with financing, including financial transactions that include company loans in risk of default. Therefore, risk analysts can use the proposed loss distributions in this study to predict their financial loss and further estimate the risk associated with the losses. Associated risk factors should be taken into consideration while predicting the loss risk with these loss distributions. Insurance companies may also use loss distributions to draw their risk management policy towards their loss on investment and return levels on their losses.

Banks may also use the findings to generally predict their investment risk. For their daily operations, the loss distribution together with their associated risk measures can be used to predict their daily operational risk. For their credit risk, the findings might also be useful particularly the ones selected in this study. Future studies may also adopt multivariate loss distributions and multivariate copula methods to test or check the interdependence and extreme relationships within the banks of companies in the stock market.

The findings of this study diverge from other previous studies when predicting financial risk. Studies such as of Chinhamu et al. (2015a) for instance, use only VaR and ES. In order to avoid biases that may be caused by using only two risk measures, researchers and scholars should engage more risk measures such as the ones used in this study and other like Tail conditional median, expected proportional shortfall, Wang's risk measure etc. as these measures and many others are available in the work of Chan and Nadarajah (2018). Also, future studies should add one more backtesting procedure known as quantile dynamic test as seen in Jeremić (2015), which is not considered.

This study is a challenge in a sense that no similar study in the context of South Africa has used EVT to model the financial risk of FTSE/JSE closing banking indices: the closing stock prices of the five major banks that trade on the JSE, namely, ABSA, Capitec, First National Bank (abbreviated to FNB in this study), Nedbank, and Standard Bank. Most studies focus on the gold index, mining index, and all-share price index. In particular, the study is unique in terms of uniting extreme value theory methods in modeling extreme quantiles of the stock returns and predicting the tail risk of the returns.

Furthermore, numerous studies that develop EVT-VaR and EVT-ES distributions do not focus on the backtesting techniques which are crucial in establishing the reliability of the model Beytell (2016). Therefore, backtesting techniques are used for all the risk measures and further uses regulatory backtesting methods, where few studies that have used backtesting methods did not utilize this method.

Acknowledgments A very special gratitude to Johannesburg stock exchange (JSE) for providing us with the high-frequency 5-day data which has realized volatility for the five banks studied in this study. The researchers are thankful to the editor and anonymous referees.

Key Terms and Definitions

Extreme Value Theory A branch of statistics dealing with the extreme deviations from the median of probability distributions.

MS(2)-EGARCH(p,q) Markov-switching exponential generalized autoregressive conditional heteroscedasticity.

Fat-Tail A probability distribution that exhibits a large skewness or kurtosis, relative to that of either a normal distribution or an exponential distribution.

Volatility Clustering The tendency of large changes in prices of financial assets to cluster together which results in the persistence of these price changes.

Generalized extreme value A family of a continuous distribution developed with extreme value theory to combine the Gumbel, Fréchet, and Weibull families.

Generalized Pareto Distribution A family of continuous distributions.

Independently and Identically Distributed A collection of random variables that has the same probability distribution as the others and all are mutually independent.

Block Minima Method A method of extreme value theory that divides a data sample into equal minimum extreme observations.

Maximum Likelihood estimation A method estimating the parameters by maximizing the likelihood function so that under the assumed statistical model, the observed data is most probable.

Peak-Over-Threshold A way of modeling extreme values. The method uses a threshold to seclude values considered extreme to the rest of the data and create a model for the extreme values by modeling the tail of all the values that exceed this threshold.

Appendix (Author's Creation) (Tables 15, 16, and 17)

Table 11 Backtesting of ES

Banks	Model	*P*-values for Kupiec test				*P*-values for Christoffersen test			
		Risk measure	Level	0.95	0.99	Risk measure	Level	0.95	0.99
ABSA	GEV	ES	Losses	0.950	0.822	ES	Losses	0.776	0.129
	GPD	ES	Losses	0.991	0.932	ES	Losses	0.892	0.899
Capitec	GEV	ES	Losses	0.950	0.722	ES	Losses	0.792	0.479
	GPD	ES	Losses	0.750	0.872	ES	Losses	0.862	0.880
FNB	GEV	ES	Losses	0.150	0.122	ES	Losses	0.992	0.129
	GPD	ES	Losses	0.958	0.982	ES	Losses	0.702	0.828
Nedbank	GEV	ES	Losses	0.657	0.322	ES	Losses	0.108	0.988
	GPD	ES	Losses	0.875	0.723	ES	Losses	0.876	0.934
Standard Bank	GEV	ES	Losses	0.979	0.332	ES	Losses	0.692	0.229
	GPD	ES	Losses	0.879	0.953	ES	Losses	0.702	0.969

Table 12 Backtesting of CTE

Banks	Model	*P*-values for Kupiec test				*P*-values for Christoffersen test			
		Risk measure	Level	0.95	0.99	Risk measure	Level	0.95	0.99
ABSA	GEV	CTE	Losses	0.559	0.256	CTE	Losses	0.229	0.843
	GPD	CTE	Losses	0.524	0.495	CTE	Losses	0.417	0.733
Capitec	GEV	CTE	Losses	0.255	0.407	CTE	Losses	0.204	0.734
	GPD	CTE	Losses	0.588	0.513	CTE	Losses	0.279	0.535
FNB	GEV	CTE	Losses	0.397	0.331	CTE	Losses	0.378	0.397
	GPD	CTE	Losses	0.596	0.612	CTE	Losses	0.509	0.420
Nedbank	GEV	CTE	Losses	0.794	0.112	CTE	Losses	0.325	0.428
	GPD	CTE	Losses	0.931	0.885	CTE	Losses	0.393	0.647
Standard Bank	GEV	CTE	Losses	0.509	0.341	CTE	Losses	0.473	0.137
	GPD	CTE	Losses	0.644	0.706	CTE	Losses	0.213	0.542

Table 13 Backtesting of Glue VaR

Banks	Model	*P*-values for Kupiec test				*P*-values for Christoffersen test			
		Risk measure	Level	0.95	0.99	Risk measure	Level	0.95	0.99
ABSA	GEV	Glue VaR risk	Losses	0.225	0.144	Glue VaR risk	Losses	0.627	0.789
	GPD	Glue VaR risk	Losses	0.599	0.382	Glue VaR risk	Losses	0.325	0.301
Capitec	GEV	Glue VaR risk	Losses	0.172	0.130	Glue VaR risk	Losses	0.654	0.779
	GPD	Glue VaR risk	Losses	0.426	0.413	Glue VaR risk	Losses	0.328	0.774
FNB	GEV	Glue VaR risk	Losses	0.141	0.137	Glue VaR risk	Losses	0.626	0.770
	GPD	Glue VaR risk	Losses	0.355	0.409	Glue VaR risk	Losses	0.333	0.291
Nedbank	GEV	Glue VaR risk	Losses	0.156	0.128	Glue VaR risk	Losses	0.159	0.262
	GPD	Glue VaR risk	Losses	0.362	0.422	Glue VaR risk	Losses	0.334	0.756
Standard Bank	GEV	Glue VaR risk	Losses	0.157	0.143	Glue VaR risk	Losses	0.165	0.283
	GPD	Glue VaR risk	Losses	0.353	0.389	Glue VaR risk	Losses	0.323	0.281

Table 14 Basel II zones results

Banks	Zone	250 days VaR	250 days ES	250 days CTE	250 days Glue VaR
ABSA	Green zone	3	3	5	6
	Yellow zone	2	2	1	3
	Red zone	2	1	0	1
	Average annual penalty	0.287	0.343	0.255	0.654
Capitec	Green zone	5	3	4	4
	Yellow zone	3	1	1	3
	Red zone	1	1	1	0
	Average annual penalty	0.272	0.376	0.25	0.35
FNB	Green zone	3	4	5	7
	Yellow zone	1	2	3	2
	Red zone	1	0	1	1
	Average annual penalty	0.27	0.24	0.24	0.279
Nedbank	Green zone	5	6	5	6
	Yellow zone	2	2	3	1
	Red zone	2	0	0	1
	Average annual penalty	0.279	0.249	0.248	0.279
Standard	Green zone	5	4	5	6
	Yellow zone	1	1	2	4
	Red zone	1	0	1	1
	Average annual penalty	0.34	0.766	0.234	0.276

Source: Authors' creation

Table 15 MS-EGARCH(1,1) ABSA and Capitec

ABSA					Capitec				
Coefficients	Estimate	Std. error	*t*-value	*P*-value	Coefficient	Estimate	Std. error	*t*-value	*P*-value
Regime 1					**Regime 1**				
δ	0.247	0.003	77.774	0.000	δ	0.434	0.003	149.707	0.000
γ	0.115	0.001	136.427	0.000	γ	0.281	0.001	279.686	0.000
α	0.089	0.001	179.954	0.000	α	0.034	0.001	71.097	0.000
β	0.933	0.001	1082.608	0.000	β	0.878	0.001	1089.077	0.000
μ	6.877	0.019	357.847	0.000	μ	4.950	0.011	435.329	0.000
δ	1.038	0.001	1624.553	0.000	δ	1.055	0.001	1933.326	0.000
Regime 2					**Regime 2**				
δ	0.158	0.002	87.127	0.000	δ	0.359	0.003	109.476	0.000
γ	0.137	0.001	102.351	0.000	γ	0.467	0.002	213.174	0.000
α	0.028	0.001	35.783	0.000	α	0.062	0.001	49.069	0.000
β	0.931	0.001	1168.652	0.000	β	0.816	0.002	519.596	0.000
μ	26.141	0.623	41.978	0.000	μ	4.485	0.022	202.026	0.000
δ	0.907	0.001	788.106	0.000	δ	1.009	0.001	1099.231	0.000
Transition matrix					**Transition matrix**				
	P11	0.998	P12	0.002		P11	0.9960	P12	0.0040
	P21	0.008	P22	0.992		P21	0.001	P22	0.999

Table 16 MS-EGARCH(1,1) FNB and Nedbank

FNB					Nedbank				
Coefficient	Estimate	Std. error	*t*-value	*P*-value	Coefficient	Estimate	Std. error	*t*-value	*P*-value
Regime 1					**Regime 1**				
δ	0.096	0.001	143.451	0.000	δ	0.214	0.001	203.638	0.000
γ	0.121	0.001	247.059	0.000	γ	0.165	0.001	259.032	0.000
α	0.069	0.000	220.309	0.000	α	0.039	0.000	103.104	0.000
β	0.969	0.000	4606.444	0.000	β	0.942	0.000	3310.505	0.000
μ	8.309	0.025	328.836	0.000	μ	9.235	0.029	317.781	0.000
δ	1.058	0.001	1733.225	0.000	δ	1.025	0.001	1434.543	0.000
Regime 2					**Regime 2**				
δ	1.702	0.014	121.015	0.000	δ	0.043	0.001	50.401	0.000
γ	0.158	0.003	49.319	0.000	γ	0.012	0.000	62.200	0.000
α	0.184	0.002	89.015	0.000	α	0.136	0.001	112.574	0.000
β	0.195	0.010	19.518	0.000	β	0.984	0.000	2789.303	0.000
μ	100.000	0.000	0.000	0.000	μ	17.449	0.086	202.295	0.000
δ	1.083	0.003	317.781	0.000	δ	1.035	0.002	637.453	0.000
Transition matrix					**Transition matrix**				
	P11	0.999	P12	0.001		P11	0.999	P12	0.002
	P21	0.006	P22	0.994		P21	0.007	P22	0.994

Table 17 MS-EGARCH (1,1) Standard Bank

Standard Bank				
Coefficient	Estimate	Std. error	*t*-value	*P*-value
Regime 1				
δ	0.077	0.000	324.056	0.000
γ	0.061	0.000	139.307	0.000
α	0.047	0.000	153.789	0.000
β	0.981	0.000	16288.209	0.000
μ	19.194	0.044	433.183	0.000
δ	1.042	0.001	1369.814	0.000
Regime 2				
δ	0.004	0.000	78.577	0.000
γ	0.005	0.000	75.550	0.000
α	0.044	0.000	102.159	0.000
β	0.998	0.000	56295.710	0.000
μ	9.773	0.022	440.607	0.000
δ	0.987	0.001	885.453	0.000
Transition matrix				
	P11	0.992	P12	0.008
	P21	0.022	P22	0.978

References

Acharya VV, Pedersen LH, Philippon T, Richardson M (2017) Measuring systemic risk. Rev Financ Stud 30(1):2–47

Agresti A, Kateri M (2011) Categorical data analysis, vol 1, 2nd edn. Springer, Hoboken, NJ

Ardia D, Bluteau K, Boudt K, Catania L, Trottier D-A (2016) Markov-switching GARCH models in R: the MSGARCH package. J Stat Softw. https://doi.org/10.18637/jss.v091.i04

Arnold BC (2015) Pareto distribution. Wiley, New York

Assaf A (2009) Extreme observations and risk assessment in the equity markets of MENA region: tail measures and value-at-risk. Int Rev Financ Anal 18(3):109–116

Baixauli JS, Alvarez S (2006) Evaluating effects of excess kurtosis on VaR estimates: evidence for international stock indices. Rev Quant Finan Acc 27(1):27–46

Basel Committee (2019) Minimum capital requirements for market risk. Routledge, Bank for International Settlements

Bauwens L, De Backer B, Dufays A (2014) A Bayesian method of change-point estimation with recurrent regimes: application to GARCH models. J Empir Financ 29:207–229

Bee M (2012) Dynamic value-at-risk models and the peaks-over-threshold method for market risk measurement: an empirical investigation during a financial crisis. J Risk Model Validation 6 (2):3

Bee M, Trapin L (2018) Estimating and forecasting conditional risk measures with extreme value theory: a review. Risks 6(2):1–16

Beirlant J, Goegebeur Y, Segers J, Teugels J (2006) Statistics of extremes: theory and applications. Wiley, New York

Bernard C, Rüschendorf L, Vanduffel S (2017) Value-at-risk bounds with variance constraints. J Risk Insur 84(3):923–959

Beytell D (2016) The effect of extreme value distributions on market risk estimation, Mathesis, Faculty of Finance and Economic Science, University of Johannesburg

Bollerslev T (1986) Generalized autoregressive conditional heteroskedasticity. J Econ 31(3):307–327

Brabson BB, Palutikof JP (2000) Tests of the generalized Pareto distribution for predicting extreme wind speeds. University of East Anglia, Norwich

Brodin E, Klüppelberg C (2014) Extreme value theory in finance. Wiley, New York

Calabrese R, Giudici P (2015) Estimating bank default with generalised extreme value regression models. J Oper Res Soc 66(11):1783–1792

Chan KS (2016) Statistical modeling of extreme values for dependent variables

Chan S, Nadarajah S (2018) Risk: an R package for financial risk measures. Comput Econ 13 (2):218–244

Chikobvu D, Chifurira R (2015) Modelling of extreme minimum rainfall using generalised extreme value distribution for Zimbabwe. S Afr J Sci 111(9–10):01–08

Chinhamu K, Huang C-K, Huang C-S, Chikobvu D (2015a) Extreme risk, value-at-risk and expected shortfall in the gold market. Int Bus Econ Res J 14(1):107

Chinhamu K, Huang CK, Huang CS, Hammujuddy J (2015b) Empirical analyses of extreme value models for the South African Mining Index. S Afr J Econ 83(1):41–55

Christoffersen P, Pelletier D (2004) Backtesting value-at-risk: a duration-based approach. J Financ Econom 2(1):84–108

Coles S, Bawa J, Trenner L, Dorazio P (2001) An introduction to statistical modeling of extreme values, vol 208. Springer, New York

Cox V (2017) Translating statistics to make decisions. Springer, New York, pp 47–74

Cruz CJF, Mapa D (2013) An early warning system for inflation in the Philippines using Markov-switching and logistic regression models. Theor Pract Res Econ Fields 4(2):137–152

Danielsson J, de Vries C (1997) Tail index and quantile estimation with very high frequency data. J Empir Financ:241–257

Davison AC, Smith RL (1990) Models for exceedances over high thresholds. J R Stat Soc Ser B 52:393–442

Dombry C (2013) Maximum likelihood estimators for the extreme value index based on the block maxima method. arXiv preprint arXiv:1301.5611

Dombry C (2015) Existence and consistency of the maximum likelihood estimators for the extreme value index within the block maxima framework. Bernoulli 21(1):420–436

Ferreira A, Haan L (2015) On the block maxima method in extreme value theory: PWM estimators. Ann Stat 43(1):276–298

Fisher RA, Tippett LHC (1928) Limiting forms of the frequency distribution of the largest or smallest member of a sample. In: Mathematical proceedings of the Cambridge philosophical society. Cambridge University Press, Cambridge, pp 180–190

Gaye GH, Demiralay S (2016) Volatility modeling and value-at-risk (VaR) forecasting of emerging stock markets in the presence of long memory, asymmetry, and skewed heavy tails. Emerg Mark Financ Trade 52(3):639–657

Hosking JR, Wallis JR (1987) Parameter and quantile estimation for the generalized Pareto distribution. Technometrics 29(3):339–349

Hung J-C, Lee M-C, Liu H-C (2008) Estimation of value-at-risk for energy commodities via fat-tailed GARCH models. Energy Econ 30(3):1173–1191

Jenkinson AF (1955) The frequency distribution of the annual maximum (or minimum) values of meteorological elements. Q J R Meteorol Soc 81(348):158–171

Jeremić Z (2015) Methods of validating the models for measuring market risk – backtesting. Contemp Financ Manag. https://doi.org/10.15308/finiz-2015-161-166

Jocković J (2016) Quantile estimation for the generalized pareto distribution with application to finance. Yugoslav Journal of Operations Research 22(2)

Juárez SF, Schucany WR (2004) Robust and efficient estimation for the generalized Pareto Distribution. Extremes 7(3):237–251

Kallah-Dagadu G (2013) Modelling Ghana stock exchange Indicies and exchange rates with stable distributions. University of Ghana, Accra

Khula A, Moroke ND (2016) The performance of maximum likelihood factor analysis on South African stock price performance

Klaassen F (2002) Advances in Markov-switching models. Springer, New York, pp 223–254

Korkpoe CH, Junior PO (2018) Behaviour of Johannesburg stock exchange all share index returns - an asymmetric GARCH and news impact effects approach. SPOUDAI J Econ Bus 68(1):26–42

Kourouma L, Dupre D, Sanfilippo G, Taramasco O (2010) Extreme value at risk and expected shortfall during financial crisis

Kupiec PH (1995) Techniques for verifying the accuracy of risk measurement models. J Deriv 3 (2):73–84

Luceño A (2006) Fitting the generalized Pareto distribution to data using maximum goodness-of-fit estimators. Comput Stat Data Anal 51(2):904–917

MacDonald AE (2011) Extreme value mixture modelling with medical and industrial applications

Maghyereh AI, Al-Zoubi HA (2008) The tail behavior of extreme stock returns in the Gulf emerging markets: an implication for financial risk management. Stud Econ Finance 25 (1):21–37

Makatjane K, Moroke N (2018) Application of multivariate generalised autoregressive score model on JSE and SSE All-share index: A Copula approach. In: Proceedings of the 60th Annual Conference of SASA organised by University of South Africa: South African Statistical Association, pp 25–32

Maposa D (2016) Statistics of extremes with applications to extreme flood heights in the lower Limpopo River basin of Mozambique

Maposa D, Cochran JJ, Lesaoana M (2016) Modelling non-stationary annual maximum flood heights in the lower Limpopo River basin of Mozambique. Jàmbá J Disaster Risk Stud 8(1):185

Massacci D (2016) Tail risk dynamics in stock returns: links to the macroeconomy and global markets connectedness. Manag Sci 63(9):3072–3089

McNeil AJ, Frey R, Embrechts P (2015) Quantitative risk management: concepts, techniques and tools. Princeton University Press, Princeton

Mills TC, Markellos R (2008) The econometric modelling of financial time series

Mokoena T (2016) The ability of GARCH models in forecasting stock volatility on the JSE Limited. University of Johannesburg, Johannesburg

Mondlane AI, Hansson K, Popov O (2013) Analysis of mathematical models and their application to extreme events. World Acad Sci Eng Technol Int J Math Comput Phys Electr Comput Eng 7 (4):720–729

Nelson DB (1991) Conditional heteroskedasticity in asset returns: a new approach. Econometrica 59(2):347–370

Nieppola O (2009) Backtesting value-at-risk models

Nleya L (2015) Estimation of value-at-risk in BRICS economies: use of multivariate GARCH models. University of Johannesburg, Johannesburg

Nortey EN, Asare K, Mettle FO (2015) Extreme value modelling of Ghana stock exchange index. Springerplus 4(1):696

Rapoo MI, Xaba D (2017) A comparative analysis of artificial neural network and autoregressive integrated moving average model on modeling and forecasting exchange rate. World Acad Sci Eng Technol Int J Math Comput Phys Electr Comput Eng 11(11):2504–2507

Rocco M (2014) Extreme value theory in finance: a survey. J Econ Surv 28(1):82–108

Saculinggan M, Balase EA (2013) Empirical power comparison of goodness of fit tests for normality in the presence of outliers. J Phys. https://doi.org/10.1088/1742-6596/435/1/012041

Sigauke C (2014) Modelling electricity demand in South Africa. University of the Free State, Bloemfontein

Sigauke C, Verster A, Chikobvu D (2012) Tail quantile estimation of heteroskedastic intraday increases in peak electricity demand. Open J Stat 2(04):435

Sigauke C, Makhwiting RM, Lesaoana M (2014) Modelling conditional heteroskedasticity in JSE stock returns using the generalised Pareto Distribution. Afr Rev Econ Finance 6(1):41–55

Šiml J (2012) Extreme value theory: empirical analysis of tail behaviour of GARCH models. Charles University, Prague
Skřivánková V, Juhás M (2012) EVT methods as risk management tools. In: Book of proceedings from 6th international scientific conference managing and modelling of financial risks, pp. 575–582
Stephens MA (1977) Goodness of fit for the extreme value distribution. Biometrika 64(3):583–588
Taylor SJ (2008) Modelling financial time series. World Scientific, Singapore
Tsay RS (2014) An introduction to analysis of financial data with R. Wiley, New York
Vee DNC, Gonpot PN (2014) An application of extreme value theory as a risk measurement approach in frontier markets. World Acad Sci Eng Technol Int J Math Comput Phys Electr Comput Eng 8(6):919–929
Verster A, De Waal D (2011) A method for choosing an optimum threshold if the underlying distribution is generalised Burr-Gamma: theory and methods. S Afr Stat J 45(2):273–292
Wang W, Vrijling J, Van Gelder PH, Ma J (2006) Testing for nonlinearity of streamflow processes at different timescales. J Hydrol 322(1–4):247–268
Wei Y, Chen W, Lin Y (2013) Measuring daily value-at-risk of SSEC index: a new approach based on multifractal analysis and extreme value theory. Phys A 392(9):2163–2174
Xaba D, Moroke N, Arkaah J, Pooe C (2015) A comparative study of stock price forecasting using nonlinear models. In: Proceedings of international academic conferences organised by International Institute of Social and Economic Sciences
Yang Y, Ignatavičiūtė E, Šiaulys J (2015) Conditional tail expectation of randomly weighted sums with heavy-tailed distributions. Stat Probab Lett 105:20–28
Zhao X (2010) Extreme value modelling with application in finance and neonatal research

Dr Katleho Makatjane has a PhD in Statistics from NWU in South Africa and is a qualified applied business statistician. His research interests are focused on quantitative time series and financial forecasting, business analytics, and risk modeling. Dr Makatjane is working as a monitoring and evaluation officer at the Christian Health Association of Lesotho (CHAL) implementing Faith and Community Initiative project. Furthermore, he is a senior member of the South African Statistical Association (SAS) since June 2018.

Ntebo Moroke is a Professor of Statistics at the North West University in South Africa. She has a PHD in Statistics from NWU in South Africa, and she is also a Deputy Dean in the Faculty of Economic and Management Sciences. She has published a large number of articles in the area of statistics and supervised a large number of doctoral students to completion, and she is a senior member of the South African Statistical Association (SAS).

Elias Munapo is a Professor of Operations Research at the North West University in South Africa. He has a PHD from NUST (Zimbabwe), a certificate in outcome-based assessment in Higher Education and Open distance learning (UNISA), and another certificate in University Education Induction Programme from UKZN. Elias Munapo is a certified SACNASP scientist. In addition Professor Munapo has published over 80 articles, supervised over 10 doctoral students to completion, and is an editor and reviewer of several international journals.

Financial Econometrics and Systemic Risk

M. Hakan Eratalay

Introduction

The financial crisis in 2008–2009 showed that there is a need for a new approach of modeling and forecasting macroeconomic risks. Indeed, after the 2008–2009 crisis, there is a big increase in the number of scientific papers on how to model and forecast systemic risk.[1] Moreover, many systemic risk centers became active, and they do research on this topic. For example, Systemic Risk Council was formed in 2012 and addresses issues regarding global systemic risk with main focus on the USA and Europe. Another example is the Systemic Risk Centre based at London School of Economics and Political Science which began its work in 2013, and its main activity is to promote research papers and seminars on systemic risk.

In essence, systemic crisis can be defined as an event in which a considerable number of financial institutions default simultaneously (Lehar 2005). Systemic risk refers to probability that such a systemic crisis will occur. There are several approaches to measure systemic risk, such as the SRISK proposed by Brownlees and Engle (2017) or the CoVaR[2] method by Adrian and Brunnermeier (2016) among many others (for survey: De Bandt and Hartmann 2000; Bisias et al. 2012; Benoit

Permission to reuse was granted for all the figures and tables used in this chapter by the journals, which published the corresponding articles.

[1] Figure 1 presents the number of research articles in different years containing the concept "systemic risk."

[2] A list of abbreviations and their meanings is given in Appendix.

M. H. Eratalay (✉)
School of Economics and Business Administration, University of Tartu, Tartu, Estonia
e-mail: hakan.eratalay@ut.ee

B. Adıgüzel Mercangöz (ed.), *Handbook of Research on Emerging Theories, Models, and Applications of Financial Econometrics*,
https://doi.org/10.1007/978-3-030-54108-8_3

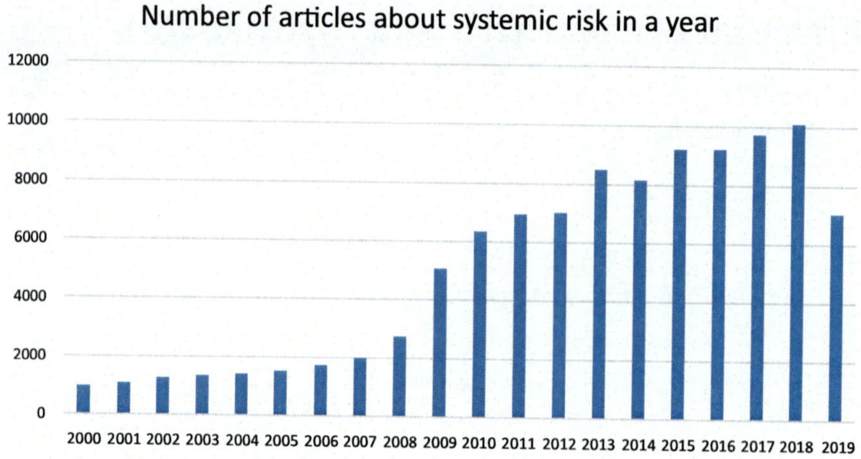

Fig. 1 Number of hits in Google Scholar upon searching the exact words "systemic risk" as of date December 31, 2019. Source: Author's calculations

et al. 2017). Some of these indicators are derived using financial econometrics and social networks methods (e.g., Eratalay and Vladimirov 2020; Anufriev and Panchenko 2015).

The literature that uses social networks approach can be further categorized into two parts. In the first one, the network of the financial institutions and their relations with each other are known. Examples for such networks are the banking networks based on the balance sheets of the banks and their lending relations to each other (e.g., Upper and Worms 2004 analyzing German banking system) and the networks of companies where the input-output relations between the companies are known (e.g., Contreras and Fagiolo 2014 analyzing input-output networks companies across European countries). Given that the network is known, the network characteristics are analyzed and some systemic risk measure based on one or more centrality measures is proposed. For example, Garratt et al. (2011) analyze the balance sheets of banking groups in 21 countries to map systemic risk. In the second approach, the data is available, but the network is not directly observed, so it has to be extracted. Examples for such cases are the networks of stocks in a stock market (e.g., Garas and Argyrakis 2007 analyzing the connections between the stocks of Greek stock market, Eratalay and Vladimirov 2020 analyzing the dynamic network of stocks in the Russian stock market) and networks of digital currencies (e.g., Ji et al. 2019 analyzing connectedness of six large cryptocurrencies). In this second approach, the network connections have to be extracted by a method. Some of the papers in the literature use methods of financial econometrics. Depending on the chosen model, it is possible to identify not only the network but also the direction of the connections.

When using financial econometrics models, one method is to use the partial correlations between the return shocks of the assets under interest. The reason why partial correlations are used is that a high ordinary correlation between two assets

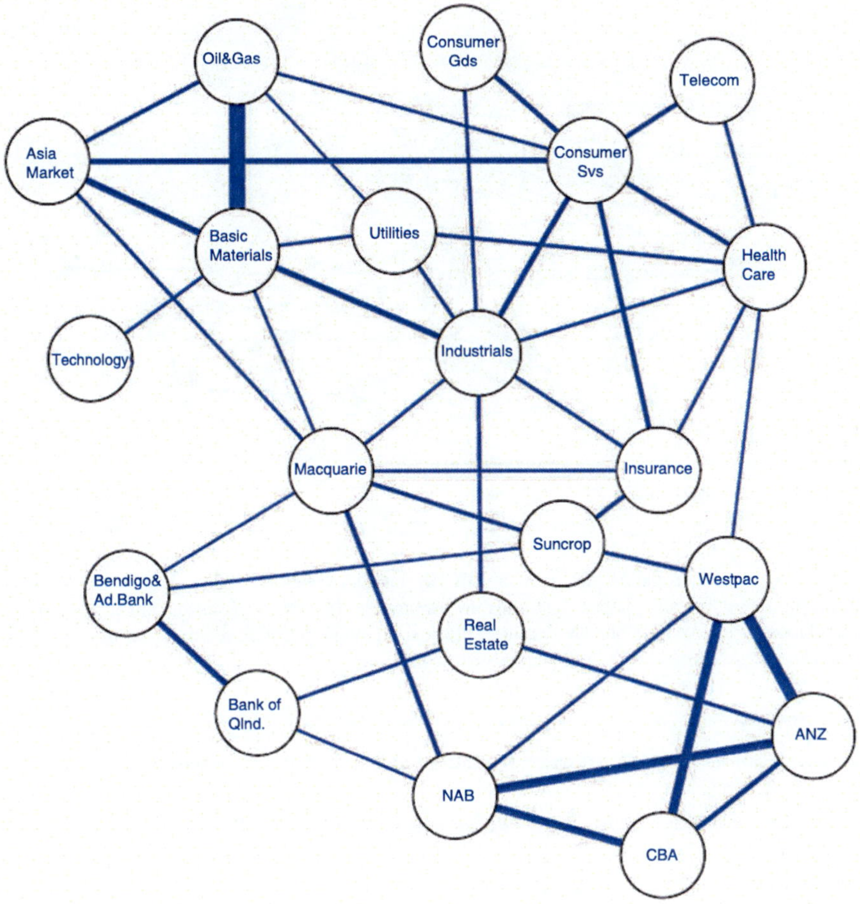

Fig. 2 Network of partial correlations of the Australian banks and other sectors. Source Anufriev and Panchenko (2015)

could be indicating a spurious relation if both assets are actually following closely a common factor. When this factor is taken out by calculating the partial correlations between these two assets, the relation in between could be weak (Barigozzi and Brownlees 2019). The partial correlations could be obtained from sample correlations of the returns, but more sophisticated ways would be to employ a constant correlation GARCH model (Bollerslev 1990) and a dynamic correlation GARCH model (Engle 2002; Aielli 2008), among others. In fact, the latter model provides dynamic partial correlations, which would allow for identifying and even forecasting the network of the assets in any given date. If partial correlations are used (e.g., Anufriev and Panchenko 2015; Eratalay and Vladimirov 2020), the connections are bidirectional, and therefore the causality relation is not given. In this approach, the

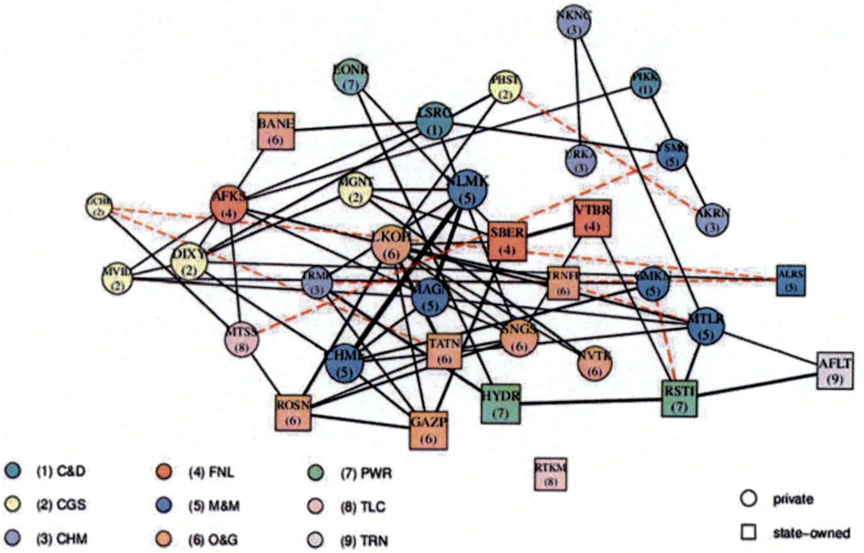

Fig. 3 Dynamic correlation network in MICEX on December 30, 2013. Nodes are colored according to sectors and shaped according to ownership. Thickness of links implies strength of the relations. Positive relations are drawn in black solid, while negative relations are drawn in red dashed style. Source: Eratalay and Vladimirov (2020)

interpretation is how the financial system reacts simultaneously when one company receives a shock.

Another approach is to use a vector autoregressive (VAR) model and Granger causality of the returns (e.g., Billio et al. 2012; Barigozzi and Brownlees 2019). Demirer et al. (2017) have shown that a VAR model would give incomplete connectedness measures as it ignores the covariance matrix of disturbances. Diebold and Yilmaz (2012, 2014) and Alter and Beyer (2014) propose to use a VAR model with variance decomposition, which would allow for capturing the direction of causality in the connections. In their approach, the strength and directions of connections are defined and are allowed to change over time. The network connections in these papers can be interpreted as how and in what strength and order a shock to one or more companies would diffuse in the financial system over time.

Although there are already a number of survey papers on systemic risk such as Benoit et al. (2017), Bisias et al. (2012), De Bandt and Hartmann (2000), and Silva et al. (2017), there is still a gap in the literature for a survey on the role of financial econometrics in measuring systemic risk. This chapter is intended to contribute to filling this gap. Since it opens a small window to the vast literature of systemic risk, it is expected that this chapter would induce interest for the readers who would like to have a general idea of systemic risk.

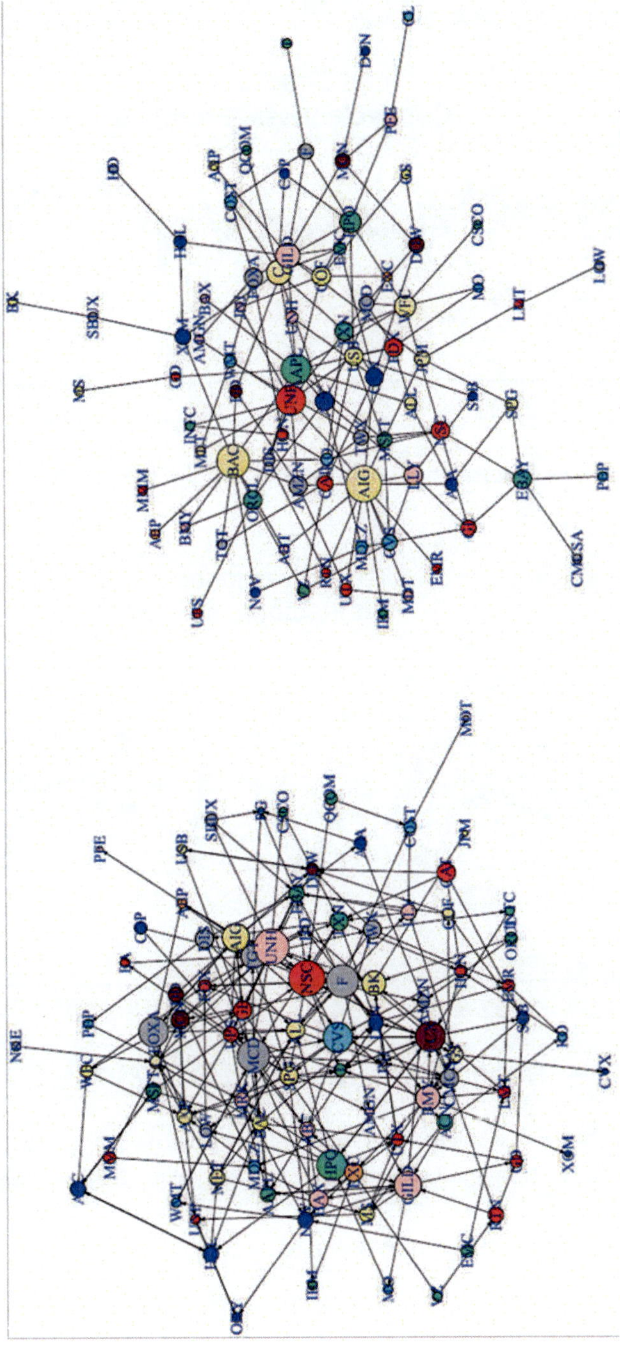

Fig. 4 SP100 Granger and contemporaneous networks. Node sizes are proportional to their degree, and colors depend on the industry sector. Source: Barigozzi and Brownlees (2019)

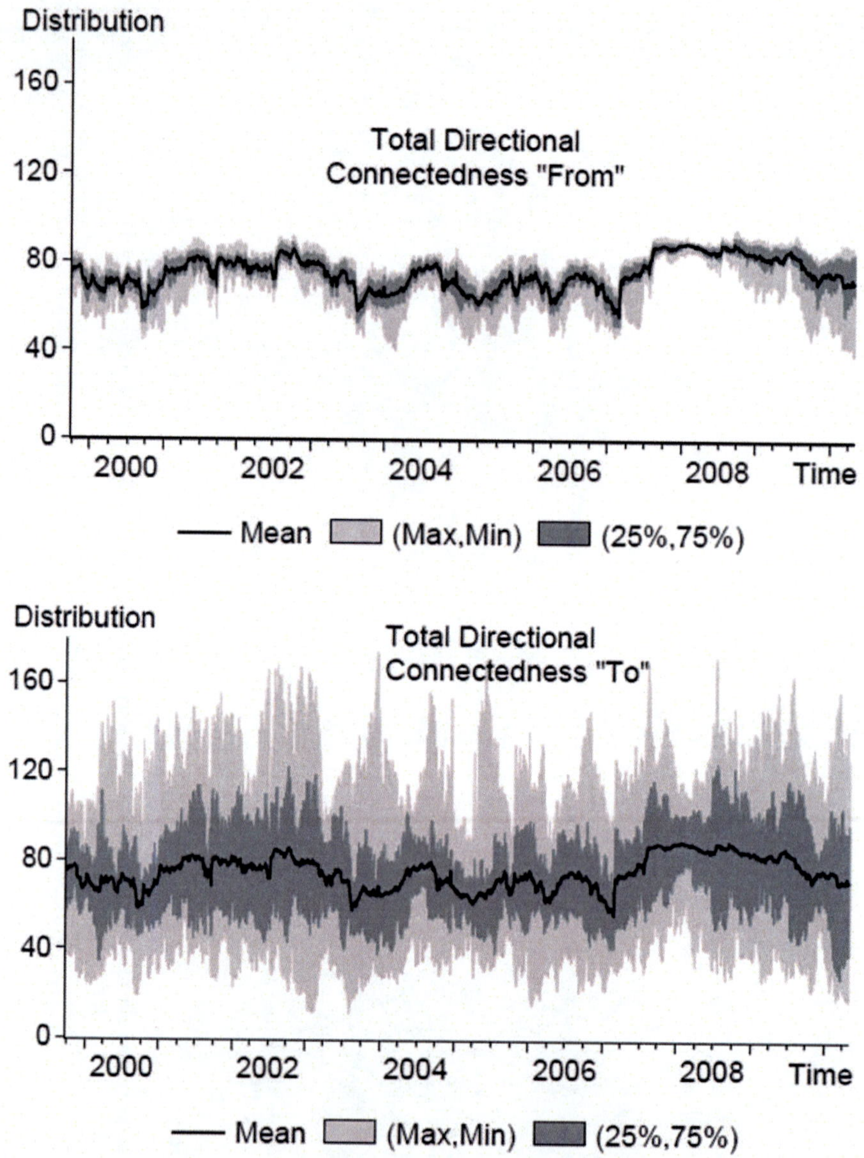

Fig. 5 Rolling distribution of total directional connectedness "from" $\left(C^H_{i\leftarrow\blacksquare}\right)$ and "to" $\left(C^H_{\blacksquare\leftarrow j}\right)$. Rolling window width is 100 days and predictive horizon H is equal to 12. Source: Diebold and Yilmaz (2014)

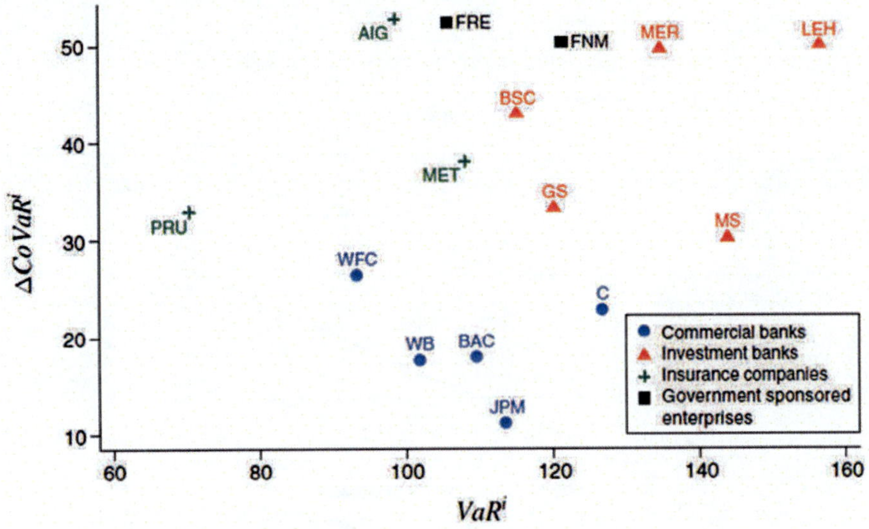

Fig. 6 Institutions' risks measured by VaR vs. institutions' contributions to systemic risk measured by $\Delta CoVaR^i$. Source: Adrian and Brunnermeier (2016)

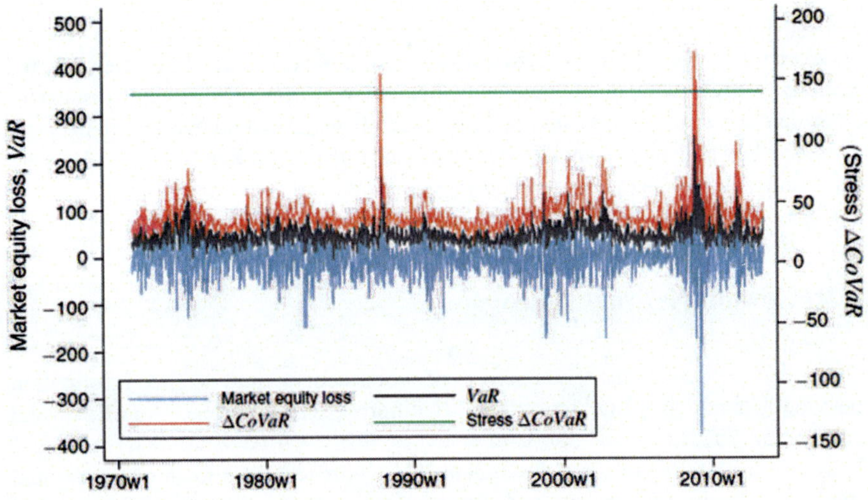

Fig. 7 Market-valued asset returns, 1% VaR, 1% ΔCoVaR for a portfolio of 20% of largest investment banks. Source: Adrian and Brunnermeier (2016)

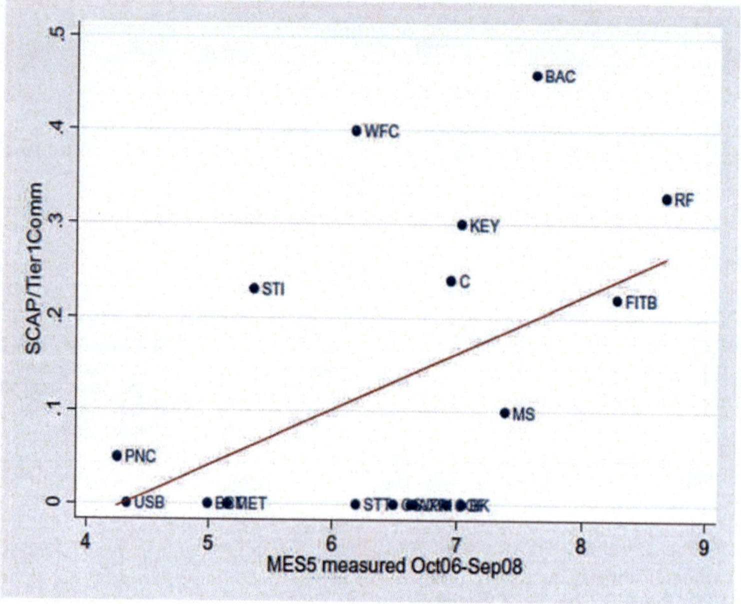

Fig. 8 MES predicts the stress tests. Marginal expected shortfall (MES) of each bank is plotted against the stress tests' assessed capital shortfall. Data period: October 2007–September 2008. Source: Acharya et al. (2017)

In what follows, first a short review on network theory is given. In the next two sections, models with undirected and directed weighted networks are discussed. After that, a section is dedicated for other models which do not use social network approach but still use financial econometrics. Finally, further research ideas are discussed, and the chapter is concluded.

A Review on Network Theory

This section reviews some terms used in network theory. More detailed information can be found in Eratalay and Vladimirov (2020) and Anufriev and Panchenko (2015).

A network graph consists of two elements: vertices (also known as nodes) and edges (also known as connections). The vertices are denoted by $V = \{1,...,n\}$ and the edges are denoted by $E = VxV$. The network is then denoted by $G = (V,E)$, and if nodes i and j are connected, then they have an edge such that $(i, j) \in E$.

The connections can be weighted or unweighted: if the connections are unweighted, then the strengths of all the connections are the same and are equal to $w_{ij} = 1$. Otherwise, the strengths of the connections are different and denoted with w_{ij}. The network can also be directed or undirected depending on the nature of the

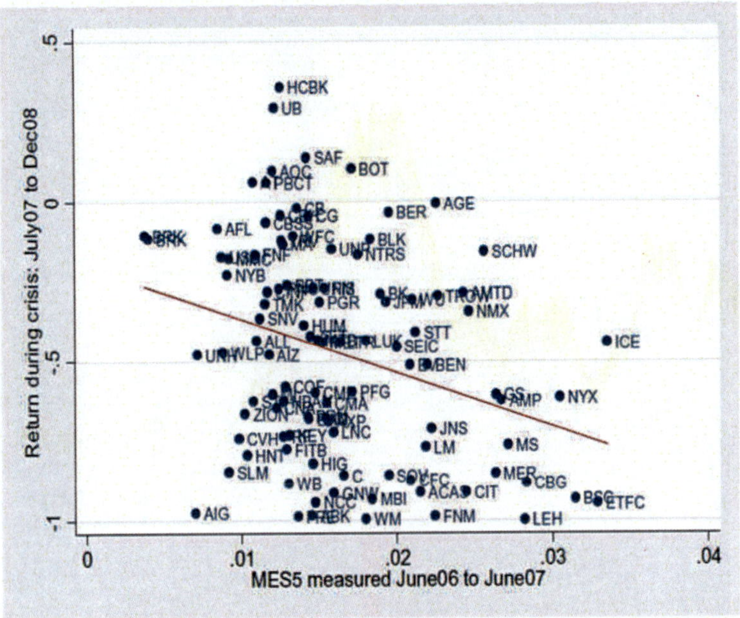

Fig. 9 MES predicts realized equity returns during the crisis. MES that is estimated over the period June 2006–June 2007 is plotted against the stock returns during the crisis July 2007–December 2008. Source: Acharya et al. (2017)

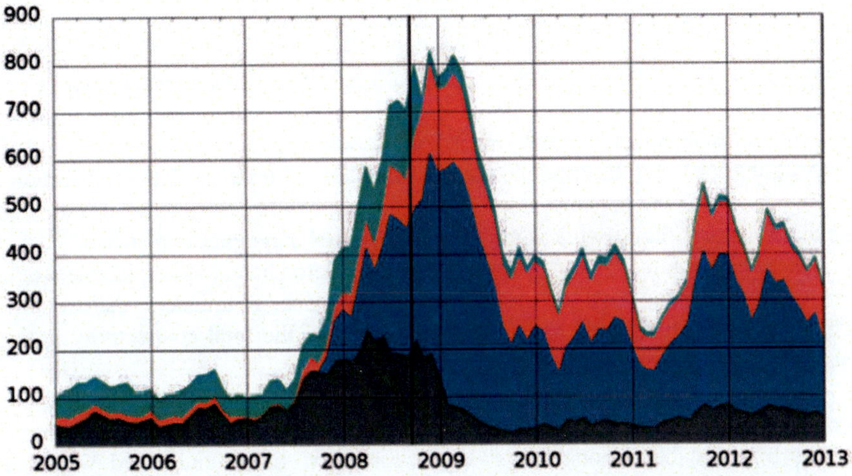

Fig. 10 Aggregate SRISK between January 2005 and December 2012 by industries (from top to bottom): Others, Insurance, Depositories, Broker-Dealers. Source: Brownlees and Engle (2017)

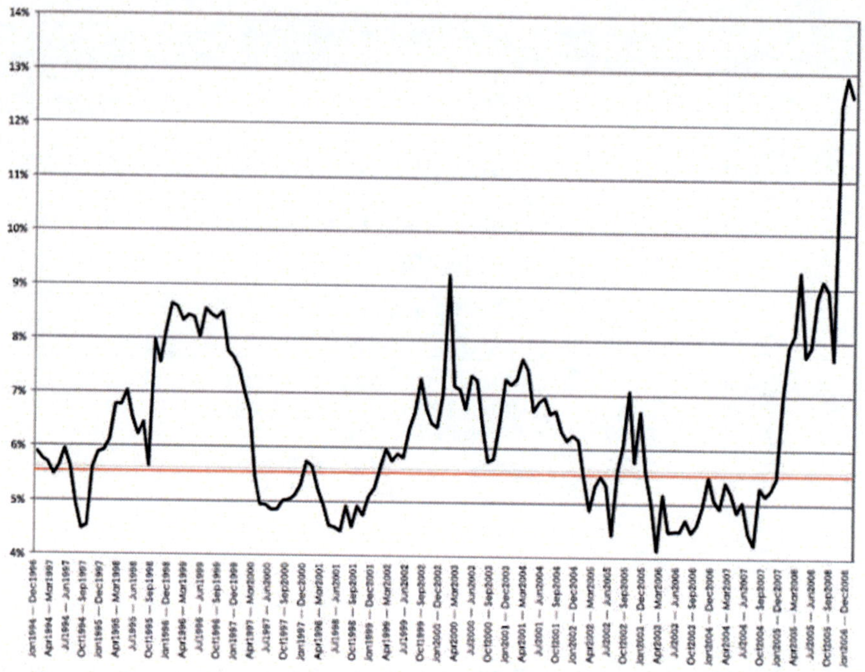

Fig. 11 Number of connections as a percentage of all possible connections. Red line indicates the chosen threshold of 5.5%. The network is derived from linear Granger causality relationships between monthly returns of the largest banks, brokers, insurers, and hedge funds. Source: Billio et al. (2012)

connections. If a network is undirected, then the nodes in this network affect each other in the same way such that the strength of connection from i to j is the same as the strength of connection from j to i, i.e., $w_{ij} = w_{ji}$. Together all the weights of connections construct the adjacency matrix A which summarizes all the connections in the network. If the network is weighted, then the off-diagonal terms of A are not equal to 1, and if the network is undirected, then A is a symmetric matrix.

It is often of interest to look at both micro and macro characteristics of a network. Micro characteristics are those that define the importance of a node in the network, while macro characteristics are those which measure the total connectivity in the network.

One of the main micro characteristics is the term called *centrality* of a node. There are many different approaches to measuring the centrality of a node. A very basic approach would be to look at its degree centrality. In an undirected weighted network, degree centrality of a node i is given by the sum of weights of each node connected with node i. However, the interpretation changes if the network has directed links or if negative weights are allowed.

Another measure of centrality is the eigenvector centrality, which states that the centrality of a node is proportional to the centrality of its neighbors. According to this measure, a node is central if its neighboring nodes are central. In terms of systemic risk, eigenvector shows how far and to what extent a shock may propagate in the system (Anufriev and Panchenko 2015).

A measure that could connect centrality to systemic risk is the so-called Bonacich centrality, also known as the beta-centrality. In this measure, the centrality of node i depends on how many nodes are affected and in what magnitude when node i is impacted by a shock. This implies that Bonacich centrality is strongly related to the propagation of shocks throughout the system. *Bonacich* centrality imposes a decay factor, β, on the strength of the shock transmitted to other nodes. When $\beta < 1$, a shock eventually dies out if there are sufficiently large amount of connections.

Macro characteristics of a network are those which measure network properties overall. The researchers are interested in how many connections there are in a network and the sum of weights in a network to measure the overall connectivity of the network. In addition to those, average path length measures the average of the smallest number of connections from one node to another, and diameter measures the longest shortest path between any two nodes. When the network becomes more connected, one would expect that the number of connections and the sum of weights would increase, while the average path length and diameter of the network would decrease. This would indicate that in a more connected network, the shocks are transmitted fast and to many nodes, compared to a less connected network. Some research papers see the increased total connectedness between the assets as a sign of distress in the financial system and exploit it to measure systemic risk (see Eratalay and Vladimirov 2020; Billio et al. 2012 among others).

Models with Undirected Weighted Networks

Gaussian graphical model (GGM) approach uses the partial correlations between series to extract the hidden network of these series. GGM model has been used, for example, by Bühlmann and Van De Geer (2011), Hastie et al. (2009), and Anufriev and Panchenko (2015). Partial correlations are correlations between two series after eliminating the indirect effect of the other series. Mathematically, a variance-covariance matrix Ω contains information about correlations: $R = D^{-1/2}\Omega D^{-1/2}$ where $D =$ diag (Ω) and R is a correlation matrix. The inverse of a non-singular covariance matrix, $K = \Omega^{-1}$, contains information about partial correlations. Bühlmann and Van De Geer (2011) discuss that the partial correlation can be derived as $\rho_{ij|\cdot} = -\frac{k_{ij}}{\sqrt{k_{ii}k_{jj}}}$ or in matrix formulation: $P = -D_K^{-1/2} K D_K^{-1/2}$ where $D_K =$ *diag* (K). Anufriev and Panchenko (2015) show that the relationship holds if $K = R^{-1}$, meaning that the partial correlations could be extracted from the regular correlation matrix.

Anufriev and Panchenko (2015) use the GGM approach to construct a network of financial dependencies between Australian banks, other Australian domestic sectors, and international markets. The authors use stock returns and assume that the returns follow an ARMA(1,1)-GARCH(1,1) model. Let $r_t = (r_{1t}, r_{2t}, \ldots, r_{nt})'$ be the *nx1* vector of returns. Then in their model:

$$\begin{aligned} r_t &= \mu_t + v_t \\ v_t &= \sqrt{H_t}\varepsilon_t \end{aligned}, \tag{1}$$

where μ_t is the econometric model for the conditional mean, v_t is the error term, and H_t is the specification for the conditional variance given in Eq. (2). The standardized error vector ε_t in Eq. (1) is assumed to be independently and identically normally distributed with zero mean and unit variance. However, the errors ε_{it} are cross-sectionally correlated with a correlation matrix R. In this model:

$$\begin{aligned} \mu_{i,t} &= c_i + \varphi_i r_{i,t-1} + v_{i,t} + \theta_i v_{i,t-1} \\ H_t &= \mathrm{diag}(h_{1t}, h_{2t}, \ldots, h_{nt}) \\ h_{i,t} &= w_i + \alpha_i v_{i,t-1}^2 + \gamma_i h_{i,t-1} \end{aligned}, \tag{2}$$

where h_{it} are the conditional variances. Together Eqs. (1) and (2) form the ARMA (1,1)-GARCH(1,1) model. Anufriev and Panchenko (2015) assume that the correlation dynamics of the error vector v_t in Eq. (1) follow a constant conditional correlation GARCH model of Bollerslev (1990). Based on this model, the correlation matrix of the errors can be estimated directly from the standardized residuals: $\widehat{R} = \frac{1}{T}\sum_{t=1}^{T} \widehat{\varepsilon}_t' \widehat{\varepsilon}_t$. Afterward, the authors extract the matrix of estimated partial correlations $\widehat{P}$ from $\widehat{R}$. In their paper, they also mention that they did a robustness analysis to see if the conditional correlations could indeed be assumed as constant. They say that their results did not change much because correlations were very close to being constant. Anufriev and Panchenko (2015) present the network of partial correlations and related centrality measures in their paper. Figure 2 presents an example from their paper where the network of Australian banks and other sectors is given.

If there are two assets such that the partial correlation between their returns is high, then one could suspect that there is a direct link between them. This link is not spurious because the indirect effect of other assets is eliminated when calculating partial correlations. However, as it can be seen from the construction of partial correlations, the effect of other events, which is not in the data set, may not be removed. Examples for such events could be political crises, economic policy changes, and trade wars, which may not even be measurable in numbers but would affect all the assets in the data set. Therefore, there could still be hidden factors driving the partial correlations between asset returns (Barigozzi and Brownlees 2019; Eratalay and Vladimirov 2020).

Eratalay and Vladimirov (2020) use the GGM model to construct the network of the stocks listed in Moscow Stock Exchange. To start with, the authors notice that there are stock-specific outliers, and they remove these outliers using a Hampel filter (Hampel et al. 1986). They keep one common outlier that was on March 3, 2014, as it affected the whole market.[3] In their paper, the conditional mean equation was given by:

$$\begin{gathered} r_t = c_1 + c_2 \mathrm{Out}_t + \beta r_{t-1} + \delta f_t + \varepsilon_t \\ f_t = \rho f_{t-1} + w_t \\ \begin{bmatrix} v_t \\ w_t \end{bmatrix} \tilde{N} \left(0, \begin{bmatrix} H_t & 0 \\ 0 & \Sigma \end{bmatrix} \right) \end{gathered}, \tag{3}$$

where Out_t is a dummy variable for March 3, 2014, and f_t is an unobservable factor. For simplicity, the authors assume that there is only one factor. The return spillovers are allowed; hence, β is non-diagonal. Therefore, the model in Eq. (3) is a VAR (1) model with an unobservable factor written in a state space form, where the errors of the observation equation and state equation are orthogonal.

The conditional variances h_{it} are given by the leading diagonal of the variance matrix H_t, i.e., $h_{it} = \mathrm{diag}(H_t)$, and they follow a GARCH(1,1) model that takes into account the effect of the common outlier:

$$h_t = w_1 + w_2 \mathrm{Out}_t + A\varepsilon_{i,t-1}^2 + Bh_{i,t-1}. \tag{4}$$

In Eq. (4), A and B coefficient matrices are assumed to be diagonal, meaning that the model does not allow for volatility spillovers. Out_t is defined as in Eq. (3). For the conditional correlation matrix, R_t, the authors follow two specifications. Similar to Anufriev and Panchenko (2015), they consider the constant conditional correlation GARCH model of Bollerslev (1990). In this model, the correlations are assumed to be constant over time: $R_t = R$. Therefore, the network implied by the constant partial correlation matrix is fixed over time. The second specification is the consistent dynamic conditional correlation GARCH model of Aielli (2008). In this model:

[3]March 3, 2014, is a date when there were large losses in Russian markets given the political tension related to the annexation of Crimea to Russian Federation.

Table 1 Correlation of network characteristics and vulnerability measures with ACRA and RTSVX indices

Correlations	ACRA FSI	RTSVX
Average of Bonacich centralities	0.3369	0.2726
Weighted average of Bonacich centralities	0.4507	0.3820
Number of edges	0.7802	0.5145
Number of negative edges	0.7844	0.5036
Sum of positive weights	0.7951	0.5552
Sum of absolute values of weights	0.8225	0.5684
Absolute values of eigenvalues	0.6764	0.5060
Average path length	−0.6570	−0.3907
Diameter	−0.3868	−0.2093
Vulnerability index	0.7639	0.5125
Weighted vulnerability index	0.7685	0.5199

Note: The table shows correlations between the ACRA and RTSVX indices and the network measures as well as the vulnerability indices. A vulnerability index is calculated as the first principal component of all the network variables listed in this table. Afterward this principal component is rescaled to [0,100]. Weights are the market capitalizations of the stocks. Missing values for the Russian Volatility Index (RTSVX) are linearly interpolated. All correlations in this table are significant at 1%

Source Eratalay and Vladimirov (2020)

$$
\begin{aligned}
R_t &= P_t Q_t P_t \\
P_t &= \operatorname{diag}(Q_t)^{-1/2} \\
Q_{t+1} &= (1-\delta_1-\delta_2)\overline{Q} + \delta_1 v_t^* v_t^{*\prime} + \delta_2 Q_t \, , \\
v_t^* &= \operatorname{diag}(Q_t)^{1/2} v_t \\
v_t &= \operatorname{diag}\left(h_t^{-1/2}\right)\varepsilon_t
\end{aligned}
\tag{5}
$$

where $\overline{Q}$ is the long-run covariance matrix. Eratalay and Vladimirov (2020) also allow for different coefficients to distinguish the cases when two assets come from the same sector or from different sectors. The network is then constructed based on the partial correlations derived from the conditional correlation matrix R_t for each day. This implies that for any given time t, the network can be derived and analyzed. Figure 3 represents the network of the stocks in MICEX on December 30, 2013, where the interconnectedness between the stocks of financial sector and the oil and gas sector is visible.

Using the dynamic partial correlations they obtained for each day, Eratalay and Vladimirov (2020) derive the micro and macro characteristics of the network, which are given in Table 1. They apply a principal components analysis approach to these network characteristics and extract the first principal component. They call this principal component as the vulnerability index. They also calculate a weighted vulnerability index, which uses the market capitalizations of the stocks as well. According to their results, the vulnerability indices they propose correlate strongly with Analytical Credit Rating Agency (ACRA) and Russian Volatility Index (RTSVX) indices. Although ACRA and RTSVX indices also measure the likelihood of financial crisis in Russia, they do not use network measures in their calculations.

Another paper that uses partial correlations is the Barigozzi and Brownlees (2019) which proposes the NETS method. The authors obtain the long-run covariance matrix between stock market returns, r_t, by:

$$\Sigma_l = \lim_{M\to\infty} \frac{1}{M} \mathrm{Cov}\left(\sum_{t=1}^{M} r_{ti}, \sum_{t=1}^{M} r_{tj} \right), \tag{6}$$

which is not equal to the covariance between the series. Barigozzi and Brownlees (2019) argue that while partial correlations capture contemporaneous dependencies, the long-run covariance matrix in Eq. (6) allows for dependencies between any leads and lags. The network implied by the long-run partial correlations is a weighted undirected network.

Using the long-run covariance matrix in Eq. (6), they derive the long-run concentration matrix, which is given by $K_L = \Sigma_L^{-1}$. To estimate the K_L, the authors use a HAC covariance estimator that approximates the return matrix r_t with an infinite order VAR:

$$r_t = \sum_{k=1}^{\infty} A_k r_{t-k} + \epsilon_t, \epsilon_t \tilde{w}.n.(0, \Gamma_\epsilon) \tag{7}$$

In Eq. (7), A_k is a coefficient matrix such that this process is stable and ϵ_t is a white noise error term. Then the long-run concentration matrix can be decomposed to:

$$K_L = \Sigma_L^{-1} = (I - G)' C (I - G), \tag{8}$$

where $G = \sum_{k=1}^{\infty} A_k$ and $C = \Gamma_\epsilon^{-1}$ are the Granger and contemporaneous components of the long-run concentration matrix. Using Lasso techniques, they estimate these components individually and construct the long-run partial correlation network estimator. The authors apply their methodology to extract Granger and contemporaneous networks of SP100 volatility, which are given in Fig. 4, in which the size of the nodes are proportional to the degree centrality of the nodes. The Granger causality network, by definition, is a directed network that shows how one stock return affects another in the next period with directed links, i.e., arrows. On the other hand, contemporaneous network shows how the simultaneous responses of the stocks will be to a shock, and it has undirected links.

Patro et al. (2013) discuss that regular correlations can be simple but effective tool for measuring systemic risk. They argue that their results are robust to the type of correlations: Pearson, Spearman, and Kendall. They calculate pairwise correlations between banks and then calculate mean and median for each bank and across banks. Authors discuss that the spikes in the correlations between the stock returns of banks indicate an increased systemic risk and these spikes are mainly ruled by the idiosyncratic risks of the banks. This approach is straightforward and avoids the complexity of econometric models of correlations, such as DCC-GARCH. However, the authors use regular correlations, which are prone to common factors, and unless filtered out they might lead to spuriously connected networks (Barigozzi and Brownlees 2019).

Models with Directed Weighted Networks

Diebold and Yilmaz (2012, 2014) construct a network of financial firms using variance decompositions. Diebold and Yilmaz (2014) argue that the correlation-based measures are commonly used although they only measure pairwise dependency and this dependency is only linear, while their method measures system-wide directed dependency. In their paper, the authors use a pth order VAR, denoted as VAR(p), for the return vector r_t:

$$r_t = \sum_{k=1}^{p} \Phi_k r_{t-k} + \epsilon_t, \epsilon_t \tilde{i}.i.d.(0, \Sigma), \tag{9}$$

where Φ_k are the non-diagonal autoregressive coefficient matrices and ϵ_t are the identically and independently distributed errors. The model in Eq. (9) can be represented in an infinite order moving average form as:

$$r_t = \sum_{k=0}^{\infty} A_k \epsilon_{t-k} \tag{10}$$

such that $A_i = \Phi_1 A_{i-1} + \Phi_2 A_{i-2} + \ldots + \Phi_p A_{i-p}$ and A_0 is an identity matrix. The authors define *own-variance share* as the fraction of H-step ahead error variance in forecasting x_i due to x_i and *cross variance shares* as the fraction of H-step ahead error variance in forecasting x_i due to x_j, such that $i \neq j$. The H-step ahead forecast error variance decomposition in Diebold and Yilmaz (2012) is given by:

$$\theta_{ij}^{g}(H) = \frac{\sigma_{jj}^{-1} \sum_{h=0}^{H-1} \left(e_i' A_h \Sigma e_j\right)^2}{\sum_{h=0}^{H-1} \left(e_i' A_h \Sigma A_h' e_i\right)}, \tag{11}$$

where e_i is the selection vector with 1 in the ith element and zeros otherwise. Given that the row sum of θ_{ij}^{g} in Eq. (11) is not equal to 1, the authors normalize θ_{ij}^{g} with its row sum and obtain $\widetilde{\theta}_{ij}^{g} = \frac{\theta_{ij}^{g}(H)}{\sum_j \theta_{ij}^{g}(H)}$. $\widetilde{\theta}_{ij}^{g}$ contains information on how assets are connected to each other and on the directions of these connections. Diebold and Yilmaz (2014) denote $\widetilde{\theta}_{ij}^{g}$ by d_{ij}^{H} and define gross pairwise directional connectedness as: $C_{i \leftarrow j}^{H} = d_{ij}^{H}$. $C_{i \leftarrow j}^{H}$ is the weight or strength of the directional connection from series j to series i. Net pairwise connectedness is then given by $C_{ij}^{H} = C_{j \leftarrow i}^{H} - C_{i \leftarrow j}^{H}$. The authors then define the total directional connectedness measures. The total directional connectedness from others to i is defined as $C_{i \leftarrow \blacksquare}^{H} = \sum_{\substack{j=1 \\ j \neq i}}^{N} d_{ij}^{H}$ and the total directional connectedness to others from j as $C_{\blacksquare \leftarrow j}^{H} = \sum_{\substack{i=1 \\ i \neq j}}^{N} d_{ij}^{H}$, where N is the number of nodes. Net total connectedness of node i is then given by $C_i = C_{\blacksquare \leftarrow i}^{H} - C_{i \leftarrow \blacksquare}^{H}$. Finally, total connectedness is given by $C^H = \frac{1}{N} \sum_{\substack{i,j=1 \\ i \neq j}}^{N} d_{ij}^{H}$. The authors apply their methodology to 13 US financial institutions, which survived 2007–2008 crisis. In Fig. 5, an example of total directional connectedness from Diebold and Yilmaz (2014) is given. In this figure total connectedness "from" and "to" are presented with their mean, maximum, minimum, and first and third quartiles. The same forecast variance decomposition methodology is also used in Demirer et al. (2017) where the authors estimate the network of global banking system using data from world's top 150 banks in the period 2003–2014.

Other Models

Adrian and Brunnermeier (2016) propose the ΔCoVaR approach. While the VaR stands for Value at Risk, the "Co" prefix denotes conditional, contagion, or comovement. The authors base their method on VaR that is given by the qth quantile such that $Pr\left(X^i \leq \mathrm{VaR}_q^i\right) = q$, where X^i is a variable of institution i. The CoVaR is then defined as the VaR of the institution j conditional on a certain event $C(X^i)$ of institution i, and it is given by:

$$Pr\left(X^j \leq \mathrm{CoVaR}_q^{j|C(X^i)} | C\left(X^i\right)\right) = q. \tag{12}$$

In Eq. (12), the CoVaR is the quantile for which the probability of observing a value for variable X^j that is less than this quantile conditional on a certain event of institute i is equal to q. The contribution of institution i to the conditional Value at Risk (CoVaR) of institution j is then given by:

$$\Delta\mathrm{CoVaR}_q^{j|i} = \mathrm{CoVaR}_q^{j|X^i=\mathrm{VaR}_q^i} - \mathrm{CoVaR}_q^{j|X^i=\mathrm{Median}^i}. \tag{13}$$

Equation (13) can be read as the difference between the VaR of institution j conditional on that the institution i is in financial distress and the VaR of the institution j conditional on the median state of the institution i. The authors use quantile regression method for estimating the CoVaR. If $\widehat{X}_q^{\mathrm{system},i}$ is the prediction from a quantile regression of financial sector variable $X_q^{\mathrm{system},i}$ on a variable of institution or portfolio i, X^i:

$$\widehat{X}_q^{\mathrm{system},i} = \widehat{\alpha}_q^i + \widehat{\beta}_q^i X^i \tag{14}$$

and by definition of Value at Risk:

$$\mathrm{VaR}_q^{\mathrm{system}} \mid X^i = \widehat{X}_q^{\mathrm{system},i}. \tag{15}$$

Equations (14) and (15) together imply that the predicted value $\widehat{X}_q^{\mathrm{system},i}$ from the quantile regression actually gives the Value at Risk of the financial system conditional on X^i. The CoVaR_q^i can be obtained with Eq. (16) by setting $X^i = \mathrm{VaR}_q^i$:

$$\mathrm{CoVaR}_q^{\mathrm{system}|X^i=\mathrm{VaR}_q^i} = \mathrm{VaR}_q^{\mathrm{system}} \mid \mathrm{VaR}_q^i = \widehat{\alpha}_q^i + \widehat{\beta}_q^i \mathrm{VaR}_q^i. \tag{16}$$

After calculating this, $\Delta\mathrm{CoVaR}_q^i$ is obtained by:

$$\Delta\mathrm{CoVaR}_q^{\mathrm{system}|i} = \widehat{\beta}_q^i\left(\mathrm{VaR}_q^i - \mathrm{VaR}_{50\%}^i\right). \tag{17}$$

Equation (17) shows the contribution of a distress in institution i to the Value at Risk of the system. Similarly $\Delta\mathrm{CoVaR}_q^{i|\mathrm{system}}$ could also be defined, and it would show the increase in the Value at Risk of institution i if there would be a financial crisis.

Adrian and Brunnermeier (2016) show in Fig. 6 that the cross-sectional relationship is loose between the isolated risk of institutions, measured by VaR_q^i, and the institutions' contribution to systemic risk, measured by $\Delta\mathrm{CoVaR}^\mathrm{i}$. However, cross-sectional averages of VaR_q^i and $\Delta\mathrm{CoVaR}^\mathrm{i}$ show a close time-series relationship which can be seen in Fig. 7. This would mean that at any given time, Value at Risk of an institution is not informative enough about its contribution to systemic risk but over time the cross-sectional averages of Value at Risks over the institutions could be informative about the average contributions of these institutions to systemic risk.

Finally, Adrian and Brunnermeier (2016) extend the ΔCoVaR methodology to estimate the conditional distribution using lagged state variables such as VIX index, short-term liquidity spread, changes in 3-month T-bill rates, change in the slope of the yield curve, and change in the credit spread between BAA-rated bonds and treasury rate.

Lopez-Espinosa et al. (2015) extend the model of Adrian and Brunnermeier (2016) to include asymmetric responses in the financial industry. In particular, the authors consider the asymmetric responses of the banking system to positive and negative shocks in the market.

Acharya et al. (2017) define the marginal expected shortfall (MES) of a firm as the expected loss of its equity in the short run when the market that it belongs to experiences a loss greater than its Value at Risk at $\alpha\%$. Following the notation of Idier et al. (2014), MES of firm i at time t is given by:

$$\mathrm{MES}_{i,t} = E_t\left(r_{i,t+1} | r_{m,t+1} < q_{\alpha,t}(r_{t+1})\right). \tag{18}$$

In Eq. (18), $r_{i,\, t+1}$ is the return of firm i's stock, $r_{m,\, t+1}$ is the return in the market that it belongs to, and $q_{\alpha,\, t}(r_{t+1})$ is the Value at Risk at time t. In Fig. 8, the authors show that MES is positively related to the stress tests of financial institutions for their capital shortfall, while in Fig. 9 they show that MES measured between June 2006 and June 2007 is negatively related to the stock returns during the crisis July 2007–December 2008.

Acharya et al. (2017) note that MES is for moderately bad days and it can be extended to accommodate extreme losses. Using independent normalized power law distributions for the idiosyncratic and market shocks, they derive the systemic expected shortfall, SES. The authors argue that the measure of how much a firm is exposed to aggregate tail shocks (MES) and the leverage of the firm has a significant explanatory power on which firms contribute to a potential crisis, namely, SES. To improve the predictive power of MES, Acharya et al. (2017) also discuss two extensions of MES, namely, weighted MES (W-MES) and dynamic MES (D-MES). W-MES uses exponentially declining weights on the past observations, while D-MES uses a DCC-GARCH model with fat idiosyncratic tails.

Idier et al. (2014) analyze the claims of Acharya et al. (2017) that the MES approach would have been able to predict the cross-sectional data of losses of US financial firms during the crisis of 2007–2009. Based on the panel data for 65 large US banks for 1996–2010, Idier et al. (2014) found that MES is broadly correlated with the balance sheet indicators of the banks' weaknesses in normal times (before a crisis). However, in extreme times it is not the best indicator for identifying which institutions are likely to suffer very severely. Therefore, the authors suggest caution in using MES for supervisory purposes.

Acharya et al. (2012) assess the dynamic MES (D-MES) of Acharya et al. (2017) that it could be an indicator for short run, and they propose two indicators which might not be as short sighted: long-run MES (LRMES) and SRISK, which is an extension of LRMES.

Brownlees and Engle (2017) use the method SRISK that is calculated based on capital shortfall, denoted by CS. It is defined as the difference between the amount of capital reserves a firm is obliged to hold by regulations and the firm's equity:

$$\mathrm{CS}_{it} = kA_{it} - W_{it} = k(D_{it} + W_{it}) - W_{it} = kD_{it} - (1-k)W_{it}, \tag{19}$$

where W_{it} is the market value of the firm's equity, D_{it} is the value of the standing debt and therefore A_{it} is the value of assets, and k is the prudential capital fraction, which is set to be 8%. According to Eq. (19), the authors state that capital shortfall can be thought of as the negative of the working capital. A systemic event occurs when the market return over a time horizon h declines below a threshold C. If this market return between periods $t + 1$ and $t + h$ is denoted as $R_{mt+1:t+h}$, then the systemic event occurs when $R_{mt+1:t+h} < C$. The authors fix h to be 20 days (equivalent to 1-month period) and $C = -10\%$. SRISK is then defined as:

$$\begin{aligned}\mathrm{SRISK}_{it} &= E_t(CS_{it+h}|\, R_{mt+1:t+h} < C) \\ &= kE_t(D_{it+h}|\, R_{mt+1:t+h} < C) - (1-k)E_t(W_{it+h}|\, R_{mt+1:t+h} < C).\end{aligned} \tag{20}$$

Equation (20) defines SRISK as the conditional expectation of the capital shortfall h periods ahead conditional on that a systemic event occurs over the time horizon $t + 1$ and $t + h$. The authors assume that the debt is fixed when there is a systemic even; therefore, $E_t(D_{it+h}| R_{mt+1:t+h} < C) = D_{it}$. In that case, the SRISK_{it} can be calculated as:

$$\begin{aligned}\mathrm{SRISK}_{it} &= kD_{it} - (1-k)W_{it}(1 - \mathrm{LRMES}_{it}) \\ &= W_{it}[\mathrm{kLVG}_{it} + (1-k)\mathrm{LRMES}_{it} - 1],\end{aligned} \tag{21}$$

where LVG_{it} stands for quasi leverage ratio $(D_{it} + W_{it})/W_{it}$ and the LRMES_{it} is the long-run marginal expected shortfall. The latter is calculated as the expectation of h period return of firm equity conditional on the systemic event:

$$\mathrm{LRMES}_{it} = -E(R_{it+1:t+h}|R_{mt+1:t+h} < C). \tag{22}$$

Equations (21) and (22) show that SRISK is directly described by the firm's size, its leverage, and the decrease in its equity value conditional on a systemic event. Firms, which are larger, with higher leverage, and with higher sensitivity to market, have higher SRISK.

Aggregate systemic risk is the sum of SRISK_{it} over all the firms, i. It can be thought of as the amount of money a government would need to save the financial system when there is a systemic event. $\mathrm{LRMES}_{\mathrm{it}}$ is calculated using a DCC-GARCH approach. If the log-returns from firm i and from the market are denoted as r_{it} and r_{mt}, respectively, then:

$$\begin{bmatrix} r_{it} \\ r_{mt} \end{bmatrix} \mid F_{t-1}\tilde{D}\left(0, \begin{bmatrix} \sigma_{it}^2 & \rho_{it}\sigma_{it}\sigma_{mt} \\ \rho_{it}\sigma_{it}\sigma_{mt} & \sigma_{mt}^2 \end{bmatrix}\right), \tag{23}$$

where D is the conditional distribution of the returns of the firm and the market and F_{t-1} is the information available until $t-1$. The variances σ_{it}^2 and σ_{mt}^2 in Eq. (23) are assumed to follow a GJR-GARCH of Glosten et al. (1993) to capture asymmetric effects:

$$\begin{aligned} \sigma_{it}^2 &= w_{Vi} + \alpha_{Vi}r_{it-1}^2 + \gamma_{Vi}r_{it-1}^2 I_{it-1}^- + \beta_{Vi}\sigma_{it-1}^2 \\ \sigma_{mt}^2 &= w_{Vm} + \alpha_{Vm}r_{mt-1}^2 + \gamma_{Vm}r_{mt-1}^2 I_{mt-1}^- + \beta_{Vm}\sigma_{mt-1}^2 \end{aligned}, \tag{24}$$

where $I_{it-1}^- = 1$ if $r_{it-1} < 0$ and $I_{mt-1}^- = 1$ if $r_{mt-1} < 0$. The γ_{Vi} and γ_{Vm} in Eq. (24) are the asymmetry parameters, which indicate that the effect of negative returns on the future volatility would be different from that of positive returns. If $\epsilon_{it} = r_{it}/\sigma_{it}$ and $\epsilon_{mt} = r_{mt}/\sigma_{mt}$, then DCC specification of Engle (2002) for the correlations between ϵ_{it} and ϵ_{mt} is:

$$\begin{aligned} Q_{it} &= (1-\alpha_{Ci}-\beta_{Ci})S_i + \alpha_{Ci}\begin{bmatrix} \epsilon_{it} \\ \epsilon_{mt} \end{bmatrix}\begin{bmatrix} \epsilon_{it} \\ \epsilon_{mt} \end{bmatrix}' + \beta_{Ci}Q_{it-1} \\ R_t &= Cor\left(\begin{bmatrix} \epsilon_{it} \\ \epsilon_{mt} \end{bmatrix}\right) = \mathrm{diag}(Q_{it})^{-1/2}Q_{it}\mathrm{diag}(Q_{it})^{-1/2} \end{aligned}, \tag{25}$$

where S_i is the unconditional correlation between ϵ_{it} and ϵ_{mt}. After this step, LRMES is calculated through Monte Carlo simulations. Figure 10 shows the aggregate SRISK calculated by Brownlees and Engle (2017) ordered by sectors for a panel of large US financial firms for the period January 2005 and December 2012. There is a clear and steep increase in aggregate SRISK between 2008 and 2009 crisis periods.

Billio et al. (2012) propose three methods to model systemic risk. The first method they discuss is based on principal components analysis.[4] Their argument is that when there is distress in the market, the asset returns of banks, brokers, dealers, hedge funds, etc. become more correlated. This increased commonality can be detected by a principal components analysis, which looks at the correlation matrix between these return series.

Principal components analysis is a method that decomposes a return series to several orthogonal components, which can explain most of the information

[4]Kritzman et al. (2011) also use principal components analysis to measure systemic risk.

contained in the original return series. These components are calculated based on the eigenvalues of the correlation matrix of the returns such that the variance of each component is equal to the corresponding eigenvalue λ_i. These components are uncorrelated with each other and are ordered in a decreasing manner of explanatory power. Typically, the first few components explain a large amount of variation in the original return series. If the system is facing distress, then the correlations between the returns increase. Therefore the ratio of the total risk of the n chosen principal components $\left(\sum_{k=1}^{n}\lambda_k\right)$ to the total risk of the whole system $\left(\sum_{k=1}^{N}\lambda_k\right)$ increases. This ratio is denoted as h_n. If this ratio exceeds a preset threshold H, then the system is very correlated, and this correlation can be detected easily. Conditional on the fact that the first n components explain more variance than the threshold H, the contribution of an institution i to the systemic risk is a measure of connectedness $\text{PCAS}_{i,\,n}$:

$$\text{PCAS}_{i,n} = \frac{1}{2}\frac{\sigma_i^2}{\sigma_S^2}\frac{\partial\sigma_S^2}{\partial\sigma_i^2}\bigg|_{h_n>H}. \tag{26}$$

Equation (26) presents how much an institution i contributes to the systemic risk, but it can be shown that it also corresponds to the exposure of institution i to systemic risk. To represent the latter, the authors argue that Eq. (26) can be rewritten as the weighted average of the square of the loadings of institution i up to the first n principal components:

$$\text{PCAS}_{i,n} = \sum_{k=1}^{n}\frac{\sigma_i^2}{\sigma_S^2}L_{i.k}^2\lambda_k\bigg|_{h_n>H}, \tag{27}$$

where the weights are the eigenvalues λ_k, σ_i^2 is the variance of return series i, σ_S^2 is the variance of the whole system, and $L_{i,\,k}$ stands for the factor loadings.

The second approach Billio et al. (2012) introduce is the linear Granger causality approach. A variable x is said to *Granger cause* variable y if the past values of x can help predict the future values of y. If R_t^i and R_t^j are two stationary time series, then the relationship in between can be written as:

$$\begin{aligned} R_{t+1}^i &= a^i R_t^i + b^{ij} R_t^j + e_{t+1}^i \\ R_{t+1}^j &= a^j R_t^j + b^{ji} R_t^i + e_{t+1}^j \end{aligned}, \tag{28}$$

where the errors are orthogonal white noise processes and a and b are coefficients. In Eq. (28), b are the Granger causality coefficients. Each return series R_t^i is modeled to be:

$$
\begin{aligned}
R^i_{(t+1)} &= a^i R^i_t + b^i j R^j_t + e^i_{(t+1)} R^j_{(t+1)} \\
R^j_{t+1} &= a^j R^j_t + b^{ji} R^i_t + e^j_{t+1}
\end{aligned}, \tag{29}
$$

where ϵ^i_t is a white noise process with unit variance. Based on the bivariate Granger causality relationship as in Eqs. (28) and (29), the authors define the network measures such as degree of Granger causality, sector conditional connections, closeness, and eigenvector centrality. By construction, the network connections in this approach are directional. Figure 11 shows the degree of Granger causality, which is the number of connections as a percentage of all possible connections, evolving over time. It is derived from linear Granger causality relationships of returns of the largest 25 banks, broker/dealers, insurers, and banks between January 1994 and December 2008. The percentage of connections is significantly large in 1998, between 2002 and 2004, and also during the recent financial crisis of 2007–2009.

The third model that the authors propose is the nonlinear Granger causality where instead of the linear system of equations, they propose to use a Markov-switching model for the returns. They decompose the joint transition probability matrix to a multiplication of two conditional probability distributions. The Granger causality test they then propose is that if one series does not Granger cause the other series, then it disappears from the conditioning set of the conditional distribution of the latter.

Some New Directions for Research

Given the large number of systemic risk indicators, one direction of research would be to compare their performances using real crisis data. Although the number of crisis periods in the recent history is not large, when different countries are considered, there could be many cases to study. For example, Benoit et al. (2013) and Kleinow et al. (2017) compare empirically some systemic risk indicators using US financial data, while Giglio et al. (2016) consider also European financial data.

Systemic risk is also related to sentiment analysis. One could study the relation between systemic risk indicators and the sentiments indicators for different sectors. It is a valid question how realistic the sentiment indicators obtained for different sectors are about the state of the economy. The sentiment data is collected via surveys, and the sectors may not be weighting the risks accurately. In addition, one could ask how sensitive the systemic risk indicators are to the sentiments of different sectors. If the banking sector or real estate sector is pessimistic about future, then this would probably reflect in their economic activities and therefore indirectly come out in the systemic risk indicators. Perhaps, the systemic risk indicators should actually take into account the sentiment indicators of different sectors. For example, Borovkova et al. (2017) propose SenSR which is a sentiment-based systemic risk indicator, and Forss and Sarlin (2018) use sentiments to derive company and network risk indicators.

Conclusion

Systemic risk as a concept became very attractive for research especially after the 2008–2009 crisis. The focus of this research line is to understand the factors that threaten the economic and financial system and to quantify this threat. The related literature is expanding very fast, and many new papers are published every year. Although there are some survey papers reviewing this literature, there is a gap for a review with a special focus on the use of financial econometrics methods when constructing systemic risk indicators. With the aim of contributing to fill this gap, this chapter reviews some of prominent papers that use econometric methods to map networks of stocks, companies, or financial institutions and to derive systemic risk measures. These papers are broadly categorized based on their use of network theory and also on the directions of connectedness in the networks.

Depending on the econometric methodology that is used to derive the network map, the links in the network can be undirected or directed. If conditional correlations between the return shocks are used, this yields a network that is undirected. This is due to the nature of correlations, which measure pairwise and mutual relations between institutions or assets. An undirected network implied by conditional correlations shows how the whole network would react simultaneously when there is a shock to one of the nodes or the whole system. Therefore it lacks the sense of direction in the sense that one cannot point out which institute's financial instability is causing another institute's financial instability. If two institutes have positively correlated return series, these institutes suffer financial instability because they give similar reaction to some negative economic impact. On the other hand, if variance decomposition methods are used, the derived network is directed. In this case the interpretation is that the financial failure of one institute would Granger cause the financial failure of another institute.

The chapter also covers some papers, which do not use network theory but rather the financial relation of the institutes to the whole system. These methods discuss not only the contribution of one institution to the systemic risk but also the exposure of that institution to the systemic risk. In some papers, these two measures are the same.

Due to its survey nature, the chapter does not cover all the details in these papers. The reader is invited to turn to the referred papers for more thorough information on the models. It is hoped that the readers who would like to have a general idea of systemic risk or who would like to start research in systemic risk field would find it useful.

Appendix: List of Abbreviations

Abbreviation	Meaning
ACRA	Analytical Credit Rating Agency
ARMA	Autoregressive moving average
CCC-GARCH	Constant conditional correlation GARCH
CoVaR	Conditional Value at Risk
DCC-GARCH	Dynamic conditional correlations GARCH
GARCH	Generalized autoregressive conditional heteroscedasticity
GGM	Gaussian graphical model
GJR-GARCH	Glosten-Jagannathan-Runkle GARCH
HAC	Heteroscedasticity and autocorrelation consistent
RTSVX	Russian Volatility Index
SP100	Standard and Poor's 100
VaR	Value at Risk
VAR	Vector autoregression
w.n.	White noise

References

Acharya V, Engle R, Richardson M (2012) Capital shortfall: a new approach to ranking and regulating systemic risks. Am Econ Rev 102(3):59–64

Acharya VV, Pedersen LH, Philippon T, Richardson M (2017) Measuring systemic risk. Rev Financ Stud 30(1):2–47

Adrian T, Brunnermeier MK (2016) CoVaR. Am Econ Rev 106(7):1705–1741

Aielli GP (2008) Consistent estimation of large scale dynamic conditional correlations. Unpublished paper: Department of Economics, Statistics, Mathematics and Sociology, University of Messina, Working paper no. 47

Alter A, Beyer A (2014) The dynamics of spillover effects during the European sovereign debt turmoil. J Bank Financ 42:134–153

Anufriev M, Panchenko V (2015) Connecting the dots: econometric methods for uncovering networks with an application to the Australian financial institutions. J Bank Financ 61:S241–S255

Barigozzi M, Brownlees C (2019) Nets: network estimation for time series. J Appl Econ 34 (3):347–364

Benoit S, Colletaz G, Hurlin C, Pérignon C (2013) A theoretical and empirical comparison of systemic risk measures. HEC Paris Research Paper No. FIN-2014-1030

Benoit S, Colliard JE, Hurlin C, Pérignon C (2017) Where the risks lie: a survey on systemic risk. Rev Financ 21(1):109–152

Billio M, Lo AW, Getmansky M, Pelizzon L (2012) Econometric measures of connectedness and systemic risk in the finance and insurance sectors. J Financ Econ 104:535–559

Bisias D, Flood M, Lo AW, Valavanis S (2012) A survey of systemic risk analytics. Annu Rev Financ Econ 4(1):255–296

Bollerslev T (1990) Modelling the coherence in short-run nominal exchange rates: a multivariate generalized ARCH model. Rev Econ Stat 72:498–505

Borovkova S, Garmaev E, Lammers P, Rustige J (2017, April 10) SenSR: a sentiment-based systemic risk indicator. De Nederlandsche Bank Working Paper No. 553
Brownlees C, Engle RF (2017) SRISK: a conditional capital shortfall measure of systemic risk. Rev Financ Stud 30(1):48–79
Bühlmann P, Van De Geer S (2011) Statistics for high-dimensional data: methods, theory and applications. Springer, New York
Contreras MGA, Fagiolo G (2014) Propagation of economic shocks in input-output networks: a cross-country analysis. Phys Rev E 90:062812
De Bandt O, Hartmann P (2000) Systemic risk: a survey, ECB Working Paper, No. 35, European Central Bank (ECB), Frankfurt
Demirer M, Diebold FX, Liu L, Yilmaz K (2017) Estimating global bank network connectedness. J Appl Econ 33:1–15
Diebold F, Yilmaz K (2012) Better to give than to receive: predictive directional measurement of volatility spillovers. Int J Forecast 28(1):57–66
Diebold F, Yilmaz K (2014) On the network topology of variance decompositions: measuring the connectedness of financial firms. J Econ 182:119–134
Engle R (2002) Dynamic conditional correlation: a simple class of multivariate generalized autoregressive conditional heteroskedasticity models. J Bus Econ Stat 20:339–350
Eratalay MH, Vladimirov EV (2020) Mapping the stocks in MICEX: who is central in the Moscow stock exchange? Econ Transit Institut Change 28(4):581–620. https://doi.org/10.1111/ecot.12251
Forss T, Sarlin P (2018) News-sentiment networks as a company risk indicator. J Netw Theory Financ 4(1):65–86
Garas A, Argyrakis P (2007) Correlation study of the Athens Stock Exchange. Phys A 380:399–410
Garratt R, Mahadeva L, Svirydzenka K (2011) Mapping systemic risk in the international banking network, Bank of England Working Paper No 413
Giglio S, Kelly B, Pruitt S (2016) Systemic risk and the macroeconomy: an empirical evaluation. J Financ Econ 119(3):457–471
Glosten LR, Jagannathan R, Runkle DE (1993) On the relation between the expected value and the volatility of the nominal excess return on stocks. J Financ 48(5):1779–1801
Hampel FR, Ronchetti EM, Rousseeuw PJ, Stahel WA (1986) Robust statistics: the approach based on influence functions. Wiley, New York
Hastie T, Tibshirani R, Friedman J (2009) The elements of statistical learning: data mining, inference, and prediction. Springer Science & Business Media
Idier J, Lamé G, Mésonnier JS (2014) How useful is the marginal expected shortfall for the measurement of systemic exposure? A practical assessment. J Bank Financ 47:134–146
Ji Q, Bouri E, Lau CKM, Roubaud D (2019) Dynamic connectedness and integration in cryptocurrency markets. Int Rev Financ Anal 63:257–272
Kleinow J, Moreira F, Strobl S, Vähämaa S (2017) Measuring systemic risk: a comparison of alternative market-based approaches. Financ Res Lett 21:40–46
Kritzman M, Li Y, Page S, Rigobon R (2011) Principal components as a measure of systemic risk. J Portfolio Manag 37(4):112–126
Lehar A (2005) Measuring systemic risk: a risk management approach. J Bank Financ 29 (10):2577–2603
Lopez-Espinosa G, Moreno A, Rubia A, Valderrama L (2015) Symmetric risk and asymmetric responses in the financial industry. J Bank Financ 58:471–485
Patro DK, Qi M, Sun X (2013) A simple indicator of systemic risk. J Financ Stab 9(1):105–116
Silva W, Kimura H, Sobreiro VA (2017) An analysis of the literature on systemic financial risk: a survey. J Financ Stab 28:91–114
Upper C, Worms A (2004) Estimating bilateral exposures in the German interbank market: is there a danger of contagion? Eur Econ Rev 48:827

M. Hakan Eratalay is a lecturer and research fellow at the University of Tartu, Estonia, since September 2017. He is also the manager of the Innovation and Technology Management Master's Program at the University of Tartu. Previously, he worked at the European University at St. Petersburg, Russia. M. Hakan Eratalay received his Ph.D. degree in Economics from the University of Alicante (Spain) in 2012. His research focuses on univariate and multivariate modeling and estimation of volatility models, systemic risk, and financial networks.

Monetary Policy Shocks, Financial Heterogeneity, and Corporate Dynamic Investment Activity

Mahbuba Aktar, Qu Wenzhou, Hijbulla Al Mahmud, and Mohammad Zoynul Abedin

Introduction

Monetary policy is one of the important instruments through which the government deals with the economic crisis. The transmission mechanism of monetary policy is much more complicated than fiscal policy. Recent observations of monetary policies have resuscitated the issue of how monetary policies would affect firms' investment, particularly their various impacts across different industries and firms. Empirical evidence on how financial heterogeneity across firms affects the transmission of monetary and other macroeconomic shocks is, at best, scant. With different financial positions across firms, which firms are the most responsive to monetary policy shocks and why?

By using panel data of US public firms, this chapter aims to investigate the differences in firm investment decisions after a monetary policy shock, conditional

M. Aktar
Department of Finance and Banking, Hajee Mohammad Danesh Science and Technology University, Dinajpur, Bangladesh

Q. Wenzhou
Institute for Financial and Accounting Studies, Xiamen University, Xiamen, People's Republic of China
e-mail: wzqu@xmu.edu.cn

H. Al Mahmud
School of Economics, Xiamen University, Xiamen, People's Republic of China

M. Z. Abedin (✉)
Department of Finance and Banking, Hajee Mohammad Danesh Science and Technology University, Dinajpur, Bangladesh

Collaborative Innovation Center for Transport Studies, Dalian Maritime University, Dalian, People's Republic of China

B. Adıgüzel Mercangöz (ed.), *Handbook of Research on Emerging Theories, Models, and Applications of Financial Econometrics*,
https://doi.org/10.1007/978-3-030-54108-8_4

on the firm financial condition during the time of the shock. However, this chapter will focus on two financial indicators to measure financial heterogeneity which are leverage and cash holdings. The first choice of leverage as a financial heterogeneity measured by, Hennessy, and Whited (2007) implies that firms with more leverage would have the high default risk and face a higher cost of debt. The next measure is the lagged cash holdings of the firm. A firm with higher cash holdings requires less external financing to invest in investment or face a lower likelihood of default. Cash holding firms have different hedging and liquidity properties of cash and debt, which make them distinct from their borrowing. Both leverage and cash holding have been standardized in order to imply that units of each measure are standard deviations with respect to their mean value in the sample. Further, the firms are grouped into high and low category based on each financial indicator such that high-leverage (cash holding) firms are firms with a standardized leverage (cash holding) value not below the 50% percentile or 5th deciles of the standardized full-sample leverage (cash holding). So, the defined goals of this chapter are to study the differential impact of monetary policy shocks on firm investment activity through different leverage and cash holding positions. By utilizing high-frequency data on federal funds futures and measuring the interest rate shocks, this study empirically estimates the response of investment activity to monetary policy shocks. For doing so, it has been hypothesized that firms with low leverage and high cash holdings respond more to monetary policy shocks. The construction of monetary policy shocks using unexpected changes in federal funds rate within 30-min window encompassing federal reserve announcements can address the endogeneity concern. This study adds to this literature by examining how different levels of leverage and cash holding firm vary with their response to monetary policy.

The remaining parts of this chapter continue as follows. The "Background" section discusses the literature review. The "Empirical Design and Methodology" section offers and explains the empirical design and methodology. It discusses how high-frequency monetary shocks are measured. It also describes the constructions of firm-level variables that are used in this analysis and empirical strategy. The "Results and Discussion" section presents empirical results as well as discussions for investment responses to a monetary shock. Finally, the "Conclusion" section summarizes and concludes this chapter.

Background

Monetary policy shocks are best thought of as shifts to the policy rate because these are unforeseen by market participants in the presence of informational frictions. On the other hand, investment is one of the key macroeconomic variables whose fluctuations cause a large fraction of the cyclical volatility of output. A number of papers contribute to the literature about firm heterogeneity, monetary policy, and their relevance in the aggregate economies. The recent literatures (Mahathanaseth and Tauer 2019; Silva 2019; Ozdagli and Velikov 2019) analyze the firms' responses to monetary shocks with heterogeneity. Researchers are also interested in different transmission channels through which monetary policy affects corporate investment behavior at the investment level. Bernanke et al. (1997) demonstrate that corporate investment is influenced by a monetary policy through the interest rate channel as well as the level of financing constraints. Zulkhibri (2013) demonstrates that bank-dependent firms are more affected by monetary policy, and during tight liquidity conditions, internal finance is more crucial for firms. Yang et al. (2017) find that corporate investment reduced by tightening monetary policy and cash holding mitigates these adverse effects. Unfortunately, it is a difficult task to understand investment behavior as explained by Abel and Olivier Blanchard (1986). The differential reactions of firms to monetary policy have been analyzed by Bernanke and Gertler (1989), where firm heterogeneity is exogenous or does not assume a pivotal job. Onliner and Rudebusch (1996) have found that small firms, who are believed to be facing more constraints in financing, react more to a monetary shock. However, Cooley and Quadrini (1999) analyzed that the heterogeneity of the firm is endogenous and small firms react more to monetary policy shocks than larger firms. Later, Silva (2019) studies the role of heterogeneity of financial frictions, monopolistic competition, and interest rate in the transmission into investment and cash holdings. He states the cash to sales ratio augments the degree of financial restraints and increases with strength of competition for monetarily constrained industries. James Cloyne et al. (2018) assess the role of financial frictions in the responses of firm investment activity to monetary policy shocks. They show that age is a stronger predictor of capital expenditure responses besides leverage and size. They also find that the behavior of small young firms who do not pay dividends is more sensitive to monetary shocks. Saleem Bahaj et al. (2018) also demonstrate that younger firms with higher leverage show higher responses to monetary policy shocks. Jeenas (2018) studies the relevance of firm liquidity in the monetary policy transmission to investment. He shows that firms with high-leverage and low liquid assets reduce investment in response to monetary policy shocks. Ottonello and Winberry (2018) also study the role of firm heterogeneity in the transmission of monetary policy to investment channel. They used three financial positions, namely, leverage, distance to default, and credit rating. They show that firm's investment with lower default risk is more responsive to policy shocks at the short horizon. They also find that a firm with one standard deviation more leverage is less responsive than the average firm about one third after a monetary policy shock. Further, high-rated firms are also more responsive than other firms. However, in the transmission of interest rate, fluctuations to investment debt may not be a marginal source of financing; in that case, a firm's liquid funds like cash on hand plays a key role. By emphasizing the relevance of cash holding position and introducing extensive margin decision, this chapter contributes to firms' responsiveness to shocks.

In reference to this literature, this study contributes by using high-frequency identified monetary policy shocks in conjunction with quarterly firm panel data and by tracing out the full dynamic heterogeneity in firms' responses conditional on leverage and cash holdings.

Empirical Design and Methodology

Data Description

The initial samples of this study come from the Compustat database from 1990 to 2007 quarterly. The availability of high-frequency identified monetary policy shock begins in 1990Q1. In order to avoid exceptional circumstances during the great recession and the implications of zero lower bound after the crisis, this study focuses on the sample period 1990Q1 to 2007Q4. The following sectors have been considered: (i) agriculture, forestry, and fishing, sic <10; (ii) mining, sic∈(10,14); (iii) construction, sic∈(15, 17); (iv) manufacturing, sic∈(20,39); (v) transportation, communications, gas, and sanitary services, sic∈(40,49); (vi) wholesale trade, sic∈ (50,51); (vii) retail trade sic∈(52,59); (viii) services, sic∈(70, 89); and excluding the financial, insurance, and real estate firms with (SIC) codes (60,67) and utilities with SIC codes (40,49) of the United States since they have a different capital structure.

Firm-Level Variables

(1) Investment
The key dependent variable investment is $\Delta \log k_{j,\, t+1}$ which measures the change in the logarithmic investment level of firm j over two time periods $t + 1$ and t, where k_{jt+1} denotes the book value of the firm's tangible capital stock of firm j at the end of period t. The construction step of calculating investment is shown as follows:

(a) Start with the firms' reported level of plant, property, and equipment as firms' initial value of capital.
(b) Compute differences of net plant, property, and equipment to get net investment.
(c) Compute capital stocks using a perpetual inventory method which is commonly done, for instance (Mongey and Williams 2017).

(2) Leverage
The financial position is the firms' debt-to-asset ratio, i.e., leverage ratio. Here, debt is the aggregate of short-term and long-term debt, and assets are the book value of assets. For this analysis, the one-period leverage is first standardized to mitigate the impact of higher and lower variances on the firm's leverage due to the size of the firm as done by Ottonello and Winberry (2018), and then the firms are grouped into high-leverage firms ($L^{H}_{j,\, t-1}$) and low-leverage firms ($L^{L}_{j,\, t-1}$) such that high-leverage firms are firms with a standardized leverage value not below the 50% percentile or 5th deciles of the standardized full-sample leverage (significantly not different from zero). Therefore, $L^{H}_{j,\, t-1}$ ($L^{L}_{j,\, t-1}$) is the previous period high (low)-leverage firm j's leverage level. Similarly, the investment levels for high-leverage firms and low-leverage firms are denoted by $\Delta \log k^{Hl}_{j,\, t+1}$ and $\Delta\ log\ k^{Ll}_{j,\, t+1}$, respectively.

The lagged leverage variable, $L_{j,\ t\ -\ 1}$, is also standardized to a mean of 0 and a variance of 1 such as to neutralize the unequal variances in the one-period lagged leverage between firms.

(3) Cash Holding
It is estimated as the proportion between the total of cash in addition to short-term investment and total assets at time $t - 1$. For this analysis, the one-period lag cash holdings is first standardized to mitigate the impact of higher and lower variances on the firms cash holdings due to the size of the firm, and then, the firms are grouped into high cash holding firms ($\mathrm{CH}^{H}{}_{j,\ t\ -\ 1}$) and low cash holding firms ($\mathrm{CH}^{L}{}_{j,\ t\ -\ 1}$) such that high cash holding firms are firms with a standardized cash holding value not below the 50% percentile or 5th deciles of the standardized full-sample cash holdings (significantly not different from zero). Therefore, $\mathrm{CH}^{H}{}_{j,\ t\ -\ 1}$ ($\mathrm{CH}^{L}{}_{j,\ t\ -\ 1}$) is the previous period high (low) cash holdings of firm *J*'s. Similarly, the investment levels for these two categories of firms are denoted by Δ log $k^{Hch}{}_{j,\ t\ +\ 1}$ and $\Delta\ log\ k^{Lch}{}_{j,\ t\ +\ 1}$, respectively.

Identification of Monetary Policy Shocks

A key challenge in measuring changes in monetary policy is that a large portion of the deviation in the federal funds rate (*ff*) driven by the Fed's endogenous reaction to overall economic conditions. Federal funds futures are a common financial instrument to isolate the unanticipated component in FOMC press releases. One could make the assumption that measurements are uncorrelated with other structural shocks. The information, times, and dates of the FOMC public statements from Gorodnichenko and Weber (2015) and the Board of Governors of the Federal Reserve framework have been acquired. A current period monetary policy shock can be obtained in Eq. (1) and then aggregate up the identified shocks to get the quarterly measure of monetary shock:[1]

$$\varepsilon^{m_t} = \left(ff_{t+\Delta+} - ff_{t-\Delta-}\right), \tag{1}$$

where t is the point time at which the FOMC issues a declaration, $ff_{t+\Delta+}$ is the federal funds future rate not long after t, $ff_{t-\Delta-}$ is the federal funds future rate just before t, D is the number of days in the month, and $D/(D - t)$ changes for the way that the federal funds futures settle on the average effective overnight federal funds rate. The window comprises of $\Delta- = 30$ min before the declaration and $\Delta+ = 1$ h

[1]The information on times and dates of the FOMC official statements and the implied measure of shocks have been acquired from Gurkaynak et al. (2005) for the sample period 1990–1994 and from Gorodnichenko and Weber (2015) for the time frame 1994–2007.

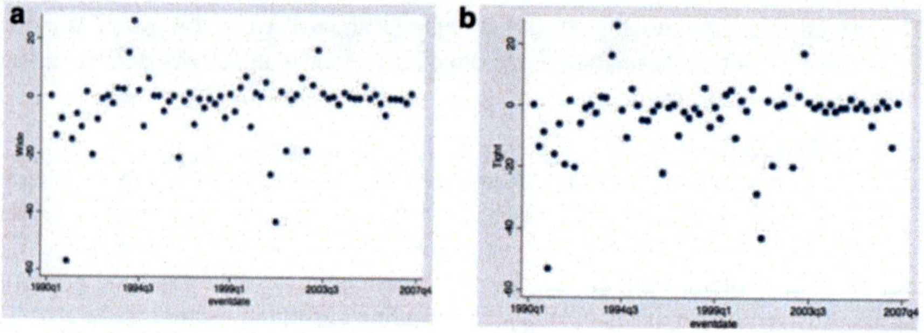

Fig. 1 Federal funds policy shocks, (a) wide window, and (**b**) tight window. Source: Author's creation

after the declaration. Here, a key assumption[2] is that there are no other factors that occurred within the window around the FOMC announcement. There are two monetary period shocks employed in this analysis. They are the wide window ($ww_{j,t}$) in Fig. 1a and tight window ($tw_{j,t}$) in Fig. 1b. The figure depicts the federal fund's policy shocks on the basis of deviations in federal funds future rates around the FOMC announcements from 1990q1 to 2007q4.

Heterogeneity by Leverage

Following Ottonello and Winberry (2018), we estimate panel regressions in order to study how firms react differently to monetary policy shock based on their financial heterogeneity. The baseline empirical specification is in Eq. (2):

$$\Delta \log k^i{}_{j,t+1} = \alpha^i + \beta^i L^i{}_{j,t-1} + \boldsymbol{\theta}^i \boldsymbol{\varepsilon}_t^{m,i} + \boldsymbol{\varphi}^i \left(L^i{}_{j,t-1} * \boldsymbol{\varepsilon}_t^{m,i} \right) + \boldsymbol{\gamma}_1^i \boldsymbol{Z}^i{}_{j,t-1} + \boldsymbol{\gamma}_2^i \boldsymbol{Y}_t + \boldsymbol{\gamma}_3^i \boldsymbol{Q}_t + u_{1jt}^i i\varepsilon(\text{High leverage firms, Low leverage firms}) \tag{2}$$

where α^i is a firm fixed effect which captures the permanent differences in investment behavior and $\varepsilon^m{}_t$ is the monetary policy shock vector of $tw_{j,t}$ and $ww_{j,t}$. Then $L_{j,t}$ is the leverage ratio of the firm; $Z_{j,t}$ is a firm-level control variable vector which incorporates the leverage ratio and the total assets; u_{1jt}^i is a residual; Y_t is a vector of controls for GDP growth, the inflation rate, and the unemployment rate; and Q_t is a vector of quarter dummy variables. The coefficient of interest φ^i indicates how the semi-elasticity of investment regarding monetary shocks relies upon the firm's leverage $L^i_{j,\ t\ -\ 1}$.

[2]The future contracts incorporate all publicly available information at the beginning of the window. Therefore, the public information will not show up as spurious variation in the monetary shock.

Table 1 Heterogeneity by leverage Hausman specification test

Models	Chi-square	p-value	Conclusion
$L^{H}_{j,\,t-1}$	280.18***	0.000	Fixed effect
$L^{L}_{j,\,t-1}$	19.01	0.2467	Fixed or random effect

*$p < 0.1$; **$p < 0.05$; ***$p < 0.01$
Source: Author's creation

Heterogeneity by Cash Holding

To study the relevance of firms' holdings of cash at the time of a monetary policy shock, the analysis has been repeated. Equation (3) estimates the following regression considering firms' cash holding, that is,

$$\Delta \log k^{i}{}_{j,t+1} = \alpha^{i} + \beta^{i}\mathrm{CH}^{i}{}_{j,t-1} + \theta^{i}\varepsilon_{t}^{m,i} + \varphi^{i}\left(\mathrm{CH}^{i}{}_{j,t-1} * \varepsilon_{t}^{m,i}\right) + \gamma_{1}^{i}Z^{i}{}_{j,t-1} + \gamma_{2}^{i}Y_{t} + \gamma_{3}^{i}Q_{t} + u_{3jt}^{i} i\varepsilon(\text{High cash holding firms, Low cash holding firms}) \tag{3}$$

where α^{i} is a firm j fixed effect which captures the permanent differences in investment behavior and $\varepsilon^{m}{}_{t}$ is the monetary policy shock vector of $tw_{j,t}$ and $ww_{j,t}$. Then, $\mathrm{CH}^{i}{}_{j,\,t-1}$ is the firm's one-period lag cash holdings; $Z_{j,t}$ is a firm-level control variable vector which incorporate the leverage ratio and the total assets; u^{i}_{1jt} is a residual; Y_t is a vector of controls for GDP growth, the inflation rate, and the unemployment rate; and Q_t is a vector of quarter dummy variables. The coefficient of interest φ^{i} measures how the semi-elasticity of investment regarding monetary policy shocks relies upon the firm's cash holdings.

Results and Discussion

It has been documented that firms with low leverage and high cash holdings are more responsive than other firms in the economy. To do so, panel regression estimation has been done. The Hausman panel data specification test has been conducted that informs the better estimation technique to estimate a panel data model based on efficiency and consistency of the panel data model through comparing the estimate differences from random effect estimation results and fixed effect estimation results.

The Hausman panel data specification test result is shown in Table 1 for model 1. Under the null hypothesis, the estimates from fixed effect are consistent, while random effect estimates are efficient. Alternatively, random effect estimation results are inefficient, but the fixed effect estimation result is consistent.

Based on the test results in Table 1, the model of high-leverage firms is estimated with fixed effect techniques given that the null hypothesis is rejected. Conversely, the low-leverage firms' model result is estimated with fixed effect even though it can be estimated using random effect since we fail to reject the null hypothesis.

Table 2 shows the fixed effect regression results of model 1. Column 1 to column 4 shows the regression result from the high-leverage firm subsample category, while column 5 to column 8 shows the fixed effect estimation results using the low-leverage firm subsample category. In column 1 and column 5, a simple linear panel data fixed effect robust regression model between the one-period lag leverage and the differenced investment level of the firms are fitted. In column 2 and column 6, the monetary policy shocks in the form of tight and wide windows are controlled for. In column 3 and column 7, the interactions between the one-period leverage lag and the two monetary policy shocks are controlled. Other firm-level and macroeconomic-level variables are also controlled in column 4 and column 8 for high-leverage and low-leverage firm subsample categories, respectively.

The causal impact conclusions, decisions, and inference are made using column 4 and column 8 for the two subsample categories which show the estimation result when firm- and macroeconomic-level characteristics are controlled for. From these columns (column 4 and column 8) in Table 4, the causal impact of leverage in the differenced investment level of the high-leverage firms is negative and about 0.231, and for the low-leverage firm, it is also negative and about 0.916. Moreover, this causal impact is significant for the high-leverage firms compared to the low-leverage firms where the one-period lag leverage is statistically insignificant in the low-leverage firms. Furthermore, the monetary policy shock, tight window, is statistically significant and negative for the high-leverage firms but not statistically significant for the low-leverage firms. On the other hand, the monetary policy shock, wide window, is statistically significant both for the high-leverage and low-leverage firm categories.

Interestingly, the interactions of the two monetary policy shock variables are statistically insignificant for the high-leverage firms, but they are statistically significant for the low-leverage firms. This empirical finding confirms the fact that the firms with low leverage respond more given the monetary policy shocks relative to firms with high-leverage level in explaining the differenced investment levels of the firms. The firm-level control variable is statistically significant for the high-leverage firm category and the low-leverage firm category. Also, the macroeconomic-level control variables are statistically significant for the low-leverage firm category relative to the high-leverage firm category. This suggests that the investment level of firms with low leverage is significantly affected by the macroeconomic policies, while the firm-level characteristics affect the investment decision of the firms with a high level of leverage. The quarter dummies are statistically significant for the low-leverage firms for all quarters, whereas only the first quarter is statistically significant to the high-leverage firms. These imply that there are other quarter-specific factors which could be unobserved or observed that is capable of explaining the variations in the level of firms' investment decision.

Based on both models' summary statistics, all the independent covariates used in the estimation explains 86.6% and 76.8% of the variations in the firms' differenced investment level for the high-leverage category and the low-leverage category,

Table 2 Regression result cf heterogeneity by leverage

	$\Delta \log k^{Hl}_{j,t+1}$	$\Delta \log k^{Hl}_{j,t+1}$	$\Delta \log k^{Hl}_{j,t+1}$	$\Delta \log k^{Hl}_{j,t+1}$	$\Delta \log k^{Ll}_{j,t+1}$	$\Delta \log k^{Ll}_{j,t+1}$	$\Delta \log k^{Ll}_{j,t+1}$	$\Delta \log k^{Ll}_{j,t+1}$
	(1)	(2)	(3)	(4)	(5)	(6)	(7)	(8)
$L^H_{j,t-1}$	−0.247***	−0.247***	−0.242***	−0.231***				
	(0.0405)	(0.0652)	(0.0674)	(0.0358)				
$L^L_{j,t-1}$					−2.223	−2.159	−2.127	−0.916
					(1.521)	(1.481)	(1.566)	(0.679)
$tw_{j,t}$		−1.026	−1.068	−0.882***		−0.0236	0.0847	0.0869
		(0.822)	(0.829)	(0.320)		(0.0487)	(0.0691)	(0.0584)
$ww_{j,t}$		1.204	1.244	0.857***		0.0445	−0.0740	−0.128**
		(0.829)	(0.836)	(0.319)		(0.0431)	(0.0613)	(0.0588)
$L^H_{j,t-1}tw_{j,t}$			−0.0171	−0.0160				
			(0.0453)	(0.0167)				
$L^H_{j,t-1}ww_{j,t}$			−0.0169	−0.0151				
			(0.0464)	(0.0171)				
$L^L_{j,t-1}tw_{j,t}$							−0.562	−0.500**
							(0.530)	(0.228)
$L^L_{j,t-1}ww_{j,t}$							−0.612	−0.545**
							(0.512)	(0.230)
$ta_{j,t}$				0.00641***				0.00550***
				(1.95e−05)				(8.18e−06)
$infl_t$				4.784***				0.826***
				(0.714)				(0.0854)
$unemp_t$				1.064				1.232***
				(0.916)				(0.111)
$gdpg_t$				1.650				1.507***
				(1.214)				(0.152)

(continued)

Table 2 (continued)

	$\Delta \log k^{Hl}_{j,t+1}$	$\Delta \log k^{Hl}_{j,t+1}$	$\Delta \log k^{Hl}_{j,t+1}$	$\Delta \log k^{Hl}_{j,t+1}$	$\Delta \log k^{Ll}_{j,t+1}$	$\Delta \log k^{Ll}_{j,t+1}$	$\Delta \log k^{Ll}_{j,t+1}$	$\Delta \log k^{Ll}_{j,t+1}$
	(1)	(2)	(3)	(4)	(5)	(6)	(7)	(8)
$Q2_t$				−0.105				−0.488**
				(1.578)				(0.199)
$Q3_t$				−0.0536				−0.377*
				(1.557)				(0.196)
$Q4_t$				−0.383				−0.753***
				(1.604)				(0.200)
Constant	24.52***	24.92***	24.91***	−46.08***	3.073***	3.119***	3.114***	−21.52***
	(0.138)	(1.557)	(1.558)	(4.356)	(0.290)	(0.327)	(0.338)	(0.535)
Observations	18,072	18,072	18,072	18,072	139,736	139,736	139,736	139,736
A. R-squared	0.010	0.011	0.011	0.866	0.013	0.013	0.014	0.768
Firms	1307	1307	1307	1307	3061	3061	3061	3061

Robust standard errors in parentheses
$^*p < 0.1$; $^{**}p < 0.05$; $^{***}p < 0.01$
Source: Author's creation

Table 3 Heterogeneity by cash holding Hausman specification test

Models	Chi-square	p-value	Conclusion
$L^{H}_{j,\,t-1}$	158.17***	0.000	Fixed effect
$L^{L}_{j,\,t-1}$	60.12**	0.0467	Fixed effect

*$p < 0.1$; **$p < 0.05$; ***$p < 0.01$
Source: Author's creation

respectively. These covariates are jointly significant, judging from the p-value of the F-statistic which is 0.000.

The Hausman panel data specification test result is shown in Table 3 for model 2. The null hypothesis is that the estimates from fixed effect are consistent and random effect estimates are efficient. Alternatively, the fixed effect estimation result is consistent, but random effect estimation results are inefficient.

Based on the test results in Table 3, the model of low cash holding firms is estimated with fixed effect techniques given that the null hypothesis is rejected. Also, the model of high cash holding firms is estimated with fixed effect techniques given that the null hypothesis is rejected.

Table 4 shows the fixed effect regression results of model 2. The high cash holding firm subsample category are shown in column 1 to column 4, while column 5 to column 8 shows the fixed effect estimation results using the low cash holding firm subsample category. A simple linear panel data fixed effect robust regression model between the one-period lag cash holding and the differenced investment level of the firms are fitted in column 1 and column 5.The monetary policy shocks in the form of tight and wide windows are controlled in column 2 and column 6. The interactions between the one-period cash holding lag and the two monetary policy shocks are controlled in column 3 and column 7, while other firm-level and macroeconomic-level variables are also controlled in column 4 and column 8 for high cash holding and low cash holding firm subsample categories, respectively.

Using column 4 and column 8, the causal impact conclusions and decisions are made where the firm- and macroeconomic-level characteristics are controlled for. From these columns, the causal impact of cash holding in the differenced investment level of the high cash holding firms is positive and about 3.598, and for the low cash holding firm, it is also positive and about 2.867. This causal impact is statistically significant both for the high cash holding firms and the low cash holding firms. Furthermore, the monetary policy shock, tight window, is statistically significant and positive for the high cash holding firms. On the other hand, the monetary policy shock, wide window, is also statistically significant for the high cash holding firms. However, they are not statistically significant for the lower cash holding firm category.

However, the interactions of the two monetary policy shock variables are statistically insignificant for the low cash holding firms, but they are statistically significant for the high cash holding firms which confirms the fact that the firms with high cash holding respond more given monetary policy shocks relative to firms with low cash holding level. The firm-level control variable is statistically significant for the high cash holding firm and the low cash holding firm category. In addition, the

Table 4 Regression result of heterogeneity by cash holdings

	$\Delta \log k^{Hc}_{j,t+1}$	$\Delta \log k^{Hc}_{j,t+1}$	$\Delta \log k^{Hc}_{j,t+1}$	$\Delta \log k^{Hc}_{j,t+1}$	$\Delta \log k^{Lc}_{j,t+1}$	$\Delta \log k^{Lc}_{j,t+1}$	$\Delta \log k^{Lc}_{j,t+1}$	$\Delta \log k^{Lc}_{j,t+1}$
	(1)	(2)	(3)	(4)	(5)	(6)	(7)	(8)
$CH^{H}_{j,t-1}$	9.076	9.066**	8.683**	3.598**				
	(6.372)	(3.790)	(3.835)	(1.426)				
$CH^{L}_{j,t-1}$					2.323	2.766	1.331	2.867*
					(6.426)	(6.505)	(6.677)	(2.777)
$tw_{j,t}$		−0.988***	−2.271***	−0.946***		0.0364	0.0239	−0.0494
		(0.289)	(0.571)	(0.215)		(0.115)	(0.169)	(0.0717)
$ww_{j,t}$		1.016***	2.333***	0.950***		0.00762	−4.32e−05	0.0273
		(0.293)	(0.577)	(0.216)		(0.116)	(0.170)	(0.0720)
$CH^{H}_{j,t-1}tw_{j,t}$			3.347***	1.517***				
			(1.281)	(0.476)				
$CH^{H}_{j,t-1}ww_{j,t}$			3.445***	1.583***				
			(1.300)	(0.483)				
$CH^{L}_{j,t-1}tw_{j,t}$							0.279	1.136
							(2.702)	(1.121)
$CH^{L}_{j,t-1}ww_{j,t}$							0.178	1.434
							(2.730)	(1.133)
$ta_{j,t}$				0.00758***				0.00551***
				(1.40e−05)				(7.76e−06)
$infl_t$				1.733***				1.014***
				(0.255)				(0.111)
$unemp_t$				0.569*				1.461***
				(0.326)				(0.144)
$gdpg_t$				0.995**				1.686***
				(0.447)				(0.196)
$Q2_t$				−0.136				−0.600**

				(0.570)				(0.259)
$Q3_t$				0.0852				−0.479*
				(0.566)				(0.255)
$Q4_t$				−0.0871				−0.904***
				(0.573)				(0.261)
Constant	9.734***	9.577***	9.420***	−20.50***	4.565***	4.737***	4.669***	−26.70***
	(2.585)	(1.634)	(1.652)	(1.640)	(0.296)	(0.375)	(0.382)	(0.683)
Observations	49,510	49,510	49,510	49,510	108,081	108,081	108,081	108,081
A. R-squared	0.011	0.011	0.011	0.862	0.013	0.014	0.014	0.828
Firms	2308	2308	2308	2308	2949	2949	2949	2949

Robust standard errors in parentheses
$*p < 0.1$; $**p < 0.05$; $***p < 0.01$
Source: Author's creation

macroeconomic-level control variables are also statistically significant for both categories of firm. This suggests that the investment level of firms with low cash holding is significantly affected by the macroeconomic policies and firm-level factors. Also, firm-level characteristics and macroeconomic-level factors affect the investment decision of the firms with a high cash holding. For high cash holding firms, only the first quarter is statistically significant which imply that some other quarter-specific factors are capable of explaining the variations in the level of firms' investment decision.

Based on the above statistics, all the independent covariates used in the estimation explains 86.2% and 82.8% of the variations in the firms' differenced investment level for the high cash holding and the low cash holding categories, respectively. These covariates are jointly significant judging from the *p*-value of the *F*-statistic which is 0.000.

Based on the abovementioned experimental results and discussions, the following findings are noted:

1. The one-period lag leverage size varies greatly relative to the high-leverage firms' category than the low-leverage firms' category.
2. The monetary policy shock windows have significant association with firms' different investment levels within the experimented period.
3. The firms with low leverage respond more on the given monetary policy shocks relative to firms with high-leverage level in explaining the different investment sizes.
4. The firms with high cash holding response more given tight monetary policy shocks relative to firms with low cash holding level in explaining the different investment levels of the firms.

Conclusion

It is well-known that investment is one of the key channels of monetary transmission in a range of standard macro-models. Despite this, there is still relatively little evidence on how firm investment is affected by monetary policy and which type firms are likely to be the most responsive to changes in monetary policy with different financial positions.

In this chapter, by combining high-frequency instrument techniques with the nonfinancial public firm-level panel data in the Unite States, it has been found that both firms with lower leverage and higher holdings at the time of a monetary shock tend to experience higher capital stock, i.e., low-leverage firm and higher cash holding firms are more reactive to monetary policy shocks. The findings suggest that firms' liquid assets on hand are playing a key role in its ability to finance investment. Therefore, the interest rate on debt becomes inconsistent as the opportunity cost of investment. Moreover, this study analyzes the effects of public policy on corporate investment which have some implications on central banks who might reconsider the monetary policy to encourage the investment activity of corporation.

High-leverage firm should have to pay more attention by monetary authorities. These results may be of independent interest to policymakers who are concerned about the distributional ramifications of monetary policy across firms. Policymakers need to make pre-judgment about the impact of various policy instruments executed by fiscal experts on investment opportunities and corporate fund. They should receive an effective reaction ahead of time to guarantee that the dimension of corporate investment can augment returns.

References

Abel AB, Blanchard OJ (1986) The present value of profits and cyclical movements in investments. Econometrica 54(2):249–273

Bernanke BS, Gertler ML (1989) Agency costs, net worth, and business fluctuations. Am Econ Rev 79(1):14–31

Bernanke BS, Gertler M, Watson M (1997) Systematic monetary policy and the effects of oil price shocks. Brook Pap Econ Act 28(1):91–157

Cloyne J, Ferreira C, Froemel M, Surico P (2018) Monetary policy, corporate finance and investment, NBER working papers 25366, National Bureau of Economic Research, Inc.

Cooley TF, Quadrini V (1999) Financial markets and firm dynamics. Am Econ Rev 91:1286–1310

Gorodnichenko Y, Weber M (2015) Are sticky prices costly? Evidence from the stock market. Am Econ Rev 106(1):165–199

Gurkaynak RS, Sack B, Swanson ET (2005) Do actions speak louder than words? The response of asset prices to monetary policy actions and statements. Int J Cent Bank 1(1):55–93

Hennessy CA, Whited TM (2007) How costly is external financing? Evidence from a structural estimation. J Financ 62(4):1705–1745

Jeenas P (2018) Monetary policy shocks, financial structure, and firm activity: a panel approach. https://doi.org/10.2139/ssrn.3043579

Mahathanaseth I, Tauer LW (2019) Monetary policy transmission through the Bank lending in Thailand. J Asian Econ 60:14–32

Mongey S, Williams J (2017) Firm dispersion and business cycles: estimating aggregate shocks using panel data. Working Paper

Oliner SD, Rudebusch GD (1996) Is there a broad credit channel for monetary policy? Econ Rev 1:3–13

Ottonello P, Winberry T (2018) Financial heterogeneity and the investment channel of monetary policy, NBER working papers 24221, National Bureau of Economic Research, Inc

Ozdagli A, Velikov M (2019) Show me the money: the monetary policy risk premium. J Financ Econ 135:320–339

Saleem B, Angus F, Gabor P, Paolo S (2018) Employment and the collateral channel of monetary policy, Discussion Papers 1832, Centre for Macroeconomics (CFM)

Silva (2019) Corporate finance, monetary policy, and aggregate demand. J Econ Dyn Control 102 (C):1–28

Yang X, Han L, Li W, Yin X, Tian L (2017) Monetary policy, cash holding and corporate investment: evidence from China. China Econ Rev 46(C):110–122

Zulkhibri M (2013) Bank-characteristics, lending channel and monetary policy in emerging markets: bank-level evidence from Malaysia. Appl Financ Econ 23(5):347–362

Mahbuba Aktar, working as an Assistant Professor, Department of Finance and Banking, Faculty of Business Studies, Hajee Mohammad Danesh Science and Technology University (HSTU), Dinajpur, Bangladesh. I believe that I am an innovative and hard worker to conduct any research activities at any level as individual or in a group.

Qu Wenzhou, is a professor of finance, institute for financial and accounting studies, Xiamen University, P. R. China. His research area includes macroeconomic policy, corporate finance, and financial economics.

Hijbulla Al Mahmud, I have completed a master's program on International Trade at the School of Economics at Xiamen University, China. In addition, I have participated in a bilateral exchange program on Business and Economics between Xiamen University and the University of Cantabria (UC), Spain. I see myself as a researcher and entrepreneur, sharing my position for any level of active research activities as an individual or in a group.

Mohammad Zoynul Abedin, an Associate professor in the Department of Finance and Banking, HSTU, Dinajpur, Bangladesh. At the moment, he is a postdoctoral fellow at the Collaborative Innovation Center for Transport Studies, Dalian Maritime University, China. Dr. Abedin's research area includes, but not limited to, Big Data Analytics, Computational Finance, Machine Learning, and Data Mining. His recent papers appeared on IEEE Access, Journal of Business Economics and Management, Journal of Credit Risk, Journal of Risk Model Validation, International Journal of Finance & Economics, Risk Management, etc.

Oil Price Scenarios: Economic and Fiscal Impacts on the Kuwait Economy

Sedat Dizmen

Introduction

Kuwait is the world's ninth-largest crude oil producer, with the seventh-largest oil reserves. It has 6% of the world's proven oil reserves and 1% of its natural gas. Kuwait is highly oil-dependent economy with crude oil reserves of about 102 billion barrels. Oil accounts for over half of GDP, 92% of export revenues and 90% of government income, and hydrocarbons continue to form the pillar of Kuwait's economy.

This shows a strong oil sector struggle to diversify its economy towards the non-oil sector. GDP and government revenues (per capita) in Kuwait show a strong link to oil price developments, with the elasticity of government revenues to oil prices being close to 1.

The fiscal impact of a decline in oil prices will depend on the persistence of low oil prices and the forces underlying the weakness in oil prices. Persistently low prices for the Kuwaiti crude oil would reduce nominal gross domestic product (GDP) below levels. Since the path for oil prices over the next 12 years is uncertain, the author has constructed three hypothetical oil price scenarios. The high oil price scenario is scenario 1, scenario 2 is the low oil price, and scenario 3 is the medium oil price.

- Scenario 1—World oil prices are assumed to increase gradually from US$74 in 2018 up to US$97 per barrel by the end of 2030 with exception of a drop of US $73 in 2020.
- Scenario 2—Low oil prices are assumed to persist through to 2019 and 2020, increasing after 2020 at their level of US$40 per barrel.

S. Dizmen (✉)
The Supreme Council for Planning and Development, Kuwait City, Kuwait

B. Adıgüzel Mercangöz (ed.), *Handbook of Research on Emerging Theories, Models, and Applications of Financial Econometrics*,
https://doi.org/10.1007/978-3-030-54108-8_5

- Scenario 3—World oil prices are assumed to decrease gradually (and linearly) from US$74 average in 2018 to US$58.7 per barrel by the end of 2030.

The author uses the "Kuwait SCPD macro model" to estimate the impact of each scenario on the forecast of oil prices from 2018 to 2030. The author computed the Kuwait SCPD macro model to estimate the impact of the various oil prices in the base scenario in Kuwait where "business is as usual" (BAU) corresponding to scenario 1. The purpose of a BAU scenario is to show what would happen if the "status quo" was maintained and highlights the associated costs and risks.

Background

The Kuwait Oil Company (KOC), the upstream arm of Kuwait Petroleum Corporation (KPC), decreased production capacity at just 2.65 million barrels per day as of August 2019, below the 3.15 mb/day it had reported in its 2017–2020 annual report.

The biggest obstacle to increasing production has been inveterated Parliament's opposition to the participation of international oil companies in Kuwait's upstream sector. Kuwait follows a conservative policy that does not offer production-sharing contracts to foreign companies. Kuwait's Parliament had previously disallowed any involvement even technical service contracts by foreign companies including Shell and BP in 2009. In 2016, the government allowed to operate as a technical service contracts to multinational oil companies, whose technical expertise is needed to boost production from fields that are in decline and develop heavy oil fields that have been awaiting development for years. However, the delay proved excessive for the country.

It is hard to achieve Kuwait's target of 3.15 mb/day of production capacity in 2020. Even the International Energy Agency Oil 2019 report through 2024 forecast downgraded its expectations of Kuwait's oil capacity growth to 2.95 mb/day. This production level is expected to keep unchanged until at least 2024. The downgrade is due to the dispute between Saudi Arabia and Kuwait over the neutral zone shared equally which has estimated a reduction of 250,000 b/day of production for Kuwait. Oil is extensively used across various sectors of Kuwait's economy, especially in power production, water sanitization, manufacturing and transportation. Gasoline and diesel prices at the pump are among the lowest in the world, and there has been little effort to introduce alternative means of transportation or more fuel-efficient vehicles. There are barriers in the electricity sector's structure and the lack of coordination between the various institutions which causes disinvolvement of private sector and the slow development and deployment of renewable energy technologies at the prospect (Dourian 2019).

The prospects of sustained low oil prices are now challenging the traditional growth and job-creation model. According to IMF (2017), "The current model has been characterized by high reliance on oil revenue and related government spending to drive economic growth and employment for nationals in Kuwait. At the same time, the private sector, which has to a large extent been driven by government contracts and spill overs from the oil boom, has relied heavily on foreign labour. With the current low oil prices expected to persist, Kuwait has to adjust to a new reality. This entails gradually increasing fiscal savings to reduce fiscal vulnerabilities and continue to save for future generations. Fiscal consolidation, in turn, is bound to slow growth. A key policy challenge is therefore to adjust the fiscal position at the least cost to economic activity. At the same time, in a constrained budgetary environment, generating higher sustainable growth, creating jobs for a growing young national population, and reducing exposure to the oil price cycle will require addressing labour market inefficiencies, encouraging private sector development and diversification into non-oil tradable sectors".

An extensive review of Kuwaiti literature relevant to the model has been made, and according to Ministry of Planning (2007), there have been a number of economy-wide macro-econometric models developed for Kuwait by Khouja and Sadler (1979), Sirageldin et al. (1986), Ahmed et al. (1997), Salih et al. (1991), MOP (2001), MOP (2004) and MOP (2007). All these models are basically demand-driven following standard Keynesian macroeconomic analytical framework. However, they also include some supply side variables. Since Ministry of Planning (MOP) (2007) model is an updated and revised version of the MOP (2004). These models are being used by MOP in the development of the 5-year plans and in the evaluation of various policy options Ministry of Planning (MOP) (2007).

Burney et al. (2017) constructed a quarterly macro-econometric model for the Kuwaiti economy estimated over the period 1979Q2–2013Q1. The exhibited real domestic output in the long run is influenced by oil revenues and foreign output. Both oil revenues and foreign output boost growth in the public sector; it proved that technological progress is the main driver for private sector real growth.

There have been a few such CGE models of Kuwait's economy that exist (Alsabah 1985; Khorshid 1990, 1991; Gelan 2018), and these do not reflect recent economic trends and market conditions. Shehabi (2017) constructed an economy-wide model in a CGE framework. Furthermore, Shehabi (2019) has extended the model further by differentiating consumer and industry-specific subsidy rates, incorporating both production and consumption subsidies in a general equilibrium model of the Kuwaiti economy (Shehabi 2019).

There are other existing Kuwait macro-econometric models—but they are not tailored nor comprehensive enough to meet the customized medium- and long-term development planning. The other models did not achieve critical mass and are not currently in use across government entities.

The government and economy's dependence on volatile oil prices has been the main driver behind the push forward with a new development plan, the Amir's State Vision New Kuwait 2035. This plan is further subdivided into 5-year medium-term plans and annual development plans to ensure proper management and execution. The current 2015–2020 5-year mid-range development plan has identified five main objectives to achieve by 2020, which are:

1. Improve the standard of living for individuals and increase their share in the gross domestic product.
2. Increase private sector contribution to the national economy.

3. Raise the standard of educational, health and social services.
4. Accelerate housing development for Kuwaiti society.
5. Improve the capabilities of governmental administration.

On a general government basis, Kuwait's public sector remains close to balance although down from double-digit surpluses a few years back. Excluding investment income from its sizable sovereign wealth fund (SWF), however, the government posted its first budget deficit in 17 years of 13.4 percent of GDP in FY 2015/2016.

1. **Model Structure**

The Kuwait SCPD macro model is a structural macro-econometric model with policy simulation and long-term planning capability. This model type has been chosen as the most appropriate to meet the project requirements and needs of SCPD.

With over 3000 equations designed for 15 thematic modules, some variables are exogenous fixed over time. Besides, some variables are global nature linked with global economic model platform and include:

- World oil and gas prices
- World nonenergy prices
- Import demand from key trading partners
- Outbound FDI from main bilateral sources of inward FDI to Kuwait

The Kuwait SCPD macro model is a macro-econometric error-correction model (ECM) which contains 3995 variables. Each variable has forecast values and sensible projections out to year 2050. Its a model that estimates the speed at which a dependent variable returns to equilibrium after a shock to one or more independent variables. Its very useful as it estimates both the short- and long-run effects of the given scenario.

The economic theory underpinning this study stems from Keynesian in the short run, e.g. output determined by demand, and monetarist in the long run, e.g. output determined by supply. Within the model, the economy returns to long-run equilibrium through Kuwaiti-specific policy rules and equilibrium forces. Some of the main Kuwaiti-specific policy "rules" incorporated into the SCPD model are as follows:

Oil sector: OPEC membership determines Kuwaiti oil production in the short to medium term.

Exchange-rate basket peg: Kuwait's exchange rate and monetary policy are determined by movements in exchange rates and monetary policies of countries that make up the basket.

Fiscal policy: Application of current prevailing individual tax rates of 10% of government revenue (excluding investment income and profit transfers from public entities) transferred each year to the Future Generations Fund (FGF) and no drawdown from the FGF unless sanctioned by law. Surplus revenue is transferred to the General Reserve Fund (GRF)—or where there is a government balance deficit, the GRF may be drawn down—but there is no formulaic rule for the annual amount transferred/drawn down to the GRF; rather it is more of a residual fiscal item.

2. **International Linkages**

The SCPD model is a globally integrated economic model. The model replicates the world economy with 80 countries. Individual country models are fully linked through global assumptions about trade volume and prices, competitiveness, capital flows, interest and exchange rates and commodity prices.

Global oil demand/supply drivers → world oil price → government oil revenue (and transfer to FGF), nominal oil GDP, nominal oil exports, domestic energy prices, domestic inflation, energy export and import deflators

OPEC production quotas → oil production → government oil revenue (and transfer to FGF), real oil GDP and oil export volumes

Global asset returns (e.g. global stock index, global bond interest rates, etc.) → FGF and GRF asset values and investment income and transfer of profits of public entities

Global exchange rates → Kuwaiti currency basket peg rate

US and ECB policy interest rates → Kuwait CBK discount rate

The Kuwait SCPD macro model exhibits the "business-as-usual" baseline scenario, which has identified significant public finances sustainability issues.

Theory behind the model:

- Eclectic macroeconomic model—partly estimated and partly calibrated, with structural features in the long term.
- Short-term dynamics follow Keynesian theory—demand shocks and price stickiness cause a deviation from long-term potential.
- Long-term properties follow monetarist approach—productive capacity of the economy is determined by population, productivity and the capital stock.

Model hosts several types of equations:

- Behavioural equations—these are key in determining scenario properties.
- Accounting identities—simple sums or products.
- Exogenous equations/variables.
- Transformations—these are only active if the variable is fixed down, i.e. imposed by the forecaster, on top of the standard model equation.
- Each equation has its residual, showing the historic/projected fit with the data.

The Kuwait SCPD macro model is an error-correction model, a form of a multiple time-series model that estimates the speed at which a dependent variable returns to its equilibrium profile after a shock to one or more independent variables. This form of model is useful as it estimates both the short- and long-run effects of variables on the given variable in question.

Equation estimation and calibration were possible, using a combination of econometrics and Kuwait specific data, including use of the latest released 2015 input-output tables.

In summary, the Kuwait SCPD macro model was built by one of the world's foremost independent global economic advisory firm in 2018 to give a good description of the historic relationship between economic variables and to capture the key linkages between those variables. Although a lot of weight is given to the fit of the model, this is not at the expense of economic theory and intuitive properties under a wide range of scenarios. The logic that underpins the model is that governments can temporarily shift the level of aggregate demand using fiscal policy. But the longer-term properties ensure that if output is driven up beyond the economy's potential, then inflation will rise, which is not sustainable. Eventually, interest rates will rise and bring the economy back to an equilibrium that is defined by the population of working age and the amount of capital they have to work with.

3. **The SCPD Model Testing: Unfixing and Solving to the Model**

In order to test the veracity and coherence of the equations on the SCPD model, the first stage in the model testing process is to unfix all equations on the model and attempt to solve the model. This process highlights issues with circularity in equations, misspecification of equations, etc.

When solving, in each period, every equation is simultaneously solved and tested for convergence over several iterations. Once convergence is achieved, it moves onto the next period and so on until the end period is reached for SCPD model. The model is said to have converged if the solution completes without a predetermined number of variables failing to converge. Variables that have failed to converge are most often due to values that are close to zero (often balancing identities), and therefore the proportional convergence can be exceeded quite easily.

4. **The SCPD Model Stability Testing**

The SCPD model went through a batch process of blank runs and unfixing for stability testing. Blank runs ensure the stability of the model when fixes are removed and into future runs, as they help to settle down the mass of simultaneous equations that are often used with contemporaneous terms. Once these blank runs are complete, the model goes through an unfixing process, which is another test that the model can be unfixed. This removes any intermediate forecast fixes that were used in the initial working of the internal model and leaves the model open and more fully endogenous to respond well to shocks.

The stability of the SCPD model were tested by first comparing the values of the unfixed databases against the fixed databases and then comparing the values of the unfixed database against further blank runs. The SCPD model is stable as evident from difference tables overleaf, which show percentage changes of zero (to a degree of one tenth).

Main Focus of the Chapter

Kuwait has a relatively undiversified economy, dominated by the oil industry and government sector, with oil accounting typically for over 50% of GDP and more than 90% of both government and export revenues.

Oil price shocks in due to demand-driven are as a result of a global economic slowdown and technology advancements. According to Sadeghi (2017), recent studies indicate that oil price shocks are more demand driven. Supply side fluctuations are not important anymore, and that they are temporary and not effective on prices.

It is highly important for Kuwait to explore how exogenous oil price shocks impact on the economy. Furthermore, Kuwait policymakers can develop policy instruments to prevent unforeseen oil turmoil in the short run. In the long run, Kuwait should diversify the economy to non-oil and private sector-driven policies.

Sadeghi (2017) illustrates that "fiscal policy is the main transmission mechanism of oil price shocks in oil-exporting countries and countercyclical policies can insulate the economy from oil price shocks and fiscal positions usually deteriorate during oil price booms (or improve when oil prices decline) owing to expansions (contractions) in government expenditure".

Oil is a high demand global commodity that shapes the world economy. The impacts of oil price fluctuations can be transmitted into the economy in both oil exporters and importers. June 2014 oil price plunge resulted in 4 years period of relative price stability. This impacted on the economic growth of the world economy.

Oil price turmoil is not only one of the most important causes of many crises in oil-exporting countries as the main source of government revenues but also the main cause of fluctuation in oil-importing countries as an important input in the production function.

The outcome of oil price plunges will affect macro-indicators such as economic growth, trade balance, inflation, exchange rates and equity market prices in oil-exporting economies (Ahmed 2016).

Therefore, the magnitude of such effects depends on the structural features of an economy. Consecutive oil price shocks either increase or decrease causes as instability for the global economy.

This chapter empirically explores and examines the effect of three oil price assumptions on selected macroeconomic variables in Kuwait.

It is crucial that Kuwait draws a target to sustainable long-term public finances as a foundation on which as envisioned in the New Kuwait Vision 2035 scenario and examines the implications for government expenditure and revenue and impacts on the macro economy.

The author investigates the potential impact on the economy and government budget; specifically, the author forecasts a range of possible economic outcomes for 2018–2030 given different potential oil prices scenarios.

Kuwait has a very high share of fuel-related sectors in the economy and shows high elasticity of both GDP and government revenues to oil price. This indicates a high specialization towards oil and a low degree of diversification of the economy towards other industries or the service sector.

According to the Institute of Banking Studies (2015), the oil price defines the proportion of the government's surplus or deficit. Whereas, government revenue is driven by oil revenues (which has made, on average, 90% of total government revenue in the past 20 years), expenditure is not adjusted to target a particular fiscal deficit or surplus. Rather, the fiscal balance is a result of fluctuating oil sector revenue and expenditure items that are performed regardless of fluctuations in the oil price before 2013. Therefore, the government kept expenditure irrespective of its revenue.

Sovereign wealth fund (SWF) investments are largely dependent on oil revenues, and the success of the SWFs (managed by the Kuwait Investment Authority (KIA)) is the first sovereign wealth fund in the world, set up in 1953, in offering a fiscal buffer which diverts resources away from sectoral and industrial growth. The KIA is an important institutional and financial feature of the Kuwaiti economy, acting as a financing cushion during oil revenue shortages. The KIA manages two funds: the Future Generations Fund, which is a long-term intergenerational fund established as an alternative source of government revenue to oil, and the General Reserve Fund, which serves a macro-stabilization objective, offering fiscal rebalancing through flows to and from the fund. Furthermore, The Future Generations Fund (FGF), which is managed by the Kuwait Investment Authority (KIA), receives as a matter of course 10% of the state's oil revenue every year. FGF constitutes 85% of KIA's total assets. The Kuwait Investment Authority (KIA) has acquired a substantial and diversified international asset portfolio, which the Sovereign Wealth Fund Institute estimated at $524 billion (Shehabi 2019).

According to Al-Kawaz (2008), economic diversification should be one of the main concerns in the process of economic development for two reasons: firstly, diversification is crucial because GDP growth feeds from the share of the oil sector, and secondly most of the economic growth comprised of factor accumulation.

Al-Kawaz (2008) explains that after a certain stage, factor accumulation turns into enforced under certain demographic and physical conditions. Thus, the potential contribution of diversification to total productivity is essential to undertake to achieve substantial growth. Kuwait has not succeeded to realize the objectives in benefiting from globalization and multilateral trade agreements. Kuwait needs to get an advantage from trade liberalization. The necessity for diversification stems from the fact that economic institutions focused on macroeconomic management issues and disregarded the sectoral issues at some point in the past.

At this point Acemoglu (2009) argues that "there is empirical support for the hypothesis that difference in economic institutions". "Institutions are a major-perhaps the most significant-fundamental cause of economic growth" (pp. 123, 140).

Acemoglu (2009) defines structural changes and transformation as follows:

> Modern economic growth and development are accompanied by a set of sweeping structural changes and transformations. These include changes in the composition of production and consumption, urbanization, financial development, changes in inequality of income and inequality of opportunity, the transformation of the social and living arrangements, changes in the internal organizational of firms and the demographic transition. While the process of economic development is multifaceted, much of its essence lies in the structural transformation of the economy and the society at large. They are also important ingredients for

> sustained growth. Lack of structural transformation not only a symptom of stagnation but it is also often one of its causes. Societies may fail to take off and benefit from the available technology and investment opportunities, partly because they have not managed to undergo the requisite structural transformation and thus lack the type of financial relations, the appropriate skills, or the types of firms that are conductive to the adoption of new technologies. (p. 863)

After 2014 oil price plunge, Kuwait lessened energy subsidies and passed economic diversification policies due to improve fiscal balance and economic sustainability. Shehabi (2019) argues that these diversification policies have not contributed to export or fiscal diversification. Shehabi (2019) tested this argument with simulations using an economy-wide general equilibrium model that embodies key features of the Kuwaiti economy including subsidies, sovereign wealth funds and industrial oligopolistic structure with collusive pricing, and labour market relies on the expatriate labour force. As an outcome, weak economic diversification is not primarily due to Dutch disease but to economic and structural constraints and economic distortions.

With high oil prices, Kuwait's economy enjoys strong growth and better fiscal and external positions. 2019–2020 forecasted lower oil prices will dampen the overall fiscal balance in Kuwait. Nevertheless, the fundamental fiscal position (non-oil balance excluding investment income) should gradually improve over the medium term due to projected introducing of new taxes, repricing of government services and spending constraint measures. Furthermore, international institutions recommended the authorities to proceed with the introduction of VAT and excises like other GCC countries.

Due to overreliant to the oil sector, the recent fall in the oil prices made economic and fiscal reform an urgent agenda for Kuwait with vision 2035. Two goals are aimed at reducing energy subsidies and boosting the economy to non-oil sector growth from oil sector growth, which have been positioned as key and complementary solutions to improve government revenues with taxes and re-establish fiscal balance (Shehabi 2019).

Fiscal financing needs will stand substantial reflecting mandatory transfers to the Future Generations Fund (FGF).

In line with Vision 2035, the private sector should lead growth and diversify the economy from oil. The magnitude of the public sector should be lessening through public-private partnerships (PPPs) and privatization. Nationals should take part in the private sector more and lower the public-private sector wage gap and improve the business environment (IMF 2019).

Institutional reforms should take place to reduce administrative burdens and achieve a more transparent and efficient governance system and institutions, including a reformed legal agenda and reduction of bureaucracy in order to improve the business climate.

The public sector is dominating the Kuwait economy. During periods of low petroleum prices, Kuwait has a budget balance issue due to high expenditure. Current expenditure, transfer and subsidies are the major spending of the total expenditure (Shehabi 2017).

According to IMF (2017), "The government's underlying fiscal position has improved on the back of spending restraint, but financing needs have remained large. While overall fiscal accounts remained broadly balanced in 2016/2017, the fiscal balance which excludes mandatory transfers to the Future Generations Fund (FGF), and investment income posted a large deficit (17.5 percent of GDP) for the second year in a row. The corresponding financing needs were covered through a drawdown in readily available General Reserve Fund (GRF) assets, domestic borrowing at various maturities, and a successful debut international sovereign bond sale. The external current account recorded its first deficit in many years in 2016".

One of the reasons is due to the huge size of the public sector as a result of the traditional policy of securing permanent, life-long employment and wealth distribution for Kuwaitis in the government. As it is not easy to find a solution for short-term planning, a step-by-step process of organizational and institutional innovations aiming at a slower future growth has to be designed and implemented to make the bureaucracy slimmer and more efficient. In a long-term planning, incentive in combination with further education and training should be developed to offer new job opportunities in the private sector (Asheim 2015).

The economy currently continues to benefit from the oil price rally, which should improve both the fiscal and current account balances. If oil prices don't fall further, the surplus will be maintained. It should also be noted that the fiscal balance figure understates the power of the government's broader financial position, since it excludes the investment income earned—via the Kuwait Investment Authority. If it is included, it would in principle push the fiscal balance to a larger surplus.

These results illustrate how the oil sector accounts for around half of GDP in real terms, and about 90% of government revenues will have a considerable impact on the outlook for both growth and the public finances in 2019 and 2020.

Burney et al. (2017) illustrate in a quarterly macro-econometric model for the Kuwaiti economy that the impact of oil price shocks and global equity turmoil on Kuwait's real GDP and public sector GDP have long-run affect. However, the impact of shocks on the private sector are not statistically significant; thus Kuwait's private sector is inelastic to price changes from the rest of the world. The institutions and economic policies might be a reason for the private sector's economic inefficiency and oligopolistic market structure.

1. The SCPD Model Features and Assumptions

The SCPD model is Keynesian in the short run, e.g. output determined by demand, and monetarist in the long run, e.g. output determined by supply. Within the model, the economy returns to long-run equilibrium through Kuwaiti-specific policy rules and equilibrium forces.

One of the key building blocks to customize a country-specific macro model is to establish the policy rules that underpin the core function of the model. Rules differ from policies in that they are predetermined and fixed and establish a principle or standard that serves as the norm for guiding behaviour within the model.

Another key model building block is establishing those variables which are exogenous.

It is typically not appropriate nor desirable to have all variables as endogenous. Variables may be exogenous because they do not tend to change in scenarios, it is not possible or desirable to develop a forecast equation for the variable, or because a more accurate/preferred forecast can be sourced from elsewhere (e.g. official Kuwaiti population projections, medium-term fiscal spending projections from the Ministry of Finance, long-term oil production projections from the Kuwait Petroleum Corporation/Ministry of Oil, etc.). Note many of the policy "rule" variables are also exogenous in nature.

Core exogenous variables for the SCPD model include:

- *GDP*: Detailed economic activity sector, public, private and mixed sector shares of GDP
- *Input-output framework*: Input-output coefficient variables (although these are variables within the model so can be dynamically changed to reflect developments such as rising export propensity/declining import propensity and the changing structure of the economy, etc.)
- *Potential output*: Broad economic activity sector human capital and capital stock production function coefficients; broad economic activity sector capital stock depreciation rates; and TFP drivers (institutional quality, R&D % GDP, government effectiveness/spending efficiency, etc.)
- *Prices*: CPI basket weights (although these are variables within the model so can be dynamically changed when the CPI is rebased)
- *Fiscal*: Gross financing source shares, privatization proceeds
- *Energy*: Oil and gas production; electricity supply mix; and energy efficiency

2. Model Levers

Both policy rule and exogenous variables are potential levers that can be adjusted for running scenarios and undertaking sensitivity analysis. Examples of other levers, in addition to policy rule and exogenous variables, include:

- Global variables: World oil and gas prices; world nonenergy prices; import demand from key trading partners; and outbound FDI from main bilateral sources of inward FDI to Kuwait
- Domestic variables: Broad economic activity sector investment and TFP; domestic energy prices (capturing the effect of energy price reforms); government expenditure allocation and pathway for core expenditure components (e.g. reform of wage bill and social welfare); government borrowing interest rates; sovereign credit rating; exchange rate; and interest rates

3. Equation Estimation

Except for transformation and identity variables, most variables in the SCPD model are endogenous and have an underlying behavioural equation. This is to reduce and minimize the number of exogenous variables and maximize linkages across the model. Where possible for the SCPD model, behavioural equations are:

- Based on economic theory
- Reflect unique Kuwaiti characteristics, including the lag structure
- As simple as possible (to help model stability and transparency)
- Estimated econometrically using Kuwaiti historic data or a cross panel of data from similar countries

That said, it is important to acknowledge the limitation of econometric estimation and recognize the benefits of calibration drawing on economic theory and other country evidence. Institutions such as the IMF and many modelers defend strongly the calibration approach.

- Poor quality and/or lack of a long historic time series and structural breaks within the data series arising from shocks can make it difficult to get robust coefficients from econometrically estimated equations using a single country's data (e.g. results with the correct sign and statistically significant values).
- Econometrically estimated equations can have a large coefficient on the lagged-dependent variable—this means the equation does not respond quickly enough in scenario.
- Even if econometrically estimated model equations provide a strong statistical fit of history, this does not guarantee the model working as a system that represents the economy and its main agents (government, business and households), nor of being a good predictor of the future where significant structural change is anticipated.

There is a trade-off between good estimated and forecasting equations (where trend variables have a higher weight) and good theoretical and scenario equations. A listing of the core equations which have been econometrically estimated or calibrated is provided below.

Econometrically estimated equations:

- GVA: Agriculture, real, LCU
- GVA: Extraction of crude petroleum and natural gas, real, LCU
- GVA: Mfg. of coke/refined petroleum products, real, LCU
- GVA: Chemical and chemical products mfg., real, LCU
- GVA: Other manufacturing, real, LCU
- GVA: Electricity, gas and water supply, real, LCU
- GVA: Construction, real, LCU
- GVA: Wholesale and retail trade, real, LCU
- GVA: Hotels and restaurants, real, LCU
- GVA: Transport and storage and communications, real, LCU
- GVA: Finance and insurance and business services, real, LCU
- GVA: Real estate and rental, real, LCU
- GVA: Public admin, sanitary, health and education, real, LCU
- GVA: Other services, real, LCU
- Claims on non-government: Local bank, deposits
- Capital adequacy ratio: Ratio of capital base to risk-weighted assets

It should be noted that the econometric analysis was also conducted on the following sets of variables but did not yield sufficiently robust results for use in the model, primarily due to small sample sizes due to a lack of sufficient quarterly time-series data.

- Private consumption expenditure
- Household spending by COICOP category shares
- Investment, private domestic, by sector
- Investment, private dwellings
- GDP deflators by broad sector
- Productivity by sector
- Exports, non-fuel goods, domestically produced
- Imports, non-fuel goods, retained

Calibrated equations use Kuwait-specific data to inform equation design and coefficients. For example, the Kuwait 2015 input-output table was used to calibrate the CPI equations.

For the behavioural equations used in the model whereby econometric estimation and/or calibration was not feasible, the global economic advisory firm drew upon its Global Economic Model and cross-panels of other country data in combination with economic theory and expert judgement to form the equations used in the model.

4. **Calibrated Equations**

- CPI by-product/service category
- Export deflator, fuels
- Import deflator, fuels
- GDP by income, other income, oil sector
- GDP by income, other income, non-oil sector
- World trade index, total
- World trade index, capital goods
- World trade index, intermediate goods
- World trade index, consumer goods
- World trade index, tourism demand
- Tourism-weighted exchange rate
- Inbound FDI demand index
- Net migration dependency ratios

5. **Modules**

The model's modular structure covers the conventional macroeconomic sectors, plus extra modules/more detailed modules to reflect Kuwait-specific characteristics (e.g. energy module, Kuwait Investment Authority assets, etc.).

(a) **Real sector modules**

- GDP
- Investment
- Input-output framework
- Potential output

- Prices
- Energy
- Demographics
- Labour market
- Household income and expenditure

(b) **Fiscal sector module**

- Fiscal

(c) **External sector modules**

- Trade
- Balance of payments
- Tourism

(d) **Monetary and financial sector module**

- Finance and banking

Each variable is either exogenous or endogenous:

- Behavioural
- Identity
- Policy rule

Behavioural equations and policy rules are a best attempt at explaining the behaviour of a variable based on other variables, it will never be perfect, and it will contain some degree of error (SCPD 2018).

6. **GDP Module Equation Overview**

$$\mathbf{GDP} = \mathrm{GVAOIL} + \mathrm{GVANOIL} + \mathrm{GVANIT} - \mathrm{FISIM} + \mathrm{SD} + \mathrm{R(GDP)}. \quad (1)$$

Total GDP is forecast as an identity which is equal to the sum of oil sector GVA and non-oil sector GVA plus net import taxes less GVA related to financial intermediaries.

GDP is gross domestic product; GVAOIL is gross value added; GVANIT is gross value added, non-oil; FISIM is GVA financial intermediaries; and SD is GVA statistical discrepancy in national accounts.

$$\mathbf{GVAOIL} = \mathrm{GVAOILMIN} + \mathrm{GVAOILREF} + (\mathrm{R(GVAOIL)}). \quad (2)$$

GVAOIL, oil sector GVA, is also an identity, which is equal to the sum of GVA from the underlying oil extraction and oil-refining sectors. Similarly, GVANOIL, non-oil GVA, is an identity equal to the sum of GVA from the 12 underlying non-oil sectors.

Several of the broad sector GVA equations link directly to the oil/gas/electricity/water production variables from the energy module.

In the short run, other broad economic activity sector GVA forecasts are a function of total demand by sector, relative GVA sector deflators and relative labour costs for tradable sectors. By contrast, in the long run, sectoral GVA growth is determined by the supply side of the economy and, specifically, broad economic activity sector potential output.

$$\mathbf{GVAOILMIN} = (\mathrm{Exp}(4.94 + \mathrm{Ln}(\mathrm{QOIL} + \mathrm{QGAS}))) * \mathrm{R}(\mathrm{GVAOILMIN}), \quad (3)$$

where GVAOILMIN is GVA extraction of crude petroleum and natural gas and GVAOILREF is manufacturing of coke/refined petroleum products/nuclear fuel.

$$\mathbf{GVAOILREF} = (\mathrm{Exp}(6.4 + \mathrm{Ln}(\mathrm{QOILREF}))) * \mathrm{R}(\mathrm{GVAOILREF}) \quad (4)$$

$$\begin{aligned}\mathbf{GVANOIL} = {} & \mathrm{GVAAGR} + \mathrm{GVAHOT} + \mathrm{GVAMINX} + \mathrm{GVAMANX} \\ & + \mathrm{GVACHEM} + \mathrm{GVAU} + \mathrm{GVACON} + \mathrm{GVADIS} \\ & + \mathrm{GVATRACOM} + \mathrm{GVAFIBU} + \mathrm{GVAGOV} + \mathrm{GVAOTHS} \\ & + \mathrm{GVAREL} + \mathrm{R}(\mathrm{GVANOIL}). \end{aligned} \quad (5)$$

GVAAGR is gross value added in agriculture and fishing, GVAHOT is GVA hotels and restaurants, GVAMINX is GVA other extraction, GVAMANX is GVA other manufacturing, GVACHEM is GVA chemical and chemical products manufacturing, GVAU is GVA electricity, gas and water supply, GVACON is GVA construction, GVADIS is GVA wholesale and retail trade, GVATRACOM is GVA transport and storage and communications, GVAFIBU is GVA financial and insurance activities and business services, GVAGOV is GVA public admin, sanitary services, health and education, GVAOTHS is GVA other services, and GVAREL is GVA real estate and rental.

$$\begin{aligned}\mathbf{GVAAGR} = {} & (\mathrm{Exp}(0 + \mathrm{Ln}(\mathrm{GVAAGR}(-1)) + 0.005 * \mathrm{TRP})) \\ & * \mathrm{R}(\mathrm{GVAAGR}) \end{aligned} \quad (6)$$

$$\begin{aligned}\mathbf{GVAHOT} = {} & (\mathrm{Exp}(0.047304 + 0.794961 * \mathrm{D}(\mathrm{Ln}(\mathrm{TDHOT})) \\ & -0.023067 * \mathrm{D}(\mathrm{Ln}(\mathrm{WCR})) - 0.314642 \\ & * \mathrm{D}(\mathrm{Ln}(\mathrm{PGDPHOT}/\mathrm{PGDPNOIL})) - 0.05 \\ & * (\mathrm{Ln}(\mathrm{GVAHOT}(-1)) - 0.497101 \\ & -\mathrm{Ln}(\mathrm{TDHOT}(-1)) + 0.15 * \mathrm{Ln}(\mathrm{WCR}(-1)) + 0.35 \\ & * \mathrm{Ln}(\mathrm{PGDPHOT}(-1)/\mathrm{PGDPNOIL}(-1))) \\ & + \mathrm{Ln}(\mathrm{GVAHOT}(-1)))) * \mathrm{R}(\mathrm{GVAHOT}) \end{aligned} \quad (7)$$

$$\begin{aligned}\mathbf{GVAMINX} = {} & (\mathrm{Exp}(0.294357 + 0.960194 * \mathrm{Ln}(\mathrm{GVAMINX}(-1)) \\ & +0.004051 * \mathrm{TRP})) * \mathrm{R}(\mathrm{GVAMINX}) \end{aligned} \quad (8)$$

$$\mathbf{GVAMANX} = (\mathrm{Exp}(0 + 0.5 * \mathrm{D}(\mathrm{Ln}(\mathrm{TDMANX})) - 0.2 * \mathrm{D}(\mathrm{Ln}(\mathrm{WCR})) \\ -0.3 * \mathrm{D}(\mathrm{Ln}(\mathrm{PGDPMANX}/\mathrm{PGDPNOIL})) \\ -0.5 * (\mathrm{Ln}(\mathrm{GVAMANX}(-1)) - \mathrm{Ln}(\mathrm{TDMANX}(-1)) \\ +0.3 * \mathrm{Ln}(\mathrm{WCR}(-1)) + 0.35 \\ * \mathrm{Ln}(\mathrm{PGDPMANX}(-1)/\mathrm{PGDPNOIL}(-1))) \\ + \mathrm{Ln}(\mathrm{GVAMANX}(-1)))) * (\mathrm{R}(\mathrm{GVAMANX})) \quad (9)$$

$$\mathbf{GVACHEM} = (\mathrm{Exp}(1.657859 + 0.821286 * \mathrm{Ln}(\mathrm{GVACHEM}(-1)) \\ +0.010552 * \mathrm{TRP})) * \mathrm{R}(\mathrm{GVACHEM}) \quad (10)$$

$$\mathbf{GVAU} = (\mathrm{Exp}(3.4 + \mathrm{Ln}(0.1 * \mathrm{WATER}/997.233 + 0.9 * \mathrm{ELEC}/211.6038))) \\ * \mathrm{R}(\mathrm{GVAU}) \quad (11)$$

$$\mathbf{GVACON} = (\mathrm{Exp}(0 - 0.013389 + 1 * \mathrm{D}(\mathrm{Ln}(\mathrm{TDCON})) \\ -0.419087 * \mathrm{D}(\mathrm{Ln}(\mathrm{PGDPCON}/\mathrm{PGDPNOIL})) - 0.055 \\ * (\mathrm{Ln}(\mathrm{GVACON}(-1)) + 1.134863 - \mathrm{Ln}(\mathrm{TDCON}(-1)) \\ +0.5 * \mathrm{Ln}(\mathrm{PGDPCON}(-1)/\mathrm{PGDPNOIL}(-1))) \\ + \mathrm{Ln}(\mathrm{GVACON}(-1)))) * \mathrm{R}(\mathrm{GVACON}) \quad (12)$$

$$\mathbf{GVADIS} = (\mathrm{Exp}(0.047304 + 0.794961 * \mathrm{D}(\mathrm{Ln}(\mathrm{TDDIS})) \\ -0.023067 * \mathrm{D}(\mathrm{Ln}(\mathrm{WCR})) - 0.314642 \\ * \mathrm{D}(\mathrm{Ln}(\mathrm{PGDPDIS}/\mathrm{PGDPNOIL})) - 0.05 \\ * (\mathrm{Ln}(\mathrm{GVADIS}(-1)) - 0.497101 - \mathrm{Ln}(\mathrm{TDDIS}(-1)) \\ +0.15 * \mathrm{Ln}(\mathrm{WCR}(-1)) \\ +0.35 * \mathrm{Ln}(\mathrm{PGDPDIS}(-1)/\mathrm{PGDPNOIL}(-1))) \\ +\mathrm{Ln}(\mathrm{GVADIS}(-1)))) * \mathrm{R}(\mathrm{GVADIS}) \quad (13)$$

$$\mathbf{GVATRACOM} = (\mathrm{Exp}(0.021039 + 0.680537 * \mathrm{D}(\mathrm{Ln}(\mathrm{TDTRACOM})) \\ -0.208856 * \mathrm{D}(\mathrm{Ln}(\mathrm{WCR})) - 0.513281 \\ * \mathrm{D}(\mathrm{Ln}(\mathrm{PGDPTRACOM}/\mathrm{PGDPNOIL})) - 0.205171 \\ * (\mathrm{Ln}(\mathrm{GVATRACOM}(-1))$$

$$-0.993294 - \mathrm{Ln}(\mathrm{TDTRACOM}(-1)) + 0.25 * \mathrm{Ln}(\mathrm{WCR}(-1)) + 0.55 * \mathrm{Ln}(\mathrm{PGDPTRACOM}(-1)/\mathrm{PGDPNOIL}(-1))) + \mathrm{Ln}(\mathrm{GVATRACOM}(-1)))) * \mathrm{R}(\mathrm{GVATRACOM}) \quad (14)$$

$$\mathbf{GVAFIBU} = (\mathrm{Exp}(0.021039 + 0.680537 * \mathrm{D}(\mathrm{Ln}(\mathrm{TDFIBU})) - 0.208856 * \mathrm{D}(\mathrm{Ln}(\mathrm{WCR})) - 0.513281 * \mathrm{D}(\mathrm{Ln}(\mathrm{PGDPFIBU}/\mathrm{PGDPNOIL})) - 0.205171 * (\mathrm{Ln}(\mathrm{GVAFIBU}(-1)) - 0.993294 - \mathrm{Ln}(\mathrm{TDFIBU}(-1)) + 0.25 * \mathrm{Ln}(\mathrm{WCR}(-1)) + 0.55 * \mathrm{Ln}(\mathrm{PGDPFIBU}(-1)/\mathrm{PGDPNOIL}(-1))) + \mathrm{Ln}(\mathrm{GVAFIBU}(-1)))) * \mathrm{R}(\mathrm{GVAFIBU}) \quad (15)$$

$$\mathbf{GVAGOV} = (\mathrm{Exp}(0 - 0.420456 + \mathrm{Ln}(\mathrm{TDGOV}) - 0 * \mathrm{TRP})) * (\mathrm{R}(\mathrm{GVAGOV})) \quad (16)$$

$$\mathbf{GVAOTHS} = (\mathrm{Exp}(0 - 1.678 + 1 * \mathrm{D}(\mathrm{Ln}(\mathrm{TDOTHS})) - 0.05 * \mathrm{D}(\mathrm{Ln}(\mathrm{PGDPOTHS}/\mathrm{PGDPNOIL})) - 0.5 * (\mathrm{Ln}(\mathrm{GVAOTHS}(-1)) - \mathrm{Ln}(\mathrm{TDOTHS}(-1)) + 0.1 * \mathrm{Ln}(\mathrm{PGDPOTHS}(-1)/\mathrm{PGDPNOIL}(-1))) + \mathrm{Ln}(\mathrm{GVAOTHS}(-1)))) * \mathrm{R}(\mathrm{GVAOTHS}) \quad (17)$$

$$\mathbf{GVAREL} = (\mathrm{Exp}(0.021039 + 0.680537 * \mathrm{D}(\mathrm{Ln}(\mathrm{TDREL})) - 0.208856 * \mathrm{D}(\mathrm{Ln}(\mathrm{WCR})) - 0.513281 * \mathrm{D}(\mathrm{Ln}(\mathrm{PGDPREL}/\mathrm{PGDPNOIL})) - 0.205171 * (\mathrm{Ln}(\mathrm{GVAREL}(-1)) - 0.993294 - \mathrm{Ln}(\mathrm{TDREL}(-1)) + 0.25 * \mathrm{Ln}(\mathrm{WCR}(-1)) + 0.55 * \mathrm{Ln}(\mathrm{PGDPREL}(-1)/\mathrm{PGDPNOIL}(-1))) + \mathrm{Ln}(\mathrm{GVAREL}(-1)))) * \mathrm{R}(\mathrm{GVAREL}) \quad (18)$$

$$\mathbf{GVANIT} = (\mathrm{Exp}(1.812834 + 0.687055 * \mathrm{Ln}(\mathrm{MG}) - 0.034386 * \mathrm{TRP})) * \mathrm{R}(\mathrm{GVANIT}) \quad (19)$$

$$\mathbf{FISIM} = \text{FISIM}(-1) * \text{GVANOIL}(-1)/\text{GVANOIL}(-2) + (\text{R}(\text{FISIM})) \quad (20)$$

$$\mathbf{SD} = \text{SD}(-1) + \text{R}(\text{SD}) \quad (21)$$

The variables and equations shown in the above are intended to provide a snapshot of the methodology underpinning the module and are not an exhaustive listing of all variables and equations relating to the module. Behavioural equations are in ECM format (log differences).

There are many linkages from the GDP module to other parts of the model. Core linkages include links to the labour market, demographics, investment, potential output and trade modules.

As in the labour market, sectoral GVA growth (along with sectoral productivity) is the core driver of sectoral employment (aside from the government and oil mining sectors which are modelled differently). That is, all else equal, faster GVA growth in a particular sector will translate to faster employment growth in that sector. In turn, assuming broadly flat levels of Kuwaitization in the labour market, this will lead to increased demand for migrant workers, which will increase net migration and so total population.

The model also assumes that faster growing economic activity sectors attract more investment than slower growing sectors, and so the relative pace of GVA growth by broad economic activity sector determines the sectoral allocation of fixed investment. In turn, sectoral investment feeds into sector capital stocks, which feeds into sectoral potential output, which dictates the pace of sectoral GVA growth in the long run (SCPD 2018).

7. Economic and Fiscal Outcomes Under Oil Price Scenarios

The author analysed a price fall particularly 2019–2020, which is a stylized representation of the oil market change over the horizon 2030. The results show that such an oil price drop has direct effects in Kuwait, unsurprisingly strongly correlated with export dependence to oil.

Figure 1 displays oil price scenarios as the high oil price scenario is scenario 1, scenario 2 is the low oil price, and scenario 3 is the medium oil price.

Economic performance has been highly susceptible to oil price swings. GDP growth is estimated at 4.0% in 2019, better than 2.7% in 2018 but still restrained by weak oil prices—further government spending cuts, tighter liquidity and sluggish regional conditions in scenario 1.

Figure 2 above suggests that a 1.3% fall in the price of oil (scenario 1 oil price assumption) could lead to a reduction of the GDP growth of Kuwait by dropping to 3.0%; a 44.4% fall in the price of oil (scenario 2 oil price assumption) could lead to a reduction of the GDP growth of Kuwait by dropping to −0.5%; and a 6.8% fall in the price of oil (scenario 3 oil price assumption) could lead to a reduction of the GDP growth of Kuwait by dropping to 2.2% in 2020.

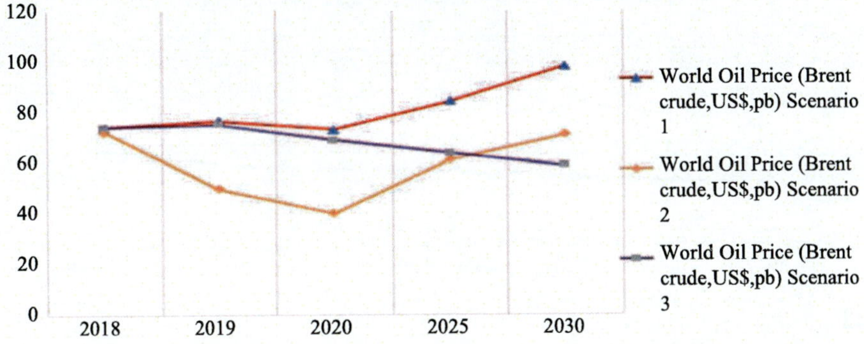

Fig. 1 World oil price scenarios (Brent crude, US$,pb). Source: The Author calculations, 2018

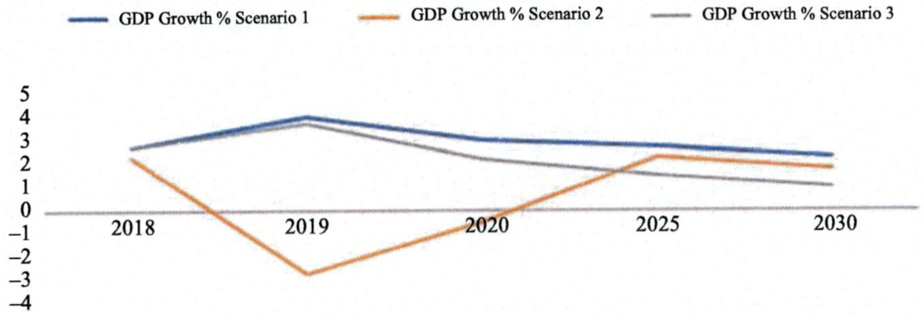

Fig. 2 GDP growth percentage (%). Source: The Author calculations, 2018

Looking forward, with further support coming from public investment spending, growth should rise close to 4 percent in 2019. Both current account and budgetary pressures should decrease on the back of a partial recovery in oil prices and rising output. Investment spending has been extremely low in recent years. However, the government is prioritizing capital spending, as part of the 2015–2020 Development Plan which includes large infrastructure projects.

A reduction in oil prices could have a direct impact on the consumer price index (CPI) as estimated in 2019 and 2020 as a negative inflation/deflation at scenario 2. As shown in Fig. 3, after 2020, inflation would pick up in all scenarios, but it keeps modest levels around 2 percent according to scenarios 1 and 3. The VAT could increase inflation in 2021 and after if it is introduced. However, this increase will depend on the price elasticities of supply and demand.

Figure 4, above, provides clear evidence that according to all scenarios, after 2020, budget balance as a percentage share of GDP declines. The government targets to balance the budget and the chances of the government responding by lowering expenditure especially public sector wages and subsidies. The government plans the

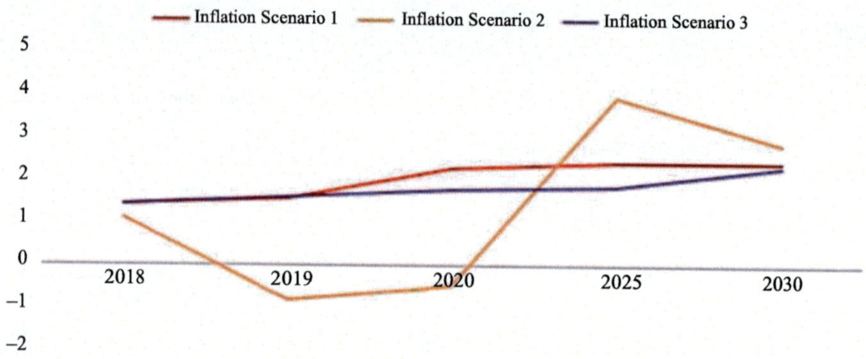

Fig. 3 Inflation year-on-year percentage. Source: The Author calculations, 2018

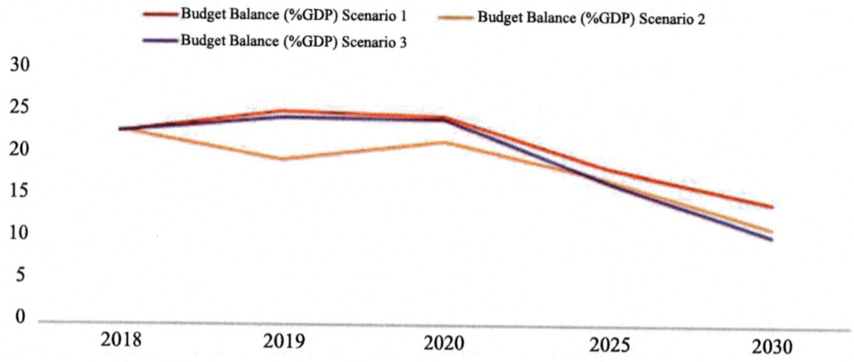

Fig. 4 Budget balance share of GDP percentage. Source: The Author calculations, 2018

introduction of excises on tobacco and sugary drinks in 2021–2022 and rational increases in fees for government services and VAT.

Figure 5 exposes that as the oil price decreases, non-oil GDP growth will climb to 5.1% in 2020 in scenario 1. The forecast exhibits that structural change in the economic diversification should start happening soon as to non-oil economy from the oil economy. Due to commitment project implementation under the mid-range plan, more effective government spending and improved confidence, non-oil GDP growth is forecasted to increase gradually to around 4 percent in medium term.

Growth will jump to 2.7% in 2018 as oil output recovers but then ease to 4 and 3.0% in 2019–20 in scenario 1 due to slower rises in oil prices. Conditions will reflect investment in infrastructure and refineries and gradually rising confidence.

Lack of diversification and modernization: this will limit both actual and potential growth, particularly as an earlier lack of oil development projects means capacity will be slow to rise despite several project contracts being awarded recently.

Figure 6 indicates in all scenarios the government revenue is higher than expenditure in the short and medium term.

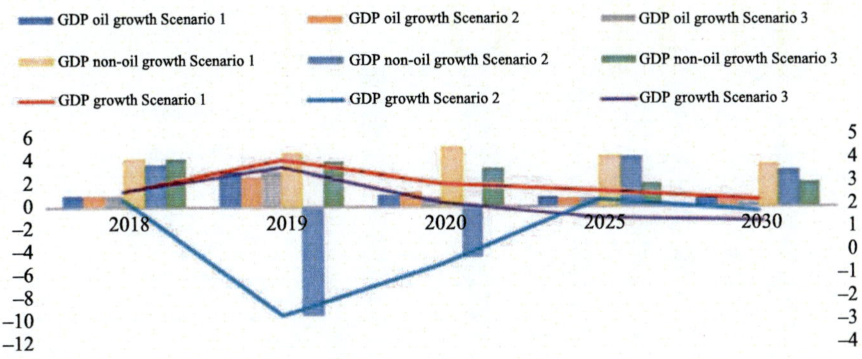

Fig. 5 GDP growth, oil growth percentage and non-oil growth percentage. Source: The Author calculations, 2018

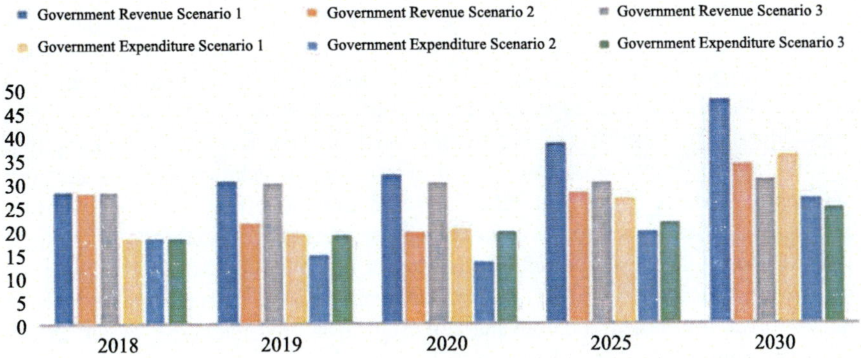

Fig. 6 Government revenue and expenditure. Source: The Author calculations, 2018

Fiscal balance is estimated to remain surplus short and medium period (it will contribute further, if the introduction of a value-added tax (VAT) and excises on tobacco and sugary drinks start), presumably with some hikes of government services and full compliance with the new 3-year expenditure ceilings. As shown in Fig. 7, in scenario 2 after 2020 and scenarios 1 and 3 after 2025, fiscal balance after FGF transfer will be negative territory.

Kuwait's government expenditure level is higher than international levels. The expenditure is the most consist of current spending, wages, subsidies and other transfers. This causes budget imbalances and labour market distortions.

Kuwaiti nationals with high wages and benefits, with quasi-guaranteed public employment, discourage them to join private sector.

Expatriates make up 69 percent of the population and 83 percent of the workforce, with most in the private sector. The majority of expatriates working in the private sector are educated to below secondary level; those who are educated to

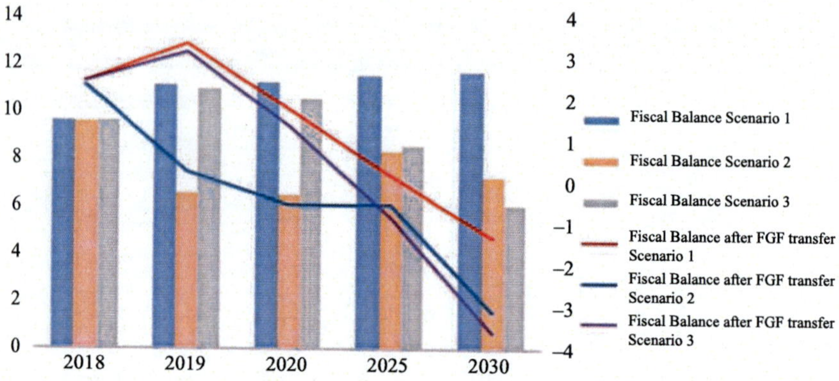

Fig. 7 Fiscal balance and fiscal balance after Future Generation Fund transfer excluding investment income (KD,bn). Source: The Author calculations, 2018

above secondary level are a minority representing only a little over 8 percent of the workforce.

Very few expatriates are employed in the categories of professional and technical workers. These skill sets represent 11 percent and 3 percent of the workforce, respectively. The majority of expatriates work in the services, manufacturing, agricultural or construction sectors. The professional and technical workers category includes scientists, engineers, architects, aircraft and ship officers, doctors, pharmacists, mathematicians, nurses, accountants, jurists, teachers and others.

Furthermore, the research reflects that lower revenues resulting from lower oil prices would decrease the government balance after Future Generation Fund (FGF) transfer (excl. investment income) share of GDP by approximately −1.7 percentage points in scenario 2 and 3.3 percentage points in scenario 3 in 2020 and 4.0 percentage points in scenario 1 in 2020.

Figure 8, above, suggests that fiscal balance after the FGF transfers and excluding investment income, a fiscal deficit between 1 and 6 percent of GDP 2020–2030 period, will generate cumulative financing needs which will continue to be financed through a limited amount of domestic borrowing, external borrowing and drawdown of the GRF assets.

Figure 9, above, clearly demonstrates that a rise in crude oil prices, therefore, widens Kuwait's trade surplus as Kuwait is a net oil exporter. Since Kuwait's main trading partners are net oil importers, lower oil prices stemming from supply factors should help boost the private sector for Kuwait's non-oil economy and its exports. However, if lower oil prices are caused by weaker global activity, demand for Kuwait's non-oil exports will be reduced. Likewise, the research reflects that a reduction in oil prices could have a direct impact on the consumer price index (CPI) as estimated in 2019 and 2020 as negative inflation/deflation.

Figure 10 reveals the strong relationship between Kuwait's annual budget relation expressed as revenue and expenditure and oil price scenarios. Thus, Kuwait's fiscal position is heavily determined by the oil price.

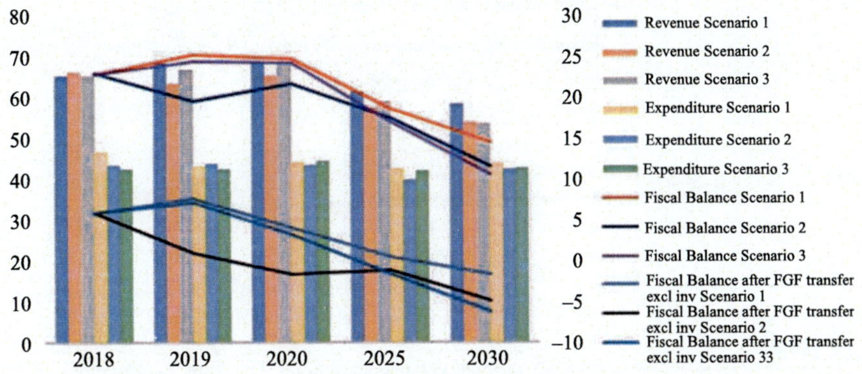

Fig. 8 Fiscal balances before Future Generation Fund and after Future Generation Fund transfer excluding investment income share of GDP percentage. Source: The Author calculations, 2018

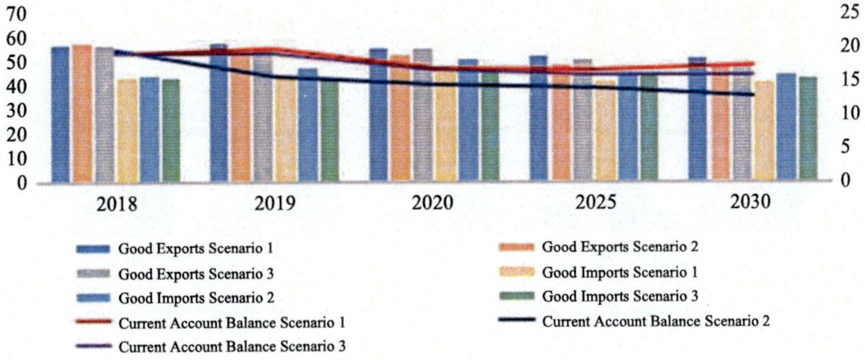

Fig. 9 Kuwait external balances share of GDP percentage. Source: The Author calculations, 2018

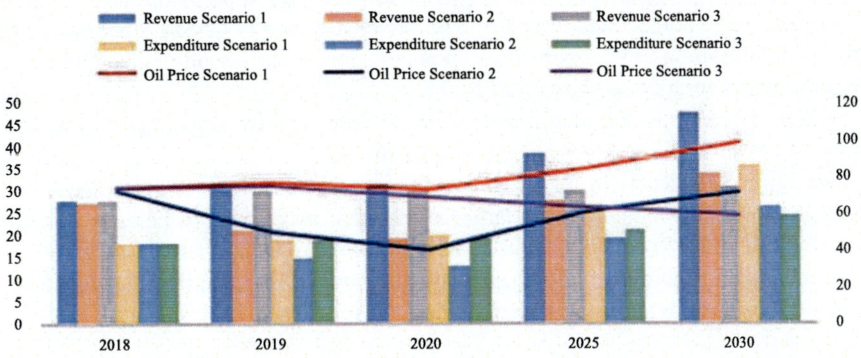

Fig. 10 Budget (KD,bn) and oil price scenarios in US$/B. Source: The Author calculations, 2018

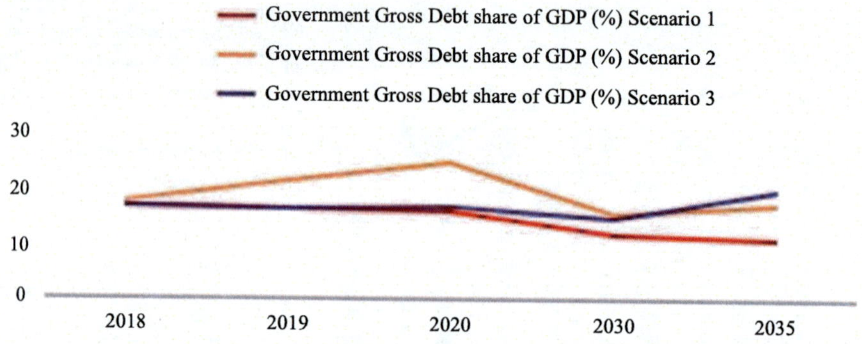

Fig. 11 Government gross debt share of GDP percentage. Source: The Author calculations, 2018

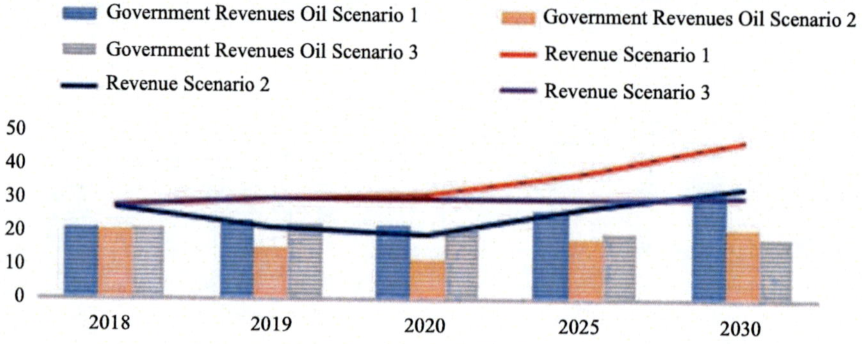

Fig. 12 Government revenue and government oil revenue (KD,bn). Source: The Author calculations, 2018

The author findings indicate that based on the scenarios above, lower oil prices would increase the total government gross debt share of GDP by approximately 25.4 percentage points under scenario 2 oil prices drop to US$40 per barrel in 2020 and 17.1 percentage points under scenario 3 oil prices decrease to US$68.9 per barrel in 2020, and dropping to 16.4 percentage points under scenario 1 oil prices fall to US $73 per barrel in 2020 as shown in Fig. 11.

Figure 12 exhibits that total revenue and oil revenue have a symmetric relationship. Oil revenue has a direct impact on total revenues.

As Fig. 13 indicates in all scenarios, the government wage bill will increase. Kuwait authorities agree that the large government wage bill (48 percent of total expenditure in 2018) would be vital on fiscal reform. Adjusting public-private wage gap and reducing public employment magnitude would increase fiscal savings and boost the private sector employment vision for nationals.

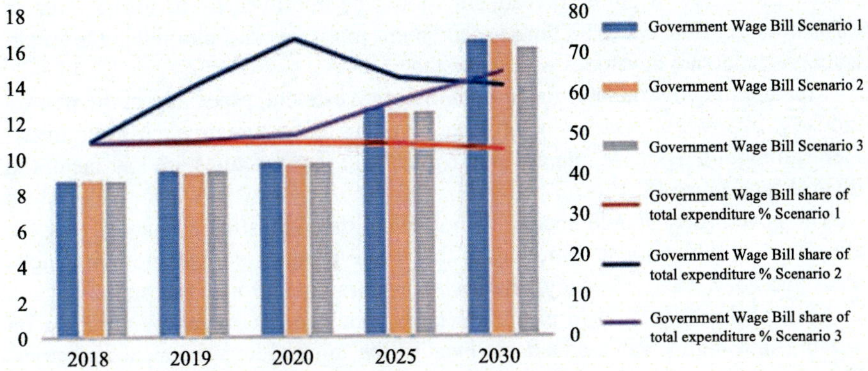

Fig. 13 Government wage bill (KD,bn) and government wage bill share of total expenditure percentage. Source: The Author calculations, 2018

Solutions and Recommendations

Economic diversification needs improve a robust fiscal agenda to help achieve short- and long-term objectives and require innovation to enhance productivity, products in order to sustain growth in new sectors and organizations due to produce more efficiently.

Restoring political stability is a necessary precondition to economic diversification as instability may disrupt economic activity and weaken investor confidence. Another macroeconomic precondition to economic diversification is to establish robust regulatory, supervisory and macroprudential frameworks to enhance the resilience of the financial sector to the volatility of oil prices.

Regulatory and institutional frameworks will boost private sector growth. Restructuring government bureaucracy is a crucial step, and moreover lessening regulatory barriers to competition, including reviewing competition policy laws and their implementation, is another precondition to private sector growth.

The channels should developed efficient creditor assessment tools and infrastructure and boost easy access to credit, especially for small and medium enterprises (SMEs).

The public sector should act as an accelerator for private sector growth. Public spending should focus on maximizing production capacity to ensure sustained development.

The government should investigate and develop labour regulations to enhance labour market freedom. One of the important issues is cutting down the magnitude of the public workforce of nationals and the premium of the public over private sector wages for comparably qualified employees. Improving labour market competitiveness will help to wage growth in line with productivity.

Improving the quality of education, including vocational training towards skills, is necessary in order to boost the private sector.

The efficiency of public investment should be improved by investing more in infrastructure. Enhancing bidding procurement processes and introducing a privatization scheme are keystones to achieve that.

Creating the environment for foreign direct investment, especially in the non-oil industry, by lowering entry requirements, relaxing the visa regime, creating investment promotion agencies and developing efficient tax structures are key factors to diverse economy.

The government should encourage horizontal diversification by intensifying the allocation of government oil revenues that make production costs down in niche areas and boost their efficiency whereas make attractive for new investors.

Vertical diversification in existing sectors should be improved by focusing on moving into higher value-added products in the mineral and chemical industries. Thus, it can be focused on vertical diversification on sectors where the countries have an immediate comparative advantage (IMF 2016).

Kuwait has a high level of welfare expenditures and social security to its citizens. These expenditures are all mandatory expenditures questioning fiscal sustainability. Revenue diversification cannot be completed in a short period of time, but reform in the spending structure or fiscal reform can be achieved to some extent in the medium term. In this respect, fiscal sector reform is essential for the promotion of long-term development. This also provides another reason for fiscal reform.

Fiscal reform should be directed to efficiently manage fiscal expenditure, as well as to diversify sources of fiscal revenue.

Two factors as non-oil revenues and to rationalize public spending are the main point for fiscal and economic reforms in Kuwait.

Transparency of the budget process should be taken. For this, the scope of the budget should be reshuffled. Off-budget activities from government funds, public enterprises, etc. should be incorporated into the on-budget process.

Furthermore, improving the efficiency of government expenditure is needed. For this, a performance-based budget system and medium-term budget planning are actual tools for this purpose.

In Kuwait, tax revenue plays a small role as a financial resource. Tax revenue is below 1 percent of GDP; the diverse channelling of fiscal revenue is essential. To achieve this, it is necessary to have a private industrial sector which financially provides to the tax base. The government and the public sector are the major contributors to economic activity.

At the present time, it is necessary to consider the gradual implementation of a modern tax system. Sectoral roles between the public and private sectors should be analysed. For this, a market test can be a necessary measure for the background argument of tax system reform.

Imposing taxes could boost government revenues and help offset public expenditures. The government needs to remain cautious when introducing taxes, however, as the literature exposed a relationship between the structure of taxes and economic growth as well as between taxes and inequalities.

Future Research Directions

This chapter empirically explored and examined the effect of three oil price assumptions on selected macroeconomic variables in Kuwait where BAU. The purpose of a BAU scenario is to show what would happen if the "status quo" was maintained and highlights the associated costs and risks.

While these BAU scenarios ignore the impact of planned and reform efforts, they also do not take into account the costs of switch from public employment as welfare to private sector employment and introduction of VAT tax.

Further research exposure can be undertaken simulating oil price assumptions as applying to different scenarios like changes on labour structure, introducing tax and excise, increasing the share of the non-oil sector and developing alternative financing tools for budget deficits for policymaking purposes.

Conclusion

Oil is the most important driver of economic growth and the main factor to sustainable development for the Kuwait economy.

The projected fall in oil prices will also weaken the fiscal position and growth. Kuwait will need fiscal adjustments in accordance with fiscal vulnerability. Therefore, fiscal policy has a crucial function in passing on or mitigation oil shocks to the economy.

The budget deficits have usually been financing through a small amount of domestic and external borrowing and a large drawdown of Kuwait's General Reserve Fund (GRF) assets. Large financial buffers that bypass budget shortfall are triggered by lower crude prices. Analysis suggests that, given the current outlook for oil prices (as BAU), current government revenue allocation rules and trends in public sector job creation for Kuwaiti nationals, by 2035 the government's general reserve fund, would be completely depleted consequently, by 2050.

The projected fall in oil prices would lead to a reduction in government spending; therefore, budget balance is an important issue for the government 2035 targets.

Kuwait should have fiscal reforms which are necessarily emphasizing the objectives. Fiscal reforms should target at step by step reducing the government deficit, decreasing financing requirements and accommodating for stimulating investment over the medium term.

The projected reduction in oil prices might lower profits in the oil-producing sector as commodity-supply, which might lead to reduced production, labour and capital in that sector.

Overall, if the oil price remains at or below the break-even fiscal oil price range of $75 to $80 per barrel for Kuwait for 2019/2020, the government may look to revise its financing and spending plans as a result.

Slow economic diversification prevents creating new private sector investment opportunities. Thus, private investment becomes reliant on for the sake of the government's grant.

Economic diversification would expose job creating; it would also broaden the base for government revenue thereby reducing the dependence on oil and making the economy more robust to oil price shocks.

As overcome Kuwait's economic and structural exposure and vulnerability to oil price volatility, policymakers and economic institutions should develop alternative long-run policy instruments. These instrument tools will contribute to managing at structural changes and transformation in order to hover unexpected shocks of energy market reliance.

The outcomes of the chapter revealed that high oil prices have a positive impact on GDP growth in Kuwait. However, oil prices shocks might cause negative macro and fiscal dynamics, with higher deficits and financing needs, and will make unstable and volatile market environments over the medium-term period.

Acknowledgements This research received no specific grant from any funding agency in the public, commercial or not-for-profit sectors.

The research was undertaken using the Kuwait SCPD macro model at GSSCPD.

Key Terms and Definitions

Business-as-usual (BAU) scenario BAU is benchmarking against other scenarios and identifying challenges/risks ahead, and likely timing of these risks, under BAU conditions.

Error-correction model (ECM) A multiple time-series model that estimates the speed at which a dependent variable returns to its equilibrium profile after a shock to one or more independent variables.

Future Generations Fund (FGF) The FGF was established in 1976 with 50 percent of the GRF balance, and each year 10 percent of all state revenues are transferred to the FGF.

General Reserve Fund (GRF) The GRF is the repository of all of the state of Kuwait's oil revenues and income earned from GRF investments.

Kuwait Investment Authority (KIA) Kuwait's sovereign wealth fund. The investment arm of the Kuwait in charge of managing the General Reserve Fund and the Future Generations Fund.

New Kuwait 2035 New Kuwait 2035 Vision is a long-term development plan in order to transform Kuwait into a lucrative business and cultural hub.

SCPD macro model Kuwait General Secretariat of the Supreme Council for Planning and Development model is the most sophisticated and large macroeconomic model which is developed for Kuwait with policy simulation and long-term planning capability.

Appendix

Oil Price Assumptions Scenarios

Table 1 Based on scenario 1 oil price projections assumption

	2018*	2019	2020	2025	2030
Oil Production (Barrels per day, millions)	2.7	2.8	2.8	3.0	3.1
World Oil price (Brent crude, US$, pb)	74	76.5	73	84	97.7
GDP growth (%)	2.7	4	3	2.7	2.3
Inflation (year on year, %)	1.41	1.56	2.24	2.4	2.4
Government oil revenue (Dinar, billions)	21.4	23.3	22.5	27.1	32.3
Kuwait National labour participation rate (%)	47	47	47	47	47
Kuwait National labour supply (000s)	371	381	391	443	497
Kuwait New labour market entrants to public sector (%)	68	67	66	61	56
Public sector employment (000s)	396	406	415	460	504
Kuwait Private sector employment share of total private sector (%)	3.01	3.1	3.1	3.41	3.71
Public sector earning growth, nominal (%)	0.9	2.5	2.7	3.5	3.3
Government wage bill (Dinar, billions)	8.8	9.3	9.7	12.8	16.5
Government wage bill share of total expenditure (%)	48.4	48.3	48.5	48	46.4
Government total expenditure (Dinar, billions)	18.3	19.2	20.1	26.6	35.7
Government total revenue (Dinar, billions)	28.0	30.5	31.5	38.4	47.5
Budget Balance (% GDP)	22.8	25.3	24.8	18.6	14.5
Fiscal Balance (Dinar, billions)	9.7	11.2	11.3	11.6	11.8
Government balance after FGF transfer excl investment income share of GDP (%)	5.9	7.6	4.0	0.4	-1.6
Government gross debt share of GDP (%)	17.4	16.8	16.4	11.9	11.1
Government interest payments (Dinar, billions)	0.17	0.21	0.25	0.33	0.44
Government interest payments share of total expenditure (%)	0.93	1.1	1.27	1.24	1.25
General Reserve Fund end of period share of GDP (%)	124.8	131.8	134.0	117.4	97.6
Current account BOP share of GDP (%)	19.2	19.7	17	16.6	17.5

Source: The SCPD Macro model, Oil price projections as constant USD
2018* is as the SCPD Macro model data and the author calculations

Table 2 Based on scenario 2 oil price projections assumptions

	2018*	2019	2020	2025	2030
Oil Production (Barrels per day, millions)	2.7	2.8	2.8	3.0	3.1
World Oil price (Brent crude, US$, pb)	74	50	40	61	71
GDP Growth (%)	2.3	−2.7	−0.5	2.3	1.8
Inflation (year on year, %)	1.19	−0.8	−0.4	3.9	2.8
Government Oil revenue (Dinar, billions)	21.4	15.3	12.3	18.4	21.3
Kuwait National labor participation rate (%)	47	47	47	47	47
Kuwait National labor supply (000s)	371	381	391	443	497
Kuwait New labor market entrants to public sector (%)	68	67	66	61	56
Public sector employment (000s)	396	406	415	460	504
Kuwait Private sector employment share of total private sector (%)	3.01	3.2	3.1	2.9	2.6
Public sector earning growth, nominal (%)	0.9	2.0	1.5	4.2	3.5
Government wage bill (Dinar, billions)	8.8	9.2	9.6	12.5	16.5
Government wage bill share of total expenditure (%)	48.4	62.4	73.8	64.4	62.2
Government total expenditure (Dinar, billions)	18.3	14.8	13.0	19.4	26.5
Government total revenue (Dinar, billions)	28.0	21.4	19.5	27.9	33.8
Budget Balance (% GDP)	23.0	19.5	21.7	17.4	11.6
Fiscal Balance (Dinar, billions)	9.6	6.6	6.5	8.4	7.3
Government balance after FGF transfer excl investment income share of GDP (%)	5.9	1.0	−1.7	−1.1	−4.9
Government gross debt share of GDP (%)	17.4	22.0	25.4	16.1	17.7
Government interest payments (Dinar, billions)	0.17	0.21	0.26	0.38	0.62
Government interest payments share of total expenditure (%)	0.93	1.4	2.0	1.9	2.3
General Reserve Fund end of period share of GDP (%)	124.8	163.5	187.0	125.9	97.4
Current account BOP share of GDP (%)	19.2	15.6	14.6	14.0	12.8

Source: The SCPD Macro model, Oil price projections as constant USD
2018* is as the SCPD Macro model data and the author calculation

Table 3 Based on scenario 3 oil price projections assumptions

	2018*	2019	2020	2025	2030
Oil Production (Barrels per day, millions)	2.7	2.8	2.8	3.0	3.1
World Oil price (Brent crude, US$, pb)	74	75.2	68.9	63.7	58.7
GDP Growth (%)	2.7	3.7	2.2	1.5	1.0
Inflation (year on year, %)	1.41	1.59	1.77	1.8	2.3
Government Oil revenue (Dinar, billions)	21.4	22.9	21.2	20.4	19.0
Kuwait National labor participation rate (%)	47	47	47	47	47
Kuwait National labor supply (000s)	371	381	391	443	497
Kuwait New labor market entrants to public sector (%)	68	67	66	61	56
Public sector employment (000s)	396	406	415	460	504
Kuwait Private sector employment share of total private sector (%)	3.01	3.07	3.13	3.41	3.68
Public sector earning growth, nominal (%)	0.9	2.5	2.6	3.1	3.3
Government wage bill (Dinar, billions)	8.8	9.3	9.7	12.6	16.1
Government wage bill share of total expenditure (%)	48.4	48.8	50.3	58.6	65.4
Government total expenditure (Dinar, billions)	18.3	19.0	19.4	21.4	24.6
Government total revenue (Dinar, billions)	28	30.1	30.0	30.1	30.8
Budget Balance (% GDP)	22.8	24.5	24.3	16.9	10.6
Fiscal Balance (Dinar, billions)	9.7	11.0	10.6	8.6	6.1
Government balance after FGF transfer excl investment income share of GDP (%)	5.9	7.1	3.3	−1.6	−6.3
Government gross debt share of GDP (%)	17.4	16.6	17.1	15.2	20.1
Government interest payments (Dinar, billions)	0.17	0.21	0.25	0.34	0.59
Government interest payments share of total expenditure (%)	0.9	1.1	1.3	1.5	1.2
General Reserve Fund end of period share of GDP (%)	124.8	130.0	138.6	134.7	118.9
Current account BOP share of GDP (%)	19.2	19.0	16.7	16.0	15.9

Source: The SCPD Macro model, Oil price projections as constant USD
2018* is as the SCPD Macro model data and the author calculations

References

Acemoglu D (2009) Introduction to modern economic growth. Princeton University Press, Princeton, NJ

Ahmed SM (2016) The impact of oil prices on the economic growth and development in the MENA countries. Munich Personal RePEc Archive (MPRA), 89073

Al-Kawaz A (2008) Economic diversification: the case of Kuwait with reference oil producing countries. J Econ Cooperation 29:23–48

Asheim BT (2015) An innovation driven economic diversification strategy for Kuwait. Kuwait Foundation for Advancement of Sciences (KFAS), Kuwait

Burney NA, Mohaddes K, Alawadhi A, Al-Musallam M (2017) The dynamics and determinants of Kuwait's long-run economic growth. Econ Model 71:289–304

Dourian K (2019) Kuwait's energy industry suffering from ministerial musical chairs. The Arab Gulf States Institute in Washington (AGSIW). Retrieved from https://agsiw.org/kuwaits-energy-industry-suffering-from-ministerial-musical-chairs/

Institute of Banking Studies (2015) What is the impact of lower oil prices in Kuwait and on the Kuwaiti banks? Kuwait

International Monetary Fund (IMF) (2016) Economic diversification in oil-exporting Arab countries. IMF, Washington, DC

International Monetary Fund (IMF) (2017) Kuwait: selected issues. IMF, Washington, DC

International Monetary Fund (IMF) (2019) Kuwait: 2019 article IV consultation. IMF, Washington, DC

Ministry of Planning (MOP) (2007) Models and the planning process: experience of the ministry of planning (Unpublished paper), Kuwait

Sadeghi A (2017) Oil price shocks and economic growth in oil-exporting countries: does the size of government matter? International Monetary Fund (IMF), Working Paper 17,287, IMF

Shehabi M (2017) Assessing Kuwaiti energy pricing reforms. OIES Paper No. MEP 17, Oxford Institute for Energy Studies, Oxford

Shehabi M (2019) Diversification in Gulf hydrocarbon economies and interactions with energy subsidy reform: lessons from Kuwait. OIES Paper No. MEP 23, Oxford Institute for Energy Studies, Oxford

The Supreme Council for Planning & Development (SCPD) (2018) Kuwait: SCPD macro model theoretical user manual (Unpublished paper). Oxford Economics, Kuwait

Sedat Dizmen is an economist and policy adviser with over 20 years of experience providing macroeconomic analysis and forecasting of regional countries at private and public sector. He worked as Econometrics and Statistics Specialist at the General Secretariat of the Supreme Council of Planning and Development (GSSCPD) in Kuwait between 2016 and 2019.He provided expert advice to the Secretary General of the Supreme Council of Planning and Development (GSSCPD) under the United Nations Development Programme (UNDP) on specific areas pertaining to specific national policies and diversification/reforms of the Kuwait economy as a pillar of national development strategies.

Exchange Rate Sensitivity of Firm Value: Evidence from Nonfinancial Firms Listed on Borsa Istanbul

İbrahim Ethem Güney, Abdullah Kazdal, Doruk Küçüksaraç, and Muhammed Hasan Yılmaz

Introduction and Literature Review

After the global financial crisis, emerging market economies have built up a significant amount of debt due to loose global financial conditions. Especially, the nonfinancial firms in these economies have tended to borrow in foreign currency in order to benefit from the low-interest rate environment. However, the monetary policy normalization in advanced economies has led to significant downward pressure on the emerging market currencies. Given the heightened levels of debt in emerging markets, this brings the question of whether these firms have sufficient buffers against the depreciation of their domestic currencies. In this regard, understanding the foreign exchange sensitivity of these firms is crucial for policymakers with respect to financial stability.

In addition to this, adverse pricing of foreign exchange (FX) risk accompanied by FX losses incurred due to short positions can put additional pressure on the financing and operational costs of manufacturing firms. This, in turn, has the potential to be transformed into cost-push inflationary pressure, which may threaten price stability.

To identify the effect of exchange rate movements on firms, the pioneering works of Dumas (1978) as well as Adler and Dumas (1984) should be brought to attention. In particular, these studies measure the exchange rate sensitivity of firms by

---

An earlier version of this chapter was prepared as a short policy note for CBRT Research Notes in Economics series. All views expressed in this chapter are authors' own and do not necessarily reflect the official views of Central Bank of the Republic of Turkey. All errors are ours.

İ. E. Güney (✉) · A. Kazdal · D. Küçüksaraç · M. H. Yılmaz
Central Bank of the Republic of Turkey, Ankara, Turkey
e-mail: ethem.guney@tcmb.gov.tr; abdullah.kazdal@tcmb.gov.tr;
doruk.kucukrasac@tcmb.gov.tr; muhammed.yilmaz@tcmb.gov.tr

B. Adıgüzel Mercangöz (ed.), *Handbook of Research on Emerging Theories, Models, and Applications of Financial Econometrics*,
https://doi.org/10.1007/978-3-030-54108-8_6

understanding the relation between stock returns and exchange rate changes, yet by overlooking the effect of other systemic risk factors. On the other hand, the seminal work of Jorion (1990) develops a two-factor model in which overall market return is included in the specification. An important criticism to the model of Jorion (1990) is made by Bodnar and Wong (2003) regarding the inclusion of market return in the estimation equation. It is stated that the coefficient of exchange rate cannot be interpreted as total sensitivity of stock returns to exchange rate changes since traditional augmented market model also includes market portfolio's currency sensitivity. Priestley and Odegaard (2007) also mention about a modification in the methodology by stating that as market portfolios are also exposed to fluctuations in exchange rate, incorporating market returns in the model without any transformation might cause spurious correlation between industry returns and exchange rate fluctuations. To mitigate this problem, market factor is orthogonalized with respect to exchange rate movements. Following this, there have been many similar empirical studies which differ by the inclusion of other systemic risk factors. There are additional attempts to include risk factors in estimations in the style of Fama and French (1992, 1993). More specifically, Fama and French (1992, 1993) develop a three-factor asset pricing model and extends on the capital asset pricing model (CAPM) by adding size and value risk factors in addition to the market risk factor. In this regard, Kolari et al. (2008) examine the relation between exchange rate fluctuations and the stock returns of US firms for the period spanning 1973 and 2002 by the inclusion of market portfolio, firm size, book-to-market ratio, and momentum factors. In a similar vein, Huffman et al. (2010) use Fama-French three-factor model to investigate the exchange rate sensitivity of US manufacturing firms for the period between 1997 and 2004.

As an earlier study conducted on developed country data, Allayannis and Ofek (2001) analyze the exchange rate exposure of S&P 500 firms in 1993 by utilizing Jorion's model. In particular, after estimating exposure levels, they are interested in whether or not real and financial hedging activities affect the course of sensitivity to currency movements. In this regard, to which extent firm sales are originated from exporting activities in the form of foreign sales is considered as a measure for natural hedging practices. On the other hand, financial hedging is defined as FX derivative holdings normalized by total assets. Their results are in line with the expectation that the more sizeable financial hedging is done, the fewer exposure levels are observed. In similar time episodes, Williamson (2001) work with the US and Japanese firms' data to check the impact of real exchange rate changes on firm value by also considering the role of competitive forces within automobile industries. Apart from showing that the sensitivity to exchange rate shock in terms of stock market pricing is profound, they also conclude that time variation in exposure is significantly related to the shifts in the competitive environment in which firms operate. To be more specific, the competition caused by foreign firms in local automobile industries exacerbates currency sensitivity.

While earlier studies are mostly concentrated on US firms, later studies are more focused on firms in emerging and other advanced economies. In this regard, Doukas et al. (1999) investigate the relation between Japanese stock returns and changes in exchange rates for 1079 firms traded at Tokyo Stock Exchange over the 1975–1995 period through a market model, which includes orthogonalized market returns and Fama-French factors. Dominguez and Tesar (2001) examine firms in advanced countries excluding the USA for the 1980–1999 period. The results obtained by the augmented CAPM-type market model show that there exists significant sensitivity at not only firm but also at the sectoral level. Parlapiano and Alexeev (2017) assess 600 European firms, which are the constituents of the Euro Stoxx Total Market Index and Euro Stoxx 50 indices. Other studies in this regard are Júnior (2011), Tomanová (2014), and Šimáková (2017), which examine the individual country cases for Brazil, Hungary, and Eastern Europe, respectively.

Few studies exist in the literature which investigate the asymmetric nature of currency exposure of firm value as it is considered in this study. In theoretical models, firm behavior stemming from pricing-to-market, hysteresis, and asymmetric hedging can create a nonlinear structure for exchange rate exposure (Goldberg 1995; Knetter 1994). By augmenting the traditional market model with an error structure and temporal dependency defined over Generalized Autoregressive Conditional Heteroskedasticity (GARCH) (1,1) process, Koutmos and Martin (2003) analyze firm exposure to currency changes in developed countries like Germany, the USA, the UK, and Japan. Their empirical results obtained from maximum likelihood estimates indicate the asymmetric structure, not only in the financial sector but also in real sector companies. Bartram and Bodnar (2007) criticize the earlier papers in terms of approaching the exchange rate exposure puzzle. While they are acknowledging the possible nonlinear effects in currency exposure, they brought attention to the issue of endogeneity of operational and formal financial hedging at the firm level. By focusing on US multinational firms between the period 1990 and 2001, Muller and Verschoor (2006) introduce nonlinearities in the modeling framework. They separate the depreciation and appreciation shocks coming to the local currency trade-weighted exchange rate index in the form of interaction dummy variables. On the top of sign asymmetries, the exposure is found to be nonuniform and statistically significant among different sizes of sensitivity. Carter et al. (2003) also evaluate the asymmetric behavior of US corporations and use an empirical setting differentiating importer/exporter status. Their analysis is rooted in a simple model of exchange rate exposure for a monopoly firm producing and selling two standardized products in two different markets. In the respective model, currency sensitivity is obtained by differentiating a profit function with respect to the spot exchange rate. In this context, they identify net importers and net exporters as well as their exposures in strong and week US dollar phases. In addition to documenting asymmetric reactions in different currency cycles, their simultaneous equation models accounting for endogeneity report that operational hedging and financial hedging practices significantly decrease the level of exposure.

As a more recent study, Bahmani-Oskooee and Saha (2016) prefer to utilize the nonlinear Autoregressive Distributed Lag (ARDL) approach within the co-integration and error-correction framework to analyze the asymmetric impact of exchange rate changes on stock market pricing in a broad sample of firms from developed and emerging markets. When nonlinear models are applied, empirical results show strong asymmetric effects in short-run dynamics which are not reported with linear ARDL model. On the other hand, results are somewhat inconclusive for rather longer-term dynamics. Moreover, Brooks et al. (2010), Cuestas and Tang (2017), and Hsu et al. (2009) are taking asymmetric approaches in country cases like Australia, China, and Japan. In this paper, as a contribution to the existing literature, the inherent asymmetry in exchange rate exposure is directly modeled, and the role of firm characteristics differing along the empirical distribution of exchange rate exposure is examined via adopting quantile regression methodology. In fact, with this approach, we can incorporate sign and size asymmetries in currency sensitivity without imposing restrictive model formations like nonlinear ARDL or GARCH-type volatility measures.

Some studies designed to obtain exchange rate exposures have been conducted for Turkish firms as well. In this context, Akay and Çifter (2014) examine the exchange rate sensitivity of Turkish manufacturing and services firms for the period between 2002 and 2010 by using sector-specific exchange rates. They find that firm-specific factors explain a substantial amount of variation concerning sensitivity. Particularly, the role of the book-to-market ratio proxy for growth opportunities is highlighted. Furthermore, Erdoğan (2016) tries to investigate the FX sensitivity of 125 nonfinancial firms in Turkey for the 1997–2011 period by incorporating the changes in the aggregate-level exchange rate in the spirit of Jorion (1990), but without applying the orthogonalization procedure. The study finds out that profitability, the degree of internationalization, and firm leverage are significant drivers of sensitivity. There are also studies like Demirhan and Atış (2013) and Kandır et al. (2015) with a narrower focus on specific sectors such as energy and textile.

Given the strong evidence provided by earlier works, this study investigates the effect of exchange rate changes on the firm value by controlling the market return and Fama-French risk factors. In this regard, this is believed to be the first attempt for the Turkish case. In doing so, firm characteristics are also included as suggested by the earlier evidence in order to account for the observed heterogeneity across firms. Hence, firm-specific variables such as the share of foreign sales in total sales, firm size, leverage/financial distress, growth opportunities, and liquidity are also controlled in this study.[1]

As another valuable contribution, this study focuses on a time period covering recent episodes, and it also includes a broader sample of nonfinancial firms listed on Borsa Istanbul (BIST) in contrast to previous works. Although the role of firm characteristics on stock market pricing of FX risk is investigated in previous works, this study embraces an asymmetric approach. Thus, whether or not the impact of firm-level variables differs depending on the sign and magnitude of sensitivities is analyzed through the quantile regression method.

The organization of the study is as follows. The next section provides detailed information about data and methodology. Then, the following section discusses both

[1]For further discussion, see Doukas et al. (1999), Li et al. (2015), Agyei-Ampomah et al. (2012), Akay and Çifter (2014), and Erdoğan (2016).

the firm-level and the sectoral-level empirical results based on the econometric analysis. The last section concludes with final remarks.

Data and Methodology

The analysis uses monthly data of 177 nonfinancial manufacturing and services firms from 17 different sectors listed on BIST for the period between January 2007 and August 2018.[2] As of September 2018, the sample constitutes 56% of market capitalization, 57% of total revenues, and 76% of the gross profit of all firms listed on BIST.

In order to estimate the sensitivity of firm stock returns to the changes in the exchange rate, the following regression is conducted by controlling risk factors pertaining to the exchange rate, market return, and Fama-French factors:

$$R_t = \beta_0 + \beta_1 \mathrm{Exchange}_t + \beta_2 \mathrm{Market}_t + \beta_3 \mathrm{SMB}_t + \beta_4 \mathrm{HML}_t + \varepsilon_t, \qquad (1)$$

where R_t represents the monthly stock returns of an individual firm, while $\mathrm{Exchange}_t$ stands for the monthly changes in the US dollar and Turkish lira (USD/TRY) exchange rate at time t.[3] On the other hand, Market_t is the orthogonalized market factor which corresponds to residuals of the regression of the BIST 100 Index on exchange rate changes.[4] Ordinary least squares (OLS) estimations are conducted with Newey-West heteroscedasticity and autocorrelation consistent standard errors.

SMB_t and HML_t denote Fama-French factors, which stand for "small minus big" and "high minus low," respectively, and these factors are empirically found to have a significant effect on firm returns besides the market factor. The derivation of these factors is based on market capitalization and the book-to-market ratio of the 177 firms in the analysis, where 6 portfolios are obtained. In this procedure, as an initial step, firms are ranked based on the median value of size (proxied by market capitalization as of June of the respective year). With these criteria, the firms are categorized as small or big according to whether their market capitalization is lower or higher than the median, respectively. In the following step, for each size portfolio, three sub-portfolios are formed by ranking individual stocks based on the book-to-market ratios (as of December of the previous year). For each size portfolio, three tranches are constituted on the basis of the value for the book-to-market ratio. In this regard, firms falling into lower 30th percentile, middle 40th percentile, and upper

[2]Due to data limitations, the period before 2007 is excluded.

[3]Stock returns are taken in gross forms in compliance with the gross return calculations for exchange rate and orthogonalized market index. Coefficients remain mostly unchanged when 2-year government bond yields are included in estimations.

[4]For the calculation of return series of individual firms, exchange rate changes, and market return, daily data is collected as an initial step. Then, weekly return series are created by taking simple averages over the month and retrieving logarithmic changes.

30th percentile are assigned to low, medium, and high portfolios, respectively. These are, namely, small-low (SL), small-medium (SM), small-high (SH), big-low (BL), big-medium (BM), and big-high (BH). The portfolio formation process is dynamic in the sense that it is revised after June of every year during the sample period. Accordingly, SMB and HML factors are formulated in the spirit of Charoenrook and Conrad (2005) as follows:

$$\mathrm{SMB} = \frac{(\mathrm{SL} + \mathrm{SM} + \mathrm{SH})}{3} - \frac{(\mathrm{BL} + \mathrm{BM} + \mathrm{BH})}{3}. \tag{2}$$

$$\mathrm{HML} = \frac{(\mathrm{SH} + \mathrm{BH})}{2} - \frac{(\mathrm{SL} + \mathrm{BL})}{2}. \tag{3}$$

As quoted in Fama and French (1996), in asset pricing literature, the Fama-French three-factor model is widely utilized to explain innovations in the short-term stock returns. Since the original capital asset pricing model (CAPM), conceptualized by Sharpe (1964) and Lintner (1965), does not explain several anomalies in asset price movements, size and market value factors are incorporated into the pricing equation. In particular, SMB and HML factors serve as proxies for latent variables governing the time variation in investment opportunity set. As stated by Fama and French (2004) among many others, the original CAPM structure is not preferred in the succeeding studies due to its poor empirical performance. Simin (2008) document the poor performance of CAPM specification regarding out-of-sample forecasting ability by utilizing US stock market data.

Generally speaking, this modeling methodology is preferred to measure the fair value return characteristics that should have been implied for risky equity instruments. Apart from obtaining cross-sectional fair value equivalents, in the empirical finance literature, such a pricing equation is also exploited on a time series dimension to explain the course of historical stock returns. On top of in-sample prediction, there exist some studies aiming to form trading strategies based on forecasts of stock return patterns implied by the three-factor pricing equation. By examining the 17 equally weighted industry portfolios defined by Fama and French (1993) over the relatively longer sample period (1954–2001), Hu (2007) presents findings pointing out trading strategies generating positive returns with zero investment. Lee and Swaminathan (2000) and Ammann et al. (2011) are among the other studies in the finance literature using the Fama-French pricing equation for trading strategies.

From another perspective, especially after the global financial crisis accompanied by considerable losses in asset portfolios, downward movements in asset prices, and rising volatilities, investors have increased awareness about the exposure of stock returns to risk factors. In this context, Fama-French methodology has been revisited by some studies assessing financial stability, contagion, and spillover. For instance, Allegret et al. (2016) document the contagion between financial firms and sovereign financial products by applying the Fama-French model in the European case throughout recent crises. Similarly, Bessler and Kurmann (2014) adopt the

Fama-French method to empirically explore the capital market assessment of risk exposures of banks. Other than these usage areas of the Fama-French method in literature, we utilize this specification to separate the exchange rate impact on asset prices from fundamental pricing factors in the same spirit of studies like Aggarwal and Harper (2010).

As mentioned above, the first step of the study is to figure out whether firms have statistically significant sensitivity to the changes in the exchange rate. In this regard, Eq. (1) is estimated as rolling regressions within 36-month intervals for firms whose exchange rate sensitivity (measured by β_1) is found to be statistically significant. Time series values for the exchange rate sensitivity are estimated for all firms with significant overall sensitivities, and then, they are combined to form the data structure with annual frequency covering the period between 2009 and 2017.[5]

The empirical studies in the literature generally aim to assess the firm-level determinants of FX sensitivity by composing the dependent variable by taking absolute values and/or square roots of coefficients (β_1). However, this approach might ignore the asymmetries in the sense that a particular firm characteristic might have a different impact on FX sensitivity of firm value depending on the magnitude and direction. Hence, this study implements a quantile regression approach to investigate what role firm-level characteristics play on the determination of FX sensitivity with the caveat that these impacts might vary across the different spectrum of sensitivity levels (and signs), in particular over quantiles of the conditional distribution of the dependent variable.

Unlike the standard linear regression techniques, the quantile regression method, which was firstly introduced by Koenker and Bassett (1978), can provide a better description of the data by considering the effect of covariates on the entire distribution of the response variable, not merely its conditional average. As another superiority over standard regression models, quantile regression is distribution agnostic. This implies that the regression does not assume parametric distribution for the response variable, nor does it assume a constant variance, unlike OLS. This type of methodology is also known to be robust to outliers. While linear regression aims to minimize the sum of squared errors, this model minimizes a sum that gives asymmetric penalties for overprediction and underprediction.

The estimation procedure for quantile regression deviates from linear regression. If we consider the quantile regression setting with τ and ε_t representing the quantile to be estimated and residual term, respectively, then objective function to be minimized can be defined as follows:

$$y_t = x_t'\beta_\tau + \varepsilon_t, \tag{4}$$

[5]The sample range for quantile regression estimations is shorter due to rolling regressions. Also, the data is annual as the balance sheet and income statement data obtained for creating explanatory variables are in annual frequency.

$$c_\tau(\varepsilon_t) = (\tau 1\{\varepsilon_t \geq 0\} + (1-\tau)1\{\varepsilon_t < 0\})|\varepsilon_t|, \quad (5)$$

$$c_\tau(\varepsilon_t) = (\tau 1\{\varepsilon_t \geq 0\} - (1-\tau)1\{\varepsilon_t < 0\})\varepsilon_t, \quad (6)$$

$$c_\tau(\varepsilon_t) = (\tau - 1\{\varepsilon_t < 0\})\varepsilon_t, \quad (7)$$

where 1{.} is termed as indicator or check function as mentioned by Wooldridge (2010). The slope of $c_\tau(\varepsilon_t)$ turns out to be τ when $\varepsilon_t > 0$, and it becomes $\tau - 1$ when $\varepsilon_t < 0$, while it is undefined for $\varepsilon_t = 0$. In this estimation procedure, one chooses $\widehat{\beta}_\tau$ that minimizes $c_\tau(\varepsilon_t)$, which is equivalent to finding $\widehat{\beta}_\tau$ that would create $x_t'\widehat{\beta}_\tau$, best fitting the quantiles of the distribution of explained variable conditional on the distribution of regressors.

The minimization problem is approached as a linear programming problem. It is solved with linear programming techniques as suggested by Armstrong et al. (1979), as described by Koenker (2005). At this point, slack variables u and v are considered where they are larger than zero and $(u_t)x(v_t) = 0$. The problem is reformulated as follows:

$$\min_{\beta_\tau, u, v} \{\tau 1_n' u + (1-\tau)1_n' v \mid y - X\beta_\tau = u - v\}, \quad (8)$$

where 1_n is a vector of 1s. This procedure can be described as an objective function on a polyhedral constraint set with $\binom{n}{k}$ vertices, and the aim is to obtain the vertex that minimizes $c_\tau(\varepsilon_t)$. Each step in the search is involved with a set of k observations through which the regression plane passes, also named as a basis. Each step in the iteration procedure is conducted by replacing a point in the basis to see whether the linear objective function is improved. The convergence definition is standard in the sense that iterations are not continued if no improvement is observed in the objective function. Quantile regression is somewhat utilized in the empirical finance literature, especially for the cases in which the asymmetries caused by the variable of interest are aimed to be reviewed. In terms of financial markets and asset pricing, Arfaoui and Rejeb (2016) incorporate quantile regressions with GARCH-type models to evaluate the stock market interdependence between emerging and developed markets, and they document that volatility spillover mechanism functions more excessively under bearish and bullish market outlook captured by lowest and highest quantiles. Reboredo and Uddin (2016) again, by focusing on financial market dynamics, examine the impact of financial stress on energy commodity prices and how the relationship varies across different return spectrum via quantile regression method. Their findings are in line with the argument that financial distress is significantly influencing commodity price changes on intermediate and upper quantiles. More similar to our case, quantile regression is also used for corporate finance issues. Li and Hwang (2011) analyze the effect of firm size and leverage on earnings by taking possible asymmetries into consideration.

In this context, the following specification is estimated:

$$\widehat{\beta}_{1,it} = \gamma_0 + \gamma_1 \text{Foreign Sales}_{it} + \gamma_2 \text{Net Position}_{it} + \gamma_3 \text{Size}_{it} + \gamma_4 \text{Debt}_{it} + \gamma_5 \text{Liquidity}_{it} + \gamma_6 \text{Profitability}_{it} + \gamma_7 \text{Growth}_{it} + u_{it}. \quad (9)$$

In Eq. (9), Foreign Sales_{it} is calculated as the ratio of foreign sales to total sales of firm *i* at time *t*. Net Position_{it} stands for the ratio of net FX position to total assets of firm *i* at time *t*. The net FX position covers both on-balance-sheet and off-balance-sheet FX position data, where the latter is obtained manually from the information provided by footnotes in firms' financial statements. Thus, it contains information about derivative transactions and hedging activities. Size_{it} and Debt_{it} represent the firm size and financial leverage of firm i at time t, and they are measured by the natural logarithm of total assets and financial debt to total assets ratio, respectively. While Liquidity_{it} and $\text{Profitability}_{it}$ are proxied by quick ratio[6] and return on equity (net profit to total equity), Growth_{it} variable represents the growth opportunity of firm i at time t and is measured by price-to-earnings (*P*/*E*) ratio.[7] The data with annual frequency is used to capture the trend in the balance sheet and income statement items, which represent the historical changes in operating performance and financial position of the sample.

In the data collection process, balance sheet and income statement items are obtained from the FINNET database, while *P*/*E* ratios are taken from Bloomberg. Net FX positions, on the other hand, are compiled from the footnotes in financial statements accessed in Public Disclosure Platform (PDP). As the last adjustment, since sensitivity values are coming from 36-month length rolling estimations, we calculate the averages of independent variables in the sense that it reflects the variation in values for the corresponding years. Detailed summary statistics of the data used in the estimation procedure are presented in Table 3 in the Appendix.

Empirical Results

In this section, firstly, overall FX sensitivity coefficient estimations from firm-level regressions are presented together with the sensitivity of sector portfolios to exchange rate movements. Then, quantile regression results about firm-specific determinants of time-varying FX sensitivities are discussed in a detailed manner.

[6]The quick ratio, which is also known as the acid test ratio, compares the total amount of cash, marketable securities, and accounts receivable to the amount of current liabilities.

[7]It should be noted that in order to account for outliers due to misreporting, the explanatory variables above the 99th percentile on one side or above the 0.5th and 99.5 percentiles on both sides are winsorized.

Aggregate Tendencies of FX Indebtedness and Open Positions in Turkish Real Sector

Especially since global financial crisis (GFC), we have observed an abundant level of capital flows directed into emerging economies plainly stemming from the excess liquidity in global markets caused by unconventional and expansionary policies of developed countries' monetary authorities and respective risk-seeking behavior at that time. This process has led to the easing in local financial conditions in emerging economies as well as the easy access of local EM banks to financing from abroad. Thus, credit activities in EM countries have expanded rapidly in line with boosted economic activity and lack of awareness about the accumulation of macro-financial imbalances and credit risk. Turkey stands as no exception among EMs, and FX debt has become an integral part of the financing for firm operations. Furthermore, comparably lower interest rates in FX loans have also enhanced the firm behavior of obtaining relatively cheaper financing sources.

In Fig. 1, the share of FX denominated loans in total commercial loans obtained in the Turkish economy is given. As it can be seen from this figure, because of cost advantages and the lack of limits in acquiring FX loans for corporates, this share has increased considerably and reached levels of 50%. In fact, Turkish households are forbidden to obtain FX debt as a result of legal regulation introduced in 2009. However, corporations had not been subject to such macro-prudential restrictions until 2018 when a new regulation is adopted to abandon FX-indexed loans and to associate the FX loans obtained to past FX revenues of firms. Additionally, downward pressure on FX loan interest rates in the previous decade can be observed from Fig. 2, both in terms of US dollar and euro. This process is thought to contribute to the ongoing worsening in the difference between FX assets and liabilities of Turkish

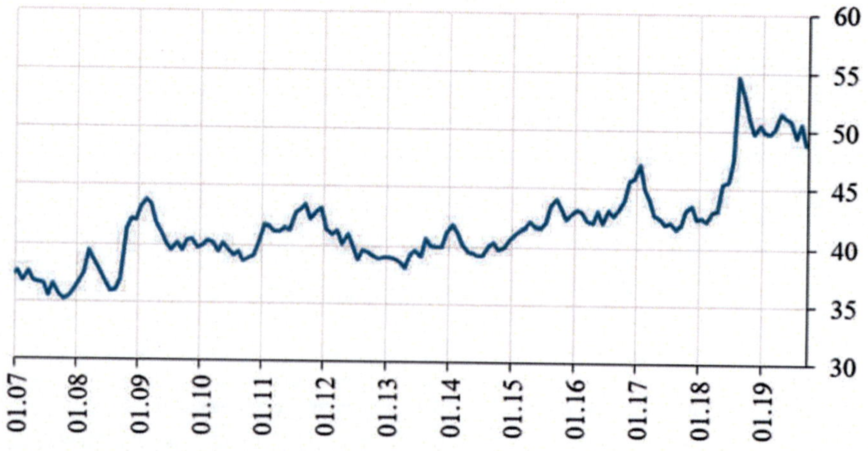

Fig. 1 The share of foreign exchange loans in total commercial loans. Data Source: BRSA

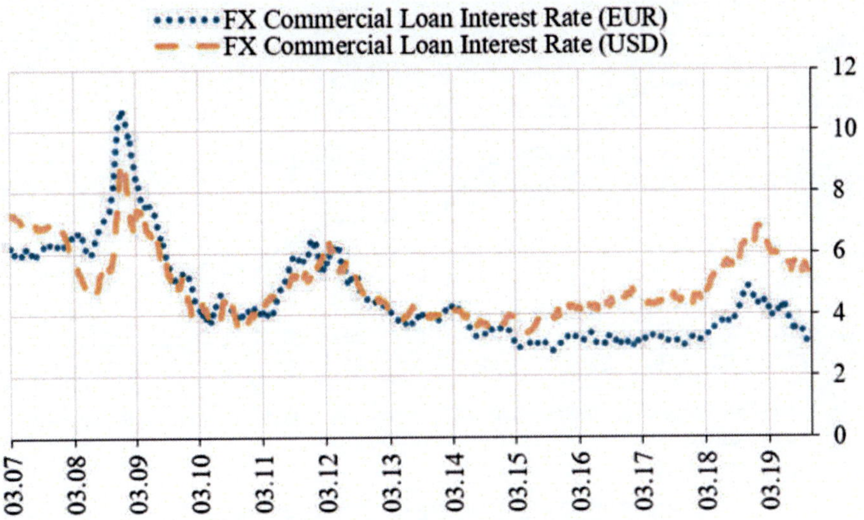

Fig. 2 Foreign exchange commercial loan interest rates. Data Source: CBRT

nonfinancial companies, which is manifested in Fig. 3 and is assessed to be a determinant of FX exposure level in our empirical setting.

Firm-Level and Sector-Level Sensitivities

Firstly, the individual firm regressions with the changes in US dollar (USD)/Turkish lira (TRY) are estimated. It is found that the changes in the exchange rate tend to influence the stock returns of 44 out of the 177 sample firms significantly. When the direction of the relation is investigated, the returns of 29 firms are found to be negatively affected by the Turkish lira depreciation.[8] The average FX sensitivity coefficient for these 44 firms is approximately −0.278. Firms whose stock returns are the most sensitive to variations in USD/TRY are reported in Figs. 4 and 5 where solid bars represent statistical significance of at least 10 percent.

The sectoral clustering of firms with positive and negative sensitivity is presented in Fig. 6. By using the sector classification codes of the sample data from the Public Disclosure Platform, sectors with a higher concentration of positive sensitivity from those of negative sensitivity can be differentiated. It seems that the stock returns of firms in sectors like holdings, utilities, retail trade, and fabricated metal are likely to be affected negatively by exchange rate depreciation. On the other hand, firms operating in sectors like chemical products and nonmetallic mineral products appear

[8] Similar results are obtained when currency basket is used instead of the USD/TRY nominal exchange rate.

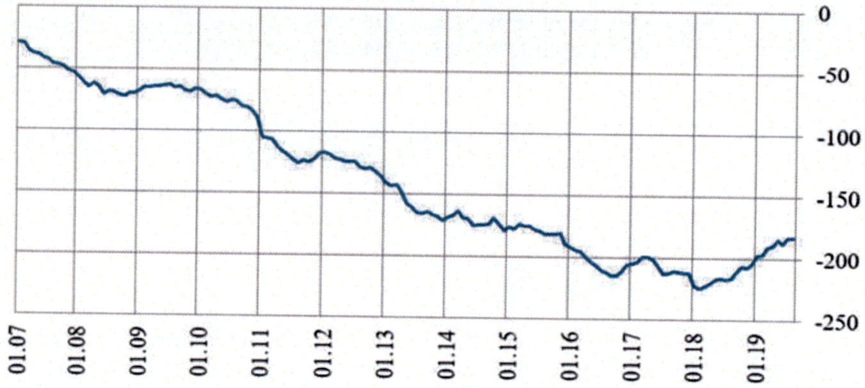

Fig. 3 Net on-balance-sheet foreign exchange open position of Turkish nonfinancial corporations. Data Source: CBRT

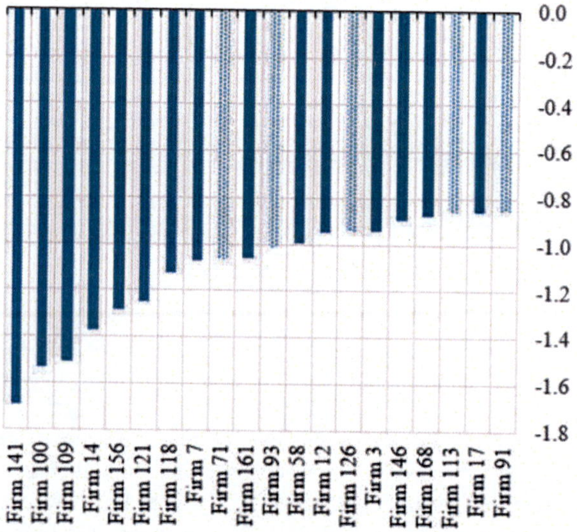

Fig. 4 Largest negative FX sensitivity coefficients for individual firms (Against USD/TRY movements) Source: Author's creation

to be immunized to adverse currency movements. One interesting finding is that, despite there is a general tendency for each sector, within-sector variation may signal the impact of firm-level characteristics in shaping sensitivities (Fig. 7).

For further empirical analysis, Eq. (1) is estimated once again using sector-level data. By using the same sector codes, 17 sector portfolios through simple averaging of individual firms' stock returns are formed. In Fig. 8, the sector-level sensitivities for USD/TRY movements are presented with solid bars corresponding to statistical significance. Results are similar to the sectoral distribution of individual firm

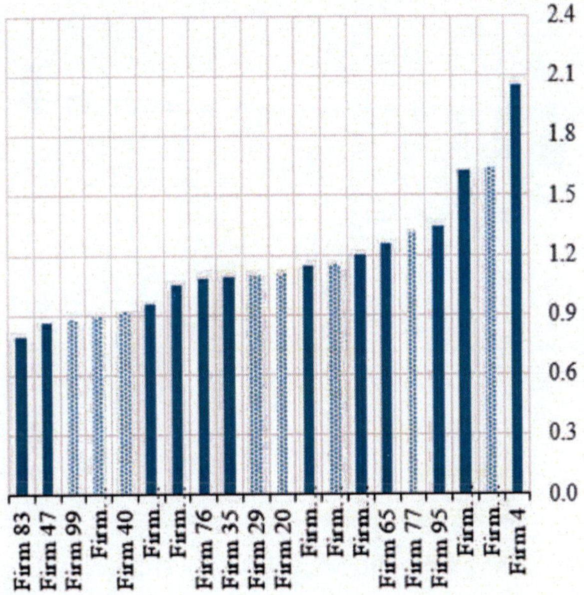

Fig. 5 Largest positive FX sensitivity coefficients for individual firms (Against USD/TRY movements) Source: Author's creation

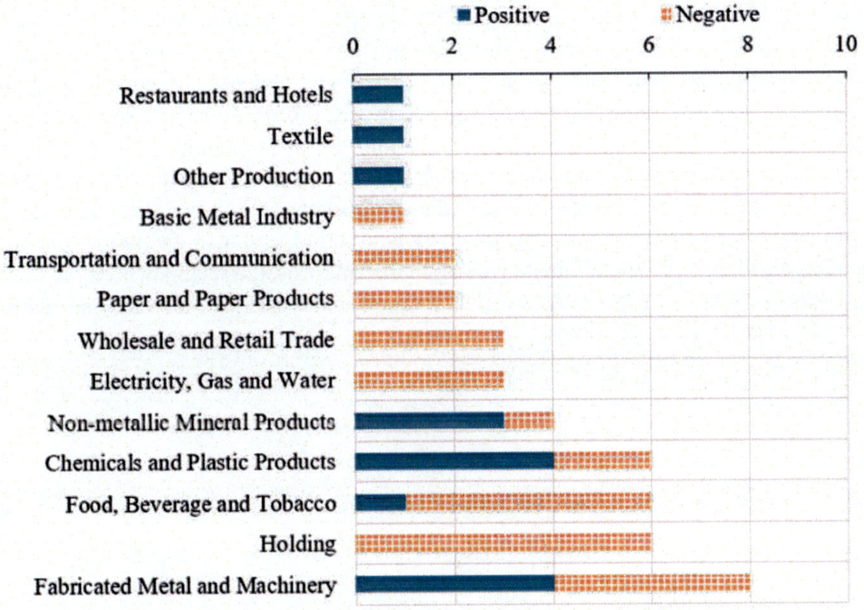

Fig. 6 Sectoral clustering of firms with significant sensitivities (Number of firms). Source: Author's creation

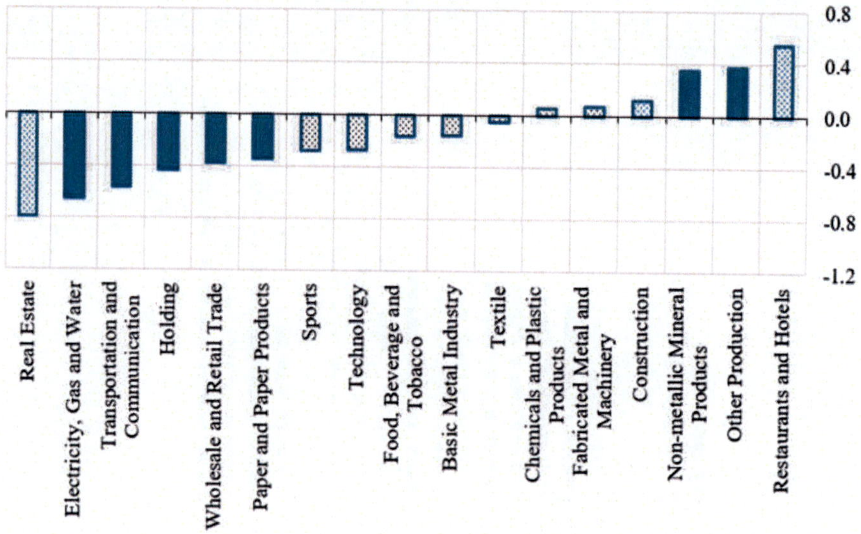

Fig. 7 Sector-level sensitivities (Against changes in USD/TRY). Source: Author's creation

sensitivities. It can be inferred that sectors such as utilities, transportation/communication, holdings, and retail trade turn out to be more vulnerable to the depreciation of the local currency.[9]

Results seem to be compatible with the previous studies about FX indebtedness of nonfinancial firms. Hülagü and Yalçın (2014) work with microdata and identify that sectors such as holdings, energy, trade, manufacturing, and transportation are characterized by elevated levels of FX debt. They also calculate a coverage ratio depending on the ability of firms to generate FX profits given FX debt service costs. When this ratio is used for classification, the abovementioned sectors also turn out to include firms with high FX risk. Çolak and Yılmaz (2017) evaluate the liability dollarization of nonfinancial firms using microdata on credits. They demonstrate that industries like energy, trade, transportation, and manufacturing hold an important share of FX-denominated loans. In that analysis, the sectors whose FX risk is found to be priced negatively in capital markets in our study are also the ones with sizeable net FX short positions.

[9]Similar results are obtained when currency basket is used instead of USD/TRY nominal exchange rate.

Quantile Regression Results

In this section, a rolling regression analysis which is described in "Data and Methodology" section is conducted. This enables to keep track of the evolution of sensitivity over time and across firms. Narrowing down our focus on only firms with significant overall sensitivity to USD/TRY, the distribution of coefficients is presented in Fig. 8. An important finding is that the distribution is left-skewed. This implies that FX risk is mostly priced negatively in stock returns. Yet, there also some firms which react positively to the depreciation of the Turkish lira with respect to firm value. Such heterogeneity leads us to examine whether or not firm-level characteristics have asymmetric effects on FX sensitivity of listed nonfinancial firms in Turkey.

Our analysis proceeds with some graphical illustrations about the direction of the relation between FX sensitivity and firm characteristics presented in Fig. 9. In particular, the vertical axis in these figures corresponds to the FX sensitivity coefficient, while the horizontal axis represents the relevant firm characteristics. Accordingly, there seems to be a positive association between net FX position and FX sensitivity. In other words, as nonfinancial firms carry more positive balances in terms of FX position (either through operational activities or off-balance-sheet transactions stemmed from financial hedging), they get more insulated against currency depreciation as indicated by the positive sensitivity. In addition, it is also observed that FX sensitivity is positively correlated with profitability, implying that highly profitable firms (firms with a higher return on equity) might not face a downturn in their stock prices given exchange rate depreciation. On the other

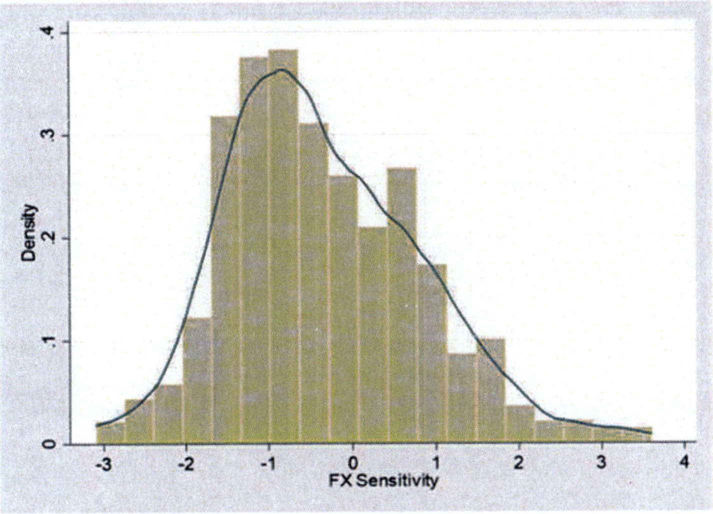

Fig. 8 The distribution of FX sensitivity coefficient (Kernel density fit). Source: Author's creation

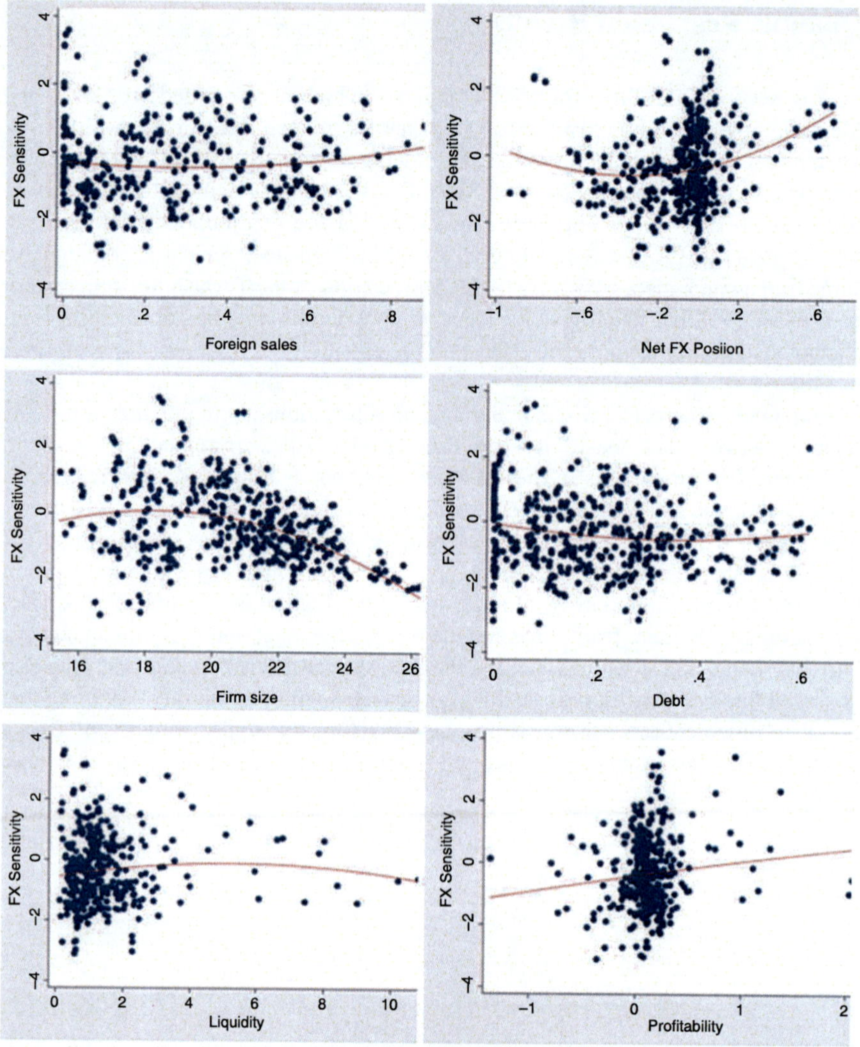

Fig. 9 Scatter plots of foreign exchange sensitivity and firm characteristics. Source: Author's creation

hand, firm size appears to be strongly and negatively correlated with FX sensitivity. In this context, it can be inferred that as the scope of firm operations grows, a possible depreciation of the Turkish lira is priced more negatively in terms of stock return. Finally, there seems to be a positive correlation between FX sensitivity and firm growth, i.e., the *P*/*E* ratio which denotes the firms' growth opportunity. The relationship of FX sensitivity with debt (leverage), liquidity (quick ratio), and foreign sales appears to be indefinite from the graphical analysis.

Table 1 Quantile regression results

Dependent variable: FX sensitivity	0.2th quantile	0.4th quantile	0.6th quantile	0.8th quantile	Pooled OLS
Foreign sales	−0.353 (0.326)	−0.772** (0.366)	−0.865** (0.336)	−1.199** (0.528)	−0.915*** (0.309)
Net FX position	0.868 (0.605)	1.701** (0.678)	1.643*** (0.624)	1.964** (0.979)	1.768*** (0.638)
Firm size	−0.161*** (0.033)	−0.217*** (0.037)	−0.265*** (0.034)	−0.422*** (0.053)	−0.254*** (0.028)
Debt	0.518 (0.681)	0.287 (0.763)	−0.361 (0.702)	−0.028 (1.101)	0.051 (0.724)
Liquidity	−0.039 (0.067)	−0.065 (0.075)	−0.165** (0.069)	−0.258** (0.109)	−0.135** (0.059)
Profitability	0.502* (0.261)	0.456 (0.292)	0.833*** (0.269)	1.492*** (0.422)	0.711*** (0.240)
Growth	0.479*** (0.183)	0.390* (0.206)	0.265 (0.189)	0.234 (0.297)	0.399*** (0.093)
Number of observations	281	281	281	281	281
Pseudo R2	0.179	0.198	0.248	0.249	

*, **, and *** display statistical significance at 10%, 5%, and 1% significance levels, respectively. Robust standard errors are provided in parentheses. Constant terms are included in the regressions
Source: Author's creation

Table 1 shows the quantile regression results according to the quantiles of FX sensitivity based on its own conditional distribution. In this case, the 0.2th and 0.4th quantiles represent larger and moderately negative sensitivities, respectively. Furthermore, the 0.6th and 0.8th quantiles are selected as they correspond to relatively smaller negative and positive ones in the respective order.

It is seen that the degree of internationalization in the operations proxied by the share of foreign sales in total revenues appears to have a decreasing impact on the FX sensitivity of firm value for the 0.4th, 0.6th, and 0.8th quantiles. The impact is especially more prominent in the last quantile, and it can be concluded that a firm is less sensitive to changes in the exchange rate as its sources of revenue are more diverse.

Apart from the role of internationalization of operations, the net FX position emerges as a determinant of FX sensitivity. The positive and significant coefficient for this variable (except for the 0.2th quantile) points out that firms with non-zero FX positions tend to be affected by currency movements. If the firms carry FX position surplus (deficit), the domestic currency depreciation positively (negatively) influences the firm's stock return keeping other factors constant.

Moreover, firm size is found to be statistically significant and negative across all quantiles. It can be interpreted that the firm size worsens the sensitivity of the firm value to exchange rate changes. This finding appears to be intuitive given the fact that rapid and sizeable depreciation in the local currency are mostly accompanied by rising uncertainties regarding product demand, supply-chain relation, and financing.

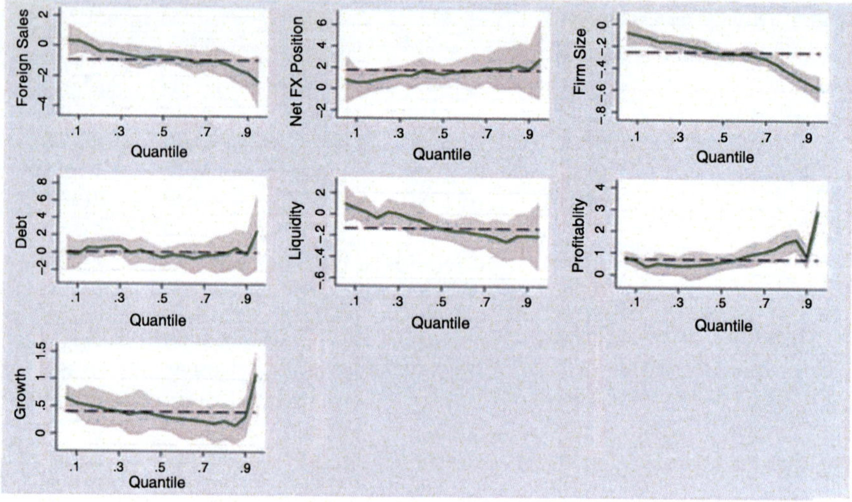

Fig. 10 Quantile process plot. Source: Author's creation

Since larger firms are prominently affected by rising uncertainty as well as volatility, a negative relation is anticipated in this context.

Apart from these, firm profitability is found out to be an important driver of FX sensitivity. It has a positive and significant coefficient across all quantiles, except for the 0.4th quantile. Strong profitability might be considered as a safeguard against adverse FX movements from the viewpoint of investors.

Growth opportunities of firms measured by *P*/*E* ratios are found to affect FX sensitivity positively for lower quantiles in which firm/year observations with negative FX sensitivities are concentrated. As the last finding, the level of liquidity is detected to put forward negative influence, albeit at only the 0.6th and the 0.8th quantiles.

The quantile process plot in Fig. 10 displays the parameter estimates denoted by the solid green line and the 95 percent confidence intervals as a function of quantile level for this model as well as the OLS coefficients shown by the dashed black lines. Considering the fact that parameter estimates exhibit variations across quantiles and deviate from the OLS estimations, this shows that firm-level characteristics have differing impacts under each quantile depending on the FX sensitivity of firms. Thus, this justifies the use of the quantile regression method.

For robustness check, quantile estimations are repeated by controlling for the time fixed effects in order to check for the effects that are not varied across firms and are subject to changes over time (Table 2). It is seen that the impact of foreign sales and net FX position stays similar to the baseline case in terms of the direction of the relationship as well as the significance. Firm size is also kept as a significant determinant of FX sensitivity of firm value across all quantiles. On the other hand,

Table 2 Quantile regression results with time fixed effects

Dependent variable: FX sensitivity	0.2th quantile	0.4th quantile	0.6th quantile	0.8th quantile
Foreign sales	−0.221 (0.347)	−0.739* (0.369)	−0.976*** (0.343)	−1.779*** (0.481)
Net FX position	0.891 (0.646)	2.092*** (0.686)	2.276*** (0.638)	2.155** (0.895)
Firm size	−0.122*** (0.035)	−0.195*** (0.038)	−0.283*** (0.035)	−0.426*** (0.049)
Debt	0.417 (0.725)	0.593 (0.770)	0.139 (0.716)	0.999 (1.005)
Liquidity	−0.032 (0.072)	−0.077 (0.076)	−0.188*** (0.071)	−0.086 (0.099)
Profitability	0.435 (0.280)	0.154 (0.297)	0.529* (0.277)	0.992** (0.388)
Growth	0.560*** (0.196)	0.392* (0.208)	0.256 (0.193)	0.257 (0.271)
Year fixed effects	Yes	Yes	Yes	Yes
Number of observations	281	281	281	281
Pseudo R2	0.179	0.198	0.248	0.249

*, **, and *** display statistical significance at 10%, 5%, and 1% significance levels respectively. Robust standard errors are provided in parentheses. Constant terms are included in the regressions
Source: Author's creation

while the signs do not change, some significance is lost for the coefficients of liquidity and profitability in the 0.6th and the 0.8th quantiles.

Solutions and Recommendations

To sum up, this study provides a detailed and up-to-date picture of the investors' behavior for pricing FX risk, not only on firm level but also regarding sectoral classifications. Moreover, the main contribution of this study is to identify factors determining to what extent FX risk is priced in stock markets. Specifically, the robust positive association between the on-balance-sheet net FX position and FX sensitivity of firm value implies the mitigating role of hedging practices. In other words, on top of natural hedging stemming from FX revenues, firms can protect themselves from adverse currency changes by taking positions in off-balance-sheet instruments. This alleviates the FX losses in accounting terms and, more importantly, also positively affects the investor sentiment. Hence, efforts to support the deepening and inclusion of FX derivative markets in Turkey would be expected to contribute to market capitalization and investor sentiment for nonfinancial firms. Although TRY is a major EM currency transacted vastly in spot markets, there is room for improvement in terms of financial hedging through instruments like forwards, futures, and swaps.

Ultimately, this may support the functioning of the expectations channel of the monetary and financial transmission mechanisms.

In recent period, some reforms were implemented to handle the FX risk and exposure to conduct sound risk management practices as well as hedging transactions. Increasing adoption of such policies will be beneficial in decreasing the dollarization and will be helpful in sustaining financial stability in emerging markets.

Moreover, this study reveals other firm-level dynamics governing the FX sensitivity of firm value. In this context, empirical results indicate that the degree of engaging in international operations, profitability, firm size, and growth opportunities are statistically significant factors. Thus, policies that would be designed to contain FX risks of nonfinancial firms can be customized and segmented to address such heterogeneities.

Future Research Directions

Especially for EMs, possible frictions and vulnerabilities of the financial sector and real sector attract the attention of investors, policymakers, and academicians in terms of financial stability framework. Considering the more and more interconnected and complicated relationship between firms and financial institutions; the importance of sound and robust real sector functioning can be understood easily. In this framework, exchange rate movements become one of the major sources of uncertainty for all agents and firms and institutions in emerging markets. Therefore, analyzing the sensitivities to shocks coming from fluctuations of exchange rates and understanding the true dynamics of the transmission channels of the shocks are of great value. However, as mentioned above due to the fragile nature of emerging markets, the analysis of such dynamics requires advanced econometric techniques that can capture possible nonlinearities and asymmetries. Otherwise, the empirical results are specific to the Turkish case, and they might give biased results and misguide policymakers when conducting policy analysis for other EM economies with differed dynamics. It should also be noted that the framework founded in this study would probably be case-specific, meaning that generalization of the results to the other countries and time periods without further examination might be misleading.

Therefore, further analysis of the fragile nature of emerging markets and sensitivities to external shocks mainly driven by exchange rate fluctuations via advanced econometric tools might give valuable insights to all related parties.

Conclusion

Given the importance of exchange rate dynamics on financial stability, it is crucial to figure out how the firms' sensitivity to exchange rate depreciation or appreciation differs. In this regard, this study investigates the reaction of the firm-level and sector-level returns to the changes in the exchange rate.

For this purpose, firstly the coefficient of sensitivity to the changes in the exchange rate is estimated at the firm level. The results suggest that the sensitivity has a wide dispersion with respect to sign and magnitude. It is also noted that the distribution is left-skewed, implying that FX risk is priced mostly negatively in stock returns. Additionally, when the same analysis is replicated at the sectoral level, sectors that are found to be more vulnerable to the depreciation of the Turkish lira are also known to carry a high level of short FX positions, which are also validated by the previous studies.

In the following step, firm-level characteristics which might have an effect on the FX sensitivity of firms are examined by allowing for possible distributional asymmetries. Few studies exist in the literature which investigate the asymmetric nature of currency exposure of firm value as it is considered in this study. In this paper, as a contribution to the existing literature, the inherent asymmetry in exchange rate exposure is directly modeled, and the role of firm characteristics differing along the empirical distribution of exchange rate exposure is examined via adopting quantile regression methodology. In fact, with this approach, possible sign and size asymmetries in currency sensitivity are incorporated without imposing restrictive model formations. As another valuable contribution, this study focuses on a time period covering recent episodes, and it also includes a broader sample of nonfinancial firms listed on Borsa Istanbul (BIST) in contrast to previous works. Although the role of firm characteristics on stock market pricing of FX risk is investigated in previous works, this study embraces an asymmetric approach.

Results seem to be compatible with the previous studies focusing on firm-level determinants of exchange rate sensitivity. The findings point out that the degree of engaging in international operations (foreign sales), profitability, firm size, and growth opportunities are statistically significant factors. As mentioned before, some of those factors are found to be significant in the previous studies, but in those studies, some of these variables controlled partially not in a compact manner adopted in this study.

Key Terms and Definitions

Exchange Rate Sensitivity It is the degree with which firm stock returns are subject to variation when spot exchange rate is fluctuating.

FX Risk A concept of exposure causing considerable changes in firm assets, equities, and projected income stream stemming from economic, transaction, and translation FX exposure.

Nonfinancial Firms: Firms with main line of business excluding activities of financial services and financial intermediation

Risk Management Taking positions in financial derivatives like swaps, forwards, and options to hedge against FX risk.

Quantile Regression Linear statistical estimation technique involving the whole distribution of dependent variable instead of just focusing on conditional mean.

Rolling Regression Simple OLS regression conducted on a rolling sample periods.

Fama-French Pricing Factors An asset pricing model developed by Fama and French (1992) that expands on CAPM by controlling for size and value risk components. In other words, it incorporates return on "small minus big" and "high minus low" portfolios obtained from firm size and book-to-market ratio.

Market Value The amount of value calculated by multiplying the price and number of shares being traded.

Appendix

Table 3 Summary statistics

Variables	Definition	Mean	Standard deviation	Max	Min	Data source
Foreign sales	The ratio of foreign sales to gross sales	0.2573	0.2207	0.8775	0.0000	FINNET
Net FX position	The ratio of balance sheet net position to total assets	−0.0817	0.2191	0.6734	−0.9336	PDP
Firm size	Natural logarithm of total assets	20.6060	2.2669	26.3076	15.4221	FINNET
Debt	The ratio of financial debt to total assets	0.2041	0.1541	0.6126	0.0000	FINNET
Liquidity	Quick ratio	1.4474	1.3904	10.8221	0.1226	FINNET
Profitability	Return on equity	0.1249	0.2840	2.0622	−1.3648	FINNET
Growth	Price to earnings ratio	0.1903	0.3250	3.1565	0.0008	Bloomberg

Source: Author's creation

References

Adler M, Dumas B (1984) Exposure to currency risk: definition and measurement. Financ Manag 13(2):41–50

Aggarwal R, Harper JT (2010) Foreign exchange exposure of "domestic" corporations. J Int Money Financ 29(8):1619–1636

Agyei-Ampomah S, Mazouz K, Yin S (2012) The foreign exchange exposure of UK non-financial firms: a comparison of market-based methodologies. Int Rev Financ Anal 29(C):251–260

Akay GH, Çifter A (2014) Exchange rate exposure at the firm and industry levels: evidence from Turkey. Econ Model 43(C):426–434

Allayannis G, Ofek E (2001) Exchange rate exposure, hedging, and the use of foreign currency derivatives. J Int Money Financ 20(2):273–296

Allegret JP, Raymond H, Rharrabti H (2016) The impact of the Eurozone crisis on European banks stocks contagion or interdependence? Eur Res Stud J 19(1):129–148

Ammann M, Moellenbeck M, Schmid MM (2011) Feasible momentum strategies in the US stock market. J Asset Manag 11(6):362–374

Arfaoui M, Rejeb AB (2016) Financial market interdependencies: a quantile regression analysis of volatility spillover. Res Int Bus Financ 36:140–157

Armstrong RD, Frome EL, Kung DS (1979) Algorithm 79-01: a revised simplex algorithm for the absolute deviation curve fitting problem. Commun Stat Simul Comput 8:175–190

Bahmani-Oskooee M, Saha S (2016) Do exchange rate changes have symmetric or asymmetric effects on stock prices? Glob Financ J 31:57–72

Bartram SM, Bodnar GM (2007) The exchange rate exposure puzzle. Manag Financ 33(9):642–666

Bessler W, Kurmann P (2014) Bank risk factors and changing risk exposures: capital market evidence before and during the financial crisis. J Financ Stab 13:151–166

Bodnar GM, Wong MF (2003) Estimating exchange rate exposures: issues in model structure. Financ Manag 32(1):35–67

Brooks RD, Di Iorio A, Faff RW, Fry T, Joymungul Y (2010) Asymmetry and time variation in exchange rate exposure: an investigation of Australian stocks returns. Int J Commer Manag 20 (4):276–295

Carter D, Pantzalis C, Simkins BJ (2003) Asymmetric exposure to foreign-exchange risk: financial and real option hedges implemented by US multinational corporations Available at SSRN 387082

Charoenrook AA, Conrad JS (2005) Identifying risk-based factors. AFA 2006 Boston meetings paper

Çolak MS, Yılmaz F (2017) Reel Sektör Döviz Pozisyonu ve Risklerin Dağılımı (in Turkish), CBT Research Notes in Economics No 2017-09

Cuestas JC, Tang B (2017) Asymmetric exchange rate exposure of stock returns: empirical evidence from Chinese industries. Stud Nonlinear Dyn Econ 4(4):21

Demirhan D, Atış AG (2013) A research on the exchange rate exposure of firms listed in Borsa Istanbul. Bus Econ Res J 4(4):25–35

Dominguez KM, Tesar LL (2001) A reexamination of exchange-rate exposure. Am Econ Rev 91 (2):396–399

Doukas J, Hall PH, Lang LH (1999) The pricing of currency risk in Japan. J Bank Financ 23 (1):1–20

Dumas B (1978) The theory of the trading firm revisited. J Financ 33(3):1019–1030

Erdoğan M (2016) Foreign exchange exposure and hedging of Turkish companies: panel data evidence. Int Bus Res 9(6):44–52

Fama EF, French KR (1992) The cross-section of expected stock returns. J Financ 47(2):427–465

Fama EF, French KR (1993) Common risk factors in the returns on stocks and bonds. J Financ Econ 33(1):3–56

Fama EF, French KR (1996) Multifactor explanations of asset pricing anomalies. J Financ 51 (1):55–84

Fama EF, French KR (2004) The capital asset pricing model: theory and evidence. J Econ Perspect 18(3):25–46
Goldberg PK (1995) Product differentiation and oligopoly in international markets: the case of the US automobile industry. Econometrica 63:891–951
Hsu CC, Yau R, Wu JY (2009) Asymmetric exchange rate exposure and industry characteristics: evidence from Japanese data. Hitotsubashi J Econ 50:57–69
Hu O (2007) Applicability of the Fama-French three-factor model in forecasting portfolio returns. J Financ Res 30(1):111–127
Huffman SP, Makar SD, Beyer SB (2010) A three-factor model investigation of foreign exchange-rate exposure. Glob Financ J 21(1):1–12
Hülagü T, Yalçın C (2014) Türkiye'de Firmaların Yabancı Para Borçluluğu ve Kur Riskine İlişkin Mikro Değerlendirmeler (in Turkish), CBT Research Notes in Economics No: 2014-13
Jorion P (1990) The exchange-rate exposure of US multinationals. J Bus 63(3):331–345
Júnior JLR (2011) Exchange rate exposure, foreign currency debt, and the use of derivatives: evidence from Brazil. Emerg Mark Financ Trade 47(1):67–89
Kandır SY, Erişmis A, Öztürk İ (2015) Investigating exchange rate exposure of energy firms: evidence from Turkey. Prague Econ Papers 24(6):729–743
Knetter MM (1994) Is export price adjustment asymmetric? Evaluating the market share and marketing bottlenecks hypotheses. J Int Money Financ 13(1):55–70
Koenker R (2005) Quantile regression. Cambridge University Press, New York
Koenker R, Bassett G Jr (1978) Regression quantiles. Econometrica 46(1):33–50
Kolari JW, Moorman TC, Sorescu SM (2008) Foreign exchange risk and the cross-section of stock returns. J Int Money Financ 27(7):1074–1097
Koutmos G, Martin AD (2003) Asymmetric exchange rate exposure: theory and evidence. J Int Money Financ 22(3):365–383
Lee CM, Swaminathan B (2000) Price momentum and trading volume. J Financ 55(5):2017–2069
Li MYL, Hwang NCR (2011) Effects of firm size, financial leverage and R&D expenditures on firm earnings: an analysis using quantile regression approach. Abacus 47(2):182–204
Li H, Ma H, Xu Y (2015) How do exchange rate movements affect Chinese exports? A firm level investigation. J Int Econ 97(1):148–161
Lintner J (1965) Security prices, risk, and maximal gains from diversification. J Financ 20 (4):587–615
Muller A, Verschoor WF (2006) Asymmetric foreign exchange risk exposure: evidence from US multinational firms. J Empir Financ 13(4–5):495–518
Parlapiano F, Alexeev V (2017) Exchange rate risk exposure and the value of European firms. Eur J Financ 23(2):111–129
Priestley R, Odegaard BA (2007) Linear and nonlinear exchange rate exposure. J Int Money Financ 26(6):1016–1037
Sharpe WF (1964) Capital asset prices: a theory of market equilibrium under conditions of risk. J Financ 19(3):425–442
Šimáková J (2017) The impact of exchange rate movements on firm value in Visegrad countries. Acta Universitatis Agriculturae et Silviculturae Mendelianae Brunensis 65(6):2105–2111
Simin T (2008) The poor predictive performance of asset pricing models. J Financ Quant Anal 43 (2):355–380
Reboredo JC, Uddin GS (2016) Do financial stress and policy uncertainty have an impact on the energy and metals markets? A quantile regression approach. Int Rev Econ Finance 43:284–298
Tomanová L (2014) Exchange rate exposure and its determinants: evidence on Hungarian firms. Eur Financ Account J 9(2):47–65
Williamson R (2001) Exchange rate exposure and competition: evidence from the automotive industry. J Financ Econ 59(3):441–475
Wooldridge JM (2010) Econometric analysis of cross section and panel data, 2nd edn. MIT Press, Cambridge, MA

Additional Reading

Adler M, Dumas B (1984) Exposure to currency risk: definition and measurement. Financ Manag 13(2):41–50

Brooks RD, Di Iorio A, Faff RW, Fry T, Joymungul Y (2010) Asymmetry and time variation in exchange rate exposure: an investigation of Australian stocks returns. Int J Commer Manag 20 (4):276–295

Fama EF, French KR (1992) The cross-section of expected stock returns. J Financ 47(2):427–465

Fama EF, French KR (1993) Common risk factors in the returns on stocks and bonds. J Financ Econ 33(1):3–56

Jorion P (1990) The exchange-rate exposure of US multinationals. J Bus 63(3):331–345

Koenker R, Bassett G Jr (1978) Regression quantiles. Econometrica 46(1):33–50

Parlapiano F, Alexeev V (2017) Exchange rate risk exposure and the value of European firms. Eur J Financ 23(2):111–129

Ibrahim Ethem Güney has a Ph.D. in Banking and Finance from the University of Zurich and Swiss Finance Institute. He is currently an Advisor at the Central Bank of the Republic of Turkey. His primary research interests include monetary policy, asset pricing, applied financial economics, mathematical finance, and big data applications.

Abdullah Kazdal is an Assistant Economist in the Research and Monetary Policy Department at the Central Bank of Turkey. He holds an M.S. in Economics from Middle East Technical University. His main research interests are applied macro-econometrics in the context of inflation dynamics and growth. The main focus of his empirical research is the exchange rate sensitivities and pass-through.

Doruk Küçüksaraç has a Ph.D. in Financial Mathematics from Middle East Technical University. He is currently the Executive Director of the Markets Department in the Central Bank of Turkey. His research areas include financial mathematics, financial economics, asset pricing, derivatives, monetary policy, and fixed-income securities.

Muhammed Hasan Yılmaz has MSc. in Finance from Bilkent University and MSc. in Economics from Middle East Technical University. He is working in the Banking and Financial Institutions Department at the Central Bank of Turkey as an Assistant Economist. His current research interests are empirical banking, financial markets, corporate finance, and applied econometrics.

Limited Dependent Variables (Logit and Probit Models) and an Application on BIST-100: Logit and Probit Models

Lokman Kantar

Introduction

Dependent (response) variables and independent (explanatory) variables can take on either quantitative values or qualitative values such as 0 and 1. Dummy variables that take on values 0 and 1 do not cause any problems in classical regression models; however, if the dependent (response) variable takes on two qualitative values, this may cause various problems. These problems include failure to meet the normal distribution requirement, varying variance of errors, and the nonlinear relationship between the dependent variable and the independent variable.

Many cases can be shown where the dependent variable has a qualitative property (whether a family can buy a house, employment status of a married couple, whether a drug is good for a disease, whether a company issues shares or not). On the other hand, the dependent variable may not be limited to two choices. For instance, if Democrat, Republican, and independent candidates are presidential candidates in the presidential election in the United States, the dependent variable will have three or more alternatives (Gujarati and Porter 2008, p. 542).

The present study focuses on the investigation of the discrete choice model which is one of the qualitative response models. This chapter will first introduce the linear probability model, one of the qualitative choice models, and then discuss in detail logit and probit models. Finally, a sample application related to logit and probit models will be presented with the help of the EViews package program.

L. Kantar (✉)
Istanbul Gelisim University, Istanbul, Turkey
e-mail: lkantar@gelisim.edu.tr

B. Adıgüzel Mercangöz (ed.), *Handbook of Research on Emerging Theories, Models, and Applications of Financial Econometrics*,
https://doi.org/10.1007/978-3-030-54108-8_7

Models with Limited Dependent Variables

Linear Probability Model

A linear probability model is a regression model where the dependent variable takes on a probability value in the range of 0–1. In other words, a linear probability model is a model where a binary dependent or independent variable or variables have a linear function (Karaoglu 2011, p. 25):

$$Y_i = \beta_1 + \beta_2 X_1 + u_i, \tag{1}$$

where Y_i denotes the dependent variable that takes on a probability value in the range of 0–1, X_1 denotes the independent variable that explains the dependent variable, β_1 denotes the probability when X variable is 0, and u_i denotes the prediction residuals (errors in the prediction model). Since the dependent variable takes on a binary value in linear probability model, the error term (u_i) takes on two values and is distributed binomially. However, because the error terms vary depending on coefficients, the assumption of homoscedasticity is not provided (Sarikovanlik et al. 2019, p. 76). In the case of changing variance, this changing variance problem is eliminated by the weighted least squares method. Since $P_i = E(Y_i|X_i) = \beta_1 + \beta_2 X_i$, $u_i = Y_i - (\beta_1 + \beta_2 X_i)$. In this case, the variance of u_i depends on the value of X and is therefore not constant. In order to eliminate the problem of changing variance, first weight (2) is determined, then both sides of the equation divided by this weight (3), and variance is made constant (Gujarati and Porter 2008, p. 545).

$$\sqrt{E(Y_i|X_i)[1 - E(Y_i|X_i)]} = \sqrt{P_i}(1 - P_i) = \sqrt{w_i} \tag{2}$$

$$\frac{Y_i}{\sqrt{w_i}} = \frac{\beta_1}{\sqrt{w_i}} + \beta_2 \frac{X_i}{\sqrt{w_i}} + \frac{u_i}{\sqrt{w_i}} \tag{3}$$

Since u_i assumes the task of weight in Eq. (3), the problem of changing variance is eliminated by the weighted least squares method. Although what is described in Eqs. (2) and (3) is correct in theory, in practice, $E(Y_i \mid X_i)$ is unknown. Therefore, firstly (1), regression equation is calculated, and then estimated $\widehat{y}_i$ is calculated to find the estimated $\widehat{w}_i$. Thus, the data is transformed as in Eq. (3), and the problem of changing variance in the linear probability model is eliminated by using the weighed least squares method.

The linear probability model is estimated according to the ordinary least squares (OLS) method. However, when it is estimated with this method, another problem arises: the errors are less than 0 or greater than 1. This causes the incorrect calculation of the probability. In the linear probability models, when X_i is the data, the conditional probability of the occurrence of Y_i is measured; therefore, $E(Y_i| X_i)$ must be between 0 and 1. Although theoretically correct, the estimators of $E(Y_i| X_i)$

does not guarantee that $\widehat{y}_i$ s meet this limitation. In the least squares method, which is used in the estimation of the linear probability model, this situation is not taken into consideration. In order to determine whether $\widehat{y}_i\, s$ are between 0 and 1, first, the linear probability model is estimated by the least squares method; then, of the estimated $\widehat{y}_i$ s, those below 0 are assumed to be 0, and those above 1 are assumed to be 1. Another method is to develop a technique that will ensure that $\widehat{y}_i\, s$ are between 0 and 1. Logit and probit models used for nonlinear regression models keep the estimates between 0 and 1 (Gujarati and Porter 2008, p. 545).

R^2, which is calculated by conventional methods, is not of much use in models with qualitative variables. Since the *Y* variable takes on values 0 or 1 according to the value of the *X*s in the models with qualitative dependent variables, all the *Y* values are located on either the *X* axis or the line at the level of 1. No linear probability model, whether bound to 0–1 values or not, conforms to the scatter plot. In most of the applications, R^2 value, calculated by conventional methods, is below 1: it is generally between 0.2 and 0.6 (Gujarati and Porter 2008). In the case where the scattering points are stacked between A and B points, R^2 value is greater than 0.8. For this reason, John Aldrich and Forrest Nelson suggest that the use of R^2 as a summarizing statistic should be avoided in models with qualitative dependent variables (Gujarati and Porter 2008, p. 546).

Logit Model

In the linear probability model, the probability of an event occurring is expressed as $P_i = \beta_1 + \beta_2 X_i + u_i$. This model is a linear model, and the occurrence of an event depends on the change in *X*. However, when calculating the probability of individuals buying a house, if *X* is accepted as the income, the increase in *X* will increase the probability of buying a house up to a point, and then the increase will come to a stop. In the case where the relationship is not linear, the linear probability model will not meet the need. In the case where the dependent variable is nominal scale, the methods that are alternative to the ordinary least squares method include discriminant and logit models. In the discriminant model of the dependent variable which consists of two or more groups, the coefficients of the model are calculated in a way that will best distinguish the groups. However, what needs to be noted here is that in order for the discriminant analysis to best distinguish the groups, the independent variables must conform to the normal distribution, and the covariances of the independent variables must be equal at each group level. In the case of nominal or ordinal scale variables among independent variables in the discriminant analysis, these assumptions cannot be met. In the logit model, on the other hand, these assumptions are not sought (Kalayci 2010, p. 273). Therefore, if we need to rearrange the equation in the linear probability model:

$$P_i = \frac{1}{1 + e^{-(\beta_1 + \beta_2 X_i)}} \tag{4}$$

$$Z_i = \beta_1 + \beta_2 X_i \tag{5}$$

$$P_i = \frac{1}{1 + e^{-(Z_i)}} = \frac{e^{Z_i}}{1 + e^{Z_i}} \tag{6}$$

Equation (6) is known as the cumulative logistic distribution function. Here, Z_i takes on values between $-\infty$ and $+\infty$, while P_i takes on a value between 0 and 1. Therefore, the relationship between Z_i and P_i can be said to be nonlinear. Therefore, in nonlinear models, P_i s cannot be estimated by the ordinary least squares method. However, the model can be linearized as follows:

In the case of buying a house, if the probability of buying a house is P_i, the probability of not buying a house is $< P_i$. In this case:

$$1 - P_i = \frac{1}{1 + e^{(Z_i)}} \tag{7}$$

$$\frac{P_i}{1 - P_i} = \frac{1 + e^{Z_i}}{1 + e^{-Z_i}} = e^{Z_i} \tag{8}$$

$P_i/1 - P_i$ is the odds ratio of buying a house. So, if this ratio is 0.90, the odds ratio of buying a house is 9 to 1 (0.90/(1 − 0.90).) When the natural logarithm of the Eq. (8) is taken:

$$L_i = \ln\left(P_i/1 - P_i\right) = \ln\left(e^{Z_i}\right) = Z_{i.}$$

$$Z_i = \beta_1 + \beta_2 X_i \tag{9}$$

So, the logarithm of the odds ratio is linear (L_i) and depends on both X and β coefficients. L is called logit, and the logit model takes its name from it (Gujarati and Porter 2008, p. 555). The logit model calculates the estimated values of the dependent variable as probability and allows the classification according to the probability rules. It is a statistical method that analyzes tabulated or raw data sets (Ozdamar 2002, p. 623). In addition to X_i values, L_i values also need to be known to be able to estimate this model. However, since it would yield meaningless results to directly place the L_i values, the maximum likelihood ML method should be used instead of the ordinary least squares (OLS) method (Sarikovanlik et al. 2019, p. 77).

The reasons why the ordinary least squares method cannot be used when the dependent variable is binary are listed as follows:

- Estimated values can be greater than 1 or below 0.
- The assumption that the estimation errors are normally distributed in the regression coefficient test is not valid since the dependent (Y) variable only takes on values 0 and 1.

- Failure to provide the constant variance assumption. In the case of maximum value of variance $((P_i) * (1 - P_i) = 0.5 * 0.5)$, that is, where 0 and 1 are equal. The variance will decrease toward extreme values ($P = 0.2$, $1 - P = 0.8$, variance $0.2 * 0.8 = 0.16$); if $P = 1$ or 0, the variance will be 0 (Orhunbilge 2010, p. 187).

Properties of the Logit Model

- Although the logits are linear with respect to *X*, their probability is not linear. This property of the logit model distinguishes it from the linear probability model.
- While the possibilities range from 0 to 1, the logit ranges from $-\infty$ to $+\infty$.
- The number of explanatory (independent) variables can be increased as many as the model requires.
- The logit model measures the change in L versus a one-unit change in *X*. For the example of buying a house, the constant term β_1 1 in the logit model is the log-odds ratio of buying a house when the income is 0.
- The linear probability model assumes that P_i is linearly related to X_i, while the logit model assumes that the log-odds ratio is linearly related to X_i.

Logit Model Estimation

To estimate the model in Eq. (9), L_i and X_i values need to be known. In the case where the data is not grouped, $P_i = 1$ if the event occurs, while $P_i = 0$ if the event does not occur. When these values are placed in the logit model:

$$\ln\left(\frac{P_i}{1-P_i}\right) = \ln\left(\frac{1}{1-1}\right) = \ln\left(\frac{1}{0}\right) \quad \text{the occurrence of the event} \tag{10}$$

$$\ln\left(\frac{P_i}{1-P_i}\right) = \ln\left(\frac{0}{1-0}\right) = \ln\left(\frac{0}{1}\right) \quad \text{non-occurrence of the event} \tag{11}$$

are meaningless. If there are ungrouped data, it is impossible to estimate the logit model by the ordinary least squares method. In this case, the maximum likelihood method needs to be used to estimate the data. However, if there are grouped data, the ordinary least squares method can be used to estimate the model (Gujarati and Porter 2008; Karaoglu 2011).

Logit Model Estimation by Ordinary Least Squares Method

When the logit model is developed with the grouped data, the relationship between the dependent variable logits and *Xs* can be estimated by the ordinary least squares method. The grouped data consists of many Y observations corresponding to each observation value in the set of external variables:

$$L_i = \ln\left(\frac{P_i}{1-P_i}\right) = \beta_1 + \beta_2 X_i + u_i$$
$$\widehat{L}_i = \ln\left(\frac{\widehat{P}_i}{1-\widehat{P}_i}\right) = \widehat{\beta}_1 + \widehat{\beta}_2 X_i \quad (12)$$

If the number of observations (N_i) is large, each X_i given is distributed independently as a binomial variable in the observation value, the logit model shows a normal distribution where the error term is u_i, mean is 0, and variance is $1/[N_i P_i(1 - P_i]$ (Gujarati and Porter 2008; Karaoglu 2011):

$$u\tilde{N}\left[0, \frac{1}{N_i P_i(1-P_i].}\right. \quad (13)$$

As in the linear probability model, the error term in the logit model faces the problem of changing variance. Therefore, instead of the ordinary least squares method, the weighted least squares method should be used. Unknown P_i is replaced by the estimated $\widehat{P}_i$, and an estimator of σ_{u^2}, i.e., $\widehat{\sigma u^2}\frac{1}{N_i P_i(1-P_i)}$ is used as the variance of the error term (u).

The following steps are applied in the estimation of the logit model Gujarati and Porter 2008; Karaoglu 2011);

1. The estimated probability of independent (explanatory) variable for each X variable is calculated as $P_i = \frac{n_i}{N_i}$ where N_i denotes the number of observations at the frequency, and n_i denotes the probability of occurrence of the event. In other words, for each X_i variable, n_i observations out of N_i observations take on the value 1 (n_i/N_i).
2. By using the calculated $\widehat{P}_i$ value for each frequency, the $\widehat{L}_i$ value for each frequency is found by Eq. (12) $\widehat{L}_i = \ln\left(\frac{\widehat{P}_i}{1-\widehat{P}_i}\right)$.
3. Since the error terms in the logit model are binomially distributed, the problem of changing variance arises. The weighted least squares method is used to solve the problem of changing variance. $L_i = \ln\left(\frac{P_i}{1-P_i}\right) = \beta_1 + \beta_2 X_i + u_i$ model is transformed as follows:

$$\sqrt{w_i L_i} = \beta_1 \sqrt{w_i} + \beta_2 \sqrt{w_i X_\mathrm{I}} + \sqrt{w_i u_\mathrm{I}} \quad (14)$$

$$L_i^* = \beta_1 \sqrt{w_i} + \beta_2 X_i^* + v_i \quad (15)$$

The scales in Eqs. (14) and (15):

w_i: $N_i \widehat{P}_i \left(1 - \widehat{P}_{ii}\right)$
L_i^*: Transformed or weighted L_i
X_i^*: Transformed or weighted X_i
v_i: Transformed or weighted error term, v_i has constant variance.

4. In this case, Eq. (14) can be estimated by the ordinary least squares method. The estimators will be effective and unbiased.
5. If the sample is large, confidence intervals and hypothesis tests will be valid. If the number of observations in logit models is not large enough ($n < 30$), obtained estimations cannot be trusted (Karaoglu 2011, p. 41).

Logit Model Estimation by Maximum Likelihood Method

In the maximum likelihood method, by using the similarity relationship between the population and the sample taken from this population, the values that maximize the probability of obtaining this sample are estimated. In this method, which can be used for grouped and ungrouped data, the distribution of error terms needs to be normal.

The likelihood function is expressed as:

$$\mathrm{LL} = (X_1, X_2, X_3, \ldots X_k; Q_1, Q_2, Q_3, \ldots, Q_k). \quad (16)$$

$Q_1, Q_2, Q_3, \ldots, Q_k$ denotes the parameters of the function to be estimated. If X has a normal distribution, the likelihood function is expressed as:

$$\mathrm{LL} = \left(X_1, X_2, X_3, \ldots, X_k; \mu, \sigma^2\right). \quad (17)$$

The maximum likelihood method is the maximization of the likelihood function. If the likelihood of occurrence of the event is P_i and the likelihood of nonoccurrence of the event is $1 - P_i$, the likelihood function is expressed as:

$$L_i = \prod_{i=1}^{N} P_i^{Y_i} (1 - P_i)^{1 - Y_i} \quad (18)$$

Here, L_i depends on the value of the parameters. Since the estimation of parameters is aimed, the likelihood function depends on β. In order to determine the $\widehat{\beta}$ coefficient to make the likelihood function maximum, the natural logarithm of both sides of the function needs to be obtained.

$$\ln L_i = \sum_{i=1}^{N} [Y_i \ln P_i + (1 - Y_i) \ln (1 - P_i)]$$

$$\ln L_i = \sum_{i=1}^{N} Y_i \ln P_i + (\ln (1 - P_i) - Y_i \ln (1 - P_i))$$

$$\ln L_i = \sum_{i=1}^{N} Y_i [\ln P_i - \ln (1 - P_i)] + \ln (1 - P_i)$$

$$\ln L_i = \sum_{i=1}^{N} Y_i \ln \left(\frac{P_i}{1 - P_i} \right) + \ln \left(\frac{1}{1 + e^{(\beta_1 + \beta_2 X_i)}} \right)$$

$$\ln L_i = \sum_{i=1}^{N} \left[Y_i (\beta_1 + \beta_2 X_i) + \ln \left(1 + e^{(\beta_1 + \beta_2 X_i)^{-1}} \right] \right.$$

$$\ln L_i = \sum_{i=1}^{N} \beta_1 Y_i + \sum_{i=1}^{N} \beta_2 X_i - \sum_{i=1}^{N} \ln \left(1 + e^{(\beta_1 + \beta_2 X_i)} \right) \tag{19}$$

The maximum likelihood method is the maximization of the likelihood function. To estimate the parameters that will maximize the log-likelihood function, the first derivative of the function is taken and equalized to zero:

$$\begin{aligned} \frac{\partial \ln L_i}{\partial \beta_1} &= \sum_{i=1}^{N} Y_i - \sum_{i=1}^{N} \ln \left(1 + e^{(\beta_1 + \beta_2 X_i)^{-1}} e^{(\beta_1 + \beta_2 X_i)} \right) = 0 \\ &= \sum_{i=1}^{N} (Y_i - P_i) = 0 \\ \frac{\partial \ln L_i}{\partial \beta_2} &= \sum_{i=1}^{N} Y_i X_i - \sum_{i=1}^{N} \left(1 + e^{(\beta_1 + \beta_2 X_i)^{-1}} e^{(\beta_1 + \beta_2 X_i)} X_i \right) \\ &= \sum_{i=1}^{N} (Y_i - P_i) X_i = 0. \end{aligned} \tag{20}$$

Estimators obtained by the maximum likelihood method are unbiased, inefficient, and not normally distributed estimators in small samples, but in large samples, they are consistent, asymptotically efficient, and asymptotic normal estimators (Guris 2005; Karaoglu 2011).

Probit Model

Another model used as an alternative to the linear probability model is the probit model. The estimation model derived from the normal cumulative distribution function is also called "probit" or "normit" model. The probit model is based on the utility theory and the rational choice theory. In this model, it is assumed that among the alternative choices, the choice which will provide the most benefit is preferred. In the nonlinear probit model, where the probability takes on a value between 0 and 1, the decision of *i*th individual is assumed to depend on an unobservable utility index (I_i). I_i index is determined by X_i *s*, which are independent variable (Karaoglu 2011, p. 41).

$$I_i = \beta_1 + \beta_2 X_i \tag{21}$$

In the Eq. (21), it is assumed that for each *i*th individual, the I_i index has a threshold value of I_i^*. This threshold value is different for each individual. For the occurrence of the Y_i event, the I_i index needs to be over the threshold value of I_i^*. In the case where the I_i index is not over the threshold value of I_i^*, ($I_i > I_i^*$) Y_i will not occur. In other words, the greater the value of the I_i index, the higher the probability of occurrence of the event (Akin 2002; Karaoglu 2011).

$$\begin{aligned} &I_i \text{If} \geq I_i^*, Y = 1 \text{ will occur} \\ &I_i \text{If} < I_i^*, Y = 1 \text{ will not occur.} \end{aligned} \tag{22}$$

Under the assumption of normality, the probability that I_i^* is less than or equal to I_i is calculated from the standardized normal CDF (cumulative distribution function) as follows:

$$P_i = P(Y = 1|X) = P\left(I_i^* \leq I_i\right) = P(Z_i \leq \beta_1 + \beta_2 X_i = F(\beta_1 + \beta_2 X_i) \tag{23}$$

$$F(I_i) = \frac{1}{\sqrt{2\pi}} \int_{-\infty}^{I_i} e^{\frac{-z^2}{2}} \mathrm{d}z$$

$$= \frac{1}{\sqrt{2\pi}} \int_{-\infty}^{\beta_1 + \beta_2 X_i} e^{-z^2/2} \mathrm{d}z$$

In Eq. (23), $P(Y = 1|X)$ refers to the probability that an event will occur when explanatory variables are X data. Z_i is standardized normal variable, that is, $Z \sim N(0, \sigma^2)$. $F(I_i)$ expresses the normal CDF (Gujarati and Porter 2008, p. 567).

As I_i $-\infty$ increases from to ∞, the probability of the occurrence of the event P_i increases by decreasing between 0 and 1 (Karaoglu 2011, p. 42).

As shown in Fig. 1, the P_i probability value is measured by the area between $-\infty$ and I_i on the standard normal distribution curve (Gujarati and Porter 2008, p. 564).

In Fig. 2, when $I_i^* \leq I_i$, the cumulative probability of the occurrence of the event is calculated from the ordinate, i.e., the vertical axis.

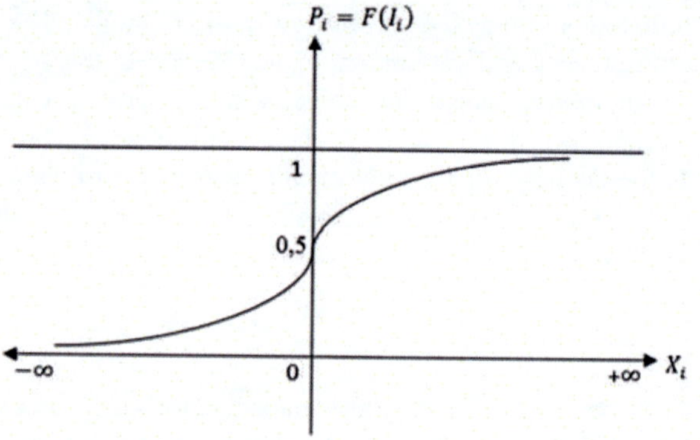

Fig. 1 Probit Model. Source: Karaoglu (2011, p. 42)

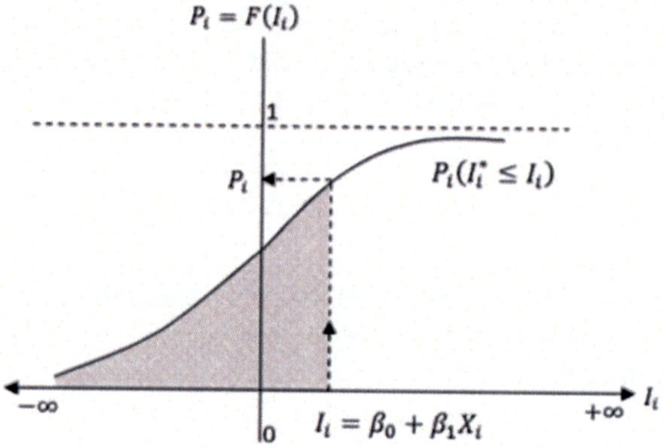

Fig. 2 Probit Model when I_i is data. Source: Gujarati and Porter (2008, p. 567)

In order to obtain information about the utility index I_i and β_1 and β_2, the inverse of $F(I_i)$ is taken. In this case:

$$I_i = F^{-1}(I_i) = F^{-1}(P_i) = \beta_1 + \beta_2 X_i \tag{24}$$

F^{-1} in Eq. (24) expresses the inverse of the normal cumulative distribution function.

In Fig. 3, when P_i is the data, I_i value is calculated from abscissa, i.e., the horizontal axis. This drawing is the inverse of figure X. Where P_i is close to 0 and 1, i.e., extreme values, equal changes in I_i causes gradually decreasing smaller changes in P_i. To be able to express this situation mathematically, the derivative of P_i according to X_i needs to be taken:

$$\begin{aligned} \frac{\mathrm{d}P_i}{\mathrm{d}X_i} &= \frac{\mathrm{d}F(\beta_1 + \beta_2 X_i)}{\mathrm{d}X_i} = \frac{\mathrm{d}F(I_i)}{\mathrm{d}X_i} = F(I_i)\frac{\mathrm{d}(I_i)}{\mathrm{d}X_i} \\ &= f(I_i)\beta_2 \end{aligned} \tag{25}$$

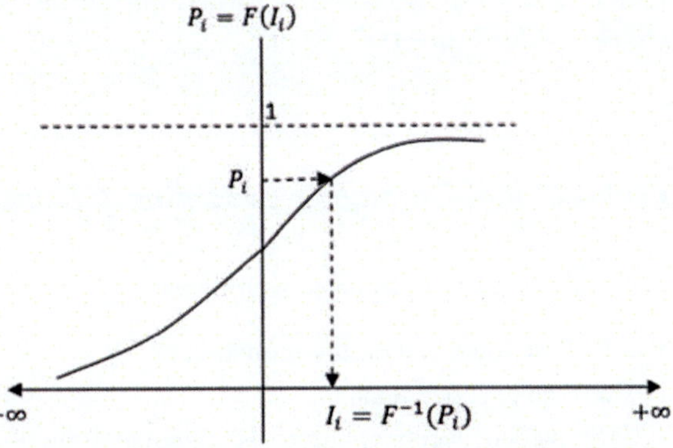

Fig. 3 Probit Model when P_i is data. Source: Gujarati and Porter (2008, p. 567)

In the probit model, the unobservable utility index I_i is called *normal equivalent deviate* (n.e.d) or normit. In Eq. (25), $f(I_i)$ refers to the standard normal distribution function of I_i. When P_i <0.5, the normal equivalent deviation or I_i will be negative, so 5 is added to I_i, and the obtained result is called probit (Gujarati and Porter 2008, p. 566).

$$\begin{aligned}\text{Probit} &= \text{n.e.d} + 5 \\ &= I_i + 5\end{aligned} \tag{26}$$

As can be seen in Eq. (26), there is a linear relationship between probit and normit. Unlike the linear probability model, in the probit model, the β_2 parameter cannot be interpreted as the effect of a one-unit change in the explanatory variable on the expected value of the dependent variable. Here, the sign of the parameters gives an idea about how the change in the independent variable will affect the dependent variable. The effect of a change in the independent (explanatory) variable on the probability of the occurrence of the event is determined by the parameter of the relevant explanatory variable and the magnitude of $f(I_i)$.

Although the probit model is more practical than the linear probability model, the number of theoretical reasons for using this model is limited. Therefore, the logit model is more practical and more widely employed than the probit model (Karaoglu 2011, p. 44).

Probit Model Estimation

In order to determine the method to be used in the estimation of the probit model, whether the data is grouped or not is checked. If ungrouped, i.e., individual data is used, the estimation is carried out by the maximum likelihood method. If grouped data is used, the estimation is carried out by the ordinary least squares method (Karaoglu 2011, p. 44).

Probit Model Estimation by Ordinary Least Squares Method

The probit model is estimated as follows:

- As in the logit model, the probability of P_i is calculated by the $\widehat{P}_i = \frac{n_i}{N_i}$ equation from the grouped data.
- $\widehat{P}_i I_i$, which accounts for it, is obtained from by the cumulative distribution function.
- Obtained $\widehat{I}$ s are used as a dependent variable in the $I_i = \beta_1 + \beta_2 X_i + u_i$ regression. If $\widehat{P}_i < 0.5$, 5 is added to $\widehat{I}$, and the obtained probits are used as dependent variables.
- As in the logit model, in the probit model, the error term u_i has a changing variance. Therefore, for the estimators to be efficient, transformation to changing variance error terms must be applied.

$$\sigma_u^2 = \frac{P_i(1 - P_i)}{N_i f_i^2} \tag{27}$$

In the transformation applied in Eq. (27), f_i is the standard normal density function found in $f^{-1}(P_i)$. Data transformation is performed by dividing the values of dependent and independent variables by the standard deviation of u_i. In the probit model, R^2 is not a good criterion for inference. Chi-square (x^2) test statistic is applied in order to have information about the functional form of the model. Test statistics:

$$X^2 = \sum \frac{N_i\left(\widehat{P}_i - P_i^*\right)^2}{P_i^*\left(1 - P_i^*\right)}, \tag{28}$$

where N_i denotes the ith observation, $\widehat{P}_i$ denotes the real possibility of the occurrence of the event, and P_i^* denotes the estimated probability. At the determined significance level and degree of freedom, X^2 table value is found. By comparing the calculated value of X^2 with the table value, it is tested whether the functional form of the model is correct (Karaoglu 2011, p. 46).

Probit Model Estimation by Maximum Likelihood Method

The likelihood function in the probit model is expressed as:

$$L = \prod_{i=1}^{N} P_i^{Y_i}(1 - P_i)^{1-Y_i}$$

$$L = \prod_{i=1}^{N} F(\beta_1 + \beta_2 X_i)^{Y_i}[1 - F(\beta_1 + \beta_2 X_i)]^{1-Y_i} \tag{29}$$

$$\ln L = \sum_{i=1}^{N} Y_i \ln F(\beta_1 + \beta_2 X_i) + \sum_{i=1}^{N} (1 - Y_i) \ln [1 - F(\beta_1 + \beta_2 X_i)].$$

Taking partial derivatives, as in the logit model, β estimators can be found to maximize L.

Comparison of Linear Probability Model, Logit Model, and Probit Model

The simplest of binary choice models is the linear probability model. Despite its ease of use, a number of problems arise in the linear probability model due to the fact that the independent variable is binary. These problems include the binominal distribution, and the changing variance of error terms, R^2 value much less than 1, the estimated probability less than 0 or greater than 1, all of which make this model difficult to use. Another problem with the linear probability model is that the constancy of the marginal effect resulting from the linearity of the model cannot be applied to real life. No solution has been found for this problem yet. For these reasons, among the binary choice models, logit and probit models are preferred more than linear probability model.

The logit model is derived from logistic cumulative distribution function, while the probit model is derived from normal cumulative distribution function. These two functions are very similar to each other.

As shown in Fig. 4, logit and probit models are very similar. Therefore, both models yield similar results. The most important difference between them is that the probit model approaches the axes more quickly than the logit model. Therefore, in cases where the data is concentrated at extreme points, probit model will yield more robust results.

In a standard normal cumulative distribution, the mean is 0, and the variance is 1, whereas in a logistic cumulative distribution, the mean is 0, and the variance is $\pi^2/3$. Therefore, the estimators obtained from the two models cannot be directly compared with each other. To compare the estimations obtained from the linear

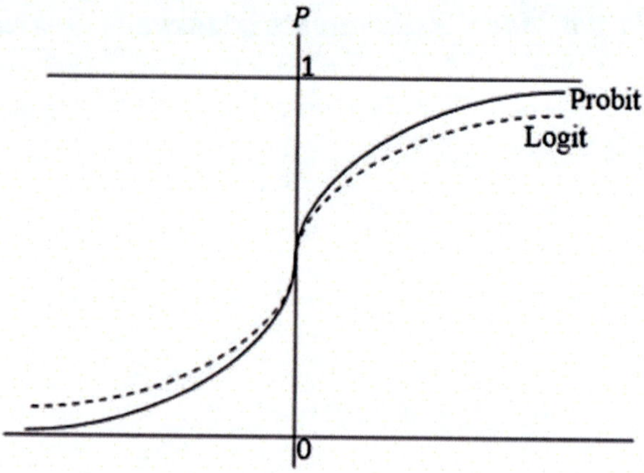

Fig. 4 Logit/probit models. Source: Karaoglu (2011, p. 42)

Table 1 The relationship between the coefficient estimators of binary choice models

Between constant terms	Between slope coefficients
$\widehat{\beta}_{\text{Probit}} \cong 0.625\,\widehat{\beta}_{\text{Logit}}$	$\widehat{\beta}_{\text{Probit}} \cong 0.625\,\widehat{\beta}_{\text{Logit}}$
$\widehat{\beta}_{\text{DOM}} \cong 0.4\widehat{\beta}_{\text{Probit}} + 0.5$	$\widehat{\beta}_{\text{DOM}} \cong 0.4\widehat{\beta}_{\text{Probit}}$
$\widehat{\beta}_{\text{DOM}} \cong 0.25\widehat{\beta}_{\text{Logit}} + 0.5$	$\widehat{\beta}_{\text{DOM}} \cong 0.25\widehat{\beta}_{\text{Logit}}$

Source: Karaoglu (2011, p. 48)

probability model, logit model, and probit model, the following transformations are employed (Table 1).

Since the normal cumulative distribution function employed for the estimation of the probit model contains integrals, it is difficult and complicated to calculate. Therefore, logit models are more widely used.

Testing the Significance of Parameters of the Estimated Model

As with the classical regression models, the statistical significance of the parameters of the estimated model needs to be tested in qualitative choice models, as well. Significance of the parameters can be tested individually or jointly.

Testing the Individual Significance of Parameters

In order to test the individual significance of the parameters, the *t*-test statistics are used. The *t*-test is performed individually for each parameter.

If the basic hypothesis for the *t*-test is:

$$H_0 : \beta_i = 0$$
$$H_1 : \beta_i \neq 0,$$

then the t-test statistics are calculated as:

$$t = \frac{\widehat{\beta_i}}{\sigma_{\widehat{\beta_i}}} \tag{30}$$

If the calculated t statistics are greater than the t table value at the significance level, the hypothesis H_0 is rejected. The rejection of the H_0 hypothesis indicates that the parameters of interest are not equal to zero, i.e., they are statistically significant.

Testing the Joint Significance of Parameters

The F test cannot be used like it is used in the classical regression model to test the joint significance of the parameters of the model estimated by the maximum likelihood method in qualitative choice models. In logit and probit models, Wald, Lagrange multiplier, and maximum likelihood ratio tests are used instead of the F test. The Lagrange multiplier only considers the estimation results of the constrained model, while the Wald test considers the estimation results of the unconstrained model. On the other hand, the likelihood ratio test is based on the results of both constrained and unconstrained models.

The hypotheses used to test the joint significance of the parameters are as follows:

$$H_0 : \beta_0 = \beta_1 = \beta_2 = \ldots \beta_k = 0$$
$$H_1 = \text{at least one of the coefficients is nonzero}$$

Wald Test

The Wald statistics is used to test the null hypothesis that each parameter of logit or probit models is zero.

Wald test statistics is expressed as:

$$W = \left(\frac{\widehat{\beta_2}}{Sh\left(\widehat{\beta}\right)}^2 \right) \tag{31}$$

Since the number of constraints will be 1, the distribution of the test statistics will fit the X^2 distribution with 1 degree of freedom. To determine whether the parameters are statistically significant, the calculated Wald test statistics are compared with the X^2 table value. If the calculated Wald test statistics are greater than X^2 table value, the hypothesis H_0 is rejected, and it is concluded that the parameters are statistically significant.

Maximum Likelihood Ratio Test

The maximum likelihood-ratio test is only used to test the significance of the parameters of models where ungrouped data is estimated by the maximum likelihood method. The significance of the parameters other than the constant term in the estimated model is similar to the F test applied in the classical regression model, where all coefficients are tested together. However, in this test, X^2 distribution is used instead of F distribution.

Maximum likelihood ratio test statistics are expressed as:

$$\mathrm{LR} = -2(\ln L_R - \ln L_{\mathrm{UR}}) \tag{32}$$

In Eq. (32), $\ln L_R$ represents the logarithm of the maximum likelihood value of the constrained model without an independent variable, and $\ln L_{\mathrm{UR}}$ represents the logarithm of the maximum likelihood value of the unconstrained model, i.e., the estimated model.

If the calculated test statistics are greater than the X^2 table value at the specified level of significance, the H_0 hypothesis, which assumes that the constraints are valid, is rejected. This result means that the constraints are invalid. In this case, at least one parameter is statistically significant. If the calculated test statistics are less than X^2 table value, the H_0 hypothesis cannot be rejected. In this case, all constraints are valid.

Lagrange Multiplier Test

The Lagrange multiplier test is used to determine whether the coefficients of all explanatory variables are different from zero.

Lagrange multiplier test statistics are expressed as:

$$\mathrm{LM} = nRU^2 \tag{33}$$

In Eq. (33), RU^2 represents the coefficient of determination of the constrained model. The test statistics fit the distribution of X^2 with the $(k - 1)$ degree of freedom. If the calculated test statistics are greater than the X^2 table value, it is concluded that the parameters are statistically significant.

Table 2 Pseudo-R^2 goodness of fit measures

Measures	Formulas
[a]Estrella R^2	$R^2_{\text{EST}} = 1 - \left[\frac{L_1}{L_0}\right]^{\frac{-2L_0}{N}}$
Maddala R^2	$R^2_{\text{MAD}} = 1 - \left[\frac{L_0}{L_1}\right]^{\frac{2}{n}}$
Cox-Snell R^2 (maximum likelihood R^2)	$R^2_{\text{CS}} = 1 - \exp\left(-\frac{LRT}{N}\right)$
[b]Nagelkerke R^2	$R^2_N = \frac{R^2_{cs}}{1-L_0^{2/N}}$
Cragg-Uhler R^2	$R^2_{\text{CU}} = \frac{1-\left[\frac{L_0}{L_1}\right]^{\left(\frac{2}{n}\right)}}{1-L_0{}^{\left(\frac{2}{n}\right)}}$
[c]Aldrich-Nelson R^2	$R^2_{\text{AN}} = \frac{LRT}{LRT+n}$
Vell-Zimmerman R^2	$R^2_{\text{VZ}} = \frac{2(L_1-L_0)}{2[L_1-L_0]+n} \, R^2_{\text{VZ}} = \frac{\frac{n}{2L_0}}{\frac{n}{2L_0}-R^2_{\text{MF}}} R^2_{\text{MF}}$
Mc Fadden R^2	$R^2_{\text{MF}} = 1 - \frac{L_1}{L_0}$
[d]Efron's R^2	$R^2_E = 1 - \frac{\sum_{i=1}^{n}(Y_i-H_i)^2}{\sum_{i=1}^{n}\left(Y_i-\overline{Y}\right)^2}$
[e]Mc Kelvey-Zavoina R^2	$R^2_{\text{MKZ}} = \frac{\text{Var}\left(\widetilde{Y^*}\right)}{\text{Var}\left(\widetilde{Y^*}\right)+\text{Var}(\varepsilon)}$

Source: Caglayan and Astar (2010, p. 4)
[a]L_0 represents the similarity ratio of only the constant parameter, while L_1 represents the similarity ratio of the entire model
[b]This measure represents an adjusted version of Cox-Snell R^2 value
[c]Represents LRT= $2[L_1 - L_0] = LR(m)$ value
[d]H_i, $Y = 1$ is the estimated probability value for
[e]Is 3.29 for the logit model and 1 for the probit model

The Goodness of Fit Measures for Logit and Probit Models

R^2, which is a coefficient of determination, gives information about the goodness of fit of the model. This coefficient expresses how much the explanatory variables explain the dependent (response) variable in linear models. However, in nonlinear models, the R^2 coefficient is a weak measure. This is because, in nonlinear models, R^2 can be other than (0,1) values. The reason for this is that in nonlinear models, the mean and variance of the dependent variable are P and $(1 - P)$, respectively (Tatoglu 2005, p. 77). Therefore, the logit and probit models, which are nonlinear models, require the goodness of fit measures that show the explanatory power of the model and can be interpreted as R^2. Therefore, it is recommended to use various R^2 measures called Pseudo-R^2 for binary choice models (Caglayan and Astar 2010, p. 3). Different Pseudo-R^2 measures proposed for the goodness of fit measures are shown in Table 2.

Most of the different Pseudo R^2 measures in Table 2 were developed to measure the change in similarity rates, not the variance, as shown. Therefore, the values obtained from formulas should not be interpreted as R^2 values obtained in classical regression models.

Literature Review (Background)

Hagle and Mitchell (1992) compared the R^2 value obtained by the ordinary least squares method with the Pseudo-R^2 values commonly used in logit and probit models. They examined the Pseudo-R^2 values proposed by McKelvey and Zavoina (1975), Achen (1979), Aldrich and Nelson (1984), and Dhrymes (1986) and OLS R^2 values using the simulation technique. They found that R^2 values best suited to theoretical expectations were those proposed by McKelvey and Zavoina and Aldrich and Nelson.

Nagler (1994) proposed the scobit (skewed-logit) model as an alternative to logit and probit models. In the study, which examined the voting possibilities of voters with low and high levels of education, it was concluded that the scobit method was more effective than other methods in testing the interaction effect in heterogeneous groups.

Kamstra et al. (2001) discussed the bond ratings of the transport and industry firms listed by Moody's, an international rating agency, between 1989 and 1992, using the sequential logit regression method proposed by Kamstra and Kennedy (1998). The findings of the study showed that the Kamstra and Kennedy (1998) model yielded more quantitative and significant estimates than the logit and probit models.

Chunrong and Norton (2003) emphasized that the magnitude of the interaction effect in nonlinear models (logit-probit) is not equal to the marginal effect of the interaction term. They, therefore, concluded that one must be cautious when interpreting the statistical significance, magnitude, and sign of the coefficient of interaction in nonlinear models.

Edward et al. (2004) analyzed the marginal effect of a change in two variables in the linear model and nonlinear models through the example of health-care expenditures in 2000. They concluded that the calculation and interpretation of interaction effects in nonlinear models are very complicated.

Hahn and Soyer (2005) reported that logit and probit models yield similar results with regard to the selection of link function in binary response models. They also stated that this situation is valid for univariate models, and if there is more than one variable, the same interpretation cannot be made. They noted that in the presence of extreme independent variables in multivariate link function models, the logit link fits better, while if a moderate data set is selected in random effect models, the model fit can be improved with the employment of the probit link.

Hoetker (2007) examined the strategic management journals for the studies conducted with logit and probit models and the success of the goodness of fit of the studies. They found out that logit and probit methods were not included in the articles published in strategic management journals in the 1980s, while, in the issues released in the 1990s and 2000s, the number of publications using these methods was more than 10% of the total publications. They also concluded that in nonlinear models, the R^2 value calculated according to the OLS method should not be overtrusted. They emphasized that Pseudo-R^2 value is more reliable than this value. Finally, they argued that although nonlinear methods are complex, statistical package programs can handle this complexity.

Ege and Bayrakdaroglu (2009), in the study, which tested the financial performance of the companies included in the Bist30 Index, covering 2005, was accepted as the dependent variable financial performance criterion for companies with positive 2005 stock returns. The relationship between this dependent variable and financial ratios (cash ratio, price/earnings ratio, etc.) was examined by logistic regression method. According to the results obtained from the research, price-earnings ratio (F/C), cash ratio (CR), and turnover rate of total assets (TRTA) are considered as important independent variables in explaining the stock returns considering the relevant period market to book value ratio was not seen as an important independent variable according to the estimated logit model.

Caglayan and Astar (2010) aimed to calculate different goodness of fit measures and to compare the results of both logit and probit models. The results of their study showed that different measures of goodness of fit yielded different results. The authors emphasized that it is very important to calculate and use the same measure of goodness of fit to compare the models.

Chen and Tsurumi (2011) conducted Monte Carlo experiments to compare the Bayesian and sample theory model selection criteria in choosing the univariate probit and logit models. They used five criteria: the deviance information criterion (DIC), predictive deviance information criterion (PDIC), Akaike information criterion (AIC), weighted, and unweighted sums of squared errors. The first two criteria are Bayesian, while the others are sample theory criteria. The authors examined the relationship between returns on S&P500 and crude oil prices according to the logit and probit models. Their results showed that if data are balanced, none of the model selection criteria can distinguish the probit and logit models. They also found that if data are unbalanced, the deviance information criterion and Akaike information criterion choose the correct models better than the other criteria. Finally, they concluded that if unbalanced binary data are generated by a leptokurtic distribution, the logit model is preferred over the probit model.

Cebeci (2012) examined the capacity of macroeconomic variables in Turkey in the 1998–2009 period to explain crises with the probit model. They also calculated the marginal effects of variables and examined to what extent these variables affected the crises. Their findings revealed that interest rate and import variables were statistically insignificant, while inflation, exchange rate, unemployment rate, gross national product, and manufacturing production index variables were significant.

Kliestik et al. (2015) focused on the use of logit and probit methods for the prediction of bankruptcy. Their findings showed that logit and probit models yield similar results, but the probit model has a steeper slope. The authors also noted that logarithmic distribution has variance equal to $\pi^2/3$, while the normal distribution function used in the probit model has variance equal to 1; therefore, it is necessary to perform a logit transformation in order to make a comparison between the estimates.

Celik (2017) aimed to determine the factors affecting the development levels of 38 countries by the logit model using the 2015 data. The authors used the variables of adult literacy rates, purchasing power parity, adjusted gross national product per capita, the share of the population aged 0–4 in the total population, and participation rate of women in the parliament to determine the factors affecting the development levels of countries. As a result, the share of the population aged 0–4 of the total population, gross national product per capita, and adult literacy rates were found to be statistically significant, while the participation rate of women in the parliament was found to be insignificant.

Akkaya and Kantar (2018) used the logit and probit method to identify leading indicators for the financial crisis using monthly data between 2005 and 2017. According to the findings of their study, gross reserves, domestic debt stock, and monthly Turkish Lira deposit interest rates are the leading indicators for financial crises.

Atay (2018), in his study covering the period of January 2006–December 2017, tested the macroeconomic variables that affect the stock returns in the ISE100 Index by Logistic regression method. According to the findings of the study, a macroeconomic variable which has an effect on the returns of stocks of any bank has the same effect (positive/negative) on the returns of other bank stocks.

Application: Method, Data, and Findings

The most important indicator of capital markets and economic developments in Turkey is ISE100 (Istanbul Stock Exchange) index. Therefore, the macroeconomic factors affecting the ISE100 index and how these factors affect it will be discussed with logit and probit models.

In this study, monthly data for February 2009–April 2019 obtained from the Central Bank of Turkey (CBRT), Electronic Data Distribution System (EDDS), were used. As a dependent variable, ISE100 index was tried to be estimated with the help of macroeconomic variables, and EViews 9 package program was used in estimation models. Variables used in the study and their abbreviations are as follows:

The macroeconomic variables in Table 3 were chosen among those found to be statistically significant in previous studies in the literature. Variables must not contain a unit root, i.e., must be stationary, before they are included in the model. Otherwise, the problem of pseudo-regression arises among variables. In such a case, there seems to be a relationship between the variables which, in fact, does not exist, and the problem of misinterpretation of the data arises. For this reason, stationarity tests should be performed on the data, and nonstationary data should be made stationary. The stationarity of the variables was tested according to the Augmented Dickey-Fuller Test results and Schwarz information criterion. According to the test results, all variables except the IPI variable are stationary at level values and do not

Table 3 Variables and their abbreviations[a]

Variable	Abbreviation
Istanbul stock exchange 100 index (dependent variable)	ISE100
Gold price per ounce	GOLD
Deposit interest	INTEREST
Euro-Dollar currency basket	EXC. R
Industrial production index	IPI

[a] The % change in the independent variables will be included in the model
Data source: Developed by the author

Table 4 Estimation results by the logit method

Variable	Coefficient	Std. Error	Prob.
Gold	3.732221	5.852475	0.5237
Interest	0.299282	4.797523	0.9503
Exc. rate	−0.228593	0.096183	0.0175
Industrial product index	0.883064	1.092732	0.4190
C	0.553774	0.216127	0.0104
Mc Fadden R-squared	0.077233	Mean dependent yes	0.581967
Akaike Info Criterion	1.336283	Sum Squared Resid	26.41248
Schwarz Criterion	1.451202	Log likelihood	−76.51325
Prob (LR statistic)	0.012254		
Obs with Dep = 0	51	Total Obs	122
Obs with Dep = 1	71		

Dependent Variable: ISE100 Index
Method: ML-Binary Logit
Data source: Developed by the author

contain a unit root. Also, the first-order difference of the IPI variable was taken, and the IPI variable was made stationary.

In nonlinear models where the dependent variable is a binary qualitative variable, the dependent variable must be defined correctly. In this study, the value of 1 was assigned if the return on the ISE100 index was positive, and the value of 0 if it was negative. Thus, the dependent variable ISE100 index was transformed into a qualitative variable. The logit model that transforms the dependent variable into a binary one is:

$$L_i(0, 1) = \beta_1 + \beta_2 \text{gold} + \beta_3 \text{interest} + \beta_4 \text{Exc.rate} + \beta_5 \text{ipi} + u_i. \tag{34}$$

L_I value indicates the probability that the return on the ISE100 index is positive or negative (0–1).

In Eq. (34), macroeconomic variables explaining the return on the ISE100 index are formed according to the nonlinear model. The results of the model estimated by the logit method are shown in Table 4.

It can be inferred from the results in Table 4 that, when the factors that affect the positive return on the ISE100 index are examined, it is seen that the variables of Gold, Interest, and Industrial Production Index are statistically insignificant. A negative and statistically significant relationship was found between the change in the return on the currency basket and the return on the ISE100 index. The results obtained by the logit method indicate the direction of the relationship, and the relationship between them cannot be interpreted as in the classical regression method. For the correct interpretation of the relationship between variables, the marginal effects of the variables must be calculated. Since marginal effects cannot be calculated in the EViews package program, they need to be mathematically calculated and interpreted.

$$L_i(0,1) = 0.55 + 3.73\text{gold} + 0.30\text{interest} - 0.2285\text{exc.rate} + 0.88ipi$$

L_i value indicates the probability that the return on the ISE100 index is positive or negative (0–1).

For the interpretation of the coefficients in the logit model, means of independent variables should be included in the evaluation.

The mean values of the independent variables were calculated as:

$$\text{Gold} : 0.0031 \quad \text{Exc.R.} : 0.0052 \quad \text{Exc.rate} : 0.9619 \quad \text{IPI} : 0.000188.$$

Accordingly, marginal effects are:

$$Z = 0.55 + (3.73 * 0.0031) + (0.30 * 0.0052) - (0.2285 * 0.9619) + (0.88 * 0.000188).$$

$$Z = 0.3435 \quad e^{-z} = e^{-(0.3435)} = 0.7093$$

$$f(Z) = \frac{dp}{dZ} = \frac{e^{-z}}{(1 + e^{-z})^2} = 0.2428$$

In this case, the marginal effects obtained considering the means are:

$f(Z)\beta_{GOLD} = 0.2428 * 3.73 = 0.9056$: When gold prices increase, the return on the ISE100 index increases with a probability of 90.91%.

$u(Z)\beta_{INTEREST} = 0.2428 * 0.30 = 0.0728$: When interest rates increase, the return on the ISE100 index increases with a probability of 7.28%.

$(Z)\beta_{EXC.\ RATE} = 0.2428 * (-0.2285) = -0.00555$: When the return on the currency basket increases, the return on the ISE100 index decreases with a probability of 0.555%.

$(Z)\beta_{IPI} = 0.2428 * 0.88 = 0.2137$: When the return on the industrial production index increases, the return on the ISE100 index increases with a probability of 21.37%.

Table 5 Logit model goodness of fit test results

H-L Statistic	6.5410	Prob.Chi-Sq(8)	0.5869
Andrews Statistic	9.8429	Prob.Chi-Sq(8)	0.4544

Data source: Developed by the author

Table 6 Logit model estimation table

	Dep = 0	Dep = 1	Total
Total	51	71	122
Correct	32	50	82
%correct	62.75	70.42	67.21
%incorrect	37.25	29.48	32.79

Data source: Developed by the author

According to the marginal effect results, the probabilities of the logit model were between 0 and 1: the most important condition of the nonlinear models was fulfilled.

To determine the goodness of fit of the model, the Hosmer-Lemeshow test needs to be performed in the EViews package program. The results of the goodness of fit tests are shown in Table 5.

According to the results shown in Table 5, Prob.Chi-Sq (8) value is greater than 0.01, 0.05, and 0.10, but Prob.Chi-Sq value is less than 0.01, 0.05, and 0.10; therefore, a clear decision cannot be made as to whether the model being created is appropriate.

To find out whether the logit model correctly estimates values 0 and 1, an estimation table must be created. The results of the estimation table obtained from the EViews package program are shown in Table 6.

According to the model results presented in Table 5, 32 of 51 observations assigned 0, and 50 of 71 observations assigned 1 were estimated correctly. In total, 82 of 122 observations were estimated correctly.

Probit Model

The probit model explaining the returns on the ISE100 with the help of macroeconomic variables is expressed as follows:

$$I_i = \beta_1 + \beta_2 \text{gold} + \beta_3 \text{interest} + \beta_4 \text{exc.rate} + \beta_5 \text{ipi} + u_i. \tag{35}$$

The results of the model estimated by the probit method are shown in Table 7.

According to the model results in Table 7, the variables of gold, interest, and IPI variables were not statistically significant. There is an inverse significant relationship between the exchange rate variable and returns on the ISE100 index. The probit model yielded similar results as the logit model. The constant coefficient of the model and the whole model were found to be statistically significant. According to the estimation results, the model is expressed as follows;

Table 7 Probit model results

Variable	Coefficient	Std.Error	Prob.
Gold	2.371312	3.520407	0.5006
Interest	0.133292	2.618664	0.9594
Exc. rate	−0.129718	0.052051	0.0127
Industrial product index	0.572739	0.673397	0.3950
C	0.330665	0.129415	0.0106
Mc Fadden R-squared	0.074777	Mean dependent yes	0.581967
Akaike info criterion	1.339621	Sum squared resid	26.52365
Schwarz criterion	1.454540	Log likelihood	−76.71689
Prob (LR statistic)	0.014608		
Obs with Dep = 0	51	Total Obs	122
Obs with Dep = 1	71		

Dependent Variable: ISE100 Index
Method: ML-Binary Probit
Data source: Developed by the author

$$I_i(0,1) = 0.33 + 2.37\text{gold} + 0.13\text{interest} - 0.13\ \text{exc.rate} + 0.57\text{ipi}.$$

For the interpretation of the variables of the model as in the classical regression model, marginal effects need to be calculated.

The mean values of the independent variables were calculated as

$$\text{Gold} : 0.0031 \quad \text{Interest.} : 0.0052 \quad \text{Exc.rate} : 0.9619 \quad \text{IPI} : 0.000188$$

Accordingly, marginal effects are:

$$Z = 0.33 + (2.37 * 0.0031) + (0.13 * 0.0052) - (0.13 * 0.9619) \\ + (0.57 * 0.000188)$$

$$Z = 0.2131$$

$$f(Z) = \frac{1}{\sqrt{2\pi}} e^{-\left(\frac{z^2}{2}\right)} = 0.3899$$

In this case, the marginal effects obtained considering the means are:

$f(Z)\beta_{\text{GOLD}} = 0.3899 * 2.37 = 0.9243$: When gold prices increase, the return on the ISE100 index increases with a probability of 92.43%.

$u(Z)\beta_{\text{INTEREST}} = 0.3899 * 0.13 = 0.0507$: When interest rates increase, the return on the ISE100 index increases with a probability of 5.07%.

$(Z)\beta_{\text{EXC. RATE}} = 0.3899 * (-0.13) = -0.0507$: When the return on the currency basket increases, the return on the ISE100 index decreases with a probability of 5.07%.

Table 8 Logit model goodness of fit test results

H-L Statistic	6.1311	Prob.Chi-Sq(8)	0.6325
Andrews Statistic	17.9214	Prob. Chi-Sq(10)	0.0563

Data source: Developed by the author

Table 9 Probit model estimation table

	Dep = 0	Dep = 1	Total
Total	51	71	122
Correct	32	49	81
%correct	62.75	69.01	66.39
%incorrect	37.25	30.99	33.61

Data source: Developed by the author

$(Z)\beta_{\text{IPI}} = 0.3899 * 0.57 = 0.2222$: When the return on the industrial production index increases, the return on the ISE100 index increases with a probability of 22.22%.

According to the marginal effect results, the results of the probit model were similar to those of the logit model. Probit model yielded a higher probability for the exchange rate than the logit model did. Therefore, after determining the results of the goodness of fit test of the probit model and estimation results, it is necessary to compare logit and probit models to select the most suitable model.

The results of the goodness of fit test of the probit model are shown in Table 8.

According to the results shown in Table 8, Prob.Chi-Sq(8) value is greater than 0.01, 0.05, and 0.10, and Prob. Chi-Sq(10) value is less than 0.10; therefore it can be concluded that the model is appropriate.

Table 9 presents the estimation table indicating whether the 0 and 1 values assigned to the dependent qualitative variable in the probit model are correctly estimated.

According to the model results presented in Table 9, 32 of 51 observations assigned 0, and 49 of 71 observations assigned 1 were correctly estimated. In total, 81 out of 122 observations were correctly estimated.

Comparison of Logit and Probit Models

Both logit and probit models are nonlinear regression models, and both models use different function tables. In order to understand which model is more efficient and more suitable for the application, it is necessary to compare the models according to the results of the goodness of fit measures such as pseudo R^2. Table 10 presents the comparison of logit and probit models.

As can be inferred from Table 10, logit and probit models yielded similar results; however, according to the Hosmer-Lemeshow goodness of fit test and goodness-of-fit test statistic of Andrews, the probit model better describes whether returns on the ISE100 index are positive or negative.

Table 10 Summary of logit and probit models

Models	β = EQUATION $\{P_i = 1/1 + e^{-(\beta)}\}$	McFadden R-squared	Prob(LR statistic)	Log likelihood	Hosmer-Lemeshow
Logit model	0.55 + 3.73gold + 0.30interest − 0.2285exc.r. + 0.88IPI	0.0772	0.0123	−76.5133	0.5869
Probit model	0.33 + 2.37gold + 0.13interest − 0.13exc.r. + 0.57IPI	0.0748	0.0146	−76.7169	0.6325

Data source: Developed by the author

Conclusion

Binary independent variables do not cause any problems in classical regression models; however, if the dependent variable takes on values 0 and 1 (dummy variable), this may cause various problems in the regression model. If the dependent variable takes on a value between 0 and 1, the errors of the model will also take on a value between 0 and 1, and the errors will not show normal distribution. If the dependent variable takes on two values (0 and 1), instead of using linear regression models, it would be more appropriate to use models in which the relationship between the dependent variable and the independent variables is nonlinear. The most important nonlinear models are logit and probit models. In logit and probit models, the relationship between dependent variables and independent variables is examined by logistic distribution function and normal cumulative distribution function, respectively.

If the data is not grouped in the logit model, the data cannot be estimated by the ordinary least squares method. The maximum likelihood method should be used instead. If the data is grouped, the model can be estimated by the ordinary least squares method. In the maximum likelihood method, by using the similarity relationship between the population and the sample taken from this population, the values that maximize the probability of obtaining this sample are estimated.

The probit model is based on the utility theory and the rational choice theory. In this model, it is assumed that among the alternative choices, the choice which will provide the most benefit is preferred. Ungrouped data in the probit model is estimated by the maximum likelihood method. In the probit model, R^2 is not a good criterion for inference. Chi-square test statistic is applied in order to have information about the functional form of the model.

Although the easiest to use one of the binary choice models is the linear probability model, the binominal distribution, and the changing variance of error terms, R^2 value much less than 1, the estimated probability less than 0 or greater than 1 make this model difficult to use. Another problem with the linear probability model is that the constancy of the marginal effect resulting from the linearity of the model cannot be applied to real life. For these reasons, among the binary choice models, logit and probit models are preferred more than the linear probability model.

The logit model is derived from logistic cumulative distribution function, whereas the probit model is derived from normal cumulative distribution function. Therefore, the two models yield similar results. The most important difference between them is that the probit model approaches the axes more quickly than the logit model. Where the data is concentrated at extreme points, the probit model will yield more robust results.

It is recommended to use the pseudo-R^2 measure for the goodness of fit of logit and probit models. The Pseudo-R^2 measure does not measure the variances of the model but changes in similarity rates; therefore, it is not appropriate to interpret it as the R^2 value in classical regression models.

In this chapter, logit and probit models, which are nonlinear models, have been studied, and whether returns on the ISE100 index can be explained by macroeconomic variables have been examined using logit and probit methods. According to the findings of the study, the increase and the decrease in the returns on the ISE100 index were accepted as 1 and 0, respectively. Also, it was found that the returns on the ISE100 index had a statistically significant relationship only with the return on the currency basket, one of the macroeconomic variables included in the study. The marginal effects of the variables were calculated for the correct interpretation of the results. According to the calculated marginal effects, the increase in the return on the currency basket decreases the probability of the increase in the return on the ISE100 index. Both the logit and probit model produced similar results. According to the goodness of fit test results, the model created by the probit method is more appropriate.

Since the relationships between variables are not always linear in real life, it is more appropriate to prefer nonlinear models. One needs to be careful when choosing nonlinear models. Interpretation of the results as in the classical regression leads to an incorrect evaluation of the possibilities. Therefore, marginal effects need to be calculated before interpreting the obtained results. Also, the Hosmer-Lemeshow test and the Pseudo-R^2 measure should be used when choosing the most appropriate nonlinear model.

References

Achen CH (1979) Alternate measures of association in the Probit Model. Unpublished manuscript. University of California, Berkeley

Akin F (2002) Kalitatif Tercih Modelleri Analizi. Bursa. Ekin Kitabevi

Akkaya M, Kantar L (2018) Finansal Krizlerin Tahmininde Oncu Gostergelerin Logit-Probit model İle Analizi: Turkiye Uygulamasi [An analysis of leading indicators with Logit-Probit model to estimate financial crisis: the case of Turkey]. Uluslararasi Yonetim İktisat ve İsletme Dergisi 14 (3):575–590. https://doi.org/10.17130/ijmeb.2018343111

Aldrich J, Nelson F (1984) Linear probability, Logit and Probit Models. Sage, Beverly Hills

Atay A (2018) Banka Hisse Senetleri Getirilerinin Makroekonomik Degiskenlerle İliskisinin Lojistik Regresyon Yontemiyle İncelenmesi, Yuksek Lisans Tezi. Baskent Universitesi Sosyal Bilimler Enstitusu, Ankara

Caglayan E, Astar M (2010) Logit ve Probit Modellerinde Uyum İyiligi Olculeri [Goodness of fit measures in Logit and Probit]. Trakya Universitesi Sosyal Bilimler Dergisi 12(2):1–12

Cebeci İ (2012 Krizleri İncelemede Kullanilan Nitel Tercih Modelleri: Turkiye İcin Bir Probit Model Uygulamasi: (1998-2009). http://hdl.handle.net/123456789/129

Celik K (2017) Secilmis Turk ve Avrupa Ulkelerinin Kalkinmislik Duzeylerini Etkileyen Faktorlerin İkili Logit Modeli ile İncelenmesi. Kirklareli Universitesi Sosyal Bilimler Dergisi 1:133–144

Chen G, Tsurumi H (2011) Probit and Logit model selection. Commun Stat Theory Methods 40:159–175

Chunrong A, Norton EC (2003) Interaction terms in Logit and Probit models. Econ Lett 80:123–129

Dhrymes PJ (1986) Limited dependent variables. In: Griliches Z, Intriligator MD (eds) Handbook of econometrics, vol 3. North-Holland, Amsterdam

Edward CN, Wang H, Chunrong A (2004) Computing interaction effects and standard errors in Logit and Probit models. Stata J 4(2):154–167
Ege İ, Bayrakdaroglu A (2009) İmkb Sirketlerinin Hisse Senedi Getiri Basarılarinin Lojistik Regresyon Teknigi ile Analizi. ZKU Sosyal Bilimler Dergisi 5(10):139–158
Gujarati ND, Porter CD (2008) Basic econometrics, 5th edn. McGraw-Hill Irwin, New York
Guris B (2005) Ulkelerin Kalkinmislik Duzeyini Etkileyen Faktorlerin Cok Secenekli Tercih Modelleri ile Analizi, Yuksek Lisans Tezi. Marmara Universitesi Sosyal Bilimler Enstitusu, İstanbul
Hagle TM, Mitchell GE (1992) Goodness-of-fit Meusures for Probit and Logit. Am J Polit Sci 36:762–784
Hah DE, Soyer R (2005) Probit and Logit models: differences in the multivariate realm. https://pdfs.semanticscholar.org/c45e/142a45851c8b4da074ac38fd56bb5ff78749.pdf
Hoetker G (2007) The use of Logit and Probit models in strategic management research: critical issues. Strateg Manag J 28:331–343
Kalayci S (2010) SPSS Uygulamalı Cok Degiskenli İstatistik Teknikleri., 5th edn. Asil Yayın Dagıtım, Ankara
Kamstra M, Kennedy P, Suan KT (2001) Combining bond rating forecasts using Logit. Financ Rev 37:75–96
Kamstra M, Kennedy P (1998) Combining qualitative forecasts using logit. Int J Forecast 14:83–93
Karaoglu N (2011) Karacabey ve Mustafa Kemal Pasa İlcelerindeki Goc Hareketlerinin İki Durumlu Tercih Modelleriyle Analizi (Yuksek Lisans Tezi). Uludag Universitesi Sosyal Bilimler Enstitusu, Bursa
Kliestik T, Kocisova K, Misankova M (2015) Logit and Probit model used for prediction of financial health of company. Proc Econ Financ 23:850–855
McKelvey R, Zavoina W (1975) A statistical model for the analysis of ordinal level dependent variables. J Math Sociol 4:103–120
Nagler J (1994) Scobit: an alternative estimator to Logit and Probit. Am J Polit Sci 38(1):230–255
Orhunbilge N (2010) Cok Degiskenli İstatistik Yontemler. İstanbul
Ozdamar K (2002) Paket Programlar ile İstatistiksel Veri Analizi 1. Kaan Kitabevi, Eskisehir
Sarikovanlik V, Koy A, Akkaya M, Yildirim HH, Kantar L (2019) Finans Biliminde Ekonometri Uygulamalari. Seckin Yayinevi, Ankara
Tatoglu Yerdelen F (2005) Sermaye Piyasası'nda Riskin Sınırlı Bağımlı Değişkenli Panel Veri Modelleri ile Analizi (Doktora Tezi). İstanbul Üniversitesi Sosyal Bilimler Enstitüsü, İstanbul

Lokman Kantar completed his master's degree in Finance at Istanbul University in 2010. He completed his PhD at the same school in 2017. Between 2005 and 2017, he worked as a teacher in Trade High Schools in the fields of Accounting and Finance. Since 2017, he started working as an Assistant Professor in Istanbul Gelişim University, School of Applied Sciences, Department of Banking and Insurance. Since 2018, he has been working as the head of the department in the Banking and Insurance department. He continues his academic studies in the fields of International Finance, Portfolio Management, and Risk Management.

Vector Autoregressive Model and Analysis

Murat Akkaya

Introduction

The complexity and versatility of the interaction between economic parameters necessitate the use of simultaneous systems of equations. Furthermore, the difficulties encountered in the determination of the dependent and independent variables, which are a natural consequence of the interaction between economic parameters, have a significant effect on the consistency of the analysis. Therefore, in simultaneous systems of equations, some constraints are sometimes required on the structural model to overcome the problem of determination (Adrian and Darnell 1990). This problem is solved by vector autoregressive (VAR) models which is developed for the solution of this complex table which includes simultaneous equation systems. VAR models are often preferred in terms of time series since dynamic relationships can be given to the structural model without any restriction (Keating 1990).

This model has been developed by Sims (1980). VAR model is a regression model that can be considered as a kind of hybrid among univariate time series models. VAR models are generally defined as alternatives to structural models of large-scale simultaneous equations. This model differs from the systems of simultaneous equations in that it does not require internal-external distinction of variables from any economic theory. In addition, the presence of lagged values of the dependent variables in VAR models makes it possible to make strong predictions for the future (Kumar et al. 1995). When examining the relationship between variables, it is necessary to first determine whether the variables are internal or external. Granger and Sims, by examining causality between variables, suggest that when two

M. Akkaya (✉)
T.C. İstanbul Arel University, İstanbul, Turkey
e-mail: muratakkaya@arel.edu.tr

B. Adıgüzel Mercangöz (ed.), *Handbook of Research on Emerging Theories, Models, and Applications of Financial Econometrics*,
https://doi.org/10.1007/978-3-030-54108-8_8

time series mutually cause each other, causality creates a mutual and feedback relationship (Granger and Newbold 1986). Since the variables are not separated internally and externally in the VAR model, there is no problem of determination. In this model, all variables are considered internal, and one variable is defined as the function of the lagged values of itself and other variables in the model (Gujarati 2009).

VAR models have three basic principles (Watson and Teelucksingh 2002):

- There are no internal and external presuppositions in the system.
- There is no zero-type restriction.
- There is no rigorous basic economic theory on which the model is based.

The VAR model is an econometric model that generalizes univariate autoregressive (AR) models. All variables in the model are treated symmetrically with an equation for each variable explaining the development of the variable, depending on the lags of the variable in the model and the lags of all other variables.

The main purpose of VAR modeling is not only to determine the one-way relationship between variables but also to reveal linkage between variables in terms of lags (Kearney and Monadjemi 1990). Proponents of VAR emphasize the advantages of the method (Kinal and Ratner 1982):

- The method is simple; it is not necessary to determine which variables are internal and which are external. All variables in VAR are endogenous.
- Prediction is simple; that is, the ordinary LS method can be applied to each equation separately.
- Estimates obtained in this method are, in many cases, better than those obtained from more complex simultaneous equation models.

VAR models have several advantages over univariate time series models and structural models in simultaneous equations (Brooks 2008):

- The VAR model does not require any restrictions
- It is not necessary to specify which variables are endogenous or exogenous—all are endogenous. This is very important because the predictability of structural models in concurrent equations depends on the definition of all variables in the system.
- VAR models allow the value of a variable to depend more than just its own lagged values or combinations of noise terms, so VAR models are more flexible than single variable AR models.
- Estimates generated by VAR models are generally better than traditional structural models.

However, the VAR model has some problems (Gujarati 2009):

- VAR model is atheistic because it uses less prior knowledge.
- The biggest practical challenge in VAR modeling is choosing the appropriate lag length. When the sample size is not too high, all the problems with which many

parameters are related will consume too much degree of freedom, so the estimation will be problematic.

- Certainly, in an m-variable VAR model, all m variables must be stationary. If this is not the case, we must transform the data appropriately (e.g., with first-order differences).
- Since the interpretation of individual coefficients in predicted VAR models is often difficult, practitioners of this technique often predict impulse-response function (IRF).

Methodology

Vector autoregressive (VAR) models eliminate the problem of complexity in concurrent models. These models are preferred over time series because they do not impose any restrictions on the model and they can be given dynamic relationships (Keating 1990).

Selection and Sequencing of Variables

For the VAR model example, the variables that affect the consumer confidence index are analyzed by using EViews. In this study, there are 23 variables and 184 months of observation covering the periods 2004: 01 and 2019: 04. Monthly changes are used in the analysis. In this study, it is aimed to determine the macroeconomic factors affecting consumer confidence by vector autoregressive (VAR) analysis. In addition, Gold Price, Borsa İstanbul 100 return index, USD/TRL rate, Turkish Lira 1-month interest rate (TLLIBOR), volatility index (VIX), and USD index are added to the study as the control variables. In addition, the lagged effects of the variables and the causality relationship have been examined. The data are gathered from the Turkey Statistical Institute (TSI), T.R. Central Bank electronic data system, and Federal Reserve sites (Table 1).

Vector autoregression (VAR) model developed by Sims (1980) is chosen as the method. This model doesn't specify variables as endogenous or exogenous—all are endogenous. In the VAR analysis, variables are assessed both by their own lags and by the lagged values of other variables (Sarıkovanlık et al. 2018). The simplest case is a VAR with only two variables (y1t ve y2t). Each of these valid values depends on different combinations of previous k values of both variables and error conditions (Brooks 2008):

$$y_{1t} = \beta_{10} + \beta_{11} y_{1t-1} + \cdots + \beta_{1k} y_{1t-k} + \alpha_{11} y_{2t-1} + \cdots + \alpha_{1k} y_{2t-k} + u_{1t} \quad (1)$$

Table 1 Variables

Variables		Variables	
Gold price	GOLD	Net international reserve	NR
Bloomberg consumer confidence index	BCI	Portfolio investments	PI
Borsa İstanbul 100 return index	BIST	Real exchange rate index (CPI based)	RERI
Banking sector domestic loans volume	BSLV	Industrial production index	IPI
Current deficit	CD	Consumer price index	CPI
Foreign trade balance	FTB	TLLIBOR	TLLIBOR
Direct investments	DI	TSI consumer confidence index	TSICCI
Domestic debt stock	DDS	USD index	USDİNDEX
Export import rate	EIR	USD/TRL rate	USDKUR
Production capacity rate	PCR	VIX volatility index	VIX
Unemployment rate	UR	Non-residents' stock portfolio	NRSP
Net error and omissions	NEO		

Source: Author

$$y_{2t} = \beta_{20} + \beta_{21} y_{2t-1} + \cdots + \beta_2 k\, y_{2t-k} + \alpha_{21} y_{1t-1} + \cdots + \alpha_{2k} y_{1t} - k + u_{2t} \quad (2)$$

In the equation, *uit* is the white noise disturbance term when *uit*, *E*(*uit*) = 0, (*i* = 1, 2), *E*(*u*1*u*2*t*) = 0.

The important features of the VAR model are flexibility and ease of generalization. For example, the model can be expanded to include moving average errors, which is a multivariate version of an autoregressive moving averages (ARMA) model known as a VARMA. Instead of having only two variables, *y*1*t* and *y*2*t*, the system g variables can be extended to include *y*1*t*, *y*2*t*, *y*3*t*.

Another useful aspect of VAR models is the effective expression in representation. For example, given the case of $k = 1$ above, each variable depends only on just the values of *y*1*t* and *y*2*t* and an error duration. In this case, the equation can be written as

$$y_{1t} = \beta_{10} + \beta_{11}\, y_{1t-1} + \alpha_{11}\, y_{2t-1} + u_{1t} \quad (3)$$

$$y_{2t} = \beta_{20} + \beta_{21}\, y_{2t-1} + \alpha_{21}\, y_{1t-1} + u_{2t} \quad (4)$$

or

$$\begin{pmatrix} y_{1t} \\ y_{2t} \end{pmatrix} = \begin{pmatrix} \beta_{10} \\ \beta_{20} \end{pmatrix} + \begin{pmatrix} \beta_{10} \alpha 11 \\ \beta_{20} \;\; \alpha 21 \end{pmatrix} \begin{pmatrix} y_{1t-1} \\ y_{2t-1} \end{pmatrix} + \begin{pmatrix} u_{1t} \\ u_{2t} \end{pmatrix} \quad (5)$$

or openly

$$\begin{aligned} y_t = \quad & \beta_0 \quad + \beta_1 y_{t-1} \cdots + u_t \\ g \times 1 g & \times 1 \cdots g \times g g \times 1 \cdots g \times 1 \end{aligned} \tag{6}$$

there are $g = 2$ variables in the system. In each equation, using the following notation, the expansion of the model can be easily performed in cases where each variable has a k lag:

$$\begin{aligned} & y_t = \beta_0 + \beta_1 y_{t-1} + \beta_2 y_{t-2} + \cdots + \beta_k y_{t-k} + u_t \\ & g \times 1 \;\; g \times 1 \cdots g \times g g \times 1 \cdots g \times g \, g \times 1 \cdots g \times g \, g \times 1 \cdots g \times 1. \end{aligned} \tag{7}$$

The model can be further extended to the case where the model includes initial difference terms and cointegration relationships (a vector error correction).

Unit Root Test and Stationary

Time series should be stationary in finance and economic studies, that is, it should not carry a unit root because it causes false regression and misleading results. The most widely used is the augmented Dickey-Fuller (ADF) unit root test developed by Dickey and Fuller (1981). In this study, augmented Dickey-Fuller (ADF) unit root test developed by Dickey and Fuller (1981) is applied. It is observed that the series, excluding the industrial production index and the USD/TRL rate, do not have unit root at 1% significance level, that is, they are stationary (Table 2). The industrial

Table 2 Augmented Dickey-Fuller (ADF) unit root test

Augmented Dickey-Fuller test statistic					
Null hypothesis: BIST has a unit root					
	t-Statistic	Prob.*		*t*-Statistic	Prob.*
GOLD	−1.130.148	0.0000	NIR	−1.230.668	0.0000
BCI	−1.066.783	0.0000	PI	−1.333.203	0.0000
BIST	−1.317.616	0.0000	RERI	−1.121.885	0.0000
BSLV	−1.062.182	0.0000	IPI (first difference)	−1.190.427	0.0000
CD	−9.293.115	0.0000	CPI	−9.849.234	0.0000
FTB	−1.168.423	0.0000	TLLIBOR	−1.212.996	0.0000
DI	−1.492.702	0.0000	TSICCI	−1.035.806	0.0000
DDS	−1.246.540	0.0000	USDİNDEX	−1.368.030	0.0000
EIR	−1.348.340	0.0000	USD/TRL (second difference)	−1.492.899	0.0000
PCR	−1.637.240	0.0000	VIX	−1.595.966	0.0000
UR	−4.483.632	0.0003	NRSP	−1.209.771	0.0000
NEO	−1.362.762	0.0000			

Econometrically, a probabilistic process whose mean and variance do not change over time and whose common variance between two periods depends only on the distance between the two periods is said to be stationary. This type of stationarity is also called a weak stationary probabilistic process, and for most analyzes, this kind of stationarity is sufficient (Gujarati, 2009).
Source: Author

production index is stationary in the first difference, and the USD/TRL rate is stationary in the second difference and the transformations are made.

Determination of Lag Lengths

The ideal lag length should be determined first when using VAR analysis. The optimal lag length for the VAR model needs to be determined according to different criteria. Since the lag length to be added to the VAR analysis is generally unknown, it is necessary to determine the lag by a suitable method (Katos et al. 2000).

There are two methods to achieve the optimal lag length for VAR: cross-equation constraints and information criteria. The best approach to selecting the appropriate VAR lag length is to use an information criterion. Akaike information criteria (AIC), Hannan-quinn information criteria (HQ) and FPE are used to determine the lag lengths. The model with the smallest information criteria is the best model.

According to FPE and Akaike information criteria (AIC), the lag length is 2 (two) (Table 3).

The VAR model is as follows (Table 4).

() means standard errors and [] is the statistical values of t on the Table 4.

The validity of the assumptions of the OLS method should also be examined in the VAR model. These assumptions include the absence of autocorrelation, heteroscedasticity, and multiple linear relationships in normality and error terms.

The assumptions are analyzed one by one from the view/residual test on the model output (Table 4). The model does not have autocorrelation, varying variance, and multiple linear connections.

It takes a long time to compare the output results presented in Table 4 with the *t* test results. Hence, VAR Granger causality/block externality Wald test is performed.

The VAR Granger causality/block externality Wald test is applied separately for TSI consumer confidence index and Bloomberg consumer confidence index. Model results for TSI consumer confidence index are significant for 5%. The results show that foreign trade balance (FTB), net international reserve (NIR), and volatility index (VIX) variables are exogenous and other variables are not. In other words, the lagged values of other independent variables, except the foreign trade balance (FTB), net

Table 3 VAR lag length criteria

Lag	LogL	LR	FPE	AIC	SC	HQ
0	−15282.76	NA	1.42e+47	171.0029	171.3946*	171.1617*
1	−14757.91	914.8098	9.26e+46	170.5465	179.5567	174.2001
2	−14316.21	661.3280	1.83e+47*	171.0191*	188.6476	178.1673
3	−13834.64	602.6258*	3.43e+47	171.0463	197.2933	181.6892

Source: Author

Table 4 Vector autoregression estimates

Vector Autoregression Estimates	
Sample (adjusted): 2004M05 2019M04	
Included observations: 180 after adjustments	
Standard errors in () and *t*-statistics in []	
	TUIKTGE
ALTIN (−1)	7.921983
	(9.51214)
	[0.83283]
ALTIN (−2)	5.675666
	(9.63207)
	[0.58925]
BIST100 (−1)	−0.025094
	(0.08494)
	[−0.29541]
BIST100 (−2)	0.017608
	(0.08786)
	[0.20042]
BYKH (−1)	−0.041414
	(0.19808)
	[−0.20908]
BYKH (−2)	−0.045370
	(0.19792)
	[−0.22924]
CA (−1)	−0.000697
	(0.00082)
	[−0.85151]
CA (−2)	0.000735
	(0.00087)
	[0.84305]
DSUE (−1)	0.046564
	(0.02548)
	[1.82773]
DSUE (−2)	0.007314
	(0.02411)
	[0.30337]
DTD (−1)	−0.013565
	(0.00595)
	[−2.27960]
DTD (−2)	0.009272
	(0.00596)
	[1.55553]
DUSDKUR (−1)	−0.000992
	(0.00139)

(continued)

Table 4 (continued)

Vector Autoregression Estimates	
Sample (adjusted): 2004M05 2019M04	
Included observations: 180 after adjustments	
Standard errors in () and *t*-statistics in []	
	TUIKTGE
	[−0.71497]
DUSDKUR (−2)	0.002123
	(0.00122)
	[1.74476]
DY (−1)	−0.000234
	(0.00092)
	[−0.25443]
DY (−2)	−0.000116
	(0.00090)
	[−0.12831]
IBS (−1)	−0.186248
	(0.34668)
	[−0.53723]
IBS (−2)	0.280640
	(0.35967)
	[0.78027]
IHRITHKO (−1)	−0.065170
	(0.03286)
	[−1.98323]
IHRITHKO (−2)	0.021241
	(0.03335)
	[0.63698]
IKKO (−1)	0.112843
	(0.10383)
	[1.08681]
IKKO (−2)	0.023372
	(0.10340)
	[0.22604]
IO (−1)	0.136395
	(0.13409)
	[1.01719]
IO (−2)	0.214519
	(0.13573)
	[1.58046]
NHN (−1)	6.56E-06
	(5.5E-05)
	[0.11970]
NHN (−2)	1.05E-05

(continued)

Table 4 (continued)

Vector Autoregression Estimates	
Sample (adjusted): 2004M05 2019M04	
Included observations: 180 after adjustments	
Standard errors in () and *t*-statistics in []	
	TUIKTGE
	(5.5E-05)
	[0.18889]
NUR (−1)	−0.291936
	(0.08934)
	[−3.26779]
NUR(−2)	0.126612
	(0.09104)
	[1.39074]
PY (−1)	−0.000476
	(0.00023)
	[−2.07259]
PY (−2)	−0.000182
	(0.00023)
	[−0.77996]
REELKUR (−1)	0.351087
	(0.19638)
	[1.78777]
REELKUR (−2)	−0.021750
	(0.17622)
	[−0.12342]
TFFE (−1)	−0.226080
	(0.43191)
	[−0.52344]
TFFE (−2)	−0.648366
	(0.45179)
	[−1.43509]
TLLIBOR (−1)	0.033572
	(0.04181)
	[0.80293]
TLLIBOR (−2)	0.080700
	(0.04021)
	[2.00701]
USDINDEX (−1)	−0.157411
	(0.14631)
	[−1.07588]
USDINDEX (−2)	−0.057101
	(0.15069)
	[−0.37893]

(continued)

Table 4 (continued)

Vector Autoregression Estimates	
Sample (adjusted): 2004M05 2019M04	
Included observations: 180 after adjustments	
Standard errors in () and *t*-statistics in []	
	TUIKTGE
VIX (−1)	−0.030137
	(0.01615)
	[−1.86577]
VIX (−2)	0.020574
	(0.01620)
	[1.27017]
YYHSP (−1)	0.083635
	(0.07282)
	[1.14850]
YYHSP (−2)	0.035990
	(0.07110)
	[0.50621]
C	0.271469
	(0.82602)
	[0.32865]
R-squared	0.184679
Adj. *R*-squared	1824.942
Sum sq. resids	3.676696
S.E. equation	1.921487
F-statistic	−463.8801
Log likelihood	5.654224
Akaike AIC	6.452463
Schwarz SC	−0.150111
Mean dependent	4.071865

Source: Author (Eviews Output)

international reserve (NIR), and volatility index (VIX) variables, are not significant on the TSI consumer confidence index (Table 5).

VAR analysis is also subject to the assumptions of regression analysis. In this study, the assumptions have been tested and the assumptions are significant.

Impulse-Response Analysis

In VAR analysis, the impulse-response functions have a significant role in determining the dynamic interaction between the variables examined and in determining the symmetrical relations. Impulse-response functions are a standard in one of the

Table 5 VAR Granger causality/block exogeneity Wald test

Dependent variable: TSICCI			
Excluded	Chi-sq.	*df*	Prob.
GOLD	1.167.287	2	0.5579
BIST	0.179435	2	0.9142
BSLV	0.114305	2	0.9444
CD	1.398.278	2	0.4970
DIPI	4.421.859	2	0.1096
FTB	7.184.430	2	0.0275%5
DUSD/TRL	3.160.005	2	0.2060
DI	0.072575	2	0.9644
DDS	0.968946	2	0.6160
EIR	5.586.712	2	0.0612%10
PCR	1.188.905	2	0.5519
UR	4.858.536	2	0.0881%10
NEO	0.049983	2	0.9753
NIR	1.269.421	2	0.0018%5
PY	4.936.302	2	0.0847%10
RERI	3.212.000	2	0.2007
CPI	2.676.114	2	0.2624
TLLIBOR	4.707.651	2	0.0950%10
USDINDEX	1.205.564	2	0.5473
VIX	6.910.219	2	0.0316%5
NRSP	1.353.255	2	0.5083
All	7.254.886	42	0.0024%5

Source: Author

random error terms. It reflects the effect of deviant shock on the present and future values of internal variables. Whether it can be used as an intermediary is determined by the effect-response functions.

Since the interpretation of coefficients calculated by VAR model is quite complex and difficult, impulse-response analysis and variance decomposition methods are generally applied (Gacener 2005).

The predictions from the VAR models are quite flexible. With VAR models, structural inferences and policy analyzes can be performed other than forecasting and data identification. When certain assumptions are made about the interaction structure of data, structural analysis can summarize how an unexpected shock or change in a given variable will affect other variables. This effect is usually reported by impulse-response functions.

The results of the *F*-test assume whether changes in the value of a given variable positively or negatively affect the other variables in the model or how long it takes for the variable to run through the model. Impulse-response results monitor the response of dependent variables in VAR by shocking each of the variables. Therefore, for each variable separately from each equation, one unit of shock is applied to the error, and its effects over the VAR system over time are noted. Thus, if a system

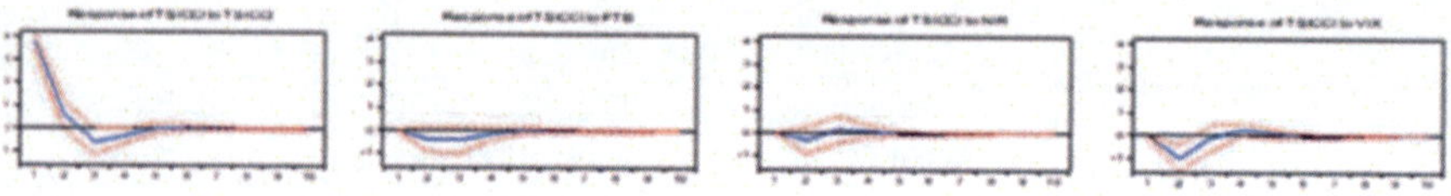

Fig. 1 The impulse-response test results. Source: Eviews output

Table 6 Impulse-response test results

Period	TSICCI	FTB	NIR	VIX
1	3.835207	0.000000	0.000000	0.000000
	(0.20102)	(0.00000)	(0.00000)	(0.00000)
2	0.627426	−0.392732	−0.332995	−1.019653
	(0.30225)	(0.29812)	(0.30095)	(0.29299)
3	−0.589337	−0.423036	0.146106	−0.109848
	(0.29645)	(0.29991)	(0.30618)	(0.29201)
4	−0.312047	−0.123604	0.106266	0.277940
	(0.16469)	(0.14997)	(0.13471)	(0.13818)
5	0.013246	0.030317	−0.013933	0.115280
	(0.11044)	(0.07359)	(0.06569)	(0.09578)
6	0.073549	0.034029	−0.037327	−0.021951
	(0.07260)	(0.03783)	(0.03648)	(0.05122)
7	0.023679	0.002371	−0.013603	−0.031222
	(0.03115)	(0.02045)	(0.01475)	(0.02801)
8	−0.007413	−0.006921	0.002583	−0.006619
	(0.02237)	(0.01024)	(0.00829)	(0.01548)
9	−0.007674	−0.003175	0.003357	0.004426
	(0.01109)	(0.00500)	(0.00476)	(0.00919)
10	−0.001119	0.000276	0.000541	0.003004
	(0.00511)	(0.00300)	(0.00193)	(0.00434)

Source: Author

has g variables, the total g2 impulse-response can be generated. This is the VAR model as a VMA—the vector autoregressive model written as the vector moving average. The shock will gradually disappear, provided the system is stationary and stable (Brooks 2008).

The impulse-response analysis graphs of TSI consumer confidence index are presented in Fig. 1.

According to the impulse-response analysis shown in Fig. 1., foreign trade balance (FTB) and VIX react to decrease by a shock applied to the TSI consumer confidence index at the first moment and there is an increase in net international reserve (NIR). The impact of shock in FTB and VIX decreases and becomes ineffective at the end of the fifth month. Inversely, the impact of shock in NIR increases and becomes ineffective at the end of the fifth month. Impulse-response analysis results of TSICCI are presented in Table 6.

Table 7 Variance decomposition test results

Period	S.E.	TSICCI	FTB	NIR	VIX
1	3.835207	100.0000	0.000000	0.000000	0.000000
2	4.050592	92.04733	0.940061	0.675830	6.336774
3	4.119100	91.05798	1.963803	0.779352	6.198861
4	4.143450	90.55805	2.029779	0.835994	6.576180
5	4.145209	90.48224	2.033407	0.836415	6.647943
6	4.146227	90.46927	2.039144	0.844109	6.647481
7	4.146436	90.46344	2.038972	0.845101	6.652484
8	4.146454	90.46296	2.039232	0.845132	6.652679
9	4.146466	90.46277	2.039279	0.845192	6.652754
10	4.146467	90.46273	2.039278	0.845194	6.652803

Source: Author

Variance Decomposition

Variance decomposition separates the change in one of the endogenous variables into separate shocks that affect all endogenous variables. In this sense, variance decomposition provides information about the dynamic structure of the system. The purpose of variance decomposition is to reveal the effect of each random shock on the predicted error variance for future periods. Variance decomposition, on the other hand, investigates how much of the variation in variance of each of the studied variables is explained by its own lags and how many is explained by other variables (Tarı 2012).

Variance decomposition provides a slightly different way to examine VAR system dynamics. It is the ratio of the changes in the dependent variables by a shock against other variables, depending on their shocks. A shock to variable will directly affect this variable, but the dynamic structure of VAR transmits the shock to all other variables in the system. Variance decomposition determines how much of the pre-s-step prediction error variance of a given variable is explained by changes in each descriptive variable for $s = 1, 2$.

According to Runkle (1987), it is very difficult to interpret the impulse-response analysis and variance decomposition correctly. Confidence groups around impulse-response results and variance decompositions should always be established. However, even then, confidence intervals are typically so large that certain inferences are impossible.

Variance decomposition results of TSICCI are presented in Table 7.

According to the variance decomposition results presented in Table 6, it is seen that 90.46% of the error variance in the TSI consumer confidence index (TSICCI) is explained by itself and 6.65% is explained by the VIX. FTB explains only 2.04%. The NIR is 0.85.

Granger Causality Test

Re-emergence and evaluation of the concept of Granger causality within the framework of cointegration analysis as a result of error correction mechanism led to the emergence of causality concepts in the literature in the long and short term. The causality tests developed by Clive W. Granger in his 1969 article published in *Econometrica* are widely used not only in economics and econometrics but also in basic sciences, engineering, and medical sciences. In Granger's original analysis and subsequent variants, the concept of causality is not distinguished as a short- and long-term effect. However, in recent years short- and long-term Granger-causation concepts have been put forward in another way.

Granger causality test is a test used to determine the direction of causality of the relationship in the presence of delayed relationship between two variables. By definition, if the history of a random X variable, considering all possible other relevant factors and non-random information, allows a better prediction of the future of another random Y variable, the X variable is called the Granger cause of Y. If Y's prediction is more successful when X's historical values are used than when X's historical values are not used (while other terms do not change), X is the Granger cause of Y.

For the Granger causality test, variables must be stationary. In the Granger causality test of stationary time series, level values of variables are used. The first (or higher) difference of non-stationary variables should be converted. Converted values should be used. The number of lags in the test should be selected using the Akaike, FPE, or Schwarz info criteria.

The word causality is a misnomer, because Granger causality is really just a correlation between the present value of one variable and the past values of others; the movements of one variable do not mean that it causes the movements of another. VAR equations can be expressed as follows (Brooks, 2008):

$$y_{1t} = \alpha_{10} + \beta_{11}\, y_{1t-1} + \beta_{12}\, y_{2t-1} + \gamma_{11}\, y_{1t-2} + \gamma_{12}\, y_{2t-2} + \delta_{11}\, y_{1t-3} + \delta_{12}\, y_{2t-3} + u_{1t}.$$

$$y_{2t} = \alpha_{20} + \beta_{21}\, y_{1t-1} + \beta_{22}\, y_{2t-1} + \gamma_{21}\, y_{1t-2} + \gamma_{22}\, y_{2t-2} + \delta_{21}\, y_{1t-3} + \delta_{22}\, y_{2t-3} + u_{2t}.$$

The tests given above can be called causality tests. These tests are developed by Granger (1969) and Sims (1972) with small differences. Causality tests try to answer the questions whether the changes in y1 cause changes in y2. This shows that if y1 causes y2, the lag of y1 is significant in the equation y2. That means, y1 is the Granger cause of y2 or there is or one-way causality from y1 to y2.

On the other hand, if y2 is the Granger cause of y1, the lags of y2 should be significant in the equation for y1. If both lag sequences are important, it can be said that there is a two-way causality or two-way feedback. If y1 is found to be the

Table 8 Granger causality test results (TSICCI)

Pairwise Granger Nedensellik test					
Observation		182			
Variables	*F*-statistic	Prob.	Variables	*F*-statistic	Prob.
GOLD-TSICCI	409.332	0.0183	RERI-TSICCI	819.971	0.0004
TSICCI-GOLD	0.84259	0.4323	TSICCI-RERI	0.74771	0.4749
BIST-TSICCI	426.961	0.0155	VIX-TSICCI	464.438	0.0108
TSICCI-BIST	0.22045	0.8024	TSICCI-VIX	0.57122	0.5659
BSLV-TSICCI	402.017	0.0196	NRSP-TSICCI	725.984	0.0009
TSICCI-BSLV	415.502	0.0172	TSICCI-NNSP	0.61973	0.5393
USDTRL-TSICCI	197.793	0.1414			
TSICCI-USDTRL	410.937	0.0180			

Source: Author

Granger cause of y2, and not vice versa, y1 is strongly said to be exogenous to y2. If both variables are not statistically significant in the equation for the other variable, y1 and y2 can be said to be independent.

In the example study, Granger causality test is applied to determine the short-term relationship between the variables. This test provides information about the direction of relationships. The causality test results between the TSI consumer confidence index and the variables are presented in Table 8.

According to the results in Table 7, there is one-way Granger causality from gold price (GOLD), Borsa İstanbul 100 return index (BIST), real effective exchange rate (RERI), volatility index (VIX), and non-residents' stock portfolio (NRSP) to TSICCI. Granger causality test results show that changes in gold price (GOLD), Borsa İstanbul 100 return index (BIST), real effective exchange rate (RERI), volatility index (VIX), and non-residents' stock portfolio (NRSP) are significant on changes of TSICCI. Moreover, there is a two-way causality between TSICCI and the banking sector domestic credit volume (BSLV). In addition, there is a one-way causality from the TSI consumer confidence index to the USD/TRL rate (USD/TRL).

Solutions and Recommendations

VAR model is frequently used in economic and finance studies. In this study, VAR model is explained in general. There are also improved versions of the model such as structural VAR (SVAR), a factor-augmented vector autoregressive (FAVAR), and threshold vector autoregression (TVAR).

Future Research Directions

The aim of this study is to explain vector autoregressive (VAR) models and Granger causality. VAR is an econometric model that generalizes univariate autoregressive (AR) models. Since the variables are not separated endogenously and exogenously in the VAR model, there is no problem of determination. In this model, all variables are considered internal, and one variable is defined as a function of delayed values of variables. The VAR model is easy to apply and interpret. Researchers interested in this subject can use the improved version of the model such as structural VAR (SVAR), a factor-augmented vector autoregressive (FAVAR), and threshold vector autoregression (TVAR) in their studies.

Conclusion

The VAR model is a systemic approach to reveal dynamics in multivariate time series analysis. Vector autoregressive (VAR) models are multidimensional linear models that are defined on the lagged values of each variable and other variables, unlike the one-dimensional linear models. Unlike other models, VAR models also allow to investigate the effects of shocks on variables and investigate how much of the variation in variance of each of the studied variables is explained by its own lags and how many is explained by other variables. Accurate determination of lag lengths is very important in VAR model application. The degree of freedom decreases when the lag length is selected longer than necessary. On the other hand, when the lag length is selected shorter than it should be, the model is underdefined.

Short-term and long-term Granger causality was first defined within the framework of error correction models that may arise as a result of cointegration analysis. Granger causality test is used to determine the direction of causality of the relationship in the presence of delayed relationship between two variables.

VAR model is used frequently in economic and finance studies. The VAR model has significant advantages. It is remarkable for being easy to use statistically. Granger causality test is also is easy to apply and interpret.

Key Terms and Definitions

Vector Autoregressive (VAR) Models VAR model is an econometric model that generalizes univariate autoregressive (AR) models. All variables in the model are treated symmetrically with an equation for each variable explaining the development of the variable, depending on the lags of the variable in the model and the lags of all other variables.

Impulse-Response Analysis It reflects the effect of deviant shock on the present and future values of internal variables. Whether it can be used as an intermediary is determined by the effect-response functions.

Variance Decomposition Variance decomposition separates the change in one of the endogenous variables into separate shocks that affect all endogenous variables.

Granger Causality Test Granger causality test is a test used to determine the direction of causality of the relationship in the presence of delayed relationship between two variables. By definition, if the history of a random X variable, considering all possible other relevant factors and non-random information, allows a better prediction of the future of another random Y variable, the X variable is called the Granger cause of Y. If Y's prediction is more successful when X's historical values are used than when X's historical values are not used (while other terms do not change), X is the Granger cause of Y.

References

Adrian C, Darnell A (1990) Dictionary of econometrics. Edward Elgar, London

Brooks C (2008) Introductory econometrics for finance, 2nd edn. New York, Cambridge University

Dickey DA, Fuller WA (1981) Likelihood ratio statistics for autoregressive time series with a unit root. Econometrica 49:1057–1072

Gacener A (2005) Türkiye Açısından Wagner Kanunu'nun Geçerliliğinin Analizi. Dokuz Eylül Üniversitesi, İktisadi ve İdari Bilimler Fakültesi Dergisi 20(1):103–122

Granger CW (1969) Investigating causal relations by econometric models and cross-spectral methods. Econometrica 37:424–438

Granger C, Newbold P (1986) Forecasting economic time series, economic theory, econometrics and mathemathical economics, 2nd edn. Harcourt Brace Jovanovich, New York

Gujarati DN (2009) Basic econometrics, 5th edn. McGraw-Hill, New York

Katos A, Kevin L, Seddighi H (2000) Econometrics: a practical approach. Taylor and Francis Group, Routledge, London

Kearney C, Monadjemi M (1990) Fiscal policy and current account performance: international evidence on the twin deficits. J Macroecon 12(2):197–219

Keating JW (1990) Identifying VAR models under rational expectations. J Monet Econ 25:453–476

Kinal T, Ratner JB (1982) Regional forecasting models with vector autoregression: the case of New York State, discussion paper, 155, Department of Economics, State University of New York at Albany

Kumar V, Leone RP, Gaskins JN (1995) Aggregate and disaggregate sector forecasting using consumer confidence measures. Int J Forecast 11(3):361–377

Runkle DE (1987) Vector autoregressions and reality. J Bus Econ Stat 5(4):437–442

Sarıkovanlık V, Koy A, Akkaya M, Yıldırım HH, Kantar L (2018) Finans Biliminde Ekonometri Uygulamaları. Seçkin Yayıncılık, Ankara

Sims CA (1972) Money, income, and causality. Am Econ Rev:540–552

Sims CA (1980) Macroeconomics and reality. Econometrica 48:1–48

Tarı R (2012) Ekonometri. Umuttepe Kitapevi, 8.Baskı, Kocaeli

Watson PK, Teelucksingh SS (2002) A practical introduction to econometric methods: classical and modern. University of West Indies Press, Jamaica

Additional Reading

Bayracı S, Ari Y, Yildirim Y (2011) A vector auto-Regressıve (VAR) model for the Turkish financial markets. University Library of Munich, Munich, Germany

Campbell JAL, MacKinlay C (1997) The econometrics of financial markets. Princeton University Press, Princeton, NJ

Hamilton JD (1994) Time series analysis. Princeton University Press, Princeton, NJ

Lütkepohl H (1993) Introduction to multiple time series analysis. Springer, Berlin, Heidelberg

Mills TC (1999) The econometric modeling of financial time series, 2nd edn. Cambridge University Press, Cambridge

Tsay RS (2013) Multivariate time series analysis: with R and financial applications. Wiley, Hoboken, NJ

Watson M (1994) Vector autoregressions and cointegration. In: Engle RF, MacFadden D (eds) Handbook of econometrics, IV. Elsevier, Amsterdam

Murat Akkaya graduated from the Faculty of Educational Sciences, Middle East Technical University in 1991. In addition, he is a graduate of T.C. Ziraat Bank MT—Banking School (1992). He worked as a fund management and capital market specialist, marketing directorate, and branch manager at Ziraat Bank. He worked also as a foreign trade manager at Azer Türk Bank, Baku, Azerbaijan, and branch manager at Ziraat Bank International A.G. and Stuttgart of Germany. He completed his master's degree in business management from Beykent University in 2011 and PhD from Istanbul University, Department of Finance in 2015. His master thesis is on "Innovation in Banking" and doctoral thesis is on "Impact of Expectation and Confidence Surveys on Financial Markets." He works at the Department of International Trade Finance (English) at T.C. Istanbul Arel University. He speaks English, German, and Russian. He works in the fields of education and consultancy. He has Behavioral Finance and Econometrics Applications in Financial Science books and many articles.

Construction of the Monetary Conditions Index with TVP-VAR Model: Empirical Evidences for Turkish Economy

Coşkun Akdeniz

Introduction

Substantial changes have been experienced in the implementation of monetary policy which have been in line with structural changes occurring in central banks. Thus, the central banks, which acquired instrument independence, became more transparent and consequently, independent in the implementation of monetary policies. In this process, the definition of central bank tasks and the scope of policy instruments in time, underwent crucial changes, due to endogenous economic conditions and global economic developments. In operating monetary policies, central banks may use policy instruments, such as short-term interest rates to reach their final targets, namely inflation and production. Due to the indirect links and extensive lags between monetary policy instruments and final targets, several central banks have adopted intermediate targets (such as monetary aggregates and exchange rates). In order to implement effective policies, these intermediate targets should respond to changes in policy instruments (Kesriyeli and Koçaker 1999: 1).

The ultimate goal of central banks in the 1990s was transformed to ensuring price stability. The Reserve Bank of New Zealand (RBNZ) and the Bank of Canada (BOC) started to implement an inflation targeting regime for the first time, in order to ensure price stability. Accordingly, the central banks that implemented the inflation targeting regime employed short-term interest rates as the main policy

This paper is an extended version of the paper entitled "A Monetary Conditions Index for Turkish Economy: Evidences from TVP-VAR Model" which was presented at the European Congress on Economic Issues-V.

C. Akdeniz (✉)
Tekirdağ Namık Kemal University, Tekirdağ, Turkey
e-mail: cakdeniz@nku.edu.tr

B. Adıgüzel Mercangöz (ed.), *Handbook of Research on Emerging Theories, Models, and Applications of Financial Econometrics*,
https://doi.org/10.1007/978-3-030-54108-8_9

instrument. Due to perfect capital mobility as a result of financial liberalization, the real exchange rate has become an important indicator for those economies that implement inflation targeting, as well as short-term interest rates. A change in the monetary policy stance in the inflation targeting regime, in other words, a change in the short-term interest rate, may affect domestic demand conditions through household investment and saving decisions. In addition, a change in the monetary policy stance may affect the real exchange rate and the competitiveness of domestic companies set against foreign businesses, thus changing external demand conditions (Goodhart and Hofmann 2001: 2).

In this context, there is a need to develop an index that reflects both changes in the short-term interest rate and the real exchange rate for the inflation targeting regime. This index which has been called the monetary conditions index (MCI), was calculated by the RBNZ and the BOC in 1990. The index, derived from the weighted sum of short-term interest and real exchange rates, is used as an operational target at the RBNZ and BOC and has also been used as an indicator index at Riksbank, Norges Bank, the Bank of Finland and the Central Bank of Iceland (Goodhart and Hofmann 2002: 2). An increase (decrease) in the MCI, demonstrates the implementation of contractionary (expansionary) monetary policies (Gauthier et al. 2004: 16). The index, calculated with the weighted sum approach, can be written as follows, based on Montagnoli and Napolitano (2006):

$$\mathrm{MCI} = w_r(r_t - r_{\text{base}}) + w_e(e_t - e_{\text{base}}). \tag{1}$$

In the model above, r_t and e_t reflect the short-term interest and exchange rate in the period t, respectively. w_r and w_e, calculated using the coefficients obtained with price level and aggregate demand equations, indicate the index components, such as the weighted short-term interest rate and exchange rate, respectively. In the weighted sum approach, the index component weights are constant. The index, which reflects the changes in monetary conditions, is calculated with constant coefficients, based on the model above. However, the fact that there is no constant relationship between the short-term interest rate and exchange rate may increase the risk of policy error. This relationship differs over the course of time, due to structural economic changes, different policy regimes and crises. Due to the index weights which change over the time period, this allows the index to provide more accurate information as an indicator.

Literature Review

Nowadays, MCIs are calculated by the financial institutions, as well as central banks. Previous literature has focused primarily on developed economies; however, the number of studies of emerging economies has increased substantially. Moreover, the majority of studies have adopted a weighted sum approach, in which the index weights do not change over time.

Duguay (1994), who investigated the interest rate and exchange rate transmission channels for Canada, reported the relative weights of the aforementioned variables, based on the coefficients obtained with aggregate demand equations. The findings of the study that investigated the 1975Q1–1990Q4 and 1980Q1–1990Q4 periods demonstrated that the relative interest rate and real exchange rate weights were around 3:1. In other words, a 1% increase in the interest rate tightens the monetary conditions three-fold, compared to a 1% increase in the Canadian dollar. Freedman (1994) who conducted the first study that calculated the MCI for the Canadian economy analysed the 1980Q1–1993Q4 periods with the weighted sum approach. The weights of the index components, calculated in this study, supported the study by Duguay (1994). Similar results have been obtained by Ericsson et al. (1998), who calculated alternative MCIs, based on different weights for Canada in their study. Batini and Turnbull (2000) developed a dynamic index, which covered the period of 1984Q4–1999Q3 for the UK. They utilized small-scale macro-econometric models in their analysis.

In a study on developing economics, Knedlik (2005) analysed South Africa, based on the 1994Q1–2003Q4 period. He demonstrated that the impact of real interest rates on monetary conditions is much higher when compared to the exchange rate. Kannan et al. (2006) calculated narrow and broad alternative indexes for India. In addition to the interest and exchange rates, bank credits are used in the development of the broad index. The MCI, calculated for the time period between 1996Q2 and 2007Q1, was found to be a good indicator of economic activity and price level. Furthermore, it has been found that the weight of the interest rate in the index is higher when compared to the exchange rate. Poon (2010) calculated the augmented monetary conditions index for the ASEAN-5 country group, for the period 1980Q1–2004Q4. MCIs calculated with different time periods, due to the availability of data, have been extended to include credits and asset prices. It has been determined that interest rate, exchange rate and asset price channels were significant for monetary transmission in Indonesia and Thailand while interest rate, exchange rate and credit channels were found to be significant in Malaysia and Singapore. Lastly, interest rate, exchange rate, loan and asset price channels were deemed significant for monetary transmission in the Philippines.

Abubabkar and Yaaba (2013) analysed the Nigerian economy and calculated the MCI for the period 1989Q1–2012Q2. In the study, which used the autoregressive distributed lag (ARDL) model, index weights were calculated using the bounds testing approach to co-integration. Private sector loans have been included as an index component. The findings revealed that the interest rate transmission channel is more effective when compared to the exchange rate and credit channels. Memon and Jabeen (2018) who examined the Gulf countries estimated the vector autoregressive (VAR) model and principal component analysis with utilized annual data. Index calculations were conducted for Bahrain (1986–2014), Iraq (2004–2011), Kuwait (1986–2015), Oman (2000–2015), Qatar (1980–2015) and Saudi Arabia (1999–2016). They showed that the MCIs calculated for Bahrain and Qatar could be used as a good indicator for long-term price levels and economic activity. They also demonstrate that the index calculated for Oman could be used as a predictor of total production in the medium and long term; the MCIs failed to provide an accurate estimate of the price level and economic activity in Kuwait and Saudi Arabia.

It has been observed that there are a limited number of studies relating to monetary conditions in Turkey. The real effective exchange rate and the real interest rate are used as components of the index calculated by Kesriyeli and Koçaker (1999). The index weights for 1988:01–1999:03 are obtained using price level equations. The estimated weight of the exchange rate is higher compared to the interest rate. This implies that the price level is more sensitive to exchange rates than interest rates. Şıklar and Doğan (2015) calculated the MCI for the period covering 1991:01–2013:12, utilizing the Kalman filter algorithm. They found that index weights have changed over time and the effect of interest rates on prices is stronger than the effect of the exchange rate. They also showed that the highest values of the index occurred during the 1994 and 2001 crises. Açcı and Tasar (2016) calculated the MCI for the period 2006:01–2015:09 using a structural VAR model. In their study, the industrial production index reflected the economic activity. They found that the index weight of the interest rate was higher than the exchange rate. Moreover, there were expansionary monetary conditions with the exception of late 2010 and the first half of 2011 within the sample period. Süslü and Dişbudak (2012) compared the effectiveness of basic instruments that affected aggregate demand, using the ARDL model. In the study, the period 2002Q1–2011Q2 was analysed with quarterly data, and the index was calculated to reflect the monetary conditions. The exchange rate weight was found to be 0.96, and it was determined that the basic instrument rule that affected aggregate demand in the long-term was not the Taylor Rule but the index with the integrated exchange rate and interest rate components.

A review of literature revealed that index weights are generally obtained with linear models. With the exception of a study by Şıklar and Doğan (2015), it has been observed that a time-varying parameter index calculation has not been used for the Turkish economy. This study aims to fill this gap in the literature by obtaining time-varying impulse-response functions with time-varying parameter vector autoregressive (TVP-VAR) models. Thus, the time-varying nature of the developed index weights will allow for a more accurate analysis of the crisis periods and structural changes.

Data and Methodology

In this article MCI is constructed based on the time-varying responses of TVP-VAR model. The VAR model used to calculate monetary conditions can be written in linear form as follows:

$$Y_t = C_i + \sum\nolimits_{i=1}^{p} \beta_i Y_{t-i} + \varepsilon_t. \tag{2}$$

In this model, Y_t and C_i indicate vectors of endogenous variables and vectors of intercepts, respectively. β_i and ε_t represent parameter matrices and idiosyncratic shocks, respectively. Endogenous variables vector can be more clearly written as follows:

$$Y'_t = [\text{int}_t \ \ \text{realer}_t \ \ \text{gap}_t], \tag{3}$$

where int_t, realer_t and gap_t represent the short-term interest rate, real exchange rate and output gap, respectively. In this study, overnight interbank rate is used to represent the short-term interest rate. The real exchange rate is obtained with the nominal exchange rate multiplied by the ratio of domestic and global price indexes. Industrial production index is used to represent the economic activity. The available monthly data for the period of 1986:05–2018:10 is used for the index. The variables used in the analysis are obtained from the IMF and OECD databases.

Before the estimation of the TVP-VAR model, several transformations are performed to make the series usable for analysis. However, the short-term interest rate is used in level. The real exchange rate has been calculated by taking the logarithm of the multiplication of Turkish and US consumer price indices by the nominal exchange rate. The logarithm of the industrial production index is used for representing the output. Hodrick-Prescott (HP 1997) filter is applied in order to obtain the long-term trend of industrial production index. The difference between industrial production index and its long-term trend value is calculated to determine the output gap. Finally, short-term interest rate, real exchange rate and output gap variables are standardized similar to the studies by Koop (2012), Koop and Korobilis (2013), Simo-Kengne et al. (2015) and Akdeniz and Çatık (2019).

After the transformations of the variables used in the TVP-VAR model, the stationarity of the series is examined by conventional and structural break unit root tests. The conventional unit root tests, namely, augmented Dickey-Fuller (ADF 1981) and Phillips-Perron (PP 1988) tests, are used in the study, and the Zivot and Andrews (1992) test that allows endogenous breaks is used. The conventional and structural break unit root test statistics are presented in Appendix Tables 1 and 2, respectively.[1]

In the calculation of the index weights by weighted sum methodology, a similar approach to the methods described by Goodhart and Hofmann (2001), Gauthier et al. (2004), Swiston (2008), Kara et al. (2012, 2015) and Akdeniz and Çatık (2017) has

[1] ADF test results presented in Table 1 demonstrated that the short-term interest rate is stationary at 5% significance level and doesn't include unit root in the model without intercept and trend. In the PP test, the real exchange rate is stationary at 5% significance level in the model with intercept and trend. The other series are stationary in all models in both unit root tests at 1% significance level. Based on the results of the Zivot-Andrews unit root test, which allows structural break, as presented in Table 2, the real exchange rate is stationary at the 10% significance level in the model with trend. The test of the series in the study are stationary at 1% significance level in all models and don't include unit roots. On the other hand, when the break dates are analysed, it has been observed that the break dates of the series are generally experienced during the economic crisis periods.

been adopted. Thus, cumulative responses of economic activity to short-term interest rate and real exchange rate shocks after 24 months are used. More clearly, the index weight of any components is obtained by dividing the sum of the absolute value of the cumulative responses of the output gap to the related variable shocks by the sum of absolute values of cumulative responses of the output gap to the all index component shocks (Goodhart and Hofmann 2001: 18).

Since the index weights obtained with linear models are constant, the relevant indexes may not accurately reflect the economies with structural changes and experience economic crises. Therefore, indexes calculated with time-varying parameter models could better demonstrate general monetary conditions. The general structure of the TVP-VAR model used in the calculation of time-varying responses can be written as mentioned in a study by Nakajima (2011) as follows:

$$Y_t = C_t + B_{1t}y_{t-1} + \cdots + B_{pt}y_{t-p} + \varepsilon_t, \quad \varepsilon_t\tilde{N}(0, \Omega_t), \tag{4}$$

where Y_t, C_t and B_{pt} are observed variables, vector of constants and time-varying coefficient matrices, respectively. Ω_t reflects the time-varying variance-covariance matrix. The variance-covariance matrix could be reduced to a lower-triangular form with the standard recursive identification method $\left(\Omega_t = A_t^{-1}\Sigma_t\Sigma_t'(A_t^{-1})'\right)$. In this reduction, $\sum_t =$ diag $(\sigma_{1t}, \ldots, \sigma_{kt})$ is the diagonal matrix for idiosyncratic shocks, and A_t is the lower-triangular matrix of covariance components. Similar to Nakajima and Watanabe (2011), β_t that consists of a combination of $X_t = I_k \otimes \left(1, y_{t-1}', \ldots, y_{t-p}'\right)$, vector of constants and time-varying coefficient matrices could be defined, and TVP-VAR model could be written as follows:

$$y_t = X_t\beta_t + A_t^{-1}\sum\nolimits_t \varepsilon_t, \quad \varepsilon_t \sim N(0, I). \tag{5}$$

Similar to the study by Primiceri (2005), it is assumed that the time-varying β_t, A_t^{-1} and $\sum_t$ parameters follow a random walk process. The parameter vector of A_t lower-triangular matrix, $h_{it} = \log \sigma_{it}^2$ and variance-covariance matrices of time-varying residuals are defined as $\alpha_t = (\alpha_{21}, \alpha_{31}, \alpha_{41}, \ldots, \alpha_{k,\ k\ -\ 1})'$ and $h_t = (h_{1t}, \ldots h_{kt})'$ for $j = 1, \ldots, k$ and $t = p + 1, \ldots, n$, respectively. Under these assumptions, time-varying structure of the β_t, α_t and h_t parameters is written as follows:

$$\beta_{t+1} = \beta_t + u_{\beta t}, \quad \alpha_{t+1} = \alpha_t + u_{\alpha t}, \quad h_{t+1} = h_t + u_{ht}$$

$$\begin{pmatrix} \varepsilon_t \\ u_{\beta_t} \\ u_{\alpha_t} \\ u_{h_t} \end{pmatrix} \sim N\left(0, \begin{pmatrix} I & 0 & 0 & 0 \\ 0 & \mathrm{V}_\beta & 0 & 0 \\ 0 & 0 & \mathrm{V}_\alpha & 0 \\ 0 & 0 & 0 & \mathrm{V}_h \end{pmatrix}\right). \tag{6}$$

It is assumed that the parameters in the equation system are normally distributed over time for $t = p+1, \ldots, n$: $\beta_{p+1} \sim N\left(\mu_{\beta_0}, \mathrm{V}_{\beta_0}\right)$, $\alpha_{p+1} \sim N\left(\mu_{\alpha_0}, \mathrm{V}_{\alpha_0}\right)$ and $h_{p+1} \sim N\left(\mu_{h0}, \mathrm{V}_{h_0}\right)$. The simultaneous correlation between the variables is reflected by the V_a matrix. The assumption of V_a matrix is that block diagonal allows the parameters in β_t matrix to change independently and hence improves efficiency of the Markov chain Monte Carlo (MCMC) algorithm of the model that employed in the Bayesian estimation process.[2]

In the construction of the index based on the weighted sum approach, time-varying impulse-response functions that have been obtained with the TVP-VAR model are used. The weights are calculated with the relative magnitude of the cumulative responses of output gap to index components. Thus, the time-varying weights of short-term interest rate and real exchange rate are calculated with equations $w_{\text{int},t} = \frac{|\beta_{\text{int},t}|}{\left(|\beta_{\text{int},t}| + |\beta_{\text{realer},t}|\right)}$ and $w_{\text{realer},t} = \frac{|\beta_{\text{realer},t}|}{\left(|\beta_{\text{int},t}| + |\beta_{\text{realer},t}|\right)}$, respectively. The index is constructed based on the time-varying weight sums of related variables by calculating the differences between index components and base year values. Thus, the obtained index could be expressed with the equation below:

$$\mathrm{MCI}_t = \sum_{i=1}^{n} w_{i,t}\left(y_{i,t} - y_{i,\text{base}}\right). \tag{7}$$

Empirical Findings

In this study that aimed to estimate the TVP-VAR model and scrutinize the index based on impulse-response functions, the cumulative responses of the output gap to the shocks were initially applied to short-term interest rates and real exchange rates. In calculating the joint posterior distribution of the TVP-VAR model parameters, 1000 iterations were conducted.[3] A three-dimensional graph of time-varying

---

[2]See Carlin and Chib (1995) and Chib (2001) for detailed explanations about the MCMC algorithm.

[3]The joint posterior distributions of the parameters are calculated with a priori distribution reported by Nakajima (2011).

impulse-response functions is presented in Fig. 1.[4] Here, one of the horizontal axes represents time span, and the other reflects the period following short-term interest rate and real exchange rate shocks where $h = 0, 1, 2, \ldots, 24$. An analysis of the responses of economic activity to the short-term interest rate shock, presented in Fig. 1a, demonstrated that all responses following the occurrence of the three periods of shocks and thereafter were negative. A comparison of the magnitude of the responses demonstrated that the responses of the output gap began to decline in the fifth period after the shock and neared zero. The highest positive response of the output gap to short-term interest rate change in the sample period was around 30%, corresponding to the 2001 crisis period. With the adoption of the fully fledged inflation targeting regime by the Central Bank of the Republic of Turkey (CBRT), the interest rate transmission channel to economic activity was functioning efficiently. The reactions of economic activity after the real exchange rate shock are presented in Fig. 1b. An increase in the price-adjusted real exchange rate means a decrease in the nominal exchange rate. Except for the first period, it has been observed that the responses of economic activity to real exchange rate changes are quantitatively lower, compared to interest rate shocks. The negative response of economic activity to the real exchange rate shocks for the entire sample period implied that the exchange rate channel is functioning effectively. It has been determined that the responses of economic activity to real exchange rate shocks decreased in the third period and thereafter. The highest response to the real exchange rate change was observed in 2018 with a decrease of 25%.

It has been observed that the time-varying responses of economic activity to short-term interest rates and real exchange rate shocks are generally sensitive to crisis periods and the CBRT's policy regime changes. The results obtained with the impulse-response functions are consistent with the findings by Çatık and Martin (2012), Sarac and Ucan (2013), Akdeniz and Çatık (2019) and Çatık and Akdeniz (2019).

In the study in which a weighted sum approach was adopted, the time-varying index weights obtained with the TVP-VAR model are presented in Fig. 2. Due to the definition of the weighted sum methodology, the sum of the index weights should be 1. Therefore, the index component weights have to be between 0 and 1. When the index weights are compared, the sum of the index weights of short-term interest rates is higher than that of the exchange rates for the entire period, and this confirms the time-varying impulse-response functions. The index weights obtained are consistent with Şıklar and Doğan (2015) and Açcı and Tasar (2016). However, the weights are not consistent with Süslü and Dişbudak (2012), who found that the relative weight of the exchange rate is higher.

It has been observed that the weight of the interest rate increased after the adoption of the implicit inflation targeting regime. With the liberalization of capital movements in the early 1990s, the weight of the real exchange rate reached the

[4]The lag order in the VAR model is determined based on Akaike information criteria.

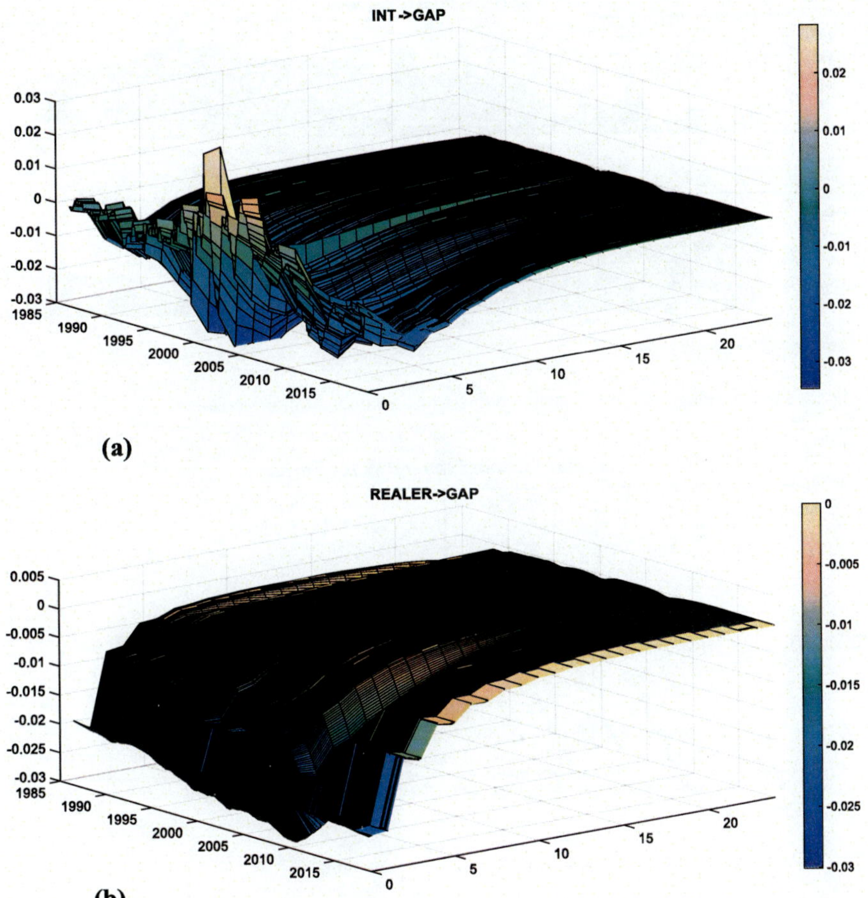

(a)

(b)

Fig. 1 Time-varying cumulative responses of output. Source: Author's creation. (**a**) Time-varying responses of output to interest rate shocks. (**b**) Time-varying responses of output to exchange rate shocks

highest level in the index. In the same period, the index weight of interest rates was quite low.

The MCI based on the weighted sum approach, using the impulse-response functions obtained using the TVP-VAR model, is presented in Fig. 3. The base year value of the index, using the base year of 2006, when the implicit inflation targeting regime was adopted, is 2006 = 100. An upward movement in the index reflects periods of monetary tightening, and a downward movement reflects periods of monetary easing. In Fig. 3, the shaded areas demonstrate that the index has exceeded the base year value and, therefore, the periods of monetary tightening. Light-coloured areas show that the index is below the base year value, indicating monetary easing periods. Moreover, the MCI captures the crisis periods

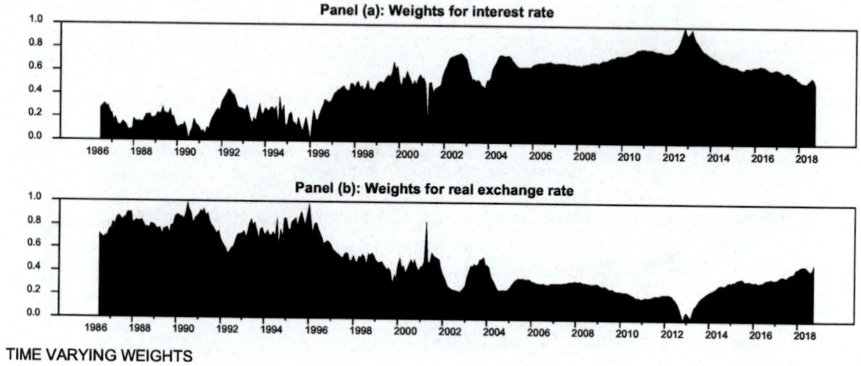

Fig. 2 Time-varying weights of index components. Source: Author's creation

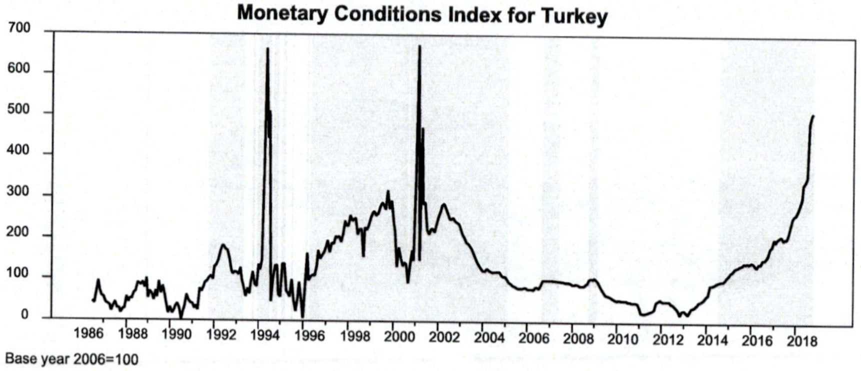

Fig. 3 Monetary conditions index. Source: Author's creation

significantly. Accordingly, the index reached its highest values during the 1994 and 2001 crises, as reported in the study by Şıklar and Doğan (2015). This is mainly due to depreciation of the real exchange rate and hikes in interest rates, in order to defend the domestic currency. During the 1994 crisis, when the fixed exchange rate regime was adopted, the budget and current account imbalances and the serious losses in the real exchange rate led the index to reach its second highest level during the sample period. The highest index value was observed during the February 2001 crisis, due to the overnight borrowing rate that reached 400% and a depreciation in real exchange rates.

Following the 2001 crisis, adopting implicit inflation targeting, switching to a floating exchange rate regime and decreasing risk premiums were the main factors influencing the easing monetary conditions. The transition to a flexible exchange rate regime decreased the exchange rate pass-through while increasing the effectiveness of monetary transmission channels, such as interest and credit channels. Besides global liquidity abundance, structural reforms, carried out within the framework of the 'Transition to the Strong Economy Program', contributed to the easing of monetary conditions. During the period of the 2008 global financial crisis, despite major decreases experienced in economic activity, there were no striking peaks in exchange and interest rates, unlike the previous crises. On the other hand, the expansionary monetary policies, implemented by the developed countries to recover from the crisis, led to an acceleration in capital inflows. Increasing capital flows also caused an appreciation of real exchange rates and a decrease in interest rates.

In December 2015, the Federal Reserve (FED) started to implement a monetary tightening policy which was signalled from May 2013. The Turkish economy exposed a series of negative domestic and external shocks in the second half of 2016 (İlhan 2019: 59–62). In addition to this, a sharp depreciation in exchange rates from the second quarter of 2018 resulted in a re-tightening of monetary conditions. Thus, the index reached the third highest level during the sample period.

Conclusion

In calculating the MCI, developed with the weighted sum methodology for the Turkish economy, time-varying impulse-response functions obtained from the TVP-VAR model were used. The present study that uses the overnight interbank rate and real exchange rate as index components covers the period of 1986:05–2018:10. The TVP-VAR model enables index weights to be changed over time and provides a better reflection of the changes in monetary conditions during economic crises, regime changes and structural arrangements. An analysis of the time-varying structure of the index components demonstrates that the transmission from interest rate to economic activity is quantitatively higher, compared to the exchange rate transmission channel.

The MCI values successfully captured the 1994 and 2001 crisis periods and the monetary tightening experienced during recent periods. Prior to the 2001 crisis, CBRT lacked instrument independence and depreciations of the real exchange rate occurred. Thus, it was observed that, in general, tight monetary conditions prevailed until that time. The index started to decrease from 2001 because of the structural reforms, the adopted implicit inflation targeting regime and global liquidity excess. Signals that the FED would put an end to expansionary monetary policies as of 2013 led the MCI to increase again.

It was observed that the index components of short-term interest rates and real exchange rates changed markedly, due to domestic and external economic developments during the sample period. According to the findings, the interest rate and exchange rate channels were sensitive to the crises and regime changes. This is consistent with the findings reported by Çatık and Martin (2012), Sarac and Ucan (2013), Akdeniz and Çatık (2019) and Çatık and Akdeniz (2019). The index that was constructed in this study could be used as an important indicator to reflect monetary conditions.

Appendix

Table 1 ADF and PP unit root test results

Series	ADF			PP		
	Intercept	Trend and intercept	None	Intercept	Trend and intercept	None
int_t	−4.850***	−6.359***	−2.228**	−8.313***	−10.566***	−4.584***
$realer_t$	−5.653***	−4.401***	−3.469***	−6.682***	−3.915**	−5.339***
gap_t	−7.274***	−7.265***	−7.283***	−14.007***	−13.994***	−14.019***

Notes: ***, ** and * indicate that the null hypothesis is rejected in 1%, 5% and 10% significance levels, respectively. Lag length is determined by the Schwarz information criterion. Bartlett Kernel method is used for spectral estimation in the PP test, and the bandwidth is determined by the Newey-West method

Source: Author's creation

Table 2 Zivot-Andrews unit root test results

Series	Intercept	Breakpoint	Trend	Breakpoint	Trend and intercept	Breakpoint
int_t	−6.944***	2003:05	−6.977***	1994:03	−7.676***	2001:03
$realer_t$	−4.671*	1999:11	−6.546***	1991:04	−6.176***	1990:09
gap_t	−7.508***	2008:10	−7.260***	1998:01	−7.616***	2008:10

Notes: ***, ** and * indicate that the null hypothesis is rejected in 1%, 5% and 10% significance levels, respectively. Lag length is determined by the Akaike information criterion

Source: Author's creation

References

Abubabkar M, Yaaba BN (2013) Post market reform analysis of monetary conditions index for Nigeria. J Econ Sustain Dev 4(14):1

Açcı Y, Tasar İ (2016) An analysis on monetary condition index in Turkey by using structural VAR analysis. Ecoforum 5(9):119–124

Akdeniz C, Çatık AN (2017) Türkiye İçin Finansal Koşulların Bir Analizi: Faktör ve VAR Modellerinden Bulgular [An analysis of financial conditions for Turkey: evidences from factor and VAR models]. Eskişehir Osmangazi Üniversitesi İktisadi ve İdari Bilimler Dergisi 12:99–120

Akdeniz C, Çatık AN (2019) Parasal Aktarım Mekanizmalarının İşleyişinde Finansal Koşulların Önemi: TVP-VAR Modellerinden Bulgular [The importance of financial conditions on the functioning of monetary transmission mechanisms: evidences from TVP-VAR models]. Pamukkale Üniversitesi Sosyal Bilimler Enstitüsü Dergisi 39:73–96

Batini N, Turnbull K (2000) Monetary conditions indices for the UK: a survey, discussion papers 01. Monetary Policy Committee Unit, Bank of England

Carlin BP, Chib S (1995) Bayesian model choice via Markov chain Monte Carlo methods. J R Stat Soc Ser B 57(3):473–484

Çatık AN, Akdeniz C (2019) The evolution of the monetary transmission channels in Turkey: evidence from a TVP-VAR model. Appl Econ Lett 26(13):1072–1079

Çatık AN, Martin C (2012) Macroeconomic transitions and the transmission mechanism: evidence from Turkey. Econ Model 29(4):1440–1449
Chib S (2001) Markov chain Monte Carlo methods: computation and inference. In J. J. Heckman, and E. E. Leamer, Handbook of econometrics. Elsevier, New York 5(57), 3569–3649
Dickey DA, Fuller WA (1981) Likelihood ratio statistics for autoregressive time series with a unit root. Econometrica 49:1057–1072
Duguay P (1994) Empirical evidence on the strength of the monetary transmission mechanism in Canada: an aggregate approach. J Monet Econ 33(1):39–61
Ericsson NR, Jansen ES, Kerbeshian NA, Nymoen R (1998) Interpreting a monetary conditions index in economic policy. In: Bank for International Settlements Conference Papers, vol 6
Freedman C (1994) The use of indicators and of the monetary conditions index in Canada. In: Baliño TJT, Cottarelli C (eds) Frameworks for monetary stability: policy issues and country experiences. International Monetary Fund, Washington, DC, pp 458–476
Gauthier C, Graham C, Liu Y (2004) Financial conditions indexes for Canada. Bank of Canada Working Paper, No: 2004–22
Goodhart C, Hofmann B (2001) Asset prices, financial conditions and the transmission of Monetary Policy. In: Paper prepared for the conference on asset prices, exchange rates, and Monetary Policy, Stanford University
Goodhart C, Hofmann B (2002) Asset prices and the conduct of Monetary policy. Royal Economic Society Annual Conference, No. 88
Hodrick RJ, Prescott EC (1997) Postwar U. S. business cycles: an empirical investigation. J Money Credit Bank 29(1):1–16
İlhan A (2019) Türkiye'de Para Politikası ve Makro İhtiyati Politikanın Karşılıklı Etkileşimi [The interaction between Monetary Policy and Macroprudential Policy in Turkey]. TESAM Akademi Dergisi, Türkiye Ekonomisi Özel Sayısı, 43–71
Kannan R, Sanyal S, Bhoi BB (2006) Monetary conditions index for India. Reserve Bank of India Occasional Papers 27(3):57–86
Kara H, Özlü P, Ünalmış D (2012) Financial conditions indices for the Turkish economy. CBT Research Notes in Economics, No. 2012-31
Kara H, Özlü P, Ünalmış D (2015) Türkiye için Finansal Koşullar Endeksi [Financial conditions indices for the Turkey]. TCMB Çalışma Tebliği, No: 15/13
Kesriyeli M, Koçaker İİ (1999) Monetary conditions index: a monetary policy Indicator for Turkey. The Central Bank of the Republic of Turkey Research Department, Discussion Paper, No: 9908
Knedlik T (2005) Estimating the monetary conditions index for South Africa. Exchange Rate Econometrics Conference, Luxemburg
Koop G (2012) Using VARs and TVP-VARs with many macroeconomic variables. CEJEME 4 (3):143–167
Koop G, Korobilis D (2013) Large time-varying parameter VARs. J Econ 177(2):185–198
Memon IA, Jabeen H (2018) Monetary condition index and its changing transmission on macroeconomic variables. Arab Econ Bus J 13(2):111–124
Montagnoli A, Napolitano O (2006) Financial condition index and interest rate settings: a comparative analysis. Department of Economic Studies, University of Naples "Parthenope", Discussion Paper, No: 2
Nakajima J (2011) Time-varying parameter VAR model with stochastic volatility: an overview of methodology and empirical applications. Monetary Econ Stud 29:107–142
Nakajima J, Watanabe T (2011) Bayesian analysis of time-varying parameter vector autoregressive model with the ordering of variables for the Japanese economy and monetary policy. Global COE Hi-Stat Discussion Paper Series, No: 196, Institute of Economic Research, Hitotsubashi University
Phillips PC, Perron P (1988) Testing for a unit root in time series regression. Biometrika 75 (2):335–346
Poon WC (2010) Augmented MCI: an indicator of monetary policy stance for ASEAN-5? Monash University. Department of Economics Discussion Paper 25(10):1–19

Primiceri GE (2005) Time varying structural vector autoregressions and monetary policy. Rev Econ Stud 72(3):821–852

Sarac TB, Ucan O (2013) The interest rate channel in Turkey: an investigation with Kalman filter approach. Int J Econ Financ Issues 3(4):874–884

Şıklar İ, Doğan B (2015) Monetary condition index with time varying weights: an application to Turkish data. Bus Econ Res 5(1):117–132

Simo-Kengne BD, Miller SM, Gupta R, Aye GC (2015) Time-varying effects of housing and stock returns on U.S. consumption. J Real Estate Financ Econ 50(3):339–354

Süslü B, Dişbudak C (2012) TCMB'nin Para Politikası Duruşunun Alternatif Açıklaması: Parasal Durum Endeksi (MCI) [Alternative Explanations for the Monetary Stance of CBRT: Monetary Condition Index (MCI)]. Yönetim ve Ekonomi 19(2):67–85

Swiston A (2008) A U.S. financial conditions index: putting credit where credit is due. IMF Working Paper Western Hemisphere Department, No: 08/161

Zivot E, Andrews DWK (1992) Further evidence on the great crash, the oil-price shock, and the unit-root hypothesis. J Bus Econ Stat 10(3):251–270

Coşkun Akdeniz is a research assistant at Tekirdağ Namik Kemal University Department of Economics, Turkey. He received his Ph.D. degree in Economics from Ege University. His main research area is non-linear analysis of time series. He has written in indexed journals such as Applied Economic Letters and Resources Policy.

Monetary Policy Regimes, Fiscal Implications, and Policy Interactions Among Developing Economies

Antonio Pacifico

Introduction

Macroeconomic financial linkages and policy evaluations have given new stimulus to the study of business cycles, international spillover effects, and policy-making. In addition, the evaluation of interdependencies, heterogeneities, and co-movements among different sectors and countries has become a modern requirement. Recently, there has been a considerable amount of analysis of the performance of monetary policy rules, prompted in part by the adoption of explicit inflation targets and the granting of independence to central banks in a number of countries [see, e.g., Bernanke and Mihov (1998), Clarida et al. (1999, 2000), Eichenbaum and Evans (1995), and Lubik and Schorfheide (2004)]. Even economic-financial interdependencies, often not directly observed, and the transmission of certain shocks, often idiosyncratic, now need to be evaluated from a global perspective and in a unified framework for either developed or developing economies [see, e.g., Canova and Ciccarelli (2009), Canova et al. (2012), Ciccarelli et al. (2018), Pacifico (2019a, b)]. Later, with the participation of emerging markets in global finance, the literature on international transmission of shocks and on business cycles synchronization now occupies a very large share of the field of international finance and macroeconomics.

From a methodological point of view, this study aims to contribute to the literature on multicountry (dynamic) panel data models for applied macroeconomic-financial analysis and the effects of monetary policy and fiscal implications in emerging market economies. In recent years, several theoretical and applied models have been designed to infer and evaluate idiosyncratic shocks

A. Pacifico (✉)
Department of Political Science & CEFOP-LUISS, LUISS Guido Carli University, Rome, Italy
e-mail: apacifico@luiss.it

B. Adıgüzel Mercangöz (ed.), *Handbook of Research on Emerging Theories, Models, and Applications of Financial Econometrics*,
https://doi.org/10.1007/978-3-030-54108-8_10

across units and time periods [see, e.g., Lane and Milesi-Ferretti (2007), Mastrogiacomo et al. (2017), Canova and Marrinan (1998), and Ciccarelli and Rebucci (2007)] and study the dynamic effects of different monetary policy regimes on financial markets, inflation, personal consumption, and real economic growth during the most recent recession and postcrisis consolidation [see, e.g., Banbura et al. (2010), Bernanke et al. (2005), Forni et al. (2005), Obstfeld et al. (2005), Shambaugh (2004), Uribe (1997), and Fredj et al. (2016)]. These studies have generated four main findings. First, there are relevant macroeconomic-financial interdependencies among countries, which have relinquished independent monetary and exchange rate policies. Second, there may still be a substantial degree of heterogeneity, with some common behaviors, in economic financial linkages among countries, and those linkages may have changed over time due to different transmission channels. Third, there is a need to allow for serious structural reforms for the entire socioeconomic system to deal with the ineffectiveness of monetary policy during the recent financial crisis. Finally, different monetary policy regimes lead to different equilibrium levels of real economic growth, and thus they need to be evaluated with care. Nevertheless, most of these studies have ignored several issues that need to be considered when dealing with multicountry setups, such as the behavior of fiscal policy when accounting for macroeconomic-financial linkages, the causality between real and financial variables, relevant interactions between monetary and fiscal policy, and the reasons underlying heterogeneous dynamics and reactions among countries due to an unexpected shock. Such carelessness has rendered functional form misspecification and heterogeneity issues topics that need to be implemented with care.

The approach and the empirical implementation aim to give a valid contribution to such topics. More precisely, the author builds on Pacifico (2019b) and extends the time-varying Structural Panel Bayesian Vector Autoregressive (SPBVAR) model in order to deal with model misspecification and unobserved heterogeneity problems when jointly modeling and quantifying multicountry data using the information contained in a large set of endogenous macroeconomic-financial variables. The author defines a hierarchical prior specification strategy [see, e.g., Koop (1996), Canova and Ciccarelli (2004,2009), and Ciccarelli et al. (2018)] and Markov Chain Monte Carlo (MCMC) implementations [see, e.g., Chib (1995, 1996), Chib and Albert (1993), Chib and Jeliazkov (2001), and Pesaran and Shinb (1998)] to calculate posterior distributions of Conditional Generalized Impulse Response Functions (CGIRFs) and Conditional Forecasts (CFs) reacting to unexpected perturbations in the innovations of the factors in the system. Bayesian methods are used to reduce the dimensionality of the model, structure the time variations, and evaluate issues of endogeneity. The author also uses a Structural Normal Linear Regression (SNLR) model in order to work with smaller systems in which the regressors are endogenous, directly measured, and time-varying linear combinations of the right-hand variables of the time-varying Extended Structural Panel Bayesian Vector Autoregressive (ESPBVAR) model. The author also accounts for structural bilateral net spillover effects (BNSEs) and systemic contributions (SCs) in order to quantify structural spillovers and thus to evaluate interdependencies, co-movements, and heterogeneities among different countries and sectors [see, e.g., Pacifico (2019a, b) and Pacifico (2020)]. The former incorporate feedback effects from the impulse variables and temporary or persistent long-run effects of a potential shock. The SC index represents the amplification contribution of an impulse variable to the response variable, and the index is able to capture sequential features associated with systemic events.

An empirical application is developed by accounting for a pool of emerging market countries, with particular emphasis to the recent recession and postcrisis consolidation. In this study, the author focuses on the latest two alternative monetary policy regimes that have been in place since the 1990 [see, for instance, Kallianiotis (2019)]: (1) the inflation stabilization era (ISE) from 1994 to 2008 and (2) the zero interest rate era (ZIRE) from 2008 to 2015. The author also considers two additional periods: (1) 2006–2009 to investigate possible commonality between financial markets and real economy during the recent crisis and (2) 2010–2016 to evaluate fiscal implications during postcrisis consolidation. The analysis focuses on three main questions. First, the author investigates how interactions between fiscal and monetary policy regimes affect the benefits of consolidation among countries. Second, the author investigates how additional shock transmissions affect the spread and intensification of structural spillovers in the real economy and financial markets. Third, the author assesses the extent to which economic financial linkages matter when evaluating the effectiveness of monetary policy regimes and fiscal implications.

The empirical analysis is robust and consistent with the more recent international business cycle studies, which recognize the importance of (1) accounting for both group-specific and global factors when evaluating cross-country spillovers [see, e.g., Canova and Marrinan (1998) and Forni et al. (2005)], (2) separating common shocks from the propagation of country-specific and variable-specific shocks when dealing with multicountry setups [see, e.g., Ciccarelli et al. (2018) and Canova et al. (2012)], and (3) the relevance of additional transmission channels and economic-financial issues when studying co-movements and interdependencies among different countries and sectors [see, e.g., Pacifico (2019a, b) and Pacifico (2020)].

The remainder of this paper is organized as follows. "Background Review" section presents a background literature on emerging economies. "Econometric Model" section introduces the econometric model and the estimation procedure. "Dynamic Analysis" section outlines the dynamic analysis and the structural spillovers' framework. "Data Description and Empirical Model" section presents the data and the empirical analysis. "International Business Cycles and Shock Transmission" section evaluates the transmission of international shocks among countries and sectors by accounting for both monetary policy regimes and fiscal implications. "Heterogeneity and Policy Interactions During the Great Recession and Post-Crisis Consolidation" section outlines the evolution of structural spillover effects during the recent recession and postcrisis consolidation highlighting policy implications for decision-makers. The final section contains some concluding remarks.

Background Review

The most promising markets for doing business in the future, for the world's most competitive companies, are the so-called emerging market economies (EMEs). According to the US government estimates, the EMEs are going to double their share of global GDP in next 20 years, from 10.2% to 20.7%. As industrialized countries continue to mature (estimated growth at average of 2% per year), EMEs, which express high rate of growth (12% per year), have huge room for extreme growth, and have become increasingly more attractive and promising for Western multinational companies.

Even though the word "Emerging Market Economies" is an often used word in the international business literature, there is not a clear definition of them. For example, Cavusgil (1997) refers to EMEs as all high-growth developing countries representing attractive business opportunities for Western firms and sharing remarkable features in terms of economic potentials. Miller (1998) defines that all EMEs are similar in their potential for future growth, where these forms of economic stimulus (attracting new technologies, foreign investment, or external participation in their commercial affairs) occur only in countries with policies conductive to increased growth. Thus, it is this opportunity for future market expansion that most distinguishes an emerging economy from one normally associated with less developed countries. Arnold and Quelch (1998) highlight that an emerging market is a country making an effort to change and improve its economy with the goal of raising its performance to that of the world's more advanced nations.

Generally speaking, emerging market economies (EMEs) represent each country characterized by the following criteria: (i) lower level of economic development (less-developed country), expressed in GDP per capita; (ii) transitional economy, in which a government does an attempt to create a framework of a market economy through an adequate economic and political reforms; (iii) high rate of growth, expressed through GDP growth rate; and (iv) a huge room for future growth, expressed through difference between obtained level of economic development and an average GDP of developed countries.

The Morgan Stanley Capital International Emerging Market Index (MSCI Index) lists 24 countries. They are Brazil, Chile, China, Colombia, Czech Republic, Egypt, Greece, Hungary, India, Indonesia, Korea, Malaysia, Mexico, Morocco, Peru, Philippines, Poland, Russia, South Africa, South Korea, Taiwan, Thailand, Turkey, and United Arab Emirates. Other sources also list another seven countries as falling into the emerging market category. They include Argentina, Hong Kong, Jordan, Kuwait, Saudi Arabia, Singapore, and Vietnam. The main emerging market powerhouses are China and India. Together, these two countries are home to 40% of the world's labor force and population. In 2017, their combined economic output was greater than either the European Union or the United.

In the past few decades, there has been a significant process of international financial integration characterized by the rising importance of international financial flows and larger gross external assets and liabilities. Following the extraordinarily expansionary monetary policies of major advanced countries in the aftermath of the Global Financial Crisis from 2007, many emerging market economies experienced a large surge of capital inflow. They are moving away from their traditional economies that have relied on agriculture and the export of raw materials. Thus, emerging market economies are expected to play a crucial role in international trade and finance as well as to contribute significantly to the global economic growth. Assets issued by emerging financial markets have been selected by both individual and professional investors to design dedicated investment portfolio strategies. However, while it is common that emerging market economies can provide substantial diversification benefits at international level, their financial characteristics and links to the global economy tend to be country specific, owing to an important degree of heterogeneity across these markets in terms of market size, financial depth, and international investment barriers, among others. The disparity between regional and global integration processes is also a source of differences in the functioning of emerging markets economies and the behavior of their financial markets.

Econometric Model

Model Estimation

The author extends a time-varying SPBVAR model developed by Pacifico (2019b) including lagged endogenous variables, a set of not directly observed variables, a set of proxy[1] variables, and an additional set of lagged endogenous variables in order to highlight policy interactions when studying international macroeconomic-financial linkages. The model has the form:

$$Y_{i,t}^{m} = A_{i,0} + \sum_{\lambda=1}^{l} \times \left[A_{it,j}^{m}(L) Y_{i,t-\lambda}^{m} + B_{it,j}^{q}(L) W_{i,t-\lambda}^{q} + \widetilde{\ddot{B}_{it,j}^{q}}(L) \widetilde{\ddot{W}_{i,t-\lambda}^{q}} + C_{it,j}^{\xi}(L) Z_{i,t-\lambda}^{\xi} \right] + \varepsilon_{it}, \quad (1)$$

where the subscripts $i, j = 1, 2, \ldots, N$ are country indices, $t = 1, 2, \ldots, T$ denotes time, L stands for the lag operator, and $A_{i,\,0}$ is a [NM $*$ 1] vector of intercepts for each i. Here, $A_{it,\,j}$, $B_{it,\,j}$, and $C_{it,\,j}$ are matrices of coefficients for each pair of countries (i, j) for a given m, q, and ξ, respectively, $Y_{i,\,t\,-\,\lambda}$, $W_{i,\,t\,-\,\lambda}$, and $Z_{i,\,t\,-\,\lambda}$ are vectors of lagged variables of interest, directly observed variables, and not directly observed variables for each i for a given m, q, and ξ, respectively, and $\varepsilon_{it} \sim i.\ i.\ d.\ N(0, \Sigma)$ is a

[1] A proxy variable is an easily measurable variable that is used in place of a variable that cannot be (directly) measured or is difficult to measure.

vector of disturbance terms.[2] The additional term $\ddot{B}^{\widetilde{q}}_{it,j}(L)\,\ddot{W}^{\widetilde{q}}_{i,t-\lambda}$ denotes the main implementation in this study including a set of further lagged directly observed variables in order to investigate policy interactions and interconnections among real economy and financial markets. More precisely, $\ddot{B}_{it,j}$ is an $[N\widetilde{Q} * N\widetilde{Q}]$ matrix of coefficients for each pair of countries (i, j) for a given $\widetilde{q}$, and $\ddot{W}_{i,t-\lambda}$ is an $[N\widetilde{Q} * 1]$ vector including the additional lagged variables for each i for a given $\widetilde{q}$. Finally, the subscripts $\lambda = 1, 2, \ldots, l$ are lags for each of the $m = 1, 2, \ldots, M$ endogenous variables, $q = 1, 2, \ldots, Q$ (directly) observed variables to account for additional transmission channels, $\widetilde{q} = 1, 2, \ldots, \widetilde{Q}$ (directly) observed variables to account for monetary and fiscal policy interactions and macroeconomic financial linkages, and $\xi = 1, 2, \ldots, \Xi$ proxy variables to account for economic-financial interdependencies and macroeconomic imbalances during fiscal consolidation. Here, all variables in the system are endogenous and time-varying.

In Eq. (1), the dynamic relationships are allowed to be unit specific, and all coefficients vary over time. In addition, whenever the matrices $A_{it,\,j}(L)$, $B_{it,\,j}(L)$, $\ddot{B}_{it,j}(L)$, and $C_{it,\,j}(L)$ differ[3] for some L, cross-unit lagged interdependencies matter, and thus dynamic feedback and interactions among countries and variables are possible. Thus, the framework of the model (1) makes it able to connect the empirical results to the existing literature and contemporaneous developments when quantifying international business cycles and evaluating policy interactions and conditional forecasting. Nevertheless, even if this feature adds flexibility to the specification, it is very costly. Indeed, the number of coefficients is increased by $N\left(M + Q + \widetilde{Q} + \Xi\right)l$ factors.

Let $k = N[M + Q + \widetilde{Q} + \Xi]\ l$ be the number of all matrix coefficients in each equation of the ESPBVAR model for each pair of countries (i, j). A $[1 * k]$ vector $X_t = \left(I, Y'^{m}_{i,t-1}, Y'^{m}_{i,t-2}, \ldots, Y'^{m}_{i,t-l}, W'^{q}_{i,t-1}, W'^{q}_{i,t-2}, \ldots, W'^{q}_{i,t-l}, \ddot{W}'^{\widetilde{q}}_{i,t-1}, \ddot{W}'^{\widetilde{q}}_{i,t-2}, \ldots, \ddot{W}'^{\widetilde{q}}_{i,t-l}, Z'^{\xi}_{i,t-1}, Z'^{\xi}_{i,t-2}, \ldots Z'^{\xi}_{i,t-l}\right)'$ can be defined, and it contains all lagged variables in the system for each i. Then, I define an $[NMk * 1]$ vector $\gamma^{k}_{it,j} = vec\left(g^{k}_{it,j}\right)$ containing all columns, stacked into a vector,[4] of the matrices $A_t(L), B_t(L), \ddot{B}_t(L)$, and $C_t(L)$ for each pair of countries (i, j) for a given k, with $g^{k}_{it,j} = \left(A'_{i,0}, A^{1'}_{it,j}, A^{2'}_{it,j}, \ldots, A^{M'}_{it,j}, B^{1'}_{it,j}, B^{2'}_{it,j}, \ldots, B^{Q'}_{it,j}, \ddot{B}^{1'}_{it,j}, \ddot{B}^{2'}_{it,j}, \ldots, \ddot{B}^{\widetilde{Q}'}_{it,j}, C^{1'}_{it,j}, C^{2'}_{it,j}, \ldots, C^{\Xi'}_{it,j}\right)'$, and $\gamma_t = \left(\gamma'_{1t}, \gamma'_{2t}, \ldots, \gamma'_{Nt}\right)'$ denoting the time-varying coefficient vectors, stacked

[2]See, for instance, Pacifico (2019b).

[3]More precisely, if the elements of $A_t(L), B_t(L), \ddot{B}_t(L)$, and $C_t(L)$ are stacked over i, it is possible to obtain matrices that are not block diagonal for at least some l.

[4]The vec operator transforms a matrix into a vector by stacking the columns of the matrix, one underneath the other.

for i, for each country-variable pair. With these specifications, the author can express the model (1) in a simultaneous equation form:

$$Y_t = \left(I_{NM} \bigotimes X_t\right)\gamma_t + E_t, \tag{2}$$

where $Y_t = \left(Y_{1t}^{m'}, \ldots, Y_{Nt}^{m'}\right)'$ and $E_t = \left(\varepsilon'_{1t}, \ldots, \varepsilon'_{Nt}\right)'$ are $[NM * 1]$ vector containing the observable variables of interest and the random disturbances of the model for each i for a given m, respectively. In model (2), there is no subscript i since all lagged variables in the system are stacked in X_t.

Now, because the coefficient vectors in γ_t vary in different time periods for each country-variable pair and there are more coefficients than data points, it is impossible to eliminate γ_t. To cope with the problem of dimensionality, the author adapts the framework in Pacifico (2019b) and assumes γ_t to have the following factor structure:

$$\gamma_t = \sum_{f=1}^{F} G_f * \beta_{ft} + u_t \quad \text{with} \quad u_t\tilde{N}(0, \Sigma_u), \tag{3}$$

where $F \ll NMk$ and $\dim(\beta_{ft}) \ll \dim(\gamma_t)$ by construction; $G_f = [G_1, G_2, \ldots, G_F]$ are $[NMk * \kappa^f]$ matrices obtained by multiplying the matrix coefficients $(g_{it,j}^k)$ stacked in the vector γ_t by conformable matrices D_f with elements equal to zero and one, where κ^f is a numerical index that depends on the typology of the factorization, u_t is an $[NMk * 1]$ vector of unmodeled variations present in γ_t, $E\left(u_t u_t'\right) = \Sigma_u = \Sigma_e \otimes \mathrm{V}$, where Σ_e is the covariance matrix of the vector E_t, and $V = (\sigma^2 I_k)$ as in Kadiyala and Karlsson (1997). In the framework, unobserved heterogeneity and model specification are absorbed in the $[\kappa^f * 1]$ time-varying coefficient vectors β_{ft}. They are observable smooth linear functions of the lagged variables and thus can be easily estimated with a gain in efficiency.

The idea is to shrink γ_t to a much smaller dimensional vector β_t, with $\beta_t = \left(\beta'_{1t}, \beta'_{2t}, \ldots, \beta'_{Ft}\right)'$, containing all regression coefficients stacked into a vector. In this way, further investigations (e.g., additional idiosyncratic shock transmission, economic-institutional linkages, and unobserved heterogeneity among countries and sectors due to unexpected shock) can be performed. Finally, the factorization of γ_t becomes exact as long as σ^2 converges to zero.

In Eq. (3), all factors are permitted to be time-varying, and thus time-variant structures can be obtained via implementations of MCMC algorithms. Moreover, time variations in the variance of shocks u_t to the factors β_{ft} are also allowed so that Y_t can capture possible heterogeneity among countries and variables. Running Eqs. (2) and (3) for Eq. (1), the factorization is:

$$\sum_{f=1}^{F} G_f * \beta_{ft} = G_1 * \beta_{1t} + G_2 * \beta_{2t} + \ldots + G_F * \beta_{Ft}. \tag{4}$$

The conformation of the ESPBVAR model and the exact form of the β_{ft}'s and the G_f's are explained in "Model Features" subsection.

The structural framework targets the potential addition of any and countless time-varying coefficient vectors to any time period, depending on the needs of the investigation. More precisely, according to the empirical implementations, one may be interested in adding (i) a set of lagged observable variables to the matrix $B_{it,j}(L)$ to account for the role of transmission channels, which allow shocks to spill over; (ii) an additional set of lagged observable variables to the matrix $\ddot{B}_{it,j}(L)$ to jointly investigate monetary policy effects and fiscal implications among countries and sectors; and (iii) a set of lagged proxy variables in the matrix $C_{it,j}(L)$ to account for economic-institutional implications when identifying shock transmission.

Given the factorization in Eq. (4), the reduced-form ESPBVAR model in Eq. (2) can be transformed into a Structural Normal Linear Regression model with an error covariance matrix of Inverse-Wishart (IW) distribution.[5] By Eqs. (2) and (3), the SNLR model can be written as:

$$Y_t = \Theta_t \left(\sum_{f=1}^{F} G_f \beta_{ft} + u_t \right) + E_t \equiv \chi_{ft} \beta_{ft} + \eta_t \quad \text{with} \quad \Theta_t = \left(I_{NM} \bigotimes X_t \right), \tag{5}$$

where Θ_t contains all lagged time-varying variables in the system by construction, $\chi_{ft} \equiv \Theta_{ft} G_{ft}$ is an $[NM * \kappa^f]$ matrix that stacks all coefficients and their possible interactions in the ESPBVAR model in Eq. (1), with $\chi_t = \text{diag}\left(\chi'_{1t}, \chi'_{2t}, \ldots, \chi'_{Ft}\right)$, and $\eta_t \equiv \Theta_{ft} u_t + E_t \sim N(0, \sigma_t * \Sigma_u)$ has a particular heteroskedastic covariance matrix that needs to be taken into account, with $\sigma_t = \left(I_N + \sigma^2 \Theta'_t \Theta_t\right)$. If the factorization in Eq. (4) is exact, $\eta_t \tilde{N}\left(0, \ddot{\Sigma}\right)$, with $\ddot{\Sigma} = \text{diag}\left(\Sigma'_e, \Sigma'_e, \ldots, \Sigma'_e\right)$, depends on the only disturbances contained in E_t. Thus, it is uncorrelated with the regressors, and classical OLS can be used to estimate the vector β_t and thus the vector γ_t. The correlation tends to decrease as k increases, and consistency is ensured as T grows.

Model Features

To illustrate the conformation of the time-varying ESPBVAR and the exact form of the β_{ft}'s and the D_f's in Eq. (3), suppose there are $M = 2$ endogenous variables,

[5] See, for instance, Pacifico (2019b).

$Q = \Xi = 2$ observable and hidden variables, and $\widetilde{Q} = 2$ additional (directly) observable variables that vary over time for every $N = 2$ countries. For convenience, the author supposes one lag and no intercept. Thus, the ESPBVAR in Eq. (1) assumes the form:

$$\begin{pmatrix} Y_{11,t} \\ Y_{21,t} \\ Y_{12,t} \\ Y_{22,t} \end{pmatrix} = \begin{pmatrix} A_{11,11} & A_{11,21} & A_{11,12} & A_{11,22} \\ A_{21,11} & A_{21,21} & A_{21,12} & A_{21,22} \\ A_{12,11} & A_{12,21} & A_{12,12} & A_{12,22} \\ A_{22,11} & A_{22,21} & A_{22,12} & A_{22,22} \end{pmatrix} \begin{pmatrix} Y_{11,t-1} \\ Y_{21,t-1} \\ Y_{12,t-1} \\ Y_{22,t-1} \end{pmatrix}$$
$$+ \begin{pmatrix} B_{11,11} & B_{11,21} & B_{11,12} & B_{11,22} \\ B_{21,11} & B_{21,21} & B_{21,12} & B_{21,22} \\ B_{12,11} & B_{12,21} & B_{12,12} & B_{12,22} \\ B_{22,11} & B_{22,21} & B_{22,12} & B_{22,22} \end{pmatrix} \begin{pmatrix} W_{11,t-1} \\ W_{21,t-1} \\ W_{12,t-1} \\ W_{22,t-1} \end{pmatrix}$$
$$+ \begin{pmatrix} \ddot{B}_{11,11} & \ddot{B}_{11,21} & \ddot{B}_{11,12} & \ddot{B}_{11,22} \\ \ddot{B}_{21,11} & \ddot{B}_{21,21} & \ddot{B}_{21,12} & \ddot{B}_{21,22} \\ \ddot{B}_{12,11} & \ddot{B}_{12,21} & \ddot{B}_{12,12} & \ddot{B}_{12,22} \\ \ddot{B}_{22,11} & \ddot{B}_{22,21} & \ddot{B}_{22,12} & \ddot{B}_{22,22} \end{pmatrix} \begin{pmatrix} \ddot{W}_{11,t-1} \\ \ddot{W}_{21,t-1} \\ \ddot{W}_{12,t-1} \\ \ddot{W}_{22,t-1} \end{pmatrix}$$
$$+ \begin{pmatrix} C_{11,11} & C_{11,21} & C_{11,12} & C_{11,22} \\ C_{21,11} & C_{21,21} & C_{21,12} & C_{21,22} \\ C_{12,11} & C_{12,21} & C_{12,12} & C_{12,22} \\ C_{22,11} & C_{22,21} & C_{22,12} & C_{22,22} \end{pmatrix} \begin{pmatrix} Z_{11,t-1} \\ Z_{21,t-1} \\ Z_{12,t-1} \\ Z_{22,t-1} \end{pmatrix} + \begin{pmatrix} \varepsilon_{11,t} \\ \varepsilon_{21,t} \\ \varepsilon_{12,t} \\ \varepsilon_{22,t} \end{pmatrix} \quad (6)$$

Let $\gamma_{it,j}^{k} = \left(vec\left(A'_{im,j\rho}\right), vec\left(B'_{iq,j\varpi}\right), vec\left(\ddot{B}'_{\widetilde{iq},j\ddot{\varpi}}\right), vec\left(C'_{i\xi,j\varphi}\right)\right)$ be the [64 $*$ 1] vector containing all columns (stacked) of the matrices $A_t(L)$, $B_t(L)$, $\ddot{B}_t(L)$, and $C_t(L)$ for each pair of countries (i, j), with $(\rho, \varpi, \ddot{\varpi}, \varphi)$ denoting the variables in each equation observed for j and independent of i, and let $X_t = \left(Y'_{im,t-1}, W'_{iq,t-1}, \ddot{W}'_{\widetilde{iq},t-1}, Z'_{i\xi,t-1}\right)' = (Y'_{11,t-1}, Y'_{21,t-1}, Y'_{12,t-1}, Y'_{22,t-1}, W'_{11,t-1}, W'_{21,t-1}, W'_{12,t-1}, W'_{22,t-1}, \ddot{W}'_{11,t-1}, \ddot{W}'_{21,t-1}, \ddot{W}'_{12,t-1}, \ddot{W}'_{22,t-1}, Z'_{11,t-1}, Z'_{21,t-1}, Z'_{12,t-1}, Z'_{22,t-1})'$ be the [1 $*$ 16] vector containing all lagged variables in the system for each i for a given k, with $k = 2$ [2 + 2 + 2 + 2].

According to the more recent studies of international business cycles and spillover effects [see, e.g., Ciccarelli et al. (2018), Canova and Marrinan (1998), and Canova et al. (2012)], it is typical for authors to define a country-specific indicator for Y_t for each i, a variable-specific indicator for Y_t for each m, and a common indicator for Y_t for each pair of countries and variables (i, m).

In this example, according to the empirical implementation in this study, the author assesses three additional terms in the factorization: (i) an indicator to account for the role of additional transmission channels (e.g., in $W_{iq,\ t\ -\ 1}$), the impact of international macroeconomic-financial interdependencies (e.g., in $Z_{i\xi,\ t\ -\ 1}$) in driving the transmission of country-specific shocks, and monetary and fiscal policy interactions (e.g., in $\ddot{W}_{i\tilde{q},t-1}$) when studying dynamic macroeconomic-financial data; (ii) an indicator to investigate heterogeneity, interdependence, and commonality among all lagged variable $(Y_{m,t-1}, W_{q,t-1}, \ddot{W}_{\tilde{q},t-1}, Z_{\xi,t-1})$ that affect shock transmission; and (iii) an indicator to highlight different reactions and co-movements among countries and variables $(Y_{im,t-1}, W_{iq,t-1}, \ddot{W}_{i\tilde{q},t-1}, Z_{i\xi,t-1})$ due to unexpected shock.

The factorization in Eq. (3) becomes:

$$\gamma_t = \sum_{f=1}^{5} G_f * \beta_{ft} + u_t = \sum_{f=1}^{5} \left(g_{it,j}^k * D_f\right)\beta_{ft} + u_t, \tag{7}$$

where u_t is a [64 $*$ 1] vector capturing unaccounted features, $g_{it,j}^k$ is a [64 $*$ 1] vector containing all matrix coefficients, stacked in the vector γ_t, for each pair of countries (i, j) for a given k, and, stacking for t, $\beta_f = (\beta_1', \beta_2', \beta_3', \beta_4', \beta_5')$ is a [15 $*$ 1] vector containing all time-varying coefficient vectors to be estimated. Thus, the factors $\beta_{1t} = (\beta_{1t,\ 1}, \beta_{1t,\ 2})$, $\beta_{2t} = (\beta_{2t,\ 1}, \beta_{2t,\ 2})$, and $\beta_{3t} = (\beta_{3t,\ 1}, \beta_{3t,\ 2})$ are [N $*$ 1] mutually orthogonal vectors capturing movements in γ_t that are country-specific; the factor $\beta_{4t} = (\beta_{4t,\ 1}, \beta_{4t,\ 2}, \beta_{4t,\ 3}, \beta_{4t,\ 4}, \beta_{4t,\ 5}, \beta_{4t,\ 6})$ is an [M_υ $*$ 1] mutually orthogonal vector capturing movements in γ_t that are variable-specific, where $M_\upsilon = (M_{\upsilon1}, M_{\upsilon2}, M_{\upsilon3}, M_{\upsilon4}, M_{\upsilon5}, M_{\upsilon6}) = 6$ denotes the number of variable groups; the factor $\beta_{5t} = (\beta_{5t,\ 1}, \beta_{5t,\ 2}, \beta_{5t,\ 3})$ is an [M_c $*$ 1] mutually orthogonal vector capturing movements in γ_t that are common among countries and variables, where $M_c = (M_{c1}, M_{c2}, M_{c3}) = 3$ denotes the number of common groups. Letting $i_1 = (1, 0, 1, 0)'$, $i_2 = (0, 1, 0, 1)'$, $i_3 = (1, 1, 1, 1)'$, $i_4 = (0, 0, 0, 0)'$, $i_5 = (1, 1, 0, 0)'$, and $i_6 = (0, 0, 1, 1)'$, the conformable matrices D_f in Eq. (7) can be constructed in this way:

$$D_1 = \begin{pmatrix} i_1 & i_2 \\ i_1 & i_2 \\ i_1 & i_2 \\ i_1 & i_2 \\ i_4 & i_4 \\ i_4 & i_4 \\ i_4 & i_4 \\ i_4 & i_4 \\ i_4 & i_4 \\ i_4 & i_4 \\ i_4 & i_4 \\ i_4 & i_4 \\ i_4 & i_4 \\ i_4 & i_4 \\ i_4 & i_4 \\ i_4 & i_4 \end{pmatrix}; D_2 = \begin{pmatrix} i_1 & i_2 \\ i_1 & i_2 \\ i_1 & i_2 \\ i_1 & i_2 \\ i_1 & i_2 \\ i_1 & i_2 \\ i_1 & i_2 \\ i_1 & i_2 \\ i_4 & i_4 \\ i_4 & i_4 \\ i_4 & i_4 \\ i_4 & i_4 \\ i_1 & i_2 \\ i_1 & i_2 \\ i_1 & i_2 \\ i_1 & i_2 \end{pmatrix}; D_3 = \begin{pmatrix} i_1 & i_2 \\ i_1 & i_2 \\ i_1 & i_2 \\ i_1 & i_2 \\ i_1 & i_2 \\ i_1 & i_2 \\ i_1 & i_2 \\ i_1 & i_2 \\ i_1 & i_2 \\ i_1 & i_2 \\ i_1 & i_2 \\ i_1 & i_2 \\ i_1 & i_2 \\ i_1 & i_2 \\ i_1 & i_2 \\ i_1 & i_2 \end{pmatrix};$$

$$D_4 = \begin{pmatrix} i_5 & i_6 i_5 & i_6 i_5 & i_6 \\ i_5 & i_6 i_5 & i_6 i_5 & i_6 \\ i_5 & i_6 i_5 & i_6 i_5 & i_6 \\ i_5 & i_6 i_5 & i_6 i_5 & i_6 \\ i_4 & i_4 i_5 & i_6 i_5 & i_6 \\ i_4 & i_4 i_5 & i_6 i_5 & i_6 \\ i_4 & i_4 i_5 & i_6 i_5 & i_6 \\ i_4 & i_4 i_5 & i_6 i_5 & i_6 \\ i_4 & i_4 i_4 & i_4 i_5 & i_6 \\ i_4 & i_4 i_4 & i_4 i_5 & i_6 \\ i_4 & i_4 i_4 & i_4 i_5 & i_6 \\ i_4 & i_4 i_4 & i_4 i_5 & i_6 \\ i_4 & i_4 i_5 & i_6 i_5 & i_6 \\ i_4 & i_4 i_5 & i_6 i_5 & i_6 \\ i_4 & i_4 i_5 & i_6 i_5 & i_6 \\ i_4 & i_4 i_5 & i_6 i_5 & i_6 \end{pmatrix}; D_5 = \begin{pmatrix} i_3 & i_3 & i_3 \\ i_3 & i_3 & i_3 \\ i_3 & i_3 & i_3 \\ i_3 & i_3 & i_3 \\ i_4 & i_3 & i_3 \\ i_4 & i_3 & i_3 \\ i_4 & i_3 & i_3 \\ i_4 & i_3 & i_3 \\ i_4 & i_4 & i_3 \\ i_4 & i_4 & i_3 \\ i_4 & i_4 & i_3 \\ i_4 & i_4 & i_3 \\ i_4 & i_3 & i_3 \\ i_4 & i_3 & i_3 \\ i_4 & i_3 & i_3 \\ i_4 & i_3 & i_3 \end{pmatrix}. \tag{8}$$

Thus, following some arrangements (as described in "Econometric Model" section), the SNLR model in Eq. (5) becomes:

$$\begin{pmatrix} Y_{11,t} \\ Y_{21,t} \\ Y_{12,t} \\ Y_{22,t} \end{pmatrix} = \begin{pmatrix} \chi_{1t,1} & 0 \\ 0 & \chi_{1t,2} \\ \chi_{1t,1} & 0 \\ 0 & \chi_{1t,2} \end{pmatrix} \begin{pmatrix} \beta_{1t,1} \\ \beta_{1t,2} \end{pmatrix} + \begin{pmatrix} \chi_{2t,1} & 0 \\ 0 & \chi_{2t,2} \\ \chi_{2t,1} & 0 \\ 0 & \chi_{2t,2} \end{pmatrix} \begin{pmatrix} \beta_{2t,1} \\ \beta_{2t,2} \end{pmatrix}$$

$$+ \begin{pmatrix} \chi_{3t,1} & 0 \\ 0 & \chi_{3t,2} \\ \chi_{3t,1} & 0 \\ 0 & \chi_{3t,2} \end{pmatrix}$$

$$\times \begin{pmatrix} \beta_{3t,1} \\ \beta_{3t,2} \end{pmatrix} + \begin{pmatrix} \chi_{4t,1} & 0 & \chi_{4t,3} & 0 & \chi_{4t,5} & 0 \\ 0 & \chi_{4t,2} & 0 & \chi_{4t,4} & 0 & \chi_{4t,6} \\ \chi_{4t,1} & 0 & \chi_{4t,3} & 0 & \chi_{4t,5} & 0 \\ 0 & \chi_{4t,2} & 0 & \chi_{4t,4} & 0 & \chi_{4t,6} \end{pmatrix} \begin{pmatrix} \beta_{4t,1} \\ \beta_{4t,2} \\ \beta_{4t,3} \\ \beta_{4t,4} \\ \beta_{4t,5} \\ \beta_{4t,6} \end{pmatrix}$$

$$+ \begin{pmatrix} \chi_{5t,1} & \chi_{5t,2} & \chi_{5t,3} \\ \chi_{5t,1} & \chi_{5t,2} & \chi_{5t,3} \\ \chi_{5t,1} & \chi_{5t,2} & \chi_{5t,3} \\ \chi_{5t,1} & \chi_{5t,2} & \chi_{5t,3} \end{pmatrix} \begin{pmatrix} \beta_{5t,1} \\ \beta_{5t,2} \\ \beta_{5t,3} \end{pmatrix} + \eta_t. \tag{9}$$

Therefore, the author obtains five matrices χ_{ft} containing all coefficients (stacked), and their possible interaction in the SNLR model in Eq. (9). (i) $\chi_{1t} = (\chi_{1t,\ 1}, \chi_{1t,\ 2})$ is an observable country-specific indicator for Y_t that captures the information contained in the lags of variable M for country *1* ($\chi_{1t,\ 1}$), and country 2 ($\chi_{1t,\ 2}$), with $\chi_{1t,1} = \sum_m y_{1mt-1}$ and $\chi_{1t,2} = \sum_m y_{2mt-1}$. (ii) $\chi_{2t} = (\chi_{2t,\ 1}, \chi_{2t,\ 2})$ is an observable country-specific indicator for Y_t that captures the information contained in a set of lagged variables $\ddot{M}$ for country *1* ($\chi_{2t,\ 1}$), and country 2 ($\chi_{2t,\ 2}$), with $\chi_{2t,1} = \sum_{\ddot{M}} y_{1\ddot{M}t-1}$ and $\chi_{2t,2} = \sum_{\ddot{M}} y_{2\ddot{M}t-1}$, with $\ddot{M}$ denoting all possible interactions between the lags of variables M, Q, and Ξ. (iii) $\chi_{3t} = (\chi_{3t,\ 1}, \chi_{3t,\ 2})$ is an observable country-specific indicator for Y_t that captures the information contained in a set of lagged variables $\ldots M$ for country *1* ($\chi_{3t,\ 1}$) and country *2* ($\chi_{3t,\ 2}$), with $\chi_{3t,1} = \sum_{\ldots M} y_{1\ldots Mt-1}$ and

$\chi_{3t,2} = \sum_{...M} y_{2...Mt-1}$, with $...M$ denoting all possible interactions between the lags of variables M, Q, $\widetilde{Q}$, and Ξ. (iv) $\chi_{4t} = (\chi_{4t,\ 1}, \chi_{4t,\ 2}, \chi_{4t,\ 3}, \chi_{4t,\ 4}, \chi_{4t,\ 5}, \chi_{4t,\ 6})$ is an observable cross-country variable-specific indicator for Y_t that captures, stacked for six groups (M_v), the information contained in the lags of variable $m = 1$ ($\chi_{4t,\ 1}, \chi_{4t,\ 3}, \chi_{4t,\ 5}$) and variable $m = 2$ ($\chi_{4t,\ 2}, \chi_{4t,\ 4}, \chi_{4t,\ 6}$). Here: $\chi_{4t,1} = \sum_i \sum_{M_{v1}} y_{iM_{v1}t-1}$ and $\chi_{4t,2} = \sum_i \sum_{M_{v2}} y_{iM_{v2}t-1}$ capture movements between the lags of the only variables M that are specific for variable $m = 1$ and $m = 2$, respectively; $\chi_{4t,3} = \sum_i \sum_{M_{v3}} y_{iM_{v3}t-1}$ and $\chi_{4t,4} = \sum_i \sum_{M_{v4}} y_{iM_{v4}t-1}$ capture movements between the lags of all variables M, Q, and Ξ that are specific for variable $m = 1$ and $m = 2$, respectively; $\chi_{4t,5} = \sum_i \sum_{M_{v5}} y_{iM_{v5}t-1}$ and $\chi_{4t,6} = \sum_i \sum_{M_{v6}} y_{iM_{v6}t-1}$ capture movements between the lags of all variables M, Q, $\widetilde{Q}$, and Ξ that are specific for variable $m = 1$ and $m = 2$, respectively. (v) $\chi_{5t} = (\chi_{5t,\ 1}, \chi_{5t,\ 2}, \chi_{5t,\ 3})$ is an observable common indicator for Y_t that captures, stacked for three groups (M_c), the information contained among countries and variable M ($\chi_{5t,\ 1}$), among countries and variables M, Q, and Ξ ($\chi_{5t,\ 2}$), and among countries and variables M, Q, $\widetilde{Q}$, and Ξ ($\chi_{5t,\ 3}$), with $\chi_{5t,1} = \sum_i \sum_{M_{c1}} y_{iM_{c1}t-1}$, $\chi_{5t,2} = \sum_i \sum_{M_{c2}} y_{iM_{c2}t-1}$, and $\chi_{5t,3} = \sum_i \sum_{M_{c3}} y_{iM_{c3}t-1}$.

Dynamic Analysis

Prior Assumptions

Given the assumptions of the error terms in Eqs. (3) and (5), the Eqs. (3) and (4) are estimable, and thus prior assumptions can be specified, and Bayesian computations are feasible. The reparametrized ESPBVAR model in (5) has a state-space structure:

$$Y_t = (\Theta_t * G)\beta_t + \eta_t \quad \text{with} \quad \eta_t = (\Theta_t * u_t + E_t)\tilde{N}\left(0, \sigma_t^2 * \Sigma_u\right) \tag{10}$$

$$\beta_t = \beta_{t-1} + v_t \quad \text{with} \quad v_t\tilde{N}(0, H_t), \tag{11}$$

where $\beta_t = (\beta_{1t}, \beta_{2t}, \ldots)'$, $H_t = \text{diag}\left(\overline{H}_{1t}, \overline{H}_{2t}, \ldots, \overline{H}_{Ft}\right)$ is a block diagonal matrix, and $\overline{H}_{ft} = \left(h_{ft} * I\right)$, where h_{ft} controls the tightness (stringent conditions) of the factorization (f) of the time-varying coefficient parameter (β_t) in order to make it estimable. The errors E_t, u_t, and v_t are mutually independent. The random walk assumption in Eq. (11) is very common in the time-varying VAR literature and has the advantage of focusing on permanent shifts and reducing the number of parameters in the estimation procedure. Moreover, with the hierarchical strategy used to construct the ESPBVAR in Eq. (1), one would be able to investigate any type of coefficient factors via their interactions.

Given the hierarchical structure in Eq. (1), Bayesian estimation requires prior distributions for Σ_u, E_t, σ^2, and β_0. These joint prior densities can be specified so that the posterior distribution for the quantities of interest can be computed numerically using MCMC methods [see, for instance, Canova and Ciccarelli (2009)]. Finally, since the state-space structure in Eqs. (10) and (11) is linear, variations of the Kalman filter algorithm can be used to construct the likelihood function, which then can be maximized with respect to the relevant parameters [see, e.g., Litterman (1986)].

Supposing exact factorization, in order to complete the model, one needs to define the prior moments on $(\Sigma_e^{-1}, h_{f0}, \beta_0)$. Thus, collecting them in a vector ϕ_0, with $\phi_0 = (\Sigma_e^{-1}, h_{f0}, \beta_0)$ be the prior densities, the likelihood function can be derived from the sampling density $p(Y|\phi_0)$ by using a mixture hierarchical distribution. In other words, (i) a normal distribution for factors β, (ii) a Wishart distribution for Σ_e^{-1}, and (iii) an Inverse-Gamma distribution for h_f, where $h_f = vec(H_t)$. That is,

$$\beta \mid \Sigma_e^{-1}, Y\tilde{N}\left(\widehat{\beta}, \Sigma_e^{-1} \otimes (\chi'\chi)^{-1}\right), \tag{12}$$

$$\Sigma_e^{-1} \mid Y\tilde{W}\left(S^{-1}, T-k-1\right), \tag{13}$$

$$\mathrm{h}_f^{-1} \mid Y\tilde{G}\left(\frac{\varpi}{2}, \frac{S}{2}\right), \tag{14}$$

where $\widehat{\beta} = \left(\sum_t \chi_t'\chi_t\right)^{-1} \left(\sum_t \chi' Y_t\right)$ is the OLS estimate of β, $S = \left(Y_t - \widehat{\beta}\chi_t\right)'\left(Y_t - \widehat{\beta}\chi_t\right)$ is the sum of squared errors, $\widehat{\Sigma}_e = S/(T-k)$ is the OLS estimate of Σ_e.

Whenever Σ_e is not replaced by an estimate,[6] the only fully Bayesian approach that leads to analytical results requires the use of a natural conjugate prior. Here, the prior, likelihood, and posterior come from the same family of distributions. According to Eqs. (12), (13), and (14), and assuming time-variant factors, the natural conjugate prior has the form:

$$\beta_t \mid \Sigma_e^{-1}, Y^T\tilde{N}\left(\overline{\beta}_{t|t}, \overline{R}_{t|t} + H_t\right) \text{ or } p(\beta_t|\Sigma_e^{-1}, Y^T) = N\left(\overline{\beta}_{t|t}, \overline{R}_{t|t} + H_t\right), \tag{15}$$

[6] For instance, the Minnesota priors are based on an approximation that involves replacing Σ_e with an estimate, $\widehat{\Sigma}_e$. See, e.g., Doan et al. (1984) and Litterman (1986).

$$\Sigma_e^{-1} \mid Y^T \tilde{W}(\beta_1, z_1) \quad \text{or} \quad p\left(\Sigma_e^{-1}|Y^T\right) = W(\beta_1, z_1), \tag{16}$$

where $\overline{\beta}_{t|t}$ and $\overline{R}_{t|t}$ correspond to hyperparameters.

According to the natural conjugate prior, $\beta_t \mid \Sigma_e^{-1}$ and Σ_e^{-1} have Normal and Wishart distributions, respectively. Since the prior for β_t depends on Σ_e, β_t and Σ_e are not independent of one another. Thus, to allow different equations in the ESPBVAR to have different explanatory variables, a general prior that does not involve the restrictions inherent in the natural conjugate prior is the independent Normal-Wishart prior:

$$\beta_t \mid Y^T \tilde{N}\left(\overline{\beta}_{t|t}, \overline{R}_{t|t}\right) \text{ or } p\left(\beta_t|Y^T\right) = N\left(\overline{\beta}_{t|t}, \overline{R}_{t|t}\right) \tag{17}$$

$$\Sigma_e \mid Y^T i\tilde{W}(z_1, \beta_1) \text{ or } p\left(\Sigma_e|Y^T\right) = iW(z_1, \beta_1), \tag{18}$$

where *iW()* stands for the inverse-Wishart distribution. Here, the prior allows for the prior covariance matrix, $\overline{R}_{t|t}$, to be anything the researcher chooses, rather than the restrictive $\left(\Sigma_e|Y^T \otimes \overline{\mathrm{R}}_{\mathrm{t|t}}\right)$ form of the natural conjugate prior.

Posterior Distributions and MCMC Implementations

Despite the dramatic parameter reduction obtained with Eq. (10), the analytical computation of posterior distributions $(\phi| Y^T)$ is unfeasible. Thus, through Monte Carlo techniques, a variant of the Gibbs sampler approach can be used in this framework by making use of the Kalman filter,[7] so it only requires knowledge of the conditional posterior of $\left(\beta_1, \ldots, \beta_T|Y^T, \phi_{-\beta_t}\right)$.[8] Thus, the posterior distributions for ϕ can be computed as:

$$\beta_t \mid Y^T, \phi_{-\beta_t} \tilde{N}\left(\widetilde{\beta}_{t|T}, \overline{R}_{t|T}\right) \text{ or } p\left(\beta_t|Y^T, \phi_{-\beta_t}\right) = N\left(\widetilde{\beta}_{t|T}, \overline{R}_{t|T}\right), \tag{19}$$

$$\Sigma_e \mid Y^T, \phi_{-\Sigma_e} i\tilde{W}\left(\widehat{z}_1, \widehat{\beta}_1\right) \text{ or } p\left(\Sigma_e|Y^T, \phi_{-\Sigma_e}\right) = iW\left(\widehat{z}_1, \widehat{\beta}_1\right), \tag{20}$$

[7] See, e.g., Chib and Grrenberg (1995).

[8] See, for instance, Pacifico (2019b) for further specifications.

$$h_{ft} \mid Y^T, \phi_{-h_{ft}} \tilde{IG}\left(\frac{\overline{\omega}_f}{2}, \frac{\overline{S}}{2}\right) \text{ or } p\left(h_{ft} | Y^T, \phi_{-h_{ft}}\right) = IG\left(\frac{\overline{\omega}_f}{2}, \frac{\overline{S}}{2}\right), \tag{21}$$

where

$$\widetilde{\beta}_{t|T} = \widetilde{R}_{t|T}\left[\overline{R}_{t|T}^{-1}\overline{\beta}_{t|T} + \sum_{t=1}^{T}(\Theta_t G)'\Sigma_e^{-1}(\Theta_t G)\widehat{\beta}\right] \tag{22}$$

$$\widetilde{R}_{t|T} = \left[\overline{R}_{t|T}^{-1} + \sum_{t=1}^{T}(\Theta_t G)'\Sigma_e^{-1}(\Theta_t G)\right]^{-1}. \tag{23}$$

The $\widehat{\beta}$ is the generalized least squares (GLS) estimator, with $\widehat{\beta} = \left[(\Theta_t G)'\Sigma_e^{-1}(\Theta_t G)\right]^{-1} * (\Theta_t G)'\Sigma_e^{-1}Y_t$. By rearranging terms, Eq. (22) can be rewritten as:

$$\widetilde{\beta}_{t|T} = \widetilde{R}_{t|T}\left[\overline{R}_{t|T}^{-1}\overline{\beta}_{t|T} + \sum_{t=1}^{T}(\Theta_t G)'\Sigma_e^{-1}Y_t\right], \tag{24}$$

where $\widetilde{\beta}_{t|T}$ and $\widetilde{R}_{t|T}$ denote the smoothed one-period-ahead forecasts of β_t and of the variance-covariance matrix of the forecast error, respectively, $\widehat{z}_1 = z_1 + T$, $\widehat{\beta}_1 = \beta_1 + \sum_t (Y_t - (\Theta_t G)\beta_t)$, $\overline{\omega}_f = k + \overline{\omega}_0$, and $\overline{S} = S_0 + \sum_t \left(\beta_t^f - \beta_{t-1}^f\right)'\left(\beta_t^f - \beta_{t-1}^f\right)$, with β_t^f denoting the fth subvector of β_t and f referring to the factors described in Eq. (3).

The choice of correlating E_t and u_t enables conjugation between the prior and the likelihood, dealing with model misspecification and heterogeneity issues, and greatly simplifies the computation of the posterior. Finally, since the fit improves when $\sigma^2 \to 0$, the model in Eq. (5) presents an exact factorization of γ_t.

Structural Spillovers

According to Pacifico (2019b), given the benchmark model in Eq. (5), the author can assess structural spillover effects given an unexpected shock in real economy and financial markets, accounting for all lagged variables in the system. More precisely, bilateral OUT and IN spillover effects (BSE_{OUT} and BSE_{IN}, respectively) are computed as the average sum of the Impulse Responses (IRs) to and from others, respectively. Thus,

$$\begin{aligned} \mathrm{BSE}_{(\mathrm{OUT},y_i \to y_j)} &= \sum_{i=1}^{N} \mathrm{IR}_{(y_i \to y_j)} \quad \text{with} \quad i = j = 1, \ldots, N \\ \mathrm{BSE}_{(\mathrm{IN},y_j \to y_i)} &= \sum_{i=1}^{N} \mathrm{IR}_{(y_j \to y_i)} \quad \text{with} \quad i = j = 1, \ldots, N. \end{aligned} \tag{25}$$

By the same token, the author computes the systemic contribution as the ratio between the bilateral net spillover effects (BNSEs) and the total net positive spillover (TNPS) of the system in order to study the dimension and intensification of structural spillover effects. Thus,

$$\mathrm{SC}_{y_{i,j}} = \frac{\mathrm{BNSE}_{y_{i,j}}}{\mathrm{TNPS}_{y_{i,j}}}. \tag{26}$$

Here, the BNSEs are defined as the difference between the conditional impulse responses sent and received to/from another variable (Eq. 27), and the TNPS is obtained by summing the only BNSEs' positive values. Thus,

$$\mathrm{BNSE}_{y_{i,j}} = \mathrm{BSE}_{\mathrm{OUT},y_i \to y_j} - \mathrm{BSE}_{\mathrm{IN},y_j \to y_i} \quad \text{with} \quad i = j = 1, \ldots, N, \tag{27}$$

where $\sum_{i=1}^{N} \left(IR_{y_i \to y_j} - IR_{y_j \to y_i} \right) = 0.$

Data Description and Empirical Model

The model is estimated for *six* emerging market countries: Chile (CH), Czech Republic (CZ), Greece (GR), Hungary (HU), Korea (KO), and Poland (PO). The dataset contains the following collection of variables. (i) Six endogenous variables are involved to describe the real economy ($\mathrm{real}_{it,\ j}$) and financial markets ($fin_{it,\ j}$): three real variables to capture real business cycles (general government spending, gross fixed capital formation, GDP growth rate), and three financial variables representing the situation in the lending markets (bank leverage, flow of credit into economy, inflation rate). (ii) Bilateral flows of trade ($r\mathrm{weights}_{it,\ j}$) and financial transactions ($f\mathrm{weights}_{it,\ j}$) are used to capture unobserved heterogeneity among countries and variables when investigating additional transmission channels that affect shock identification and spillover effects. (iii) Three policy variables (international interest policy rate, general government debt, and current account balance) are used to investigate monetary and fiscal policy interactions ($\mathrm{policy}_{it,\ j}$) among countries and sectors. (iv) Four (directly) observed variables are used as proxy variables to evaluate economic-institutional implications ($\mathrm{structures}_{it,\ j}$) in driving the transmission of shocks among countries and variables: three indicators reflect internal imbalances (general government consumption, private sector consumption, and

Table 1 Data description

General government spending	Financial accounts for general government spending
Gross fixed capital formation	Investments of fixed assets at current prices
GDP growth rate	Change of real GDP per capita
Inflation	It is calculated from the consumer Price index
Bank leverage	It is calculated as loan (L) to deposit (D) ratio
Credit growth	It is calculated as: $100 * \{[(L_t/P_t) - (L_{t-4}/P_{t-4})]/(L_{t-4}/P_{t-4})\}$
Bilateral flows of trade	Exports and imports in goods and services
Financial transactions	Financial assets on the total economy
Interest rate	International interest policy rate
Public debt	Non-financial accounts for general government debt
Current account balance	Non-financial accounts for general government net
General government consumption	Total general government expenditure at current prices
Private sector consumption	Private consumption expenditure
Change of unemployment rate	Growth rate of the unemployment rate as percentage
Household price index	Real household per capita index
Productivity	It corresponds to logarithm of the real GDP per capita

Here, general government spending and consumption, gross fixed capital formation, bilateral flows of trade, financial transactions, public debt, current account balance, private consumption, and unemployment rate are weighted for the GDP. Source: "Author's creation"

change in unemployment rate), and one indicator monitors the probabilities of transitions between expansion/recession phases in business cycles and potential macroeconomic imbalances (house price indices). (*v*) The real GDP per capita in logarithmic form (hereafter called productivity) is used to identify and investigate shock transmission among countries in the real and financial dimensions over time. The weights$_{it,\,j}$,[9] the policy$_{it,\,j}$, and the structures$_{it,\,j}$ components are treated endogenously and used to deal with functional form misspecification and heterogeneity issues in multicountry setups.

The series are expressed in standard deviations with respect to the same quarter of the previous year (q_t/q_{t-1}) and seasonally and calendar adjusted. All variables are used in year-on-year growth rates, and all data comes from OECD (Table 1).

The estimation sample covers the period from December 1994 to June 2018. It amounts, without restrictions, to *8550* regression parameters. To be more precise, each equation of the time-varying ESPBVAR in Eq. (1) has $k = [6\,(6 + 2 + 3 + 4)] * 1 = 90$ coefficients, and there are *95* equations in the system. Since this span of data includes a sufficient number of quarters describing the recent financial crisis and postcrisis consolidation, the model, given its structural conformation, is able to capture additional cross-country heterogeneity, interdependence,

[9]The weights$_{it,\,j}$ component corresponds to the sum of *r*weights$_{it,\,j}$ and fweights$_{it,\,j}$.

and commonality due to possible macroeconomic-financial linkages, and relevant interactions between monetary policy regimes and fiscal implications.

Given the factor structure in Eq. (3), the author assumes that the coefficient vector γ_t depends on ten factors. Thus,

$$G_f\beta_{ft} = G_1\beta_{1t} + G_2\beta_{2t} + G_3\beta_{3t} + G_4\beta_{4t} + G_5\beta_{5t} + G_6\beta_{6t} + G_7\beta_{7t} + G_8\beta_{8t} + +G_9\beta_{9t} + G_{10}\beta_{10t} + u_t, \quad (28)$$

where, stacking for t, $\beta_f = (\beta_1, \beta_2, \beta_3, \beta_4, \beta_5, \beta_6, \beta_7, \beta_8, \beta_9, \beta_{10})'$ contains all time-varying coefficient vectors to be estimated. Given the factorization in Eq. (27), the SNLR model in Eq. (5) can be rewritten as:

$$Y_t = \Theta_t\left(\sum_{f=1}^{10} G_f\beta_{ft} + u_t\right) + E_t \equiv \chi_{ft}\beta_{ft} + \eta_t \text{ with } \Theta_t = (I_{NM} \otimes \mathrm{X_t}). \quad (29)$$

By diagnostic tests (Table 2), the factorization in Eq. (28) is exact. The estimates would be asymptotically consistent given the absence of serial correlations between residuals. According to time-variant factors and the Schwarz approximation, the marginal (conditional) likelihood estimation for the factorization f has been tested. The latter confirms the exact γ_t's factorization, as the p-value of the test sets to $1.64e^{-08}$. Thus, the specified factors in Eq. (29) the author assumed for the empirical analysis can be made clearer.

Indeed, $\chi_{1t}\beta_{1t}$ and $\chi_{2t}\beta_{2t}$ are $[NM * 1]$ vectors of observable country-specific indicators for Y_t, and account for the only $\text{real}_{it,\,j}$ and $\mathit{fin}_{it,\,j}$ components, respectively, in order to evaluate international transmission of shocks and the evolution of structural spillover effects among countries in real economy and financial markets.

The indicators $\chi_{3t}\beta_{3t}$ and $\chi_{4t}\beta_{4t}$ are $[NM * 1]$ vectors of observable country-specific effects for Y_t, and account for one additional component: (1) $\text{real}_{it,\,j}$ with $\text{policy}_{it,\,j}$ and (2) $\mathit{fin}_{it,\,j}$ with $\text{policy}_{it,\,j}$. They are able to investigate monetary and fiscal policy interactions in real economy and financial markets, respectively, and thus deal with model misspecification problems when studying international macroeconomic-financial linkages.

Table 2 Diagnostic tests

Tests	Test statistics	Degrees of freedom	P-value
LGB_π	7683	2430	0
P_π	312.4	451	0.54
MLE_f	60.76	12	0.00

Here, LGB_π stands for a multivariate Ljung-Box test of the series, with lags $\pi = 30$; P_π refers to the portmanteau (asymptotic) test on the residuals, with lags $\pi = 30$; MLE_f is the marginal (Conditional) likelihood estimation test obtained through the Schwartz approximation, with $f = 10$

Source: Author's creation

The indicators $\chi_{5t}\beta_{5t}$ and $\chi_{6t}\beta_{6t}$ are $[NM * 1]$ vectors of observable country-specific effects for Y_t and account for two components further: (1) real$_{it,\ j}$ with *r*weights$_{it,\ j}$ and *policy*$_{it,\ j}$ and (2) *fin*$_{it,\ j}$ with *f*weights$_{it,\ j}$ and policy$_{it,\ j}$. They are able to assess the role that additional transmission channels play in driving the spread of an unexpected shock in the real and financial dimensions, respectively, and thus deal with unobserved heterogeneity among countries when jointly investigating monetary policy effects and fiscal implications.

The indicators $\chi_{7t}\beta_{7t}$ and $\chi_{8t}\beta_{8t}$ are $[NM * 1]$ vectors of observable country-specific effects for Y_t, and account for one component further: (1) real$_{it,\ j}$ with *r*weights$_{it,\ j}$, policy$_{it,\ j}$, and structures$_{it,\ j}$ and (2) *fin*$_{it,\ j}$ with *f*weights$_{it,\ j}$, policy$_{it,\ j}$, and structures$_{it,\ j}$. They are able to investigate how additional transmission channels, macroeconomic-institutional implications, and potential macroeconomic imbalances affect the intensity and the spreading of spillover effects in the real and financial dimensions when jointly dealing with monetary and fiscal policy effects.

The indicator $\chi_{9t}\beta_{9t}$ is a $[\mathrm{NM} * M_\upsilon]$ vector of observable cross-country variable-specific effects for Y_t, where $M_\upsilon = (M_{\upsilon 1}, M_{\upsilon 2}, M_{\upsilon 3}, M_{\upsilon 4}, M_{\upsilon 5}, M_{\upsilon 6}, M_{\upsilon 7}, M_{\upsilon 8})$ denotes the number of variable groups: (i) $M_{\upsilon 1} =$ real$_{it,\ j}$; (ii) $M_{\upsilon 2} =$ *fin*$_{it,\ j}$; (iii) $M_{\upsilon 3} =$ real$_{it,\ j}$ and policy$_{it,\ j}$; (iv) $M_{\upsilon 4} =$ *fin*$_{it,\ j}$ and policy$_{it,\ j}$; (v) $M_{\upsilon 5} =$ real$_{it,\ j}$, *r*weights$_{it,\ j}$, and policy$_{it,\ j}$; (vi) $M_{\upsilon 6} =$ *fin*$_{it,\ j}$, *f*weights$_{it,\ j}$, and policy$_{it,\ j}$; (vii) $M_{\upsilon 7} =$ real$_{it,\ j}$, *r*weights$_{it,\ j}$, policy$_{it,\ j}$, and structures$_{it,\ j}$; and (viii) $M_{\upsilon 8} =$ *fin*$_{it,\ j}$, *f*weights$_{it,\ j}$, policy$_{it,\ j}$, and structures$_{it,\ j}$. The factor can be used to assess possible commonality, heterogeneity, and interdependence in the real and financial dimensions among variables, accounting for additional transmission channels, macroeconomic-institutional linkages, and monetary and fiscal interactions.

Finally, the indicator $\chi_{10t}\beta_{10t}$ is a $[NM * M_c]$ vector of observable common effects for Y_t, where $M_c = (M_{c1}, M_{c2}, M_{c3}, M_{c4})$ denotes the number of common groups: (i) $M_{c1} =$ real$_{it,\ j}$ and *fin*$_{it,\ j}$; (ii) $M_{c2} =$ real$_{it,\ j}$, *fin*$_{it,\ j}$, and policy$_{it,\ j}$; (iii) $M_{c3} =$ real$_{it,\ j}$, *fin*$_{it,\ j}$, weights$_{it,\ j}$, and policy$_{it,\ j}$; and (iv) $M_{c4} =$ real$_{it,\ j}$, *fin*$_{it,\ j}$, weights$_{it,\ j}$, policy$_{it,\ j}$, and structures$_{it,\ j}$. The factor is able to assess idiosyncratic spillover effects due to different reactions or co-movements among countries and variables for a given common unexpected shock in both the real and financial dimensions.

In this empirical application, the hyperparameters are all known.[10] More precisely, collecting them in a vector δ, where $\delta = \left(z_1, \overline{\omega}_0, S_0, \beta_1, \overline{\beta}_0, \overline{R}_0\right)$, they are treated as fixed and are either obtained from the data to tune the prior to the specific applications (this is the case for $\overline{\beta}_0$, $\overline{\omega}_0$, and β_1) or selected a priori to produce relatively loose priors (this is the case for z_1, $\overline{R}_0$, and S_0). The values are $z_1 = N * (M + M_\upsilon + M_c)$, $\overline{\omega}_0 = 10^{M_\upsilon + M_c}$, $S_0 = 1.0$, $\overline{\beta}_0 = \widehat{\beta}_0$, where $\widehat{\beta}_0$ is obtained with the OLS version of Eq. (29), $\overline{R}_0 = \widetilde{R}_0$, where $\widetilde{R}_0$ is the OLS variance-covariance matrix in Eq. (29), and $\beta_1 =$ diag $(Q_{11}, \ldots, Q_{1N})$, where Q_{1i} is the estimated covariance matrix according to the estimates of all the $\widehat{\beta}_t$'s in Eq. (29) for each i.

[10]Own computations.

Dynamic analyses[11] have been conducted via accurate MCMC simulations and implementations on the period from *1994q4* to *2018q2*.[12] The natural conjugate prior refers to four subsamples: (i) *1994q4–2008q3* and (ii) *2008q4–2015q4* in order to emphasize the impact of the two different monetary policy regimes on the dynamics of the GDP growth, and (iii) *2006q1–2009q4* and (iv) *2010q1–2018q2* in order to emphasize the impact of the recent financial crisis and fiscal consolidation periods among countries and sectors.

International Business Cycles and Shock Transmission

Given the benchmark model in Eq. (29) and the corresponding selected factors, structural spillover effects given an unexpected shock in real and financial dimensions, accounting for all variables in the system, can be assessed. To be more precise, the dimension and intensification of spillover effects are measured through the SC index, denoting the amplification contribution of the impulse variable to the response variable and is able to capture sequential features associated with systemic events.

Monetary Regimes, Financial Markets, and Fiscal Implications

In Fig. 1, where the author considers the first two country-specific indicators (χ_{1t}, χ_{2t}) for the overall sampled time-series, a consistent degree of heterogeneity among countries matters in the financial dimension and even more in the real economy. In the financial dimension (Fig. 1b), all countries are net senders of the system, and thus unexpected country-specific shocks directly affect a country's own output growth in the financial dimension and then in the real economy because of consistent cross-country interdependencies. The latter is confirmed by a relative homogeneity in the spreading of the structural spillovers in financial markets. Moreover, a relevant common component is found in real economy.

In Fig. 2, the same indicators are considered according to the two monetary policy regimes. Each regime represents an experiment associated with different policy objectives, different operating procedures, different statistical patterns in the data, and different results. In the inflation stabilization regime (Fig. 2a, b), the intensity of spillovers in financial markets tends to increase due to unexpected shocks to inflation in emerging markets. It would be confirmed because most of countries tend to be net senders (outward spillover effects), except for inflation being the response variable, and reflect in part changes in the international monetary system and inflation trends in advanced countries. More precisely, inflation has been, on average, persistently

[11] See, for instance, Pacifico (2019b) for further details.

[12] Here, a time frame of 8 quarters (2 years) has been used to compute conditional forecasts.

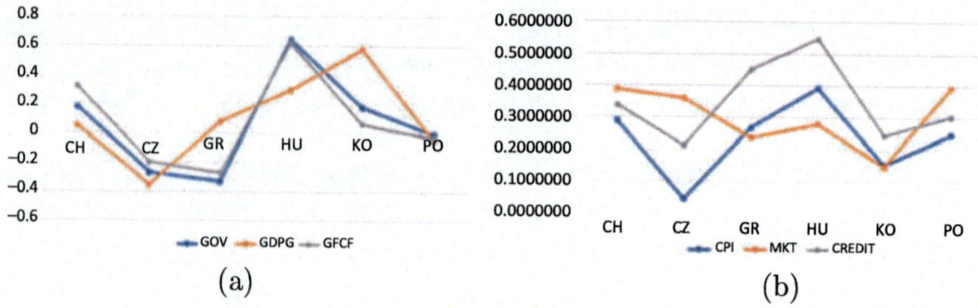

Fig. 1 Systemic contributions of the productivity given a 1% shock to real and financial dimensions are drawn as standard deviations of the variables in the system and in year-on-year growth rates. They account for $\chi_{1t}\widehat{\beta}_{1t}$ (plot **a**) and $\chi_{2t}\widehat{\beta}_{2t}$ (plot **b**) cross-country indicators, referring to the overall sampled time-series, where $\widehat{\beta}_{1t}$ and $\widehat{\beta}_{2t}$ are posterior means

high in some countries, but in others (such as Czech Republic, Poland, and Hungary), the combination of dismantling of price controls, nominal rigidities, and fiscal problems has produced brief episodes of high inflation only. The effects of inflation on the development of the financial system have been especially relevant for emerging markets. High inflation would be expected to increase the resources a country devotes to financial services, and higher unexpected inflation would raise the demand for financial sector services in order to ensure economic agents from the associated uncertainty. Thus, in real economy, most countries tend to be net receivers (inward spillover effects) with a stronger heterogeneity component due to the sudden amplification contribution of inflation (impulse variable for the real dimension).

The main concern of the zero interest rate regime, with the onset of the global financial crisis, has been the output stabilization, as output is appeared to grow along a path that has been considered to be well below the potential for GDP. It is confirmed by strong inward spillover effects in the real GDP growth rate and general consumptions (response variables). In this context, the degree of cross-country heterogeneity is stronger in the financial dimension (Fig. 2d). More precisely, during this period and mainly in the Great Recession, there have been abuses in the mortgage market due to many factors, but many are attributed to the bad debt to low interest rates. Moreover, the use of macro-prudential policies to promote financial stability and thus monitor financial markets has been emphasized in an era of low interest rates. It has been an important feature of the ZIRE meeting the failure of the economy to return to the trend in potential GDP. Conversely, the real economy tends to show a higher degree of homogeneity across countries because of spillover effects essentially inwards (Fig. 2c).

Accounting for policy$_{it,\,j}$ component, important findings and policy perspectives are derived (Fig. 3). Given the widespread view that fiscal policy is closely connected with the inflationary experience of many emerging market countries and interest rate policy is aimed at stabilizing output and targeting inflation, the relationships between fiscal implications and monetary policy effects need to be accounted

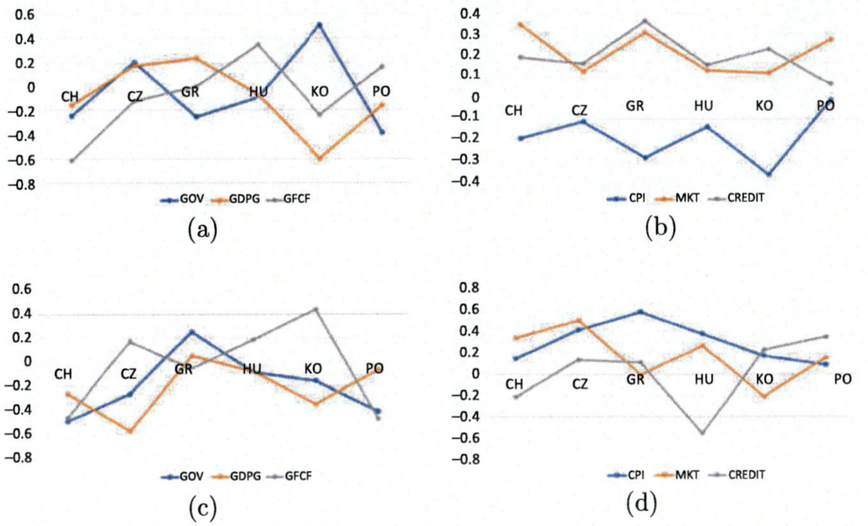

Fig. 2 Systemic contributions of the productivity given a 1% shock to real and financial dimensions are drawn as standard deviations of the variables in the system and in year-on-year growth rates. They account for $\chi_{1t}\widehat{\beta}_{1t}$ (plots **a**, **c**) and $\chi_{2t}\widehat{\beta}_{2t}$ (plots **b**, **d**) cross-country indicators, referring to the two monetary policy regimes, where $\widehat{\beta}_{1t}$ and $\widehat{\beta}_{2t}$ are posterior means

for. A significant and positive long-run relationship between the size of government deficits, debt stabilization, and inflation has been found. From a policy perspective, fiscal deficits are one of the main causes of inflation, particularly high and hyperinflation. By creating excessive aggregate demand pressures, recurrent fiscal deficits can sustain inflationary processes. Typically, governments facing persistent fiscal imbalances are unwilling (or incapable) to create the political consensus needed to increase taxes and/or reduce expenditures and find borrowing increasingly difficult.[13] In addition, a large number of emerging economies have focused on economic stabilization instead of debt stabilization by using several fiscal stimulus packages and pursuing an active expansionary fiscal policy. Thus, a stronger homogeneity component among countries is found in the financial dimension (Fig. 3b, d). A similar pattern, jointly with a relevant common component, is found for real economy due to dynamic interdependence across countries (Fig. 3a, c). Overall, most countries tend to be net receivers, and consistent co-movements also matter among countries in the financial dimension.

In Fig. 4, the author considers the first four group variable factors in order to investigate the presence of heterogeneity, interdependency, and commonality between real economy and financial markets without and with policy interactions according to the two monetary policy regimes.

---

[13]See, e.g., Dornbusch and Fischer (1993) and Fischer et al. (1996).

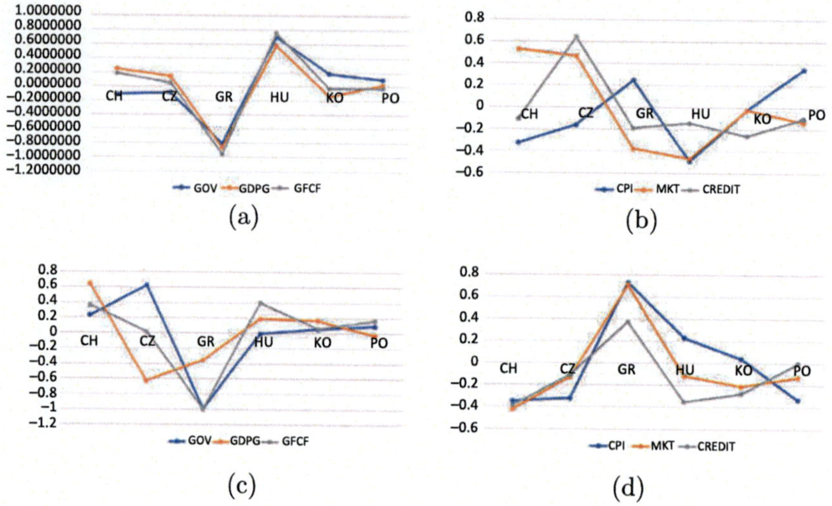

Fig. 3 Systemic contributions of the productivity given a 1% shock to real and financial dimensions, dealing with policy interactions, are drawn as standard deviations of the variables in the system and in year-on-year growth rates. They account for $\chi_{3t}\widehat{\beta}_{3t}$ (plots **a**, **c**) and $\chi_{4t}\widehat{\beta}_{4t}$ (plots **b**, **d**) cross-country indicators, referring to the two monetary policy regimes, where $\widehat{\beta}_{3t}$ and $\widehat{\beta}_{4t}$ are posterior means

During the ISE Regime, accounting for the real and financial variables only (Fig. 4a), on average, most countries in real and financial dimensions have been inward (net receivers) and outward (net senders), respectively. Inward spillover effects in financial markets have been observed for Czech Republic and Poland only due to the absence of persistent episodes of high inflation. Moreover, the spreading of the structural spillovers among countries tends to show a larger homogeneity component in financial markets than in real economy because of stronger cross-country interdependencies among sectors. Same results have been found according to the ZIRE Regime (Fig. 4b). To be more precise, there is an increasing number of inward and outward spillover effects in the real and financial dimensions, respectively. However, on average, significant co-movements between real and financial variables matter more during this regime because of financial measures implemented to comply with the output stabilization.

In Fig. 4c, d, significant policy interactions matter. Co-movements in the real and financial dimensions tend to be quite large, with a consistent volatility's decrease in the output responses (lower spillover effects). They are stronger during the ZIRE Regime where, especially in the aftermath of the global financial crisis, a large number of emerging economies has focused on economic stabilization instead of debt stabilization by using several fiscal stimulus packages and pursuing an active expansionary fiscal policy. The empirical results show that the behavior of fiscal authority is as important as the monetary authority in conducting desirable monetary policy rules involving inflation targeting and output stabilization. However, because

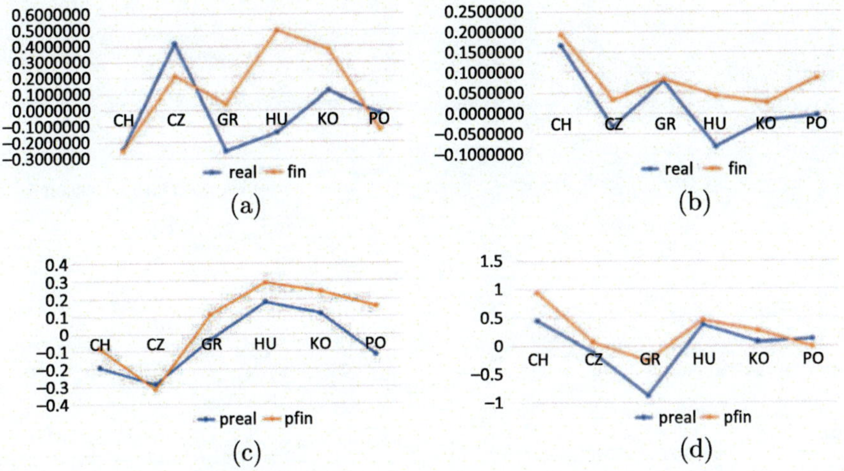

Fig. 4 Systemic contributions of the productivity given a 1% shock to real and financial dimensions are drawn as standard deviations of the variables in the system and in year-on-year growth rates. They account for the variable-specific indicators $\chi_{9t,1}\widehat{\beta}_{9t,1}$ and $\chi_{9t,2}\widehat{\beta}_{9t,2}$ (plots **a**, **b**), without dealing with policy interactions, and $\chi_{9t,3}\widehat{\beta}_{9t,3}$ and $\chi_{9t,4}\widehat{\beta}_{9t,4}$ (plots **c**, **d**), dealing with policy interactions, where $\widehat{\beta}_{9t,M\ddot{v}}$'s are posterior means with $\ddot{v} = v1, v2, v3, v4$

of a persistent degree of heterogeneity in the country's responses in either real or financial variables and greater extent of impulse variables (outward spillover effects) in the financial dimension, expansionary fiscal policy would affect monetary policy and lead to deviations from policy targets in the emerging economies. It is well-known that several emerging markets have started to pursue inflation targeting policies at early phase of ISE Regime. For example, monetary authorities in the Czech Republic and Poland have pursued inflation targeting regimes since *1998*. Hungary has started to conduct an inflation targeting regime as a monetary policy rule in *2001*. These findings highlight some main elements for successful inflation targeting: central bank instrument independence, transparent policies to build accountability and credibility, a well-developed financial system, a reasonable degree of macroeconomic stability, and a reasonable understanding of transmission channels and economic-institutional issues between policy instruments and inflation.

International Macroeconomic Financial Linkages Accounting for Transmission Channels and Economic Institutional Issues

Accounting for weights$_{it,\ j}$ component, relevant empirical results and policy perspectives are derived (Fig. 5).

During ISE Regime (Fig. 5a, b), the intensity of the structural spillovers tends to increase in the real dimension and even more in the financial dimension because of

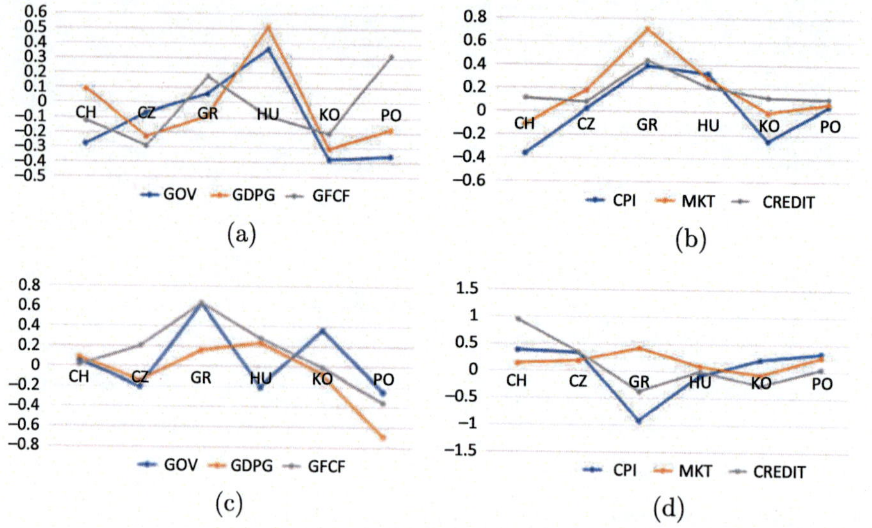

Fig. 5 Systemic contributions of the productivity given a 1% shock to real and financial dimensions, dealing with policy interactions and additional transmission channels, are drawn as standard deviations of the variables in the system and in year-on-year growth rates. They account for $\chi_{5t}\widehat{\beta}_{5t}$ (plots **a**, **c**) and $\chi_{6t}\widehat{\beta}_{6t}$ (plots **b**, **d**) cross-country indicators, referring to the two monetary policy regimes, where $\widehat{\beta}_{5t}$ and $\widehat{\beta}_{6t}$ are posterior means

stronger dynamic interdependence according to capital flows. In addition, most countries in the financial dimension follow to be net senders of the system, and thus capital income flows would matter more than trade exposures in driving shock transmission. Indeed, the degree of commonality tends to decrease among countries in their real economy but not in their financial dimension. Stronger homogeneity is found among countries, except for Czech Republic, Hungary, and Poland because of financial instability. Opposite results are observed during ZIRE Regime (Fig. 5c, d). The commonality component tends to increase among countries in their financial dimension and even more in their real economy because of lower heterogeneities among countries. Because of higher trade flows in real economy, most countries tend to be net senders of the system with greater magnitude of spillover effects (larger volatility) behind more intense shock transmission.

According to fiscal implications, larger exposures of capital flows would be usually associated with rapid movements in idiosyncratic shock transmission, which can be particularly disruptive for countries that are relatively open to trade or are large borrowers. In an inflation targeting framework, clear explanations by the central bank of the rationale underlying its policy stance would help to ensure that such idiosyncratic shocks are not compounded by uncertainty regarding the conduct of monetary policy. Over time, a proven track record of attaining the inflation targets should help financial markets to develop greater confidence in the motivations underpinning monetary actions and establish the credibility of an inflation targeting

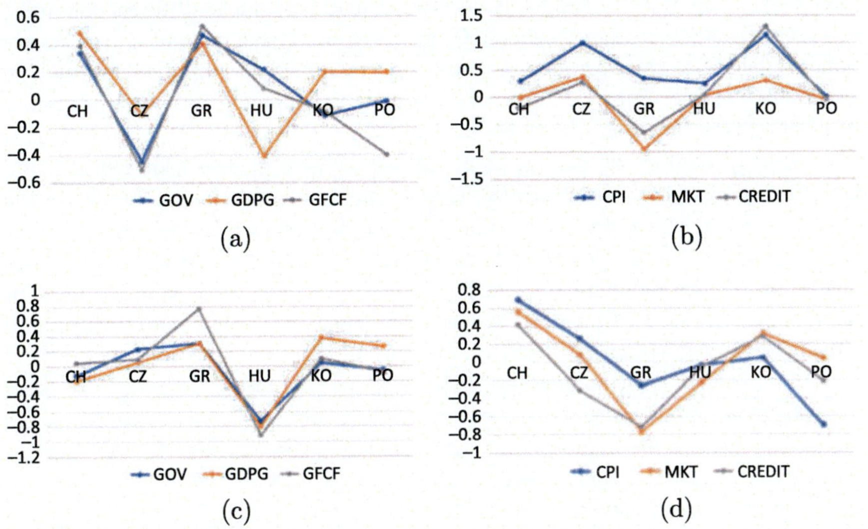

Fig. 6 Systemic contributions of the productivity given a 1% shock to real and financial dimensions are drawn as standard deviations of the variables in the system and in year-on-year growth rates. Here, policy interactions, additional transmission channels, and economic-institutional issues are accounted for. They account for $\chi_{7t}\widehat{\beta}_{7t}$ (plots **a**, **c**) and $\chi_{8t}\widehat{\beta}_{8t}$ (plots **b**, **d**) cross-country indicators, referring to the two monetary policy regimes, where $\widehat{\beta}_{7t}$ and $\widehat{\beta}_{8t}$ arc posterior means

framework, particularly in cases where there are large fiscal debt burdens or an inadequate track record of entrenched macroeconomic stability.

Similar results are found for the two monetary policy regimes when accounting for either the weights$_{it,\ j}$ or structures$_{it,\ j}$ components (Fig. 6). More precisely, the spillover effects tend to be larger in both the real and financial dimensions, and thus the intensity (volatility) and the spreading (contagion) of the structural spillovers are driven by the structures$_{it,\ j}$ and the weights$_{it,\ j}$ components, respectively. Their spreading is similar among countries in either real economy or financial markets, with larger common and homogeneous behaviors. Indeed, the countries tend to be either net senders or net receivers of the system and thus an unexpected shock affects countries' economy in a similar way because of the presence of stronger economic institutional linkages, mainly in financial markets. These findings would confirm a relevant presence of cross-country interdependencies when dealing with not directly observed economic issues during ISE Regime and even more during ZIRE Regime. The commonality component mainly matters in real economy among countries because of larger trade exposures.

From a policy perspective, cross-country homogeneity and interdependency tend to be driven by stringent international institutional constraints and pressures in both the monetary regimes. Thus, without dealing with unobserved heterogeneity, policy interactions would seem to be likely decreasing over time due to different countries' reactions given an unexpected shock. Conversely, policy interactions and monetary policy effects are relevant among emerging markets. The empirical results also suggest that emerging markets need more formal institutional frameworks in support of inflation targeting than advanced economies [see, for instance, Pacifico (2019a)]. They usually modify the central bank legal framework before adopting inflation targeting and explicitly limit central bank financing of government deficits in the primary market. The more formal inflation targeting frameworks in emerging economies compared to their advanced counterparts would reflect histories of greater government intervention in monetary policy, higher and more variable rates of inflation, less developed financial systems, and greater vulnerability to inflationary monetization of government debt.

Finally, in Fig. 7, the author compares the $real_{it,\,j}$ and $fin_{it,\,j}$ variables with either the $weights_{it,\,j}$ or $structures_{it,\,j}$ components. The analysis shows the ability of the model to deal with unobserved heterogeneity. Indeed, whether economic-institutional issues matter more in reflecting changes in the magnitudes of structural shocks, international trade and financial exposures tend to mainly affect changes in the response of the economies.

Accounting for the only $weights_{it,\,j}$ component (Fig. 7a, b), during ISE Regime, most spillover effects associated to the real and financial dimensions are inward and

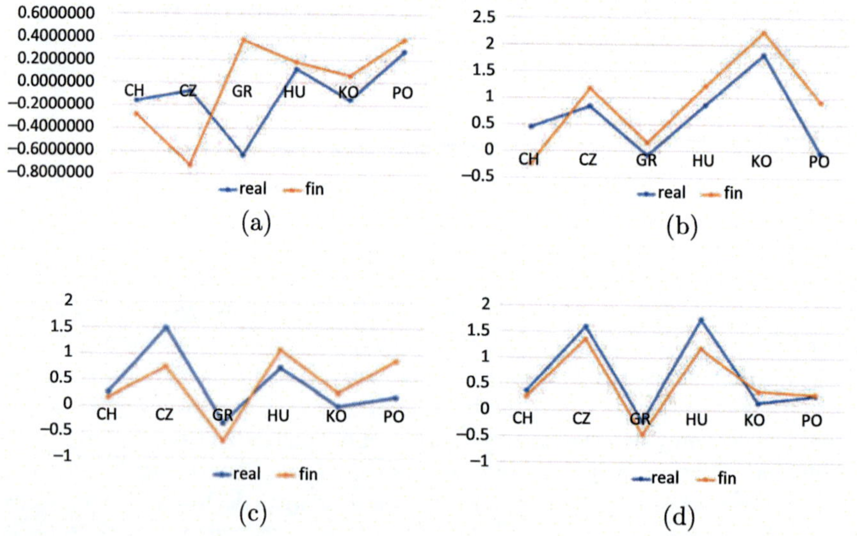

Fig. 7 Systemic contributions of the productivity given a 1% shock to real and financial dimensions are drawn as standard deviations of the variables in the system and in year-on-year growth rates. They account for the variable-specific indicators $\chi_{9t,5}\widehat{\beta}_{9t,5}$ and $\chi_{9t,6}\widehat{\beta}_{9t,6}$ (plots **a**, **b**), dealing with additional transmission channels only, and $\chi_{9t,7}\widehat{\beta}_{9t,7}$ and $\chi_{9t,8}\widehat{\beta}_{9t,8}$ (plots **c**, **d**), dealing with both transmission channels and economic institutional issues, where $\widehat{\beta}_{9t,M\ddot{\upsilon}}$'s are posterior means with $\ddot{\upsilon} = \upsilon 5, \upsilon 6, \upsilon 7, \upsilon 8$

outward, respectively. During ZIRE Regime, because of larger idiosyncratic shocks in the aftermath of the Great Recession, spillover effects tend to be larger in real economy and even more in financial markets behind stronger cross-country interdependencies among sectors.

The results are different by accounting for both the components (Fig. 7c, d). Most spillover effects would be outward among real and financial sectors because of stronger policy interactions when dealing with not directly observed economic issues. The commonality component tends to be stronger during ISE Regime and even more during ZIRE Regime behind more coordinated fiscal actions in the aftermath of the Great Recession. The intensity (volatility) of the structural spillovers tends to increase in both the real and financial dimensions due to highly stringent economic-institutional linkages among sectors.

The empirical results show that the combination of additional shock transmission, mainly financial resources, with economic-institutional issues creates a scope for a coordination between monetary and cyclical macroprudential policies. More precisely, if a cyclical tax on foreign currency borrowing by banks, combined with a relatively strict inflation targeting, enhances welfare; the same inflation targeting, without macroprudential policies, would reduce it. Thus, high expected inflation would lead households to make smaller cash withdrawals with greater frequency and then the banks will need to make more investments in technology in order to satisfy increased customer activity. In this context, the banks would correspond to agents who have access to foreign financial markets and engage in financial intermediation.

Heterogeneity and Policy Interactions During the Great Recession and Postcrisis Consolidation

Previous section provides evidence of significant co-movements in real economy and consistent dynamic interdependence in financial markets among emerging economies. Moreover, the author finds that there is a quite homogeneity in the spreading of the spillover effects among real variables and even more among financial sectors. Thus, unexpected country-specific shocks directly affect a country's own output growth in the financial dimension and then in the real economy because of consistent cross-country interdependencies. When dealing with not directly observed economic issues, the author shows that there is a large common component in the real and financial dimensions because of consistent interactions between monetary and fiscal policy, mainly during in the aftermath of the Great Recession. Accounting for additional transmission channels, the author highlights that they mainly affect the real economy where commonality and homogeneity matter more because of relevant international trade exposures.

The aim of this section is to gauge the relative weight of these findings in investigating the evolution of the structural spillovers among sectors and countries over time ("Empirical Results" section). Policy implications and suggestions for decision-makers are also accounted for ("Purposes, Implications, and Lessons for Policy Making" section). Thus, the author provides to deepen the knowledge about the interactions between fiscal and monetary policy during different phases of financial cycles since it is rather limited in the existing literature.

Empirical Results

Although fundamental factors (e.g., macroeconomic imbalances and internal or external shocks) are often observed, many questions remain about the exact causes of crises. Financial crises sometimes appear to be driven by not directly observed factors, including contagion and spillovers among financial markets, limits to arbitrage during times of stress, and other aspects of financial turmoil. The structural framework of the model allows to provide quantitative estimates of such factors. For example, are they domestic or international in origin? Do they reflect changes in the magnitudes of structural shocks or, rather, changes in the response of the economies to those shocks? How additional transmission channels and economic-institutional issues affect country's responses due to an unexpected shock during triggering events?

The empirical results suggest important heterogeneity in the shape and the dynamics of spillover effects during the Great Recession, with countries endogenously reacting to foreign impulses (Fig. 8a, b). Conversely, during postcrisis period, there have been deeper co-movements and larger degrees of homogeneity in the real dimension and even more in the financial dimension (Fig. 8c, d). These results translate into three main findings. First, interdependencies due to strongly common economic-institutional linkages are relevant during triggering events and even more in successive postcrisis consolidation behind stronger interactions between fiscal and monetary policy. Second, coordinated fiscal actions do not necessarily yield better outcomes. More precisely, although recent theoretical studies suggest that a significant improvement in fiscal sustainability has been achieved, the strong and nonlinear reaction of markets, the risk of a cascade of policy errors, and adverse political economy incentives are additional reasons for early and determined fiscal consolidation. Thus, they suggest a need for great caution in efforts to fine-tune the economy via fiscal structures. Third, the persistent common component among countries in real economy and even more in financial markets in the aftermath of the global crisis highlights more active interactions between fiscal and monetary policy in the last few decades.

By accounting for the variable-specific indicator (Fig. 9), I confirm that trade channels matter less than capital linkages in driving the spreading of spillover effects. Indeed, most countries tend to be net senders in the financial dimension and net receivers in the real economy (Fig. 9a). Conversely, during postcrisis consolidation, larger trade exposures among countries would support a persistent common component over time. Moreover, the intensity of spillover effects sufficiently decreases behind more coordinated fiscal actions, mainly in the financial

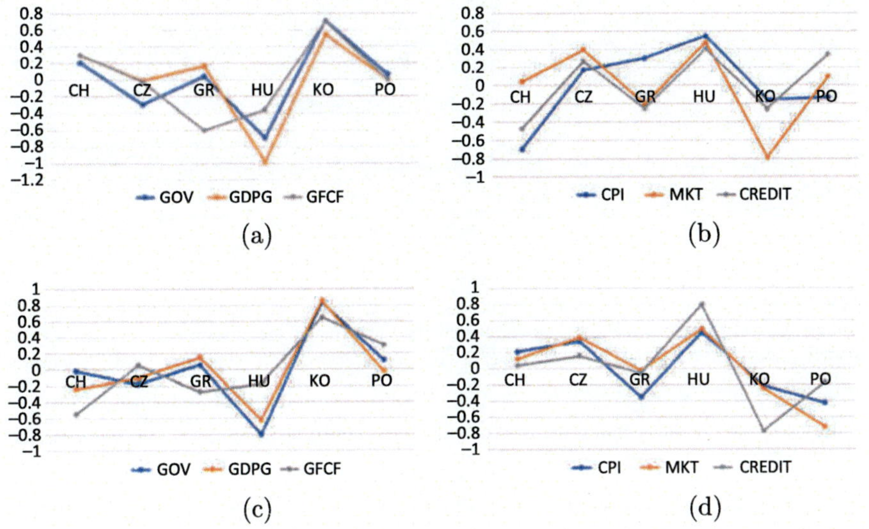

Fig. 8 Systemic contributions of the productivity given a 1% shock to real and financial dimensions are drawn as standard deviations of the variables in the system and in year-on-year growth rates. Here, policy interactions, additional transmission channels, and economic-institutional issues are accounted for. They account for $\chi_{7t}\widehat{\beta}_{7t}$ (plots **a**, **c**) and $\chi_{8t}\widehat{\beta}_{8t}$ (plots **b**, **d**) cross-country indicators, referring to the crisis period and postcrisis consolidation, where $\widehat{\beta}_{7t}$ and $\widehat{\beta}_{8t}$ are posterior means

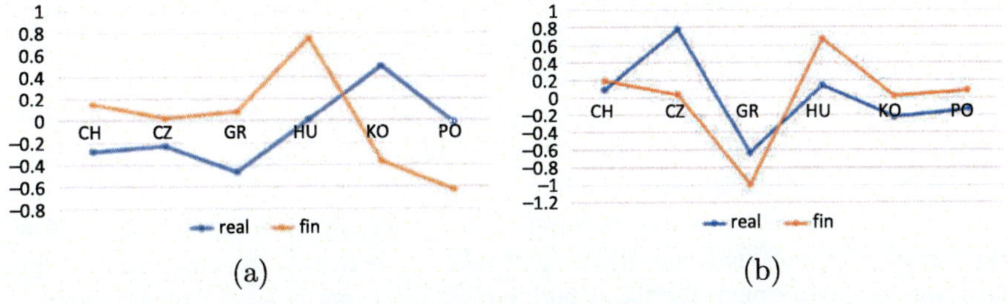

Fig. 9 Systemic contributions of the productivity given a 1% shock to real and financial dimensions are drawn as standard deviations of the variables in the system and in year-on-year growth rates. They account for the variable-specific indicators $\chi_{9t,7}\widehat{\beta}_{9t,7}$ and $\chi_{9t,8}\widehat{\beta}_{9t,8}$ dealing with both additional transmission channels and economic-institutional issues, during crisis period (plot **a**) and postcrisis consolidation (plot **b**), where $\widehat{\beta}_{9t,M\ddot{v}}$'s are posterior means with $\ddot{v} = v7, v8$

dimension because of stronger cross-country interdependencies (Fig. 9b). This suggests that there would be significant benefits from fiscal consolidation without delay and that there is a need for caution against excessive faith in fiscal structures. To achieve the full short-run and long-run benefits, it should be part of an ambitious,

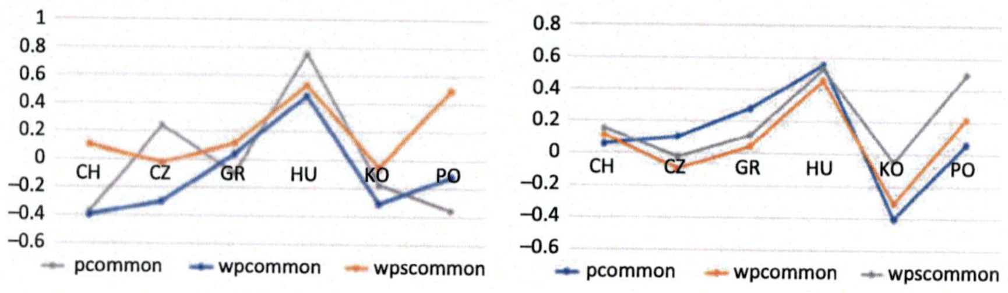

(a) (b)

Fig. 10 Systemic contributions of the productivity given a 1% shock to real and financial dimensions are drawn as standard deviations of the variables in the system and in year-on-year growth rates. Here, policy interactions, additional transmission channels, and economic-institutional issues are accounted for. They account for the common indicator $\ddot{\chi}_{10t}\widehat{\beta}_{10t}$, referring to the crisis period (plot **a**) and postcrisis consolidation (plot **b**), where $\widehat{\beta}_{10t}$'s are posterior means

comprehensive, and credible reform strategy which will indeed reap a significant improvement in fiscal sustainability.

Finally, the common factor $\ddot{\chi}_{10t}\widehat{\beta}_{10t} = \chi_{10t,2}\widehat{\beta}_{10t,2}, \chi_{10t,3}\widehat{\beta}_{10t,3}, \chi_{10t,4}\widehat{\beta}_{10t,4}$ is used to investigate commonality among sectors and countries in real economy and financial markets accounting for policy$_{it,j}$, weights$_{it,j}$, and structures$_{it,j}$ components (Fig. 10).

The common indicator shows that economic-institutional interdependencies matter more than different transmission channels in driving the intensity and, mainly in the last few decades, the spread of common unexpected shocks. It is proved because of larger spillover effects by accounting for both the weights$_{it,j}$ and structures$_{it,j}$ components. Nevertheless, a degree of heterogeneity persists among countries, especially during crisis period (Fig. 10a). On the contrary, a consistent degree of homogeneity tends to matter more during the last few decades (Fig. 10b). From a policy perspective, these different country's reactions highlight a need for reducing unsustainable public liabilities with their deleterious effects on long-term growth and confidence. Consolidation is needed to underpin confidence in fiscal solvency at the country level and prevent adverse international externalities. Then, the chances of successful and sustained consolidation would be increased by strengthening the institutional environment for fiscal policy-making at the national and the international level. Consolidation should also be generally based on expenditure reduction, which could provide additional support to long-term growth via reduced distortions in the economy. The analysis is robust and consistent with the more recent business cycle studies, which recognize the importance of (1) accounting for both group-specific and global factors when evaluating cross-country spillovers, (2) separating common shocks from the propagation of country- and variable-specific shocks when studying economic-financial linkages, and (*3*) accounting for additional transmission channels and economic-institutional issues when using multicountry dynamic data.

Purposes, Implications, and Lessons for Policy-Making

In summary, even if the gradual increase in the persistence of inflation, combined with the associated removal of external constraints on accommodative monetary policies, has made possible to push world inflation to unprecedented peacetime levels in the past, the adoption of sounder macroeconomic policies and institutional and operational changes, put in place to foster monetary and fiscal policy discipline, has helped to bring inflation in emerging markets back under control. Following the decline in inflation in emerging markets during the overall ZIRE Regime with a humble increase in recent years, a widespread consensus has emerged among policymakers and the public that one of the key policy challenges is to preserve these gains in the future. It is agreed that inflation, especially high inflation, harms economic efficiency and growth, but the nature and magnitude of these costs are not yet entirely understood. Likewise, the empirical analysis has identified several costs associated with high inflation, such as (i) distortion in relative prices of different goods and services, lowering economic efficiency; (ii) higher uncertainty about future inflation, forcing people to spend time and resources protecting themselves from future changes in inflation; and (iii) interference with the financial system's ability to allocate resources effectively, for example, because of distortions to accounting and tax rules.

The empirical results highlight that fiscal consolidation has also played a central role in the disinflation process. Nevertheless, according to the structural framework used in this analysis, a number of other forces, not directly captured in standard dynamic econometric models, have also contributed, although their impact likely is varied considerably among different countries. More precisely, the analysis highlights three main forces. (i) Economic institutional reforms. In most emerging markets, the independence of the central bank is enhanced, helping to bring inflation in emerging markets back under control and address the output stabilization problem. (ii) Structural reforms. Most countries have undertaken wide-ranging structural reforms in trade, product, and labor markets, which tend to reduce inflationary pressures. One outcome of these reforms has been the substantial rise in trade openness for emerging markets as a group (larger commonality among real sectors). (iii) Access to global capital markets. Capital flows to emerging markets is substantially increased, mainly during the ISE Regime behind larger inward spillovers, as well as to a number of emerging European countries, such as Hungary and Czech Republic. Whether it would theoretically be beneficial for disinflation, it would also contribute to overheating and inflationary pressures in countries with fixed exchange rate regimes or where the authorities have been reluctant to let the exchange rate appreciate.

Following the notably expansionary monetary policies of major advanced countries in the aftermath of the Great Recession, many emerging market economies have experienced a large surge of capital inflow. Emerging market economies have adopted a variety of policy tools aimed at curbing credit growth. Ongoing postcrisis consolidation, there has been a significant process of international financial integration characterized by the rising importance of international financial flows and larger gross external assets and liabilities. More precisely, many emerging economies have experienced sharp capital flow reversals intensifying and causing significant local currency depreciation in financial markets. These sharp retrenchments of capital flows, known as sudden stops, have posed a different policy tradeoff for these economies. They would create pressure for countries to depreciate their currencies, which can boost inflation. Thus, fighting inflation would require tighter monetary policy, which could lower growth assessment. In addition, currency depreciations reduce the net worth of sectors in home country which have outstanding debts denominated in foreign currencies. When emerging economies are vulnerable to shocks, especially to shocks to the international interest rate, it is often argued that banks should be discouraged from borrowing in foreign currency. Another policy recommendation would be to discourage banks from holding too much risky assets relative to their net worth by imposing bank capital requirement.

Concluding Remarks

This chapter provides new empirical insights in order to give a relevant contribution to the more recent literature on international macroeconomic-financial linkages when evaluating idiosyncratic shock transmission and investigating policy interactions in multicountry dynamic panel setups. An extended time-varying Structural Panel Bayesian Vector Autoregressive model is developed to jointly deal with model misspecification and unobserved heterogeneity problems in panel data. The author defines a hierarchical prior specification strategy and compute MCMC implementations to calculate posterior distributions of conditional generalized impulse response functions and conditional forecasts reacting to unexpected perturbations in the innovations of factors in the system. Bayesian methods are used to reduce the dimensionality of the model, structure the time variations, and evaluate issues of endogeneity.

The approach and the empirical implementation focus on a pool of emerging market countries by using the information contained in a large set of endogenous macroeconomic-financial variables, with particular attention to the most recent recession and postcrisis consolidation. The author focuses on the latest two alternative monetary policy regimes that have been in place since the *1990*: (1) the inflation stabilization era from *1994* to *2008* and (2) the zero interest rate era from *2008* to *2015*. The author also considers two additional periods: (1) *2006–2009* to investigate possible commonality between financial markets and real economy during the recent crisis and (2) *2010–2016* to evaluate fiscal implications and lessons for policymaking during postcrisis consolidation. The analysis is robust and consistent with the more recent business cycle studies, which recognize the importance of (1) accounting for both group-specific and global factors when evaluating cross-country spillovers, (2) separating common shocks from the propagation of country- and variable-specific shocks when studying economic-financial linkages, and

(3) accounting for additional transmission channels and economic-institutional issues when using multicountry dynamic data.

From a modeling perspective, there has been evidence of significant co-movements in real economy and significant dynamic interdependence in financial markets among emerging economies. A relevant degree of homogeneity in the spreading of the spillover effects matters among real variables and even more among financial sectors. Thus, unexpected country-specific shocks directly affect a country's own output growth in the financial dimension and then in the real economy because of consistent cross-country interdependencies. When dealing with not directly observed economic issues, the common component in the real and financial dimensions tends to matter more because of consistent interactions between monetary and fiscal policy, mainly during the aftermath of the Great Recession. Accounting for additional transmission channels, they would mainly affect the real economy where commonality and homogeneity matter more because of relevant international trade exposures. During postcrisis consolidation, the intensity of spillover effects sufficiently decreases behind more coordinated fiscal actions, mainly in the financial dimension because of stronger cross-country interdependencies. This suggests that there would be significant benefits from fiscal consolidation without delay and that there is a need for caution against excessive faith in fiscal structures.

From a policy perspective, the empirical results highlight that fiscal consolidation has played a central role in the disinflation process. Nevertheless, a number of other forces have also contributed, although their impact likely is varied considerably among different countries, such as economic-institutional reforms, structural reforms, and access to global capital markets. Ongoing postcrisis consolidation, many emerging market economies have experienced a significant process of international financial integration characterized by the rising importance of international financial flows and larger gross external assets and liabilities. More precisely, many emerging economies have experienced sharp capital flow reversals causing significant local currency depreciation in financial markets. When emerging economies are vulnerable to shocks, especially to shocks to the international interest rate, it is often argued that banks should be discouraged from borrowing in foreign currency and from holding too much risky assets relative to their net worth by imposing bank capital requirement. Finally, further reforms in goods, service, and labor markets, that improve economic efficiency, will boost the output at the potential growth, in turn serving as important tools in the fiscal adjustment process.

References

Arnold JD, Quelch AJ (1998) New strategies in emerging markets. Sloan Manag Rev 40(1):7–20

Banbura M, Giannone D, Reichlin L (2010) Large Bayesian vector auto regression. J Appl Econ 25:71–92

Bernanke B, Mihov I (1998) Measuring monetary policy. Q J Econ 113(3):869–902

Bernanke B, Boivin J, Eliasz P (2005) Measuring the effects of monetary policy: a Factor-Augmented vector autoregressive (FAVAR) approach. Q J Econ 120:387–422

Canova F, Ciccarelli M (2004) Forecasting and turning point predictions in a Bayesian panel VAR model. J Econ 120(2):327–359
Canova F, Ciccarelli M (2009) Estimating multicountry VAR models. Int Econ Rev 50(3):929–959
Canova F, Marrinan J (1998) Sources and propagation of international output cycles: common shocks or transmission? J Int Econ 46(1):133–166
Canova F, Ciccarelli M, Ortega E (2012) Do institutional changes affect business cycles? J Econ Dyn Control 36(10):1520–1533
Cavusgil ST (1997) Measuring the potential of emerging markets: an indexing approach. Bus Horiz 40(1):87–97
Chib S (1995) Marginal likelihood from the Gibbs output. J Am Stat Assoc 90(432):1313–1321
Chib S (1996) Calculating posterior distributions and model estimates in Markov mixture models. J Econ 75(1):79–97
Chib S, Albert JH (1993) Bayes inference via Gibbs sampling of autoregressive time series subject to Markov mean and variance shifts. J Bus Econ Stat 11(1):1–15
Chib S, Grrenberg E (1995) Understanding the metropolis-hasting algorithm. Am Stat 49 (4):327–335
Chib S, Jeliazkov I (2001) Marginal likelihood from the metropolis-hastings output. J Am Stat Assoc 96(453):270–281
Ciccarelli M, Rebucci A (2007) Measuring contagion using a Bayesian time-varying coefficient model. J Financ Econ 5(2):285–320
Ciccarelli M, Ortega E, Valderrama MT (2018) Commonalities and cross-country spillovers in macroeconomic-financial linkages. J Macroecon 16(1):231–275
Clarida R, Gali J, Gertler M (1999) The science of monetary policy: a new Keynesian perspective. J Econ Lit 37:1661–1707
Clarida R, Gali J, Gertler M (2000) Monetary policy rules and macroeconomic stability: evidence and some theory. Q J Econ 115:147–180
Doan T, Litterman R, Sims C (1984) Forecasting and conditional projection using realistic prior distributions. Econ Rev 3(1):1–100
Dornbusch R, Fischer S (1993) Moderate inflation. World Bank Econ Rev 7(3896)
Eichenbaum M, Evans CL (1995) Some empirical evidence of shocks to monetary policy on exchange rates. Q J Econ 110(4):975–1010
Fischer S, Sahay R, Végh CA (1996) Stabilization and growth in transition economies: the early experience. J Econ Perspect 10(2):45–66
Forni M, Hallin M, Lippi M, Reichlin L (2005) The generalized factor models: one-sided estimation of forecasting. J Am Stat Assoc 100(471):830–840
Fredj J, Sushanta KM, Ricardo MS (2016) Fiscal and monetary policies in the BRICS: a panel VAR approach. Econ Model 58:535–542
Kadiyala RK, Karlsson S (1997) Numerical methods for estimation and inference in Bayesian VAR models. J Appl Econ 12(2):99–132
Kallianiotis IN (2019) Monetary policy, real cost of capital, financial markets, and the real economic growth. J Appl Financ Bank 9(1):75–118
Koop G (1996) Parameter uncertainty and impulse response analysis. J Econ 72(1–2):135–149
Lane PR, Milesi-Ferretti GM (2007) The external wealth of nations Mark II: revised and extended estimates of foreign assets and liabilities, 1970-2004. J Int Econ 73(2):223–250
Litterman RB (1986) Forecasting with Bayesian vector autoregressions - five years of experience. J Bus Econ Stat 4(1):25–38
Lubik T, Schorfheide F (2004) Computing sunspost equilibria in linear rational expectations models. J Econ Dyn Control 28(2):273–285
Mastrogiacomo M, Bosch NM, Gielen MD, Jongen EL (2017) Heterogeneity in labour supply responses: evidence from a major tax reform. Oxf Bull Econ Stat 79(4):769–796
Miller RR (1998) Selling to newly emerging markets. Quorum Books, New York, pp 324–326
Obstfeld M, Shambaugh J, Taylor A (2005) The Trilemma in history: tradeoffs among exchange rates, monetary policies, and capital mobility. Rev Econ Stat 87(3):423–438

Pacifico A (2019a) International co-movements and business cycles synchronization across advanced economies: a SPBVAR evidence. Int J Stat Probab 8(4):68–85
Pacifico A (2019b) Structural panel Bayesian VAR model to deal with model misspecification and unobserved heterogeneity problems. Econometrics 7(1):1–24
Pacifico A (2020) Fiscal implications, misspecified dynamics, and international spillover effects across Europe: a time-varying multicountry analysis. Int J Stat Econ 21(2):18–40
Pesaran HM, Shinb Y (1998) Generalized impulse response analysis in linear multivariate models. Econ Lett 58(1):17–29
Shambaugh J (2004) The effect of fixed exchange rates on monetary policy. Q J Econ 119 (1):301–352
Uribe M (1997) Exchange-rate-based inflation stabilization: the initial real effects of credible plans. J Monet Econ 39(2):197–221

Antonio Pacifico I am Professor on contract since 2015 in Applied Statistics and Micro-econometrics at the Department of Political Science of the LUISS University (Rome), and in Financial Econometrics and Time-Series Analysis at the Departments of Business and Management and Economics and Finance of the LUISS and Tor Vergata Universities (Rome).

I hold a Ph.D. and a Postdoctoral Program in Applied Statistics and Econometrics.

My primary research interests are in the fields of High Dimensional Time-Series, Bayesian Statistics, Forecasting, Dynamic Panel VAR Models, MCMC Integrations and Implementations, Big Data Analytics, and Machine Learning Techniques for Data Mining.

The Impacts of Transportation Sector and Unemployment on Economic Growth: Evidence from Asymmetric Causality

Sultan Kuzu Yıldırım

Abbreviations

ADF	Augmented Dickey–Fuller
AIC	Akaike Information Criteria
AR	Autoregressive
ARCH	Autoregressive Conditional Heteroscedasticity
BTS	Bureau of Transportation Statistics
DF-GLS	Dickey–Fuller-Generalized Least Square
DOT	Department of Transportation
FPE	Final Prediction Error
GDP	Gross Domestic Product
HJC	Hatemi J Criteria (lag length)
HQ	Hannan–Quinn Information Criteria
KPSS	Kwiatkowski and Phillips and Schmidt and Shin
LM	Lagrange Multiplier
LR	Likelihood Ratio
PP	Phillips and Perron
SIC	Schwarz Information Criteria
TSI	Transportation Services Index
UR	Unemployment Rate
US	United States
VAR	Vector Autoregressive
ZA	Zivot and Andrews

S. Kuzu Yıldırım (✉)
School of Business, Quantitative Methods Department, Istanbul University, Istanbul, Turkey
e-mail: sultan.kuzu@istanbul.edu.tr

B. Adıgüzel Mercangöz (ed.), *Handbook of Research on Emerging Theories, Models, and Applications of Financial Econometrics*,
https://doi.org/10.1007/978-3-030-54108-8_11

Importance of the Chapter

There are many studies in the econometrics literature regarding these variables. The relationships between economic growth, unemployment, and the transport sector were mostly examined through Granger causality tests. However, in recent years, there have been major developments in causality analysis. With the asymmetric causality analysis developed by Hatemi in 2012, the causal relationship between the variables can be examined in more detail. With this test, it is determined in which direction the negative or positive shock occurring in one variable changes the other variable. In the literature, applications of asymmetric causality analysis are encountered. However, asymmetric causality analysis of the variables in this study has never been done before. The study is quite unique in this respect.

Introduction

Transportation sector has been increasingly recognized as one of the important driving forces for economic growth. This sector also creates employment due to its relations with sectors such as insurance, warehouse, customs clearance, and packaging (Deniz 2016). Transportation sector also plays an important role in the country's competitive advantage due to its contribution to economic growth and employment. High level of economic growth, rapid urbanization, increasing disposable income, diversity of social and leisure activities, rapid growth in the number of private vehicles and unequal distribution of materials and energy resources have increased transportation demand (Saboori et al. 2014). As can be seen, it is not possible to think independently of the concepts of the transport sector, economic growth, and unemployment. In this study, the relationship between the transportation sector, economic growth, and unemployment will be examined. But first, these three concepts will be explained in detail.

Transportation sector regulates the flow of goods, establishes connections with different countries and ensures the continuity of this process. There is no single definition of *transportation* in the literature. But the most commonly used definition is Pegrum's (1973) "Movement of people and goods from one place to another." Transport is a key economic sector, supporting economic and social development, allowing efficient allocation of materials and resources and mobility for people (Saboori et al. 2014). Transport plays a vital role in world commerce. This industry may not seem like an obvious economic driver but, without transport, manufacturers would not have products and components, consumers would not receive goods, and businesses would not be able to trade internationally. The existence of indirect and direct impact of transport sector and infrastructure investments on economic growth has been demonstrated by many studies. An efficient transport network reduces logistics and production costs and facilitates market integration. Integrated markets bring economic opportunities and communication networks are developing.

Transportation and transportation-related industries employ over 13.3 million people, accounting for 9.1% of workers in the USA. Employment in these industries rose steadily from 2011 to 2015 to 13.6 million, exceeding prerecession levels, then declined to 13.3 million in 2017.

In this study, Transportation Services Index (TSI) data were used to represent growth in the US transportation sector. TSI, created by the US Department of Transportation (DOT), Bureau of Transportation Statistics (BTS), measures the movement of freight and passengers. This index, which is seasonally adjusted, combines available data on freight traffic, as well as passenger travel, that have been weighted to yield a monthly measure of transportation services output.

Our second variable, economic growth, has been of great interest since the Second World War. Economic growth is the increase in the market value of the goods and services produced by an economy over time. Economic growth, by its nature, is about aggregate and macro outcomes. It is conventionally measured as the percent rate of increase in real gross domestic product, or real GDP. When the current statistics on the USA are examined, it is seen that the Gross Domestic Product is 20,494,099.85 by 2018. And it increased by 2.2% compared to a year ago.

Unemployment, which is the last variable we are interested in, is one of the most important problems of the whole economy in macro and micro scale. It causes economic and social problems as well. In economic terms, the cost of unemployment, both to the individual and to the collective, is extremely high (Jahoda 1982). It is a widely accepted view in economics that the growth rate of the GDP of an economy increases employment and reduces unemployment (Kreishan 2011). In addition to economic growth, the transport sector also contributes to employment. Transport infrastructure increases foreign trade and tourism and therefore leads to demand for qualified labor in these sectors. The US unemployment rate stood at 3.7% in July 2019, unchanged from the previous month's figure and in line with market expectations. The number of unemployed increased by 88 thousand to 6.1 million while employment went up by 283 thousand to 157.3 million.

Literature Review

The literature research is basically divided into two parts. In the first part, studies on unemployment, economic growth, and transportation sector are compiled. In the second part, similar studies with the methodology used are examined.

Part 1

The terms economic development and economic growth refer to long-term increases in economic activities. In many studies, it has been determined that transportation investments have a positive relationship with economic growth and it has been proposed to give priority to the transportation sector in public fund allocation (Banister and Berechman 2001). Aschauer (1989a, b, c) determined the positive effect of infrastructure investments on production and economy. In his study, Aschauer (1991) found that transportation expenditures have the potential to have a positive impact on economic growth more than highway investment expenditures in the long run. Mohmand et al. (2017) have argued that the direct and indirect effects of transport infrastructure have a positive impact on the economic growth and development of a country. Pradhan and Bagchi (2013) suggested that the expansion of transport infrastructure (both road and rail) along with gross capital formation will lead to substantial growth of the Indian economy.

Fernald (1999) found that when growth in roads which is the largest component of infrastructure changes, productivity growth changes unproportioned in the United States (US) industries with more vehicles. In study reported also a causality relationship from changes in road stock to changes in productivity in the US industries from 1953 to 1989. Sturm et al. (1999) found a positive impact of transport infrastructure investment on the Netherlands GDP in their study. In study this strong evidence interpreted as a quantitative underpinning of the claim that infrastructure induced economic growth. Lean et al. (2014) investigated the causal relationship between logistics development and economic growth in both the short and long-term run. In study researches found a long-run relationship between logistics development and economic growth in the total output and disaggregate output models. The short-run causality runs from Real output of transportation, warehouse service, and telecommunications industry to Real GDP for the total output mode. Banerjee et al. (2012) estimated the effect of access to transportation networks on regional economic outcomes in China over a 20 period of rapid income growth. Their results show that proximity to transportation networks has a moderate positive causal effect on per capita GDP levels across sectors, but no effect on per capita GDP growth.

The transport infrastructure investments are local specific and growth effects on local economies. For this reason, to actually identify and measure the economic growth resulting from such investment, analysis must take place at locally.

Wang (2010) investigated the relation between regional Logistics of Anhui/Eastern China province and economic growth by Granger causality tests and Logistic model. According to the study, coordinated development of economic growth and regional logistics and healthy development of regional logistics is till to be the direction of Anhui in the next period of time. Chu (2012) examined the long-run relationship between logistics investment and economic growth investigated with conditional convergence model with dynamic panel data approach. The dataset covering 30 provinces over the period from 1998 to 2007 in China investigated. As a result, higher initial per capita GDP does not lead to a lower economic growth in coastal provinces significantly. Hong et al. (2011) examined the relationship between transportation investments and regional economic growth for 31 cities in China within the period of 1998–2007 with panel data analysis. As a result of the study, it has been determined that transportation infrastructure investments play an important role in regional economic growth. Yu et al. (2012), in their studies conducted on Granger causality and panel cointegration in spatial clusters scale between 1978 and 2008 in China, it was determined that transportation investments in spatial clusters with low-income, level of development were not the main factors of economic growth and it was suggested that policy makers contribute to the development of these regions with additional factors.

In the literature, apart from the studies that examine the relationship between economic growth and transportation infrastructure investments, there are studies on the relationship between the transportation and logistics sector and sectoral expenditures and economic growth. Chu (2012) examined the long-term relationship between logistics investments and economic growth and analyzed the 1998–2007 period for 30 regions in China with the Conditional convergence model with dynamic panel data approach. As a result of the study, a significant and positive relationship was found between logistics investments and regional economic growth. Achour and Belloumi (2016) examined the 1971–2012 period using the Johansen multivariate cointegration approach. In their studies in which they examined the relationship between energy consumption and economic growth as well as transport investment expenditures for Tunisia. In their study, Saboori et al. (2014) examined the relationship between economic growth and energy consumption and CO2 emissions in road transport for OECD countries. In this study, Fully Modified Ordinary Least Squares cointegration method was used and as a result, a long-term positive correlation was determined between the selected variables.

It is possible to come across studies that examine the effects of other transport modes on economic growth besides road transport. From these studies, Marazzo et al. (2010), in their study examining the relationship between air transport demand and economic growth in Brazil, the relationship between passenger-km (PAX) and GDP was analyzed for the period 1966–2006. According to the results of the study, the variables examined were co-integrated, but the effect of GDP on PAX was found to be slower and moderated. Yamaguchi (2007) examined the impact of interregional air transport accessibility on the economy in Japan.

Part II

Kim (2003) used a modified Granger-(non)causality in reviewing the negative correlation between stock returns and inflation in Germany. The results show that the hypothesis of Granger-noncausality from stock returns to real activity is significant. Hristu-Varsakelis and Kyrtsou (2008) proposed an asymmetric version of a Mackey-Glass causality model in their study. They have demonstrated the relationship between inflation and metal returns series and found that the bidirectional causality identified is mainly due to positive movements of metal prices and negative movements of inflation. Yıldırım et al. (2013) examined the relation between financial development and economic growth from the asymmetry perspective using a dataset covering emerging European economies over the period from 1990 to 2012. As a result, they found that negative shocks in economic growth are the cause of negative shocks in financial development. Akbaş et al. (2014) tested the validity of the triplet deficit in Turkish economy. As a result of the asymmetric causality test, bidirectional causality was found between the current account deficit and the budget deficit and between the current account deficit and savings gap. Alper and Oguz (2016) used asymmetric causality test approach and autoregressive distributed lag (ARDL) approach to examine the causality among economic growth, renewable energy consumption, capital, and labor for new EU member countries for the period of 1990–2009. The empirical results support that renewable energy consumption has positive impacts on economic growth for all investigated countries. Destek (2016) investigated the relationship between renewable energy consumption and economic growth in newly industrialized countries is examined for the period from 1971 to 2011. According to the results of his study that negative shocks in renewable energy consumption cause positive shocks in real GDP for South Africa and Mexico; negative shocks in renewable energy consumption causes negative shocks in real GDP for India. Besides, the neutrality hypothesis is approved for Brazil and Malaysia. Hatemi et al. (2017) applied an asymmetric causality test in each G7 countries and they found that increasing oil prices cause stock prices to rise in the world, the USA and Japan while decreasing oil prices cause stock prices to fall in Germany. Hatemi et al. (2018) applied asymmetric causality tests, to revisit military expenditures-growth nexus for the world's top six defense spenders during the period of 1988–2013. Their empirical results show that the military expenditure-led hypothesis is supported in China and Japan. Tuna and Tuna (2019) analyzed the causality between energy consumption and economic growth for ASEAN-5 countries. They used Hacker and Hatemi (2006) test's and Hatemi (2012) test's together. The result of the Hatemi (2012) tests put forward the presence of a significant relationships between non-renewable economic growth and energy consumption. They observed different interactions according to the situation of positive and negative shocks.

Methodology

- Unit Root Tests
  There are many unit root tests in the literature. In this study, Augmented Dickey–Fuller (ADF) (Dickey and Fuller 1979), Phillips–Perron (PP) (Phillips and Perron 1988), Kwiatkowski–Phillips–Schmidt–Shin (KPSS) (Kwiatkowski et al. 1992), and Dickey–Fuller-GLS unit root test were applied. The hypotheses of ADF, PP, and DF-GLS unit root tests are established in the same way. In these tests, the null hypothesis suggests that the unit root exists in the series;

$$H_0 : \rho = 1 \text{ (Non – Stationary)}.$$

$$H_1 : |\rho|\langle 1 \text{ (Stationary)}$$

But hypotheses are inversely established in the KPSS unit root test.

$$H_0 : |\rho|\langle 1 \text{ (Stationary)}$$

$$H_1 : \rho = 1 \text{ (Non} - \text{Stationary)}$$

Furthermore, ADF and KPSS unit root tests are parametric tests, PP is a nonparametric alternative. It is recommended to compare at least the values obtained from these three tests for the validity of the stability results. It is also important to determine the presence or absence of structural breaks in the long-term time series. If there is a structural break, conventional unit root tests give inconsistent results. In order to solve this problem, unit root tests have been developed considering structural breaks.

In this book section, the tests recommended by Perron and Zıvot & Andrews (ZA) unit root tests will be applied. These tests are used when the date of fracture is unknown (endogenous break). It is one of testing for a unit root against the alternative of stationarity with structural change at some unknown point.

- Granger Causality Test

In order to perform the Granger causality analysis, the appropriate Vector autoregressive (VAR) model should be established. VAR is a stochastic process model used to capture the linear interdependencies among multiple time series. VAR models generalize the univariate autoregressive model (AR model) by allowing for more than one evolving variable. VAR model was developed by Sims (1980). VAR models are frequently used to examine the relationships between economic variables. This model does not impose any restrictions on the structural model of the endogenous–exogenous variables that do not require separation.

Let X_t, Y_t be two stationary time series with zero means. The simple causal model is,

$$X_t = \sum_{j=1}^{m} a_j X_{t-j} + \sum_{j=1}^{m} b_j Y_{t-j} + \varepsilon_t \tag{1}$$

$$Y_t = \sum_{j=1}^{m} c_j X_{t-j} + \sum_{j=1}^{m} d_j Y_{t-j} + \eta_t \tag{2}$$

where ε_t, η_t are taken to be two uncorrelated white-noise series. The definition of causality given above implies that Y_t is causing X_t provided some b_j is not zero. M can equal infinity but in practice, of course, due to the finite length of the available data, m will be assumed finite and shorter than the given time series (Granger 1969). Information criteria are considered when determining the number of lag length. Of these criteria, frequently used LR (sequential modified LR test statistic),
FPE (Final prediction error), AIC (Akaike information criterion),
SIC (Schwarz information criterion), HQ (Hannan–Quinn information criterion). When determining the number of delays, it is not enough to look at the information

criteria. It is important that the model is stable and provides assumptions in the number of delays selected.

- Asymmetric Causality Tests

In classical causality analysis, the effect of positive or negative shocks is not considered separately. However, these tests may be insufficient in the financial markets due to the existence of asymmetric information and the fact that the participants in the market are not homogeneous and that the participants do not respond to the same magnitude negative and positive shocks with the same intensity. Granger and Yoon (2002) argued that, apart from examining two series, cointegration could also occur between the components of the series. In other words, the response of the series to positive and negative shocks may be different from the relationship between the variables. Hatemi (2012) developed the Granger and Yoo approach for causality analysis.

$Y_{1t}$and Y_{2t} causality relationship get two series to be examined. Random walking processes of this series;

$$Y_{1t} = Y_{1t} + \varepsilon_{1t} = Y_{1,0} + \sum_{i=1}^{t} \varepsilon_{1i} \tag{3}$$

$$Y_{2t} = Y_{2t} + \varepsilon_{2t} = Y_{2,0} + \sum_{i=1}^{t} \varepsilon_{2i} \tag{4}$$

where t = 1,2,...T, the constants $Y_{1,\,0}$ and $Y_{2,\,0}$ are the initial values, and ε_{1i} ε_{2i} signify white-noise disturbance terms. Positive shocks; $\begin{matrix}\varepsilon_{1i}^{+} = \max(\varepsilon_{1i}, 0)\\ \varepsilon_{2i}^{+} = \max(\varepsilon_{2i}, 0)\end{matrix}$ negative shocks; $\begin{matrix}\varepsilon_{1i}^{-} = \max(\varepsilon_{1i}, 0)\\ \varepsilon_{2i}^{-} = \max(\varepsilon_{2i}, 0)\end{matrix}$ as defined $\varepsilon_{1i} = \varepsilon_{1i}^{+} + \varepsilon_{1i}^{-}$ ve $\varepsilon_{2i} = \varepsilon_{2i}^{+} + \varepsilon_{2i}^{-}$ is expressed as. Positive and negative shocks are expressed cumulatively as follows.

$$Y_{1t}^{+} = \sum_{i=1}^{t} \varepsilon_{1i}^{+}, Y_{1t}^{-} = \sum_{i=1}^{t} \varepsilon_{1i}^{-}, Y_{2t}^{+} = \sum_{i=1}^{t} \varepsilon_{2i}^{+}, Y_{2t}^{-} = \sum_{i=1}^{t} \varepsilon_{2i}^{-} \tag{5}$$

Assuming that $Y_t^{+} = \left(Y_{1t}^{+}, Y_{2t}^{+}\right)$the test for causality can be implemented by using the following vector autoregressive model of order p, VAR (p):

$$Y_t^{+} = \upsilon + A_1 Y_{t-1}^{+} + \ldots + A_p Y_{t-1}^{+} + u_t \tag{6}$$

Y_t^{+} vector of variables (2×1), υ vector of constant, (2×1), u_t^{+} vector of error terms (2×1) The matrix A_r is a 2×2 coefficient matrix of parameters. The HJC criterion developed by Hatemi is used in order to find the optimal delay number.

$$HJC = \ln\left(\left|\widehat{\Omega}\right|\right) + j\left(\frac{n^2 \ln T + 2n^2 \ln(\ln T)}{2T}\right) \quad (7)$$

In this equation, T, is the number of observations; n, is the number of VAR models equation, $\left|\widehat{\Omega}\right|$, is determinant of variance covariance matrix of error terms. After determining the appropriate number of delay, the null hypothesis is tested to show that there is no causality. The hypothesis is tested through the Wald Test statistic. The Wald test shows the asymptotic χ^2 distribution with the degree of freedom as the number of constraints under the assumption that the series is normally distributed. However, financial data does not usually follow a normal distribution. Therefore, the effects of Autoregressive Conditional heteroscedasticity (ARCH) are seen in the series. Critical (table) values are obtained by bootstrap simulations to resolve this problem. The bootstrap simulations are applied by using statistical software components written in GAUSS.

Data and Empirical Results

In order to investigate the relationship between transportation, economic growth, and unemployment we use quarterly data on Transportation Service Index (TSI), Gross Domestic Product (GDP), and Unemployment Rate (UR) over the period from 2000/Q1 through 2018/Q4. The graphs of these series are given in Figs. 1, 2, and 3. The analyzes were applied with the help of Gauss and WinRats programs.

When the graphs are examined, it is seen that the series are not stationary in general. Even in some periods, the impression of structural breaks occurs. To

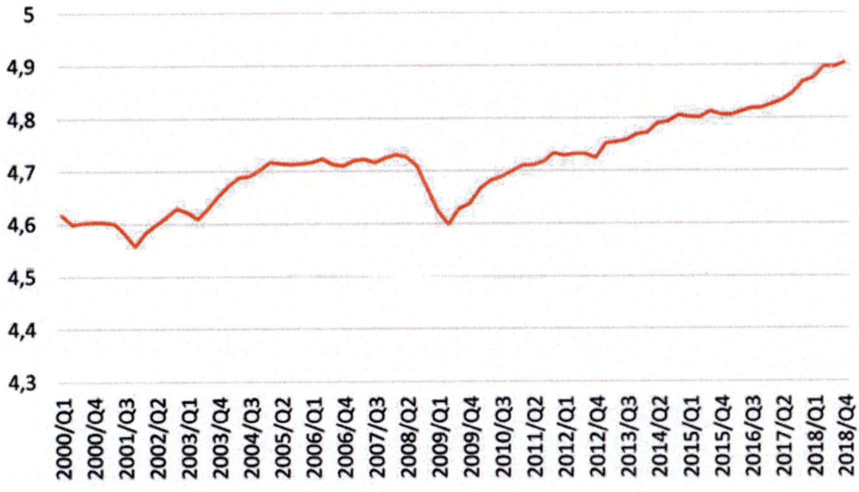

Fig. 1 Transportation Service Index. Source: Author's creation

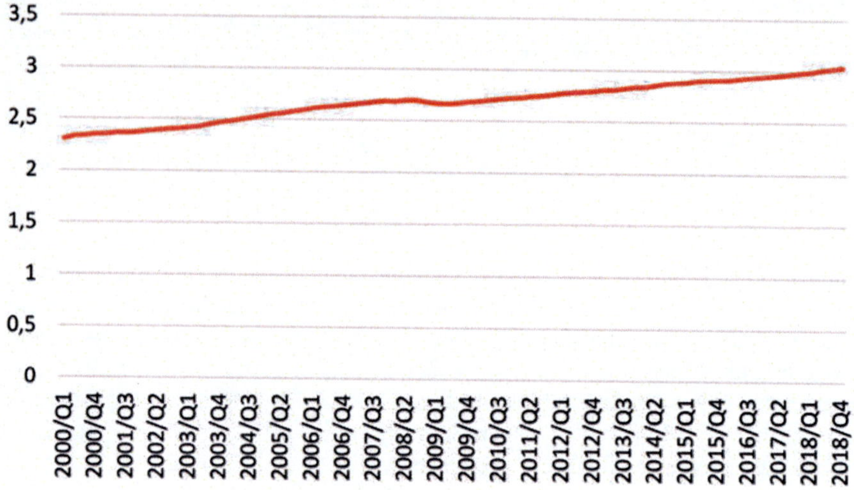

Fig. 2 Gross Domestic Product. Source: Author's creation

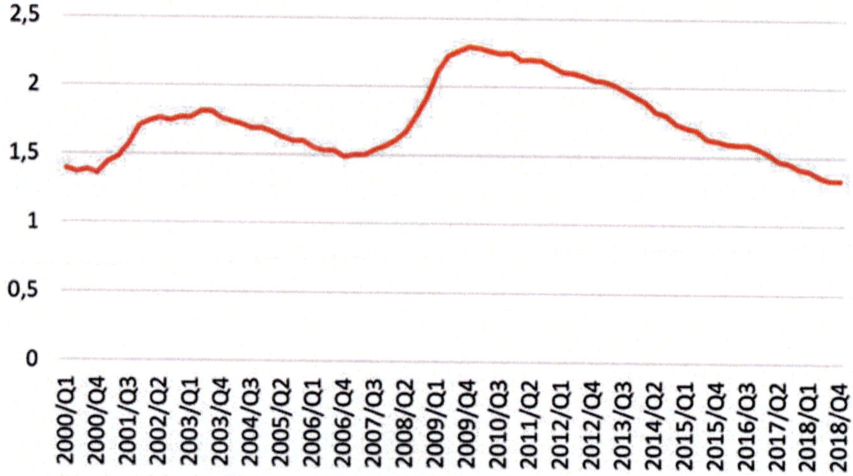

Fig. 3 Unemployment Rate. Source: Author's creation

determine this, unit root tests were performed. Before the analysis, we convert the data into the natural logarithmic form and the data are seasonally adjusted. As a first step of the analysis conventional unit root tests are Augmented Dickey–Fuller (ADF) and Philips and Perron (PP), Kwiatkowski–Phillips–Schmidt–Shin (KPSS) and DF-GLS unit root tests. The results are tabulated in Tables 1, 2, and 3.

When the maximum lag number is selected 6, the result of unit root tests for Transportation Service Index is given in Table 1.

When the maximum lag number is selected 6, the result of unit root tests for Gross Domestic Product is given in Table 2.

Table 1 Seasonally adjusted logarithmic "TSI" series and their first differences

	Model A				Model B				Model C			
	t-stat.		Sig.		t-stat.		Sig.		t-stat.		Sig.	
ADF	−0.48	−5.66'	0.89	0.00'	−2.19	−5.66'	0.49	0.00'	1.69	−5.34'	0.98	0.00'
PP	0.02	−5.66'	0.95	0.00'	−1.89	−5.66'	0.65	0.00'	1.82	−5.35'	0.98	0.00'
	Model A						Model B					
KPSS	0.99			0.13'			0.12			0.06'		
DF-GLS	0.30			−3.94'			−2.23			−5.15'		

Source: Author's creation

Table 2 Seasonally adjusted logarithmic "GDP" series and their first differences

	Model A				Model B				Model C			
	t-stat.		Sig.		t-stat.		Sig.		t-stat.		Sig.	
ADF	0.19	−5.64'	0.93	0.00'	−1.59	−5.58'	0.78	0.00'	4.42	−1.39'	1.00	0.15'
PP	−0.71	−5.87'	0.83	0.00'	−1.88	−5.82'	0.65	0.00'	7.59	−2.82'	1.00	0.00'
	Model A						Model B					
KPSS	1.17			0.12'			0.15			0.09'		
DF-GLS	1.99			−2.03'			−1.54			−4.45'		

Source: Author's creation

Table 3 Seasonally adjusted logarithmic "UR" series and their first differences

	Model A				Model B				Model C			
	t-stat.		Sig.		t-stat.		Sig.		t-stat.		Sig.	
ADF	−2.49	−3.43'	0.12	0.01'	−2.33	−3.79'	0.41	0.02'	−0.27	−3.45'	0.58	0.00'
PP	−1.46	−3.48'	0.54	0.01'	−1.09	−3.89'	0.92	0.02'	−0.29	−3.50'	0.57	0.00'
	Model A						Model B					
KPSS	0.22			0.31'			0.20			0.07'		
DF-GLS	−1.49			−3.29'			−2.19			−3.49'		

': It indicates the values after the first differences of the series are taken.
Source: Author's creation

Table 4 Structural break unit root test

		TSI		GDP		UR	
		Break P.	t-stat.	Break P.	t-stat.	Break P.	t-stat.
Zivot and Andrews	Model A	2008/Q3	−5.18	2008/Q4	−3.67	2008/Q2	−4.67
	Model B	2012/Q2	−2.81	2005/Q1	−3.37	2011/Q4	−3.74
	Model C	2008/Q3	−5.26	2008/Q4	−5.80	2008/Q3	−6.24
Perron	Model A	2008/Q2	−5.38	2008/Q2	−3.54	2008/Q1	−4.31
	Model B	2008/Q2	−5.39	2008/Q3	−5.85	2008/Q2	−6.07
	Model C	2012/Q2	−2.85	2008/Q4	−5.80	2013/Q2	−2.58

Source: Author's creation

Table 5 VAR lag order selection criteria

Lag	LogL	LR	FPE	AIC	SC	HQ
0	592.5616	NA	7.60e-12	−17.08874	−16.99161	−17.05021
1	632.0303	74.36130	3.15e-12	−17.97189	−17.58335*	−17.81775*
2	639.9471	14.22735	3.25e-12	−17.94050	−17.26055	−17.67074
3	651.6086	19.94275	3.02e-12	−18.01764	−17.04629	−17.63227
4	661.7763	16.50407	2.94e-12	−18.05149	−16.78873	−17.55051
5	669.3139	11.57957	3.11e-12	−18.00910	−16.45494	−17.39251
6	684.2486	21.64451*	2.66e-12*	−18.18112*	−16.33555	−17.44892

Source: Author's creation

Finally, the results of unemployment rates are given in Table 3. When the conventional unit root tests (ADF, PP, KPSS, DF-GLS) are examined for TSI, GDP, and UR, it has seen that they are not stationary at the level but the first-order differences are taken, the series becomes stationary. Although these tests have generally yielded consistent results, at the same time stationary tests have been performed considering structural breaks. In this study, we applied Zivot and Andrews (1992) and Perron (1989) structural break unit root test. The results are tabulated in Table 4.

According to the results in Table 4, the break in 2008 was found to be significant in both tests. Especially in the second, third, and fourth quarter of 2008, significant breaks were observed. This period coincides with the beginning of the world crisis. Therefore, it is an expected result. However, when the structural breaks in the series were taken into consideration, it was found that the series was not stationary at the level. In order to establish the appropriate VAR model, first differences of the series were taken and Granger causality analysis was performed. For VAR model to be valid, firstly this model must be stable and provide assumptions. In order to determine the lag number of the VAR model, the information criteria were examined.

Table 5. shows lag length criteria and results. All models with 1 lag to 6 lag have been tried and a suitable model has been selected with at least 4 delays. (The model was found to be unstable with smaller delays.) The stability of this model is given in Fig. 4.

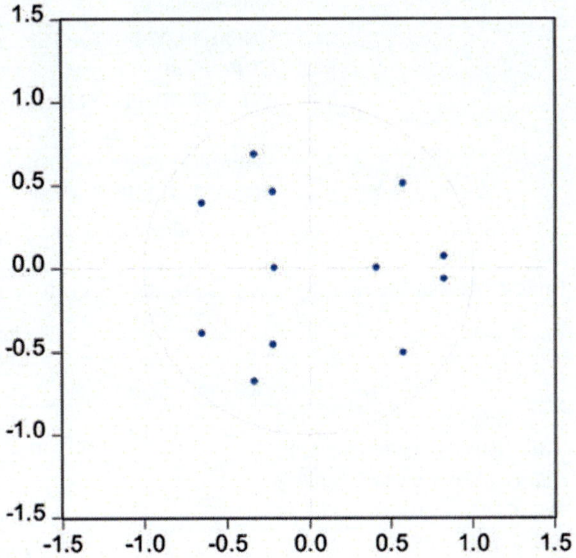

Fig. 4 VAR model stability test: inverse root of AR characteristic polynomial source: Author's creation

Table 6 LM Autocorrelation test

	Model	
L	LM-Stat	Prob.
1	10.3060	0.3263
2	16.7057	0.0535
3	13.6647	0.1348
4	7.7808	0.5564
5	11.7596	0.2278
6	12.2842	0.1978

Source: Author's creation

All of the inverse roots were found to be within the unit circle. So the established VAR model is stable. Since the model is stable, hypothesis examinations can now be performed. Firstly LM test was used to determine if errors were auto correlated. The results are given Table 6.

There was no autocorrelation problem in the error terms. Secondly, the assumption of homoscedasticity was examined. According to VAR Residual Heteroscedasticity Tests (No Cross Terms), there is no heteroscedasticity. The Chi-square value was found 153.02 (prob = 0.28). Thus, the model was also found to be homoscedasticity.

When Table 7 is examined, it is seen that Granger causation is only from transportation to unemployment. That is, there is a one-way relationship. No causal relationship was found between the other variables. The contribution of the transport sector to employment is also an appropriate result for the literature. As the one-way causality relationship was not sufficient, asymmetric causality was investigated.

Table 7 Granger causality test

Null Hypothesis	Chi-sq	df	Prob.
UNEMPLOYMENT→ TSI	7.0036	4	0.1357
GDP → TSI	7.6035	4	0.1072
TSI → UNEMPLOYMENT	10.1978	4	*0.0372*
GDP → UNEMPLOYMENT	2.8709	4	0.5797
UNEMPLOYMENT→ GDP	4.8415	4	0.3040
UNEMPLOYMENT→ TSI	1.7851	4	0.7752

Source: Author's creation

Table 8 Asymmetric causality tests between TSI and GDP

			Critical values for the Leveraged Bootstrap Test		
	MWALD	Asymptotic chi-sqaure p-value	1%	5%	10%
TSI+ GDP+	3.302	0.192	15.359	9.229	6.997
TSI+ GDP-	1.532	0.216	8.317	4.218	2.905
TSI- GDP-	*6.950*	*0.008*	*19.159*	*13.882*	*11.512*
TSI- GDP+	0.635	0.425	9.671	4.697	3.197
GDP+ TSI+	*13.083*	*0.001*	*13.490*	*8.561*	*6.591*
GDP+ TSI-	6.478	0.039	18.883	12.771	10.417
GDP- TSI-	2.512	0.113	19.248	11.397	8.492
GDP- TSI+	1.349	0.510	14.005	9.506	7.051

Source: Author's creation

Table 9 Asymmetric causality tests between TSI and unemployment

			Critical values for the Leveraged Bootstrap Test		
	MWALD	Asymptotic chi-square p-value	1%	5%	10%
TSI+ UNEMP+	3.844	0.146	15.641	10.504	8.004
TSI+ UNEMP -	*13.158*	*0.000*	*16.084*	*10.976*	*9.255*
TSI- UNEMP -	3.344	0.188	19.240	11.507	8.880
TSI- UNEMP +	*5.704*	*0.017*	*10.032*	*5.812*	*3.853*
UNEMP + TSI+	2.202	0.333	15.372	10.299	8.101
UNEMP + TSI -	*6.239*	*0.044*	*21.656*	*15.716*	*12.855*
UNEMP–TSI -	3.639	0.162	15.241	8.614	6.075
UNEMP–TSI +	0.742	0.690	13.248	8.111	5.611

Source: Author's creation

Asymmetric causality analyzes evaluate the negative and positive shocks separately. According to Table 8, the decrease in GDP is the cause of the decrease in Transportation Service Index. At the same time, it is seen that the growth in transportation sector is the reason for the growth in GDP. That is, causal relationships between the transport sector and economic growth are meaningful only when they are in the same direction (Table 9).

When the asymmetrical causality between unemployment and transportation sector is examined, the decline in unemployment rates triggered growth in the transport sector. According to Table 9, it is seen that the increase in unemployment rates caused the shrinkage in transportation sector. Therefore, the causality relationship between unemployment and the transport sector is asymmetrical. This can be said clearly. At the same time, the shrinkage in the transportation sector increases unemployment rates. Studies in the literature generally argue that the transport sector contributes to employment. For this reason, the study produced appropriate results for the literature.

Conclusion

Techniques in econometrics are increasing day by day and econometric analyzes/tests are being updated rapidly. In addition to classical unit root tests, unit root tests that take structural breaks into consideration are also applied frequently. It is known that these tests give better results even in the case of series breakage. For this reason, unit root tests, which are both traditional and considering breaks, were applied in the study. However, in both cases, the series was found to be non-stationary and VAR models were established by taking the first differences. Then, classical causality analyzes were performed and no causality was found among the variables. However, no causal relationship was found with this test. In this test, there is no separation between the causal impact of positive and negative shocks. This is a very restrictive assumption and in many cases, there is an asymmetric structure of causal effects. Hatemi (2012) suggests taking into account this asymmetric behavior in causality testing by constructing the cumulative sums of positive and negative shocks. In this study, causality has been examined as suggested by Hatemi and significant causal relationships were determined with this test. The relations between the transport sector and economic growth and unemployment are examined separately. When the causal relationship between the transportation sector and economic growth is analyzed, it is found that a negative shock in the transport index causes a negative shock in the GDP, but a positive shock in the transport index has no effect on growth. The positive shock observed in the GDP is both positive and negative for the transport index. However, negative shocks that occur in growth have no effect on the transport index. When the relationship between unemployment and transportation index is examined, it is found that the positive shock in transportation causes a negative shock in unemployment rates. Conversely, the positive shock in unemployment is the cause of the negative shock in the transport index. This is an indication that the causality in the unemployment and transport sector is asymmetrical. This study is a proof of the contribution of the transportation sector to employment and economic growth.

Acknowledgment No funding was provided from any institution for writing this book section. The data was obtained free of charge from the official web sites of the US ministries.

References

Achour H, Belloumi M (2016) Investigating the causal relationship between transport infrastructure, transport energy consumption and economic growth in Tunisia. Renew Sust Energ Rev 56:988–998

Akbaş YE, Lebe F, Zeren F (2014) Testing the validity of the triplet deficit hypothesis for Turkey: asymmetric causality analysis. J Bus Econ 7(14):137–154

Alper A, Oguz O (2016) The role of renewable energy consumption in economic growth: evidence from asymmetric causality. Renew Sust Energ Rev 60:953–959

Aschauer DA (1989a) Is public expenditure productive? J Monet Econ 23(2):177–200

Aschauer DA (1989b) Does public capital crowd out private capital? J Monet Econ 24(2):171–188

Aschauer DA (1989c) Public investment and productivity growth in the Group of Seven. Econ Perspect 13(5):17–25

Aschauer DA (1991) Transportation spending and economic growth: the effects of transit and highway expenditures

Banerjee A, Duflo E, Qian N. (2012) On the road: access to transportation infrastructure and economic growth in China (No. w17897). National Bureau of Economic Research

Banister D, Berechman Y (2001) Transport investment and the promotion of economic growth. J Transp Geogr 9(3):209–218

Chu Z (2012) Logistics and economic growth: a panel data approach. Ann Reg Sci 49(1):87–102

Deniz T (2016) Türkiye'de Ulaşım Sektöründe Yaşanan Değişimler ve Mevcut Durum. Doğu Coğrafya Dergisi 21(36):135–156

Destek MA (2016) Renewable energy consumption and economic growth in newly industrialized countries: evidence from asymmetric causality test. Renew Energy 95:478–484

Dickey DA, Fuller WA (1979) Distribution of the estimators for autoregressive time series with a unit root. J Am Stat Assoc 74(366a):427–431

Fernald JG (1999) Roads to prosperity? Assessing the link between public capital and productivity. Am Econ Rev 89(3):619–638

Granger CW (1969) Investigating causal relations by econometric models and cross-spectral methods. J Econ Soc, Econometrica, pp 424–438

Granger CW, Yoon G (2002) Hidden cointegration. Department of Economics Working Paper. University of California, San Diego, pp 1–48

Hacker RS, Hatemi JA (2006) Tests for causality between integrated variables using asymptotic and bootstrap distributions: theory and application. Appl Econ 38(13):1489–1500

Hatemi JA (2012) Asymmetric causality tests with an application. Empir Econ 43(1):447–456

Hatemi JA, Al Shayeb A, Roca E (2017) The effect of oil prices on stock prices: fresh evidence from asymmetric causality tests. Appl Econ 49(16):1584–1592

Hatemi JA, Chang T, Chen WY, Lin FL, Gupta R (2018) Asymmetric causality between military expenditures and economic growth in top six defense spenders. Qual Quant 52(3):1193–1207

Hong J, Chu Z, Wang Q (2011) Transport infrastructure and regional economic growth: evidence from China. Transportation 38(5):737–752

Hristu-Varsakelis D, Kyrtsou C (2008) Evidence for nonlinear asymmetric causality in US inflation, metal, and stock returns. Discret Dyn Nat Soc 2008

Jahoda M (1982) Employment and unemployment. Cambridge University Press

Kim JR (2003) The stock return-inflation puzzle and the asymmetric causality in stock returns, inflation and real activity. Econ Lett 80(2):155–160

Kreishan FM (2011) Economic growth and unemployment: an empirical analysis. J Soc Sci 7 (2):228–231

Kwiatkowski D, Phillips PC, Schmidt P, Shin Y (1992) Testing the null hypothesis of stationarity against the alternative of a unit root: how sure are we that economic time series have a unit root? J Econ 54(1–3):159–178

Lean HH, Huang W, Hong J (2014) Logistics and economic development: experience from China. Transp Policy 32:96–104

Marazzo M, Scherre R, Fernandes E (2010) Air transport demand and economic growth in Brazil: a time series analysis. Transportation Research Part E: Logistics and Transportation Review 46 (2):261–269

Mohmand YT, Wang A, Saeed A (2017) The impact of transportation infrastructure on economic growth: empirical evidence from Pakistan. Transportation Letters 9(2):63–69

Pegrum DF (1973) Transportation: economics and public policy. Richard D. Irwin. Inc., Homewood, Illinois, p 1973

Perron P (1989) The great crash, the oil price shock, and the unit root hypothesis. Journal of the Econometric Society, Econometrica, pp 1361–1401

Phillips PC, Perron P (1988) Testing for a unit root in time series regression. Biometrika 75 (2):335–346

Pradhan RP, Bagchi TP (2013) Effect of transportation infrastructure on economic growth in India: the VECM approach. Res Transp Econ 38(1):139–148

Saboori B, Sapri M, bin Baba M (2014) Economic growth, energy consumption and CO2 emissions in OECD (Organization for Economic CO-operation and Development)'s transport sector: a fully modified bi-directional relationship approach. Energy 66:150–161

Sims CA (1980) Macroeconomics and reality. Econometrica:1–48

Sturm JE, Jacobs J, Groote P (1999) Output effects of infrastructure investment in the Netherlands, 1853–1913. J Macroecon 21(2):355–380

Tuna G, Tuna VE (2019) The asymmetric causal relationship between renewable and non-renewable energy consumption and economic growth in the ASEAN-5 countries. Resources Policy 62:114–124

Wang A (2010) Research of logistics and regional economic growth. iBusiness 2(04):395–400

Yamaguchi K (2007) Inter-regional air transport accessibility and macro-economic performance in Japan. Transportation Research Part E: Logistics and Transportation Review 43(3):247–258

Yıldırım S, Ozdemir BK, Dogan B (2013) Financial development and economic growth nexus in emerging European economies: new evidence from asymmetric causality. Int J Econ Financ Issues 3(3):710–722

Yu N, De Jong M, Storm S, Mi J (2012) Transport infrastructure, spatial clusters and regional economic growth in China. Transp Rev 32(1):3–28

Zivot E, Andrews DWK (1992) Further evidence on the great crash, the oil-price shock, and the unit-root hypothesis. J Bus Econ Stat 10(3):251–270

Sultan Kuzu Yıldırım received her PhD degree in Quantitative Methods from Istanbul University, Institute of Social Sciences in 2016. She is currently working as Assistant Professor at Business School, Istanbul University. Her research interests are Time Series Analysis, Financial Econometrics, Statistical Analysis, and Multivariate Statistical Methods. She has many articles and papers in these fields.

ARCH Models and an Application on Exchange Rate Volatility: ARCH and GARCH Models

Lokman Kantar

Introduction

Due to rising inflation and oil prices since the 1970s, financial liberalization began in the world in the early 1980s. With the financial liberalization, the barriers between the countries were eliminated and intensive capital movements emerged between the countries. The acceleration of financial liberalization increased the importance of the financial sector along with the real sector. These developments that have emerged since the 1980s and sudden movements in asset prices have introduced the concept of volatility to the world agenda.

Accurate calculation of asset prices is related to the correct determination of the risk for that asset. The measure of the risk of the asset is the volatility of that asset. With the development of information technologies and derivative products, accurate determination of the volatility of assets has become extremely important in the financial markets.

There are two main reasons why accurate modeling and estimation of volatility have become extremely important in financial time series. These are:

- Determination of the riskiness of an asset is of great importance for the determination of the price of that asset and volatility is the greatest determinant of risk.
- For a conditional mean to make significant inferences about the price of an asset, it is necessary to define the conditional variance of that asset correctly (Ertuğrul 2012: 5).

L. Kantar (✉)
Istanbul Gelisim University, Istanbul, Turkey
e-mail: lkantar@gelisim.edu.tr

B. Adıgüzel Mercangöz (ed.), *Handbook of Research on Emerging Theories, Models, and Applications of Financial Econometrics*,
https://doi.org/10.1007/978-3-030-54108-8_12

This chapter will discuss the models that best measure stability and volatility, which are the most important prerequisite for the determination of volatility, an indicator of risk. Exchange rate volatility in Turkey will be examined with GARCH models.

Garch Models

Autoregressive Conditional Heteroskedasticity (ARCH) Model

One of the most widely used models in finance is the ARCH model, which deals with nonlinear variances. In a classical regression model, the variance of errors is assumed to be homoscedastic. If the variance of errors is heteroscedastic, the classical regression model (CLRM) will make biased estimates, and the standard error will miscalculate the estimates.

One of the most important properties of financial asset returns is volatility cluster or volatility pooling (Brooks 2008). In such a case, major changes in asset prices are followed by major changes, and minor changes are followed by minor changes. ARCH models are the best models of such movements, not classical regression models.

In the ARCH model, an error term (u_t) is required to define the conditional variance of a random variable. The distinction between conditional and unconditional variances of a random variable and the distinction between conditional and unconditional variances of errors are the same. In the model, the conditional variance of $u_t\left(\sigma_t^2\right)$ is as follows:

$$\sigma_t^2 = var\Big((u_t|u_{t-1},u_{t-2},u_{t-3....,}) = E\Big[(u_t - E(u_t))^2|u_{t-1},u_{t-2},u_{t-3....,}\Big] \tag{1}$$

Since $E(u_t) = 0$

$$\sigma_t^2 = var\big((u_t|u_{t-1},u_{t-2},u_{t-3....,}) = E\big(u_t^2|u_{t-1},u_{t-2},\ldots]. \tag{2}$$

According to Eq. (1), the conditional variance of the normally distributed u_t random variable with a mean of 0 is equal to the square of the conditional expected value of u_t. Therefore, in the ARCH model, σ_t^2 depends on the value of the error squares in the previous period. If the model depends only on the previous delay value, it is referred to as ARCH (1); in this case, the conditional variance depends only on the error square of the previous period. The model shown in (2) is a partial model and does not yet mention anything about the conditional average. Therefore, the whole model can be expressed as follows;

$$y_t = \beta_t + \beta_2 X_{2t} + \beta_3 X_{3t} + \beta_4 X_{4t} + \mathrm{u_t} u_t \tilde{N}(0, \sigma_t^2) \tag{3}$$

$$\sigma_t^2 = \alpha_0 + \alpha_1 u_{t-1}^2 \tag{4}$$

As shown in formulas (3) and (4), the model can be expanded according to the delay length (q) of the error squares. In this case, the model is called ARCH (q). The model can be represented as:

$$\sigma_t^2 = \alpha_0 + \alpha_1 u_{t-1}^2 + \alpha_2 u_{t-2}^2 + \alpha_3 u_{t-3}^2 + \alpha_q u_{t-q}^2 \tag{5}$$

In the literature, conditional variance is usually represented by h_t notation. Therefore, we can write the model as follows (Brooks 2008):

$$y_t = \beta_t + \beta_2 X_{2t} + \beta_3 X_{3t} + \beta_4 X_{4t} + \mathrm{u_t} u_t \tilde{N}(0, h_t) \tag{6}$$

$$h_t = \alpha_0 + \alpha_1 u_{t-1}^2 + \alpha_2 u_{t-2}^2 + \alpha_3 u_{t-3}^2 + \alpha_q u_{t-q}^2 \tag{7}$$

Constraints of the ARCH (Q) Model

ARCH models provide a framework for the analysis of volatility in time series in the literature on finance. However, it has not been preferred recently due to a number of constraints, and its advanced models have become more widely used. The various constraints and difficulties that the ARCH model has can be listed as follows (Brooks 2008):

- Determination of the number of delays (q) of the squares of errors.
- Since the number of delays indicates dependence in the model, a very high q number will reduce the efficiency of the model.
- Negligence of the non-negativity of the coefficients (α, β).
- The model gives equal importance to negative and positive shocks (ignores asymmetry).

GARCH Models

The GARCH model was developed by Bollerslev (1987) and Taylor (1986). In this model, the delay value of the conditional variance is added to the model. In this case, the model is represented as

$$\sigma_t^2 = \alpha_0 + \alpha_1 u_{t-1}^2 + \beta\sigma_{t-1}^2 \quad (8)$$

This model is expressed as the GARCH (1,1) model. The advantages of the GARCH model over the ARCH model is that it better predicts the volatility as the delay value of the conditional variance is included in the model as a condition and the delay values of an infinite number of squares of errors are included in the model. Apart from the GARCH(1,1) model, the GARCH (p, q) model can be created; however, the GARCH(1,1) model is a highly competent model to capture the volatility cluster for financial data (Brooks 2008).

Estimation of ARCH/GARCH Models

Since the ARCH and GARCH models are generally used for the estimation of nonlinear models, the Maximum Likelihood (ML) method is applied instead of the Least Squares method (LSM) which minimizes error squares. Maximum Likelihood estimation helps us find parameters in both linear and nonlinear models. On the other hand, the Least Squares method (LSM) estimates linear models better.

Extensions of GARCH Models

Since GARCH models have several constraints and disadvantages, a number of improvements were needed. Some of these disadvantages are (Sarıkovanlık et al. 2019):

- The model neglects the non-negativity condition when estimating.
- It does not take into account the leverage effect, although it considers as fat tails (leptokurtosis) and volatility clustering.
- It cannot establish a direct relationship between conditional mean and conditional variance and does not consider asymmetry in volatility.

Various variants of the model have been developed considering these constraints.

Asymmetric GARCH Models

One of the most important constraints of GARCH models is that they do not take into account the effect of signal in negative and positive shocks since they employ squares of errors. It has been observed in the literature on finance that negative shocks cause more volatility in time series than positive shocks of the same size. Therefore, it was needed to develop models that take them into account. These models include the GJR model (Glosten et al. 1993) and the Exponential GARCH (EGARCH–Nelson 1991) model.

GJR Model (TARCH)

The GJR model is a simple extension of the GARCH model: a variable that takes positive asymmetry into consideration is added to the GARCH model. In this case, the conditional variance is defined as follows:

$$\sigma_t^2 = \alpha_0 + \alpha_1 u_{t-1}^2 + \beta \sigma_{t-1}^2 + \gamma u_{t-1}^2 I_{t-1} \tag{9}$$

$$I_{t-1} = 1; if\ u_{t-1} < 0$$

$I_{t-1} = 0$; otherwise, we add a dummy variable to the model; in this case, to ensure the non-negativity condition,

$\alpha_0 > 0$, $\beta > 0$, $\alpha_1 + \gamma \geq 0$ thus, even if $\gamma < 0$, the model will meet the non-negativity condition and will be accepted (Brooks 2008).

EGARCH Model

The exponential GARCH model was developed by Nelson in 1991 and has been represented in various ways. Most commonly used formula is as follows:

$$\ln\left(\sigma_t^2\right) = \omega + \beta \ln\left(\sigma_{t-1}^2\right) + \gamma \frac{u_{t-1}}{\sqrt{\sigma_{t-1}^2}} + \alpha \left[\frac{|u_{t-1}|}{\sqrt{\sigma_{t-1}^2}} - \sqrt{\frac{2}{\pi}}\right] \tag{10}$$

One of the most important advantages of the EGARCH model over the GARCH model is that it takes the logarithm of the variance and meets the non-negativity condition. Secondly, if there is a negative relationship between returns and volatility γ, may be negative, i.e., the model will allow asymmetry (Brooks 2008).

Literature Review (Background)

Studies on exchange rate volatility became further important after the industrialized countries allowed their national currencies to fluctuate after the collapse of the Bretton-Woods system in 1973.

Using the GARCH (1,1) t model, Bollerslev (1987) better estimated daily exchange rates and volatility in stock prices in the 1980–1985 period.

Using daily data for the period 1974–1983, Hsieh (1989) examined the volatility between the US dollar and Canadian, Swiss, German, English, and Japanese currencies with the help of ARCH and GARCH models and the best result in explaining volatility was determined by EGARCH (1,1) model.

Engel and Hamilton (1990) examined the volatility between the US dollar and German, French and British currencies during the 1973–1988 period with the Markov Switching model and found that this model produced better estimates than the random walk model.

Heynen and Kat (1994) estimated the volatility between the US dollar and five national currencies in the 1980–1992 period with GARCH (1,1), EGARCH (1,1), and Stochastic volatility models and found that the best result was yielded by the GARCH (1,1) model.

Engle (1994) examined the volatility of 18 different exchange rates in the 1973–1986 period with the Markov model and the random walk model and he succeeded in estimating the direction of the change in the exchange rates with the help of the Markov model.

Using five bilateral weekly exchange rates for the dollar for the 1973–1989 period, West and Cho (1995) compared autoregressive integrated moving average (ARIMA) model, GARCH (1,1), and IGARCH (1,1) models and found that none of the models performed well in a conventional test of forecast efficiency.

Fong (1997) applied the SWARCH model to weekly DM/£ exchange rates for the period of March 1987–December 1994. The author found that since the model takes structural breaks into account, it captured the ERM crisis of 1992 well.

Beine et al. (2003) tried to estimate the volatility between Dollar and DM and Dollar and Japanese Yen exchange rates in two different periods (1985–1995 and 1991–1995) using the GARCH model and the SWARCH model that considers structural breaks. They concluded that the SWARCH model which takes structural breaks into consideration is more successful than the GARCH model.

Fidrmuc and Horvath (2008) examined the exchange rate volatilities of the new member states of the EU, such as the Czech Republic, Hungary, Poland, Slovakia, and Romania for the period 1999–2006, using the GARCH model and the TARCH model that considers asymmetry. The authors concluded that since there is asymmetry in the currencies of these countries, the TARCH model, which takes asymmetry into consideration, yields better results.

Çağlayan and Dayıoğlu (2009) examined the volatility in the exchange rates of OECD countries for the period 1993–2006 with the ARCH, GARCH, EGARCH, and APARCH models. The authors concluded that asymmetric ARCH models provided better results than symmetric models for most countries.

Oduncu et al. (2013) created a currency basket of 0.5 * Euro/TL and 0.5 * Dollar/TL for the period of 2010–2012 and examined the effect of ROM on exchange rate volatility by using the GARCH (1,1) model.

The authors concluded that the ROM reduces exchange rate volatility. Altuntaş Taşpunar and Deniz (2015) examined the effect of uncertainty in financial markets on the ISE100 index[1] by using symmetric and asymmetric conditional variance models. The authors concluded that symmetrical conditional variance models were appropriate for the 1994 and 2001 years when there was an economic crisis in Turkey while for the 2002–2009 period when there were no economic crises, both symmetric and asymmetric conditional variance models were appropriate.

Güç et al. (2016) tested the day of the week effect in the ISE100 index with OLS, ARCH, and GARCH models. The authors concluded that daily returns on Fridays and Thursdays were significant and higher than the average compared to other days.

Kuzu (2018) analyzed the return volatility of the BIST100 Index by the ARCH, GARCH, EGARCH, and TGARCH models using the daily closing values of the 2011–2017 period. The author concluded that the TGARCH model gave the most successful results in revealing ISE100 index return volatility.

Application: Method, Data, and Findings

Since GARCH models are used to determine volatility and volatility clustering, by using the daily data of September 16, 2011 and September 16, .2016 period, the present study will examine the variables that are thought to affect the volatility of exchange rate returns with GARCH models in EViews nine package program. The dependent variable of the model is the return on the daily currency basket of 0.50 USD/TL and 0.50 Euro/TL. The volatility in the return of the currency basket will be examined and the effect of Reserve Option Mechanism (ROM—a mechanism designed by the Central Bank of the Republic of Turkey that allows banks to keep a certain ratio of their Turkish lira reserve requirements in foreign exchange and/or gold) on exchange rate volatility will be tested.

Variables to Be Used in the Model and their Abbreviations

Rt	Return on the currency basket (Dependent Variable)
DMS	The amount of foreign exchange sold by the Central Bank through direct interventions
EPS	Additional monetary tightening implemented by the Central Bank (Control variable)
VIX	Change in global capital movements
ROM	Amount of foreign exchange kept for Turkish Lira Reserve Requirements (Kantar 2017)

[1]ISE: Istanbul Stock Exchange

Identification of Variables in the Model

$$R_t = \ln(P_t/P_{t-1}) * 100 \quad (11)$$

$$\Delta VIX = \ln(VIX_t/VIX_{t-1}) * 100 \quad (12)$$

$$DMS = \left\{ \frac{\text{The amount of foreign exchange sold by CBRT by intervention or tender}}{\text{Gross foreign exchange reserve of the CBRT}} \right. \quad (13)$$

$$EPS = \begin{array}{l} 0, \text{otherdays} \\ 1, \text{days when additional monetary tightening was implemented} \end{array} \quad (14)$$

$$ROM = \frac{\text{Amount of foreign exchange kept for TL reserve requirements under ROM}}{\text{Gross foreign exchange reserve of the CBRT}} \quad (15)$$

Model:

$$R_t = \beta_0 + \beta_1 R_{t-1} + \beta_2 R_{t-2}{}^2 + \beta_3 \Delta VIX_t + \beta_4 DMS_t + \beta_5 D_{EPS} + \beta_6 ROM_t + \varepsilon_t \quad (16)$$

$$\varepsilon_t N(0, h_t) \quad (17)$$

$$h_t = \alpha_0 + \alpha_1 \varepsilon_{t-1}^2 + \alpha_2 h_{t-1} + \alpha_3 \Delta VIX_t + \alpha_4 DMS_t + \alpha_5 D_{EPS} + \alpha_6 ROM_t + u_t \quad (18)$$

$$h_t = \alpha_0 + \alpha_1 \varepsilon_{t-1}^2 + \alpha_2 h_{t-1} + \alpha_3 \Delta VIX_t + \alpha_4 DMS_t + \alpha_5 D_{EPS} + \alpha_6 ROM_t + \alpha_7 D_{ROMt}{}^3 + u_t \quad (19)$$

ADF Unit Root Test

According to the ADF unit root results, all variables were stationary and did not contain any unit roots. Since the EPS variable was a dummy variable, no stationary test was required.

Table 1 GARCH (1,1) variance equation

Variables	Coefficients	*P* value
c	0,147,084	0,0000
ε_{t-1}^2	0,127,005	0,0000
h_{t-1}	0,509,321	0,0000
ΔVIX_t	–,003997	0,0000
DMS_t	−6,548,730	0,0000
D_{EPS}	−0,042819	0,0000
ROM_t	−0,173,839	0,0018

Data Source: Developed by the author

Table 2 GARCH (1,1) model adjusted variance equation

Variables	Coefficients	*P* value
c	0,164,116	0,0000
ε_{t-1}^2	0,123,536	0,0000
h_{t-1}	0,539,482	0,0000
ΔVIX_t	−0,003868	0,0001
DMS_t	−4,099,848	0,1402
D_{EPS}	−0,027864	0,0144
ROM_t	−0,110,093	0,1466
D_{ROMt}	−0,269,960	0,0000

Data Source: Developed by the author

Estimation and Results of Models

In order to test the effect of ROM on exchange rate volatility, GARCH (1,1), GJR, or TGARCH (1,1), and EGARCH (1,1) models will be applied. The model with the lowest AIC, SIC values, and the highest Log Likelihood value will be considered the best model. Since the effect of ROM on volatility is measured, the results are interpreted through the variance equation.

As can be seen in Table 1, the ROM_t variable in the GARCH (1,1) model variance equation has a decreasing effect on volatility. However, it does not give an idea as to whether it reduces volatility in positive or negative shocks. Therefore, if we add a control variable to the variance equation of GARCH (1,1) model, which can give an idea about the response of ROM to negative shocks and retest the model.

As shown in Table 2, when we add the D_{ROMt} control variable to the variance equation, ROM is more effective in negative shocks. Therefore, this model seems to be more useful than the previous variance equation.

According to Table 3, it is understood from the negative coefficient of variable $\varepsilon_{t-1}^2{}_* I_{t-1}$ that positive shocks affect exchange rate volatility more.

According to Table 4, although the model has advantages over other models and correctly determines the effect of ROM on volatility, the results were not statistically significant.

According to the model results presented in Table 5, the model with the lowest AIC and SIC, and the highest Log Likelihood value is accepted as the best model.

Table 3 GJR/TGARCH (1,1) model variance equation

Variables	Coefficients	*P* value
c	0,165,249	0,0000
ε_{t-1}^2	0,129,459	0,0000
$\varepsilon_{t-1*}^2 I_{t-1}$	−0,072647	0,0299
h_{t-1}	0,542,539	0,0000
ΔVIX_t	−0,004588	0,0000
DMS_t	−4,031,068	0,3967
D_{EPS}	−0,027901	0,0232
ROM_t	−0,105,995	0,1686
D_{ROMt}	−0,257,562	0,0000

Data Source: Developed by the author

Table 4 EGARCH (1,1) model variance equation

Variables	Coefficients	*P* value
ω	−0,089681	0,6021
$\left\lvert \frac{\varepsilon_{t-1}}{\sqrt{h_{t-1}}} \right\rvert$	0,113,444	0,0000
$\varepsilon_{t-1}/\sqrt{h_{t-1}}$	0,052502	0,0000
$logh_{t-1}$	0,977,748	0,0000
ΔVIX_t	−0,013406	0,0000
DMS_t	−13,13,530	0,0008
D_{EPS}	0,047476	0,0039
ROM_t	−0,040183	0,2892
D_{ROMt}	−0,139,106	0,1300

Data Source: Developed by the author

Accordingly, although the EGARCH (1,1) model seems to be the best model, the GARCH (1,1) model has been accepted as a more suitable model because some variables are insignificant in the variance equation in the EGARCH(1,1) model.

When standardized errors and squares of errors are examined in order to determine the goodness of fit of the data, it can be concluded that Q statistics are insignificant at the level of 1% in all delayed periods in errors and in the first two delay periods in squares of errors. In other words, the model was found to be a valid model.

When we test whether the ARCH effect exists in the errors in the GARCH (1,1) model,

H_0: The ARCH effect exists in the errors.
H_1: The ARCH effect does not exist in the errors.

According to the model results presented in Table 6, H_0 hypothesis was accepted at 5% significance level (*p* value 0,0523); thus, no ARCH effect was found in the errors.

Examining whether the errors show normal distribution, it was found that the errors are not normally distributed and the kurtosis value is 8,266,613, that is, there is a fat-tailed distribution. This result is frequently encountered in volatility models and

Table 5 GARCH models for the currency series in Turkey

GARCH(1,1)	TGARCH(1,1)	EGARCH(1,1)		
Variance model				
α_0	Coefficient	0,164,116	0,165,300	−0,089367
	p value	*0,0000*	*0,0000*	*0,0000*
α_1	Coefficient	0,123,536	0,129,334	
	p value	0,00000	0,0000	
β_1	Coefficient	0,539,474	0,543,263	0,977,849
	p value	0,0000	0,0000	0,00000
γ	Coefficient		−0,072855	
	p value		0,0291	
δ_1	Coefficient			0,113,051
	p value			*0,0000*
δ_2	Coefficient			0,052550
	p value			*0,0000*
Criteria				
AIC criterion		*1,173,915*	*1,177,468*	*0,998,226*
SIC criterion		*1,219,197*	*1,225,769*	*1,046,527*
Log likelihood		*−1056,197*	*−1058,440*	*−894,8816*

Data Source: Developed by the author

Table 6 Correlogram of standardized errors and squares of errors

Standardized Errors			Squares of Standardized Errors		
Period	Q Statistics	*p* value	Period	Q Statistics	*p* value
1	12,965	0,255	1	37,749	0,052
2	45,582	0,102	2	74,418	0,024
3	48,361	0,184			
4	48,388	0,304			
5	49,596	0,421			

Data Source: Developed by the author

nonlinear models. According to the obtained findings and results, the conditional variance equation suitable for the series is as follows;

$$h_t = 0.164116 + 0,123536\varepsilon_{t-1}^2 + 0,539474\, h_{t-1}\text{-}0,003868\Delta \mathrm{VIX}_t\text{-}4,099838\mathrm{DMS}_t \text{-}0,027863\, D_{\mathrm{EPS}}\text{-}0110093\ \mathrm{ROM}_t - 0,269959\ \mathrm{D}_{\mathrm{ROMt}}$$

Conclusion

Financial liberalization was initiated in the world since the early 1980s due to reasons such as high inflation and high oil prices since the 1970s. With financial liberalization, barriers between countries have been removed and intensive capital flows have moved among countries. The acceleration of financial liberalization has rapidly increased the importance of the financial sector along with the real sector in the economy.

These developments and sudden movements in asset prices that have been encountered since the 1980s brought the concept of volatility to the agenda. The correct calculation of asset prices is related to the correct determination of the risk related to that asset. As a measure of the risk of the asset, it is the volatility of that asset. With the development of information technologies and derivative products, it is extremely important to determine the volatility of the asset correctly in financial markets.

For the correct pricing of financial assets and accurate estimations, there should be low volatility in the price movements of an asset. Therefore, the volatility of any financial asset must be calculated accurately. Volatility, an indicator of risk, is calculated by various models. Since changes in asset prices are not linear, volatility in asset prices is determined by the ARCH model, not by the classical regression method. Nevertheless, the ARCH model has a number of constraints such as the number of delays of squares of errors, negligence of the non-negativity of the coefficients, and that the model gives equal importance to negative and positive shocks. Due to these constraints, the GARCH model was developed by Bollerslev (1987) and Taylor (1986). In this model, the delay value of the conditional variance is added to the model. On the other hand, one constraint of GARCH models is that they do not take into account negative and positive effects of signal since they employ squares of errors. In order to eliminate this constraint, EGARCH by Nelson (1991) and TARCH (GJR) by Glosten et al. (1993) were developed.

The exchange rate volatility in Turkey is quite high. In the present study, the exchange rate volatility in Turkey for the period September 16, 2011–September 16, 2016 was analyzed with the help of GARCH models. The study concludes that the exchange rate volatility in Turkey can be determined by GARCH models. Among GARCH models, it is the GARCH (1,1) model that best describes the exchange rate volatility.

Exchange rate volatility must be monitored very carefully by investors, companies, and countries. High volatility is very important for predicting the future and pricing the assets.

References

Altuntaş Taşpunar S, Çolak Deniz F (2015) Bist-100 Endeksine Volatilitenin Modellenmesi ve Öngörülmesinde ARCH Modelleri. İstanbul Üniversitesi İşletme Fakültesi İşletme İktisadı Enstitüsü Yönetim Dergisi 26(79):208–223

Beine M, Laurent S, Lecourt C (2003) Official central Bank interventions and exchange rate volatility: evidence from a regime-switching analysis. Eur Econ Rev 47:891–911

Bollerslev T (1987) A conditionally Heteroskedastic time series model for speculative prices and rates of return. Rev Econ Stat 69:542–547

Brooks C. (2008). Introductory econometrics for finance. Second Edition

Çağlayan E, Dayıoğlu T (2009) Döviz Kuru Getiri Volatilitesinin Koşullu Değişen Varyans Modelleri ile Öngörüsü. İstanbul Üniversitesi İktisat Fakültesi Ekonometri ve İstatistik Dergisi 9:1–16

Engel C, Hamilton JD (1990) Long swings in the Dollar: are they in the data and do Markets know it? Am Econ Rev 80(4):689–713

Engle C (1994) Can the Markow switching model forecast exchange rates? J Int Econ 36:151–165

Ertuğrul HM (2012) Türkiye'de Döviz Kuru Volatilitesi ve Enflasyon İlişkisi Doktora Tezi. Ankara Hacettepe Ü, Sosyal Bilimler Enstitüsü

Fidrmuc J, Horvath R (2008) Volatility of exchange rates in selected new EU members: evidence from daily data. Econ Syst 32(1):103–118

Fong WM (1997) Volatility persistence and switching ARCH in Japanese stock returns. Asia-Pasific Financial Market 4(1):37–57

Güç E, Saçan E, Kaplan Yıldırım R (2016) Borsa İstanbul'da Haftanın Günü Anomalisinin ARCH, GARCH ve OLS modelleri ile Test Edilmesi. J Int Soc Res 9(44):1084–1094

Glosten LR, Jagannathan R, Runkle DE (1993) On the relation between the expected value and the volatility of the nominal excess return on stocks. J Financ 48(5):1779–1801

Heynen RC, Kat HM (1994) Volatility prediction: a comparison of stochastic volatility, GARCH (1,1) and EGARCH(1,1) models. J Deriv 2(2):50–65

Hsieh DA (1989) Modeling Heteroskedasticity in daily foreign exchange rates. J Bus Econ Stat 7:307–317

Kantar L (2017) Rezerv Opsiyon Mekanizması ve Döviz Kuru Volatilitesi: Türkiye Üzerine Bir Uygulama. Doktora Tezi. İstanbul. İ.Ü, Sosyal Bilimler Enstitüsü

Kuzu S (2018) Borsa İstanbul Endeksi (Bist 100) Getiri Volatilitesinin ARCH ve GARCH Modeli ile Tahmin Edilmesi, Muhasebe ve Vergi Uygulamaları Dergisi, Nisan 2018 Özel Sayı 608–624

Nelson DB (1991) Conditional heteroskedasticity in asset returns: a new approach. Econometrica 59(2):347–370

Oduncu A, Ermişoğlu E, Akçelik Y (2013) Merkez Bankasının Yeni Enstrümanı Rezerv Opsiyonu Mekanizması ve Kur Oynaklığı. Bankacılar Dergisi 86:43–52

Sarıkovanlık V, Koy A, Akkaya M, Yildirim HH, Kantar L (2019) Finans Biliminde Ekonometri Uygulamaları, 1st edn

Taylor SJ (1986) Forecasting the volatility of currency exchange rates. Int J Forecast 3:159–170

West KD, Cho D (1995) The predictive ability of several models of exchange rate volatility. J Econ 69:367–391

Lokman Kantar completed his master's degree in finance at Istanbul University in 2010. He completed his PhD at the same school in 2017. Between 2005 and 2017, he worked as a teacher in Trade High Schools in the fields of Accounting and Finance. He has been working since 2017 as an Assistant Professor in the Department of Banking and Insurance, School of Applied Sciences, Istanbul Gelişim University,. Since 2018, he has been working as the head of the department in the Banking and Insurance department. He continues his academic studies in the fields of International Finance, Portfolio Management, and Risk Management.

Using COGARCH-Filtered Volatility in Modelling Within ARDL Framework

Yakup Arı

Introduction

Autoregressive Distributed Lags (ARDL) is one of the two subjects of this chapter since it is a popular model to determine the short-run and long-run relationships or cointegration between macroeconomic variables. In addition, a new proposal is introduced in this chapter to reveal the short and long-run relationship between the volatility of financial variables and other macroeconomic variables using Continuous Generalized Autoregressive Conditional Heteroscedastic (COGARCH) model. This proposal is that the volatility of financial time series such as foreign exchange rates, the stock market indices are determined by COGARCH model and then to point out the relationship between volatility and other macroeconomic variables. Therefore, the ARDL model, which demonstrates the short-run and long-run relationship between variables that are stationary at different orders, is applied.

The COGARCH model is introduced by Klüppelberg et al. (2004). They proposed a continuous-time GARCH (COGARCH) process driven by a Lévy process, which is an analog of discrete-time GARCH process and is further generalized to solutions of Lévy driven stochastic differential equations. Like in the discrete-time case, the COGARCH model cannot model this stylized fact of time series. Therefore, the extensions of the COGARCH model are developed that are based on the extensions of the discrete-time GARCH models. But, the COGARCH is successful to filter the volatility of both equally spaced and unequally spaced time data. The impact of the volatility of financial time series on other macroeconomic variables

Y. Arı (✉)
Alanya Alaaddin Keykubat University, Alanya, Turkey
e-mail: yakup.ari@alanya.edu.tr

B. Adıgüzel Mercangöz (ed.), *Handbook of Research on Emerging Theories, Models, and Applications of Financial Econometrics*,
https://doi.org/10.1007/978-3-030-54108-8_13

and the cointegration between these variables are determined by utilizing bounds tests to be followed in the ARDL cointegration method.

The general way to examine the long-run relationship between variables is to apply the cointegration tests. The most usual cointegration tests such as Engle and Granger (1987) and Johansen (1988, 1991) need that the variables should be uniformly integrated at the same order. The fact that the variables included in the test are stationary at the same order can be considered as a constraint of the mentioned methods. The ARDL approach to eliminate this constraint was proposed by Pesaran et al. (1996). Later, Pesaran and colleagues developed this approach with their works, Pesaran and Pesaran (1997), Pesaran and Smith (1998), Pesaran and Shin (1999) and Pesaran et al. (2001) respectively. The least-squares method is a basis for the ARDL approach which is not required unit root tests in advance since the variables do not need to be classified as I(1) and I(0). Pesaran and Pesaran (1997) proposed that the ARDL approach to cointegration gives a meaningful interpretation even if the variables are I(1) or I(0). The requirement of the integration order of the variables should not be the same can be regarded as an advantage of the ARDL approach over other methods. However, if there are variables integrated at I(2), the ARDL approach cannot be applied. Another advantage of the ARDL approach is that it can be applied to samples with small sizes. In the studies respectively Pesaran and Shin (1998), Pesaran et al. (2001), and Adom et al. (2012), it has shown that the method gives consistent results for sample sizes ranging from 80 to 190.

The further advantage of ARDL can be considered by comparing, e.g., Vector Autoregressive (VAR) with ARDL. If the VAR is applied to series that are required to be stationary. If they are not stationary VAR can be utilized after taking the difference of the series. In most cases, long-run relations between series may disappear when the series are stationary at the first difference (Brooks 2014). In contrast, in an ARDL framework, it is not necessary to make an adjustment to the data, and hence long-run relationships still remain possible to calculate.

The aim of this chapter is to propose a method to use the GOGARCH filtered volatility modeling within the ARDL framework. The structure of the method is to determine the cointegration between the macroeconomic series and the volatility of financial time series, filtered by the COGARCH process, using the ARDL bounds test. In this context, the outline of the chapter is designed as follows;

The definition and properties of the COGARCH process are given in Sect. 2. Then, the properties of the Distributed-Lag (DL) models and the Autoregressive (AR) models are discussed in Sect. 3 and Sect. 4 since these mentioned models are the basics of the ARDL model. In Sect. 5, the ARDL bounds test is discussed in details and furthermore, the features and estimation method for ARDL are given. In the last section, the real-life data application is given for illustrative purposes.

Continuous-Time Garch Process

The derivation of the COGARCH process and second-order properties of the volatility process are explained depending on the studies Klüppelberg et al. (2004, 2011) in this part. There is only one source of uncertainty (two of the same kind) is the main difference or the advantage of the approach of Klüppelberg et al. (2004). In the COGARCH process, the increments of a Lévy process replaces the innovations of a discrete-time GARCH model. According to the approach of Klüppelberg and her colleagues while the COGARCH model is deriving the main features of a discrete-time GARCH model are maintained. In addition, the discrete-time GARCH(1,1) process is utilized by Klüppelberg et al. (2004) to construct a continuous-time analog.

Let $a_n = \sigma_n \epsilon_n$ where $\epsilon_n \sim f_v(0, 1)$ and $\sigma_n^2 = \alpha_0 + \alpha_1 a_{n-1}^2 + \beta_1 \sigma_{n-1}^2$ be a discrete-time GARCH(1,1) process where α_0, α_1 and β_1 are constant parameters. The idea is to replace the white noise sequence of the discrete equation with the increments of a Lévy process. So, the continuous-time GARCH process $(G_t)_{t \geq 0}$ can be defined by replacing the $\beta = \alpha_0$, $\eta = -\log \beta_1$ and $\varphi = \frac{\alpha_1}{\beta_1}$ in the discrete-time GARCH(1,1) the volatility process as following

$$(G_t)_{t \geq 0} = \int_0^t \sigma_{s-} dL_s \tag{1}$$

and the variance process $\sigma^2 = \left(\sigma_t^2\right)_{t \geq 0}$ are defined by the stochastic differential equations

$$dG_t = \sigma_{t-} dL_t \tag{2}$$

$$d\sigma_t^2 = (\beta - \eta \sigma_{t-})dt + \varphi \sigma_{t-} d[L, L]_t^d \tag{3}$$

for $t \geq 0$ and $G_0 = 0$, $\beta > 0$, $\eta > 0$, $\varphi \geq 0$ and $[L, L]_t^d$ is the discrete part of the quadratic variation Lévy process.

One can infer from the definition of COGARCH that the number of jumps the process G is the same as in L. Furthermore, the size of jumps of G can be defined as $\Delta G_t = \sigma_t \Delta L_t$ for $t \geq 0$. Thus, it is understood that ΔL_t in the COGARCH model has taken its place in the model such as innovations in the GARCH model.

Since introducing COGARCH and its extensions models, there are various proposed parameter estimation methods in the literature. Although one can find a number of frequentists and Bayesian estimation methods, only two methods the Method of Moments (Haug et al. 2007) and Pseudo-Maximum Likelihood (Maller et al. 2008) for COGARCH are mentioned in this chapter. The log-returns of the series are utilized to estimate the parameters in the Method of Moments (MM) procedure. The first step of the method is that the empirical autocorrelation function and moments are fitted to their theoretical counterparts. The assumption that the driving Lévy process has finite variance is only satisfied when the processes area

Compound Poisson process with normally distributed jumps or a Variance-Gamma process. With respect to the MM procedure, the driving Lévy process is not required to be enumerated. However, it can only be applied to equally spaced observations, and accordingly, in many intriguing contexts it is not pertinent. Furthermore; although this moment method has been demonstrated as being consistent, it is not very efficient for many other models. The Pseudo-Maximum Likelihood (PML) includes an approximation in which Maller et al. (2008) fitted the model to unequally spaced time data. They derived a pseudo-maximum likelihood (PML) function and numerically maximizing it in order to estimate the corresponding parameters. They suppose that the observations are $G(t_i)$, $0 = t_0 < t_1 < \ldots < t_N = T$, on the integrated COGARCH $(G_t)_{t \geq 0} = \int_0^t \sigma_{s-} dL_s$ and assumed to be stationary. The $\{t_i\}$ are assumed fixed time points. Let $a_i = Y_i = G(t_i) - G(t_{i-1})$ denote the observed returns and $\Delta t_i := t_i - t_{i-1}$. So, the observed return can be written as following $Y_i = \int_0^t \sigma_{s-} dL_s$ where L is a Lévy process with $E[L(1)] = 0$ and $E[L^2(1)] = 1$.

The purpose is to estimate (β, η, φ) from the observed $Y_1, Y_2, \ldots, Y_N$ using PML method. Y_i is conditionally independent of $Y_{i-1}, Y_{i-2}, \ldots$ given information set F_{t-1} since σ is Markovian. So, $E(Y_i | F_{t-1}) = 0$ for the conditional expectation of Y_i, and, for the conditional variance,

$$\rho_i^2 = , E\left(Y_i^2 | F_{t-1}\right) = \left(\sigma^2(t_{i-1}) - \frac{\beta}{\eta - \varphi}\right)\left(\frac{e^{(\eta - \varphi)\Delta t_i}}{\eta - \varphi}\right) + \frac{\beta \Delta t_i}{\eta - \varphi} \tag{4}$$

$E(\sigma^2(0)) = \frac{\beta}{\eta - \varphi}$, with $\eta > \varphi$ and $E[L^2(1)] = 1$ satisfy the stationarity of the model. The pseudo-maximum likelihood function for $Y_1, Y_2, \ldots, Y_N$ can be written as following with the assumption of Y_i, are conditionally $N\left(0, \rho_i^2\right)$

$$L = L(\beta, \eta, \varphi) = \sum_{i=1}^{N} \left(-\frac{1}{2} \log (2\pi) - \frac{1}{2} \ln \rho_i^2 - \frac{1}{2} \frac{Y_i^2}{\rho_i^2}\right) \tag{5}$$

Above Eq. (5) needs a calculable quantity for ρ_i^2. Hence $\sigma^2(t_{i-1})$ should be substituted by $\sigma_i^2 = \beta \Delta t_i + e^{-\eta \Delta t_i} \sigma_{i-1}^2 + \varphi e^{-\eta \Delta t_i} Y_i^2$. After substituting σ_i^2 for $\sigma^2(t_{i-1})$ and resulting modified ρ_i^2, pseudo-maximum likelihood function can be found for fitting a GARCH model to the unequally spaced series. The recursion of σ_i^2 can be easily done taking $\sigma^2(0) = \frac{\beta}{\eta - \varphi}$ as an initial value. The maximization of $L = L(\beta, \eta, \varphi)$ gives PMLEs of (β, η, φ). One can see the study of Arı (2019) for detail information about the COGARCH process and the estimation methods of the model. In this study, the PMLE method is used for parameter estimation of the COGARCH model.

Lag Distributed Models

In this section, the properties and the structure of distributed-lag models will be discussed as the basics of the ARDL model. The effect of a regressor x on y can be observed during the time interval in a dynamic model such as distributed-lag model since with DL models, the effect of a shock in the explanatory variable lasts more. In the DL model, there is not only the current value of the explanatory variable but there is also its past value(s). The parameters of DL models can be estimated with Ordinary Least Square (OLS) method since the lags of the explanatory variable are also non-stochastic. One can also apply the Almon's Method (1965) which is based on Weierstrass's Approximation Theorem is a pretty neat way of re-formulating the model prior to its estimation. DL models can be written as follows

$$DL(0) : y_t = \beta_0 + \beta_1 x_t + u_t \tag{6}$$

$$DL(1) : y_t = \beta_0 + \beta_1 x_t + \beta_2 x_{t-1} + u_t \tag{7}$$

$$DL(q) : y_t = \beta_0 + \sum_{i=0}^{q} \beta_i x_{t-i} + u_t \tag{8}$$

where u_t is a stationary error term. The form defined in Eq. (8) has a very similar structure with the infinite-moving-average representation of an AR process which will be discussed briefly in Sect. 4. The coefficients βs show the lag weights of the explanatory variable that defines the pattern of how x affects y over time.

The finite distributed lag models have two disadvantages which are multicollinearity and having a long lag length in small samples. Even if x is stationary, x and lag values of x have strongly correlated that causes multicollinearity. The way of dealing with multicollinearity is to restrict the estimated β coefficients to satisfy prior assumptions of smoothness. In conclusion, the finite distributed lag model is most suitable for estimating dynamic relationships when lag weights decline to zero relatively quickly, when the regressor is not highly autocorrelated, and when the sample is long relative to the length of the lag distribution.

Autoregressive Models

The stationarity, dynamic dependence, autocorrelation function, modeling, and forecasting are the main discussion part of the theories of linear time series. The simple autoregressive (AR) models are introduced as econometric models that are utilized for modeling and forecasting the financial time series. (see: Tsay 2012 Chap. 2) AR models are important to understand the logic behind the ARDL models. AR models can be defined as follows

$$AR(0): y_t = \alpha_0 + u_t \tag{9}$$

$$AR(1): y_t = \alpha_0 + \alpha_1 y_{t-1} + u_t \tag{10}$$

$$AR(p): y_t = \alpha_0 + \sum_{i=0}^{p} \alpha_i y_{t-i} + u_t \tag{11}$$

where p is nonnegative integer and u_t is white noise series with mean 0 and variance σ_u^2. Under the stationarity condition, $E(y_t) = E(y_{t-1}) = \ldots = E(y_{t-p}) = \mu$ and hence

$$E(y_t) = \mu = \frac{\alpha_0}{1 - \sum_{i=0}^{p} \alpha_i} \tag{12}$$

The Eq. (12) has two implications for y_t. First, the mean exists if $\sum_{i=0}^{p} \alpha_i \neq 1$. Second is that the mean is zero if and only if $\alpha_0 = 0$. Using the independence of the series u_t, $Var(y_t) = Var(y_{t-1}) = \ldots = Var(y_{t-p})$, so that

$$Var(y_t) = \frac{\sigma_u^2}{1 - \sum_{i=0}^{p} \alpha_i^2} \tag{13}$$

The Eq. (13) implies that $\sum_{i=0}^{p} \alpha_i^2 < 1$ to satisfy the variance is positive. Consuquently, the weak stationarity of an AR(p) model implies that $-1 < \sum_{i=0}^{p} \alpha_i < 1$.

The past value(s) of the dependent variables becomes an explanatory variable in AR models. The OLS method cannot be applicable in an autoregressive model since the presence of stochastic explanatory variables and the possibility of serial correlation. Therefore, the conditional maximum likelihood method or conditional least square method is used.

Autoregressive Distributed-Lag Models

The correlation analysis is performed to indicate the direction and strength of the linear relationship between two independent variables. In general statistical use, the correlation shows how far away from the state of independence is. Although it does not give a definitive conclusion about the cause-effect relationship between the variables, it is important in terms of being a preliminary finding. Before the cointegration and causality concepts, stationarity of time series is briefly discussed. The stationarity of time series has two important parts. First, the regression analysis of time series can give a statistically significant regression coefficient between two variables. If there is a trend in both time series, the relationship may be spurious rather than real. This situation raises the problem of false regression. Whether regression reflects a real relationship or a false relationship is closely related to whether the time series data are stationary or not. The concept of stationarity, which can be expressed as the mean, variance, and autocovariance of a stochastic or random variable is constant over time, which means that the values of the series fluctuate around a certain value or fluctuate around its expected value. Most of the time series studies are aimed at making accurate predictions about the uncertain and unknown future. If a stochastic process is not stationary, the behavior of the series is valid only for the forecast period under consideration. However, no generalization can be made about the series for other periods and the shock to the variable will be permanent. In a time series, it is important that the impacts of the shocks are transient and that this effect disappears after a while. Because if the effect of shocks is permanent and does not diminish with time, the series cannot return to the mean. The use of non-stationary variables in econometric modeling prevents the existing relationships between variables to be explained in a healthy way. The non-stationary problem in economic variables leads to misinterpretation of Ordinary Least Square (OLS) results (Enders 1995). There are significant differences between stationary and non-stationary series. In stationary series, shocks are temporary, their effects disappear over time and return to their average level over the long term. The unit root tests are used in the stationary analysis of time series. Dickey and Fuller (1981) and Phillips and Perron (1988) are the most commonly used systematic tests investigating the presence of unit root in a time series.

Although Dickey–Fuller test approach has a very important role in finding the unit root, the deficiencies in the test are found and these deficiencies are solved by auxiliary tests. These missing aspects; The AR process is not known exactly and the number of lags to be created, the decision whether the constant term and time trend is in the regression, the existence the structural breakage, the presence of the seasonality effect in the series and the presence of partial stationarity can be listed. Dickey–Fuller Test assumes that error terms are statistically independent and have constant variance. When using this method, it is necessary to ensure that there is no correlation between error terms and that they have constant variance. Phillips and Perron expanded (1988) Dickey–Fuller's hypothesis about error terms.

The reason why Phillips-Perron abandoned the Dickey–Fuller test's limiting assumptions about error terms is that they use error terms or the historical values of these error terms as a moving average (MA-Moving Average). In this respect, the AR process in the Dickey–Fuller test was transformed into the ARMA process in the Phillips–Perron test. The introduction of the MA process allows the testing of the trend stationary concept to be more powerful. The Phillips-Perron test is more powerful than the Dickey–Fuller test, especially in the case of trend-series. If MA processes are negative, ADF tests are more powerful than Phillips-Perron. (If the MA processes are negative or decreasing, the expected mean of the error terms approaches zero.)

It is not always correct to evaluate the cases as "cause" or "result." A phenomenon that is the result of one event may be the cause of another event. In this case, it can be said that instead of investigating the causes of the cases, it is more accurate to investigate the observed and unchanging causal relationships between the cases. If the causal relationships between variables in economics are determined, it will be possible to classify the variables in economic models and test economic theory. In other words, as a result of determining the causality relationship between variables, the classification of variables as internal or external in the economic study is easily passed. For example, if a one-way causal relationship from X to Y is determined, X is called internal and Y is called external.

The first definition of causality in the context of time series was made by the famous mathematician Norbert Wiener (1956). This definition was reconsidered by Granger-Hatanaka study, and it was taken further by Granger (1969) to allow the existence and direction of causality to be determined. Since Granger makes the greatest contribution to this definition, it is called Granger causality in the literature. If past and present information about one of the variables causes an improvement in the prospective estimate of the other variable, the variable that provides the improvement is defined as the Granger cause of the other. Before starting the causality analysis, the variables should be cleared of trend, seasonal effects and stationarity should be provided. Granger's concept of causality is a two-variable VAR (Vector Auto Regressive) model with the appropriate lag length. In the Granger causality test, it is tested whether one variable regularly affects the other.

Later, Granger and Newbold (1974) showed that spurious regression problems may be encountered when working with non-stationary time series. In this case, the result obtained by regression analysis does not reflect the real relationship. Because these test statistics do not have a standard distribution, they lose their validity. Regression analyzes with non-stationary time series can only reflect the real relationship if there is a cointegration relationship between these series.

The error correction model (ECM) developed by Engle and Granger (1987) has been used quite frequently in case of cointegration between non-stationary series which become stationary after taking first order difference. In the error correction model which is a limited VAR model, the F-test is used for the analysis of causality. But test statistic of the cointegration of the series may not be valid because it does not conform to the standard distribution.

In the causality analysis with a lagged VAR method developed by Toda and Yamamoto (1995), the cointegration relationship between the series is not important, but it is sufficient to determine the model correctly and to know the maximum degree of integration of the variables in the model.

There are cointegration tests in literature introduced by Engel and Granger (1987), Johansen (1988, 1991), Johansen and Juselius (1990) to determine the short-run and long-run relationships or cointegration between macroeconomic variables. These tests cannot be applied in cases of different levels of stationarity of variables. The bounds test developed by Paseran et al. (2001) allows the cointegration analysis in case of different levels of stationarity of variables.

In cointegration analysis, the problem arising from the failure to perform cointegration analysis on time series with different degrees of cointegration is eliminated by the bounds test approach developed by Pesaran et al. (1996), Pesaran and Shin (1995) and Pesaran et al. (2001). This method is called the ARDL (Autoregressive Distributed-Lag) approach. This model is used to analyze the existence of long- and short-run relationships by eliminating the difficulties of predetermining the stationary properties of the series in cointegration tests. In a multivariate model, this method is used when some of the series are stationary at the level (I (0)) and others are stationary at the first differences (I (1)). This method consists of two stages. In the first stage, it is tested whether there is a long term relationship between the variables. In the second stage, short and long term parameters are derived and estimated.

According to stationary levels of variables, the ARDL bounds test for cointegration analysis can be applied. In the ARDL models, both AR and DL part are in one regression and is written

$$ARDL(p,q) : y_t = \beta_0 + \sum_{i=0}^{p} \alpha_i y_{t-i} + \sum_{i=0}^{q} \beta_i x_{t-i} + u_t \tag{14}$$

where $u_t \tilde{d}(0, \sigma_u^2)$ and $\beta_0 \in \mathbb{R}$.The explanatory variables are represented by x_t which is a $kX1$ vector. The lag values of the dependent and independent variables are also included in the ARDL approach. Thus, the ARDL approach consists of two parts, AR and DL. The AR part includes the lags of the dependent variable, and the DL part includes the lags of the explanatory variables. Depending on this feature of the model, it can be concluded whether the effect of a change in independent variables will be instantaneous. The parameters of the ARDL model are estimated by the OLS method. But, OLS is usually biased since the model includes the lagged values of the dependent variable. Moreover, if there is autocorrelation between error terms, The OLS method is inconsistent. Therefore, the Instrumental Variables Estimation method is often applied to estimate the parameters of ARDL.

Based on the standard regression model, ARDL Bounds test equation is established to determine the cointegration relationship between the variables in the model as follows:

$$\begin{aligned} \Delta\, ln\, y_t = \alpha_0 + \sum_{i=1}^{p} \alpha_{1i} \Delta\, ln\, y_{t-i} + \sum_{i=0}^{q} \alpha_{2i} \Delta\, ln\, (vol)_{t-i} + \beta_1\, ln\, y_{t-1} \\ + \beta_2\, ln\, (vol)_{t-1} + e_t \end{aligned} \tag{15}$$

where the dependent variable is denoted by "y_t" and the COGARCH-filtered volatility is denoted by "*vol.*" The short-run and the long-run dynamics are represented by the alpha and beta coefficients in Eq. (15) respectively. The first step of the ARDL approach is to determine the optimal lag lengths. The information criteria are used to determine the optimal lag lengths (p, q) of the variables in the

Eq. (15). Thus, the stability conditions of the estimation are satisfied. After determining the appropriate lag, the bounds test is carried out from the model. The null hypothesis of the bounds test is that there is no long-run relationship between the variables which is tested by F-test. This null hypothesis is tested by whether the coefficients of the lag values of the dependent and independent variables in Eq. (15). are equal to zero. Respectively, in this research, the null hypothesis for F-test is ($H_0 : \beta_1 = \beta_2 = 0$), the alternative hypothesis ($H_0 : \beta_i \neq 0$ for at least one i; $i = 1, 2$). To conclude the hypothesis test, the calculated F-test statistic is compared with asymptotic critical values at certain confidence levels. These asymptotic critical values are given in the study of Pesaran et al. (2001). ARDL method is applied in order to investigate the long-run relationship between the variables, given the fact that there is a long-run relationship between the level values of the variables by the bounds test. In this study, the ARDL model to be estimated to examine the long-run relationship between variables is as follows;

$$ln\, y_t = \alpha_0 + \sum_{i=1}^{p} \alpha_{1i}\, ln\, y_{t-i} + \sum_{i=0}^{q} \alpha_{2i}\, ln\, (vol)_{t-i} + e_t \tag{16}$$

The short-run relationship between the variables is examined with the error correction model based on the ARDL method. This model is as follows;

$$\Delta\, ln\, y_t = \alpha_0 + \sum_{i=1}^{p} \alpha_{1i} \Delta\, ln\, y_{t-i} + \sum_{i=0}^{q} \alpha_{2i} \Delta\, ln\, (vol)_{t-i} + \delta ECT_{t-1} + e_t \tag{17}$$

where ECT is an error correction term that shows how soon it is possible to correct a short-run equilibrium between dependent and explanatory variables in the model. For the error correction mechanism to work, the coefficient of this variable is expected to be negative and statistically significant.

Illustration

In this section, the real-life data are used for illustrative purposes. The volatility of the financial time series is filtered by the COGARCH process using the R package "yuima" by Iacus et al. (2018). ARDL bounds test is done using the R package "dLagM" by Demirhan (2019). Moreover, the R codes of the application are given in every steps.

The application is adapted from Brockwell et al. (2006), where the relationship between GARCH and COGARCH is also checked on the estimates from data for these two models.

The data is downloaded from "finance.yahoo.com" via "quantmod" package (Ryan and Ulrich 2018) in R and a GARCH(1,1) process is fitted to the de-trended

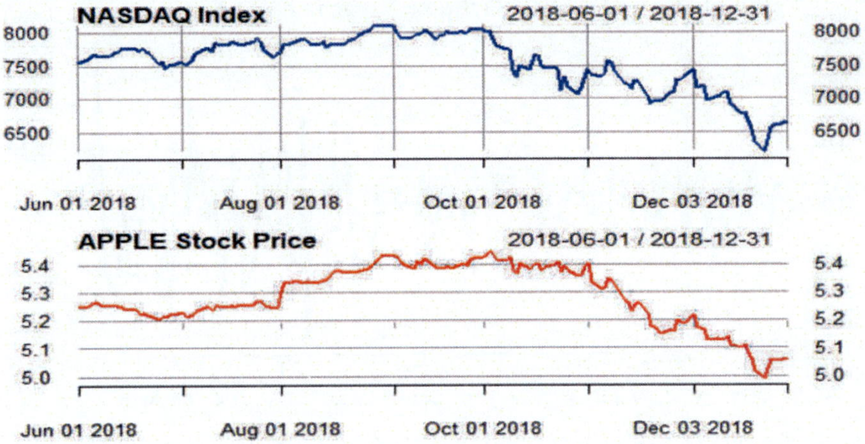

Fig. 1 The plots of NASDAQ index data and apple stock price data. Source: "finance.yahoo.com" via "quantmod" package in R

log-returns of Nasdaq Index using the rugarch package (Ghalanos 2020) and later a COGARCH(1,1) by yuima.

```
#Libraries
library(yuima)
library(rugarch)
library(quantmod)
library(FinTS)
library(zoo)
library(dLagM)
library(vars)

#DATA MERGING
getSymbols("^IXIC", from="2018-06-01", to="2019-01-01")
getSymbols("AAPL", from="2018-06-01", to="2019-01-01")
ns<-IXIC$IXIC.Close
apl<-AAPL$AAPL.Close
md<-merge(ns,apl)
na.md<-na.omit(md)

par(mfrow=c(2,1))
plot(ns, main="NASDAQ Index", col="blue")
plot(apl,main="APPLE Stock Price", col="red" )
```

The data is given in the Fig. 1.

Then, we apply the GARCH model to fit to the log-returns of Nasdaq Index data, which has ARCH effect according to Engle's LM test is stationary according to Augmented Dickey–Fuller and Philips–Perron tests. The parameters of the GARCH model satisfy the stationary conditions of the model.

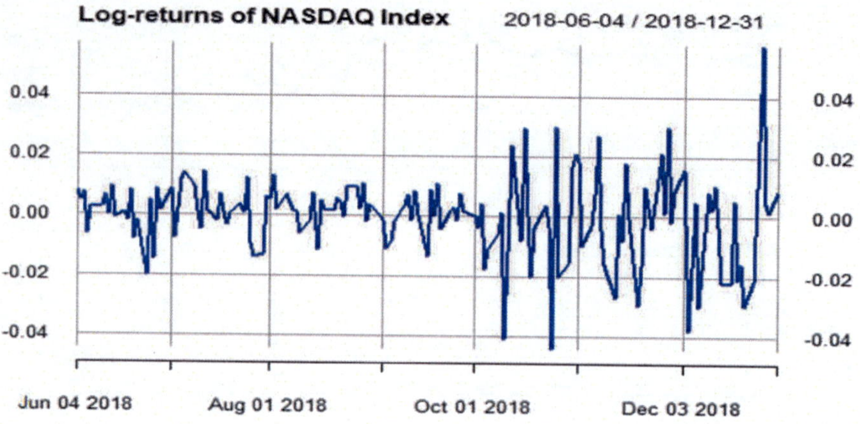

Fig. 2 The Plot of log-returns of NASDAQ Index Data. Source: Author's creation

```
#Log Returns of Nasdaq data
S<-na.md$IXIC.Close
X <- na.omit(diff(log(S)))
mX <- mean(X)
X <- X - mX
plot(X, main="Log-returns of NASDAQ Index",col="blue")

# Engle's LM test for ARCH effect
arch.effect<-ArchTest(X)

#stationarity test for log-returns of Nasdaq Index = X
pp.x<-stationary.test(X, method = "pp")
adf.x<-stationary.test(X, method = "adf")

#GARCH(1,1) fit
spec <- ugarchspec(variance.model =
list(model = "sGARCH", garchOrder = c(1, 1)),
mean.model = list(armaOrder = c(0, 0), include.mean = FALSE))

fitGARCH <- ugarchfit(data = X, spec = spec)
names(fitGARCH@fit)
plot(fitGARCH, which="all")
fitGARCH
```

The plot of log-returns of NASDAQ Index Data and the plot of GARCH(1,1) fit are given in Figs. 2 and 3 respectively. The diagnostics of the GARCH(1,1) model shows that the model is adequate according to results of the following tests; The Ljung–Box test for autocorrelation within the GARCH model's standardized residuals, the ARCH LM test for serial dependence, the Nyblom stability test for structural change within a time series and the sign bias test for misspecification of conditional volatility models. Furthermore, the adjusted Pearson goodness-of-fit test

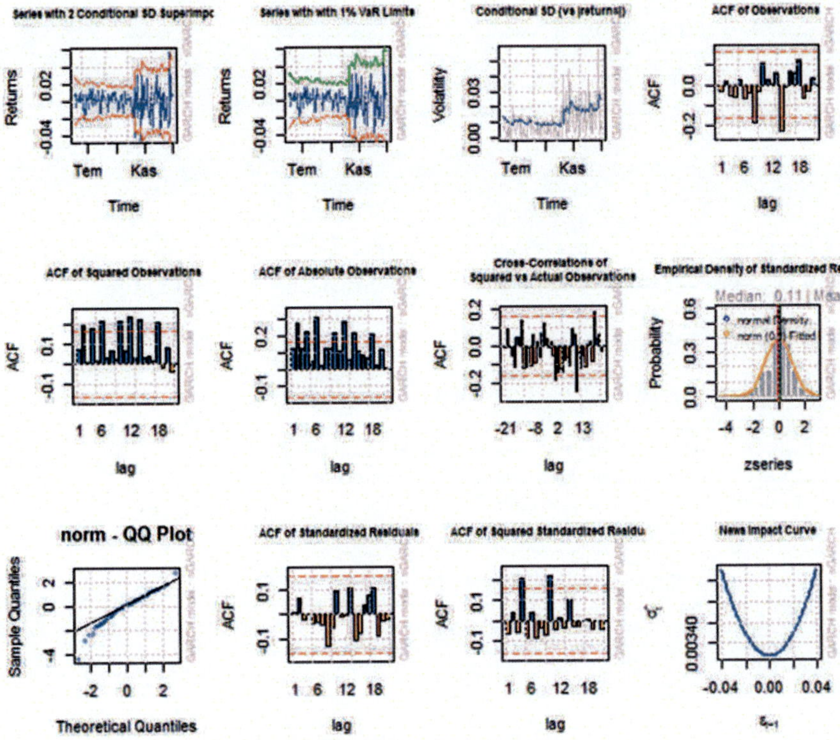

Fig. 3 The plot of GARCH(1,1) fit. Source: Author's creation

for comparing the empirical distribution of the standardized residuals with the selected theoretical distribution is acceptable.

In the following part of illustration, the codes in the book of Iacus and Yoshida (2018) that is a well-written handbook for stochastic processes with YUIMA is followed. Iacus et al. (2018; Iacus and Yoshida 2018) define the relationship between discrete GARCH process and the COGARCH process via Euler approximation where the increments of the Lévy process are a sequence of i.i.d. standard Gaussian distribution. So, the following function is used to convert the parameters from a GARCH(1,1) to a COGARCH(1,1) model.

```
# a function to convert the parameters from GARCH(1,1) to COGARCH(1,1)
model

Delta <- 1/252
ParGarToCog<- function(GARCH11param, dt, names=NULL){
if(is.null(names))
names <- names(GARCH11param)
my.omega <- GARCH11param["omega"]
my.alpha <- GARCH11param["alpha1"]
my.beta <- GARCH11param["beta1"]
```

```
a1 <- my.alpha/dt
b1 <- -log(my.beta)/dt
a0 <- my.omega/(b1*dt^2)
qmleparInGARCH <- c(a0, a1, b1)
names(qmleparInGARCH) <- c("a0", "a1", "b1")
return(qmleparInGARCH)

}


#use the converted values as initial point of the qmle optimizer

ParGarToCog(GARCH11param, Delta)

start <- as.list(ParGarToCog(GARCH11param, Delta))
modCog11 <- setCogarch(p=1, q=1, measure = list(intensity="1",
df=list("dnorm(z, 0, 1)")), measure.type="CP")
volatility.data <- setData(cumsum(X), delta = Delta)
Cog11 <- setYuima(data = volatility.data, model = modCog11)
Cog11.fit <- qmle(yuima = Cog11, grideq=TRUE,
start = c(start, y1 = 0.1),
aggregation = FALSE, method = "Nelder-Mead",
Est.Incr = "Incr")

v=simulate(Cog11.fit)
vol.cogarch<-v@data@zoo.data$`Series 2`

plot(v, main="COGARCH Model Fit by Compound Poisson")

COGARCH11par <- coef(Cog11.fit)
COGARCH11par
Cog11.fit@vcov

summary(Cog11.fit)

#diagnostics
check11<-Diagnostic.Cogarch(Cog11, param=COGARCH11par)
```

The summary of the COGARCH(1,1) model is given below.

```
Coefficients:
Estimate Std. Error
a0 0.007964285 0.003278197
a1 33.274698874 16.414936487
b1 40.976523028 19.170666945

Log.objFun PseudoLogLik: -433.2198

Number of increments: 146
Average of increments: -0.000140
```

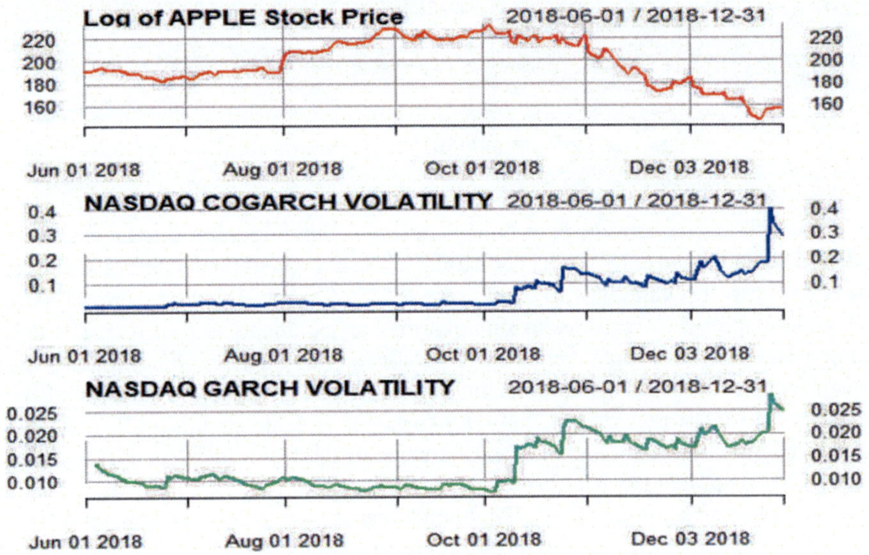

Fig. 4 The plot of Log of Apple stock price and COGARCH-filtered volatility. Source: Author's creation

```
Standard Dev. of increments: 0.068218
Summary statistics for increments:
Min. 1st Qu. Median Mean 3rd Qu. Max.
-0.297570 -0.031473 0.006945 -0.000140 0.038898 0.201473

The variance and covariance matrix

a0 a1 b1
a0 1.074657e-05 3.048447e-03 0.0139478
a1 3.048447e-03 2.694501e+02 305.5607473
b1 1.394780e-02 3.055607e+02 367.5144711
```

It can be concluded that the process is strictly stationary and the unconditional first moment of the Variance process exists according to COGARCH diagnostics. Moreover, another result of diagnostics is that the variance is a positive process.

The data, logarithm of Apple stock price and the COGARCH-filtered volatility of NASDAQ index, that are used in the ARDL bounds test are shown in the following Fig. 4 with the GARCH filtered volatility of NASDAQ index.

```
#ARDL data

plot.data<-merge(apl,vol.cogarch,vol.garch,X)

par(mfrow=c(3,1))
plot(plot.data$AAPL.Close , main="Log of APPLE Stock Price",
col="red")
```

```
plot(plot.data$vol.cogarch,main="NASDAQ COGARCH VOLATILITY",
col="blue" )
plot(plot.data$vol.garch,main="NASDAQ GARCH VOLATILITY",
col="green" )

last.data<-merge(apl,vol.cogarch)
dat.ardl<- data.frame(last.data)
```

The well-known advantage of bounds testing is that it requires that the variables should be integrated at I(0) or I(1) or I(0)/I(1). The computed F-statistics of ARDL is useless when the variables are stationary at I(2). Therefore, the stationarity tests should be applied to variables to sure that they are stationary I(0) or I(1). The unit root tests show that both variables are stationary at I(1). So, the variables are stationary at their first differences. In general, it can be reviewed in most of the studies on ARDL bounds test that the dependent variable should be I(1) and the independent variable should be I(0). But, some of the researchers such as Shahbaz et al. (2013) applied the ARDL bounds test to variables that are stationary at I(1).

The optimum lag orders for ARDL bounds test are $p = 7$ for autoregressive order, $q = 1$ distributed-lag order with the minimum statistics -16705.29 according to the Akaike and Bayes Information criteria. The ARDL bounds test results are given in the following R-output.

```
#ARDL Model and Bounds test

optim.lag<-ardlBoundOrders(data = dat.ardl ,
formula = AAPL.Close ~ vol.cogarch,
ic = c("AIC", "BIC", "MASE","GMRAE"),
max.p = 8, max.q = 8, FullSearch = FALSE )
optim.lag

ardlboundstest<-ardlBound(data = dat.ardl,
formula = AAPL.Close ~ vol.cogarch,
case = 1 , max.p = 7, max.q =1,ECM = TRUE, stability = TRUE)

model.ardlDlm = ardlDlm(formula = AAPL.Close ~ vol.cogarch,
data = dat.ardl , p = 7 , q = 1)

summary(ardlboundstest)
summary(model.ardlDlm)
```

The output of ARDL model and ARDL bounds test is given below.

```
Orders being calculated with max.p = 7 and max.q = 1 ...

Autoregressive order: 2 and p-orders: 8
----------------------------------------------------

Breusch-Godfrey Test for the autocorrelation in residuals:
```

```
Breusch-Godfrey test for serial correlation of order up to 1

data: modelFull$model
LM test = 1.4968, df1 = 1, df2 = 127, p-value = 0.2234

-------------------------------------------------------

Ljung-Box Test for the autocorrelation in residuals:

Box-Ljung test

data: res
X-squared = 0.026887, df = 1, p-value = 0.8698

-------------------------------------------------------

Breusch-Pagan Test for the homoskedasticity of residuals:

studentized Breusch-Pagan test

data: modelFull$model
BP = 27.54, df = 10, p-value = 0.002138

The p-value of Breusch-Pagan test for the homoskedasticity of
residuals:
0.002137605 < 0.05!
-------------------------------------------------------

Shapiro-Wilk test of normality of residuals:

Shapiro-Wilk normality test

data: modelFull$model$residual
W = 0.96876, p-value = 0.002826

The p-value of Shapiro-Wilk test normality of residuals: 0.002825923 <
0.05!
-------------------------------------------------------

PESARAN, SHIN AND SMITH (2001) COINTEGRATION TEST

Observations: 146
Number of Regressors (k): 1
Case: 1

-------------------------------------------------------
- F-test -
-------------------------------------------------------
<------- I(0) ------------ I(1) ----->
10% critical value 2.44 3.28
```

```
5% critical value 3.15 4.11
1% critical value 4.81 6.02

F-statistic = 3.34545560563242

------------------------------------------------------------
F-statistic note: Asymptotic critical values used.

------------------------------------------------------------

Ramsey's RESET Test for model specification:

RESET test

data: modelECM$model
RESET = 0.1935, df1 = 2, df2 = 127, p-value = 0.8243

------------------------------------------------------------
------------------------------------------------------------
Error Correction Model Output:

Time series regression with "ts" data:
Start = 8, End = 146

Call:
dynlm(formula = as.formula(model.text), data = data)

Residuals:
Min 1Q Median 3Q Max
-0.058804 -0.009736 0.000662 0.009567 0.070277

Coefficients:
Estimate Std. Error t value Pr(>|t|)
ec.1 0.0004428 0.0001705 2.597 0.0105 *
dvol.cogarch.t 0.0006854 0.0683780 0.010 0.9920
dvol.cogarch.1 0.1075625 0.0838549 1.283 0.2019
dvol.cogarch.2 0.1158932 0.0852127 1.360 0.1762
dvol.cogarch.3 0.2570448 0.1146414 2.242 0.0267 *
dvol.cogarch.4 0.2039107 0.1178214 1.731 0.0859 .
dvol.cogarch.5 0.1414597 0.1169045 1.210 0.2285
dvol.cogarch.6 0.0339789 0.1164307 0.292 0.7709
dvol.cogarch.7 -0.1462743 0.1117352 -1.309 0.1928
dAAPL.Close.1 -0.0512518 0.0877476 -0.584 0.5602
---
Signif. codes: 0 '***' 0.001 '**' 0.01 '*' 0.05 '.' 0.1 ' ' 1

Residual standard error: 0.01953 on 129 degrees of freedom
Multiple R-squared: 0.09678, Adjusted R-squared: 0.02676
F-statistic: 1.382 on 10 and 129 DF, p-value: 0.1954
```

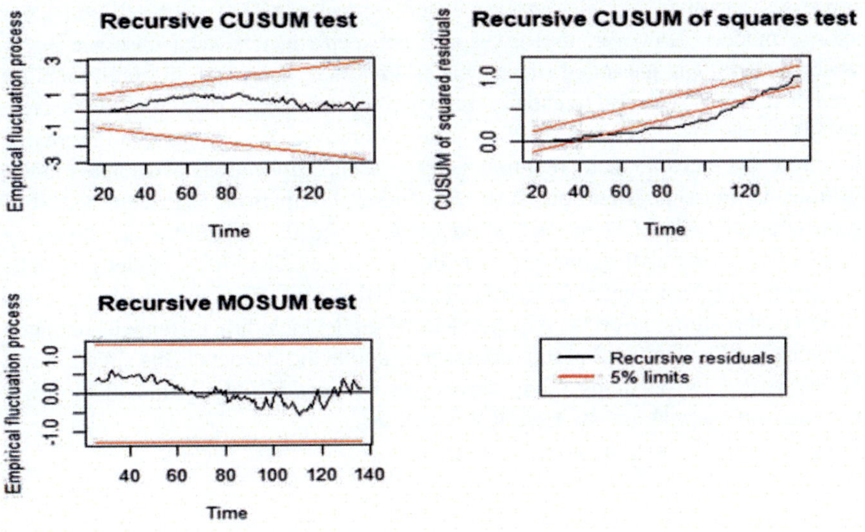

Fig. 5 The plot of CUSUM and MUSUM test. Source: Author's creation

```
------------------------------------------------------
Long-run coefficients:
vol.cogarch.1
-0.08251874
```

The ARDL bounds test F-statistics is greater than the critical values at 10%. It leads to reject the hypothesis of no cointegration. So, it can be concluded that there is one cointegrating vector to define the long-run relationship between the COGARCH-filtered volatility of NASDAQ index and Apple stock prices. Breusch–Godfrey Test and Ljung–Box tests indicate that there is no autocorrelation. But, the p-value of Breusch–Pagan test for the homoskedasticity of residuals is less than 0.05 that indicates heteroskedasticity of residuals. The Shapiro-Wilk normality test result shows that the residuals are not normally distributed may be ignored in most of the studies. The ECM coefficient is not in the interval between −1 and 0. So, it indicates that it cannot be examined marginal impacts of volatility on stock prices.

The recursive CUSUM of square tests in Fig. 5 shows the coefficients are out of the boundaries, which is an evidence of structural break in the data. It may be fixed adding dummy variable into the model.

A Brief Discussion

The purpose of this book section is to show how to use the volatility data obtained from the COGARCH model in the ARDL bounds test approach. In the current studies in literature, the effect of volatility data obtained from discrete GARCH processes on other variables was analyzed by using ARDL approach and other similar models. However, the time-space between financial data observations in which volatility is measured in real life is irregular. Therefore, discrete volatility models may not be useful to capture the volatility in financial data. But, the discrete volatility models have various extensions. Moreover, it is understood from the literature that there are many real-time and successful applications of discrete models in financial markets. Therefore, in future studies, comparison of discrete GARCH models and COGARCH model should be done and the volatility data should be obtained by selecting the appropriate model. Even the COGARCH model should be compared with Exponential COGARCH and GJR-COGARCH models. In the illustration of this study, Levy Driven COGARCH model including increments obtained by using the Compound Poisson process was applied to the data. This situation can be diversified by obtaining many derivatives of the COGARCH model by using Gamma and Normal Inverse Gaussian processes.

References

Adom PK, Bekoe W, Akoena SKK (2012) Modelling aggregate domestic electricity demand in Ghana: an autoregressive distributed lag bounds cointegration approach. Energy Policy 42:530–537

Almon S (1965) The distributed lag between capital appropriations and net expenditures. Econometrica 33:178–196

Arı Y (2019) COGARCH models: an explicit solution to the stochastic differential equation for variance. In: Alparslan Gök S, Aruğaslan Çinçin D (eds) Emerging applications of differential equations and game theory. IGI Global, Hershey, PA, pp 79–97. https://doi.org/10.4018/978-1-7998-0134-4.ch005

Brooks C (2014) Introductory econometrics for finance. Cambridge university press, New York

Brockwell P, Chadraa E, Lindner A (2006) Continuous-time GARCH processes. Ann Appl Probab 16(2):790–826

Demirhan H (2019) Package 'dLagM': time series regression models with distributed lag models. https://cran.rstudio.com/web/packages/dLagM/dLagM.pdf

Dickey DA, Fuller WA (1981) Likelihood ratio statistics for autoregressive time series with a unit root. Econometrica 49:1057

Enders W (1995) Applied econometric time series. Wiley and Sons

Engle RF, Granger CWJ (1987) Co-integration and error-correction: representation, estimation, and testing. Econometrica 55:251–276

Granger CWJ (1969) Investigating causal relations by econometrics models and cross-spectral methods. Econometrica:424–438

Ghalanos A (2020) Rugarch: univariate GARCH models. R package version 1.4–2. Available at: https://cran.r-project.org/web/packages/rugarch/rugarch.pdf

Granger CWJ, Newbold P (1974) Spurious regressions in economics. J Econ:111

Haug S, Klüppelberg C, Lindner A, Zapp M (2007) Moment estimating the COGARCH (1,1) model - a first go. Econ J 10(2):320–341

Iacus SM, Mercuri L, Rroji E (2015) Estimation and simulation of a COGARCH(p,q) model in the YUIMA project. arXiv preprint arXiv:1505.03914

Iacus SM, Mercuri L, Rroji E (2018) Discrete-time approximation of a cogarch(p,q) model and its estimation. J Time Ser Anal 39:787–809. https://doi.org/10.1111/jtsa.12406

Iacus SM, Yoshida N (2018) Simulation and inference for stochastic processes with YUIMA: a Comprehensive R Framework for SDEs and other Stochastic Processes. Springer International Publishing, pp. 254–256

Johansen S (1991) Estimation and hypothesis testing of cointegration vectors in Gaussian vector autoregressive models. Econometrica 59:1551–1580

Johansen S, Juselius K (1990) Maximum likelihood estimation and inference on Cointegration with applications to demand for money. Oxf Bull Econ Stat 52:169–210

Johensen S (1988) Statistical analysis of Cointegration vectors. J Econ Dyn Control 12:231–254

Klüppelberg C, Lindner A, Maller RA (2004) Continuous time GARCH process driven by a Lévy process: stationarity and second order behavior. J Appl Probab 41(3):601–622

Klüppelberg C, Maller R, Szimayer A. (2011) The COGARCH: a review, with news on option pricing and statistical inference. In Surveys in Stochastic Processes. Proc. Of the 33rd SPA Conference in Berlin, pages 29–58. EMS Series of Congress Reports, EMS Publishing House

Maller RA, Mueller G, Szimayer A (2008) GARCH modelling in continuous time for irregularly spaced time series data. Bernoulli 14(2):519–542

Pesaran MH, Pesaran B (1997) Working with microfit 4.0: interactive econometric analysis. Oxford University Press, Oxford

Pesaran MH, Shin Y (1995) An autoregressive distributed lag modelling approach to cointegration analysis. Cambridge working papers in economics 9514, Faculty of economics, University of Cambridge

Pesaran MH, Shin Y (1998) An autoregressive distributed-lag modelling approach to cointegration analysis. Econ Soc Monographs 31:371–413

Pesaran MH, Shin Y (1999) An autoregressive distributed lag modelling approach to cointegration analysis. http://www.econ.cam.ac.uk/faculty/pesaran/ardl.pdf

Pesaran MH, Shin Y, Smith R (1996) Testing for the existence of a longrun relationship. University of Cambridge, DAE Working Paper No. 9622

Pesaran MH, Shin Y, Smith RJ (2001) Bounds testing approaches to the analysis of level relationships. J Appl Econ 16(3):289–326

Pesaran MH, Smith R (1998) Structural analysis of Cointegrating VARs. J Econ Survey 12 (5):471–505

Phillips B, Perron P (1988) Testing for a unit Root in Time Series Regression. Biometrika 75:335–346

Ryan J A , Ulrich JM (2018) Quantmod: quantitative financial Modelling framework. R package version 0.4–13. https://CRAN.R-project.org/package=quantmod

Shahbaz M, Khan S, Tahir MI (2013) The dynamic links between energy consumption, economic growth, financial development and trade in China: fresh evidence from multivariate framework analysis. Energy Econ 40:8–21.

Toda HY, Yamamoto T (1995) Statistical inference in vector autoregression with possibly integrated processes. J Econ:225–250

Tsay RS (2012) Analysis of financial time series. Wiley and Sons

Wiener N (1956) Nonlinear prediction and dynamics. Proceedings of the third berkeley symposium on mathematical statistics and probability. In: Contributions to astronomy and physics, vol 3. University of California Press, Berkeley, pp 247–252

Yakup Arı is an Assistant Professor in the Department of Economics and Finance, Alanya Alaaddin Keykubat University. Having graduated with a bachelor's degree in Mathematics, he pursued an MBA degree in Finance and a PhD degree in Financial Economics—all of which at Yeditepe University. He worked as a statistical consultant at several private consultancy firms in Istanbul. He teaches courses in time series analysis, mathematical economics, technical analysis, probability and statistics, biostatistics, and econometrics. His primary research interest lies in the area of Time Series Analysis, Lévy Driven Stochastic Processes, the Bayesian Approach in Statistics and Econometrics, in addition to statistical methods in Engineering and Social Sciences.

Performance of MS-GARCH Models: Bayesian MCMC-Based Estimation

Lawrence Diteboho Xaba, Ntebogang Dinah Moroke, and Lebotsa Daniel Metsileng

Introduction

Modeling volatility of financial markets is central in risk management. Some contribution to this field has been a development of generalized autoregressive conditional heteroscedasticity (GARCH) model which was firstly developed by Bollerslev (1986) in which volatility is a function of past asset returns. According to Ardia et al. (2016), the GARCH model is today a widespread tool in risk management. However, recent studies show that estimates of GARCH models can be biased because of structural breaks in the dynamics of volatility (Bauwens et al. 2014). These structural breaks ordinarily happen during times of financial turmoil. Assessing a GARCH model on data showing structural break yields a nonstationary evaluated model and infers poor hazard forecasts. According to Ardia (2008), an approach to adapt to this issue is given by Markov-switching GARCH models MS (k) − GARCH(p, q) whose parameters fluctuate after some time as per an inert discrete Markov process. These models can rapidly adjust to variations in the unconditional volatility level, which enhances hazard forecasts. The accumulated evidence from empirical research suggests that the volatility of financial markets displays some type of persistence that cannot be appropriately captured by classical GARCH models. Bauwens et al. (2006), has shown that these models usually indicate high persistence in conditional volatility. This persistence, as was noted by Klaassen (2002), is not compatible with the poor forecasting results of these models.

L. D. Xaba (✉) · N. D. Moroke · L. D. Metsileng
North West University, Mafikeng, South Africa
e-mail: Diteboho.Xaba@nwu.ac.za; Ntebo.Moroke@nwu.ac.za

B. Adıgüzel Mercangöz (ed.), *Handbook of Research on Emerging Theories, Models, and Applications of Financial Econometrics*,
https://doi.org/10.1007/978-3-030-54108-8_14

Hamilton and Susmel (1994) were among the first authors to discuss the MS-GARCH model and they noted that the estimation of this path-dependent model is a challenging task because the exact computation of the likelihood is infeasible in practice. Furthermore, the computation method based on the maximum likelihood (ML) procedure has shown some convergence problems and it has a problem of local maxima (Ardia 2008). Hamilton and Susmel (1994) and Cai (1994) reported that the disadvantage of MLE approach becomes computationally unfeasible for MS-GARCH models. This led to some authors such Dueker (1997), Gray (1996), Haas et al. (2004), and Klaassen (2002) to propose modified estimation versions of the MS-GARCH model that avoids the path dependence problem which is often experienced when using the ML estimation method. Bauwens et al. (2007) suggested an alternative estimation method called Bayesian Markov Chain Monte Carlo (MCMC) algorithm. Authors (Bauwens et al. 2010, 2011, 2014; Henneke et al. 2011) resorted to the Bayesian framework because the MCMC methods are powerful tools for the numerical computation of integrals. Furthermore, the Bayesian MCMC algorithm is able to circumvent the problem of path dependence by including the state variables in the parameter space and simulating them by Gibbs sampling.

The current work aims at finding the best estimation method for the MRS (k) − GARCH(p, q) model. This empirical analysis is in two stages. Firstly, MRS (k) − GARCH(p, q) model is estimated using both the Maximum likelihood estimation (MLE) method and Bayesian estimation method. Lastly, a comparative analysis is directed to survey whether the MLE method successfully represents the volatility estimation contrasted with Bayesian estimation method.

Literature Review

There is a great deal of interest to Markov-Switching models (MSM) in financial econometrics literature. However, most of the current literature focuses on the stock market, interest, and exchange rates. Generally, studies in the literature suggest the superiority of the MSM. Following the seminal study of Hamilton (1989), many analyses are conducted for different markets by using MSM. Besides, some modifications are presented and the power of the models is improved. Rashid and Kocaaslan (2013) state that the Markov Regime-Switching (MRS) model has a significant explanatory power for the behavior of Gross Domestic Products (GDP) volatilities. Billio et al. (2013) improve a new Bayesian multichain Markov-Switching Regime Generalized Autoregressive Conditional Heteroskedastic MRS-GARCH model for the dynamic hedging in energy futures. Likewise, Zainudin (2013) shows that when regime switching is taken into account, more successful hedging performance can be obtained. Kritzman et al. (2012) explain how MRS models can be used in the prediction of regimes in market turbulence, inflation, and economic growth and obtain a dynamic process that outperforms static asset allocation for the risk-averse investors. Naeini and Fatahi (2012) compared

GARCH models and MS-GARCH models in their ability to estimate and forecasting the volatility of the Tehran stock market on some horizon of forecasting. The study using daily data for the period 1995–2011. The results, also, show that MS-GARCH models can remove the high persistence of GARCH models and separately in each regime of volatility, the persistence is high. This shows the priority of SW-GARCH models. Another implication is that there is evidence of regime clustering.

Günay (2015) demonstrated the ability of Markov regime-switching GARCH (MRS-GARCH) compared to generalized autoregressive conditional heteroskedastic (GARCH), exponential GARCH, Glosten–Jagannathan–Runkle GARCH models. Günay (2015) used the return volatility of Brent oil returns to obtain a reliable forecasting model. The volatility models were formed under normal, generalized error distribution and Student's t distributions. The best model was selected based on the Akaike information criterion (AIC) and Bayesian information criterion (BIC) values, MRS-GARCH model outperforms all other alternative models. Yadavalli and Matlou (2015) conducted an empirical analysis of the daily returns of the All-Share Index (Alsi) of South Africa using different variants of the Generalized Autoregressive Conditional Heteroskedasticity (GARCH) model. The objective of the study was to estimate and compare the standard GARCH and nonlinear GARCH models. The analysis demonstrated that MRS-GARCH models outperform the standard GARCH models in forecasting volatility at short horizons.

Marcucci (2005) compared different GARCH models in terms of their ability to describe and forecast financial time series volatility. The author used Standard & Poor (S&P 500) stock market daily closing price index, the sample is from January 1988 to October 2003 for a total of 4095 observations all obtained from DataStream. The main objective of the study is to compare different volatility forecasts of GARCH models and measure the number of times a given model can correctly predict the directions of change of the actual volatility. In terms of evaluating the best model between different GARCH models, the study used error metrics such as MSE, QLIKE, R2LOG, MAD1, MAD2, and HMSE. The empirical analysis demonstrated that Markov Regime-Switching GARCH (MSR-GARCH) models outperformed all the standard GARCH models for forecasting volatility at shorter horizons according to a broad set of statistical loss functions. But at the longer horizons, standard asymmetric GARCH models performed better than MSR-GARCH model. The finding of the study revealed that no model clearly outperformed the other at all horizons under this risk-management evaluation criterion.

Similarly, Naeini and Fatahi (2012) comparing GARCH models and Markov-switching GARCH models in their ability to estimate and forecasting the volatility of the Tehran stock market on some horizon of forecasting. The study provided an analysis of regime switching in volatility and out-of-sample forecasting of the IRAN using daily data for the period 1995–2011 for a total of 2480 observations all obtained from DataStream. The study modeled volatility regime switching within a univariate Markov-Switching framework. Then the study provided out-of-sample forecasts of the TEHRAN daily returns using two competing nonlinear models, the GARCH Markov-Switching model, and the uniregime GARCH Model. The comparison of the out-of-sample forecasts is done on the basis of forecast accuracy such MSE, QLIKE, R2LOG, MAD1, MAD2, and HMSE. The results, of forecast accuracy, revealed that MSR-GARCH models performed better than standard GARCH.

Zhang et al. (2015) in their study tried to find a reasonable and reliable forecast method for crude oil price volatility. In their study, they evaluated the forecast performance of single-regime GARCH models (including the standard linear GARCH model and the nonlinear GJR-GARCH and EGARCH models) and the two-regime Markov Regime-Switching GARCH (MRS-GARCH) model for crude oil price volatility at different data frequencies and time horizons.

Bildirici and Ersin (2014) incorporated fractional integration and asymmetric power properties to MS-GARCH in modeling the daily stock returns in the emerging market, the Istanbul Stock Index (ISE100). The author proposed Markov-switching MS-ARMA-FIGARCH, APGARCH, and FIAPGARCH processes are further augmented with MLP, Recurrent-NN, and Hybrid NN type neural networks. The author used daily stock returns in the emerging market, the Istanbul Stock Index (ISE100), the sample is from July 07, 1986 to December 2010 for a total of 5852 observations. The aim of the study was to compare the MS-ARMA-FIGARCH, APGARCH, and FIAPGARCH using MAE, MSE, and RMSE error criteria and Diebold-Mariano equal forecast accuracy tests. The results of the study suggested that the fractionally integrated and asymmetric power counterparts of Gray's MS-GARCH model provided promising results, while the best results are obtained for their neural network-based counterparts. Further, among the models analyzed, the models based on the Hybrid-MLP and Recurrent-NN, the MS-ARMA-FIAPGARCH-Hybrid MLP, and MS-ARMA-FIAPGARCH-RNN provided the best forecast performances over the baseline single-regime GARCH models and further, over the Gray's MS-GARCH model. Therefore, the models are promising for various economic applications.

Crawford and Fratantoni (2003) compare the forecasting performance of three types of univariate time series models ARIMA, GARCH, and regime-switching. The underlying intuition behind regime-switching models is that the series of interest behave differently depending on the realization of an unobservable regime variable. Regime-switching models are a compelling choice for real estate markets that have historically displayed boom and bust cycles. However, we find that, while regime-switching models can perform better in-sample, simple ARIMA models generally perform better in out-of-sample forecasting.

Alemohammad et al. (2017) proposed a Markov-switching asymmetric GARCH model that follows a logistic smooth transition structure between the effects of positive and negative shocks. The study applied the MCMC method through Gibbs and Griddy Gibbs sampling to parameters of the model. Alemohammad et al. (2017) made a demonstration by using S&P 500 indices to show the competing performance of in-sample fit and out-of-sample forecast volatility and value at risk of the proposed model. The Diebold-Mariano test shows that the proposed model outperforms all competing models in forecast volatility.

Ardia et al. (2018) in their study used MS-GARCH models the stock price and forex market of Latin American countries using both the Monte Carlo Expectation-

Maximization (MCEM) and Monte Carlo Maximum Likelihood (MCML) algorithms. The study compared the abilities of estimation methods under standard GARCH, MS-GARCH. The results show that the volatility persistence is captured differently in the MS-GARCH models. The estimated parameters with a standard GARCH model exacerbates the volatility in almost double compared to MS-GARCH model. There is different behavior of the coefficients and the variance according to the two-regimes (high and low volatility) by each model in the Latin American stock and Forex markets. There are common episodes related to global international crises and also domestic events producing different behavior in the volatility of each time series.

Shiferaw (2018) applied the three-state Markov-switching (MS) regression, the standard single-regime GARCH, and the Markov-switching GARCH (MS-GARCH) models. To choose the best fit model, the log-likelihood function, Akaike information criterion (AIC), Bayesian information criterion (BIC), and deviance information criterion (DIC) are employed under different distributions for innovations. The results indicated that the price of agricultural commodities was found to be significantly associated with the price of coal, the price of natural gas, the price of oil, and the exchange rate. In addition, the MS-GARCH models under the MCMC approach outperformed the standard single-regime GARCH models in measuring VaR.

Methodology

The section discusses the methods ranging from nonlinearity tests to nonlinear GARCH models. We investigate the best estimation method and distribution that can be used under MRS-GARCH models of the exchange rates of BRICS countries.

Nonlinearity and Nonlinear Unit Root Tests

In this section, researchers listed nonlinearity and nonlinear unit root tests. In order to apply the nonlinear methods needed to address the objectives of the chapter, the data was first tested for nonlinearity and nonstationarity. Since nonlinearity in time series may occur in several ways, it is imprudent to rely solely on single test (Ismail and Isa 2006). In that case to test for nonlinearity in the data sets, the Regression Specification Error Test (RESET), ARCH test, the McLeod and Li test, Keenan's test, Tsay test, Brock–Dechert–Scheinkman (BDS), and CUSUM test were used. In the case of testing nonlinear unit root, the Bierens Nonlinear ADF (B-NLADF) was used to determine the existence of nonlinear dependence in the data.

Markov Regime-Switching Approach

The Markov-switching regime model adopted relies on two assumptions: (1) the volatility process is characterized by two regimes, high volatility, and low volatility; (2) the high volatility regime is associated with large stock price deviations (high values of the mean process) and the low volatility regime is associated with small stock price movements (low values of the mean process). The presence of two regimes low volatility versus high volatility motivates the Markov-switching approach adopted. Brunetti et al. (2008) documented that it is also evident that within the two regimes; volatility is not constant. Hence the need for GARCH approaches. Following the study of Sajjad et al. (2008), the MS (k) – GARCH(p, q) is presented as:

Let Y_t be the first difference in the log nominal stock prices. According to Hamilton (1989), Hamilton and Raj (2013) and Cruz and Mapa (2013), the simple Markov-Switching model which was firstly derived by Hamilton (1989) is as follows:

$$Y_t - \alpha(S_t) = \Phi_1[Y_{t-1} - \alpha(S_{t-1})] + \cdots + \Phi_p[Y_{t-p} - \alpha(S_p)] + \varepsilon_t \quad (1)$$

when re-parameterized yields:

$$Y_t = C + \Phi_1 Y_{t-1} + \Phi_2 + \cdots + \Phi_p Y_{t-p} + \varepsilon_t \quad (2)$$

Which it is further simplified to:

$$Y_t = \sum\nolimits_{i=1}^{p} \Phi_i Y_{t-1} + \varepsilon_t \quad (3)$$

According to Marcucci (2005), the general GARCH (p, q) model for the conditional variance of innovations Y_t is:

$$\widehat{\varepsilon_t^2} = \alpha_0 + \sum_{t=1}^{p} \Phi_i \widehat{\varepsilon_{t-i}^2} + \sum_{i=1}^{q} \Theta_j \widehat{\varepsilon_{t-i}^2} \quad (4)$$

Then the N-state Markov chain with p_{ij} as transition probabilities is a process in which the probability that unobserved S_t equals some particular value j depends on the past only through the most recent value S_{t-1}. That is:

$$P_r\{S_t = i | S_{t-1} = j, S_{t-2} = N, ..\} = P_r\{S_t = i | S_{t-1} = j\} = p_{ij} \quad (5)$$

The process of one regime changing to the other and vice versa is been administered by the first order MC R state with the flowing transition probabilities which are being administered by Cruz and Mapa (2013), Chkili, and Nguyen (2014).

$$P = \begin{bmatrix} P_{11} & P_{12} \\ P_{21} & P_{22} \end{bmatrix} = \begin{bmatrix} P_{11} & 1 - P_{11} \\ 1 - P_{22} & P_{22} \end{bmatrix} \tag{6}$$

and $P_{11} + P_{12} + P_{21} + P_{22} = 1$ which are also known as the transition probabilities and are estimated from the two-regime Markov-Switching model. The ergodic probability (that is the unconditional probability) of being in state $S_t = 1$ is given by $P_1 = \frac{(1-P)}{(2-p-q)}$. For further details on regime-switching models, see Hamilton (2010). Combining (4) and (5) together, then the whole MS (k) – GARCH(p, q) model which is the extended vision of standard GARCH model which was extended by Klaassen (2002) and Marcucci (2005) is represented in the following mathematical expression:

$$Y_t = \alpha_0 + \sum_{t=1}^{p} \Phi_i(S_t)\widehat{\varepsilon}_{t-i}^2 + \sum_{i=1}^{q} \Theta_j(S_t)\widehat{\varepsilon}_{t-i}^2 \tag{7}$$

whereas S_t is the latent state component that takes the values of 1 for high regime period or 0 for low regime period. The MS (k) – GARCH(p, q) approach allows the estimation of the high and low volatility structures of stock prices. Cifter (2013) has emphasized that the MS (k) – GARCH(p, q) model likewise the GARCH model is estimated with Gaussian Bollerslev (1986), Student-t Bollerslev (1987), and Skewed Student-t. The reason for including the Student-t and the skewed Student-t distribution is that most of the financial time series changes are not normally distributed. Therefore, Marcucci (2005) has revealed that the MS (k) – GARCH(p, q) consists of four elements: the conditional mean, the conditional variance, the regime process, and the conditional distribution. The conditional mean equation, which is generally modeled through a random walk with or without drift, here is simply modeled as:

$$Y_t = \mu_t^i + \varepsilon_t = \delta^i + \varepsilon_t \tag{8}$$

where $i = 1, 2$ and $\varepsilon_t = \eta_t \sqrt{\widehat{\varepsilon}_t^2}$ and η_t is a zero mean, unit variance process. For this chapter, the series is the exchange rates of BRICS countries.

Parameter Estimation

The parameter estimation is the method that can be used to estimate the parameters of the linear or nonlinear models. For the present study, to estimate the parameters of MRS-GARCH model, the study used both Maximum Likelihood and Bayesian MCMC estimation methods. The estimation methods are discussed in the following subsections.

Maximum Likelihood Estimation Method

Maximum likelihood method is the most popular procedure used to estimate one or more parameters of the given model (Harris and Stocker 1998). The specification causes difficulties in estimation since the Conditional variance at time t depends on the entire regime path S_t. To underline this dependence, Augustyniak (2014), denoted that the notation $(s_t)\varepsilon_{t-i}^2$ is used, but for simplicity, ε_t^2 is used to represent $(s_t)\varepsilon_{t-i}^2$. Furthermore, letting y and s to represent Y_t and (S_t) and the probability mass function (PMF) by $f(p)$, then the computation of the likelihood of the observations, denoted by $f(y|\theta)$ can be proficient by integrating out all possible regime paths:

$$
\begin{aligned}
f(y|\theta) &= \sum_{S} f(y|\theta) \sum_{S} f(y|\theta) p(s|\theta) \\
&= \sum\nolimits_{S} \left[\prod\nolimits_{t-1}^{T} \varepsilon_t^{-1} \frac{1}{\sqrt{2\pi}} e^{\left(-\frac{y_t - \mu_{s_t}}{2\varepsilon_t^2} \right)} \right] p(s|\theta)
\end{aligned} \tag{9}
$$

when T is large, the integration in the equation is numerically infeasible because it contains N^t terms that quickly increases exponentially. Therefore, Bauwens et al. (2014) had shown that it is possible to accurately estimate the log-likelihood by:

$$
\log f(y|\theta) = \log f(y|\theta) + \sum_{t=1}^{T-1} \log \left(y_{t+1} | y_{1:t}\theta \right), \tag{10}
$$

and also estimating $f(y_{t+1} | y_{1:t}, \theta)$, $t = 1, \ldots, T-1$ successively with the support of particle filters. For a parsimonious expression of the likelihood function, we define the vector $y = (y_1, \ldots, y_T)^{`}$, $\varpi = (\varpi_1, \ldots, \varpi_T)^{`}$, $s = (s_1, \ldots, s_T)^{`}$ and $\alpha = \left(\alpha_0^{`}, \alpha_1^{`}, \alpha_2^{`}\right)^{`}$. Finally, the diagonal matrix is $\sum = \sum \Theta = \mathrm{diag}\left(\left\{\varpi_t \varrho e_t^{`} \varepsilon^t\right\}_{t=1}^{T}\right)$. Note that ϱ, e_t and ε_t are the model parameter functions respectively. Therefore the likelihood function of Θ is as follows (Bauwens et al. 2014):

$$
l(\Theta|y) \propto \left(\det \sum\right)^{\frac{-1}{2}} e^{\left[\frac{-1}{2} y \sum_{y}^{-1}\right]} \tag{11}
$$

Bayesian MCMC Estimation Method

Estimating the MRS-GARCH model with Bayesian methods have more advantage over the classical approach. Firstly, proper computation methods are based on Markov Chain Monte Carlo (MCMC) procedures and circumvent the common problem of local maxima encountered in MLE of this class of models Ardia (2008). Secondly, exploring the posterior joint distribution gives a comprehensive picture of the uncertainty of parameters that is not achievable with classical approach. For the model considered in this study, the asymptotic distribution theory of the MLE is inoperable because of the threshold parameters. Third, constraints on the model parameters can be incorporated through prior specifications. Finally, the likelihoods and Bayes factors can be used to achieve discrimination between models. In the classical framework, testing the null of K versus K′ states is not possible (Frühwirth-Schnatter 2006).

Following Frühwirth-Schnatter (2006), Ardia (2008, 2009), Bauwens et al. (2014) and Ardia (2016), the normal, Student-t, and generalized error distribution specification are nested in Bayes factor and the following posterior distribution is constructed using Bayes rule:

$$\begin{aligned} P(\Theta, S|Y) &\propto P(\Theta, S)P(Y|\Theta, S), \\ &\propto P(\Theta)P(S|\Theta)P(Y|\Theta, S) \end{aligned} \tag{12}$$

where, $\Theta = (Y, \alpha, \beta, \mu_1, \mu_2, P_{11}, P_{22})$, $S = (S_1, S_T)$ and $Y = (y_1, y_T)$. The Bayes' rule is applied in the first line. The second line comes from the definition of conditional probability. The posterior parameters are denoted by $P(\Theta)$. Under the assumption of independence, the prior density is chosen as:

$$P(\Theta) = P(Y)P(\mu_1)P(\mu_2)P(\alpha)P(\beta)P(P_{11})P(P_{22}) \tag{13}$$

Furthermore, the likelihood function of S is given by:

$$\begin{aligned} P(S|\Theta) &= P(S|P_{11}, P_{22}) \\ &= \prod\nolimits_{t=1}^{T} P(S_{t+1}|S_t, P_{11}, P_{22}\ ) \\ &= P_{11}^{\eta_{11}}(1 - P_{11})^{\eta_{12}} P_{22}^{\eta_{22}}(1 - P_{22})^{\eta_{21}} \end{aligned} \tag{14}$$

where the number of transitions from state i to j are denoted by η_{ij}. The second line is due to the Markov property of S. The last term, $P(Y| \Theta, S)$ is the likelihood function Θ and S.

$$P(Y|\Theta, S) = \begin{aligned} &\prod\nolimits_{t=1}^{T} P(y_t|Y_{t-1}, S_t, S_1, \Theta) \\ &= \prod\nolimits_{t=1}^{T} \frac{1}{\sqrt{2\pi\sigma_t^2}} e^{\left[-\frac{\varepsilon_t^2}{2\sigma_t^2}\right]} \end{aligned} \tag{15}$$

Forecast Evaluation

This section discusses the evaluation based forecasting which depends on the three error metrices. According to Marcucci (2005), the commonly used error metrices for forecast evaluation are Mean Squared Error (MSE), Root Mean Square Error (RMSE), and Mean Absolute Error (MAE). The three error metrices are used in the current study in order to select the appropriate models for BRICS exchange rates using MS-GARCH model.

Model Forecasting Accuracy

This section discusses the test used to determine the accuracy of the forecasts. Diebold-Mariano's (1995) (DM) test is used to compare the forecasting ability of two or more competing models. Diebold and Mariano (1995) are of the view that comparing the forecasting ability of competing models built for a given data is very important. Although the lower the forecast measure, the better the forecasting performance, it does not necessarily imply superior forecasting ability since the difference between error measures from competing models may not be significantly different from zero (Diebold and Mariano 1995). One simple approach to compare the forecast accuracy of competing models is the DM test, which evaluates the fairness of forecast accuracy of pairs of competing models built for a particular data.

Empirical Analysis

This section discusses the empirical analysis of data. The results are summarized using tables and figures and the graphical presentations assist in determining the behavior of the data. The aim is to explore the possibility of estimating empirical models capable of describing and forecasting each of the exchange rates of BRICS countries. We sought to explore the performance of the hybrid models using the two estimation methods namely Maximum Likelihood estimation and Bayesian Markov Chain Monti Carlo (MCMC) estimation.

Preliminary Data Analyses Results

This section discusses the preliminary analysis of data with the aim to identify the broad behavior of the measured variables. We conducted descriptive statistics, nonlinearity tests, and nonstationary tests to assess the characteristics of exchange rates of BRICS countries.

Descriptive Statistics

The descriptive statistics used are Skewness, Kurtosis, and Jarque–Bera test to assess the characteristics of the five (5) variables (Brazil, Russia, India, China, and South Africa). Prior to executing the primary analysis of data, researchers also addresses a few very important issues such as the normality of the actual data as suggested by Vavra (2011) as well as Kline (2005). The normality test gives an indication of which appropriate methods (linear or nonlinear) to be used. Furthermore, the test gives the indication whether it is appropriate to use normal distribution to estimation MRS-GARCH model or not. Table 1 gives summary results for descriptive statistics of the data.

Table 1 presents the descriptive statistics of the five (5) variables (Brazil, Russia, India, China, and South Africa). Most of the exchange rates were negatively Skewed (India, Russia, and RSA) except Brazil and China. It is also noted that the series have excess kurtosis of less than three. These values indicate that the exchange rates of BRICS countries are not normally distributed. The assertion was also confirmed by the Jarque–Bera (JB) test. This indicates that exchange rates of BRICS can only be estimated and forecasted using nonlinear models. These results are consistent with those obtained by Liu and He (2010), Sattayathama et al. (2012) as well as Naeini and Fatahi (2012).

Figure 1 presents the results of the time series plots of the BRICS given separately. This is aimed at identifying the broad characteristics of the variables used

A graphic examination of the plot reveals different kinds of patterns for BRICS countries. Figure 1 indicates that there was a high and consistent increase in the exchange rates after the period 2007–2008 global financial crises. India and China appear to be the two countries with strong currencies as evidenced by an upward sloping trend after recovery from the crises. On the other hand, Brazil, Russia, and South Africa experienced the increasing pattern in the exchange rates until the period 2015–2011 when the data shows a plateau or constant slow increase. The five countries have nonstationary exchange rates by eye inspection. Further empirical analysis was conducted by employing the nonlinear tests to confirm the graphical presentation.

Table 1 Descriptive statistics of exchange rates

	Brazil	China	India	Russia	South Africa
Mean	25.45582	25.83268	25.53752	25.52313	23.48393
Median	25.22723	25.61887	25.87703	26.41118	23.87066
Std. Dev.	0.951398	0.512947	0.936779	1.450933	0.929245
Skewness	0.032629	0.222667	−0.599311	−0.692757	−0.439318
Kurtosis	1.288816	1.581710	1.769979	1.957169	1.675854
Jarque–Bera	29.44629	22.19075	29.61936	30.19678	25.35885
Probability	0.000000	0.000015	0.000000	0.000000	0.000003

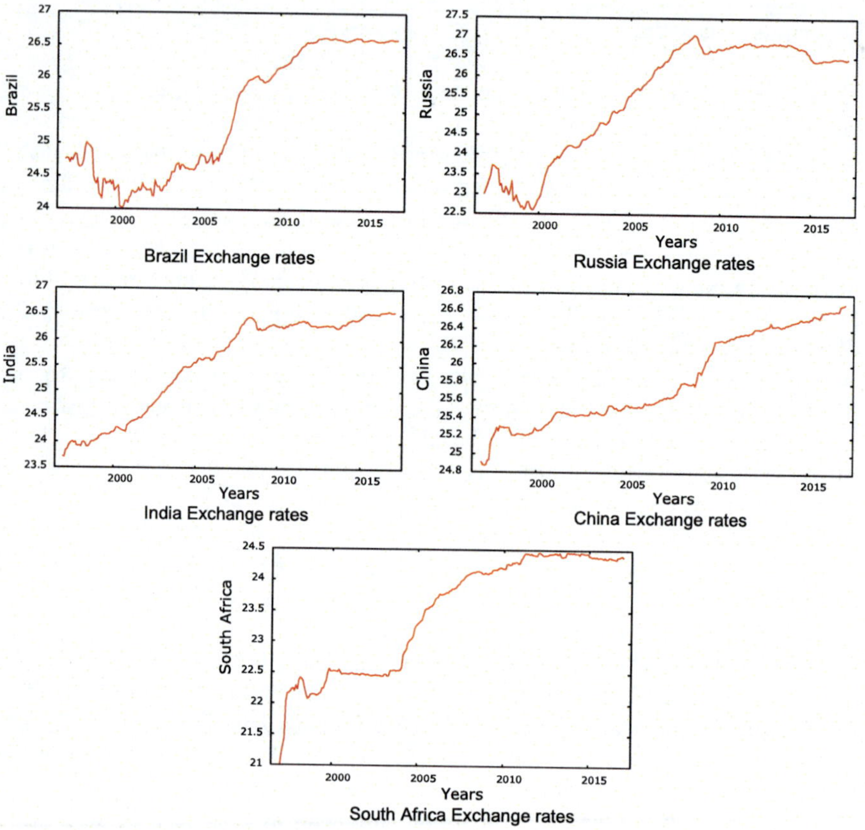

Fig. 1 Graphical representation of the exchange rates

Results of Nonlinearity Tests

This section presents the nonlinear test to confirm the use of nonlinear MRS-GARCH model. We used several nonlinearity tests such as the Regression Specification Error Test (RESET), the McLeod and Li test, Keenan's test, the Tsay test, Brock–Dechert–Scheinkman (BDS), the CUSUM test for parameters instability, and the Engle LM test for detecting the presence of nonlinearity. According to Ismail and Isa (2006), it is unwise to rely solely on a single test, since nonlinear behavior can be detected differently. Based on the advice by Ismail and Isa (2006), several nonlinearity tests to detect nonlinear behavior in the exchange rates series were computed. The results of the test are summarized in Table 2.

The results from RESET, McLeod and Li, Keenan and Tsay tests revealed that the linear model is inadequate in capturing the stochastic properties of the BRICS exchange rates. The results also showed that all the above tests conducted are significant (the p-values are less than 1%, 5%, and 10%) for each of the series. It

Table 2 Test for nonlinearity

Test/Variable	Brazil	Russia	India	China	South Africa
RESET test for specification	3.328 [0.0156]	2.694 [0.0696]	3.805 [0.0236]	7.3397 [0.0008]	25.9658 [0.0000]
McLeod and Li test	203.629 [0.0000]	219.993 [0.0000]	219.760 [0.0000]	161.036 [0.0000]	957.84 [0.0000]
Keenan's test	2.573 [0.0981]	22.347 [0.0000]	17.436 [0.0000]	17.436 [0.0000]	18.743 [0.0000]
Tsay test	9.078 [0.0028]	15.92 [0.0000]	11.650 [0.0008]	11.650 [0.0008]	3.625 [0.0581]

Note: Parentheses [.] indicate *p*-values

implies that the exchange rates of BRICS countries are nonlinear in nature and could be better characterized by nonlinear models. Similar results were reported in the studies of Ashley and Patterson (2006), Chan (2011), and Chan (2014).

CUSUM Tests Results

The CUSUM test was conducted to demonstrate the existence of parameters instability. This test assists us to find the best suitable model for exchange rates of BRICS countries. Figure 2 below presents the graphical presentation of the CUSUM test results.

The results of the CUSUM test presented in Fig. 2 reveal that the exchange rates of the BRICS countries are outside the bends. The study concluded that there is an existence of nonlinear behavior in exchange rates of the BRICS countries. These results are in agreement with studies by Ismail and Isa (2006), and Ardia et al. (2016).

Brock–Dechert–Scheinkman (BDS) Test Results

Nonlinearity tests on exchange rates using a BDS test were conducted. The test was conducted to assess if data is iid or not. The results of the BDS test are summarized below in Table 3.

Following the work of Gooijer and Yuan (2016), a dimension m from 2 to 6 and distance (ϵ) of 0.7 was selected to complete the BDS test. The quest is to test the null hypothesis that the exchange rates are iid against the alternative hypothesis of nonlinearly. The BDS test indicates that exchange rates with *p*-values less than 5% are significant for all countries. Thus, authors strongly reject the null hypothesis of iid. The results clearly suggest that BRICS exchange rates are nonlinearly dependent. These results are in agreement with those reported by Cheteni (2016).

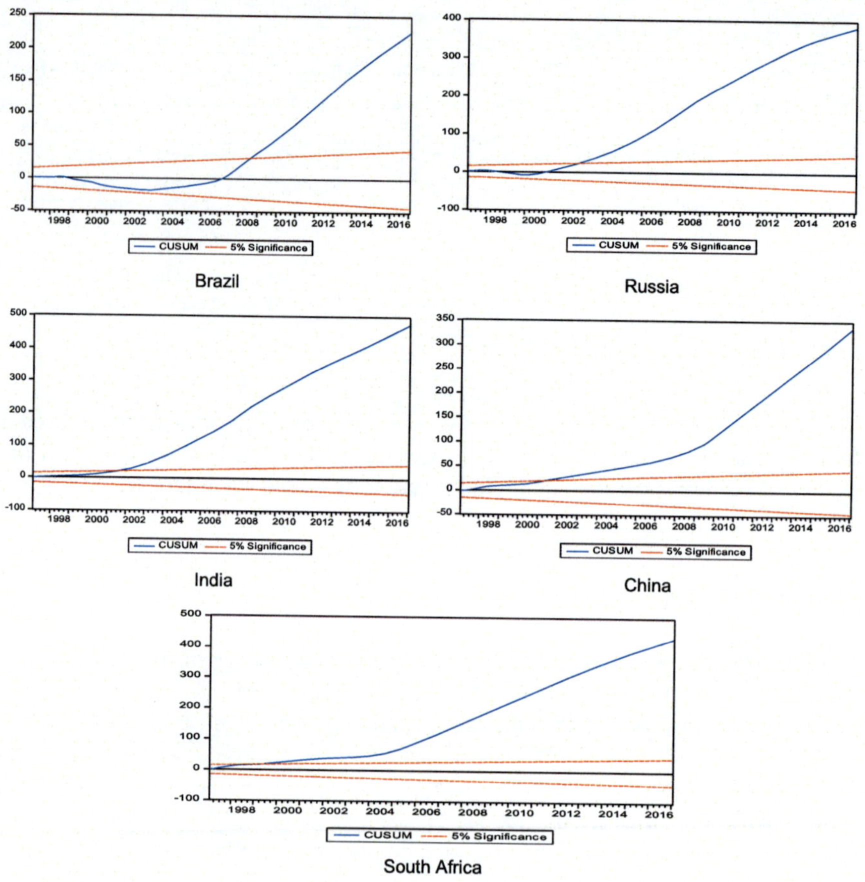

Fig. 2 CUSUM test for stability

LM Test Results

In this section, the presence of nonlinear using LM test was assessed. The LM test is utilized to detect the presence of ARCH effects in exchange rates of BRICS countries. The results of the test are summarized in Table 4.

The results in Table 4 above show that there is evidence of ARCH effects in the exchange rates of BRICS countries as *p*-values are less than 5% significant level. Therefore, authors strongly reject the null hypothesis that the exchange rates are iid and then conclude that the exchange rates are nonlinearly dependent. Similar results were reported in the studies by Zhang (2002) and Cheteni (2016).

Table 3 BDS tests results

Variable	Dimension	BDS statistic	Std. error	z-statistic	Normal prob.
Brazil	2	0.184827	0.005436	34.00340	0.0000
	3	0.311352	0.008652	35.98423	0.0000
	4	0.397733	0.010321	38.53627	0.0000
	5	0.454402	0.010776	42.16732	0.0000
	6	0.490482	0.010411	47.11356	0.0000
Russia	2	0.195461	0.006352	30.77084	0.0000
	3	0.329959	0.010145	32.52570	0.0000
	4	0.421976	0.012143	34.74983	0.0000
	5	0.484647	0.012725	38.08739	0.0000
	6	0.528197	0.012338	42.80903	0.0000
India	2	0.197887	0.003054	64.78753	0.0000
	3	0.333542	0.004793	69.59105	0.0000
	4	0.426467	0.005632	75.71631	0.0000
	5	0.490329	0.005792	84.65417	0.0000
	6	0.534366	0.005510	96.97522	0.0000
China	2	0.193145	0.003046	63.40764	0.0000
	3	0.325900	0.004825	67.54717	0.0000
	4	0.417053	0.005723	72.87172	0.0000
	5	0.479473	0.005941	80.71139	0.0000
	6	0.521592	0.005705	91.43478	0.0000
South Africa	2	0.189819	0.002970	63.91627	0.0000
	3	0.321221	0.004717	68.09580	0.0000
	4	0.411922	0.005611	73.41182	0.0000
	5	0.473761	0.005841	81.11613	0.0000
	6	0.515437	0.005624	91.64955	0.0000

Nonlinear Unit Root Test Result

This section presents nonlinear unit root test. The test is used to assess the presence of the nonlinearity in the exchange rates of BRICS countries. The test is used to confirm if it is appropriate to apply MRS-GARCH model in the study. The nonlinear unit root test was conducted to support nonlinearity tests in section "Brock–Dechert–Scheinkman (BDS) Test Results" nonlinear unit root was tested using the Bierens Nonlinear Augmented Dickey–Fuller (B-NADF) unit root tests. The results of the B-NADF test are summarized in Table 5.

The results of the B-NLADF unit root tests for various Chebyshev polynomial orders were computed. The optimal lag length for each variable was chosen using the AIC, while the test statistics were obtained using Gaussian AR (*m*) process. The results showed that the null hypothesis of nonlinear unit root cannot be rejected at 5% significance level. The *t*-test, Am-test, and *F*-test statistics are all greater than their corresponding critical values. This indicates that the exchange rates of BRICS countries are nonstationary. Since various tests confirmed the presence of

Table 4 LM Test results

Variable	Engle test	F-statistic	Prob.
Brazil	Using up to lag 1	5851.97	0.0000
	Using up to lag 2	3078.35	0.0000
	Using up to lag 3	2046.24	0.0000
	Using up to lag 4	1529.89	0.0000
Russia	Using up to lag 1	6247.88	0.0000
	Using up to lag 2	3153.68	0.0000
	Using up to lag 3	2095.34	0.0000
	Using up to lag 4	1568.96	0.0000
India	Using up to lag 1	21564.65	0.0000
	Using up to lag 2	11041.88	0.0000
	Using up to lag 3	7333.67	0.0000
	Using up to lag 4	5479.42	0.0000
China	Using up to lag 1	11226.46	0.0000
	Using up to lag 2	5676.92	0.0000
	Using up to lag 3	3770.39	0.0000
	Using up to lag 4	2817.36	0.0000
South Africa	Using up to lag 1	11617.18	0.0000
	Using up to lag 2	6009.25	0.0000
	Using up to lag 3	3995.08	0.0000
	Using up to lag 4	2994.13	0.0000

Note: ***Represents that p-value at 5% level of significance. The null hypothesis that time series is iid

nonlinearity and nonstationarity in the exchange rates of BRICS countries, the researchers proceeded to estimate the MS-GARCH models using different estimation methods.

Model Estimation Results

This section presents the results of the MS-GARCH model using Maximum likelihood estimation method. MRS-GARCH models were estimated using three various error distributions (normal, student-t, and GED). The subsequent section "Brazil Results" presents the results of MS-GARCH where MLE is used to estimate the best-fitted models of the exchange rates of BRICS countries.

Brazil Results

The parameter estimates and unconditional probability of these models are presented in Table 6 below for Brazil exchange rate.

According to the results, all the parameter estimates are significant at 1%, 5%, and 10% of levels of significant. The two regimes (from the columns), first with low

Table 5 Bierens nonlinear unit root test results

		t-TEST		Am		*F*-Test	
Variables	*M*	Statistic	5% critical value	Statistic	5% critical value	Statistic	5% critical value
Brazil	2	−1.608	−3.97	−6.117	−27.2	1.744	1.08
	5	−4.496	−5.16	−41.408	−48.7	3.757	1.83
	10	−4.605	−6.67	−43.744	−80.3	2.727	2.15
	15	−6.452	−7.89	−90.703	−112.4	3.783	2.36
	20	−7.609	−9.00	−131.096	−145.7	4.214	2.52
Russia	2	−6.14	−3.97	0.66	−27.2	3.1916	1.08
	5	−4.4372	−5.16	−43.3766	−48.7	4.0562	1.83
	10	−6.8818	−6.67	−89.6121	−80.3	4.8848	2.15
	15	−7.3307	−7.89	−103.0385	−112.4	3.9183	2.36
	20	−8.6817	−9.00	−137.5241	−145.7	4.0834	2.52
India	2	−2.2387	−3.97	−12.6037	−27.2	2.2546	1.08
	5	−4.1939	−5.16	−33.9801	−48.7	3.6163	1.83
	10	−4.4909	−6.67	−41.3511	−80.3	2.5293	2.15
	15	−7.2159	−7.89	−97.3750	−112.4	4.1744	2.36
	20	−7.4247	−9.00	−104.5964	−145.7	3.3754	2.52
China	2	−2.6593	−3.97	−12.7934	−27.2	2.9569	1.08
	5	−5.2442	−5.16	−54.5963	−48.7	4.9939	1.83
	10	−6.2399	−6.67	75.2555	−80.3	3.8577	2.15
	15	−7.4658	−7.89	−104.1044	−112.4	3.7836	2.36
	20	−7.8911	−9.00	−113.3282	−145.7	3.3911	2.52
South Africa	2	−4.2306	−3.97	−30.0178	−27.2	6.3504	1.08
	5	−6.0093	−5.16	−67.1012	−48.7	79.0804	1.83
	10	−7.4250	−6.67	−103.2396	−80.3	5.5080	2.15
	15	−8.4151	−7.89	−130.5011	−112.4	4.5205	2.36
	20	−9.3462	−9.00	−158.2898	−145.7	4.5205	2.52

volatility and second with high volatility can be identified from the estimates. The transition probabilities are all significant, implying that almost all regimes are particularly persistent in MS-GARCH models. The results also reported the unconditional probabilities for each MS-GARCH model. The unconditional probability π_1 is the first regime representing low volatility and it ranges between 58% (Student-t) and 89% (GED) for different MS-GARCH models. Similarly, the unconditional probability π_2 is the second regime representing high volatility and it ranges between 11% (normal) and 42% (student-t and GED) for different MS-GARCH models. The subsection "Russia Results" below presents the results for Russia.

Russia Results

The parameter estimates and unconditional probability of these models are presented in Table 7 below for the Russia exchange rate.

The results in Table 7 above show that all the estimated parameters are significant at all levels of significance. The estimates confirmed the existence of two regimes;

Table 6 Maximum likelihood estimates of MS-GARCH models for Brazil

Brazil						
	Normal		Student-t		GED	
Model	Low volatility	High volatility	Low volatility	High volatility	Low volatility	High volatility
μ			5.2817	2.9103	1.3396	0.9521
P-value			0.0000	0.0000	0.0000	0.0000
α_0		0.2051	0.0000	0.0991	0.0000	0.0947
P-value	0.0000	0.0000	0.0000	0.0000	0.0000	0.0000
α_1	0.0000	0.0415	0.0026	0.0001	0.0010	0.0010
P-value	0.0000	0.0000	0.0000	0.0000	0.0000	0.0000
β_1	0.7948	0.9584	0.9007	0.6969	0.9051	0.8593
P-value	0.0000	0.0000	0.0000	0.0000	0.0000	0.0000
P_{00}	0.8708		0.9864		0.9864	
P-value	0.0000		0.0000		0.0000	
P_{11}	1.0000		0.0188		0.0188	
P-value	0.0000		0.0000		0.0000	
Persistence	0.7948	0.9999	0.9033	0.6970	0.9061	0.8603
π_1 (Low volatility)	0.89		0.58		0.59	
π_2 (High volatility)	0.11		0.42		0.42	

Table 7 Maximum likelihood estimates of MS-GARCH models for Russia

Russia						
	Normal		Student-t		GED	
Model	Low volatility	High volatility	Low volatility	High volatility	Low volatility	High volatility
μ			99.2939	11.8796	3.5139	1.5859
P-value			0.0000	0.0000	0.0000	0.0000
α_0	0.0000	0.0087	0.0000	0.0086		0.0089
P-value	0.0000	0.0000	0.0000	0.0000	0.0000	0.0000
α_1	0.0001	0.0663	0.0001	0.0812	0.0001	0.2650
P-value	0.0000	0.0000	0.0000	0.0000	0.0000	0.0000
β_1	0.9679	0.9322	0.9667	0.9174	0.9668	0.7347
P-value	0.0000	0.0000	0.0000	0.0000	0.0000	0.0000
P_{00}	0.9276		0.9397		0.7848	
P-value	0.0000		0.0000		0.0000	
P_{11}	0.1393		0.0970		0.1550	
P-value	0.0000		0.0000		0.0000	
Persistence	0.9680	0.9985	0.9668	0.0898	0.9669	0.9997
π_1 (Low volatility)	0.66		0.62		0.42	
π_2 (High volatility)	0.34		0.38		0.58	

the first regime is regarded as low volatility and second as high volatility. The persistence of the regimes can be illustrated by p00 and p11 which are commonly referred to as the staying probabilities of regimes. These transition probabilities are found significant in all cases showing the persistence of both regimes. Table 7 also reported unconditional probabilities for each model. The unconditional probability of the first regime ranges between 42% (GED) and 66% (normal) whereas the unconditional probability of being in the second regime ranges between 34% (normal) and 58% (GED). The subsequent subsection "India" presents the results for India.

India

The parameter estimates and unconditional probability of these models are presented in Table 8 below for the India exchange rate.

Table 8 presents the results for MS-GARCH models using normal, student-t, and GED. The estimated parameters of the models together with their respective probability values were reported. All the parameters estimates in MS-GARCH are significant at 1%, 5%, and 10% of levels of significance. These estimates can be identified from both the first regime (low volatility) and the second regime (high volatility). Staying probabilities of regimes which are p00 and p11 are used to assess the persistence of the regimes. Reported results show that for the first regime in all

Table 8 Maximum likelihood estimates of MS-GARCH models

India						
	Normal		Student-t		GED	
Model	Low volatility	High volatility	Low volatility	High volatility	Low volatility	High volatility
μ			89.9671	2.7826	1.4146	1.2667
P-value			0.0000	0.0000	0.0000	0.0000
α_0	0.0006	0.0001	0.0002	0.0001		
P-value	0.0000	0.0000	0.0000	0.0000	0.0000	0.0000
α_1	0.0000	0.1179	0.0000	0.0315	0.0000	0.1005
P-value	0.0000	0.0000	0.0000	0.0000	0.0000	0.0000
β_1	0.5342	0.8820	0.8096	0.9684	0.9952	0.8994
P-value	0.0000	0.0000	0.0000	0.0000	0.0000	0.0000
P_{00}	0.9872		0.9771		0.9874	
P-value	0.0000		0.0000		0.0000	
P_{11}	0.0085		0.0079		0.0070	
P-value	0.0000		0.0000		0.0000	
Persistence	0.5342	0.9999	0.8096	0.9684	0.9952	0.9999
π_1 (Low volatility)	0.40		0.26		0.36	
π_2 (High volatility)	0.60		0.74		0.64	

three error distributions the probabilities are found to be significant for all the distributions. Furthermore, the unconditional probabilities for each model which ranges between 26% (student-t) and 40% (normal) for the first regime whereas the unconditional probability of the second regime ranges between 60% (GED) and 74% (normal) were reported. The subsequent subsection "China" presents the results for China.

China

The results presented in Table 9 present the parameter estimates and unconditional probability of these models below for the China exchange rate.

The parameter estimates for MS-GARCH models for China are presented in Table 9 above. According to the results, all the parameter estimates are significant at three levels of significance. The estimates confirmed the existence of two regimes. The transition probabilities are all significant, showing that all regimes are particularly persistent in MRS-GARCH models. The unconditional probability π_1 of the first regime ranges between 61% (normal and student-t) and 64% (GED) for different MRS-GARCH models. The unconditional probability π_2 of the second regime ranges between 36% (GED) and 39% (normal and student-t) for different MS-GARCH models. The subsequent subsection "South African" presents the results for South Africa.

Table 9 Maximum likelihood estimates of MRS-GARCH models

China						
	Normal		Student-t		GED	
Model	Low volatility	High volatility	Low volatility	High volatility	Low volatility	High volatility
μ			99.6867	67.0870	1.7261	0.7000
P-value			0.0000	0.0000	0.0000	0.0000
α_0	0.0001	0.0000	0.0001	0.0000	0.0001	0.8438
P-value	0.0000	0.0000	0.0000	0.0000	0.0000	0.0000
α_1	0.0003	0.6593	0.0002	0.5583	0.0001	0.2548
P-value	0.0000	0.0000	0.0002	0.0000	0.0000	0.0000
β_1	0.0008	0.3406	0.0003	0.4413	0.0004	0.7441
P-value	0.0000	0.0000	0.0000	0.0000	0.0000	0.0000
P_{00}	0.8217		0.8263		0.7916	
P-value	0.0000		0.0000		0.0000	
P_{11}	0.2766		0.2717		0.3652	
P-value	0.0000		0.0000		0.0000	
Persistence	0.0011	0.9999	0.0005	0.9996	0.0005	0.9989
π_1 (Low volatility)	0.61		0.61		0.64	
π_2 (High volatility)	0.39		0.39		0.36	

South Africa

The parameter estimates and unconditional probability of these models are presented in Table 10 below for the South African exchange rate.

The estimated results and summary statistics of MRS-GARCH models are presented in Table 10 above. All parameter estimates are significant at 1%, 5%, and 10% of significant levels. The estimates confirmed the existence of two regimes. The persistence of the regimes can be illustrated by p_{00} and p_{11} which are commonly referred to as the staying probabilities of regimes. These transition probabilities are found significant in all cases showing the persistence of both regimes. The unconditional probability of the first regime ranges between 42% (GED) and 66% (normal) whereas the unconditional probability of the second regime ranges between 34% (normal) and 58% (GED). The next section "In-Sampling Evaluation Using Maximum Likelihood Estimation (MLE)" presents the in-sampling evaluation using the maximum likelihood estimation method.

Table 10 Maximum likelihood estimates of MRS-GARCH models

South Africa						
	Normal		Student-t		GED	
Model	Low volatility	High volatility	Low volatility	High volatility	Low volatility	High volatility
μ			3.1816	2.6406	4.0017	0.7000
P-value			0.0000	0.0000	0.0000	0.0000
α_0	0.0001	0.1381	0.0000	0.0048		0.3051
P-value	0.0000	0.0000	0.0000	0.0000	0.0000	0.0000
α_1	0.0012	0.7569	0.0001	0.1312	0.0001	0.2134
P-value	0.0000	0.0000	0.0000	0.0000	0.0000	0.0000
β_1	0.2511	0.2430	0.8321	0.8681	0.1356	0.7861
P-value	0.0000	0.0000	0.0000	0.0000	0.0000	0.0000
P_{00}	0.6884		0.7617		0.5507	
P-value	0.0000		0.0000		0.0000	
P_{11}	0.6434		0.1064		0.2462	
P-value	0.0000		0.0000		0.0000	
Persistence	0.2523	0.9999	0.8322	0.9993	0.1357	0.9995
π_1 (Low volatility)	0.67		0.31		0.35	
π_2 (High volatility)	0.33		0.69		0.65	

In-Sampling Evaluation Using Maximum Likelihood Estimation (MLE)

The section presents the in-sampling results of MRS-GARCH using the MLE method. Various model including selection criterions and error metrices statistics to compare in-sampling evaluation between MRS-GARCH-MLE using normal, student-t, and GED innovation distributions were used. The results are presented in Table 11.

In Table 11 above, the results of the model section criteria and error metrices for all volatility models are presented. According to the BIC, AIC, LOGL, MSE, RMSE, and MAE, the MRS-GARCH model with the t-distribution performed better in modeling the exchange rates of Brazil, India, and South Africa. However, Russia and China were modeled using different distributions. In the case of Russia model section criteria and error metrices chose the MRS-GARCH with normal distribution while China's exchange rate was modeled with MRS-GARCH using GED-distribution. The next section "Model Estimation Results Using Bayesian MCMC" presents the model estimation results using Bayesian MCMC.

Model Estimation Results Using Bayesian MCMC

This section provides the results of the MRS-GARCH using the Bayesian MCMC estimation method. The parameter estimates for MRS-GARCH models are presented in Tables 12, 13,14, 15, and 16.

Brazil Results

This section presents the summarized results of MRS-GARCH models for Brazil's exchange rate. Various distributions under MRS-GARCH model to estimate the best model were used.

The results in Table 12 shows that the parameters estimated are significant at 1%, 5%, and 10% level of significance. The first regime of the two existing regimes is characterized by low volatility, whereas the second one reveals high volatility. The transition probabilities are all significant, showing that all regimes are particularly persistent in MRS-GARCH models. The unconditional probability of the first regime ranges between 52%(norm) and 84% (student-t) for different MRS-GARCH models. The unconditional probability of the second regime ranges between 16% (norm) and 48%(student-t) for different MRS-GARCH models. Table 13 presents the Bayesian estimates of MRS-GARCH models for Russia.

Table 11 In-sample results using MRS-GARCH models for BRICS countries

Model	Maximum likelihood estimation method							
	No. of Par.	BIC	AIC	Log(L)	MSE	RMSE	MAE	Conclusion
Brazil								
MRS-GARCH-N	5	−865.614	−893.459	454.729	0.7989	0.8983	0.624	MRS-GARCH-t
MRS-GARCH-t	6	−872.625	−907.431	463.715	0.6566	0.8103	0.548	
MRS-GARCH-GED	6	−868.152	−902.959	461.479	0.7709	0.8780	0.589	
Russia								
MS-GARCH-N	5	−753.534	−781.38	398.690	1.0315	1.0157	0.757	MRS-GARCH-N
MS-GARCH-t	5	−741.648	−776.454	398.227	1.0888	1.0434	0.7742	
MS-GARCH-GED	6	−741.547	−776.353	398.177	1.1471	1.0710	0.8131	
India								
MS-GARCH-N	5	−993.667	−1021.513	518.756	0.9269	0.96277	0.7161	MRS-GARCH-t
MS-GARCH-t	6	−995.875	−1030.682	525.341	0.727	0.853	0.635	
MS-GARCH-GED	6	−991.770	−1026.577	523.289	0.911	0.954	0.709	
China								
MS-GARCH-N	5	−1255.931	−1290.737	655.474	0.9689	0.9843	06848	MRS-GARCH-GED
MS-GARCH-t	6	−1256.427	−1291.233	655.369	0.9626	0.9811	0.6812	
MS-GARCH-GED	6	−1267.103	−1294.948	655.617	0.870	0.932	0.649	
South Africa								
MS-GARCH-N	5	−1016.372	−1044.217	530.108	1.050	1.024	0.657	MRS-GARCH-t
MS-GARCH-t	6	−1020.007	−1054.813	537.406	0.784	0.885	0.545	
MS-GARCH-GED	6	−1018.835	−1053.641	536.821	0.874	0.934	0.592	

Table 12 Bayesian MCMC estimates of MRS-GARCH models for Brazil

Brazil						
	Normal		Student-t		GED	
Model	Low Volatility	High volatility	Low volatility	High volatility	Low volatility	High volatility
μ			6.9680	3.1274	1.1603	1.2283
Std. err.			0.2958	0.2488	0.0439	0.0521
α_0	0.0000	0.0122	0.0057	0.0135		0.3255
Std. err.	0.0000	0.0135	0.0004	0.0035		0.0350
α_1	0.0060	0.0417	0.0011	0.0518	0.0041	0.2209
Std. err.	0.0005	0.0120	0.0004	0.0035	0.0002	0.0219
β_1	0.9461	0.5148	0.3975	0.8382	0.5885	0.2384
Std. err.	0.0021	0.013	0.0335	0.0331	0.0439	0.0332
P_{00}	0.9751		0.9485		0.9864	
Std. err.	0.0013		0.0032		0.0011	
P_{11}	0.0664		0.0105		0.0347	
Std. err.	0.0037		0.0031		0.0028	
π_1 (Low volatility)	0.84		0.52		0.66	
π_2 (High volatility)	0.16		0.48		0.34	

Table 13 Bayesian MCMC model estimates of MRS-GARCH models for Russia

Russia						
	Normal		Student-t		GED	
Model	Low volatility	High volatility	Low volatility	High volatility	Low volatility	High volatility
μ	–	–	19.8070	88.2912	2.6101	1.7385
Std. err.	–	–	4.1827	4.1781	0.1302	0.0427
α_0	0.0001	0.0807	0.0001	0.1946	–	0.0282
Std. err.	0.0000	0.0017	0.0000	0.0054	–	0.0018
α_1	0.0002	0.1187	–	0.1374	0.0003	0.1491
Std. err.	0.0000	0.0334	–	0.0058	0.0000	0.0041
β_1	0.7758	0.8765	0.6860	0.8564	0.8461	0.8308
Std. err.	0.0062	0.0044	0.0115	0.0078	0.0062	0.0053
P_{00}	0.8559		0.8639		0.9594	
Std. err.	0.0106		0.0034		0.0022	
P_{11}	0.2052		0.0947		0.0387	
Std. err.	0.0085		0.0037		0.0014	
π_1 (Low volatility)	0.73		0.48		0.29	
π_2 (High volatility)	0.27		0.52		0.71	

Table 14 Bayesian MCMC model estimates of MRS-GARCH models for India

India						
	Normal		Student-t		GED	
Model	Low volatility	High volatility	Low volatility	High volatility	Low volatility	High volatility
μ			62.6217	29.9564	7.4348	3.1757
Std. err.			3.4992	5.0842	1.0157	0.7916
α_0	0.0002	0.2154	0.0002	0.2434	0.0013	0.0788
Std. err.	0.0000	0.0225	0.0000	0.0207	0.0001	0.0192
α_1	0.0009	0.0001	0.0002	0.1377	0.0005	0.2592
Std. err.	0.0001	0.0000	0.0001	0.0193	0.0001	0.0230
β_1	0.0424	0.4234	0.4029	0.7435	0.1099	0.5228
Std. err.	0.0057	0.0313	0.0205	0.0324	0.0273	0.0366
P_{00}	0.9481		0.3020		0.8363	
Std. err.	0.0096		0.0364		0.0229	
P_{11}	0.0716		0.5082		0.1292	
Std. err.	0.0143		0.0439		0.0189	
π_1 (Low volatility)	0.20		0.90		0.51	
π_2 (High volatility)	0.80		0.10		0.49	

Table 15 Bayesian MCMC model estimates of MRS-GARCH models for China

China						
	Normal		Student-t		GED	
Model	low volatility	High volatility	Low volatility	High volatility	Low volatility	High volatility
μ			95.7979	3.5539	1.5416	1.0514
Std. err.			0.3569	0.0964	0.0391	0.0376
α_0	0.0001	0.1610	0.0001	0.0335	0.0001	0.4072
Std. err.	0.0000	0.0046	0.0000	0.0047	0.0000	0.0297
α_1	0.0003	0.5330	0.0014	0.5943	0.0018	0.2415
Std. err.	0.0000	0.0099	0.0001	0.0197	0.0002	0.0238
β_1	0.0005	0.4638	0.0758	0.1900	0.0063	0.3436
Std. err.	0.0000	0.0096	0.0122	0.0126	0.0005	0.0201
P_{00}	0.8777		0.8725		0.9216	
Std. err.	0.0016		0.0080		0.0063	
P_{11}	0.3182		0.2461		0.2865	
Std. err.	0.0073		0.0086		0.0145	
π_1 (Low volatility)	0.75		0.79		0.97	
π_2 (High volatility)	0.25		0.21		0.03	

Table 16 Bayesian MCMC model estimates of MRS-GARCH models for South Africa

South Africa						
	Normal		Student-t		GED	
Model	Low volatility	High volatility	Low volatility	High volatility	Low volatility	High volatility
μ			4.1866	3.1138	0.9004	15.5730
Std. err.			0.2251	0.2214	0.0112	0.3731
α_0	0.0001	0.0189	0.0001	0.3226	0.0003	0.6930
Std. err.	0.0000	0.0010	0.0000	0.0251	0.0000	0.0207
α_1	0.0016	0.6398	0.0028	0.3386	0.3243	0.8092
Std. err.	0.0001	0.0154	0.0003	0.0373	0.0414	0.0197
β_1	0.3633	0.3568	0.3682	0.5500	0.2104	0.1061
Std. err.	0.0102	0.0152	0.0188	0.0448	0.0191	0.0128
P_{00}	0.8685		0.8785		0.9877	
Std. err.	0.0050		0.0070		0.0007	
P_{11}	0.3466		0.4181		0.3800	
Std. err.	0.0114		0.0308		0.0179	
π_1 (Low volatility)	0.66		0.69		0.41	
π_2 (High volatility)	0.40		0.31		0.59	

Russia Results

The section presents the results of the Russian exchange rate.

The parameter estimates for MRS-GARCH models are presented in Table 13 above. All the parameter estimates are significant at 1%, 5%, and 10% level of significance. The estimates confirmed the existence of two regimes: the first regime is regarded as low volatility and whereas the second one reveals high volatility. The transition probabilities are all significant at 1%, 5%, and 10% level of significance, showing that all regimes are persistent in MRS-GARCH models. The unconditional probability of the first regime ranges between 29% (GED) and 73% (norm) for different MS-GARCH models. The unconditional probability of the second regime ranges between 27% (norm) and 71% (GED) for different MRS-GARCH models. The next section "India Results" presents the Bayesian estimates of MRS-GARCH models for India.

India Results

The section presents the Indian exchange rate results. The estimation results and summary statistics of MRS-GARCH models are presented in Table 14.

The parameter estimates for MRS-GARCH models are presented in Table 14 above. All the parameter estimates are significant at 1%, 5%, and 10% level of significance. The two regimes were identified from the estimated models. All the transition probabilities were found to be significant at 1%, 5%, and 10% level of significance, showing that regimes are persistent in MRS-GARCH models. The unconditional probability of the first regime ranges between 20% (norm) and 90% (student-t) for different MRS-GARCH models. The unconditional probability of the second regime ranges between 10% (student-t) and 80% (norm) for different MRS-GARCH models. The subsequent Section presents the Bayesian estimates of MRS-GARCH models for China.

China Results

This section presents the results of China's exchange rate use Bayesian MRS-GARCH models. Table 15 below shows the summarized results of estimated MRS-GARCH models.

The parameter estimates for MRS-GARCH models are presented in Table 15 above. The results revealed that the estimated parameters are significant at 1%, 5%, and 10% level of significance. The estimates confirmed the existence of two regimes: The first regime is categorized by low volatility, whereas the second one reveals high volatility. The transition probabilities are all significant. This means that all regimes are persistent in MRS-GARCH models for China's exchange rate. The unconditional probability of the first regime ranges between 75% (norm) and 97% (GED) for different MRS-GARCH models. The unconditional probability of the second regime ranges between 3% (GED) and 25% (norm) for different MRS-GARCH models. The next subsection "South Africa Results" presents the Bayesian estimates of MRS-GARCH models for South Africa.

South Africa Results

This section presents the results of the South African's exchange rate. The summary of the results is presented in Table 16.

Table 16 presents the parameter estimates for MRS-GARCH models. The results revealed that the parameters estimated are significant at 1%, 5%, and 10% levels of significance. The estimates showed that the two regime's existence, the first regime is regarded as the low volatility and the second regime as the high volatility. The transition probabilities are all significant at 1%, 5%, and 10% levels of significance. This means that the two regimes are persistent in MRS-GARCH models. The unconditional probability of the first regime ranges between 41% (GED) and 69% (student-t) for different MRS-GARCH models while the second regime ranges between 31% (student-t) and 59% (GED) for different MRS-GARCH models. The next section "In-Sampling Evaluation Using Bayesian MCMC" presents the in-sampling results of Bayesian MCMC estimates of MRS-GARCH models.

In-Sampling Evaluation Using Bayesian MCMC

In Table 17, the results of model selection and error metrices for all volatility models are presented.

Researchers conducted in-sampling evaluation to identify the best-fitted models for exchange rates of BRICS countries. The competing models are compared based on model section criterion and error metrices. The results revealed that the MRS-GARCH model with the t-distribution performed better in modeling the exchange rates of Brazil, Russia, India, and South Africa as opposed to other distributions. The MRS-GARCH models with t-distribution are regarded as the best-fitted models. The next section "Model Comparison Results of MRS-GARCH Model" presents the model comparison results.

Model Comparison Results of MRS-GARCH Model

Table 18 presents the MRS-GARCH model in-sampling results for model comparison.

Table 17 MS-GARCH: in-sample results using Bayesian MCMC estimator

Model	Bayesian MCMC estimation method					
	No. of Par.	DIC	MSE	RMSE	MAE	Best
Brazil						
MRS-GARCH-N	5	−888.79	0.9376	0.9682	0.6089	MRS-GARCH-t
MRS-GARCH-t	6	−927.51	0.4608	0.6788	0.4657	
MRS-GARCH-GED	6	−901.80	0.7688	0.8768	0.5817	
Russia						
MRS-GARCH-N	5	−771.63	1.0970	1.0474	0.8043	MRS-GARCH-t
MRS-GARCH-t	6	−776.11	0.9694	0.9846	0.7400	
MRS-GARCH-GED	6	−769.26	1.0744	1.0365	0.7847	
India						
MRS-GARCH-N	5	−1016.62	0.9686	0.9842	0.7246	MRS-GARCH-t
MRS-GARCH-t	6	−1028.78	0.8223	0.9069	0.6587	
MRS-GARCH-GED	6	−998.63	0.8580	0.9263	0.6713	
China						
MRS-GARCH-N	5	−1291.22	0.8816	0.9389	0.6463	MRS-GARCH-t
MRS-GARCH-t	6	−1300.67	0.7668	0.8757	0.5726	
MRS-GARCH-GED	6	−1293.39	1.1010	1.0493	0.6689	
South Africa						
MRS-GARCH-N	5	−1038.47	0.9579	0.9787	0.6159	MRS-GARCH-t
MRS-GARCH-t	6	−1045.39	0.8684	0.9319	0.5707	
MRS-GARCH-GED	6	−1036.91	0.9511	0.9752	0.5927	

Table 18 MRS-GARCH: in-sample results for model comparison

Variable	Maximum likelihood estimation				Bayesian MCMC estimation				Best MODEL
	Model	MSE	RMSE	MAE	Model	MSE	RMSE	MAE	
Brazil	MRS-GARCH-t	0.657	0.810	0.549	MRS-GARCH-t	0.461	0.679	0.466	MRS-GARCH-t
Russia	MRS-GARCH-N	1.032	1.016	0.757	MRS-GARCH-t	0.969	0.985	0.740	MRS-GARCH-t
India	MRS-GARCH-t	0.727	0.853	0.635	MRS-GARCH-t	0.822	0.907	0.659	MRS-GARCH-t
China	MRS-GARCH-GED	0.870	0.933	0.649	MRS-GARCH-t	0.767	0.876	0.573	MRS-GARCH-t
South Africa	MRS-GARCH-t	0.784	0.886	0.546	MRS-GARCH-t	0.868	0.932	0.571	MRS-GARCH-t

This section compares the forecast ability of the estimated models under MLE and Bayesian MCMC estimation methods as presented in Table 18 above. The aim of the section is to find the best-estimated methods that can be used to estimate MRS-GARCH models. The results from the data deduced 30 models (15 from MLE and 15 from Bayesian MCMC). From the 30 models, 10 models were selected as the best models. These models are deemed accurate and can be used for further forecasting. The three criteria MSE, RMSE, and MAE are used to measure forecast accuracy of the models.

The best model for each of the BRICS countries is presented as follows; Brazil, Russia, and China were better produced from the Bayesian MCMC estimation method and India and South Africa were better produced from the ML estimation method. To test the accuracy of the five selected models, the DM test for predictive accuracy was employed. The subsequent section "Comparing Predictive Accuracy of Models" presents the results of the DM test for in-sampling on testing the accuracy of the models.

Comparing Predictive Accuracy of Models

This section predicts the accuracy of the models. According to Harris and Sollis (2003), the model with the lowest MSE, RMSE, and MAE do not necessarily suggest a superior forecasting ability of a model since the difference between error metrices for two different models may not be significantly different from zero. Therefore, in order to assess the predictive accuracy of the two estimated models, DM test for pairs of models for exchange rate were performed using the absolute error loss differential, and the results summarized in Table 19.

These results, the null hypothesis of the paired models MRS-GARCH-t (ML) versus MRS-GARCH-t (MCMC), MRS-GARCH-t (ML) versus MRS-GARCH-GED (MCMC), MRS-GARCH-GED (ML) versus MRS-GARCH-t (MCMC), and MRS-GARCH-t (ML) versus MRS-GARCH-t (MCMC) for exchange rates having equal predictive accuracy is rejected since their respective p-values (0.0013, 0.0194, 0.0008 and 0.0000) of the test statistics are less than 1%, 5%, and 10% levels of significance. Therefore, it can be concluded that the estimated

Table 19 Comparison of model accuracy: Diebold-Mariano absolute error test

HAC standard errors and covariance (Bartlett kernel, Newey-West fixed bandwidth = 6.0000)			
Absolute error loss differential			
Variable	Hypothesis	t-Statistic	Prob.
Brazil	MRS-GARCH-t versus MRS-GARCH-t	3.0357	0.0013
Russia	MRS-GARCH-N versus MRS-GARCH-t	0.7721	0.2204
India	MRS-GARCH-t versus MRS-GARCH-t	2.0776	0.0194
China	MRS-GARCH-GED versus MRS-GARCH-t	3.1743	0.0008
South Africa	MRS-GARCH-t versus MRS-GARCH-t	3.1770	0.0000

MRS-GARCH-t (MCMC), MRS-GARCH-GED (MCMC), MRS-GARCH-t (MCMC), and MRS-GARCH-t (MCMC) models for exchange rate are more accurate than their counterpart where ML is used to estimate the models. However, the null hypothesis that the paired model MRS-GARCH-N (ML) versus MRS-GARCH-t (MCMC) for Russia having the same predictive accuracy is not rejected since the *p*-value (0.2204) of the test statistic is great than 1%, 5%, and 10% levels of significance. This indicates that the accuracy of the pair of models is equal. Based on the error metrices and DM Absolute error tests, the appropriate conditional distribution to be used is student-t distribution and the best estimation method is Bayesian (MCMC) for in-sample evaluation.

Conclusions

Researchers sought to determine the best estimating method for $MRS(k) - GARCH$ (p, q) which is suited for the exchange rates of BRICS countries. $MS(k) - GARCH$ (p, q) is estimated with two different estimation methods which are the maximum likelihood and Bayesian estimation and their results were compared. The results have indicated that the Bayesian MCMC estimation is the best method as compared to the Maximum likelihood estimation method. According to the error metrices and DM Absolute error tests, the appropriate conditional distribution to be used is student-t distribution and the best estimation method is Bayesian (MCMC) for in-sample evaluation. The study recommended that the Monti Carlo Maximum Likelihood estimator and/or Monti Carlo Expected Maximization estimator can be used to improve the Maximum Likelihood estimation method.

The chapter contributes to the existing literature on the performance of MRS-GARCH models using in-sample volatility forecasts where the parameters are estimated using Maximum Likelihood and Bayesian MCMC estimation methods. This study is an attempt to bridge this gap, specifically, as used in the investigation of the behaviors of the exchange rates of BRICS countries. By using one of the most powerful nonlinear modeling technique, this study also provides a skillful guideline for modeling the different dynamic patterns of exchange rates of BRICS countries in general as well as the art involved in capturing the nonlinear attributes of exchange rates. Overall, this chapter provided appropriate distribution and estimation method that can be used under MRS-GARCH to understand the patterns and movements of exchange rates. This chapter recommends studies could use MRS-GARCH model with GE distribution under Bayesian MCMC estimation utilizing different data sets. This could help establish if similar results will be found using a different data set.

References

Alemohammad N, Rezakhah S, Alizadeh SH (2017) Markov switching component GARCH model: stability and forecasting. Commun Stat Theory and Methods 45(15):4332–4348

Ardia D (2008) Financial risk management with bayesian estimation of GARCH models: theory and applications. In: Lecture notes in economics and mathematical systems, vol 612. Springer, Heidelberg

Ardia D (2009) Bayesian estimation of a Markov switching threshold asymmetric GARCH model with Student-t innovations. Econ J 12(2):105–126

Ardia D, Bluteau K, Boudt K, Trottier DA (2016) Markov-switching GARCH models in R: the MSGARCH package

Ardia D, Bluteau K, Boudt K, Catania L (2018) Forecasting risk with Markov-switching GARCH models. Elsevier, Issue 34, 733–747

Ashley RA, Patterson DM (2006) Evaluating the effectiveness of state-switching time series models for U.S. real output. J Bus Econ Stat 24(3):266–277

Augustyniak M (2014) Maximum likelihood estimation of the Markov-switching GARCH model. Comput Stat Data Anal 76(2014):61–75

Bauwens L, Preminger A, Rombouts JV (2006) Regime switching GARCH models. CORE Discussion Paper 2006/11, Universite catholique de Louvain, Louvain La Neuve

Bauwens L, Hafner CM, Rombouts JVK (2007) Multivariate mixed normal conditional heteroskedasticity. Comput Stat Data Anal 51:3551–3566

Bauwens L, Preminger A, Rombouts JVK (2010) Theory and inference for a Markov switching GARCH model. Econ J 13:218–244

Bauwens L, Dufays A, Rombouts JVK (2011) The marginal likelihood for Markov-switching and change-point GARCH models. CORE Discussion Papers 2011013. Universite Catholique de Louvain, Center for Operations Research and Econometrics (CORE)

Bauwens L, De Backer B, Dufays A (2014) A Bayesian method of change-point estimation with recurrent regimes: application to GARCH models. J Empir Financ 29:207–229

Bildirici M, Ersin O (2014) Modeling Markov switching ARMA-GARCH neural networks models and an application to forecasting stock returns. Sci World J 2014:1. https://doi.org/10.1155/2014/497941

Billio M, Getmansky M, Pelizzon L (2013) Dynamic risk exposures in hedge funds. Comput Stat Data Anal 56:3517–3532

Bollerslev T (1986) Generalized autoregressive conditional heteroskedasticity. J Econ 31 (3):307–327

Bollerslev T (1987) A conditionally heteroskedastic time series model for speculative prices and rates of return. Rev Econ Stat 69:542–547

Brunetti C, Scotti C, Mariano RS, Tan AH (2008) Markov switching GARCH models of currency turmoil in Southeast Asia. Emerg Mark Rev 9(2):104–128

Cai J (1994) A Markov model of switching-regime ARCH. J Bus Econ Appl 37(7):482–493

Chan SW (2011) Are current account deficits really sustainable in the G-7 countries? Jpn World Econ 23(3):190–201

Chan SW (2014) Smooth transition, non-linearity and current account sustainability: Evidence from the European countries. Econ Model 38:541–554

Cheteni P (2016) Stock market volatility using GARCH models: evidence from South Africa and China stock markets. J Econ Behav Stud 8(6):237–245

Chkili W, Nguyen DK (2014) Exchange rate movements and stock market returns in a regime-switching environment: Evidence for BRICS countries. Res Int Bus Financ 31:46–56

Cifter A (2013) Forecasting electricity price volatility with the Markov-switching GARCH model: evidence from the Nordic electric power market. Electr Power Syst Res 102:61–67

Crawford G, Fratantoni M (2003) Assessing the forecasting performance of regime-switching, ARIMA and GARCH models of house prices. Real Estate Econ 31(2):223–243

Cruz CJF, Mapa DS (2013) An early warning system for inflation in the Philippines using Markov-switching and logistic regression models. Theor Pract Res Econ Fields (TPREF) 2(8):137–152

Diebold FX, Mariano RS (1995) Comparing predictive accuracy. J Bus Econ Stat 13:253–263

Dueker MJ (1997) Markov switching in GARCH processes and mean-reverting stock-market volatility. J Bus Econ Stat 15:26–34

Frühwirth-Schnatter S (2006) Finite mixture and markov switching models. Springer, New York, p 492. isbn:10:0-387-32909-9

Gooijer JGD, Yuan A (2016) Non parametric portmanteau tests for detecting nonlinearities in high dimensions. Commun Stat Theory Methods 45:385–399

Gray SF (1996) Modeling the Conditional Distribution of Interest Rates as a Regime-Switching Process. J Financ Econ 42:27–62

Günay S (2015) Markov regime switching generalized autoregressive conditional heteroskedastic model and volatility modeling for oil returns. Int J Energy Econ Policy 5(4):979–985

Haas M, Mittnik S, Paolella M (2004) A new approach to Markov switching GARCH models. J Financ Economet 2:493–530

Hamilton JD (1989) A new approach to the economic analysis of nonstationary time series and the business cycle. Econometrica 57:357–384

Hamilton JD (2010) Regime switching models. In: Macroeconometrics and time series analysis. Springer, London, pp 202–209

Hamilton JD, Raj B (2013) Advances in Markov-switching models: applications in business cycle research and finance. Springer Science & Business Media, Berlin

Hamilton JD, Susmel R (1994) Autoregressive conditional heteroscedasticity and changes in regime. J Econ 64:307–333

Harris R, Sollis R (2003) Applied time series modelling and forecasting. John Wiley, New York

Harris JW, Stocker H (1998) Maximum likelihood method. 21.10.4 in Handbook of mathematics and computational science. Springer, New York, p 824

Henneke JS, Rachev S, Fabzozzi FJ, Nikolov M (2011) MCMC-based estimation of Markov switching ARMA-GARCH models. Appl Econ 43(3):259–271

Ismail MT, Isa Z (2006) Modelling exchange rates using regime switching models. Sains Malaysiana 35(2): 55–62

Klaassen F (2002) Improving GARCH volatility forecasts with regime-switching GARCH. In: Advances in markov-switching models. Springer, Heidelberg, pp 223–254

Kline RB (2005) Principles and practice of structural equation modelling, 2nd edn. Guilford, New York

Kritzman M, Page S, Turkington D (2012) Regime shifts: Implications for dynamic strategies. Financ Anal J 68(3):22–39

Liu CC, He L-Y (2010) KSS unit root test of nonlinearity and nonstationarity in China's agricultural futures markets. Phys Procedia 3(5):1753–1756. https://doi.org/10.1016/j.phpro.2010.07.015

Marcucci J (2005) Forecasting stock market volatility with regime-switching GARCH models. Stud Nonlinear Dyn Econom 9(4):1–53

Nazifi M, Fatahi S (2012) Regime switching GARCH models and GARCH Models, in stock market of the developing countries (SSRN Scholarly Paper No. ID 1987428). Social science Research Network, Rochester, NY

Rashid AP, Kocaaslan OK (2013) Does energy consumption volatility affect real GDP volatility? An empirical analysis for the UK. Int J Energy Econ Policy 3(4):384–394

Sajjad R, Coakley J, Nankervis JC (2008) Markov-switching GARCH modelling of value-at-risk. Stud Nonlinear Dyn Econom 12(3):7

Sattayathama P, Sopipana N, Premanode B (2012) Forecasting volatility and price of the SET50 index using the Markov regime switching. Procedia Econ Finance 2:265–274

Shiferaw Y (2018) The bayesian MS-GARCH model and value-at-risk in South African agricultural commodity price markets, Conference, July 28–August 2, 2018, Vancouver, British Columbia 275991, International Association of Agricultural Economists

Vavra M (2011) Testing normality in time series. Department of Economics, Mathematics and Statistics University of London (Birkbeck College) United Kingdom
Yadavalli L, Matlou K (2015) Regime switching model of stock market volatility
Zainudin R (2013) The effect of regime shift in minimum variance hedging ratio: The evidence of the crude palm oil market. Invest Manage Financ Innov 10(4):83–92
Zhang Y (2002) Testing for nonlinearities in time series with application to exchange rates. Doctoral dissertation, Lowa State University
Zhang Y-J, Yao T, He LY, Ripple R (2015) Volatility forecasting of crude oil market: can the regime switching GARCH model beat the single-regime GARCH models? Internat Rev Econom Financ

Lawrence Diteboho Xaba is an Operations Research Analyst with more than five years of research and teaching experience. He is currently working on his PhD in Operations Research at the North-West University. He has wide-ranging knowledge in Optimization, Nonlinear Models, and Stochastic Models.

Ntebogang Dinah Moroke is a Professor of Statistics at the North-West University, South Africa. Professor Moroke received her PhD degree in 2014 and published in accredited local and international journals and conference proceedings. Professor Moroke is a reviewer for several journals and conferences. Her research interest is drawn to analyzing real-life high-dimensional data applying Multivariate Data Analysis methods. She currently serves as a Dean of the Faculty of Economic and Management Sciences.

Lebotsa Daniel Metsileng holds a PhD in Statistics and poses a vest experience teaching the subject. His interest is in Multivariate techniques, Econometrics, and Time Series. He published several articles in international journals. He believes team goals are better scored than individual goals. He is more concerned about details and more results driven.

Volatility Spillovers Between Oil Prices and BIST (Borsa Istanbul) Dividend Indexes

Barış Kocaarslan

Introduction and Theoretical Background

Traditional finance theories focus on the valuation of an asset. The present value model argues that the fundamental value of an asset is determined by a stream of expected cash flows (e.g., dividend yields) discounted at a specified rate (a discount rate) (Campbell et al. 1997). In this respect, expected cash flows should be properly estimated and it is of immense importance in determining the appropriate discount rate to carefully value the cash flows. Therefore, a better understanding of the impact of common risk factors on cash flows and discount rate helps to more accurately predict the current value of an asset. Among these risk factors, oil prices might play a key role in influencing both cash flows and discount rates via the negative impacts on economic activities and monetary conditions (Brown and Yucel 1999, 2002; Edelstein and Kilian 2009; Dohner 1981; Jones and Kaul 1996; Mork 1994; Pierce et al. 1974; Tang et al. 2010).

Bird-in-the-hand theory is one of the main finance theories regarding dividend policy suggested by Gordon (1963) and Lintner (1962). The basic argument of this theory is that risk-averse investors prefer certain incomes (dividend payments) to uncertain future capital gains because they consider the capital gains to be highly risky and hence require higher returns due to increased risks. For this reason, the value of a firm is significantly affected by its dividend policy, which has an impact on the cost of capital of the firm.

Companies that pay high-dividends aim to both reward existing shareholders and to encourage other investors to invest in their shares (Black 1976). Sudden changes in dividend policy give market players an insight into the financial situation of

B. Kocaarslan (✉)
Yalova University, Yalova, Turkey

B. Adıgüzel Mercangöz (ed.), *Handbook of Research on Emerging Theories, Models, and Applications of Financial Econometrics*,
https://doi.org/10.1007/978-3-030-54108-8_15

companies. For example, if companies increase dividend payout, this will ensure that the prospects for the future of the companies are perceived as positive (Black 1976). Therefore, on the contrary, the reduced dividend distribution is not good news for investors in global markets and it is highly probable that this will cause a decrease in the prices of the stocks with high-dividend yield. In this context, investors need to closely monitor macroeconomic developments which have a negative impact on the dividend payout ratio of companies. Hence, investors should gain a better understanding of the impact of the changes in economic activities on the dividend policy of firms.

Benartzi et al. (1997) show that changing dividend payout policy by companies has information content regarding the current earnings of companies. Based on this information, it could be argued that the macroeconomic risks that adversely affect the dividend distribution policy of companies will also affect their cash flows and profitability. These effects are likely to have a negative impact on the stock prices of companies that distribute high dividends. Therefore, market conditions that affect the dividend distribution policy are of great importance in terms of forming global portfolios.

According to the present value model, the expected dividend payments are considered as the expected cash flows to take into account in the valuation of stock prices. Therefore, the factors affecting the dividend policies of companies and the causes of fluctuations in these factors need to be carefully analyzed. Among these factors, liquidity, cash flows, profitability, and operating income are the main factors on the dividend policy of a firm (Amidu and Abor 2006; Gill et al. 2010; Jensen et al. 1992; Baker et al. 2001; Koch and Shenoy 1999). Observed negative changes in these factors (e.g., unstable cash flows, reduced profitability, reduced operating income) cause a widespread fear about dividend cuts. As mentioned above, rising oil prices may lead to these unfavorable developments due to the adverse effects on the whole economy.

This research is grounded on some theoretical assertions on various transmission channels through which oil price fluctuations have a striking impact on economic activities. The adverse effects of oil prices on the overall economy have been clearly evidenced by a great number of studies during the last decades.

On the production side of the economy, the reduced availability of a vital input (oil) associated with increasing oil prices gives rise to rising production costs, which leads to less productivity for many industries (Brown and Yucel 1999, 2002). These increased costs result in declining company profits and hence in reducing cash flows (Jones and Kaul 1996). On the consumption side of the economy, rising oil prices cause declining income levels of individuals and ultimately generate less consumption expenditure in the economy (Edelstein and Kilian 2009). Another important issue on the impact of oil price increases on economic activity is the wealth transfer effect from oil-importing to oil-exporting countries (Dohner 1981). This transmission channel points out that rising oil prices lead to less consumer demand for services and goods in oil-importing countries than that in oil-exporting countries. Therefore, the GDP (gross domestic product) growth of oil-importing countries is considerably and negatively influenced by this economic mechanism stemming from rising oil prices.

The effect of oil price fluctuations on macroeconomic indicators is readily observed via the changes in monetary conditions. For example, the real-balance effect is due to that an increase in oil prices leads individuals to demand more money for transaction purposes (Mork 1994; Pierce et al. 1974). If the monetary authorities fail to satisfy this increasing demand, an increase in interest rates is observed, giving rise to worsening economic conditions. Also, there is an inflation effect emphasizing the link between oil prices and inflation. Oil price increases cause growing inflation rates due to increased costs. During high-inflation periods, contractionary monetary policy is utilized by the monetary authorities to increase interest rates (to curb inflation). The use of this policy results in a deteriorated investment climate (Tang et al. 2010).

The above-mentioned transmission channels distort the cash flows of the firms and influence interest rates (discount rates) especially in an oil-importing country (e.g., Turkey). Jones and Kaul (1996) demonstrate that the effect of oil price shocks on the stock markets can be explained through the effects of these shocks on cash flows. In light of this information, one might argue that the sensitivity of the stock prices of companies with high-dividend yields to oil price shocks should be pretty high. The main reason behind this argument is that companies distributing a high amount of cash dividends are expected to have stable cash flows and thereby are vulnerable to increased costs (hence reduced cash flows) and increased interest rates due to oil price shocks. Based on the above discussion and arguments, the following two hypotheses are suggested:

Hypothesis 1 There is a significant volatility spillover effect from oil prices to BIST Dividend and BIST Dividend 25 indexes.

Hypothesis 2 The statistical significance of this effect is more pronounced for the BIST Dividend 25 index than for the BIST Dividend index since the BIST Dividend 25 index includes 25 stocks based on higher ranking with respect to dividend yield (and thus has more sensitivity to the variation in cash flows and interest rates caused by oil price shocks).

Related Literature and Contribution of this Chapter

A vast number of studies on the relationship between oil and stock markets have been carried out in the relevant literature. Most of the previous studies reveal the negative relationship between these markets (e.g., Jones and Kaul 1996; Sadorsky 1999; Park and Ratti 2008; Basher et al. 2012). However, some others find a positive relationship between them. (e.g., Narayan and Narayan 2010; Silvapulle et al. 2017; Zhu et al. 2014). Smyth and Narayan (2018) imply that the effect of oil price fluctuations on stock markets differs depending on the varying characteristics of the stocks in aggregate stock markets. The level of oil dependence of a country (or a sector) could play a crucial role in this effect (Kocaarslan et al. 2019; Smyth and Narayan 2018).

A line of research focuses on the impact of oil price dynamics on oil-importing and oil-exporting countries. Park and Ratti (2008) find a positive effect of rising oil prices on the stock market returns in Norway, which is an oil-exporter. The analysis of Bjørnland (2009) confirms this finding. Park and Ratti (2008) also show the depressing impact of increased oil price volatility on stock returns for many European countries. Cunado and de Gracia (2014) provide supportive evidence for the negative impact of oil price fluctuations on stock market returns of many European countries. Using a Vector Error-Correction Modeling, Masih et al. (2011) conclude that oil price volatility is a dominant factor in stock returns in South Korea. Silvapulle et al. (2017) point out the crucial role of stock market fundamentals in the link between oil and stock prices. Arouri and Rault (2012) demonstrate the positive impact of oil price hikes on stock prices in the Gulf Cooperation Council (GCC) countries, except in Saudi Arabia. Mohanty et al. (2011) and Demirer et al. (2015) present similar findings to those of Arouri and Rault (2012). Filis et al. (2011) concentrate on the time-varying dynamic correlations between oil and stock market prices for oil-exporting and oil-importing countries and demonstrate that oil is not a good hedge against the stock market risks during a period of recession. Ramos and Veiga (2013) indicate the negative and positive impacts of oil price increases on the stock markets of oil-importing and oil-exporting countries, respectively. Wang et al. (2013) find that the magnitude and direction of oil price shocks on the stock market depend on the oil dependence characteristics of countries. Overall, previous literature emphasizes that the direction of the impact of oil price shocks on stock market returns depends on whether a country is an oil-exporter or an oil-importer.

Some studies focus on the impact of oil price shocks on sector stock returns and volatility for the developed markets. Narayan and Sharma (2011) demonstrate that the heterogeneous impact of oil price fluctuations on the US firm returns depends on the sector that the firm belongs to. In support of this evidence, Arouri (2011) shows the differentiated sensitivity of Europe sector stock returns to oil price changes. Using a bivariate GARCH–in-mean VAR model, Alsalman (2016) do not find a significant impact of oil price volatility on US sector stock returns. Elyasiani et al. (2011) utilize the GARCH (1,1) model to investigate the impact of oil price returns and volatility on US industry-level stock returns and volatility and reveal that, compared to oil price volatility, oil futures returns strongly influence some sectors including the oil-related and oil-substitute sectors. The opposite of this result holds for the oil-user industries. Using a double-threshold FIGARCH model, Elyasiani et al. (2013) find that oil price fluctuations significantly affect ten major US sector returns and/or volatility. Arouri et al. (2012) indicate that the intensity of volatility spillovers between oil prices and Europe sector stock returns changes from one sector to another and hence these changes are of utmost importance for investment and hedging strategies. Moya-Martínez et al. (2014), for the Spanish stock market, examine the sensitivity of the industry-level stock returns to oil price movements and show that Basic Resources, Energy, Food and Beverages, Construction, and

Banking sector returns are highly sensitive to oil price risk. Xu (2015) concludes that the lagged and contemporaneous oil price changes are the significant predictors of the UK industry-level stock returns. This study points out the presence of asymmetric interactions between oil and stock prices. Lee et al. (2012) concentrate their effort on the impact of oil price shocks on the industry-level stock returns for the G-7 countries. Their results suggest that the information technology sector returns appear to be most influenced by oil price movements compared to other sector returns.

Some other studies turn scientific attention to the link between oil price shocks and sector stock returns for the Chinese market. Cong et al. (2008), employing multivariate vector auto-regression, find that oil price shocks have explanatory power for the manufacturing index returns. Utilizing a panel cointegration method, Li et al. (2012) provide evidence of the positive effect of the oil price on the Chinese sector stocks in the long-run. Caporale et al. (2015) show the different impacts of oil price uncertainty on the Chinese sector stocks in the period of demand-side shocks. Also, they do not find a significant impact of oil price uncertainty on the sector stocks in the period of precautionary demand shocks. Zhu et al. (2016) use a quantile regression framework and reveal that the Chinese sector stock returns response heterogeneously to oil price movements depending on the conditional distribution of the returns. Peng et al. (2017) find a lagged impact of oil price shocks on Chinese oil firms.

The impact of oil price fluctuations on the oil and gas firms' stock returns has attracted attention in the related literature. Sadorsky (2001) indicates the positive impact of oil price rises on the Canadian oil and gas firms' stock returns. Boyer and Filion (2007) obtain a similar result to Sadorsky (2001). Nandha and Faff (2008) show the negative impact of oil price fluctuations on all global sectors' stock returns except for oil and gas and mining sectors. Gupta (2016) demonstrates that oil price shocks have a positive effect on the oil and gas stock returns at the firm-level. Using a multi-factor model, El-Sharif et al. (2005) conclude that rising oil prices lead to an increase in the UK-listed oil and gas companies' returns. Kang et al. (2017) present evidence of the positive impact of oil demand-side shock on oil and gas firms' returns. As for the adverse impacts of oil prices on some related sectors, an increase in oil prices is expected to have a negative impact on some sectors (e.g., manufacturing and transport sectors) returns since oil is a vital input for the production in these sectors. Some studies imply that oil price increases negatively impact the returns of the transport sector stocks (Nandha and Faff 2008; Aggarwal et al. 2012). Furthermore, Cameron and Schnusenberg (2009) find an adverse impact of oil prices on the automobile manufacturer sector stock returns. Also, a strand of literature has investigated the link between oil prices and renewable energy stocks. The results of a few studies suggest that oil price changes explain variation in clean energy stock prices (Henriques and Sadorsky 2008; Kumar et al. 2012). Some studies point out that the impact of oil price movements on renewable energy stocks varies in the short- and long-run (Reboredo et al. 2017; Kocaarslan and Soytas 2019). Also, previous research reveals that the relationship between oil prices and renewable energy stocks has strengthened since 2007 (Managi and Okimoto 2013; Inchauspe et al. 2015).

During a financial turmoil, the high-volatility of asset classes is frequently observed (Bloom 2014). Therefore, the presence of financial contagion between various financial and commodity markets can be better explained by investigating volatility spillovers between the markets. Previous research emphasizes the significance of the impact of oil price volatility on stock prices (Masih et al. 2011; Arouri et al. 2011).

There are a limited number of studies on the effect of oil prices on the Turkish stock market. Using the generalized impulse response and generalized forecast error variance decomposition approaches, Sari and Soytas (2006) do not find a significant impact of oil price changes on Turkish stock market returns. Some studies concentrate on the impact of oil price changes on the subindexes of the Turkish stock market index. Soytas and Oran (2011) utilize the Cheung and Ng (1996) approach and demonstrate the causality-in-variance from oil prices and ISE (Istanbul Stock Exchange) electricity index returns, but this causality is not observed for the ISE 100 index returns. Using an ARMA-GARCH model, Çelik et al. (2015) do not find a significant impact of oil prices on the BIST chemical-petroleum-plastic subindex and BIST industrial subindexes. Converse to this finding, using the Granger causality method, Gencer and Demiralay (2013) find a one-way causality from oil prices to the BIST chemical-petroleum-plastic subindex. More recently, Ordu and Soytaş (2016) use an augmented VAR approach and find that there is no Granger causality from oil prices to electricity and market indexes returns in Turkey. In another empirical investigation, utilizing the generalized impulse response approach, Akkaya and Sari (2019) demonstrate that increased oil prices positively influence the Turkish banking stock returns.

Our study differs from the literature in the following aspects. First, we use the causality-in-variance test procedure developed by Hafner and Herwartz (2006) to investigate volatility spillovers between oil prices and BIST (Borsa Istanbul) dividend indexes due to the various advantages of this procedure, which are explained in the following parts. Second, there is no empirical study that tests the causality-in-variance between oil prices and BIST (Borsa Istanbul) dividend indexes returns. Third, as mentioned in the preceding section, we take into consideration two dividend indexes to better understand the sensitivity of the companies with high-dividend yields to oil price shocks.

Data Sources and Characteristics

This study uses the daily closing prices of the two dividend indices (BIST Dividend Index and BIST Dividend 25 Index) for the Turkish stock market. BIST Dividend Index (BISTDIV hereafter) includes the stocks of companies listed in Borsa Istanbul (BIST) that have paid cash dividends in the last 3 years. BIST Dividend 25 index (BISTDIV25 hereafter) includes 25 stocks based on the higher ranking with respect to the dividend yield. To represent oil prices, Brent crude oil futures prices, which are widely preferred in the related literature, are used for the empirical investigations.

Table 1 Summary statistics of the data

	DLBISTDIV	DLBISTDIV25	DLBRENT
Mean	0.0002	0.0004	−0.0003
Median	0.0005	0.0011	0.0003
Maximum	0.0686	0.0625	0.1042
Minimum	−0.1114	−0.1054	−0.0886
Std. Dev.	0.0145	0.0139	0.0194
Skewness	−0.4917	−0.5585	0.0784
Kurtosis	6.6823	6.5755	5.9245
Jarque–Bera	1213.5750	1172.2140	716.5450
Probability	0.0000	0.0000	0.0000

Note: Table 1 shows the summary statistics of the data. D and L refer to the first difference and log operators, respectively. DLBISTDIV, DLBISTDIV25, and DLBRENT refer to the daily returns of the BIST dividend indexes (BISTDIV and BISTDIV25) and oil prices, respectively. Source: Author's creation

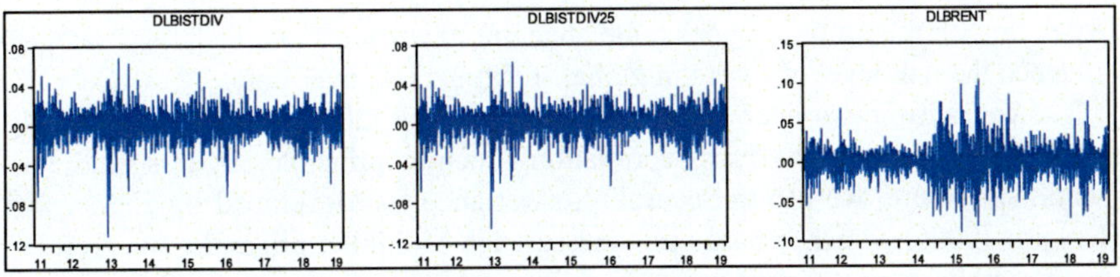

Fig. 1 Evolution of the returns of the variables over the test period. Note: D and L refer to the first difference and log operators, respectively. DLBISTDIV, DLBISTDIV25, and DLBRENT refer to the daily returns of the BIST dividend indexes (BISTDIV and BISTDIV25) and oil prices, respectively. Source: Author's creation

The stock and oil data are obtained from investing.com. The sample period ranges from July 4, 2011 to July 22, 2019. The availability of the BIST dividend indexes data restricts the sample period because the BISTDIV and BISTDIV25 have no data prior to July 4, 2011. The first differences of the logarithm of the time series are used to represent the return of the BIST dividend indexes and oil prices.

Table 1 reports the summary statistics of the returns of the BIST dividend indexes and oil prices. The reported statistics indicate the excess kurtosis and skewness for the data set (see Table 1). The Jarque–Bera statistics confirm these deviations from the normality assumption, rejecting the null hypothesis of normality. As seen in Table 1, oil price returns have a higher standard deviation indicating higher volatility than the returns of the BIST dividend indexes.

Figure 1 shows the evolution of the returns of the BIST dividend indexes and oil prices over the analysis period. The presence of volatility clustering and heteroscedasticity is clearly observed in this illustration (see Fig. 1). Based on this, the use of GARCH models is highly convenient to investigate the risk spillovers between the BIST dividend indexes and oil prices.

The volatility spillover analysis requires that variables should be stationary. To control for this requirement, this study utilizes the Dickey–Fuller GLS detrended test (DF-GLS unit root test) (Elliott et al. 1996). Also, for robustness, the modified augmented Dickey–Fuller (MADF) test (Kim and Perron 2009) is applied to account for a structural breakpoint. The tests are conducted by considering intercept and both intercept and trend. Table 2 reports the unit root test results. The findings reported in Table 2 demonstrate that the variables are stationary.

Methodology

This research aims to examine the causality-in-variance between the BIST dividend indexes and oil prices. This analysis leads to an understanding of volatility linkages between these variables. The key role of oil price fluctuations in global markets is quite important for the investment and hedging strategies of global investors. Depending on the oil price shocks, the changing investment and hedging strategies influence the risk level of assets in global stock markets over time.

The causality-in-variance tests suggested by Hong (2001) and Cheung and Ng (1996) are based on the cross-correlation function principle. In this study, as mentioned before, we use the causality-in-variance test developed by Hafner and Herwartz (2006), which is based on the Lagrange-Multiplier principle. We prefer to use this test because it overcomes some serious problems (e.g., significant oversizing in small samples in the existence of leptokurtic volatility process and a high-sensitivity to the order of lags and leads) that other causality-in-variance tests (e.g., tests developed by Hong (2001) and Cheung and Ng (1996)) encounter.

For the first step of the volatility spillover analysis, univariate GARCH models are estimated to describe the variations in the conditional means and variances. A standard GARCH model (Bollerslev 1986) is applied for the conditional variance. The AR(1) autoregressive term in the mean equation is used to consider the impact of lagged market information on the BIST dividend indexes and oil prices and to reduce serial correlation in data series. The mean and variance equations are specified as below, respectively:

$$R_t = \mu + \mathrm{AR}(1) + \varepsilon_t \tag{1}$$

$$\sigma_t^2 = \omega + \alpha\varepsilon_{t-1}^2 + \beta\sigma_{t-1}^2 \tag{2}$$

R_t refers to the daily returns of each time series. AR(1) represents the lagged market returns (the lagged returns of the BIST dividend indexes and oil prices). The α (ARCH parameter) indicates the impact of lagged squared errors (previous shocks) on current conditional variance as the β (GARCH parameter) indicates the impact of lagged conditional variance (previous conditional variance) on current conditional variance. The sum of the GARCH and ARCH parameters (β + α) shows the persistence of the conditional volatility series. For stationarity and stability, several

Table 2 Unit root test results

		DF-GLS	MADF		DF-GLS	MADF
		Statistics	Statistics		Statistics	Statistics
Variables						
DLBISTDIV	Intercept	−6.217897[a]	−46.41308[a]	Intercept	−22.07216[a]	−46.40299[a]
DLBISTDIV25		−3.905770[a]	−45.60980[a]	And trend	−6.567763[a]	−45.59676[a]
DLBRENT		−2.264294**	−48.57719[a]		−6.529243[a]	−48.77551[a]

Note: D and L refer to the first difference and log operators, respectively. DLBISTDIV, DLBISTDIV25, and DLBRENT refer to the daily returns of the BIST dividend indexes (BISTDIV and BISTDIV25) and oil prices, respectively. DF-GLS and MADF represent the Dickey–Fuller GLS detrended (DF-GLS) and modified augmented Dickey–Fuller (MADF) unit root tests, respectively

Source: Author's creation

[a]Significant at the 1% level

**Significant at the 5% level

conditions ($\alpha + \beta < 1$; $\alpha \geq 0$; $\beta \geq 0$; $\omega > 0$) should be satisfied for the variance equations.

For the second step of the analysis, the following null hypothesis of non-causality-in-variance between the BIST dividend indexes (series i) and oil prices (series j) is tested.

$$H_0 : \mathrm{Var}\left(\varepsilon_{it} \mid F_{t-1}^{(j)}\right) = \mathrm{Var}\left(\varepsilon_{it} \mid F_{t-1}\right) \quad j = 1, \ldots, N, i \neq j, \tag{3}$$

where $F_t^{(j)} = F_t/\sigma(\varepsilon_{j\tau}, \tau \leq t)$ and ε_{it} are the residuals derived from the traditional GARCH model. The below equation is employed to test the null hypothesis:

$$\varepsilon_{it} = \xi_{it}\sqrt{\sigma_{it}^2\left(1 + z_{jt}'\pi\right)}, \quad z_{jt} = \left(\varepsilon_{jt-1}^2, \sigma_{jt-1}^2\right)' \tag{4}$$

σ_{it}^2 and ξ_{it} represents the conditional variance (conditional volatility) and the standardized residuals for the series i, respectively, while σ_{jt-1}^2 and ε_{jt-1}^2 represents the conditional variance (conditional volatility) and the squared standardized residuals for the series j, respectively. The null hypothesis H_0: $\pi = 0$ (no causality-in-variance) is tested against H_1: $\pi \neq 0$ (the alternative hypothesis), which states the presence of the causality. The score of the Gaussian log-likelihood function of ε_{it} is given by $x_{it}\left(\xi_{it-1}^2\right)/2$, where the derivatives are $x_{it} = \sigma_{it}^{-2}\left(\partial\sigma_{it}^2/\partial\theta_i\right)$, $\theta_i = (\omega_i, \alpha_i, \beta_i)'$. Hafner and Herwartz (2006) suggest the following LM (Lagrange-multiplier) test to uncover volatility transmissions between the variables of interest.

$$\lambda_{LM} = \frac{1}{4T}\left(\sum_{t=1}^{T}\left(\xi_{it}^2 - 1\right)z_{jt}'\right)V(\theta_i)^{-1}\left(\sum_{t=1}^{T}\left(\xi_{it}^2 - 1\right)z_{jt}\right), \tag{5}$$

Where

$$V(\theta_i) = \frac{K}{4T}\left(\sum_{t=1}^{T} z_{jt}z_{jt}' - \sum_{t=1}^{T} z_{jt}x_{it}' - \left(\sum_{t=1}^{T} x_{it}x_{it}'\right)^{-1}\sum_{t=1}^{T} x_{it}z_{jt}'\right),$$

$$K = \frac{1}{T}\left(\sum_{t=1}^{T}\left(\xi_{it}^2 - 1\right)^2\right).$$

The asymptotic distribution of the test statistic λ_{LM} in Eq. (5) relies on the number of misspecification indicators in z_{jt}. The existence of two misspecification indicators in λ_{LM} equation necessitates the obtainment of an asymptotic chi-square distribution with two degrees of freedom for the applied models. Rejecting the null hypothesis implies that there is a volatility spillover from series j to series i. A similar test procedure can be applied to explore volatility spillover from series i to series j.

Empirical Results

As explained in the preceding section, for the first step of the test procedure, univariate GARCH (1,1) models are applied to identify the volatility characteristics of oil prices and BIST dividend indexes returns. Tables 3 and 4 present the empirical findings for the mean and variance equations of the univariate GARCH (1,1) models, respectively. A careful analysis requires us to test whether the stability conditions ($\alpha \geq 0; \beta \geq 0; \omega > 0; \alpha + \beta < 1$) are met or not. The results reported in Table 4 show that there is no stability problem with respect to the estimated GARCH models. To ensure that the conditional variance process fits well with the time-series data, various diagnostic tests (e.g., tests on the residuals and squared residuals and ARCH-LM tests for chosen models) are conducted. The diagnostic test results do not indicate a significant problem for the used model specifications (see Table 4). As shown in Table 3, a marginally significant AR(1) term in the mean equation for Brent crude oil prices means that Brent crude oil price returns are negatively affected by lagged changes in itself. The statistically significant parameters reported in Table 4 for the variance equations demonstrate the presence of conditional

Table 3 Mean equation results

Independent variables		Dependent variables	
	DLBISTDIV	DLBISTDIV25	DLBRENT
Constant	0.000592[a]	0.000747[a]	−4.89E-05
AR(1)	−0.00601	0.005168	−0.042376[a]

Note: Table 3 provides the mean equation results for the return series. D and L refer to the first difference and log operators, respectively. DLBISTDIV, DLBISTDIV25, and DLBRENT refer to the daily returns of the BIST dividend indexes (BISTDIV and BISTDIV25) and oil prices, respectively. Dependent variables are the DLBISTDIV, DLBISTDIV25, and DLBRENT. Independent variables are the lagged changes (AR(1) term)
Source: Author's creation
[a]Significant at the 10% level

Table 4 Variance equation results

Parameters and model diagnostics		Market returns	
	DLBISTDIV	DLBISTDIV25	DLBRENT
ω	7.20E-06[a]	1.08E-05[a]	2.67E-06[a]
α	0.060178[a]	0.084671[a]	0.064576[a]
β	0.906495[a]	0.861516[a]	0.929587[a]
Q(10)	0.14	0.099	0.333
SRQ(10)	0.575	0.169	0.921
ARCH(10)	0.5498	0.1543	0.9151

Note: Table 4 provides the variance equation results for the chosen GARCH (1,1) models
Source: Author's creation
[a]Significant at the 1% level. α and β refer to the ARCH and GARCH parameters, respectively. The p-values for the Ljung–Box Q statistics and for ARCH-LM test statistics for the 10 lags are reported. SR represents the squared residuals

Table 5 Causality-in-variance test results

	DLBISTDIV	DLBISTDIV25	DLBRENT
DLBISTDIV			7.457803[a]
DLBISTDIV25			10.03082[b]
DLBRENT	3.440507	2.781218	

Note: Table 5 presents the volatility spillover test results. D and L refer to the first difference and log operators, respectively. DLBISTDIV, DLBISTDIV25, and DLBRENT refer to the daily returns of the BIST dividend indexes (BISTDIV and BISTDIV25) and oil prices, respectively. Significance indicates Granger causality-in-variance running from column variable to row variable

Source: Author's creation

[a]Significant at the 5% level

[b]significant at the 1% level

heteroscedasticity for oil prices and BIST dividend indexes returns. As seen in Table 4, compared to the short-run (ARCH) effects, the greater long-run (GARCH) effects are revealed for the variables of interest. These results point to the strong impact of long-run volatility on oil prices and BIST dividend indexes returns.

The observed strong long-run volatility motivates us to test volatility spillovers between oil prices and BIST (Borsa Istanbul) dividend indexes returns. In the second part of the causality-in-variance test, the LM test statistics (the causality-in-variance test results) are reported to understand whether there is a significant volatility spillover effect from oil prices to BIST Dividend and BIST Dividend 25 indexes. Table 5 presents the causality-in-variance test findings. The findings reported in Table 5 suggest a significant one-way volatility spillover effect from oil prices to BIST dividend and BIST Dividend 25 indexes returns. The statistical significance of this effect is more apparent for the BIST Dividend 25 index than for the BIST Dividend index (see Table 5). These findings clearly confirm our hypotheses.

Discussion

In this study, using a causality-in-variance approach developed by Hafner and Herwartz (2006), volatility spillovers between oil prices and BIST (Borsa Istanbul) dividend indexes returns are uncovered. As expected, the BIST Dividend 25 index appears to be more vulnerable to oil price fluctuations compared to the BIST Dividend index. The main reason behind this vulnerability is that the BIST Dividend 25 index contains 25 stocks based on the higher ranking with respect to dividend yield and thus is more sensitive to fluctuations in cash flows and interest rates caused by oil price shocks. The overall assessment suggests that the increased sensitivity to the variation in cash flows and interest rates makes the stocks with high-dividend yield more vulnerable to oil price shocks.

The findings of this study provide important implications with respect to various economic mechanisms by which volatility in oil prices can have an impact on the stocks of companies that distribute high dividends. Firms need a regular stream of cash flows in order to fulfill debt obligations and provide dividends to their shareholders. Determining the appropriate investment strategies requires investors to make an assessment of how the ability of companies to generate cash flows is affected by fluctuations in the economy when making decisions about stock investments. This assessment provides investors with an idea of the extent to which companies are adapting to changing conditions in the economy and gives information on the liquidity and solvency of the companies. In this respect, when evaluating stock prices, the potential of companies to create cash should be taken into consideration. The fluctuations in oil prices have a strong impact on the cash flows of the companies in oil-dependent countries (such as Turkey) through negative effects on economic activities. Therefore, volatility in oil prices is expected to significantly increase the riskiness of stocks with high-dividend yields in the Turkish stock market. The results of this study strongly support this expectation.

Another important issue for companies that distribute high dividends is the factors that affect their profitability. We find support for the expectation that falling profitability leads to a negative impact on the dividend distribution policy of companies and thus negative effects on the stock prices of these companies prevail in global markets. If there is uncertainty about the profitability of a company with high-dividend yields, the risk perception of the company increases. The profitability of companies, as is known, depends on the balance of income and costs (expenditures). Therefore, the effect of the factors influencing the supply-demand balance in the market on profitability comes to the fore. At this point, it could be argued that the volatility in oil prices will play an important role in the profitability of companies by affecting both production costs and consumption expenditures. In support of this argument, the findings of the analyses conducted in this study show that the volatility in oil prices plays a crucial role in the volatility of the stocks with high-dividend yields.

In order to realize a sustainable dividend stream, the liquidity position of companies is highly important. Due to the low demand during recession periods, companies have difficulty in marketing their goods or services. These economic conditions reduce the incomes of firms from their main activities and therefore make their liquidity position weak. Therefore, the liquidity position of firms considerably affects their dividend distribution policies. The oil price volatility, especially in oil-dependent countries (such as Turkey), is likely to have a strong impact on the liquidity position of a company through negative effects on market demand. In particular, the companies that distribute high dividends will be most affected by these adverse conditions. The main reason for this is that the irregularity of the cash flows of the companies, due to the weak liquidity position, creates a negative perception of the investors. The findings of this study show a significant risk transfer from oil prices to dividend indices. This finding confirms the above arguments.

As mentioned in the preceding sections, the interest rate is an important indicator to value an asset. According to the present value model, increasing interest rates are expected to affect stock prices negatively. Another important role of oil price volatility is to change monetary conditions (hence interest rates). For example, as mentioned in the introduction section, rising oil prices result in an increase in money demand. Consequently, increasing interest rates, due to increased money demand that cannot be met by monetary authorities, negatively affect the economy. In addition, rising costs caused by rising oil prices cause inflation to rise. These economic conditions lead the monetary authority to increase interest rates by conducting contractionary policies. A conducted contractionary policy to curb inflation might worsen economic conditions and hence badly affect the supply and demand balance in global markets. It is inevitable that these transmission channels have a great impact on the stocks of companies that distribute high dividends due to the deterioration in cash flows. In sum, the overall assessment points out that the strong volatility spillovers from oil prices to dividend indices may be due to the above economic mechanisms through which oil price volatility plays a central role in influencing monetary conditions.

Conclusion

Careful scrutiny of the impact of oil price volatility on financial markets via various transmission channels is crucial for market participants. With the increasing financialization of commodities (such as oil) in recent years, the effects of changes in oil market conditions on global markets have started to play a key role in determining the decisions of all actors in the economy. Macroeconomic risks should be carefully considered before making investment decisions in stock markets. Investments in the stocks of companies that distribute high dividends are more attractive for high risk-averse investors to hedge price risk since there is a guaranteed income. However, uncertainty in the dividend policy due to unfavorable developments in the economy (e.g., a substantial deterioration in cash flows, reduced liquidity, and reduced profitability) adversely affects the prices of the stocks with high-dividend yield. In oil-dependent countries (e.g., Turkey), one of the reasons for this negative effect may be a negative impact of oil price volatility on the whole economy. Hence, this study aims to investigate the risk spillovers between oil prices and dividend indices.

The baseline findings suggest that there is a significant one-way causality-in-variance from oil prices to BIST Dividend indexes. The statistical significance of this causality is more observed for the BIST Dividend 25 index compared to the BIST Dividend index. It appears to be due to the higher sensitivity of the BIST Dividend 25 index (which contains 25 stocks based on the higher ranking with respect to dividend yield) to fluctuations in cash flows and interest rates caused by oil price shocks. The volatility spillovers between different asset classes are expected to be stronger in the presence of financial contagion, especially during bad times. Detailed information on the risk spillovers between oil prices and dividend indexes is necessary to determine optimal investment and hedging strategies. From this perspective, the findings of this research are of immense importance for fund managers, investors, and speculators as well as policy makers.

The implications of the analyses point out that global investors change their asset allocations in an optimal portfolio depending on the fluctuations in oil price volatility. Therefore, the volatility of the stocks with high-dividend yield shows an increase. The main reason behind this increase is that, as explained in the discussion part, oil price volatility increases the riskiness of the stocks with high dividends through various economic mechanisms. According to the results, it appears that changes in oil market conditions influence the degree of global risk aversion and hence result in rebalancing the portfolio holdings of global investors, especially during high-volatility periods. Overall, investors investing in the stocks of companies that pay high dividends should closely follow the price fluctuations in the oil market. To be able to hedge the risks arising from these fluctuations, global investors should revise their portfolio structures by accounting for oil price volatility.

For future research, the impact of oil price volatility on stocks with a high-dividend yield in the stock markets of developed countries might be examined. In addition, future studies investigate volatility spillover between oil prices and sectoral and thematic indexes returns considering the characteristics of other oil-importing and oil-exporting countries. This investigation may provide a better understanding of the transmission mechanisms through which oil price volatility affects the stocks with different characteristics.

References

Aggarwal R, Akhigbe A, Mohanty SK (2012) Oil price shocks and transportation firm asset prices. Energy Econ 34(5):1370–1379

Akkaya BMO, Sari R (2019) Oil prices and banking stocks nexus: evidence from an oil-dependent country. Dumlupınar Üniversitesi Sosyal Bilimler Dergisi 59:34–47

Alsalman Z (2016) Oil price uncertainty and the US stock market analysis based on a GARCH-in-mean VAR model. Energy Econ 59:251–260

Amidu M, Abor J (2006) Determinants of dividend payout ratios in Ghana. J Risk Financ 7 (2):136–145

Arouri MEH (2011) Does crude oil move stock markets in Europe? A sector investigation. Econ Model 28(4):1716–1725

Arouri MEH, Rault C (2012) Oil prices and stock markets in GCC countries: empirical evidence from panel analysis. Int J Financ Econ 17(3):242–253

Arouri MEH, Jouini J, Nguyen DK (2011) Volatility spillovers between oil prices and stock sector returns: implications for portfolio management. J Int Money Financ 30(7):1387–1405

Arouri MEH, Jouini J, Nguyen DK (2012) On the impacts of oil price fluctuations on European equity markets: volatility spillover and hedging effectiveness. Energy Econ 34(2):611–617

Baker HK, Veit ET, Powell GE (2001) Factors influencing dividend policy decisions of Nasdaq firms. Financ Rev 36(3):19–38

Basher SA, Haug AA, Sadorsky P (2012) Oil prices, exchange rates and emerging stock markets. Energy Econ 34(1):227–240

Benartzi S, Michaely R, Thaler R (1997) Do changes in dividends signal the future or the past? J Financ 52(3):1007–1034

Bjørnland HC (2009) Oil price shocks and stock market booms in an oil exporting country. Scott J Polit Econ 56(2):232–254

Black F (1976) The dividend puzzle. J Portf Manag 2(2):5–8

Bloom N (2014) Fluctuations in uncertainty. J Econ Perspect 28(2):153–176
Bollerslev T (1986) Generalized autoregressive conditional heteroskedasticity. J Econ 31 (3):307–327
Boyer MM, Filion D (2007) Common and fundamental factors in stock returns of Canadian oil and gas companies. Energy Econ 29(3):428–453
Brown SP, Yucel MK (1999) Oil prices and US aggregate economic activity: a question of neutrality. Econ Financ Rev (Q II):16–23
Brown S, Yucel M (2002) Energy prices and aggregate economic activity: an interpretative survey. Quart Rev Econ Financ 42(2):193–208
Cameron K, Schnusenberg O (2009) Oil prices, SUVs, and Iraq: an investigation of automobile manufacturer oil price sensitivity. Energy Econ 31(3):375–381
Campbell JY, Lo AW, Ve MacKinlay AC (1997) The econometrics of financial markets, vol 2. Princeton University Press, Princeton, NJ, pp 149–180
Caporale GM, Ali FM, Spagnolo N (2015) Oil price uncertainty and sectoral stock returns in China: a time-varying approach. China Econ Rev 34:311–321
Çelik İ, Özdemir A, Gülcan N (2015) Petrol fiyat dalgalanmalarının getiri oynaklığı üzerine etkisi: Türkiye'de alt endeksler üzerine bir uygulama. Muhasebe ve Finansman Dergisi 10:157–169
Cheung YW, Ng LK (1996) A causality-in-variance test and its application to financial market prices. J Econ 72(1–2):33–48
Cong RG, Wei YM, Jiao JL, Fan Y (2008) Relationships between oil price shocks and stock market: an empirical analysis from China. Energy Policy 36(9):3544–3553
Cunado J, de Gracia FP (2014) Oil price shocks and stock market returns: evidence for some European countries. Energy Econ 42:365–377
Demirer R, Jategaonkar SP, Khalifa AA (2015) Oil price risk exposure and the cross-section of stock returns: the case of net exporting countries. Energy Econ 49:132–140
Dohner RS (1981) Energy prices, economic activity and inflation: survey of issues and results. In: Mork KA (ed) Energy prices, inflation and economic activity. Ballinger, Cambridge, MA
Edelstein P, Kilian L (2009) How sensitive are consumer expenditures to retail energy prices? J Monet Econ 56(6):766–779
Elliott G, Rothenberg T, Stock J (1996) Efficient tests for an autoregressive unit root. Econometrica 64(4):813–836
El-Sharif I, Brown D, Burton B, Nixon B, Russell A (2005) Evidence on the nature and extent of the relationship between oil prices and equity values in the UK. Energy Econ 27(6):819–830
Elyasiani E, Mansur I, Odusami B (2011) Oil price shocks and industry stock returns. Energy Econ 33(5):966–974
Elyasiani E, Mansur I, Odusami B (2013) Sectoral stock return sensitivity to oil price changes: a double-threshold FIGARCH model. Quant Finan 13(4):593–612
Filis G, Degiannakis S, Floros C (2011) Dynamic correlation between stock market and oil prices: the case of oil-importing and oil-exporting countries. Int Rev Financ Anal 20(3):152–164
Gencer G, Demiralay S (2013) The impact of oil prices on sectoral returns: an empirical analysis from Borsa Istanbul. Theoret Appl Econ 18(12(589)):7–24
Gill A, Biger N, Tibrewala R (2010) Determinants of dividend payout ratios: evidence from United States. Open Bus J 3(1):8
Gordon MJ (1963) Optimal investment and financing policy. J Financ 18(2):264–272
Gupta K (2016) Oil price shocks, competition, and oil & gas stock returns—global evidence. Energy Econ 57:140–153
Hafner CM, Herwartz H (2006) A Lagrange multiplier test for causality in variance. Econ Lett 93 (1):137–141
Henriques I, Sadorsky P (2008) Oil prices and the stock prices of alternative energy companies. Energy Econ 30(3):998–1010
Hong Y (2001) A test for volatility spillover with application to exchange rates. J Econ 103 (1–2):183–224

Inchauspe J, Ripple RD, Trück S (2015) The dynamics of returns on renewable energy companies: a state-space approach. Energy Econ 48:325–335
Jensen GR, Solberg DP, Zorn TS (1992) Simultaneous determination of insider ownership, debt, and dividend policies. J Financ Quant Anal 27(2):247–263
Jones CM, Kaul G (1996) Oil and the stock markets. J Financ 51(2):463–491
Kang W, de Gracia FP, Ratti RA (2017) Oil price shocks, policy uncertainty, and stock returns of oil and gas corporations. J Int Money Financ 70:344–359
Kim D, Perron P (2009) Unit root tests allowing for a break in the trend function at an unknown time under both the null and alternative hypotheses. J Econ 148(1):1–13
Kocaarslan B, Soytas U (2019) Asymmetric pass-through between oil prices and the stock prices of clean energy firms: new evidence from a nonlinear analysis. Energy Rep 5:117–125
Kocaarslan B, Soytas U, Sari R, Ugurlu E (2019) The changing role of financial stress, oil price, and gold price in financial contagion among US and BRIC markets. Int Rev Financ 19(3):541–574
Koch PD, Shenoy C (1999) The information content of dividend and capital structure policies. Financ Manag 28:16–35
Kumar S, Managi S, Matsuda A (2012) Stock prices of clean energy firms, oil and carbon markets: a vector autoregressive analysis. Energy Econ 34(1):215–226
Lee BJ, Yang CW, Huang BN (2012) Oil price movements and stock markets revisited: a case of sector stock price indexes in the G-7 countries. Energy Econ 34(5):1284–1300
Li SF, Zhu HM, Yu K (2012) Oil prices and stock market in China: a sector analysis using panel cointegration with multiple breaks. Energy Econ 34(6):1951–1958
Lintner J (1962) Dividends, earnings, leverage, stock prices and supply of capital to corporations. Rev Econ Stat 64:243–269
Managi S, Okimoto T (2013) Does the price of oil interact with clean energy prices in the stock market? Jpn World Econ 27:1–9
Masih R, Peters S, De Mello L (2011) Oil price volatility and stock price fluctuations in an emerging market: evidence from South Korea. Energy Econ 33(5):975–986
Mohanty SK, Nandha M, Turkistani AQ, Alaitani MY (2011) Oil price movements and stock market returns: evidence from gulf cooperation council (GCC) countries. Glob Financ J 22 (1):42–55
Mork KA (1994) Business cycles and the oil market. Energy J 15:15–38
Moya-Martínez P, Ferrer-Lapeña R, Escribano-Sotos F (2014) Oil price risk in the Spanish stock market: an industry perspective. Econ Model 37:280–290
Nandha M, Faff R (2008) Does oil move equity prices? A global view. Energy Econ 30(3):986–997
Narayan PK, Narayan S (2010) Modelling the impact of oil prices on Vietnam's stock prices. Appl Energy 87(1):356–361
Narayan PK, Sharma SS (2011) New evidence on oil price and firm returns. J Bank Financ 35 (12):3253–3262
Ordu BM, Soytaş U (2016) The relationship between energy commodity prices and electricity and market index performances: evidence from an emerging market. Emerg Mark Financ Trade 52 (9):2149–2164
Park J, Ratti RA (2008) Oil price shocks and stock markets in the US and 13 European countries. Energy Econ 30(5):2587–2608
Peng C, Zhu H, Jia X, You W (2017) Stock price synchronicity to oil shocks across quantiles: evidence from Chinese oil firms. Econ Model 61:248–259
Pierce JL, Enzler JJ, Fand DI, Gordon RJ (1974) The effects of external inflationary shocks. Brook Pap Econ Act 1974(1):13–61
Ramos SB, Veiga H (2013) Oil price asymmetric effects: answering the puzzle in international stock markets. Energy Econ 38:136–145
Reboredo JC, Rivera-Castro MA, Ugolini A (2017) Wavelet-based test of comovement and causality between oil and renewable energy stock prices. Energy Econ 61:241–252
Sadorsky P (1999) Oil price shocks and stock market activity. Energy Econ 21(5):449–469

Sadorsky P (2001) Risk factors in stock returns of Canadian oil and gas companies. Energy Econ 23 (1):17–28
Sari R, Soytas U (2006) The relationship between stock returns, crude oil prices, interest rates, and output: evidence from a developing economy. Empir Econ Lett 5(4):205–220
Silvapulle P, Smyth R, Zhang X, Fenech JP (2017) Nonparametric panel data model for crude oil and stock market prices in net oil importing countries. Energy Econ 67:255–267
Smyth R, Narayan PK (2018) What do we know about oil prices and stock returns? Int Rev Financ Anal 57:148–156
Soytas U, Oran A (2011) Volatility spillover from world oil spot markets to aggregate and electricity stock index returns in Turkey. Appl Energy 88(1):354–360
Tang W, Wu L, Zhang Z (2010) Oil price shocks and their short-and long-term effects on the Chinese economy. Energy Econ 32:S3–S14
Wang Y, Wu C, Yang L (2013) Oil price shocks and stock market activities: evidence from oil-importing and oil-exporting countries. J Comp Econ 41(4):1220–1239
Xu B (2015) Oil prices and UK industry-level stock returns. Appl Econ 47(25):2608–2627
Zhu HM, Li R, Li S (2014) Modelling dynamic dependence between crude oil prices and Asia-Pacific stock market returns. Int Rev Econ Financ 29:208–223
Zhu H, Guo Y, You W, Xu Y (2016) The heterogeneity dependence between crude oil price changes and industry stock market returns in China: evidence from a quantile regression approach. Energy Econ 55:30–41

Baris Kocaarslan received his bachelor's degree in Aircraft Electrical and Electronics from Erciyes University in 2007. He worked as a research assistant in the Department of Business Administration, Middle East Technical University (METU) between 2011 and 2018. He received his MBA degree in 2013 and his PhD degree in 2018, both from the Department of Business Administration of Middle East Technical University (METU). *Journal of Commodity Markets*, *Energy Economics*, *Energy Reports*, *Emerging Markets Finance and Trade*, and *International Review of Finance* are some journals in which his studies are published. His research interests include financial markets, asset pricing, financial econometrics, quantitative methods, energy economics, environmental economics and finance.

Panel Data Analysis

Hasan Huseyin Yıldırım

Panel Data Analysis

Econometric data are defined as cross-sectional (unstructured/undated), time series (dated—regular frequency), and mixed (panel) data (Gujarati and Porter 2012: 22). Cross-sectional data are data used to show changes of any variable in a fixed time period according to different units (Tatoğlu 2012: 2). Time series, however, are series that show changes in values of variables collected according to their frequency values over a series of time intervals (year, month, week, day, hour, etc.) (Orhunbilge 1999: 2). In contrast to the two data types above, panel data contain both the *horizontal* and *vertical* (time) dimensions of the data together. Panel data are both space-dimensional and time-dimensional data (Gujarati 2016: 406). Therefore, researchers who wish to examine changes of a group (of each observation value in a cross section) over time with econometric tests frequently require panel data analysis. By using panel data methods, more reliable and positive results can be obtained.

Panel data are defined with different names according to the type of data. If each unit is observed over all periods, this is known as a balanced panel, whereas if data for some units at certain periods are missing or lost, this is known as an unbalanced panel. In other words, if the unit dealt with in the panel data set is equal to the same number of observations, it is called a balanced panel, whereas if it is not equal, it is called an unbalanced panel (Tatoğlu 2012: 5). Another distinction made in panel data is that if the cross section of the panel data set is greater than the time dimension, it is known as a short panel, while if the opposite is the case, it is known as a long panel.

H. H. Yıldırım (✉)
Balikesir University, Balikesir, Turkey
e-mail: hhyildirim@balikesir.edu.tr

B. Adıgüzel Mercangöz (ed.), *Handbook of Research on Emerging Theories, Models, and Applications of Financial Econometrics*,
https://doi.org/10.1007/978-3-030-54108-8_16

Since time and units are dealt with together when using panel data models, a wider number of observations can be worked with. This situation raises the degree of freedom and increases the strength and reliability of the tests conducted. Moreover, in cases where time series are used separately, the problem of multicollinearity that may occur can be solved with panel data. Results of models estimated with cross-sectional or time series data may be biased. In this case, the heterogeneity of units cannot be checked (Tatoğlu 2017: 2), whereas in panel data models, since both cross-sectional and time series data can be examined together, the heterogeneity of units can be checked. However, in addition to the benefits and convenience of panel data models, a number of difficulties and weaknesses also exist. The most important of the problems encountered in panel data models are data collection and data location. In cases where data cannot be fully obtained, certain changes in the research may become necessary. When the unit dimension in panel data models is longer than the time dimension, problems related to the degree of freedom and asymptotic estimation may arise.

The regression relationship between the Y and X variables based on the panel data set can be expressed as follows:

$$Y_{it} = \beta_0 + \beta_1 X_{it} + u_{it} \quad i = 1, 2, \ldots, N \quad t = 1, 2, \ldots, T \tag{1}$$

When the variables are expressed, the index i for the cross section and the index t for the time series are mostly used. In panel data, however, since changes are shown according to both unit and time, a double index is used. On an Excel page, a sequence is shown first according to units of cross-sectional observations (i), and then according to the time variable (t). An example of a panel data set is shown in Table 1.

In panel data models, the time-constant variables that reflect the characteristic of each unit are called *unit effects*, and the unit-constant variables that reflect the characteristic of each time are called *time effects*.

If there is a correlation between the error term and the independent variables in the model, this is a case of *endogeneity*, whereas if there is no correlation in the same period, this is called *weak exogeneity*, and if no correlation exists with past/future values, this is a case of *strict exogeneity*. Endogeneity mainly occurs when variables excluded from the model, measurement error, dynamic models, and simultaneous models are worked with. Correlation between units indicates that there is a correlation between the error terms of the units.

For conducting panel data studies, software programs such as EViews, Stata, SAS, and PcGive are used.

Estimation Methods in Panel Data Analysis (Fixed Effects and Random Effects)

In panel regression estimation, there are two important estimation approaches, namely *fixed effects* and *random effects* (Lopez 2015: 15–16). Choosing between fixed effects and random effects constitutes an important problem in panel regression

Table 1 Arrangement of a panel data set in an excel worksheet

i	t	Y_{it}	X_{it}	...	Z_{it}
1	2015	$Y_{1\ 2015}$	$X_{1\ 2015}$	...	$Z_{1\ 2015}$
1	2016	$Y_{1\ 2016}$	$X_{1\ 2016}$	...	$Z_{1\ 2016}$
1	2017	$Y_{1\ 2017}$	$X_{1\ 2017}$	...	$Z_{1\ 2017}$
1	2018	$Y_{1\ 2018}$	$X_{1\ 2018}$	...	$Z_{1\ 2018}$
1	2019	$Y_{1\ 2019}$	$X_{1\ 2019}$	...	$Z_{1\ 2019}$
2	2015	$Y_{2\ 2015}$	$X_{2\ 2015}$	...	$Z_{2\ 2015}$
2	2016	$Y_{2\ 2016}$	$X_{2\ 2016}$	...	$Z_{2\ 2016}$
2	2017	$Y_{2\ 2017}$	$X_{2\ 2017}$	...	$Z_{2\ 2017}$
2	2018	$Y_{2\ 2018}$	$X_{2\ 2018}$	...	$Z_{2\ 2018}$
2	2019	$Y_{2\ 2019}$	$X_{2\ 2019}$	...	$Z_{2\ 2019}$
.	.	.	.	...	.
.	.	.	.	...	.
.	.	.	.	...	.
N	2015	$Y_{N\ 2015}$	$X_{N\ 2015}$	...	$Z_{N\ 2015}$
N	2016	$Y_{N\ 2016}$	$X_{N\ 2016}$	...	$Z_{N\ 2016}$
N	2017	$Y_{N\ 2017}$	$X_{N\ 2017}$	...	$Z_{N\ 2017}$
N	2018	$Y_{N\ 2018}$	$X_{N\ 2018}$	...	$Z_{N\ 2018}$
N	2019	$Y_{N\ 2019}$	$X_{N\ 2019}$	...	$Z_{N\ 2019}$

Source: Author's creation

estimation. When using panel data models, the presence of unobservable unit-specific effects may occur for each unit. If the effects are treated as a random variable such as error term, this is a case of *random effects*, whereas if each cross section is treated as a parameter estimated for observation, then *fixed effects* are in question. If the cross-sectional units are selected randomly from a large universe, then it will be logical to consider a random effects approach, whereas if the units make up the whole universe, then a fixed effects approach will be more reasonable. To the fixed effects and random effects approaches, which are panel data estimation methods, can be added the *pooled ordinary least squares model* (*pooled OLS model*). In the estimation of a pooled panel model, cross-sectional and time series characteristics are not taken into consideration.

Hausman Test

It is necessary to determine whether the fixed effects or random effects approach is more suitable for models. At this point, the Hausman (1978) test statistic is utilized to determine selection of the suitable model. One of the most important differences between the fixed and random effects models is whether or not the unit effects are correlated with the independent variables. If there is no correlation between them, the random effects model is more suitable. The hypotheses of the Hausman test statistic are as follows:

Null Hypothesis	=> H_0:	Random effects model is more suitable
Alternative hypothesis	=> H_1:	Fixed effects model is more suitable

When calculating the Hausman test statistic, the H statistic (H) is calculated by utilizing the difference between the variance–covariance matrices of the generalized least squares estimator and the estimator for the group. The Hausman test tests whether this difference is equal to zero. The test statistic is as follows:

$$H = \left(\widehat{\beta}_{\mathrm{SE}} - \widehat{\beta}_{\mathrm{TE}}\right)' \left[A\ \mathrm{var}\left(\widehat{\beta}_{\mathrm{SE}}\right) - A\ \mathrm{var}\left(\widehat{\beta}_{\mathrm{TE}}\right)\right]^{-1} \left(\widehat{\beta}_{\mathrm{SE}} - \widehat{\beta}_{\mathrm{TE}}\right) \tag{2}$$

The SE subindex in this equation shows the estimators of the fixed effects model, while the TE subindex indicates the estimators of the random effects model. $A\ \mathrm{var}\widehat{\beta}_{\mathrm{SE}}$ and $A\ \mathrm{var}\widehat{\beta}_{\mathrm{TE}}$ express the asymptotic variance–covariance matrices obtained in the estimation of the fixed and random effects models, respectively. The asymptotic variance–covariance matrices and the difference between them are as follows:

$$A\ \mathrm{var}\widehat{\beta}_{\mathrm{SE}} = \frac{\sigma_u^2\left[E\left(\ddot{X}_i'\ddot{X}_i\right)\right]^{-1}}{N} \tag{3}$$

$$A\ \mathrm{var}\widehat{\beta}_{\mathrm{TE}} = \frac{\sigma_u^2\left[E\left(\check{X}_i{}'\check{X}_i\right)\right]^{-1}}{N} \tag{4}$$

$$\ddot{X} = X_{it} - \overline{X}_i \text{ ve } \check{X} = X_{it} - \theta\overline{X}_i \tag{5}$$

$$E\left(\check{X}_i{}'\check{X}_i\right) - E\left(\ddot{X}_i'\ddot{X}_i\right) = E\left[X_i'(I_T - \theta P_T)X_i\right] - E\left[X_i'(I_T - P_T)X_i\right] \tag{6}$$

$$= (1-\theta)\, E\left[X_i'P_TX_i\right] \tag{7}$$

$$= (1-\theta)\, E\left[\overline{X}_i'\overline{X}_i\right] \tag{8}$$

The H statistic is distributed asymptotically as x^2 with degrees of freedom equal to the number of parameters in $\widehat{\beta}_{\mathrm{SE}}$ and $\widehat{\beta}_{\mathrm{TE}}$. The Hausman test is applied for models created with the random effects approach.

Wald Test

The *Wald test* is used to determine whether the fixed effects approach or pooled panel approach is more suitable for panel regression estimation. The equation for the Wald test statistic is as follows:

$$W = \left(R\widehat{\beta} - r\right)'\left(R\widehat{V}R'\right)^{-1}\left(R\widehat{\beta} - r\right) \tag{9}$$

Here, $\widehat{V}$ is the asymptotic variance matrix of β. This test statistic is distributed as X^2 with $Q(N\text{-}K)$ degrees of freedom. The hypotheses of the Wald test statistic are:

Null Hypothesis	=>	H_0:	Pooled panel approach is more suitable.
Alternative hypothesis	=>	H_1:	Fixed effects approach is more suitable.

Cross-Sectional Dependence for Panel Data

Cross-sectional independence is expected to be realized in panel data models for the reliability of the estimates. Cross-sectional independence is tested for the independence of the error term. The main purpose of testing horizontal section independence in panel data models is to determine whether all units are equally affected by a series shock when the series is shocked. Friedman (1937) Test, Breusch Pagan Lagrange Multiplier (LM) Test (1980) and Pesaran CD (2004) Test are used to test Cross-sectional independence (Un 2018: 88). If the panel data set is a long panel ($T > N$), BP-LM test is suitable. If the data set is a short panel ($T < N$), the CD test is suitable.

It is commonly assumed that disturbances in panel data models are cross-sectionally independent, especially when the cross-section dimension (N) is large. There is, however, considerable evidence that cross-sectional dependence is often present in panel regression settings. Ignoring cross-sectional dependence in estimation can have serious consequences, with unaccounted for residual dependence resulting in estimator efficiency loss and invalid test statistics (IHS 2015: 872).

Cross-sectional dependence test hypotheses are as follows:

H_0: There is no cross-sectional dependence for panel data.
H_1: There is cross-sectional dependence for panel data.

The panel equation must be created before the test of cross-section dependency. After creating the equation, we click on View/Residual Diagnostics/Cross-section Dependence Test.

If the Prob. values of the LM and CD tests are less than 5% as a result of the tests, the H_0 hypothesis is rejected. H_1 hypothesis is accepted. In other words, if the Prob.

value is less than 5%, there is a cross-section dependency. Prob. value is requested to be greater than 5% in the analysis results. Cross-sectional dependence is not desired in panel data models.

Panel Unit Root Tests

A panel data set contains both cross-sectional (unit values/observations) and time series values. Since the time dimension is included in the panel data set, it is necessary to examine whether or not the series is stationary over time. If the variance and means of the series are time independent and covariance also occurs based on the difference between times, then the series can be said to be stationary. Stationary series are series that do not contain unit roots. As in time series analyses, in panel data analyses, too, it is desirable that series should be stationary. If econometric analyses are made with series that are non-stationary (containing unit roots), the problem of spurious regression arises (Sevüktekin and Nargeleçekenler 2010). Accordingly, the unit root weakens the reliability and validity of the analysis results obtained. In other words, the t, F and R^2 values obtained produce biased results. For this reason, the assessment regarding the data that primarily needs to be made by researchers wishing to work with panel data sets is to determine whether or not there is stationarity (Sarıkovanlık et al. 2019: 185).

Since panel data unit root tests contain both unit and time dimensions, the data have asymptotic characteristics (Şak 2018: 261).

Tests developed to determine whether or not panel data are stationary over time are shown in Fig. 1. In classification of panel unit root tests, the question of whether or not there is a correlation between units is examined. For panel data, the existence of correlation between units affects the asymptotic characteristics of the tests. The first-generation unit root tests were developed for cases where there is no correlation between units. For situations where there is a correlation between units and cross-sectional dependence, however, the second-generation unit root tests were developed. Unit root tests with structural breaks were propounded in the study by Perron, with the main finding that in cases where there is a structural break, unit root tests produce results in favor of accepting the unit root hypothesis.

Levin, Lin, and Chu Panel Unit Root Test

The Levin, Lin, and Chu panel unit root test is based on the t test, and was developed to analyze the effect of a deterministic trend in balanced panel data sets only. The Levin, Lin, and Chu panel unit root test was developed in 1992. In 1993, the unit root analyses were generalized according to heteroscedasticity and autocorrelation, and with the additions they made in 2002, they completed the missing parts of the test they had developed for panel unit roots.

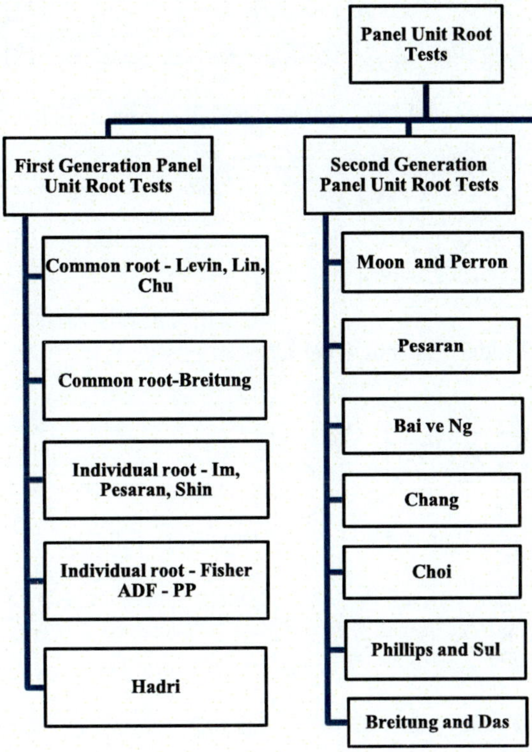

Fig. 1 Classification of panel unit root tests. Source: Sarıkovanlık et al. (2019: 186)

The Levin, Lin, and Chu panel unit root test hypotheses are as follows:

H_0: There is a unit root in the series. The series is not stationary. (H0: $\rho_i = \rho = 1$)
H_1: There is no unit root in the series. The series is stationary. (H1: $\rho_i = \rho < 1$)

The Levin, Lin, and Chu panel unit root test H_0 hypothesis includes the proposition that the panel data set contains a unit root. If the data set contains a unit root, however, the series must be stationarized. For this purpose, the series can be stationarized with a number of transformations (taking the difference, logarithmic transformations, etc.). Since the results of tests performed without stationarization will be inaccurate, this can cause the researcher to reach the wrong conclusions (Sarıkovanlık et al. 2019: 187).

The procedure of the Levin, Lin, and Chu panel unit root test is as specified in the 3 models below:

$$\text{Model 1}: \quad \Delta Y_{it} = \rho Y_{i,t-1} + \varepsilon_{it} \tag{10}$$

$$\text{Model 2}: \Delta Y_{it} = \alpha_{0i} + \rho Y_{i,t-1} + \varepsilon_{it} \tag{11}$$

$$\text{Model 3}: \Delta Y_{it} = \alpha_{0i} + \alpha_{1i}t + \rho Y_{i,t-1} + \varepsilon_{it} \tag{12}$$

The autoregressive parameter ρ in Model 1 is calculated with the formula below:

$$\widehat{\rho} = \frac{\sum_{i=1}^{N} \sum_{t=1}^{T} Y_{it} Y_{it-1}}{\sum_{i=1}^{N} \sum_{t=1}^{T} Y_{it-1}^{2}} \tag{13}$$

The t test statistic formula of Model 1 is shown below:

$$t_p = \left[\sum_{i=1}^{N} \sum_{t=1}^{T} Y_{it-1}^{2} \right]^{1/2} \frac{(\widehat{\rho} - 1)}{\widehat{\sigma}} \tag{14}$$

The standard error ($\widehat{\sigma}$) of the panel data regression is calculated as follows:

$$\widehat{\sigma} = \left[\frac{1}{NT} \sum_{i=1}^{N} \sum_{t=1}^{T} (Y_{it} - \widehat{\rho} Y_{it-1})^2 \right]^{1/2} \tag{15}$$

In the analysis results, when T and N tend to $\rightarrow\infty$, unit root estimations with normal distribution can be obtained.

Breitung Unit Root Test

Used with balanced panel data, the Breitung (2000) unit root test determines stationarity for the data set by utilizing the following regression equation that has a clustering and deterministic trend:

$$Y_{it} = \mu_i + \beta_i t + X_{it} \quad t = 1, \ldots, T \tag{16}$$

The X_{it} in the above panel data regression Eq. (16) has an autoregressive function. The expansion of X_{it} is like this:

$$X_{it} = \sum_{k=1}^{p+1} \alpha_{ik} X_{i,t-k} + \varepsilon_{it} \tag{17}$$

The hypotheses of the Breitung panel unit root test are as follows:

H_0: There is a unit root in the series. The series is not stationary. $\left(H_0\colon \rho_i \equiv \sum_{k=1}^{p+1} \alpha_{ik} = 0\right)$

H_1: There is no unit root in the series. The series is stationary. $\left(H_1\colon \rho_i \equiv \sum_{k=1}^{p+1} \alpha_{ik} < 0\right)$

Im, Pesaran, and Shin Panel Unit Root Test

In the Im et al. (IPS) (1997) unit root test, in which a balanced panel data condition is not sought, there should be no gaps in the time series for the units. The simplest model of the IPS unit root test is shown below:

$$\Delta Y_{it} = (\rho_i - 1)Y_{i,t-1} + \mu_{it} \tag{18}$$

The hypotheses of the IPS unit root test are as follows:

H_0: There is a unit root in the series. The series is not stationary. $(H_0\colon \rho_i = 1)$
H_1: There is no unit root in the series. The series is stationary. $(H_1\colon \rho_i < 1)$

Fisher-ADF & Phillips Perron (PP) Unit Root Tests

In the Fisher-ADF and PP tests, the condition for the panel data set to be a balanced panel is not sought. Moreover, there can also be gaps in the time series for the units. The Fisher-ADF and PP tests for the panel data set are the application of the ADF and PP unit root tests undertaken for the time series for each unit. The regression model applied for the Fisher-ADF and PP unit root tests for the panel data set is as follows:

$$Y_{it} = d_{it} + X_{it} \; (i = 1, \ldots, N; t = 1, \ldots, T) \tag{19}$$

$$d_{it} = \beta_{i0} + \beta_{i1}t + \ldots + \beta_{im_i}t^{m_i} \tag{20}$$

$$X_{it} = \alpha_i X_{it-1} + \mu_{it} \tag{21}$$

The hypotheses of the Fisher-ADF and PP unit root tests are as follows:

H_0: There is a unit root in the series. The series is not stationary. $(H_0\colon \rho_i = 0)$
H_1: There is no unit root in the series. The series is stationary. $(H_1\colon |\rho_i| < 0)$

Hadri Unit Root Test

The Hadri unit root test applied to a balanced panel data set assumes that the error terms are normally distributed. In contrast to the other panel unit root tests, the Hadri (2000) test tests the H_0 hypothesis which is stationary against a non-stationary alternative.

$$\text{Model 1 (Fixed effects)} : Y_{it} = r_{it} + \varepsilon_{it} \tag{22}$$

$$\text{Model 2 (Fixed effects with trend)} : Y_{it} = r_{it} + \beta_i t + \varepsilon_{it} \tag{23}$$

$$r_{it} = r_{it-1} + \mu_{it} \text{ ve } \mu_{it}\tilde{(}0, \sigma_u^2) \tag{24}$$

The r_{it} in the Eq. (24) corresponds to the random walk and r_{it} and μ_{it} are uncorrelated.

The hypotheses of the Hadri unit root test are as follows:

H_0: There is a unit root in the series. The series is not stationary. (H_0: $\lambda = 0$)
H_1: There is no unit root in the series. The series is stationary. (H_1: $\lambda > 0$)

Panel Cointegration Analysis

As with time series analysis, a cointegration approach is also utilized in panel data series for examining long-term relationships. Financial and economic variables containing unit roots in level values can be correlated over a long period, and cointegration tests are utilized to examine this relationship. A precondition for a panel cointegration test is the variables should not be stationary in the level values, whereas all variables should be stationary in the first difference.

To examine long-term relationships between panel series, the Pedroni (1999), Kao (1999), McCoskey and Kao (1998), Larsson et al. (2001) and Westerlund (2007) tests are used. In the literature, Pedroni (1999) and Kao (1999) analyses are widely used for cointegration analysis.

Pedroni Panel Cointegration Test

The Pedroni (1999) panel cointegration test includes 7 panel cointegration tests, of which 4 are panel tests (within-group tests) and 3 are group tests (between-group tests). According to the 11 outcomes obtained from these 7 tests, a decision is made as to whether or not there is cointegration between the variables. If a situation exists in which there is cointegration in 6 of the 11 outcomes while there is no cointegration in 5 of them, then when making the decision, it is concluded that there is a majority.

The model to be examined with the Pedroni panel cointegration test is designed according to whether or not there is a trend and mean. The equation for a cointegration test in which there is a mean and trend is given below:

$$Y_{it} = \alpha_i + \delta_t t + \beta_{1i} X_{1i,t} + \ldots + \beta_{ki} X_{ki,t} + \varepsilon_{it} \tag{25}$$

The hypotheses of the Pedroni (1999) panel cointegration test are as follows:

H_0: There is no cointegration between variables. (H_0: $\rho_i = 1$)
H_1: There is cointegration between variables. (H_1: $\rho_i < 1$)

The statistics for the 7 panel cointegration tests forming the within-group tests and between-group tests of the Pedroni panel cointegration test are as follows:

- Panel v-statistic:

$$T^2 N^{3/2} Z_{\widehat{v}\,N,T} \equiv T^2 N^{3/2} \left(\sum_{i=1}^{N} \sum_{t=1}^{T} \widehat{L}_{11i}^{-2} \widehat{e}_{i,t-1}^{2} \right)^{-1} \tag{26}$$

- Panel ρ-statistic:

$$T\sqrt{N} Z_{\widehat{\rho},N,T-1} \equiv T\sqrt{N} \left(\sum_{i=1}^{N} \sum_{t=1}^{T} \widehat{L}_{11i}^{-2} \widehat{e}_{i,t-1}^{2} \right)^{-1} \sum_{i=1}^{N} \sum_{t=1}^{T} \widehat{L}_{11i}^{-2} \left(\widehat{e}_{i,t-1} \Delta \widehat{e}_{i,t} - \widehat{\lambda}_i \right) \tag{27}$$

- Panel t-statistic (non-parametric):

$$Z_{t,N,T} \equiv T\sqrt{N} \left(\widetilde{\sigma}_{N,T}^{2} \sum_{i=1}^{N} \sum_{t=1}^{T} \widehat{L}_{11i}^{-2} \widehat{e}_{i,t-1}^{2} \right)^{-1/2} \sum_{i=1}^{N} \sum_{t=1}^{T} \widehat{L}_{11i}^{-2} \left(\widehat{e}_{i,t-1} \Delta \widehat{e}_{i,t} - \widehat{\lambda}_i \right) \tag{28}$$

- Panel t-statistic (parametric):

$$Z_{t,N,T}^{*} \equiv T\sqrt{N} \left(\widetilde{s}_{N,T}^{*2} \sum_{i=1}^{N} \sum_{t=1}^{T} \widehat{L}_{11i}^{-2} \widehat{e}_{i,t-1}^{*2} \right)^{-\frac{1}{2}} \sum_{i=1}^{N} \sum_{t=1}^{T} \widehat{L}_{11i}^{-2} \widehat{e}_{i,t-1}^{*} \Delta \widehat{e}_{i,t}^{*} \tag{29}$$

- Group ρ-statistic:

$$TN^{-\frac{1}{2}}Z_{\widehat{p},N,T-1} \equiv TN^{-\frac{1}{2}}\sum_{i=1}^{N}\left(\sum_{t=1}^{T}\widehat{e}_{i,t-1}^{2}\right)^{-1}\sum_{t=1}^{T}\left(\widehat{e}_{i,t-1}\Delta\widehat{e}_{i,t}-\widehat{\lambda}_i\right) \quad (30)$$

- Group $\widetilde{t}$-statistic (non-parametric):

$$N^{-1/2}Z_{t,N,T} \equiv N^{-1/2}\sum_{i=1}^{N}\left(\widetilde{\sigma}_{N,T}^{2}\sum_{t=1}^{T}\widehat{e}_{i,t-1}^{2}\right)^{-1/2}\sum_{t=1}^{T}\left(\widehat{e}_{i,t-1}\Delta\widehat{e}_{i,t}-\widehat{\lambda}_i\right) \quad (31)$$

- Group $\widetilde{t}$-statistic (parametric):

$$N^{-1/2}Z_{t,N,T}^{*} \equiv N^{-1/2}\sum_{i=1}^{N}\left(\sum_{t=1}^{T}\widehat{s}_{i}^{*2}\,\widehat{e}_{i,t-1}^{*2}\right)^{-\frac{1}{2}}\sum_{t=1}^{T}\widehat{e}_{i,t-1}^{*}\Delta\widehat{e}_{i,t}^{*} \quad (32)$$

Kao Panel Cointegration Test

Based on the Dickey-Fuller (DF) and Augmented Dickey-Fuller (ADF) tests, the Kao (1999) panel cointegration test is a panel cointegration test used to analyze long-term relationships between panel variables. The following model is utilized for the test:

$$Y_{it} = \alpha_i + \beta X_{it} + \varepsilon_{it}\ i = 1,\ldots,N\ t = 1,\ldots,T \quad (33)$$

If the dependent variable Y_{it} and independent variable or variables X_{it} in the equation are not stationary (contain a unit root), incorrect equation results appear. The equation loses reliability and validity, leading to false regression. The hypotheses of the Kao (1999) panel cointegration test are as follows:

H_0: There is no cointegration between variables. (H_0: $\rho = 1$)
H_1: There is cointegration between variables. (H_1: $\rho < 1$)

Johansen Cointegration Test

The basis of the Johansen cointegration method is to reveal the relationship between the matrix sequence and the characteristic roots. The Johansen cointegration test has two main aims. These are to determine the cointegration vector in a maximum number of examined variables and to obtain maximum likelihood estimates of the adjustment speed coefficients. To understand whether or not there was a long-term relationship between the examined variables and to determine the number of cointegration vectors, Johansen (1998) and Johansen and Juselius (1990) used *Trace* and *Maximum Eigenvalue* statistics. Table 2 includes the hypotheses for both tests (Table 3).

Panel Causality

The existence of a relationship between variables in time series is not proof of causality or of the direction of the relationship (Gujarati and Porter 2012: 653). A number of tests have been developed from past to present for determining the existence of correlation among variables. The first studies on causality were conducted by Wiener (1956). A commonly used and popular test was proposed by Granger (1969). As the basis of causality analysis, the direction of the relationship between variables is investigated. With causality tests, information about the strength of the relationship cannot be obtained (Tatoğlu 2017: 153).

As in time series, examination of causality relationships in panel data models is also based on the logic of Granger causality. As Engle and Granger (1987) showed in

Table 2 Equation output created according to pooled panel for Model 1

Dependent variable: *E*1				
Method: Panel least squares				
Sample: 2004–2018				
Periods included: 15				
Cross-sections included: 10				
Total panel (balanced) observations: 150				
Variable	Coefficient	Std. error	*t*-statistic	Prob.
C	0.067536	0.008308	8.128968	0.0000
*A*1	−0.176532	0.026465	−6.670317	0.0000
*A*2	−0.055957	0.007555	−7.406546	0.0000
*M*1	−0.362845	0.046974	−7.724406	0.0000
*M*2	0.055386	0.009290	5.961767	0.0000
*S*1	−0.036855	0.005520	−6.676306	0.0000
R-squared	0.441104	Mean dependent var.		0.018300
Adjusted *R*-squared	0.421698	SD dependent var.		0.010061
SE of regression	0.007651	Akaike info criterion		−6.868704
Sum squared resid.	0.008430	Schwarz criterion		−6.748278
Log likelihood	521.1528	Hannan-Quinn criter.		−6.819779
F-statistic	22.73014	Durbin-Watson stat.		0.988814
Prob(*F*-statistic)	0.000000			

Source: Author's creation

Table 3 Johansen Cointegration test hypotheses

	Tests	
	Trace	Maximum eigenvalue
H_0:	There is at least one cointegration vector.	There is at least one cointegration vector.
H_1:	There is one cointegration vector.	There is one cointegration vector.

Source: Author's creation

their study, if there is a cointegration relationship between variables in values at the same level, the causality relationship is revealed by the Vector Error Correction Model (VECM). If no cointegration relationship exists between variables in values at the same level, however, the causality relationship is established with VAR. In causality analyses to be made for a panel data set, the series should be stationary. The equation of the model to be used for panel causality is shown in (34) below:

$$y_{it} = \alpha_i + \sum_{k=1}^{k} y^{(k)} y_{it-k} + \sum_{k=1}^{k} \beta^{(k)} x_{it-k} + \varepsilon_{it} \tag{34}$$

In Eq. (34), "α_i" expresses the unit-specific effects, while "$y^{(k)}$" and "$\beta^{(k)}$" are also assumed to be the same for all units. Unlike Granger causality tests carried out for time series, causality tests in panel data analyses take the heterogeneity created between units into consideration. Otherwise, the outcomes obtained from the results of the analyses made can be misleading. According to Eq. (34), the basic hypothesis for the panel causality test is set as H_0: $\beta^{(k)} = 0$, and states that there is no causality from X to Y.

Application Example

In this section, the aim is to determine the relationships of the financial ratios of 10 banks trading on the Istanbul Stock Exchange (BIST) with their Return on Assets ($E1$) over the period 2004–2018. As financial ratios in the analysis, the ratios of "Non-Performing Loans to Total Assets" ($A1$) and "Total Credits to Total Assets" ($A2$) to measure asset quality; "Operating Costs to Total Assets" ($M1$) and "Total Deposits to Total Assets" ($M2$) to measure management quality; and "Foreign Currency Assets to Foreign Currency Liabilities" ($S1$) to measure sensitivity to market risks were used as variables.

After the panel data set has been made ready, the panel data type must be specified. Firstly, it is necessary to ascertain whether or not any variable in the data set is significant for data analysis by determining the variables in the model to be created.

$$\textbf{Model 1}: E1 = C(1) + C(2) \times A1 + C(3) \times A2 + C(4) \times M1 + C(5) \times M2 + C(6) \times S1$$

In the created Model 1, return on assets is specified as the dependent variable, while $A1, A2, M1, M2$, and $S1$ are determined as the independent variables. Following the *Quick/Estimate Equation* steps, after the dependent variable of the equation, $E1$, has been typed, the constant term C and then the independent variables with the abbreviations $A1$, $A2$, $M1$, $M2$, and $S1$ are selected, respectively. While the panel data equation is being created, it is necessary to specify the type of effect below the panel option. The selection of pooled panel data is completed by selecting the *None* option as the effect type.

Equation results for Model 1 are shown in Table 2. In the equation obtained according to the pooled panel model, it is seen that there is a statistically significant effect of all independent variables on the dependent variable, $E1$ (Prob. values of variables $A1$, $A2$, $M1$, $M2$, and $S1$ are less than 0.05). After the significance of an independent variable has been determined, it is necessary to ascertain whether the fixed effects or the random effects model is the more suitable model.

Determination of Fixed Effects or Random Effects

To determine the existence of a random effect for Model 1, following the *Quick/Estimate Equation* steps, after the dependent variable of the equation, E1, has been typed, the constant term C and then the independent variables with the abbreviations $A1$, $A2$, $M1$, $M2$, and $S1$ are selected, respectively. Next, by entering the *Panel Options* section, in the *cross-section* part in *Effects specification*, the "*Random*" option is selected.

The equation output created according to random effects for Model 1 is shown in Table 4. When the table is examined, it is seen that the Prob-values of the independent variables are less than 0.05. This situation indicates that the independent variables, $A1, A2, M1, M2$, and $S1$ have a statistically significant effect on the dependent variable, $E1$.

In determining the choice of a suitable model for Model 1, the *Hausman* (1978) test statistic is utilized. The *Hausman test* is applied for regression equations created on random effects. The Hausman test is used for determining whether the fixed effects or random effects approach is more suitable in panel regression estimation. The estimation output created according to random effects is carried out by following the *View/Fixed-Random Effects Testing/Correlated Random Effects-Hausman Test* steps.

Table 4 Equation output created according to random effects for Model 1

Dependent variable: *E*1				
Method: Panel EGLS (cross-section random effects)				
Sample: 2004–2018				
Periods included: 15				
Cross-sections included: 10				
Total panel (balanced) observations: 150				
Swamy and Arora estimator of component variances				
Variable	Coefficient	Std. error	*t*-statistic	Prob.
C	0.067495	0.008146	8.286154	0.0000
*A*1	−0.176494	0.025878	−6.820166	0.0000
*A*2	−0.055988	0.007392	−7.573956	0.0000
*M*1	−0.363088	0.045951	−7.901653	0.0000
*M*2	0.055488	0.009102	6.096063	0.0000
*S*1	−0.036856	0.005408	−6.814794	0.0000
	Effects specification			
			S.D.	Rho
Cross-section random			0.000211	0.0008
Idiosyncratic random			0.007472	0.9992
	Weighted statistics			
R-squared	0.440563	Mean dependent var.		0.018191
Adjusted *R*-squared	0.421138	S.D. dependent var.		0.010052
S.E. of regression	0.007648	Sum squared resid.		0.008423
F-statistic	22.68030	Durbin-Watson stat.		0.989578
Prob (*F*-statistic)	0.000000			
	Unweighted statistics			
R-squared	0.441103	Mean dependent var.		0.018300
Sum squared resid.	0.008430	Durbin-Watson stat.		0.988758

Source: Author's creation

The hypotheses of the Hausman test statistic are as follows:

Null Hypothesis => H_0: Random effects model is more suitable
Alternative hypothesis => H_1: Fixed effects model is more suitable

For evaluating the Hausman test result in Table 5, the Prob-value in the cross-section random row is examined. If the Prob-value is less than 0.05, the H_0 hypothesis, defined as the null hypothesis, is rejected. The H_1 hypothesis, which is the alternative hypothesis to this, is accepted. If the Prob-value is greater than 0.05, the H_0 hypothesis, defined as the null hypothesis, is not rejected (is accepted). That is, the H_1 hypothesis, which is the alternative hypothesis, is rejected.

In Table 5, it is seen that the H_0 hypothesis is rejected for Model 1 (Prob.: $0.0369 < 0.05$). In other words, the fixed effects approach is suitable for Model 1.

To determine the existence of a fixed effect for Model 1, following the *Quick/Estimate Equation* steps, after the dependent variable of the equation, *E*1, has been

Table 5 Hausman test result for Model 1

Correlated random effects—Hausman test			
Equation: EQ01			
Test: Cross-section random effects			
Test summary	Chi-Sq. statistic	Chi-Sq. d.f.	Prob.
Cross-section random	11.852418	5	0.0369

Source: Author's creation

typed, the constant term C and then the independent variables with the abbreviations $A1$, $A2$, $M1$, $M2$, and $S1$ are selected, respectively. Next, by entering the *Panel Options* section, in the *cross-section* part in *Effects specification*, the "*Fixed*" option is selected.

The equation output created according to fixed effects is included in Table 6. According to the fixed effects result, it is determined that all of the independent variables, $A1, A2, M1, M2$, and $S1$, respectively, have a statistically significant effect on the dependent variable, $E1$ (Prob. < 0.05). It is established that the increase in the $M2$ variable has a positive effect on $E1$, while the increase in the $A1, A2, M1$, and $S1$ variables has a negative impact on $E1$.

Testing for Stationarity (Unit Root Tests)

A unit root test is applied separately for each variable. In the application example, the $E1$ variable will be tested as to whether it is stationary or not. Firstly, after the file of the $E1$ variable has been opened, the View/Unit Root Test steps are followed. For the unit root test, moreover, the screen in which the unit root test is to be applied can be accessed by following the Quick/Series Statistics/Unit Root Test steps included on the main EViews study screen.

For establishing whether or not the $E1$ variable contains unit roots, the optimal lag value suitable for the data is selected automatically by the *lag length* program on the test screen. In the tests to be conducted for types of unit root test, summary evaluation tests that include the ideal unit root tests can be obtained by selecting the "*Summary*" option. In other words, instead of separately applying tests that include the test types, the *Summary* option can be selected for an overall summary representation. For summary representation of the $E1$ variable, the results of the Levin, Lin & Chu t*, IPS, Fisher-ADF, and PP tests, made by selecting the *Summary* option for the test type, are shown all together in Table 7.

In Table 7, the results of 4 different unit root tests of the $E1$ variable are shown. Among these tests, the results of the Levin, Lin, and Chu t* test are the main reference. Furthermore, a majority finding obtained from the results of these four tests is accepted for evaluation of stationarity. According to the results of Levin, Lin, and Chu's unit root test, the H_0 hypothesis is rejected (since the Prob. value 0.0001 < 0.05). According to the Levin, Lin, and Chu unit root test results, the $E1$

Table 6 Equation output created according to fixed effects for Model 1

Dependent variable: *E*1				
Method: Panel least squares				
Sample: 2004–2018				
Periods included: 15				
Cross-sections included: 10				
Total panel (balanced) observations: 150				
Variable	Coefficient	Std. error	*t*-statistic	Prob.
C	0.038993	0.016373	2.381625	0.0186
*A*1	−0.165078	0.030216	−5.463190	0.0000
*A*2	−0.052845	0.010026	−5.270865	0.0000
*M*1	−0.426948	0.057700	−7.399417	0.0000
*M*2	0.088441	0.016214	5.454652	0.0000
*S*1	−0.029146	0.009353	−3.116088	0.0022
	Effects specification			
Cross-section fixed (dummy variables)				
R-squared	0.500250	Mean dependent var.		0.018300
Adjusted *R*-squared	0.448424	S.D. dependent var.		0.010061
S.E. of regression	0.007472	Akaike info criterion		−6.860559
Sum squared resid.	0.007538	Schwarz criterion		−6.559495
Log likelihood	529.5419	Hannan-Quinn criter.		−6.738246
F-statistic	9.652489	Durbin-Watson stat.		1.101823
Prob(*F*-statistic)	0.000000			

Source: Author's creation

variable is stationary. However, according to the results of the Im, Pesaran, and Shin, Fisher-ADF and PP tests, the *E*1 variable does not contain a unit root and is non-stationary (Prob. > 0.05).

By performing a number of data transformation operations on non-stationary time series and panel data series, series can be stationarized. For stationarity of the *E*1 variable, the stationarity of the series is tested by taking the first differences. The unit root test must be repeated with the *Summary* option for the test type.

Examining Table 8, since the Prob-values of the Levin, Lin, and Chu, IPS, Fisher-ADF, and PP tests are below 0.05, the H_0 hypothesis is rejected and the H_1 hypothesis is accepted. In other words, when the first difference of the *E*1 variable is taken, the variable has been stationarized in all of the 4 test statistics and at the first difference, the E1 variable does not contain a unit root.

Cointegration Tests

For the panel cointegration tests, cointegration analysis of the data for "Return on Assets" (*E*1) and "Total Deposits/Total Assets (*M*2) was conducted to determine

Table 7 Results of unit root test for *E*1 variable (I0 Level)

Panel unit root test: Summary				
Series: *E*1				
Sample: 2004–2018				
Exogenous variables: Individual effects				
Automatic selection of maximum lags				
Automatic lag length selection based on SIC: 0–2				
Newey-west automatic bandwidth selection and Bartlett kernel				
Method	Statistic	Prob.[a]	Cross-Sections	Obs
Null: Unit root (assumes common unit root process)				
Levin, Lin & Chu t*	−3.63551	0.0001	10	134
Null: Unit root (assumes individual unit root process)				
Im, Pesaran, and shin W-stat.	−1.47620	0.0699	10	134
ADF—Fisher chi-square	31.3189	0.0511	10	134
PP—Fisher chi-square	30.1040	0.0682	10	140

Source: Author's creation
[a]Probabilities for fisher tests are computed using an asymptotic chi-square distribution. All other tests assume asymptotic normality

Table 8 Results of unit root test for *E*1 variable (I1—first difference)

Panel unit root test: Summary				
Series: *D*(*E*1)				
Sample: 2004–2018				
Exogenous variables: Individual effects				
Automatic selection of maximum lags				
Automatic lag length selection based on SIC: 0–2				
Newey-west automatic bandwidth selection and Bartlett kernel				
Method	Statistic	Prob.[a]	Cross-Sections	Obs
Null: Unit root (assumes common unit root process)				
Levin, Lin, and Chu t*	−15.8959	0.0000	10	127
Null: Unit root (assumes individual unit root process)				
Im, Pesaran, and shin W-stat.	−12.5979	0.0000	10	127
ADF—Fisher chi-square	139.682	0.0000	10	127
PP—Fisher chi-square	164.267	0.0000	10	130

Source: Author's creation
[a]Probabilities for fisher tests are computed using an asymptotic chi-square distribution. All other tests assume asymptotic normality

whether or not the two variables acted together over a long period, that is to say, whether or not there was a long-term relationship between them. For cointegration analysis, the two variables must not be stationary at their level values and stationarity must be enabled at their first differences.

Table 9 Pedroni (Engle-Granger based) cointegration test results

Pedroni residual cointegration test				
Series: *E*1 *M*2				
Sample: 2004–2018				
Included observations: 150				
Cross-sections included: 10				
Null hypothesis: No cointegration				
Trend assumption: No deterministic trend				
Automatic lag length selection based on SIC with a max. Lag of 2				
Newey-west automatic bandwidth selection and Bartlett kernel				
Alternative hypothesis: Common AR coeffs. (within-dimension)				
			Weighted	
	Statistic	*Prob.*	*Statistic*	*Prob.*
Panel v-statistic	1.049257	0.1470	−0.169184	0.5672
Panel rho-statistic	−1.982041	0.0237	−2.539882	0.0055
Panel PP-statistic	−3.201338	0.0007	−3.780493	0.0001
Panel ADF-statistic	−3.197349	0.0007	−3.781751	0.0001
Alternative hypothesis: Individual AR coeffs. (between-dimension)				
	Statistic	*Prob.*		
Group rho-statistic	−1.941185	0.0261		
Group PP-statistic	−5.371584	0.0000		
Group ADF-statistic	−5.491466	0.0000		

Source: Author's creation

Tables 7 and 8 include the results of stationarity tests for the *E*1 variable at level and first difference, respectively. It was determined that the *E*1 variable was non-stationary at level and stationary at first difference. It was determined that similar results applied to the *M*2 variable following the unit root tests conducted for *M*2. Consequently, it was established that both the *E*1 and the *M*2 variables were non-stationary at level and stationary at first difference.

Following the condition of stationarity at first difference, by following the *Quick/Group Statistics/Johansen Cointegration Test* steps, the *Series List*, in which the series are to be listed, appears. The steps for carrying out the panel cointegration test were begun by typing *E*1 and *M*2 in the box. Accordingly, it was first necessary to select the test type. The *Pedroni panel cointegration test* was chosen as the test type and *fixed* (*individual intercept*) was selected as the deterministic trend. To ensure the optimal lag value as the *lag length*, the automatic option was selected.

Table 9 shows 11 output results of 7 test statistics for the Pedroni cointegration test of the *E*1 and *M*2 variables. Results of weighted statistics for the first 4 tests have been added to the 7 test statistics. According to these 11 results, a majority decision will determine the finding of cointegration. When the Prob-values are examined, it is seen that the Prob-value for 9 tests is less than 0.05. In this case, the H_0 hypothesis, which is the basic hypothesis, is rejected. Consequently, it is concluded that these *E*1 and *M*2 variables acted together over a long period.

Table 10 Granger causality/block exogeneity test results

VEC granger causality/block exogeneity wald tests			
Sample: 2004–2018			
Included observations: 120			
Dependent variable: *D*(*E*1)			
Excluded	Chi-sq	*Df*	Prob.
D(*S*1)	7.737227	2	0.0209
All	7.737227	2	0.0209
Dependent variable: *D*(*S*1)			
Excluded	Chi-sq	*Df*	Prob.
D(*E*1)	0.171212	2	0.9180
All	0.171212	2	0.9180

Source: Author's creation

Causality Tests

Just as causality results can be obtained in the short term with the Wald test, they can be obtained more practically and easily by creating a Vector Error Correction Model (VECM) equation included in the VAR model to be created. For the application of causality, the *E*1 variable and *S*1 variable were dealt with. In causality analysis, an attempt is made to establish which variable is the effecter and which variable is the affected. For this purpose, firstly each of the *E*1 and *S*1 variables was selected in the EViews study file, and the VAR type VECM option was selected for the VAR model to be created. Next, in the obtained equation, the *View/Lag Structure/Granger Causality&Block Exogeneity Test* steps were followed, respectively.

According to the results included in Table 10, the first chi-square probability value (0.0209) was less than 0.05. Accordingly, the H_0 hypothesis was rejected. In this case, a short-term causality from the independent variable *S*1 to the dependent variable *E*1 was determined. The second chi-square probability value (0.9180) was greater than 0.05. Accordingly, the H_0 hypothesis could not be rejected. In this case, a short-term causality from the independent variable *E*1 to the dependent variable *S*1 could not be determined.

References

Breitung J (2000) The local power of some unit root tests for panel data. In: Baltagi BH (ed) Advance in econometrics, volume 15: nonstationary panels, panel Cointegration, and dynamic panels. JAI Press, Amsterdam, pp 161–178

Engle RF, Granger CWJ (1987) Co-integration and error correction: representation, estimation, and testing. Econometrica 55:251–276

Friedman M (1937) The use of ranks to avoid the assumption of normality implicit in the analysis of variance. J Am Stat Assoc 32(200):675–701

Granger CW (1969) Investigating causal relations by econometric models and cross-spectral methods. Econometrica: J Econ Soc 37(3):424–438

Gujarati DN (2016) Örneklerle Ekonometri, Translated by: Doç. Dr. Nasip Bolatoğlu, BB101 Yayınevi, Ankara
Gujarati DN, Porter DC (2012) Temel Ekonometri, translation of fifth edition (Ümit Şenesen, Gülay Günlük Şenesen). Literatür Yayıncılık, İstanbul
Hadri K (2000) Testing for stationarity in heterogeneous panel data. Econ J 3(2):148–161
Hausman JA (1978) Specification test in econometrics. Econometrica 46(6):1251–1271
IHS (2015) EViews 9 user's guide II, isbn:978-1-880411-27-8. IHS Global, Irvine CA
Im SK, Pesaran, MH Shin Y (1997) Testing for unit roots in heterogenous Panels, 1–30
Johansen S (1998) Statistical analysis of Cointegration vectors. J Econ Dyn Control 12:231–254
Johansen S, Juselius K (1990) Maximum likelihood estimation and inference on cointegration-with applications to the demand for money. Oxf Bull Econ Stat 52(2):160–210
Kao C (1999) Spurious regression and residual-based tests for cointegration in panel data. J Econ 90 (1):1–44
Larsson R, Lyhagen J, Löthgren M (2001) Likelihood-based cointegration tests in heterogeneous panels. Econ J 4(1):109–142
Lopez CP (2015) Econometric models with panel data, ISBN-10: 9781507644997 create space independent publishing platform
McCoskey S, Kao C (1998) A residual-based test of the null of cointegration in panel data. Econ Rev 17(1):57–84
Orhunbilge N (1999) Zaman Serileri Analizi Tahmin ve Fiyat İndeksleri. Avcıol Basım Yayın, İstanbul
Pedroni P (1999) Critical values for cointegration tests in heterogeneous panels with multiple regressors. Oxf Bull Econ Stat 61(1):653–670
Pesaran HM (2004) General diagnostic tests for cross-sectional dependence in panels. University of Cambridge, Cambridge Working Papers in Economics, p 435.
Şak N (2018) Panel Birim Kök Testleri. In: Güriş S (ed) Uygulamalı Panel Veri Ekonometrisi. Der Yayınları, İstanbul, pp 261–314
Sarıkovanlık V, Koy A, Akkaya M, Yıldırım HH, Kantar L (2019) Finans Biliminde Ekonometri Uygulamaları. Seçkin Yayıncılık A.Ş, Ankara
Sevüktekin M, Nargeleçekenler M (2010) Ekonometrik Zaman Serileri Analizi Eviews Uygulamalı, Geliştirilmiş 3. Baskı, Nobel Yayın Dağıtım Tic. Ltd. Şti., İstanbul
Tatoğlu FY (2012) Panel Veri Ekonometrisi. Beta Yayıncılık, İstanbul
Tatoğlu FY (2017) Panel Zaman Serileri Analizi (Stata Uygulamalı). Beta Yayıncılık, İstanbul
Un T (2018) Panel Veri Modellerinin Varsayımlarının Testi. In: Güriş S (ed) Uygulamalı Panel Veri Ekonometrisi. Der Yayınları, İstanbul, pp 75–105
Westerlund J (2007) Testing for error correction in panel data. Oxf Bull Econ Stat 69:709–748
Wiener N (1956) The theory of prediction. In: Beckenback EF (ed) Modern mathematics for engineers. McGraw-Hill, New York

Hasan Huseyin Yildirim received his master's degree (2011) in Finance from Marmara University and obtained a PhD degree (2016) from Istanbul University. Mr. Yildirim is an Assistant Professor at the Burhaniye School of Applied Sciences, Balikesir University. His research interests include the Economy, Finance, Banking Sector, and Renewable Energy Investments.

An Amalgamation of Big Data Analytics with Tweet Feeds for Stock Market Trend Anticipating Systems: A Review

Deepika Nalabala, M. Nirupama Bhat, and P. Victer Paul

Introduction

The main conception of Big Data Analytics (BDA) is driven by the effects of new innovations from ground level and with intellect analytic services and rousing technology advancements throughout the most recent couple of decades. The randomly coming out applications of BDA has provoked the consideration of numerous scholarly scientists, business experts, and government associations. It is an innovation motivated environment, where enhanced basic management will assist numerous associations with extracting information from data in an interpretable and suitable structure.

The organization of this research chapter is prearranged as follows. Segment 2 gives a review on Big Data, section "Big Data Analytics" lists the analytics of Big Data proceedings and application space of predicting stock market trend is talked about. A natural language processing and human opinion mining are presented in Section "Sentiment Analysis". In Section "Integrated Model", an integrated model is constructed for the prediction using Sections. "Big Data Analytics" and "Sentiment Analysis". In the next section, the findings of literature survey are discussed. This survey ends with a detailed summary and scope of work.

D. Nalabala (✉) · M. N. Bhat
Department of Computer Science and Engineering, Vignan's Foundation for Science, Technology and Research, Guntur, AP, India
e-mail: drmnb_cse@vignan.ac.in

P. V. Paul
Department of Computer Science and Engineering, Indian Institute of Information Technology Kottayam, Kottayam, Kerala, India

B. Adıgüzel Mercangöz (ed.), *Handbook of Research on Emerging Theories, Models, and Applications of Financial Econometrics*,
https://doi.org/10.1007/978-3-030-54108-8_17

Big Data

Big Data is an integrated approach, which generates the new technologies and architectures and also described to organize, process, analyze the six characteristics namely volume, variety, velocity, veracity, valence, and value to financially extricate an incentive from vast volumes of a wide assortment of data, by empowering the high-speed capture, revelation, and analysis. BDA is utilized to produce activity for conveying insightful decisions, value, measuring performance, and establishing competitive advantages.

Big Data management: Big Data is an evolving term as it provides the enormous information and it has the potential to mine the various forms of huge data can be analyzed for keen choices that lead to better choices and key business moves. These data sets are so voluminous and complex that conventional data handling application software is insufficient to manage them. Current blast of data that is being created is because of three principle reasons:

1. Many applications, for example, mobile sensors, services of social media, and other related gadgets are gathering data ceaselessly.
2. Storage ability has improved so much that gathering data is less expensive than any time in recent memory, making favorable to purchase more space of storage rather than choosing what to erase.
3. Machine Learning and information recovery approaches have achieved a huge improvement in the most recent years, thus enabling the attainment of a higher level of learning from data. Corporations know about these developments. Gaining critical business bits of knowledge by questioning and examining such enormous amounts of data is turning in to a need. This issue is known as Business Intelligence (BI), which refers to decision support systems that combine data gathering, data stockpiling, and knowledge management with analysis to give contribution as input to the decision process. With respect to previous issues, another idea shows up as an increasingly broad field, coordinating data warehousing, Data Mining (DM), and data visualization for Business Analytics. This theme is known as Data Science (Waller and Fawcett 2013). The data management and analytics carried out in regular database frameworks (and other related solutions) cannot address the Big Data challenges: data size is excessively substantial, values are changed quickly, and/or they do no longer satisfy the constraints of Database Management Systems (DBMS). As indicated by this reality, new frameworks have developed to address the past issues: (1) "Not just SQL" (NoSQL) frameworks change the capacity and recovery of key/value pairs for interactive data serving surroundings and (2) systems for extensive scale analytics dependent on the Map Reduce parallel programming model, Hadoop being the most significant usage.

Sources of Data: There are primarily nine sources of Big Data as shown in Fig. 1. Figure 1 presents multiple sources like social media, public web, machine log data, and sensor data, from where the data can be collected and information can be processed.

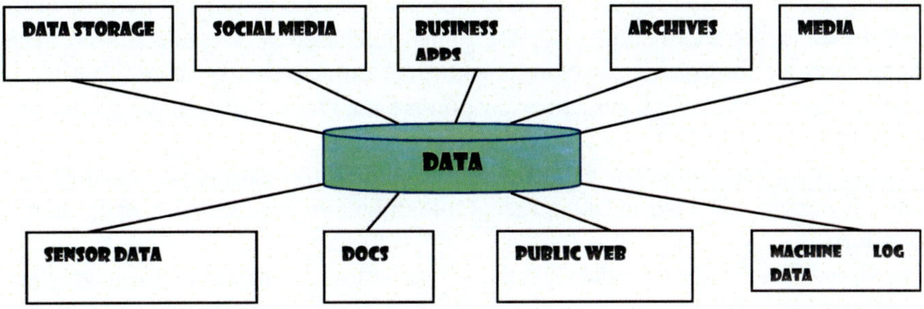

Fig. 1 Sources of data. Source: Author's creation

Kinds of data: Database data, data warehouse data, and transactional data. *Source: Author's Creation.*

Database Data

A database system, also termed as database management system (DBMS), composed of a gathering of connected data, referred as a database, and a deposit of software programs to access and deal with the data via various structuring and storing mechanisms for database and data definitions, respectively; for specification and management of simultaneous, distributed, or shared accessing of data; and for make sure reliability and safety of stored data.

Data Warehouse Data

The data warehouse is the single massive storage, consisting of data collected from various sources and maintained under unified schema as a historical data to provide information with certain operations like cleaning, integration, transformation, loading, and refreshing of periodic data. The data in a data warehouse are prearranged around most important theme to facilitate decision-making. For example, instead of each student details storage six subjects marks for all term examinations, the data warehouse may store a précis of the marks per subject, for every examination or, recapitulate to a higher level, for each subject.

Transactional Data

In a transactional database each one database record illustrates a transaction, such as a purchase made by a buyer, an activity type of any bookings, or a client's web page activity log. A typical transactional operation consists of a unique ID, list of actions performed in the transaction (e.g., the items purchased in the transaction). The supplementary information associated with the transactions like item description, sales person details, and transaction location are maintained as additional tables in transaction database.

Data Representation: The data collected from multiple sources possess different formats of data that need to be converted into unique representation namely digital data format.

Digital data: The digital data is a binary form of data, interpreted from complex structures like audio, video, or text using specific machine language systems usually 0's and 1's or "on" and "off" values. Digital data can be discrete or discontinuous representations of information. It is in contrast to uninterrupted or analog signals which carry in a continuous way, or characterize data using a ceaseless function. All kinds of complex and variety of data can be characterized as advanced information; which is a digital format with aid of binary system. Through a computerized interface, an information capture model along with smaller microchips and larger data stockpiling centers has helped agencies like businesses and government offices to investigate and represent new leading edges of data collection with noteworthy recreations. An example is the translation of a physical scene to a computerized version. Digital data records visual information into a bitmap that stores a specific color property for each bit on an exact and sophisticated grid. By utilizing this direct basic arrangement of data conversion, the computerized digital picture is made.

Different Classes of Data

In addition to foreseen kinds of data, other sorts of data can be seen in numerous applications:

1. Time-related or sequential data (e.g., Historical records, stock trade data).
2. Time-series and biological sequential data.
3. Data streams (e.g., video surveillance and sensor data, which are constantly transmitted).
4. Spatial information (e.g., maps).
5. Building plan data (e.g., the structure of buildings, framework parts, or integrated circuits).
6. Hypertext and multimedia information (including content, picture, video, and sound information).
7. Chart and networked information (e.g., social and data systems).
8. The Web (an enormous, generally disseminated data vault made accessible by the Internet).

From different kinds of generated data knowledge in various dimensions can be mined. Banking data can be mined for shifting patterns, which may assist in the bank employees' arrangement, as indicated by the volume of client traffic. Stock trade data can be mined to reveal patterns that could help in investment strategies (e.g., the best time to buy stock) (Naveen Balaji et al. 2017; Victer Paul et al. 2017; Deepika et al. 2020). We could mine network data streams of a computer to recognize interruptions dependent on the inconsistency of communication streams, which might be found by grouping. The dealings among a deposit of objects which are spatially isolated can be inspected so as to find spatial auto associability among the subsets of objects. By applying text mining on data, for example, consider the literature on data mining from the previous 10 years, we can recognize the development of intriguing issues in the field. By applying mining for the data—customer remarks on items (which are frequently submitted as short instant messages), we can survey purchaser feelings and see how well an item is grasped by a market. We are permitted to mine the pictures and video, and do labeling by applying classification on the multimedia data. For example, with video-data mining of a game hockey, we can discover video sequences relating to goals. Web mining can enable us to find out about the dissemination of data on the WWW in common, describe and arrange website pages, and reveal web-dynamics and the relationships among various substances like social pages, clients, network societies, and online web-supported actions.

Evolution of Big Data

Figure 2 presents the evolution of Big Data in a three-phase format namely data generation and storage, data utilization, data-driven phase. And also the figure explains the management and increase of data volume with respect to time in an exponential manner.

Structured, Semi-structured, and Unstructured Data with Examples

Figure 3 represents the various formats of data and their growth.

Structured data is the data stockpiled in a relational database; data is organized in rows and columns within named tables.

Semi-structured data unlike structured data, it does not have a proper data model but has a clear, self-describing pattern and structure that enable its analysis. Ex: spreadsheets and XML files.

Quasi-structured data consists of textual data with changeable data formats, which are unpredictable, and can be formatted with effort, software tools, and time. Ex: the data about user navigation order through Web Pages.

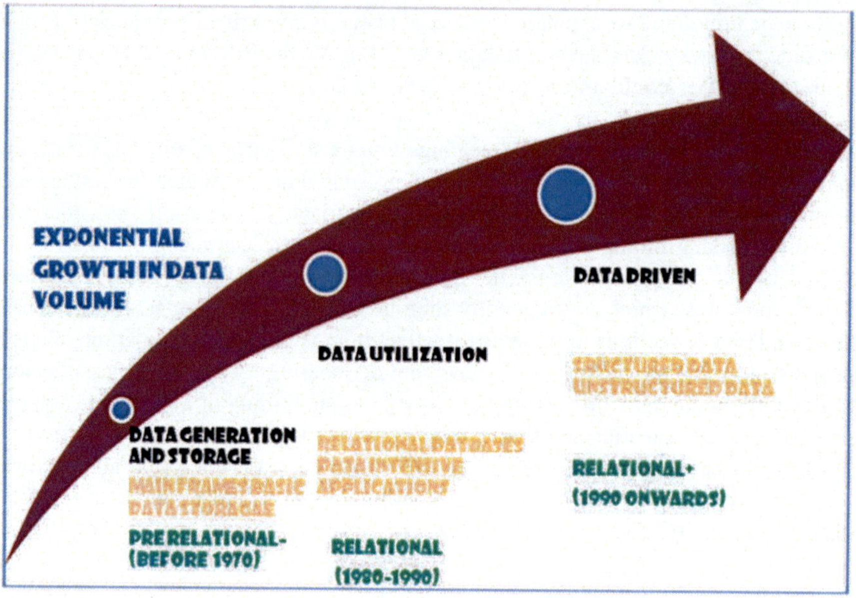

Fig. 2 Evolution of Big Data. Source: Author's creation

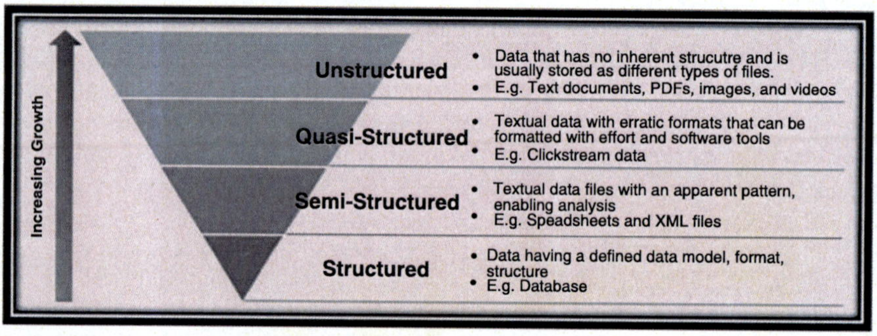

Fig. 3 Formats of data. Source: Author's creation

Unstructured data like semi-structured data it does not have a data model and like quasi structured data, it does not arrange in any format particularly. Ex: e-mails, images, PDF files, presentations, text documents, and videos.

Present days over 90%, of the data generated as nonstructured data (semi-, quasi-, and unstructured).

Characteristics: The characteristics of Big Data can be defined in terms of V's, with respect to support, fast analysis, types of data, quality of data, benefits and insights, variation, and connectivity in data.

.

The characteristics of Big Data Analytics—Seven V's:

(a) Velocity.
(b) Volume.
(c) Value.
(d) Variety.
(e) Veracity.
(f) Variability.
(g) Valence.

(a) Velocity:

It refers to the rapidness of data generation, creation, and analysis at any instance of time. It may consider the posts in social media, emails generated and the billions of texts added per day as comments or as entries, which can be accessed, edited, or written online using any of the electronic gadgets like mobile devices, and tablets. The data collected in this form can be analyzed in real-time using Big Data technology.

(b) Volume:

It refers to the quantity of data formed through online channels such as social media, mobile gadgets and online-based operations. As leaps and bounds of data have been created, with traditional databases we can no longer stockpile and analyze the data, as a result, a new type of eminent system came into existence, where chunks of data are accumulated and bring collectively by software for examination is named as distributed. As an exemplar, for every second five new profiles can be generated with 136,000 profile picture uploads and 510 comments per minute with a Facebook alone.

(c) Value:

It refers to the worth in terms of charges and gains of collecting and analyzing of the data being extracted. The data has to be treated as unequal which means that having data in endless amounts does not give high value to data. The informed business decisions can be made for a market by analyzing the data. The social media data aggregation can assist the organization to identify the influencers for driving market awareness. The activities like Cluster analysis, Data mining can be used to enhance the market strategies in order to adopt the cost-effective and quick solution for transforming collected data into value.

(d) Variety:

It is represented as forms of data that we use from various sources like Internet and social media. As technology and web evolve, information will outdate rapidly. The data collected from these mediums include difficulty in categorization as structured and labelled formats, day by day the medium like social media broadly increases data by including posts of blog, updates, profiles, pictures, videos, and audio files of social media.

(e) Veracity:

It represents the quality or dependability/trustworthiness of data collected. As quality plays a major role in Big Data analysis, the quality metrics were set to analyze the type of data and the source of the data. Another factor to be considered is the frequency of a data flow which is cooperative in identifying the sources of data to track.

(f) Variability:

It refers to data property whose value is changed quickly.

(g) Valence:

It represents the associations among the vast amount of data, in the form of graphs. The connectedness exists in Big Data known as valence.

Challenges of Big Data

The key challenges of the Big Data lie in the concepts like data capture, data storage, data analysis, information privacy, search, sharing, transfer, querying, update, and visualization. Applications and advantages of Big Data analytics are being realized in various sectors. A realism on behalf of Big Data processing brought by the development of systems namely Cloud computing (e.g., Amazon EC2), distributed file (e.g., HDFS), Cluster in-memory computing (e.g., Spark), parallel computing (e.g., Pig) and emergence of NoSQL systems, improvement and enhancement in machine learning algorithms (e.g., Auto-Encoders, Deep Learning, Random Forest, and Support Vector Machines).

Some of the challenges that are faced in day-to-day life of Big Data area are:

- Vast quantity of data utilization and understanding.
- Learning continuously emerging and complex technologies.
- Solutions based on Cloud.
- Security, privacy, and regulatory constraints and considerations.
- Archiving, maintenance, and disposal of Big Data.
- Configuration of services using the call for an IT, Data Analyst, and Management Resources.

Even though the expansion of these technologies includes numerous methodologies to handle Big Data, few constraints do exist, those are as follows:

1. Storage and scalability issues: As the generating speed of data is faster than the processing speed of data, there is a need for storage systems for storing such huge data, therefore the faster processing system needs to be developed for handling present and future needs.
2. Time-based analysis: The worth of data changes over time which may either decrease or increase with respect to time. The real-time applications like fraud detection, banking, and telecom systems include real-time data for transaction processing.
3. Heterogeneous data representation: The data retrieved or collected from various sources include varied representations like unstructured data collected from videos, pictures, and audio sequences, which cannot be processed using usual tools like SQL.

4. Data analytics system: As the RDBMS lacks expandability and scalability and lack of performance in non-relational databases a flexible system need to be developed which mixes the features of relational and non-relational databases for handling structured and unstructured data.
5. Need for skill as a pool: As the abundant data is generating, there is a need and demand of analytically skilled people. Research says that there is a need for people in huge numbers for Big Data analytics in the near future.
6. Privacy and security: As the advance of technology, with the integration of IT architectures, all the organizations providing the gateways to access the stored information for analysis, which may damage intellectual property rights of people and may cause greater risks to security.
7. Not always better data: As the data collected in various ways through various available sources we may get irrelevant data also, which is not so much useful for analysis. Again filtering of gathered data is a big challenge in Big Data analytics.
8. Out of Context: For filtering data reduction method can be used, as it is most usual and can be easily fit into a mathematical model. At the data abstraction phase, retaining context is a critical task. Out of context Data may affect meaning and value of actual data.
9. Digital Divide: Getting permission to access Big Data is one of the most significant limitations. The social data which is large can be accessed directly by data and social media companies only. Some of these companies control the data accessing permissions for the people by deciding, who can and up to what extent people can access. Few people will sell the access rights on payment basis, while others offer an open access to a portion of data sets, specifically the group of people like researchers.
10. Data errors: With incremental growth of information technology, enormous amount of data is produced. With the arrival of cloud computing for storage and retrieval of data, there is a need to use the Big Data. Unreliable models are generated due to data errors and losses prone by the bulky datasets formed from various Internet sources.

Advantages: The significance of Big Data lies on the utilization of data collected from different sources rather than data owned by company. Different companies use their own strategies in handling data efficiently for potential growth. The metrics to consider in data analysis are: Cost Savings, Time Reductions, New Product Development, Understand the economic situations, Control online notoriety.

Applications

The demand for information management specialists or data analysts has been increased in software firms specializing in data management executives and analytics due to an enormous data. Therefore, with the invention of Big Data analytics, the opportunities in business and career are increased. The usage of Big Data is trending now a day to give better competition among the peer organizations by adopting their own strategies to innovate and capture values through data analysis. These organizations have liberal information about the items and services, purchasers and providers, buyer inclinations that can be captured from previous purchases and then dissected for analysis. It also comprehends and streamlines business forms. Using the predictive models generated for applications like stock market, social network, and web search trends; weather estimates data the merchants can easily optimize their business. Therefore, Big Data can be explored as a competitive advantage for businesses.

Empirical Example

Banking and Securities

In financial market monitoring, trade analytics, pre-trade decision support analytics, sentiment measurement, predictive analytics, risk analytics, "Know Your Customer," and fraud mitigation. And to catch illegal trading activity in the Securities Exchange Commission (SEC), the technologies like network analytics and natural language processors of Big Data were used.

Healthcare Sector

Faster identification and efficient analysis of healthcare information, evidence-based medicine recommendations, also used in tracking the spread of chronic disease.

Education

Learning and Management System, used to measure teacher's effectiveness, students' behavioral classification, and click patterns are also being used to detect boredom.

Manufacturing and Natural Resources

In the natural resources industry, Big Data allows for predictive modeling to support decision making that has been utilized for ingesting and integrating large amounts of data from geospatial data, graphical data, text, and temporal data, to gain a competitive advantage.

Government

In public services, in Social Security Administration (SSA), for faster decision-making and to detect suspicious or fraudulent claims. The Food and Drug Administration (FDA) is using Big Data to detect and study patterns of food-related illnesses and diseases. This allows for a faster response, which has led to more rapid treatment and less death. Big Data is analyzed from various government agencies and is used to protect the country.

Insurance

For better customer retention, in claims management, predictive analytics used to offer faster service, Fraud detection, real-time monitoring of claims throughout the claims cycle.

Retail and Wholesale Trade

Optimized staffing, reduced fraud, timely analysis of inventory, customer prospecting, customer retention, and promotion of products.

Transportation

To understand travel behavior, traffic control, route planning, intelligent transport systems, congestion management (by predicting traffic conditions), revenue management, technological enhancements, logistics and for competitive advantage, route planning to save on fuel and time, for travel arrangements in tourism, etc.

Energy and Utilities

Smart meter readers, to analyze the consumption of utilities, for better asset and workforce management.

Communications, Media, and Entertainment

As an example, the evolving challenges of Big Data can be explained with any of the sectors mentioned above. In this section, the communications, media, and entertainment are considered and challenges are explained as follows:

- Collection, analysis, and utilization of customer opinions.

- Analyzing the impact of machine-generated data like mobile, sensors, and social media.
- Understanding the patterns hidden.
- Creation of customer profiles by understanding customer data with behavioral patterns to focus on various target audience, perform recommendations on demand basis, and scale the performance of the content for further usage.

The set of cases like music recommendations to individuals, by analyzing the data from on-demand music service providers, and prediction of games and reality shows on TV by tracking live score or information and to provide great customer experiences heavily utilizes Big Data.

Big Data Analytics

Big Data analytics is the way toward inspecting substantial and differed data sets—i.e., Big Data—to make organizations the more-informed business decisions, which leads to new opportunities, higher profits and happier customers, by revealing unseen blueprints, unnoticed correlations, and trends of market, client inclinations and other valuable data. Big Data has got an incentive in the accompanying ways: cost reduction, faster, and better decision-making, innovation of new items, and administration services (Vijayaraj et al. 2016; Thamizhselvan et al. 2015).

Importance of Data Analytics

Figure 4 explains the outcomes of using Big Data analytics. Big Data analytics aids organizations combine their data and utilize it to make out innovative chances, to perform operations in a more efficient way, to make business moves as smarter, to get a lot of profits and to make consumers happy.

Cost reduction: With respect to storing plus retrieval of vast amounts of data, for doing business in a more efficient way, Hadoop and cloud-based Big Data analytics technologies helped out in significant cost advantages.

Faster, better decision-making: An immediate information analysis along with the ability to analyze new data sources and making decisions based on what they have learned is possible via the speed of Hadoop, HDFS, and in-memory analytics.

New products and services: For the raising needs of consumers, the Big Data analytics provides innovations in creating new products to meet customers' satisfaction by enabling valid services.

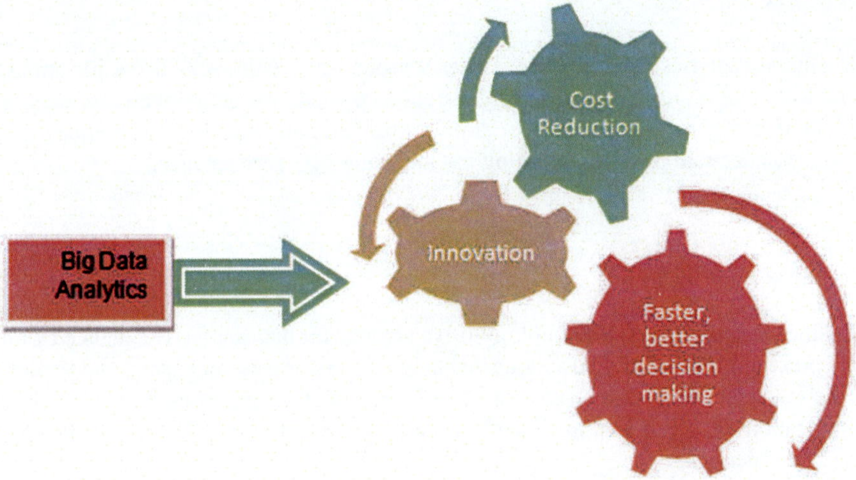

Fig. 4 Gains of Big Data analytics. Source: Author's creation

Need For Big Data Analytics

The emergence for analytic practices of immense amounts of data is due to generation of huge quantity of structured, semi-structured, unstructured forms data and with the traditional techniques data storage, retrieval and analysis at advantageous time lag is a challenging task. Hence these constraints led to the urgency appearance of the term Big Data Analytics. Though Big Data has achieved awareness as a result of the emergence of the Internet, it cannot be compared with it. It is ahead of the Internet, though, Web makes it easier to pull together and share knowledge as well as raw data. Therefore, storing, processing, and comprehending task usage for predicting the past and future course of action accurately in an acceptable time delay is termed as Big Data analytics. Different business developers focus on their respective target marketing. For example, insurance providers target is offering forth customized insurances to their clients, and healthcare providers focus on assisting in offering quality and low-cost treatment to patients. Along with the progressions in storage, accumulation, analysis of data and related forecast calculations, comprehension of fundamental driving as well as the regulating factors (advertise, law, social standards, and engineering) is essential, to help in creating business rules even on the huge data sets productively and vigorous prediction models with high accuracy. Big Data analytics is the comprehension of Business Intelligence, Data Science, and data analytics.

Business Analytics

Business Analytics can be referred to as a grouping of various skills, applications, and technologies used by various organizations to attain focus into their business by evaluating organization-wide operations using data and statistical techniques and guide to constrain business planning by analyzing past performance.

Business Intelligence

Business Intelligence is a technology-driven course for data analysis sequenced with the presentation of informed actions that helps the executives, managers, and various corporate end users. BI viewed as a basic foundation for supporting all the business application's decision-making that should yield good results in industry and, increasingly, academia.

Benefits of Business Intelligence

To make a rapid worthy decision, the interior business process needs to be optimized and operational efficiency should be enhanced that drives innovative revenue and give rivalry over business rivals by addressing market trends and business problems identified.

Data Science: Data Science is all about the creation, generation, representation of data, and creation of business and IT strategies for data storage and retrieval; through mining identify the patterns to help the organization gain the competitive advantage. The field of Data Science integrates the disciplines of computer science, statistics, and mathematics by incorporating techniques like data mining and visualization, cluster analysis, and machine learning techniques.

Applications of Data Science

Data science can be connected in different sectors to be specific; Finance, Government Policies, Human Resources, Health Care, Marketing, and each conceivable industry where data gets created. Based on customers' behavioral data, marketing agents make decisions regarding their products sale. Creating customized personal recommendations dependent on a client's survey history. Shipment business organizations locate the preeminent routes and times of delivery, in addition to the finest modes of transportation for their shipments. Human Resources (which employees are most likely to leave, evaluation of their performance, deciding their rewards), Funding sector (Credit Risk, Fraud) are effectively practiced utilizing data science in these disciplines.

Data Analytics: DA is the area of technologies and techniques applied, to examine the datasets, in turn, to depict the conclusions holding the qualitative information which can be used for more-informed future business decision-making.

Data analytics can be categorized into qualitative and quantitative approaches (Tiwari et al. 2018). The qualitative approach is easily interpretable and it deals with non-numeric data, such as pictures, text, sound, and visual contents as well as common phrases, themes, and viewpoints. The quantitative approach is estimated measurably and it deals with numerical data with quantifiable factors.

Business use of Data Analytics

Banks and credit card companies are in a position to identify and prevent fraud by monitoring and analyzing bank customers' transaction patterns. Web-based business organizations and promoting administration providers do click stream to identify website guests who are willing to purchase specifically manufactured goods and to provide services basing on navigation and page viewing patterns. To improve the CRM analytics. It is useful for Healthcare associations to evaluate and assess the adequacy of medicines for different diseases. Analytics is not new. Numerous logical methods, for example, regression analysis, simulation, machine learning, and AI, have been accessible for a long time. Indeed, even the incentive in analyzing unstructured data such as email and documents has been surely known. We should be aware of what is new at the present moment, i.e., the convergence of progress in technology and software, new data sources (e.g., social network), and market opportunities. Now and then traditional data warehousing is considered a poor fit because of high processing necessities of Big Data.

Applications of Data Analytics

1. Automobile insurance: Customer risk analysis, scam discovery, quick processing of claims.
2. Manufacturing, distribution, and retail: Tracking, rack accessibility, surveying the effect of promotional displays; evaluate the viability of promotional campaigns, stock management, and pricing, sophisticated click stream analysis.
3. Transportation and logistics: Some of the example applications are fleet management in real-time, RFID technology used for resource tracking.
4. Health care systems: Prediction of disease and trends and locations, prediction of hospital re-admissions, track of patient pathway, drug switches, etc.
5. Banking Applications: Credit card fraudulent detection, cibil score analysis, loan disbursement, etc.
6. Stock market forecasting analysis: Stock trend prediction, stock value prediction.
7. Telecommunications and gaming are the other application areas.

8. Used in stock optimization by the retailers basing generated social network data, web search movements predictions, and weather condition estimates (Shanmugam et al. 2013).
9. With sensors, delivery route, and supply chain management optimization is done for identification of geographic position and radiofrequency.
10. Big Data can be used to form smart cities, where vehicle transportation and traffic and weather conditions altogether signed up.

Kinds of Data Analytics

There is a need for distinguishing various kinds of analytics as the points differed has allegations for the advancements and structural design determination for Big Data analytics. Diverse kinds of analytics could perform preferred on a couple of platforms over others.

Descriptive Analytics: Descriptive analytics, summarization of historical data to yield valuable knowledge, and set up the data for further investigation. It is utilized to evaluate the number of relationships covered up in data. Data visualization, dashboards/scorecards, and reporting/OLAP are broadly utilized analytic strategies for some time, and are the core applications of conventional BI. Descriptive analytics is glanced in reverse (like a vehicle's rear view reflect) and uncover what has happened.

Prescriptive Analytics: Prescriptive Analytics is the region of business analytics devoted to finding the best strategy for a given circumstance.

Predictive Analytics: Technique that utilizes past or recorded information to furnish future expectations with sensible precision.

Data Analytics Algorithms

Clustering Algorithms

In the era of Big Data, usual clustering mechanisms will not function in effective way as they specifically require that whole data in the same format at a single place to acquire some knowledge. Although the difficulty of examining the datasets with high dimensions and of large scale has retained the attention of numerous researchers from diverse disciplines in the last century and in current years number of solutions have been addressed the difficulties encountered and projected new challenges in the data clustering area. One of the data clustering issues is reduction of data complexity. As the complexity and required memory for the data analysis process are declined in present days, the conventional methodologies like dimension reduction and sampling methods can also be utilized for Big Data.

Classification Algorithms

In order to serve a parallel computing environment, the conventional classification algorithms need to be enhanced or create/execute a new set of classification algorithms. The data for these classification algorithms are collected in a distributed manner which can be practiced by a diverse group of beginners.

Frequent Pattern Mining Algorithms

The association rules and sequential pattern mining set of algorithms are proposed to concentrate on taking care of voluminous datasets such as transaction data of large shopping centers.

Difficulties of Big Data Analytics

Communication Between Systems

As most of the frameworks of Big Data analytics are intended for service in parallel computing, they may work with other frameworks or work away at different frameworks. Hence the communication plays a vital role and it will unequivocally affect the entire knowledge discovery procedure performance. Instructions to decrease the cost of communication will be the absolute first thing that the data researchers need to mind.

Bottlenecks on Data Analytics System

As the conditions, frameworks, and input data have changed in current years, comparatively diverse from the conventional data analytics situations. Hence the various kinds of bottlenecks will be showed up in dissimilar areas of the Big Data analytics.

Security Issues: Since we are gathering much more amount of data we can't build a reliable system to apply Big Data analytics, without providing protection to collected data. Hence, how to guard them will also be an open issue.

Key Areas that Big Data Analytics May Influence

Data Management

There are potential savings in time and funds if offices executed more astute organization of data rehearses that were aware of the requirements of Big Data analysis. Organization's data sources and operational zones would be of more noteworthy advantage to the number of organizations and for numerous reasons if there is more prominent straightforwardness.

Personalization of Services

The Big Data analytics may deliver an incentive by revealing a clear picture of an individual user or user gathering. Big Data can realize this because of its granularity trademark (its capacity to consolidate numerous and unstable small pieces of data to generate revealing insights).

Problem Solving and Predictive Analytics

The merger of multiple datasets from divergent sources in association with advanced analytic techniques and technologies will improve significant thinking power and the ability of prescient analytics to uncover accurate and deep understandings that can successfully bolster helps in making decisions.

Productivity and Efficiency

The examination of Big Data sources can be utilized to discover expenditure reserve funds and chances to expand the effectiveness, which will legitimately add to an upgrading in production, which leads to further innovation.

Predictive Analytics

It is the process of pulling out knowledge from various datasets by uncovering the hidden behavioral patterns and forecast future outcomes. The objective of this analytics is to forecast (Waller and Fawcett 2013) the future outcomes with an acceptance level trustworthiness by including risk assessment and what-if scenarios. The key idea of predictive analytics depends on identifying associations among descriptive and forecasted variables of the earlier happenings, which reveal unknown outcomes from the existing patterns. The accuracy and quality of results are dependent on assumptions made and data analysis applied to past data. Predictive

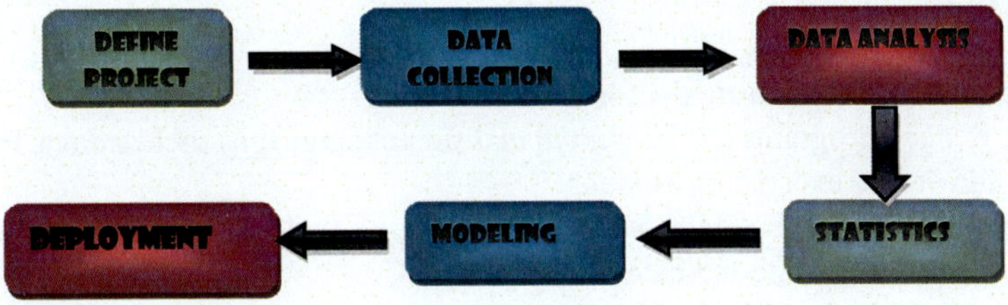

Fig. 5 Life cycle of predictive analysis. Source: Author's creation

analytics can be evolved with Big Data to provide random and efficient decisions basing on the business or application area in order to provide reasonable economic cost. The life cycle of predictive analytics, as in Fig. 5, (Waller and Fawcett 2013) includes (1). Data acquisition, (2). model construction and validation, (3). Testing the model, and (4). Deploy and enhance the model.

Tools, Techniques, and Technologies

Hadoop EcoSystem Core Components:

- HDFS: Hadoop distributed file system.
- YARN: Frame work for job scheduling and resource management.
- Map Reduce: Parallel processing mechanism for distributed data.

The subcomponents are:

- Hbase: Column oriented database for processing billions of records.
- Hive: Data warehouse for distributed file system HDFS.
- Pig: High-level programming language for distributed computations.
- Sqoop: Data migration tool from/to RDBMSs to/from HDFS, HBase, Hive.
- Flume: Data collection mechanism for Log and Event data.
- Oozie: It is a work flow management service.
- Mahout: Library of machine learning statistical algorithms used by data scientist for statistical analysis.
- Zookeeper: Configuration management and coordination service.

HDFS

- Files are stockpiled in HDFS and partitioned into blocks, which are then copied to several data nodes.
- Hadoop cluster includes only one Name Node and several Data Nodes.
- For high availability and fast access, Data blocks are needed to be replicated.

Map Reduce

- Programing execution model for data processing.
- Map Reduce programs can be written in different languages such as Java, Python, and allowed to execute on Hadoop.
- Parallel processing put Map Reduce in very large-scale data analysis.
- Mapper produces intermediate results.
- Reducer aggregates the results.

YARN

- As the Map Reduce 1.0 architecture had issues like scalability, memory usage and synchronization, YARN addresses these problems, specifically with the service namely job tracker.
- YARN splits up the job tracker's two major functionalities namely, resource management and job scheduling/monitoring, into separate daemons.
- Instead of troubling a single node with taking care of booking and resource management for the whole cluster, YARN now disseminates this responsibility over the cluster.

Brief overview of the Hadoop ecosystem subcomponents shown in Fig. 6:

(A) Data transfer components.

Hadoop deals with all kinds of data. For the data transfer in and out of Hadoop, there are two Hadoop ecosystem components Sqoop and Flume.

Sqoop:

An efficient tool, used for exchanging a large amount of structured data between HDFS and relational databases. Such as Oracle, SQL Server, and MySQL.

Sqoop basically has an import and export utility to move data in and out of Hadoop.

Sqoop's "sq" comes from SQL and "oop" comes from Hadoop.

Flume:

Flume is also known as a log collector, as it is a distributed service for gathering, combining, and moving a large amount of log data. As the existed tool Sqoop, can handle only structured data and we are allowed to have Hadoop for handling semi- and unstructured data. Typically when we go to a website, all the clicks and actions on website are recorded and fed into a log file.

Flume can access data from a log file and change it into Hadoop compatible format.

(B) API (Application programming components).

Map Reduce programming is in java and is complicated. So Hive and Pig are two components for inducing Map Reduce jobs in a more user-friendly way.

Hive:

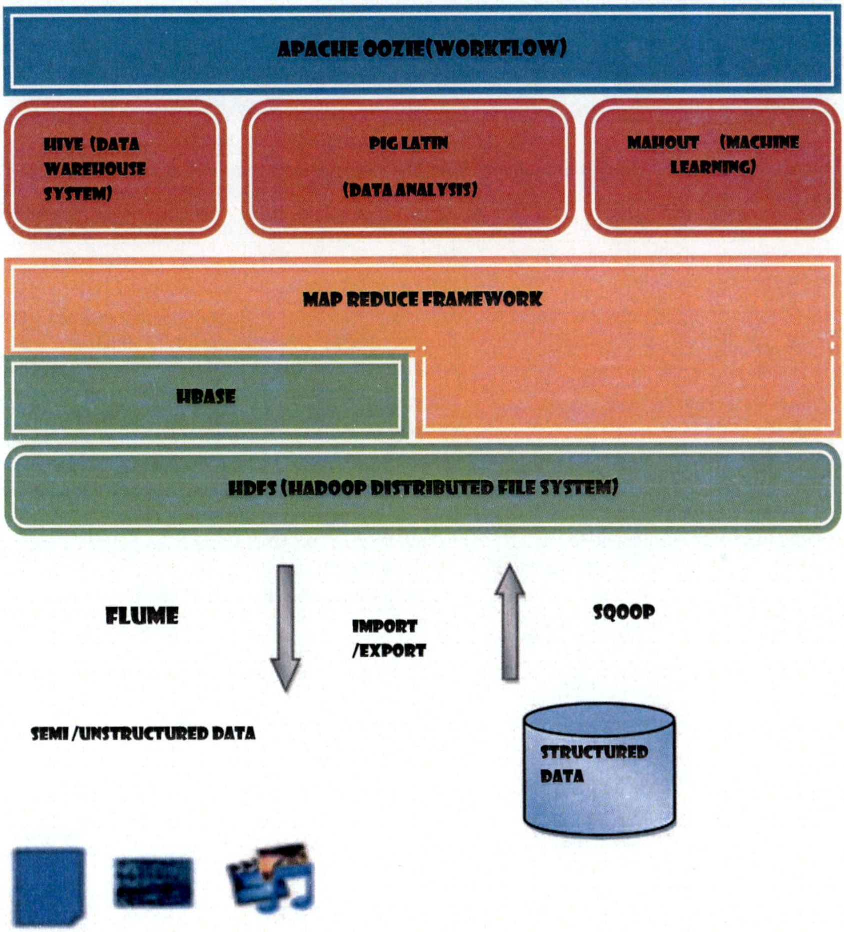

Fig. 6 Hadoop ecosystem. Source: Author's creation

As the SQL is simple all the users and analysts understand it. Hive is an API that is written in SQL recognized as HiveQL specifically for bring on Map Reduce jobs. Hive is basically a distributed data warehouse infrastructure build on top of Hadoop for proving the Big Data analysis, summarization, and query using HiveQL.

Pig:

Pig Latin is a programming query language at high level, as it is an easy and convenient way of programming; it is used for the analysis of very large datasets that run on HDFS. Hence a language layer of Pig consisting of "Pig Latin" and infrastructure layer consisting of compiler that produces a sequence of Map Reduce programs based on Pig Latin command. The comparison between the tools Pig and Hive is shown in Table 1.

Table 1 Hive versus Pig

Pig	Hive
It was developed by yahoo.	It was developed by Facebook.
Procedural data flow language.	Declarative SQL language.
Designed for programming.	Designed for generating reports.
For the most part utilized by researchers and programmers.	For the most part utilized by data analysts.
Works on the customer side of a cluster.	Works on the server side of a cluster.
Does not have a devoted metadata database.	Variation of SQL DDL language is specified by defining structure as tables in advance.
The features of pig seem to be similar to that of SQL but vary a lot.	Directly implements SQL features that can be easily interpretable by professionals of the database.
Pig sustains Avro file format.	Hive does not sustain Avro file.
Pig uses the relational flow language called Pig Latin.	Like SQL, hive uses a special query language, specifically hive query language.
Advantages of hive • Keeps queries running fast. • Takes very less time to write hive query compared to Map Reduce code. • HiveQL is a declarative language like SQL. • Provides the structure on an array of data formats. Disadvantages of hive • Useful when the data is structured. • You can do any analytical operation using MR programming. • Debugging code is very difficult..	Advantages of pig • Creates a sequence of Map Reduce jobs that run by Hadoop cluster. • Decrease in deployment time. • Easy to write and read. • Provides data operations like ordering, filters, and joins. Disadvantages of pig • Data schema is not enforced explicitly but implicitly. • Commands are not executed until you dump in an intermediate result.

Source: Author's creation

(C) Data Storage Components

HBase:

It is a disseminated, open-source, non-relational database, keeps running over HDFS. In this data is structured in columns instead of rows and it acts as a representative set for all No-SQL databases termed as columnar database. So HBase is fundamentally a distributed columnar database that utilizes HDFS for its data stockpiling. In HBase you can store data in amazingly substantial tables with variable column structure.

(D) Analysis components.

Mahout:

Mahout is a machine learning component in the open source world. It is a library of many machine learning statistical procedures. Mahout can help us write a number of algorithms in machine learning and can be exercised for Big Data analysis. It is mainly used by data scientists to do machine learning for statistical analysis.

For example, Amazon recommends products as per your taste based on your previous purchases.

(E) Workflow management.

Oozie:

It is basically a Java-based application acts as a workflow scheduler to run jobs at a specified time in the Hadoop system.

In the Hadoop ecosystem, you may write programs in Hive and Pig and you may want to run them one after the other on schedule basis which can be done by Oozie.

(F) Administration and Coordination components.

Ambari:

It has a set of Hadoop administrative tools for installing, maintaining, and monitoring, used by the administrator of the system. Hadoop is known for its multi-node cluster topology.

For example, The task of inclusion or taking away a slave node in a cluster can be done by Ambari.

Hue:

Hue is an administrative interface and also has a GUI tool for issuing Hive and Pig queries, browsing files, and creating Oozie work processes.

Zookeeper:

It is a mechanism used to perform coordination and synchronization between Hadoop ecosystem tools and components. It is used for centralized coordination of services, for example, configuration and synchronization utilized by the various distributed application.

Differences Between Hadoop Map Reduce and Spark

Even though both the frameworks are liable for data processing, the key variation lies in the processing approach which affects the speed and volume; Spark uses in-memory processing, whereas Hadoop Map Reduce uses interpret ways read from/ write to a disk processing yield an outcome there is a significant change in processing speed and volume. Spark can accelerate up to 100 times faster and Hadoop Map Reduce allows working with a huge volume of datasets than Spark.

Hadoop Map Reduce Benefits

Linear processing of huge data sets: Map Reduce can perform parallel processing on large volume of data by breaking large chunks into smaller ones, which allows us to process each individual chunk separately at various data nodes and automatic integration of the results across multiple nodes. If the data set range is bigger than the RAM then, Hadoop Map Reduce can do better than Spark.

Cost-effective solution, if no quick results are expected. If the processing speed is not critical then Hadoop Map Reduce can be considered as an efficient solution.

Spark Benefits

Quick data handling: Spark permits in-memory handling. Therefore, compared to Hadoop, Map Reduce, Spark is having faster processing.

Iterative handling: Spark's Resilient Distributed Datasets (RDDs) permit performing several map operations in memory, with no need to write temporary datasets to a disk. If the task is recursive processing: Spark defeats Hadoop Map Reduce.

Near real-time processing: Spark is an excellent tool to give a business with required prompt bits of knowledge. This conceivable gain is because of Spark's in-memory processing.

Graph processing. Iterative calculations are typical using graph processing, for which spark's computational model is used through an API namely GraphX—Apache Spark for graph calculation.

Machine learning. Spark composed of machine learning in-built library named MLlib together with out-of-the-box algorithms which likewise keep running in memory, Whereas Hadoop requires a third-party systems to enable machine learning libraries. In addition, there is a chance to change and regulate them.

Joining datasets. The arrangements were made quickly due the speed processing of spark, where as Hadoop performs better in joining large data collections that requires great attention towards arranging and rearranging.

Examples of Practical Applications

With respect to a few real-time applications, it may be concluded that spark may outperform Map Reduce for efficient real-time processing the examples are:

- *Segmentation of customers:* Investigating customer conduct and recognizing customer segments that show comparative standards of behavioral patterns will assist organizations to be aware of client inclinations and create a unique client familiarity.
- *Risk management:* Various potential situations anticipation can assist administrators with making precise decisions by picking non-risky alternatives.
- *Real-time fraud discovery:* Once the framework is prepared on past data with machine learning algorithms, it will discover a few relations within data. These discoveries can be utilized to recognize or foresee peculiarity in real time that may be considered as a flag of a probable fraud.
- *Industrial Big Data analysis:* It is also about identifying and anticipating about abnormalities, however, for this situation, these peculiarities are related to machinery breakdowns. A legitimately designed framework gathers the data from sensors to recognize pre-failure conditions.

Apache Pig: Architecture

Pig Latin is a specific high-level data processing language for analyzing data in Hadoop Pig environment. It provides a rich set of data types and operators to perform various operations on the data. A programmer who uses Pig, need to use the Pig Latin language to write a Pig script, and then execute using the execution mechanisms such as Grunt Shell, Embedded, and UDFs. Later to produce the desired output, a series of transformations need to be applied. Apache Pig helps in making the programmers' job easy by converting these scripts internally into a series of Map Reduce jobs and its complex architecture is presented in Fig. 7.

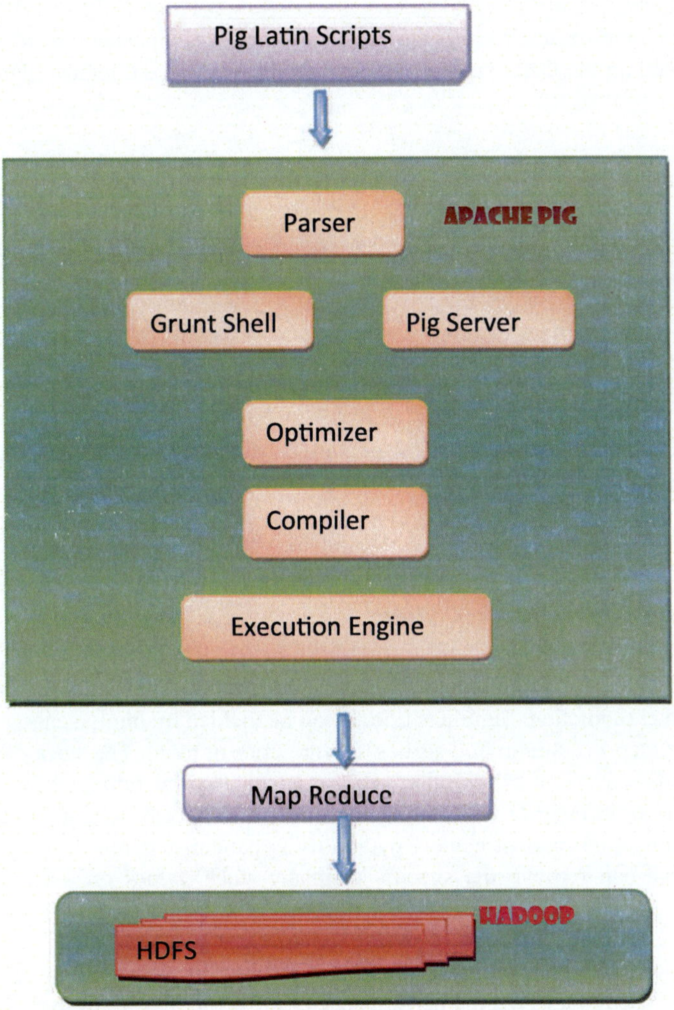

Fig. 7 Apache pig architecture. Source: Author's creation

Apache Pig Components

Parser

It handles the Pig Scripts for syntax check, type check, and other miscellaneous checks and then produces an output in the form of DAG (directed acyclic graph), which holds statements and logical operators of Pig Latin. The DAG is represented with logical operators of the script are as nodes and data flows are as edges.

Optimizer

The logical optimization techniques namely Projection and pushdown are employed in this phase on the DAG passed as input t produce optimized logical plan.

Compiler

In this phase the optimized logical plan compilation is done and a series of Map Reduce jobs are generated.

Execution Engine

In this final phase the submission of sorted Map Reduce jobs to Hadoop for execution to produce valid results.

Stock Market Trend Prediction

The act of anticipating future trends of a stock traded on an exchange is referred to as stock market prediction. Significant profit can be yielded by implementing successful prediction procedure to find a stock's future price or trend. The stock data can be retrieved directly from NSE India website. It can also be retrieved from Yahoo Finance, Google Finance by entering the ticker of a specific company. From the programming environment namely python using pandas data reader module's data package we can retrieve the specific company stock values on a day with the columnar tags Close, Date, High, Low, Open, Volume of a specific past period in a day wise format. A deposit of machine learning algorithms namely regression, classification, and clustering were adopted for handling prediction and various metrics are used to analyze the performance of different algorithms used.

Sentiment Analysis

It is also known as opinion mining that analyzes the opinions and emotions of people toward individual items, businesses, and their related attributes. In the current days, social network plays a significant role in information providing about any item from a number of posts, blogs, reviews, and comments. To acquire useful information from people's sentiments, (Tedeschi and Benedetto 2015) different machine learning techniques (supervised and unsupervised learning) are applied. G-POMS, Google N-gram, Ling motif, LIWC, POMS, Opinion Finder, and SentiStrength are the different analytical tools provide to calculate sentiment analysis of given data.

Sentiment Analysis Approaches: The sentiment classification approaches (Rachid et al. 2018) can be classified as: (a) Machine Learning and (b) Lexicon based.

(a) Machine Learning:

In three different ways, Sentiment analysis can be performed with Machine Learning.

Document (coarse) level
Sentence (intermediate) level
Aspect (Feature) level

Document or Coarse level sentiment analysis: Identifies the sentiment from the whole document or manuscript and classifies it as either positive or negative based on the views given by the user.

It is also called as binary or sentiment polarity classification.

Sentence or Intermediate level sentiment analysis: It is utilized for obtaining the refinement of opinions mentioned in the document by filtering the sentences that do not contain any opinion. In general, a sentence consists of two kinds of information; objective and subjective. An objective statement illustrates the facts in the real world, whereas subjective statements present the personal belief or view, feeling. The practice of classifying a sentence as either subjective or objective is termed as subjectivity classification. The subjective sentences can be further classified as positive or negative expressions. It is generally used for analyzing single line sentences given by the user, as reviews or comments.

The aforementioned techniques work fine if a single entity is referred. But in some cases, opinions may be about various entities and their features or aspects. The majority of opinion mining techniques gather opinions from outsized opinion holders.

Aspect or feature level sentiment analysis:

An opinion from a single person is usually inadequate and hence a summary of opinions based on aspects is advantageous.

In general, Document and Sentence level sentiment analysis can identify the overall sentiment toward a service but may not be able to capture the fundamental nature of the review. Therefore, aspect level sentiment analysis focus on recognizing all the sentiment terminologies within a specified document and the aspects or attributes to which the opinions refer.

(b) Lexicon-based approach (Appel et al. 2016):

This strategy depends on the presumption that the sum of the feeling orientation of each word makes contextual sentiment orientation. This strategy is sub-partitioned into two kinds:

Dictionary-based methodology: This methodology uses predefined lexicon of words where each word is related to explicit opinion polarity quality. Feeling of individuals, for example, cheerful, pitiful, or discouraged can be discovered by looking at words against vocabularies from lexicons.

Corpus-based methodology: Corpus-based methodology endeavors to discover co-occurrence patterns of words to decide their estimations. This methodology depends on the seeding list of assessment words and afterward finds another sentiment words which have comparative context.. This technique is utilized to allot bliss factor of words relying upon recurrence of their events in "glad" or "tragic" blog entry.

The sentiment analysis process includes polarity identification, i.e., positive, negative, or neutral sentiment. The developers and brand manager could gain insight into opinions of customers about the topic using various sentiment algorithms.

Sentiment as metrics:

The opinions of the customer could break or make a success of brands or business standards, the decision of monitoring such business can mean the difference between course corrections or opportunities that are missed. The sentiments can also provide a chance for marketing and production strategies to reframe the experiences of customer.

For calculating the scaling of customer opinions an automated sentiment analysis is used, instead of reading and evaluating large volumes of text, an algorithm are used to process and score the sentiments efficiently.

Sentiment analysis workflow steps:

1. Create a set of predetermined words with positive and negative values (or find a pre-made dictionary).
2. Write a function that parses text, checks for the presence of those words, and uses the preset sentiment values to compute the overall text sentiment.

In favor of a more data-driven opinion mining approach, a Machine learning (ML) algorithms such as the Naive Bayes Classifier can be used to build the model. When these models encounter a new piece of text, to recognizing positive, negative, and neutral opinions, these models should be trained by sample datasets fed.

By scraping data from Twitter, we can:

Know more about the newest trends worldwide.
Find out your potential customers for business.
Analyze the marketing value of hot topics.

To access and read Twitter data REST API's and to access Twitter Data in real-time streaming API's are provided by Twitter. Using Twitter's search API, we can retrieve the tweet feeds from twitter for this initially we need to register with the twitter, then register an application using Twitter app dashboard and generate the access tokens namely consumer key, consumer secret key, access token, access token secret using "Keys and Tokens" tab. But the limitation with this API is, it can process up to 180 requests for every 15 min with a maximum of 100 tweets/ request. And another limitation is it can retrieve the past 7 days' tweets only. Therefore, we can mine only 72,000 tweets/hour. With another way of retrieval, Twitter Scraper there is no such limitation on past data period. And no limit on number of tweets, it completely based on Internet speed/bandwidth and the number of instances of Twitter Scraper started. A simple script to scrape for Tweets utilizing the Python bundle, in particular, Twitter scrapper, requests to recover the content and Beautifulsoup4 to parse the recovered content. The scrapped tweets saved as .json or .csv format files. Username, Full Name, Tweet id, Tweet URL, tweet text, Tweet html, Tweet timestamp, number of likes, number of replies, number of retweets information can be scraped per Tweet. Another way to scrape is Octoparse. And also there are several modules like GetOldTweets created for scrapping the tweets via python like programming environment in an efficient manner. For working of these modules we need to install tweepy, lxml, pyquery, twitterscrapper packages.

Integrated Model

Predictive Analytics along with NLP of tweet feeds, we can build an integrated model for anticipation. Big Data is the vast amount of stored or real-time data collected from clients. It can be analyzed through predictive analytics techniques; which enables the organizations to transform the Big Data from the historical view to forward-looking perspective of the client. Among the various, the familiar Ensemble models are Bagging, Boosting, and Blending.

The strategies developed by merging several base model machine learning techniques into a single optimal predictive model are called as ensemble methods. These meta algorithms are formed in order to reduce variance (bagging), and bias (boosting), or progress predictions (stacking) and robustness over a single model. And also used to build more accurate component classifiers that are independent of each other.

There are two ideal paradigms of Ensemble techniques namely sequential, where the base learners are produced consecutively (for example, AdaBoost) and parallel, where the base learners are produced in parallel (for example, Random Forest). The notion of sequential approaches is to utilize the dependence between the base learners, contrastingly the parallel strategies are to abuse freedom between the base learners. The other way of classification is based on usage of base learning algorithm; homogeneous versus heterogeneous ensembles. Homogeneous ensembles utilize a single base learning algorithm to deliver homogeneous base learners, i.e., learners of a similar sort. Heterogeneous learners, for example, learners of various kinds, leading to heterogeneous ensembles. For having increasingly precise ensemble strategies, the base learners utilized must be as exact as would be prudent and as assorted as could reasonably be expected.

Types of constructing ensemble methods:

1. *Simple Weighted Average Voting:* It is the simplest one, uses the voting procedure to select the models in classification and performs the average in Regression.
2. *Bagging:* It is an ensemble method formed by combining Bootstrapping and AGGregating, so got the name BAGGing. Bagging adopts the procedures like bootstrap sampling, voting, and averaging to obtain the subsets of data to train base learners, classification, and regression, respectively. M various models (same algorithm) are trained in parallel for random subsamples of dataset with the policy of replacement. Finally, take average by combining them linearly to or through majority vote of obtained results. Taking the average of multiple estimates is the one way of variance reduction.

$$f(x) = \frac{1}{M}\sum_{m=1}^{M} f_m(x)$$

3. *Boosting:* This is the ensemble model, where the models are trained sequentially, where (n)th model uses the output of (n–1)th model and works on the limitation of the previous model, the process stops when result stops improving. Boosting facilitates the conversion of powerless learners to powerful learners. Through a weighted majority vote (classification) or a weighted sum (regression), the expectations are joined to produce the final prediction. The most generally utilized type of boosting algorithm is AdaBoost, which represents versatile boosting. Gradient Boosting builds the model in a sequential manner and it is a nonlinear classifier, which is a speculation of boosting to subjective differentiable misfortune capacities. It very well may be utilized for both regression and classification problems.
4. *Stacking:* It is an ensemble learning technique that combines two or more than two classification or regression models utilizing other machine learning algorithms in particular a meta-classifier or a meta-regressor. The entire training set is utilized to train the base-level models, the yields of this model utilized as features to train the meta-model.

Tools

Predictive analytic tools can be categorized into open source and commercial. Under the open-source category, the available tools are scikit learn, KNIME, OpenNN, Orange, R, RapidMiner, Weka, Octave, and Apache. And under the commercial category available tools are Alpine Data Labs, BIRT Analytics, Angoss Knowledge

STUDIO, IBM SPSS Statistics and Modeler, Modeler, Mathematica, MATLAB, Minitab, Oracle, Data, Pervasive, Software, and Revolution.

Models Adoption

The integrated models can be constructed by adopting decision and predictive models, which are explained in detail in the preceding section.

Decision Models

Decision models are the models that provide the relation among all the attributes participated in decision-making, like yields of anticipation models, the decision, and the anticipating results of the decision. These models are employed to construct decision logic and to form a set of business rules and in optimization.

Predictive Models

The hierarchy of Predictive techniques is presented in Fig. 8.

These are the models that provide the association between the specific performance of a sample unit and one or more notorious features of the unit predictive model, which performs real-time transaction calculations. The sample units with recognized features and performances are to be treated as training samples whereas the sample units with known features and unknown performances are to be treated as out of training sample units.

The two main categories of Predictive Analytics Techniques are Regression Techniques and Machine Learning Techniques. In models developed using regression concept, the interactions between the different variables represented with the mathematical equation. There are several models in the area of predictive analytics, basing on the application any model can be adopted.

Related Work

Tahir M. Nisar and Man Yeung (2018) investigated if there is a relationship between politics-related sentiment that determines the general mood of the public and FTSE 100 movement sat the market level, which influences the investment making decisions in the short term, in the United Kingdom, during local elections. For this the author wants to evaluate Twitter feeds on social networks (Benedetto and Tedeschi

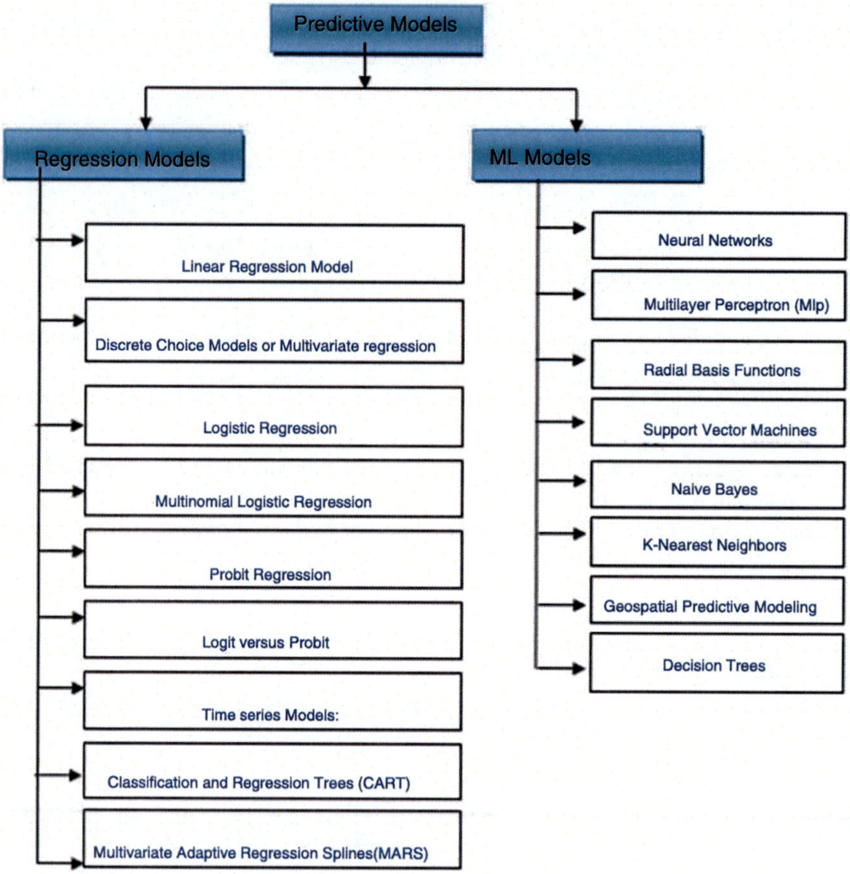

Fig. 8 Predictive models. Source: Author's creation

2016; Tedeschi and Benedetto 2015) in a political context, using the Twitter API and adopt data mining methods. The study involved performing a collection of correlation and regression analyses tests to compare the daily mood of UK population during local elections with daily changes in the price based on the FTSE 100 index and the time lag findings of MOOD and PRICE. Lexicon-based sentiment analytics was used by the author to classify data sentiment to gauge the overall population mood in relation to the nearby races and stock market indicators.

Alejandro Escobar et al. (2013), proposed a technical analysis supported indicator based on fuzzy logic with the aim of conveying accurately, the mode that a novice investor would study the stock market according to his inclinations and profile, to arrive at the reasoning for decision-making for deciding when to purchase or sell a stock. This fuzzy indicator is not a totally objective mathematical model, but incorporates subjective investor features such as his risk profile. The investigation included running of a few reproductions with chronicled time arrangement of two of the most significant loads of the Colombian financial exchange to arrive at the agents' reasoning, using a multi-agent-based simulation approach. This involved a fixed amount of agents whose performances (behavior and profits) were compared against those acquired by operators who utilized conventional pointers like MA, RSI, and MACD. They recorded the perceptions concerning specialists who utilized the fluffy marker; on a normal these specialists got more benefits. In any case, they additionally got the biggest measure of exchanges, which is an inconvenience thinking about that every exchange has a related expense in a genuine situation. There was greater changeability for these two factors with these specialists. This was, be that as it may, a normal conduct and relies upon the financial specialist's hazard inclination. The optimal threshold value for balancing mean profitability and the number of transactions was observed around 0.8. They concluded that the decision-making process can be enriched by improving the way of modelling the current variables; incorporating more input variables into the fuzzy system; including a more realistic investor's profile and by using fundamental analysis along with technical analysis.

Raut Sushrut Deepak et al. (2017) suggested a Machine Learning (ML) approach for accurate prediction of stock market. Unlike in using technical, fundamental, or the time series analysis, in this approach the learning algorithm will be trained from accessible stock information to pick up insight and afterward utilize the gained learning for precise forecast. In this methodology, Input data assumes a significant role in prediction along with machine learning strategies. The study involved the exploration of various algorithms and their fitness for various issue domains, in light of which Artificial Neural Network (ANN) was observed to be the most viable way to deal with actualize a wide number of highlights along with the cross approval sets. To get the best exact yield, supervised classifier SVM was implemented, whose outcomes are tested on the binary classification done with an alternate arrangement of a feature list on the Bombay Stock Exchange (BSE) index data set. The perceptions made are, when the data is split into train and test, the number becomes extremely less which is nothing but noise which can be completely removed from the dataset by using filtering techniques and hence better outcome can be predicted with the absence of noise. In this case, dataset can be combined to form four sets of feature list. SVM has demonstrated that an increasingly custom list of capabilities can be produced to get expectations with incredible effectiveness. Tests led utilizing non-linear RBF kernel showed extensive precision in result. They presumed that the project can be extended further by improvising feature list and with different classifiers. Future work incorporates the utilization of unsupervised preprocessor along with the supervise classifier on this data, which can be utilized in future to train classifiers in a greatly improved manner.

Mahajan Shubhrata et al. (2016) developed an application framework to automate and predict company shares purchase and sale actions. They adopted Naïve Bayes algorithm for the efficient predicting of return on investment in the share market. The adoption of automation is to give easy access to users and save time. Their work focused on predicting future stock price using prediction concept like Naïve Bayes by parsing records they calculated predicted values and sent to the user in order to automate the process of operations like purchase and sales of shares. To have an automation process, the real-time access is considered from the Yahoo Finance.

Ahmed Oussous et al. (2018) discussed and divided the technologies of Big Data into several system layers namely Data Storage Layer, Data Processing Layer, Data Querying Layer, Data Access Layer and Management Layer to help in choosing and adopting the right combination of different Big Data technologies according to their technological needs and specific applications' requirements. They illustrated both global and contrast views of Big Data technologies. Their main focus is to give detailed knowledge about Big Data technologies and tools to face the complex Big Data challenges by categorizing and discussing main technologies features, advantages, limits, and practices. They discussed about the raised challenges in Big Data area by studying the characteristics of it. They focused on several domains with respect to impact of Big Data mining. And also they presented technologies and components that are used in each layer of Big Data. The distributions and technologies used in Big Data are contrasted in terms of advantages, limits, and their capabilities. The Big Data systems were categorized based on the characteristics and services afforded to the clients.

Yuvraj M. Wadghule and Sonawane V. R. (2017) together proposed a forecasting method, in view of the supposition that key data openly accessible in the past has some prescient connections to the future stock returns. They concentrated on the research areas of Data Mining, Hidden Markov Model Neural Network, and Neuro-Fuzzy system to develop the hybrid model by combining two methods namely the Back Propagation using ANN and Regression. They suggested that the regression is a statistical method for foretelling values of any entity and it is less accurate than the Artificial Neural Network. Employing historical data into two methods is to increase accuracy and correctness which will help investors in buying or selling the stocks by providing appropriate decision-making at right time. Suitable prediction techniques need to be selected for specific domains.

Yang Jiao and Jakubowicz (2017) reviewed the performance of artificial neural network, gradient boosted trees, random forest, and logistic regression algorithms in predicting the S&P 500 stocks. They adopted and compared standard validation schemes such as single validation, sequential validation, and cross validation for each prediction algorithm. They found that the prediction of financial sector stocks is easier than other sectors. Their models are compared to Elston's algorithm and better performance is achieved in the movement direction of S&P 500 index forecasting. Other sources of information namely Macroeconomic data and trading volume data can be utilized to improve prediction accuracy.

Jadhav and Wakode (2017) presented a survey on various prediction models that can be used to predict the future value of a company stock by including sentiment score from public opinions gathered from social media and news articles and for efficient stock market prediction. They discussed time series models namely random walk, moving averages, regression method, and ARIMA model. The prediction models are evaluated using different performance metrics like Mean Absolute Error, Normalized Mean Absolute Error, Mean Absolute Percentage Error, Mean Square Root Error, Mean Square Error, and Root Mean Square Error. They adopted various classification algorithms for sentiment analysis for calculating sentiment score and also extracted the information regarding the exact location of a person, the number of retweets, the number of followers collectively applied as features to improve accuracy and to speed up the performance for proposed prediction algorithm. The parallel distributed algorithm Map Reduce was implemented to support the Big Data environment.

Checkley et al. (2017) tried to discover the ability of sentiment metrics along with Granger-causal of stock price returns, stock trading volume, and volatility to predict stock markets. The sentiment metrics have been calculated from the text extracted from microblogging sites based on sentiments' predictive time horizons. The sentiment metrics like independent bullish and bearish data are collected for major stocks in granular of two-minute intervals from the opinions of bloggers. They suggested that high volume sentiment could provide an efficient prediction of price volatility and traded volume than traditional prediction approaches. They concluded that efficient prediction is possible from the diversified environments rather than a single source of wisdom.

Pooja Singh (2014) made an attempt to inspect the association among changeable macroeconomics and the Indian stock market and, it is also observed that there exists a long-run stable relationships among the variables and the rise in industrial sector performance will increase the stock market performance. They also suggested that the gold rates are also used as investment alternatives, which could increase Indian Stock market performance. Using the Granger Causality test, they observed the casual relationships among FII to stock market. The movement in the foreign investments has a major control in stock market. The government should take initiatives such that investment in share market could improve the investors' confidence by reducing the gold consumption and enhancing the investments.

Tripathy et al. (2016) outlined the key contributions by proposing the classification of movie reviews stated generally in the form of text in an unstructured format of IMDB dataset (IMDB 2011) by specifying various machine learning algorithms using n-gram techniques like Unigram, Bigram, Trigram, hybrid techniques of unigram and bigram, unigram, bigram and trigram, bigram, and trigram. They used machine learning techniques like Support Vector Machine, Stochastic gradient Descent, Maximum entropy, Naive Bayes for the purpose of classification. The performance metrics like Precision, Recall, and F-Measure are used to analyze accuracy. In this paper, the authors presented the limitations of their work, like non-consideration of tweets of short length and consisting of special symbols (e.g., ©, §, @) and stressed words to carry their emotions like "Fineee, Greatttt." They also stated the challenges related to sentiment analysis in the context of opinion mining in determining the positive and negative type of sentiment as the opinions vary according to the state of mind of the user, which may be difficult for the machine to understand sometimes.

Goykhman and Teimouri (2018) performed research on the stock market simulation framework by defining sentiment processes. Their main focus is to develop a Markov chain model to analyze the buy/sell trading sentiment in the market environment. For the reconstruction of the probabilities matrix of the sentiment process,

Baum–Welch algorithm of Hidden Markov Model (HMM) is used and to deduce the states of sentiment at each time stamp Viterbi algorithm of the HMM, is used to recover the basic sentiment states from observed stock prices behavior. The Recurrent Neural Networks Models are used to record the sequence of states by fitting the time series by improving the accuracy. They concluded that the suggested model with long-term sentiment states could provide better results than the time series of stock prices collected in the manner of intra-day.

Sunil Tiwari et al. (2018) investigated and reported the Big Data analytics research area and supply chain management application area and its insights into industries. They found that the need for Big Data tools could highly impact the data in supply chain management.

Asur Sitaram and Bernardo A. Huberman (2010) have predicted that the box office collections of a movie, is dependent on the public sentiments related to movies before its release and expressed as chatter or social opinions from Twitter.com. Constructed linear regression model is used for prediction, they concluded that the performance of a real-world scenario can be analyzed using social media feeds that acts as an effective indicator. They recognized that the powerful model can be constructed for forecasting the revenue of the box office using the frequency of tweets collected and the predictions made by these could provide efficiently than the information market like Hollywood Stock Exchange. The box office predictions can be further improvised via sentiment analysis performed on tweets content and rates of tweets collected after the movie release. They developed the regression model and tweet rate time series for the effective prediction of box office revenue.

Borodino et al. (2012) have shown that the voluminous queries (multiple users requests submitted for the search engines) are correlated with trading volumes of stocks recorded in NASDAQ-100.

Gilbert and Karahalios (2010) observed the downfall in the movement of S&P 500 index due to hype in expressions like fear, worry. And also noticed that the weblogs could affect downward movement S&P 500 index. They used the Granger-causal framework. They confirmed the result via Monte Carlo simulation. They had taken opinions from posts made on the site *Live* journal. Their findings revealed that the mood of millions of people in an online community can be helpful in anticipation of changes in an apparently distinct system.

Bollen et al. (2011) analyzed that the collective mood of public opinions from twitter feeds directly affect the Dow Jones Industrial Index. They included self-organizing fuzzy neural network and Granger Causality analysis for effective prediction. Their research is for finding the answers for the queries like; is decision-making affected by society experiences, are the economic indicators affected by the public moods. For text content analysis in the tweets the mood tracking tools like Google-Profile of Mood States (GPOMS), Opinion Finder are used. The idea of Opinion finder is to calculate positive versus negative moods whereas GPOMS is used to analyze the mood with six factors namely Happy, Alert, Calm, Sure, Kind, and Vital. They presented the results of accuracy for DJIA predictions that were improved appreciably by considering the public mood dimensions like Happy, calm,

Anxiety but not all others. They presented the prediction accuracy of 86.7% and reduced the Mean Average Percentage Error (MAPE) up to 6%.

Chakraborty et al. (2017) worked on 1-year data of tweets extracted with "AAPL" keyword to forecast the stock indices of a company and collected tweets using keywords like "stock market," "stocktwits" for analyzing stock market movement from US database. They used sentiment140 API to collect the tweets and adapted the boosted regression tree model for prediction of DJIA stock. SVM for tweets classification. Along with unigram, bigram, trigram approaches different classification algorithms namely Logistic Regression, SVM, Decision Tree, Boosted Tree, Random Forest are applied to dataset. SVM model gave the best accuracy with the unigram approach to the test tweets. Although, SVM performs better, logistic classifier performed almost as well as SVM.

Pagolu et al. (2016) discussed that there exists a strong correlation among everyday stock prices and twitter sentiment, for this analysis they considered the year wise stock information of Microsoft Company by defining tweets, stock closing, and opening prices. They adapted a random forest algorithm for predicting nonhuman annotated tweets. Word2Vec and N-grams are the forms of textual representations used for the analysis of public sentiments collected from tweets. The Sentiment analysis and supervised learning techniques were used to analyze the stock market movements either raise or downfall correlated with public sentiments of tweets collected from twitter. The preprocessing of tweets adopts three filtering stages namely, removal of stop words, tokenization, and regex matching for pruning special characters from the tweets. The main contribution of authors includes the development of sentiment analyzer for judging sentiment in the tweet.

Conclusion

The chapter presents the outline vision of research about Big Data and its relevant applications and related disciplines connected to the Big Data research field. This chapter contains four sections where Section "Introduction" presents the introduction to Big Data analytics and in the preceding sections, i.e., from Sections "Big Data", "Big Data Analytics" and "Sentiment Analysis" present the various streaming applications operated under Big Data, Tools and Techniques, methods and approaches followed for each operating areas using Big Data like stock market analysis and sentiment analysis. The next section describes about literature survey performed by various authors on Big Data. In this chapter, the importance of Hadoop and Spark technologies and its working environment is also discussed with respect to Big Data applications.

References

Appel O, Chiclana F, Carter J, Fujita H (2016) A hybrid approach to the sentiment analysis problem at the sentence level. Knowl-Based Syst 108:110–124

Asur S, Huberman BA (2010, August) Predicting the future with social media. In: 2010 IEEE/WIC/ACM international conference on web intelligence and intelligent agent technology, vol 1. IEEE, New Jersey, pp 492–499

Benedetto F, Tedeschi A (2016) Big data sentiment analysis for brand monitoring in social media streams by cloud computing. In: Sentiment analysis and ontology engineering. Springer, Cham, pp 341–377

Bollen J, Mao H, Zeng X (2011) Twitter mood predicts the stock market. J Comput Sci 2(1):1–8

Bordino I, Battiston S, Caldarelli G, Cristelli M, Ukkonen A, Weber I (2012) Web search queries can predict stock market volumes. PLoS One 7(7):e40014

Chakraborty P, Pria US, Rony MRAH, Majumdar MA (2017 September) Predicting stock movement using sentiment analysis of twitter feed. In: 2017 6th international conference on informatics, electronics and vision & 2017 7th international symposium in computational medical and health technology (ICIEV-ISCMHT). IEEE, New Jersey, pp 1–6

Checkley MS, Higón DA, Alles H (2017) The hasty wisdom of the mob: how market sentiment predicts stock market behavior. Expert Syst Appl 77:256–263

Deepak RS, Uday SI, Malathi D (2017) Machine learning approach in stock market prediction. Int J Pure Appl Math 115(8):71–77

Deepika N, Bhat MN, Paul PV (2020). Study on Indian stock market performance based on commodities: study on Indian stock market performance based on commodities. Handbook of research on applied AI for international business and marketing applications. IGI Global, Sept 2020. Web Mar 2020, 250–275. https://doi.org/10.4018/978-1-7998-5077-9.ch0xx

Escobar A, Moreno J, Múnera S (2013) A technical analysis indicator based on fuzzy logic. Electron Notes in Theor Comput Sci 292:27–37

Gilbert E, Karahalios K (2010, May) Widespread worry and the stock market. In: Fourth International AAAI Conference on Weblogs and Social Media

Goykhman M, Teimouri A (2018) Machine learning in sentiment reconstruction of the simulated stock market. Physica A Stat Mech Appl 492:1729–1740

Jadhav R, Wakode MS (2017) Survey: sentiment analysis of twitter data for stock market prediction. Int J Adv Res Comput Commun Eng 6(3):558–562

Jiao Y, Jakubowicz J (2017, December) Predicting stock movement direction with machine learning: an extensive study on S & P 500 stocks. In: 2017 IEEE international conference on big data (big data). IEEE, New Jersey, pp 4705–4713

Mahajan Shubhrata D, Deshmukh Kaveri V, Thite Pranit R, Samel Bhavana Y, Chate PJ (2016) Stock market prediction and analysis using Naïve Bayes. Int J Recent Innov Trends Comput Commun (IJRITCC) 4(11):121–124

Naveen Balaji S, Victer Paul P, Saravanan R (2017) Survey on sentiment analysis based stock prediction using big data analytics. In: International IEEE Conference on Innovations in Power and Advanced Computing Technologies [i-PACT-2017], Chennai, pp 1–5

Nisar TM, Yeung M (2018) Twitter as a tool for forecasting stock market movements: a short-window event study. J Financ Data Sci 4(2):101–119

Oussous A, Benjelloun FZ, Lahcen AA, Belfkih S (2018) Big data technologies: a survey. J King Saud Univ Comput Inf Sci 30(4):431–448

Pagolu VS, Reddy KN, Panda G, Majhi B (2016, October) Sentiment analysis of twitter data for predicting stock market movements. In: 2016 International Conference on Signal Processing, Communication, Power and Embedded System (SCOPES). IEEE, New Jersey, pp 1345–1350

Rachid BA, Azza H, Henda BG (2018) Sentiment analysis approaches based on granularity levels

Shanmugam M, Saleem Basha MS, Victer Paul P, Dhavachelvan P, Baskaran R (2013) Performance assessment over heuristic population seeding techniques of genetic algorithm:

benchmark analyses on traveling salesman problems. Int J Appl Eng Res (IJAER) 8 (10):1171–1184. ISSN 0973-4562

Singh P (2014) An empirical relationship between selected Indian stock market indices and macroeconomic indicators. Int J Res Bus Manage 2(9):81–92

Tedeschi A, Benedetto F (2015, September) A cloud-based big data sentiment analysis application for enterprises' brand monitoring in social media streams. In: 2015 IEEE 1st International Forum on Research and Technologies for Society and Industry Leveraging a Better Tomorrow (RTSI). IEEE, New Jersey, pp 186–191

Thamizhselvan M, Raghuraman R, Manoj SG, Victer Paul P (2015 Jan) Data security model for cloud computing using V-GRT methodology. In: IEEE 9th International Conference on Intelligent Systems and Control (ISCO), India., pp 1–6. [Scopus Indexed]

Tiwari S, Wee HM, Daryanto Y (2018) Big data analytics in supply chain management between 2010 and 2016: insights to industries. Comput Ind Eng 115:319–330

Tripathy A, Agrawal A, Rath SK (2016) Classification of sentiment reviews using n-gram machine learning approach. Expert Syst Appl 57:117–126

Victer Paul P, Monica K, Trishanka M (2017) A survey on big data analytics using social media data. In: International IEEE Conference on Innovations in Power and Advanced Computing Technologies [i-PACT2017], Chennai, pp 1–5

Vijayaraj J, Saravanan R, Victer Paul P, Raju R (2016) A comprehensive survey on big data analytics tools. In: 2016 Online International Conference on Green Engineering and Technologies (IC-GET), Coimbatore, pp 1–6. [Scopus Indexed]

Wadghule MYM, Sonawane VR (2017) Stock market prediction and forecasting techniques: a survey. Int J Eng Sci Res Technol 6(1):39–42

Waller MA, Fawcett SE (2013) Data science, predictive analytics, and big data: a revolution that will transform supply chain design and management. J Bus Logist 34(2):77–84

Deepika Nalabala is a research scholar in the Department of Computer Science and Engineering, Vignan's Foundation for Science, Technology & Research (Deemed to be University), Guntur, AP, India. She received B. Tech in Computer Science & Information Technology (2005) from JNTU Hyderabad, M. Tech in Computer Science (2009) from JNTU Hyderabad. She has 10+ years of academic experience and published ten research papers in various International Journals and Conferences. Her areas of Interest are Data Analytics and Data Mining.

M. Nirupama Bhat is working as an Associate Professor in the Department of Computer Science and Engineering at Vignan's Foundation for Science, Technology & Research (Deemed to be University), Guntur, AP, India. She completed her Ph.D. in Computer Science (2015) from Sri Padmavati Mahila ViswaVidyalayam, Tirupati, India. She has 20+ years of academic experience and over 10 years of research. She published over 25 research papers in various National and International Journals and Conferences. Currently, she is working in the areas of Cryptography, Cloud Computing, and Data Analytics.

P. Victer Paul is working as assistant professor in the Department of Computer Science and Engineering, Indian Institute of Information Technology Kottayam, Valavoor P.O, Pala, Kottayam, Kerala, India. He has completed his PhD in the Department of Computer Science (2015), from Pondicherry University, Pondicherry, India. He has done his B.Tech. in Information Technology (2007) and M.Tech. in Network and Internet Engineering (2011) from Pondicherry University, Pondicherry, India. He is a recipient of an eminent INSPIRE fellowship from the Department of Science and Technology, New Delhi. He is a University Gold medalist in both B.Tech. and M.Tech. studies. He has also received "TCS Best Student Award 2010" for academic excellence from Pondicherry University, Pondicherry. He has 7+ years of academic and industrial experience and published over 90 research papers in various International Journals and Conferences. Currently, he is working in the fields of Cloud Computing, Evolutionary Computing, and Data Analytics.

Capital Structure Adjustment Speed: Evidence from Borsa Istanbul Sub-Sectors

Turhan Korkmaz and Aslı Yıkılmaz Erkol

Introduction

The determination of an optimal capital structure has been one of the most debatable issues in the financial literature since the irrelevance theorem of Modigliani and Miller (M&M) (1958). However, empirical studies have found inconsistent results with M&M's (1958) theorem. These studies have guided other studies and several theories over the past four decades have been developed to explain debt puzzle. The theoretical and empirical studies have reconciled two significant theories of capital structure: The pecking order theory developed by Myers (1984) and the trade-off theories developed by Kraus and Litzenberger (1973). The most crucial difference between these two major theories is the assumption of the existence of the optimal debt ratio. By the trade-off theory, the optimum debt level of the firms is determined by the tax shield, financial distress, bankruptcy costs, and agency costs. If each firm has a target debt ratio, any deviation from this target ought to be adjusted to return to the target debt ratio.

The dynamic trade-off theory that emerged in the 1990s is a more sophisticated and realistic approach than the static trade-off theory. Dynamic trade-off theory is an approach that criticizes the assumption of M&M (1958) that effective market and financing needs can be met without cost. If the markets are efficient and the financing needs of the firms can be met without transaction costs, then the debt/equity level of the firms represents the optimum capital structure. Moreover, this debt level is static. Fischer et al. (1989) are the most influential authors of the dynamic trade-off theory in the last 20 years and have shown that the optimum debt level has changed over

T. Korkmaz (✉) · A. Y. Erkol
Faculty of Economics and Administrative Sciences, Mersin University, Mersin, Turkey
e-mail: tkorkmaz@mersin.edu.tr; ayikilmazerkol@mersin.edu.tr

B. Adıgüzel Mercangöz (ed.), *Handbook of Research on Emerging Theories, Models, and Applications of Financial Econometrics*,
https://doi.org/10.1007/978-3-030-54108-8_18

time. The firms do not immediately adjust the deviations from the optimum debt level because of the adjustment costs and allow the debt level to fluctuate between the upper and lower limits.

Several studies have investigated the capital structure of firms (Graham and Harvey 2001; Titman and Wessels 1988; Fama and French 2002; Harris and Raviv 1991; Frank and Goyal 2002, 2009; Strebulaev 2007; Deangelo and Roll 2015). The main goal of most of these studies is revealed through the capital structures of firms. The result of these studies confirms whether the capital structure of firms supports the static trade-off theory or pecking order theory. Besides, some other studies have investigated whether firms have a target leverage ratio, and they have provided evidence supporting the trade-off theory (Leary and Roberts 2005; Fama and French 2002; Nieh et al. 2008; Flannery and Rangan 2006).

If the firms have a target debt ratio, the question of whether this target debt ratio is critical for the firm's capital structure can be answered by determining the adjustment speed of firms. The main purpose of this study is to assign the adjustment speed of BIST sub-sectors. Thus, whether the firms have a dynamic capital structure, as well as which capital structure theory is supported implicitly, will be determined. This implicit validation is expected to contribute to studies testing capital structure theories in the literature. In the macro dimension, the sub-sectors that have higher adjustment speed will be revealed and how the crisis affects the adjustment speed of the sub-sectors will be determined.

In the first section, classical capital structure theories and current capital structure theories are briefly mentioned, and the dynamic capital structure theory is examined. The study proceeds as follows. The theoretical review is presented in Secttion "Theoretical Review". The data and methodology are described in Section "Literature Review". Lastly, the results are reported with their implications in Section "Methodology".

Theoretical Review

Capital structure decisions and the existence of optimum debt ratio have been one of the most debated issues. Theories have not yet reached a consensus on whether firms operate at the optimal capital structure level.

The capital structure theories are examined under two main headings: Classical approaches and current approaches. As understood, classical approaches include the approaches that are effective in the emergence of capital structure theories. These approaches point to the existence of the relationship between firm value and capital structure. The most fundamental theorem that distinguishes between classical and current approaches is the irrelevance approach proposed by M&M in 1958. The theory of irrelevance sets the basis for many fundamental studies such as trade-off theory (Kraus and Litzenberger 1973), pecking order theory (Myers 1984), agency theory, signaling theory, free cash flow hypothesis, and dynamic trade-off theory.

The basis of the current capital structure approaches is the irrelevance theorem. According to the theorem, given a set of assumptions, the firm value and cost of capital are independent of the capital structure. M&M's proposition triggered debates and criticism, and numerous articles were published in the coming periods.

M&M's lack of consideration of financial distress and bankruptcy costs, which is a severe problem for firms in real life, has been frequently criticized in the literature. As a result of these criticisms, the static trade-off theory (Kraus and Litzenberger 1973) has been developed which suggests that excessive borrowing causes the risk of insolvency, and therefore, the effect of tax saving on increasing the firms' value will not continue permanently. Kraus and Litzenberger (1973), who developed a firm valuation model for a single period, consider two factors in evaluating the optimal capital structure of firms; these are the benefits from the tax advantage of debt (tax shield) and financial distress/bankruptcy costs. The optimal debt level of firms is suggested to be the point where the marginal tax advantage provided by the debt is equal to the marginal financial distress costs. In addition, the weighted average cost of capital is at the lowest level, and firm value is at the highest level at this point.

The static trade-off theory has been criticized in many ways. The most trenchant criticism was directed to the expected positive relationship between the debt level and the profitability. Under the assumption that firms with high profitability will have low financial distress and bankruptcy costs, it is expected that firms with high profit will want to benefit from higher tax savings by using higher debt levels (Brealey et al. 2001: 412). However, empirical studies have shown that large and successful firms have a low debt level despite the high tax rate advantage (Miller 1977; Titman and Wessels 1988; Harris and Raviv 1991; Rajan and Zingales 1995; Graham and Harvey 2001; Fama and French 2002; Frank and Goyal 2009). Besides, surveys approve the existence of a target debt ratio and the significance of the adjustment speed. Graham and Harvey (2001) and Brealey et al. (2001) have reported that more than half of the firms in their survey sample maintain a target debt ratio.

The dynamic trade-off theory investigates why and when firms adjust optimum debt levels. The cost arising from the reorganization of the capital structure is called adjustment cost, which is one of the most significant factors for capital structure behavior of firms. The adjustment costs are the costs that must be incurred to attain the optimum debt/equity ratio of firms whose target debt ratio deviates from the optimum. Firms that deviate from the target debt ratio progressively return to the target debt level over time or operate below the target debt level. The adjustment speed depends on the costs of returning to the target capital structure and the costs of deviating from the target capital structure (Faulkender et al. 2012).

However, the cost of adjusting leverage depends not only on evident transaction costs but also on the firm's encouragement to reach capital markets for other reasons (Faulkender et al. 2012). Financial managers should appraise the trade-off between the costs of being off the target debt ratio and the costs of adjustment (Drobetz and Wanzenried 2006: 937). If firms follow the dynamic trade-off theory, implying that they have target capital structures, then their adjustment speeds should be functions of the costs and benefits of adjusting their debt structures (Clark et al. 2009: 3).

The adjustment speed indicates the percentage of the firm's deflection from the target debt level in each period. In other words, it refers to the reduction percentage of the firm in the difference between the current debt and the target debt ratio in a period.

Firms with a high adjustment speed have high adaptability of capital structures, and firms with a low adjustment speed have low adaptability of capital structures. When the adjustment speeds are evaluated within this scope, firms with a high adjustment speed can adapt their capital structures faster and evaluate opportunities in case of possible shocks and investment opportunities.

The adjustment speed is directly related to the deviation from the target debt ratio and the adjustment costs. Adjustment costs are affected by the firm's institutional statutory and financial environment (Antoniou et al. 2008). Macroeconomic variables are other factors that have a significant effect on the correction rate and correction costs. In particular, the insufficiency of capital supply in the crisis period restricts firms' access to capital markets (Cook and Tang 2010).

Ease of access to capital markets is a component of the adjustment costs. In countries with restraining access to capital markets, either debt or equity is more complicated and more costly. The more advanced financial systems decrease market defects and thus can provide better financial services (Drobetz and Wanzenried 2006: 951). Therefore, firms in countries with an advanced financial system have a higher adjustment speed. According to Clark et al. (2009), higher managerial agency costs, higher expected bankruptcy costs, tax rates, and sound relation between creditor and shareholder rights cause a faster adjustment in developing countries. Overall, macroeconomic, country-level and firm-level factors are responsible for the heterogeneity in the adjustment speed of firms (Drobetz and Wanzenried 2006: 937).

Although in estimating the speed of adjustment, Fama and French (2002), Özkan (2001), and Flannery and Rangan (2006) assumed that the speed of adjustment is homogeneous for each firm, this assumption is inconsistent because each firm has different deviation costs and adjustment costs. The heterogeneity of the speed of adjustment means that the capital structures of firms are dynamic and supports the arguments of capital structure theories based upon the existence of the target debt level.

The dynamic trade-off theory implies that the optimal target debt level of firms adjusts over time; moreover, this optimal target debt level is a function of changing exogenous and endogenous factors (Getzmann et al. 2010: 2).

Literature Review

Many researchers have investigated the rate of adjustment of the target debt level. Some of them are as follows.

Like Fama and French (2002), Shyam-Sunder, and Myers (1999) have examined 157 firms between 1971 and 1989. They have rejected the pecking order against alternative trade-off hypotheses. The adjustment speed of US firms is approximately 41%.

Meanwhile, Özkan (2001) has examined a long-run optimal target debt level, which is a function of several firm characteristics and varies over time and firms. Using the generalized method of moments (GMM) estimation technique, they have estimated the adjustment speed of 390 UK firms during the period 1984–1996. Results revealed that firms' speed of adjustment is 57%.

De Miguel and Pindado (2001) have examined 133 non-financial Spanish firms from 1990 to 1997. They have developed a target adjustment model and found that the Spanish firms' adjustment speed is approximately 21%.

Fama and French (2002) have investigated to determine the rate of adjustment of target payout and target debt ratio. They have analyzed 157 nonfinancial US firms between 1971 and 1989. Their results revealed that the adjustment speeds of US firms are about 7–18% per year, which is a low level.

Moreover, Gaud et al. (2005) have examined 104 Swiss firms for the period 1991–2000 to calculate adjustment speed. They have shown that Swiss firms adjust the target debt/equity ratio, but the adjustment speed is much slower than that in other countries. The adjustment speed of Swiss firms is about 27%.

Leary and Roberts (2005) have investigated whether firms engage in a dynamic rebalancing of their capital structures. They have estimated the adjustment speed of 3494 US firms for the years 1984–2001. They estimated three different measurement methods and found that the adjustment speed of the firms is 15%, 17%, and 39% per year, respectively.

Flannery and Rangan (2006) have analyzed US firms' capital structure for the period 1965–2001. They have used general partial-adjustment model of the firm. They have pointed out that the speed of adjustment to the target debt ratio depends on the adjustment costs and the costs of deviating from the target debt level. Further, a typical firm converges to its long-term target debt level at a rate of more than 30% per year.

Meanwhile, Lemmon et al. (2008) have investigated UK non-financial firms between 1965 and 2003. Using the GMM method, they have found that the speed of adjustment of firms is approximately 22%.

In the work of Huang and Ritter (2009), their sample consists of US firms for the period 1963–2001. They have found that firms adjust to target leverage at a moderate speed. The adjustment speed of firms is 17% per year for book leverage and 23.2% per year for market leverage. Using the partial adjustment model for the 1970–2007 period, Hovakimian and Li (2011) have also investigated the speed of adjustment and found that it ranged from 5.5 to 7.4% per year.

Ghazouani (2013) analyzed 20 non-financial firms in Tunisia for the period 2004–2010. They have concluded that the adjustment costs are relatively high. They have engendered a slow adjustment toward the optimal, and the speed of adjustment is 83.6%.

Haron et al. (2013) examined the 590 Malaysian non-financial firms' debt behavior for the period 2000–2009. They have found that the adjustment speed of Malaysian firms is 57%.

Similarly, Arioglu and Tuan (2014) have investigated the adjustment speed of non-financial firms in Turkey. They have analyzed the capital structure of firms listed on Borsa İstanbul between the years 1998 and 2010. They have suggested that firms follow target capital structures and adjustment speed of about 29%.

Getzmann et al. (2014) analyzed the determinants of capital structure and speed of adjustment to target debt level for firms listed in Asian financial markets for the period 1995–2009. Using the system GMM estimation method, they have concluded that the firms in the Asian financial market have target debt and adjustment speed ranging from 24 to 45%.

Syahara and Soekarno (2015) have analyzed the capital structure characteristic of Indonesian public firms depends on firm-specific factors. They have examined 18 public firms under the LQ45 index, which starts from 2005 to 2014. By employing GMM, they have determined that Indonesian public firms have displayed 38% adjustment speed.

Finally, Kayo et al. (2018) have analyzed Brazilian firms to determine the adjustment speed. By selecting 257 firms from 19 sectors, they found that Brazilian family and non-family firms' adjustment speeds are 73% and 77%, respectively.

The summary of the studies is shown in Table 1.

Methodology

The aim of the study is to investigate the adjustment speed of the BIST 100 index sub-sectors during the pre-crisis, crisis, and post-crisis periods. The study sample is the sub-sectors of Borsa İstanbul over the three study periods: pre-crisis period (2004–2007), crisis period (2008–2012), and post-crisis period (2013–2018). Semi-annual financial statements were used for the analysis. According to Turkey's macroeconomic dynamics, six sub-sectors are determined. The sub-sectors and the total number of firms in each sector are shown in Table 2.

The firms' yearly data are used, and the accounting information is obtained from the Public Disclosure Platform (KAP) and Borsa İstanbul. Moreover, the classic dynamic partial adjustment model developed by Flannery and Rangan (2006) to estimate the target debt level of firms is used, which allows temporary diversions from the target debt level. It allows the target debt ratio to diverge over time, which is determined by a vector of particular firm variables that are related to the cost and benefit of different debt and equity combinations (He and Kyaw 2018).

Preceding studies that forecast the speed of adjustment used the ordinary least squares method, fixed effect estimation, instrumental variables techniques, GMM or longest differencing to estimate dynamic partial adjustment models. In particular, the inconsistency of the estimates in models may be derived from (1) the unbalanced panel structure of corporate financial data; (2) the inclusion of the lagged dependent

Table 1 Summary of the studies on adjustment speed

Author/Authors	Country	Speed of adjustment
Shyam-Sunder and Myers (1999)	US	59%
Özkan (2001)	UK	43%
De Miguel and Pindado (2001)	Spain	21%
Fama and French (2002)	US	Range 7–18%
Gaud et al. (2005)	Switzerland	27%
Leary and Roberts (2005)	US	15%, 17%, and 39% per year
Flannery and Rangan (2006)	US	30%
Lemmon et al. (2008)	UK	22%
Huang and Ritter (2009)	US	17% per year for book leverage and 23.2% per year for market leverage
Hovakimian and Li (2011)	US	Range 5.5–7.4%
Ghazouani (2013)	Tunisian	83.6%
Haron et al. (2013)	Malaysian	57%
Devosa et al. (2017)	US	86%
Arioglu and Tuan (2014)	Turkey	29%
Getzmann et al. (2010)	Asian countries	Range 27–39%
Syahara and Soekarno (2015)	Indonesia	38.15%
Kayo et al. (2018)	Brazilian	73%

Source: Authors' creation

Table 2 BIST sub-sectors, the number of firms and sector codes

Sub-sectors		The number of firms	Sector code
1	Food, beverage, and tobacco	19	FBT
2	Textile, wearing apparel, and leather	15	TWAL
3	Chemicals, petroleum, rubber, and plastic products	17	CPRP
4	Nonmetallic mineral products	24	NMMP
5	Fabricated metal products, machinery, and equipment	21	FMPM
6	Technology	9	TECH
	Total firms	**105**	

Source: Authors' creation

variable as an explanatory variable; (3) the presence of unobserved heterogeneity; and (4) the fractional nature of the dependent variable (Drobetz and Wanzenried 2006: 942). GMM approaches (Arellano and Bond 1991; Blundell and Bond 1998) and long difference estimation (Hahn et al. 2007) account for unobserved heterogeneity and are consistent with the dynamic model structure.

Equation (1) ensures an estimate of each firm's target leverage ratio in the absence of an imperfect market condition. In Eq. (1), the vector variables are represented by vector X, and θ is the related parameter of vector X:

$$D^*_{(i,t)} = \theta(X(i,t-1)) + \varepsilon_{it}, \quad (1)$$

where $D^*_{(i,t)}$ is the unobservable target debt level.

However, in an imperfect market, firms may not exactly adjust their actual debt ratio from the prior period to the current debt ratio. Therefore, to determine the adjustment speeds of the six BİST sub-sectors, we have estimated the partial adjustment model as used by Hovakimian et al. (2001).

Equation 2 reflects the standard partial adjustment model of firm capital structure, which estimates a regression of the form:

$$D_{(i,t)} - D_{(i,t-1)} = \lambda\left(D^*_{(i,t)} - D(i,t-1)\right) + \varepsilon_{(i,t-1)}. \quad (2)$$

Algebraically, when Eq. (1) is substituted into Eq. (2), we obtain the following:

$$D_{(\mathrm{i,t})} = \gamma X_{(\mathrm{i,t-1})} + (1-\lambda)D_{(\mathrm{i,t-1})} + \varepsilon_{(\mathrm{i,t-1})}, \quad (3)$$

where $D_{(i,t)}$ and $D_{(i,t-1)}$ are the total debt ratio at the end of the year (t) and year ($t-1$), respectively. γ is the parameter of the vector of variables, $X_{(i,t)}$ is the firm's several variables related to target debt level and $(1-\lambda)$ is the estimated speed of adjustment to the target debt level.

In Eq. (3), the speed of adjustment (soa) is the difference between 1 and the estimated coefficient of the lagged debt ratio (soa: $1-\lambda$). $(1-\lambda)$ represents the speed of adjustment and varies from 0 to 1.

The existence of adjustment costs is represented by the restriction that $(1-\lambda) < 1$, which implies that $D_{(i,t)} \rightarrow D^*_{(i,t)}$ as $t \rightarrow \infty$. In contrast, if $D_{(i,t)} = 1$, all adjustments are made instantaneously, and a firm's debt ratio is always at the target. In the presence of adjustment costs, it is expected that $(1-\lambda) < 1$; hence, a firm does not fully adjust from period $t-1$ to period t. Finally, if $(1-\lambda) > 1$, a firm adjusts more than would be necessary and is still not at its target debt level (Drobetz and Wanzenried 2006: 944). If $(1-\lambda) = 1$, then the optimal adjustment is achieved within one period, and the firm at time t is at its target leverage (Lööf 2003: 9).

The firm optimum debt level is represented by financial variables in the partial adjustment model because of unobservable nature. Each firm's optimal leverage varies according to country and the firm's characteristics (Frank and Goyal 2009). The variables used in the previous studies investigating the determinants of capital structure are shown in Table 3.

Based on previous studies, which investigate capital structure determinants, we used growth, profitability, tangibility, and the size of estimate firms' target debt level to control for firm heterogeneity. Equation (4) represents the general capital structure model.

Table 3 The literature on firm-specific determinants

Author/Authors	Variables					
Dang (2011)	Profitability	Size	Tangibility	Tax shields effect	–	–
Frank and Goyal (2009)	Profitability	Size	Tangibility	–	–	–
Lemmon et al. (2008)	Profitability	Size	Tangibility	–	–	–
Deesomsak et al. (2009)	Profitability	Size	Tangibility	Liquidity	Earning per share	–
Chen (2004)	Profitability	Size	Tangibility	Cost of financial distress	–	–
Baker and Wurgler (2002)	Profitability	Size	Tangibility	Tax shields effect	–	–
Fama and French (2002)	Profitability	Size	Tangibility	Tax shields effect	–	–
Titman and Wessels (1988)	Profitability	Size	Tangibility	Tax shields effect	Growth	Risk

Source: Authors' creation

Table 4 Firm-specific variables

	Definitions	Proxy (Abbreviation)
Independent variable	The ratio of total debt to total debt plus the market value of equity	Debt
Dependent variables	Natural logarithm of total assets	Size
	Earnings before interest and tax divided by total assets	Profitability (ROA)
	Fixed assets divided by total assets	Tangibility
	Net sales growth (%) (annual)	Growth opportunities

Source: Authors' creation

$$D^*_{(i,t)} = \beta_{(1)} + \beta_{(2)}\text{Profit} + \beta_{(3)}\text{Size} + \beta_{(4)}\text{Growth} + \beta_{(5)}\text{Tang} \quad (4)$$

The variables used in the general equation are shown in Table 4.

The descriptive statistics for six BİST sub-sectors are presented in Appendix. Table 5 demonstrates the periods (Pre crisis, Crisis, and Post- crisis) in which the variables have the highest and lowest values.

In all sectors (except TWAL), the size variable was the lowest in the pre-crisis period and the highest in the post-crisis period. The TWAL sector has grown in the opposite direction of other sectors: The size variable has the highest level in the pre-crisis period and the lowest level in the post-crisis period. If the adjustment of the capital structure involves substantial fixed costs, these costs might be relatively smaller for large firms. Therefore, they should more readily be able to adjust deviations from the target (Drobetz and Wanzenried 2006). These results show

Table 5 Highest and lowest values of the variables

	Low/High	Growth	Size	D	ROA	Tang
FBT	Lowest	Crisis	Pre-crisis	Pre-crisis	Crisis	Pre-crisis
	Highest	Post-crisis	Post-crisis	Crisis	Post-crisis	Crisis
TWAL	Lowest	Crisis	Post-crisis	Post-crisis	Crisis	Post-crisis
	Highest	Post-crisis	Pre-crisis	Pre-crisis	Pre-crisis	Crisis
CPRP	Lowest	Pre-crisis	Pre-crisis	Post-crisis	Pre-crisis	Post-crisis
	Highest	Crisis	Post-crisis	Crisis	Post-crisis	Crisis
FMPM	Lowest	Pre-crisis	Pre-crisis	Crisis	Pre-crisis	Post-crisis
	Highest	Post-crisis	Post-crisis	Pre-crisis	Post-crisis	Crisis
NMMP	Lowest	Crisis	Pre-crisis	Pre-crisis	Crisis	Pre-crisis
	Highest	Pre-crisis	Post-crisis	Post-crisis	Pre-crisis	Post-crisis
TECH	Lowest	Pre-crisis	Pre-crisis	Post-crisis	Pre-crisis	Pre-crisis
	Highest	Crisis	Post-crisis	Pre-crisis	Post-crisis	Crisis

Source: Authors' creation

that if the adjustment of the capital structure involves substantial fixed costs, the adjustment speed in all sectors is expected to be high in the post-crisis period and low in the pre-crisis period.

Growing firms can access alternative sources of financing. Therefore, they are more likely to adapt to their capital structure. The growth opportunity mean values are at the lowest level in the crisis period for the food, beverage, and tobacco (FBT), textile, wearing apparel and leather (TWAL) and nonmetallic mineral products (NMMP) sectors, but at the highest level in the post-crisis period for FBT, TWAL and fabricated metal products, machinery, and equipment (FMPM) sectors. Conversely, the technology (TECH) sector shows different result: The growth opportunities are highest in the crisis period and lowest in the pre-crisis period.

The debt ratio varies by sectors. The debt levels of FBT are at the highest in the pre-crisis period whereas the lowest level in the crisis period. The debt ratios for TWAL and TECH have shown a similar trend, which is the highest level in the pre-crisis and lowest in the post-crisis period. The debt ratio for FBT and TWAL is at the highest level in the crisis period.

For the return on asset, it is at the lowest level for FBT, TWAL, and NMMP sectors in the crisis period; similarly, it is at the lowest level for FMPM, CPRP, and TECH sectors in the pre-crisis period.

The tangibility ratio for all sectors is at the highest level in the crisis period. However, it is at the lowest level for FBT, NMMP, and TECH in the pre-crisis period whereas the lowest level for TWAL, CPRP, and FMPM in the post-crisis period.

Meanwhile, the growth opportunities, size, and profitability of the FBT sector are at the highest level after the crisis period and the lowest level in the crisis period. Similarly, for the TWAL sector, the growth opportunities and size are at the highest level after the crisis period and the lowest level in the crisis period. If the adjustment of the debt ratio includes prominent fixed costs, these costs might be relatively smaller for large firms, and therefore, they should more readily be able to adjust deviations from the target debt level.

Using the GMM of Arellano and Bond (1991), we can estimate the speed of adjustment. The GMM estimator, one of the dynamic panel models, considers heterogeneity and potential autocorrelation in residues. System-GMM combines equation in first difference and improves efficiency. In addition, there is no correlation between the series in system-GMM, and the hypothesis is tested. Therefore, the high probability value of the Arellano-Bond AR(2) test statistic is essential for the estimator to provide reliable results. If the problem persists, the lagged values of the independent variables were used. In addition, in the system-GMM estimators, the t-statistic is robust, and the validity of the tool variables used are tested by the Hansen J test. The hypothesis tested is that "all instrument variables are common." Therefore, the rejection of the hypothesis tested in the Hansen J test is vital for the validity of GMM results.

Table 6 shows the GMM results.

As presented in Table 6, in the pre-crisis period, the coefficient of FBT, TWAL, and CPRP sectors is negative and statistically significant, whereas the coefficients of other sectors are not statistically significant. The Arellano-Bond AR(2) test statistic value is high for all sectors, and Hansen J statistic was not rejected for all models.

In the crisis period, the coefficient of FBT, TWAL, FMPE, and NMMP sectors is positive and statistically significant. The coefficients of other sectors are positive but not statistically significant. The Arellano-Bond AR(2) test statistic value is high for both sectors, and Hansen J statistic is not rejected for all models.

Similar to the pre-crisis period, in the post-crisis period, the coefficient of FBT, TWAL, FMPE, and NMMP sectors is positive and statistically significant. The coefficients of other sectors are positive but not statistically significant. The Arellano-Bond AR(2) test statistic value is high for both sectors, and Hansen J statistic is not rejected for all models.

For all periods, the coefficient of FBT, TWAL, FMPE, CPRP, and NMMP sectors is positive and statistically significant except TECH sector. The sector number of instruments is higher than the number of observations; hence, the coefficient for the TECH sector has not been calculated for all periods. The Arellano-Bond AR(2) test statistic value is high for all sectors, and Hansen J statistic is not rejected for all models.

The speed of adjustment values calculated by the correlation coefficients is shown in Table 7.

Table 7 shows the speed of adjustments in all sectors. The adjustment speed is not calculated for FMPE, NMMP, and TECH sectors in the pre-crisis period, CPRP and TECH sectors in the crisis period, and CPRP and TECH sectors in the post-crisis period because the sectors' coefficient is statistically insignificant. It can be stated that there is no evidence for the existence of the target debt ratio of the sectors whose adjustment speed cannot be calculated. However, it can be claimed that sectors with a significant correlation coefficient have a target debt ratio, which may also be the evidence to deviate from this target debt ratio.

Table 6 The GMM results

Debt (t–1)	FBT	TWAL	CPRP	FMPE	NMMP	TECH
Pre-crisis period (2005–2007)						
Coefficient	−0.534529***	−0.315800**	−0.30509***	−0.79111	0.02837	0.25002
AR 1	0.1703	0.3683	0.4602	0.4630	0.0580	–
AR 2	0.3240	0.5453	0.6979	0.4145	0.1355	0.9998
J statistic	11.08159	13.07808	13.82261	9.357992	15.90180	5.792092
Probability	0.270158	0.159105	0.128777	0.404906	0.068961	0.215222
Crisis period (2008–2012)						
Coefficient	0.39258**	0.64098***	0.20224	0.53044***	0.33840***	0.365508
AR 1	0.0279	0.5115	0.5267	0.5124	0.0444	0.4705
AR 2	0.7412	0.8604	0.3154	0.0917	0.7438	0.3536
J statistic	16.10933	8.970300	11.12843	17.50343	20.52649	6.204917
Probability	0.306743	0.440020	0.432567	0.230341	0.363544	0.184359
Post-crisis period (2013–2018)						
Coefficient	0.572985***	0.581720***	0.012360	0.320232***	0.123306***	0.243296
AR 1	0.8183	0.7196	0.2922	–	0.0344	0.9363
AR 2	0.9974	0.9502	0.9568	0.6339	0.9067	0.9075
J statistic	14.91220	8.173566	16.00290	19.06582	22.40162	3.844080
Probability	0.384183	0.516754	0.191103	0.265265	0.264727	0.427518
All periods (2005–2018)						
Coefficient	0.7791***	0.5253***	0.5290***	0.6145***	0.4864***	–
AR 1	0.0803	0.8327	0.0664	0.8949	0.1522	–
AR 2	0.8452	–	0.5762	–	–	–
J statistic	18.0333	8.7807	15.7531	16.4359	21.2643	–
Probability	0.2052	0.5530	0.2028	0.4931	0.3223	–

Source: Authors' creation

***, **, and * indicate the coefficient is significant at 1%, 5%, and 10% levels, respectively

Table 7 The speed of adjustment values for BİST sub-sectors

Sectors	Pre-crisis period (2005–2007)	Crisis period (2008–2012)	Post-crisis period (2013–2018)	All periods (2005–2018)
FBT	Correlation Coefficient −0.534529 Soa = 1.53453	Correlation Coefficient 0.392580 Soa = 0.60742	Correlation Coefficient 0.572985 Soa = 0.42702	Correlation Coefficient 0.7791 Soa = 0.2209
TWAL	Correlation Coefficient −0.315800 Soa = 1.31580	Correlation Coefficient 0.640985 Soa = 0.35902	Correlation Coefficient 0.581720 Soa = 0.41828	Correlation Coefficient 0.5253 Soa = 0.4747
CPRP	Correlation Coefficient −0.315800 Soa = 1.30509	–	–	Correlation Coefficient 0.5290 Soa = 0.471
FMPE	–	Correlation Coefficient 0.530442 Soa = 0.46956	Correlation Coefficient 0.320232 Soa = 0.67977	Correlation Coefficient 0.6145 Soa = 0.3855
NMMP	–	Correlation Coefficient 0.338403 Soa = 0.66159	Correlation Coefficient 0.123306 Soa = 0.87669	Correlation Coefficient 0.4864 Soa = 0.5136
TECH	–	–	–	–

Source: Authors' creation

In the pre-crisis period, the adjustment speeds of FBT, TWAL, and CPRP are 153%, 131%, and 130% on an annual average, respectively. The sectors' adjustment speed values are more significant than one. Sector's firms overadjust by making more adjustments than necessary and are still not at its target debt level. According to Lööf (2003), overadjustment may reflect unanticipated changes in economic conditions.

In the crisis period, the adjustment speeds of each sector on an average annually are as follows: FBT 60.7%, TWAL 35.9%, NMMP 46.9%, and FMPM 66.1%. The sectors' adjustment speed value is lower than 1, indicating that these sectors do not fully adjust the debt level from period $t - 1$ to period t.

In the post-crisis period, FBT's adjustment speed is 42.7%, TWAL's adjustment speed is 41.8%, NMMP's adjustment speed is 87.6% and FMPM's adjustment speed is 67.9%. These adjustment speed values are lower than one. Observed, the adjustment speed of the firms in the sector increased in the post-crisis period compared with the crisis period.

In all periods, the following adjustment speeds are reported: FBT 22%; TWAL 47.4%; CPRP 47.1%, NMMP 51.3%, and FMPM 38.5%. The sectors' adjustment speed values are lower than 1.

Figure 1 shows the adjustment speed of the sectors.

FBT sector's adjustment speed decline over the period. In the pre-crisis period, the adjustment rate is more than one, implying more adjustments. The adjustment

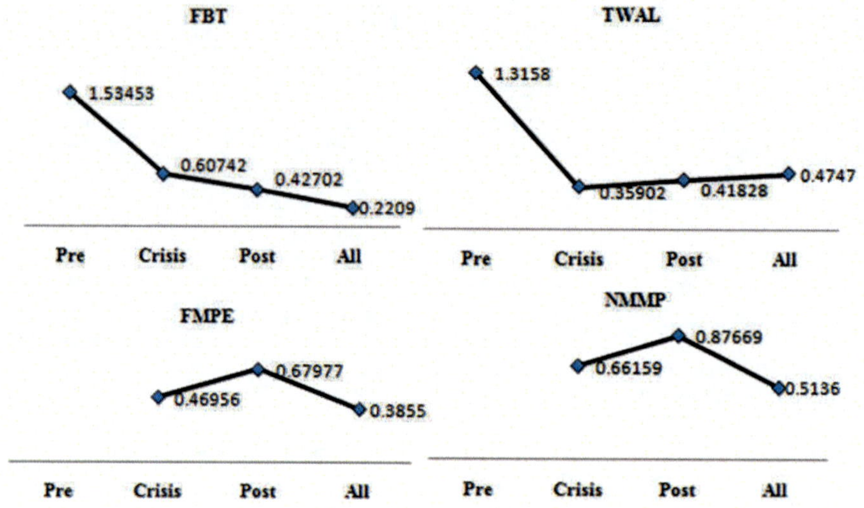

Fig. 1 The sectors' speed of adjustment in the pre-crisis, crisis, post-crisis, and all periods. Source: Authors' creation

speed in the crisis period decreased compared with that in the pre-crisis period, and this decrease continued in the post-crisis period. The adjustment speed is the lowest in the whole period. The adjustment costs of the sector have increased over time. It is observed that the opportunities encountered in the pre-crisis period and the low level of adjustment costs increase the adjustment speed of firms in the sector.

TWAL sector has shown excessive adjustment in the pre-crisis period similar to FBT. However, in the crisis period, the adjustment speed has fallen below one, and the adjustment speed has decreased. In the post-crisis period, the adjustment speed slightly increased compared with that in the crisis period. The adjustment speed of the sector is the second highest level in the entire period.

Meanwhile, the adjustment speed of NMMP and FMPM sectors has shown a steady increase from the crisis period to the post-crisis period but has shown the lowest level in the entire period.

Prior empirical studies have found that economic downturn periods limit firms' access to capital markets. These problems affect the capital structure adjustment speed negatively (Cook and Tang 2010; Hovakimian and Li 2009). Same inference can be applied to FBT and TWAL sectors for the crisis period. The adjustment speed in these sectors has decreased by more than half compared with that in the pre-crisis period. In this context, FBT and TWAL sector's ability to access capital markets appears to be significantly affected by the crisis period.

Discussion and Conclusion

This study reveals that five of the six sectors in the BIST index deviate from the target debt level in different periods and correct these deviations again at different periods and different adjustment speeds.

The adjustment speed values for all sectors with significant coefficient are similar to those found in the studies conducted in developing countries. For all the periods, the adjustment speed of the sub-sectors is below 50% (Syahara and Soekarno 2015; Ghazouani 2013; Kayo et al. 2018).

The adjustment speed is different from zero for the FBT, TWAL, CPRP, NMMP, and FMPM sectors. Therefore, it can be claimed that these sectors have a target debt ratio and support the trade-off theory for different periods.

However, the adjustment speed for the TECH sector could not be determined in any period. Therefore, it is not possible to make an inference on the target debt ratio of the TECH sector in the pre-crisis, crisis, and post-crisis periods. Moreover, it can be concluded that the trade-off theory is not supported because there is no evidence of the target debt ratio. However, it is not possible to infer whether the pecking order theory is supported.

All sectors exhibit a lower adjustment speed in the crisis period. In particular, FBT and TWAL sectors are more restricted during the crisis period. This result supports the findings of Cook and Tang (2010) who investigated the relationship between macroeconomic factors; they have claimed that firms exhibit a faster adjustment speed in good states compared with those in bad states.

In the crisis period, firms may have reduced their adjustment speed to avoid adjustment costs that limit their liquidity. Due to increased borrowing costs, firms operating under the target debt ratio may not have opted for additional debt, whereas firms above the target debt ratio may not have preferred to close the debt. There is an increase in the adjustment speed in all sectors (except for FBT sector) in the post-crisis period. This result also supports the conclusion that the ability to access capital markets is limited during the crisis, and therefore, firms have decreased the adjustment speed.

Appendix: Descriptive Statistics

		Growth	Size	D	Roa	Tang
Food, beverage, and tobacco						
Pre-crisis (2005–2007)	Mean	0.1128	18.5057	0.4593	−0.0283	0.7055
	Median	0.0707	18.1735	0.4709	−0.0014	0.7200
	Maximum	1.3432	22.1737	0.9117	0.3824	0.9934
	Minimum	−0.7688	16.5566	0.0667	−0.8733	0.1597
	Std. dev.	0.3312	1.2234	0.2104	0.1705	0.2236

(continued)

		Growth	Size	D	Roa	Tang
Crisis (2008–2012)	Mean	0.0906	18.8013	0.4294	−0.0290	0.7670
	Median	0.0829	18.5705	0.4186	0.0033	0.7798
	Maximum	2.9925	23.0675	0.9777	0.1602	0.9968
	Minimum	−0.8346	16.2374	0.0313	−1.1933	0.2801
	Std. dev.	0.3311	1.4714	0.2161	0.1714	0.1907
Post-crisis (2013–2018)	Mean	0.2189	19.3658	0.4509	0.0486	0.7398
	Median	0.1506	19.1499	0.4653	0.0066	0.7784
	Maximum	5.7992	24.4383	0.9252	5.7148	0.9930
	Minimum	−0.6510	16.3548	0.0283	−0.9495	0.2485
	Std. dev.	0.5398	1.6659	0.2404	0.5093	0.1754
All periods (2005–2018)	Mean	20.6336	19.1537	0.5235	0.1591	66.4286
	Median	13.5850	18.1467	0.4993	−1.8800	65.3750
	Maximum	299.2500	24.4383	0.9777	571.4800	99.5400
	Minimum	−83.460	16.8779	0.0392	−119.330	24.8500
	Std. dev.	49.9473	2.1723	0.2574	64.7783	20.4882
Textile, wearing apparel, and leather						
Pre-crisis (2005–2007)	Mean	0.1000	18.7608	0.5071	0.0126	0.6875
	Median	0.0765	18.8381	0.5306	0.0193	0.7233
	Maximum	1.5920	21.0176	0.9210	0.1421	0.9844
	Minimum	−0.8084	16.2696	0.0189	−0.3061	0.0982
	Std. dev.	0.3185	0.9728	0.2010	0.0746	0.2159
Crisis (2008–2012)	Mean	0.0696	18.9541	0.5453	−0.0105	0.7583
	Median	0.0391	18.8988	0.5835	0.0030	0.8340
	Maximum	4.1277	21.2542	0.9199	0.1231	0.9930
	Minimum	−0.6783	16.6911	0.0080	−0.2593	0.2992
	Std. dev.	0.4749	0.9247	0.2129	0.0684	0.1950
Post-crisis (2013—2018)	Mean	0.1397	19.5024	0.6161	0.0123	0.6465
	Median	0.1441	19.4034	0.6527	0.0119	0.6918
	Maximum	3.9616	22.2951	0.9283	0.3275	0.9990
	Minimum	−0.9415	17.3960	0.0148	−0.1580	0.0629
	Std. dev.	0.3973	0.9301	0.2275	0.0761	0.2108
All periods (2005–2018)	Mean	20.6336	19.1537	0.5235	0.1591	66.4286
	Median	13.5850	18.1467	0.4993	−1.8800	65.3750
	Maximum	299.250	24.4383	0.9777	571.480	99.5400
	Minimum	−83.460	16.8779	0.0392	−119.330	24.8500
	Std. dev.	49.9473	2.1723	0.2574	64.7783	20.4882
Chemicals, petroleum, rubber, and plastic products						
Pre-crisis (2005–2007)	Mean	0.0844	19.8024	0.4305	0.0419	0.7243
	Median	0.0834	19.5514	0.3978	0.0564	0.7532
	Maximum	0.6532	22.9275	0.8967	0.2800	0.9628
	Minimum	−0.3499	18.2531	0.0935	−0.2925	0.2284
	Std. dev.	0.1669	1.2083	0.1895	0.0905	0.1800

(continued)

		Growth	Size	D	Roa	Tang
Crisis (2008–2012)	Mean	0.1461	20.2005	0.4521	0.0477	0.7665
	Median	0.1176	19.9391	0.4128	0.0598	0.7917
	Maximum	1.3129	23.5360	0.9228	0.3732	0.9787
	Minimum	−0.4647	18.2055	0.1147	−0.2295	0.3953
	Std. dev.	0.2392	1.2674	0.2058	0.0822	0.1395
Post-crisis (2013–2018)	Mean	0.1395	20.8499	0.4274	0.0786	0.7142
	Median	0.1243	20.7746	0.3915	0.0793	0.7289
	Maximum	0.9708	24.4180	0.8636	0.3036	0.9852
	Minimum	−0.3134	18.2855	0.1298	−0.1474	0.2593
	Std. dev.	0.1791	1.4123	0.1868	0.0701	0.1764
All periods (2005–2018)	Mean	0.1301	20.3935	0.4369	0.0597	0.7350
	Median	0.1092	20.2545	0.4015	0.0645	0.7580
	Maximum	1.3129	24.4180	0.9228	0.3732	0.9852
	Minimum	−0.4647	18.2055	0.0935	−0.2925	0.2284
	Std. dev.	0.2014	1.3828	0.1943	0.0807	0.1664
Fabricated metal products, machinery, and equipment						
Pre-crisis (2005–2007)	Mean	0.1229	19.1426	0.3908	0.0360	0.7440
	Median	0.1038	18.9024	0.3796	0.0515	0.8165
	Maximum	0.8653	23.7131	0.9208	0.3638	1.0000
	Minimum	−0.3365	15.7999	0.0046	−1.2893	0.1006
	Std. dev.	0.2073	2.0108	0.2164	0.1647	0.1988
Crisis (2008–2012)	Mean	0.1486	19.4826	0.4551	0.0364	0.7752
	Median	0.1039	19.3855	0.4584	0.0330	0.7994
	Maximum	1.3142	24.1449	0.9553	0.6383	0.9989
	Minimum	−0.6177	16.6643	0.0055	−1.2225	0.4100
	Std. dev.	0.3216	1.7687	0.2117	0.1518	0.1450
Post-crisis (2013–2018)	Mean	0.1678	20.1468	0.4441	0.0702	0.7045
	Median	0.1527	19.8631	0.4429	0.0498	0.7039
	Maximum	1.8638	24.0714	0.9008	0.6517	0.9873
	Minimum	−0.6074	17.1253	0.0125	−0.3469	0.1579
	Std. dev.	0.2416	1.8103	0.2375	0.1480	0.1761
All periods (2005–2018)	Mean	0.1513	19.6944	0.4366	0.0508	0.7382
	Median	0.1260	19.4182	0.4402	0.0450	0.7543
	Maximum	1.8638	24.1449	0.9553	0.6517	1.0000
	Minimum	−0.6177	15.7999	0.0046	−1.2893	0.1006
	Std. dev.	0.2669	1.8829	0.2250	0.1537	0.1736
Non-metallic mineral products						
Pre-crisis (2005–2007)	Mean	0.1866	19.2627	0.2307	0.1481	0.6263
	Median	0.1662	19.2484	0.1730	0.1294	0.6358
	Maximum	1.1573	21.2316	0.6865	0.7199	0.9513
	Minimum	−0.2947	16.3214	0.0170	−0.1039	0.1087
	Std. dev.	0.1925	1.1472	0.1656	0.1363	0.1779

(continued)

		Growth	Size	D	Roa	Tang
Crisis (2008–2012)	Mean	0.0447	19.4730	0.2589	0.0688	0.6812
	Median	0.0484	19.4374	0.2248	0.0530	0.7030
	Maximum	0.5571	21.6888	0.9026	0.5010	0.9577
	Minimum	−0.4695	16.2952	0.0145	−0.2142	0.2595
	Std. dev.	0.1642	1.2185	0.1961	0.1047	0.1711
Post-crisis (2013–2018)	Mean	0.1532	20.0357	0.3340	0.0855	0.7013
	Median	0.1201	19.9019	0.3289	0.0839	0.7508
	Maximum	1.8643	23.0611	0.8597	0.7195	0.9840
	Minimum	−0.4586	16.7113	0.0344	−0.2137	0.1853
	Std. dev.	0.2306	1.2760	0.2085	0.0936	0.1844
All periods (2005–2018)	Mean	0.1216	19.6691	0.2850	0.0929	0.6780
	Median	0.1053	19.6218	0.2490	0.0792	0.7065
	Maximum	1.8643	23.0611	0.9026	0.7199	0.9840
	Minimum	−0.4695	16.2952	0.0145	−0.2142	0.1087
	Std. dev.	0.2090	1.2699	0.2001	0.1118	0.1804
Technology						
Pre-crisis (2005–2007)	Mean	0.0688	18.4635	0.4091	0.0404	0.8355
	Median	0.1042	18.7998	0.5259	0.0559	0.8962
	Maximum	1.4215	21.0593	0.7191	0.2762	0.9972
	Minimum	−0.5770	15.7859	0.0334	−0.2267	0.3951
	Std. dev.	0.3325	1.4543	0.2442	0.0879	0.1873
Crisis (2008–2012)	Mean	0.6002	18.6789	0.3973	0.0419	0.7825
	Median	0.1295	18.9252	0.4168	0.0337	0.8692
	Maximum	32.7236	21.9259	0.8483	0.7244	0.9986
	Minimum	−0.6565	15.6319	0.0204	−0.1246	0.2116
	Std. dev.	3.5939	1.6291	0.2683	0.1234	0.2242
Post-crisis (2013–2018)	Mean	0.2146	19.5313	0.3630	0.0711	0.8225
	Median	0.1886	19.6789	0.3086	0.0546	0.9143
	Maximum	1.5902	23.6921	0.8112	0.2877	0.9953
	Minimum	−0.9957	16.2457	0.0213	−0.1237	0.3908
	Std. dev.	0.3664	1.7697	0.2644	0.0751	0.1933
All periods (2005–2018)	Mean	0.3183	18.9655	0.3735	0.0518	0.8095
	Median	0.1554	19.1083	0.3491	0.0467	0.9073
	Maximum	32.726	23.6921	0.8483	0.7244	0.9986
	Minimum	−0.9957	15.6319	0.0107	−0.2267	0.1912
	Std. dev.	2.1689	1.7250	0.2632	0.0972	0.2060

Source: Authors' creation

References

Antoniou A, Guney Y, Paudyal K (2008) The determinants of capital structure: capital market-oriented versus bank-oriented institutions. J Financ Quant Anal 43:59–92

Arellano M, Bond S (1991) Some tests of specification for panel data: Monte Carlo evidence and an application to employment equations. Rev Econ Stud 58(2):277–297
Arioglu E, Tuan K (2014) Speed of adjustment: evidence from Borsa Istanbul. Borsa Istanbul Rev 14(2):126–131
Baker M, Wurgler J (2002) Market timing and capital structure. J Financ 57(1):1–32
Blundell R, Bond S (1998) Initial conditions and moment restrictions in dynamic panel data models. J Econ 87(1):115–143
Brealey RA, Myers SC, Marcus AJ (2001) Fundamentals of corporate finance. McGraw-Hill, New York
Chen JJ (2004) Determinants of the capital structure of Chinese-listed companies. J Bus Res 57 (12):1341–1351
Clark BJ, Francis BB, Hasan I (2009) Do firms adjust toward target capital structures? Some Int Evid. Retrieved from https://doi.org/10.2139/ssrn.1364095
Cook DO, Tang T (2010) Macroeconomic conditions and capital structure adjustment speed. J Corp Finan 16:73–87
Dang VA (2011) Leverage, debt maturity and firm investment: an empirical analysis. J Bus Financ Acc 38(1–2):225–258
De Miguel A, Pindado J (2001) Determinants of capital structure: new evidence from Spanish panel data. J Corp Finan 7(1):77–99
DeAngelo H, Roll R (2015) How stable are corporate capital structures? J Financ 70(1):373–418
Deesomsak R, Paudyal K, Pescetto G (2009) Debt maturity structure and the 1997 Asian financial crisis. J Multinatl Financ Manag 19(1):26–42
Devosa E, Rahman S, Tsang D (2017) Debt covenants and the speed of capital structure adjustment. J Corp Finan 45:1–18
Drobetz W, Wanzenried G (2006) What determines the speed of adjustment to the target capital structure? Appl Financ Econ 16(13):941–958
Fama EF, French KR (2002) Testing trade-off and pecking order predictions about dividends and debt. Rev Financ Stud 15(1):1–33
Faulkender M, Flannery MJ, Hankins KW, Smith JM (2012) Cash flows and leverage adjustments. J Financ Econ 103(3):632–646
Fischer EO, Heinkel R, Zechner J (1989) Dynamic capital structure choice: theory and tests. J Financ 44(1):19–40
Flannery MJ, Rangan KP (2006) Partial adjustment toward target capital structures. J Financ Econ 79(3):469–506
Frank MZ, Goyal VK (2002) Testing the pecking order theory of capital structure. J Financ Econ 67 (2):217–248
Frank MZ, Goyal VK (2009) Capital structure decisions: which factors are reliably important? Financ Manag 38(1):1–37
Gaud P, Jani E, Hoesli M, Bender A (2005) The capital structure of Swiss companies: an empirical analysis using dynamic panel data. Eur Financ Manag 11(1):51–69
Getzmann A, Lang S, Spremann K (2010) Determinants of the target capital structure and adjustment speed-evidence from Asian, European, and US-capital markets. Eur Financ Manag:1–41
Getzmann A, Lang S, Spremann K (2014) Target capital structure and adjustment speed in Asia. Asia Pac J Financ Stud 43(1):1–30
Ghazouani T (2013) The capital structure through the trade-off theory: evidence from Tunisian firm. Int J Econ Financ Issues 3(3):625–636
Graham JR, Harvey CR (2001) The theory and practice of corporate finance: evidence from the field. J Financ Econ 60(2–3):187–243
Hahn J, Hausman J, Kuersteiner G (2007) Long difference instrumental variables estimation for dynamic panel models with fixed effects. J Econ 140(2):574–617
Haron R, Ibrahim K, Nor FM, Ibrahim I (2013) Factors affecting the speed of adjustment to target leverage: Malaysia evidence. Glob Bus Rev 14(2):243–262
Harris M, Raviv A (1991) The theory of capital structure. J Financ 46(1):297–355

He W, Kyaw NA (2018) Capital structure adjustment behaviours of Chinese listed companies: evidence from the split share structure reform in China. Glob Financ J 36:14–22
Hovakimian A, Opler T, Titman S (2001) The debt-equity choice. J Financ Quant Anal:1–24
Hovakimian A, Li G (2009) Do firms have unique target debt ratios to which they adjust? Available at SSRN 1138316
Hovakimian A, Li G (2011) In search of conclusive evidence: how to test for adjustment to target capital structure. J Corp Finan 17(1):33–44
Huang R, Ritter JR (2009) Testing theories of capital structure and estimating the speed of adjustment. J Financ Quant Anal 44(2):237–271
Kayo EK, Brunaldi EO, Aldrighi DM (2018) Capital structure adjustment in Brazilian family firms. Revista de Administração Contemporânea 22(1):92–114
Kraus A, Litzenberger RH (1973) A state-preference model of optimal financial leverage. J Financ 28(4):911–922
Leary MT, Roberts MR (2005) Do firms rebalance their capital structures? J Financ 60 (6):2575–2619
Lemmon ML, Roberts MR, Zender JF (2008) Back to the beginning: persistence and the cross-section of corporate capital structure. J Financ 63(4):1575–1608
Lööf H (2003) Dynamic optimal capital structure and technological change. Discussion paper no. 03–06. Retrieved from https://madoc.bib.uni-mannheim.de/190/1/ZEW80.pdf
Miller EM (1977) Risk, uncertainty, and divergence of opinion. J Financ 32(4):1151–1168
Modigliani F, Miller MH (1958) The cost of capital, corporation finance and the theory of investment. Am Econ Rev 48(3):261–297
Myers SC (1984) The capital structure puzzle. J Financ 39(3):574–592
Nieh CC, Yau HY, Liu WC (2008) Investigation of target capital structure for electronic listed firms in Taiwan. Emerg Mark Financ Trade 44(4):75–87
Özkan A (2001) Determinants of capital structure and adjustment to long-run target: Evidence from UK company panel data. J Bus Financ Acc 28(1–2):175–198
Rajan RG, Zingales L (1995) What do we know about capital structure? Some evidence from international data. J Financ 50(5):1421–1460
Shyam-Sunder L, Myers SC (1999) Testing static trade-off against pecking order models of capital structure. J Financ Econ 51(2):219–244
Strebulaev IA (2007) Do tests of capital structure theory mean what they say? J Financ 62 (4):1747–1787
Syahara YR, Soekarno S (2015) The existence of target capital structure and speed of adjustment: evidence from Indonesian public firms. In: Proceedings of International Conference on Management Finance Economics, July 11–12, pp 191–199
Titman S, Wessels R (1988) The determinants of capital structure choice. J Financ 43(1):1–19

Turhan Korkmaz is a Professor of Finance at Mersin University, Turkey. He also served 14 years as a faculty member at Zonguldak Bulent Ecevit University, Turkey. He is the author or co-author of nine books, sixteen edited volumes, over 90 research articles in leading journals, and presented dozens of papers in the field of finance at national and international conferences. Turhan Korkmaz has made several important research contributions in corporate finance, capital markets, portfolio management, international asset allocation, and risk management. Professor Korkmaz completed his first degree in business administration at Bursa Uludag University, Turkey and he also holds MBA and PhD degrees in finance from Chicago Illinois Institute of Technology, USA.

Aslı Yıkılmaz Erkol is a Research Assistant at Mersin University, Turkey. She received her PhD in finance from the University of Mersin. She has worked as an expert in the Small and Medium Enterprises Development Organization of Turkey for two years. Her areas of interest are Corporate Finance, Capital Markets, and Risk Management. Doctor Yıkılmaz Erkol completed her first degree in business administration at Cukurova University, Turkey. She also holds MSc in finance from Mersin University and completed her PhD degrees with the scholarship of Scientific and Technological Research Council of Turkey.